T0295623

Social Economy Science

Social Economy Science

Transforming the Economy and Making
Society More Resilient

Edited by

Gorgi Krlev
Dominika Wruk
Giulio Pasi
and
Marika Bernhard

OXFORD
UNIVERSITY PRESS

UNIVERSITY PRESS

Great Clarendon Street, Oxford, OX2 6DP,
United Kingdom

Oxford University Press is a department of the University of Oxford.
It furthers the University's objective of excellence in research, scholarship,
and education by publishing worldwide. Oxford is a registered trade mark of
Oxford University Press in the UK and in certain other countries

Published in the United States of America by Oxford University Press
198 Madison Avenue, New York, NY 10016, United States of America

British Library Cataloguing in Publication Data

Data available

Library of Congress Control Number: 2023943785

ISBN 9780192868343

DOI: 10.1093/oso/9780192868343.001.0001

Printed and bound in the UK by
Clays Ltd, Elcograf S.p.A.

Links to third party websites are provided by Oxford in good faith and
for information only. Oxford disclaims any responsibility for the materials
contained in any third party website referenced in this work.

Contents

Preface

Everyone knows how good it feels when, after several years of work and much effort, things finally fall into place. This is such a moment. What makes this moment special is that it marks a clear departure. The publishing of *Social Economy Science* by Oxford University Press makes the underdog the winner. It moves a phenomenological area from the fringes of researchers' attention into the limelight. This book has its seeds in a small idea: the idea to organize an intimate academic exchange on issues surrounding the social economy as a sister event to the European Social Economy Summit (EUSES), which was planned for November 2020 in Mannheim and was held virtually in May 2021 due to the COVID-19 pandemic. Because of the unfolding crisis, and made possible by a strong partnership with the European Commission, we chose to move our event online too, but also to make it much bigger than initially planned by opening it up to a wider audience. What started as a gathering of eighty researchers became the Social Economy Science Conference, with more than 800 registered academics, practitioners, and policy-makers.

In the run-up to the event, when we saw that the interest was substantially larger than we had expected, we placed bets on how many participants we would reach. Even the most daring among us far underestimated how many people would want to hear about cutting-edge research on, for example, how social and solidarity organizations were buffering the effects of the crisis for society's most vulnerable groups; or how social entrepreneurship and social innovation play an essential role in addressing persistent societal problems, including the challenge of creating more democratic, equitable and participatory forms of organizing; or how impact investing and social outcomes contracting by governments change the ways in which we think about funding the common good.

The large turnout of participants was certainly not least due to a world-class line-up of academics and support for the event by the European Commission. However, it was also one of the few positive effects of the COVID-19 pandemic. The global crisis highlighted what holds society together and what really matters to people: solidarity and social relations, values and caring, collective instead of individual action. These are all traits and virtues that the social economy embodies like no other organizational field.

The crisis represented the culmination of a realization that only gradually emerged over the years: a realization that we had unduly ignored phenomena that might hold the answer to ills which society has been grappling with for ages. Such ills include social inequalities, societal polarization, and environmental degradation—and combating these has always been at the heart of the social economy. After our conference, many of the speakers thought back to their own pasts as social economy scholars. Ten years ago we were met with disbelief when we said we were studying social entrepreneurship, due to the seeming incompatibility of the two words 'social' and 'entrepreneurship' in combination; or we were asked whether our work on social impact measurement had anything to do with social media.

Today there is almost no business leader or politician who does not talk about their aim to create a positive impact for society. And countries are busy setting up national policies to stimulate social entrepreneurship and social innovations, whereby these efforts have intensified markedly during the last two years. Many societal stakeholders have come to realize that the conversation should not be along the lines of 'Oh, you're running a social economy organization. That is just like running a business, but simpler, because these organizations don't need to make a profit.' Quite the reverse is true: running social economy organizations is more complex than running a mainstream business, because social value is much harder to create than purely commercial profit. Besides, social economy organizations operate under extreme uncertainty and yet uphold cultural values and remain true to high ethical standards.

So, it is with some satisfaction that we can now say there is *more, not less* to learn from social economy organizations than from other types of organizations as regards organizational strategy, governance, management and leadership. And this is what we hope to demonstrate in *Social Economy Science*. Our focus is explicitly not inward-looking, in that we do not primarily discuss the intricacies of the social economy. Instead we look outward and provide empirical and conceptual work and essays on how social economy organizations (and scientific inquiry that takes them seriously) can help us understand how we can transform the economy into a system that is more environmentally and socially conscious and thus sustainable in the long term. We also deal with how social economy practices, processes, and values can make society more resilient to crises of the future.

We believe this is an innovative mission in itself, but see other reasons why we hope *Social Economy Science* will become an agenda-setting book. One reason is that the book bridges two separate fields of research. First, it builds on organization theory which is potent in deciphering processes and practices at the micro level of organizations and the meso level of organizational fields, which are essential for achieving stability and forming a common identity. Second, it builds on transitions theory, which has its strength in grasping processes that stretch over long periods of time and fundamentally alter social systems and structures, which are important to understand social change. Another reason is that the book brings together a strong group of scholar-practitioners as well as practitioner-scholars, that is, academics who have prioritized impact work for policy and practice for a long time *and* doers, makers, and shapers on the ground who have a solid footing in research and science. This constellation has given rise to a set of eighteen chapters, each of which has a profound research as well as policy and practice component. We believe this is unique for an edited volume, where, if present, these components are typically located in different parts of a book rather than merged in each chapter.

We would like to sincerely thank all contributors of the book for sticking with us, from initial contact for a speaking role during the Social Economy Science

Conference through to their final chapters. Not a single contributor was lost on this joint journey from event to book, and some of the author teams have grown. The chapters greatly benefited from the continuous exchange over this period of time and a gradual process of finetuning chapters against each other. We hope that those who hold the book in their hands will, when reading, be reminded of the saying that the whole is worth more than its individual parts.

We are very grateful to Ulla Engelmann (former head of Clusters, Social Economy, and Entrepreneurship), with whom we co-initiated the Social Economy Science Conference, as well as to other heads of units and directors at the European Commission who supported it passionately, namely Xabier Goenaga Beldarrain and Mikel Landabaso Alvarez (Joint Research Centre), Slawomir Tokarski (Directorate General for Internal Market, Industry, Entrepreneurship and SMEs), and Antonella Noya from the OECD.

We would also like to greatly thank Adam Swallow of Oxford University Press. We are grateful for his genuine interest and trust in the subject and in us as a team right from the start, as well as his choice of three anonymous reviewers, who provided excellent suggestions on how to further improve the book. It is rather seldom that reviewers, in unison, apply such a productive stance in their reviews, in which they focus much less on criticizing what is there and much more on what could be added to make the existing foundation even stronger. The reviewers for instance suggested we should implement additional chapters, one to provide an explicit policy perspective and one with a focus on the local level. As readers will see, we have taken these suggestions to heart and believe the book is the better for it.

Finally, we are especially pleased that we can provide the book to interested readers open access. In the absence of one big funder to cover the fees, we were able to crowd-fund the necessary amount—quite authentic to the style in which the social economy operates. We gratefully acknowledge generous support from: University of Mannheim, Social Entrepreneurship Baden-Württemberg e.V., University of Milano Bicocca, University of Valencia, Politecnico di Milano's TIRESIA group, ESADE Business School's Center for Social Impact, University of Oxford's Government Outcomes Lab at the Blavatnik School of Government, and Harvard Kennedy School's Social Innovation + Change Initiative.

Instead of closing with a description of how the book is composed, which we elaborate on in the introduction and theory chapters, we want to leave readers with a call to action. This call to action is not only probably rare for a book, but also fully in line with the social economy's ethos: do not only read the book; take the knowledge to co-create, shape, and scale new solutions. Only when science and practical action move closer together and reinforce each other do we stand a chance of solving the immense challenges that lie ahead of society.

As German chemistry professor and Scientists for Future activist Sebastian Seifert said on Twitter: 'We need to achieve transformations on three levels: the economy, society, and technology. I have come to realize technology is the easy one, and that it is the social sciences, which hold the key to overcoming the big crises of the century.'

Our stress on how the social economy transforms the economy and makes society more resilient underlines that social economy science should play an essential part in achieving this mission and vision.

Gorgi Krlev, Dominika Wruk, Giulio Pasi and Marika Bernhard
30. September 2022

List of figures

List of tables

Contributors

Nigel Ball is Director of the newly founded Social Purpose Lab at the University of the Arts London and was previously Executive Director of the Government Outcomes Lab at the Blavatnik School of Government, University of Oxford, where he led engagement with government policy-makers and practitioners. He has spent his whole career working in the social economy in different parts of the world.

Julie Battilana is Professor of Organizational Behavior at Harvard Business School and of social innovation at Harvard Kennedy School, where she is also the founder and faculty chair of the Social Innovation + Change Initiative. Her research examines the politics of change in organizations and in society and especially focuses on organizations and individuals that initiate and implement changes that break with the status quo. She has co-authored two books: *Power, For All: How It Really Works and Why It's Everyone's Business*, with Tiziana Casciaro, and *Democratize Work: The Case for Reorganizing the Economy*, with Isabelle Ferreras and Dominique Méda.

Marika Bernhard is Lead of Sustainability at DFL (the German Football Association). She is also founder and chairwoman of Social Entrepreneurship Baden-Württemberg (SocEnt BW), a network organization supporting impact-driven ventures across Germany. She initiated the Social Innovation Summit, which, after many years of running successfully as an entrepreneurial endeavour, merged existing efforts and partnerships, including with the European Commission, to become the Social Economy Science Conference in 2021.

François Bonnici is a public health physician, professor, social change practitioner, foundation leader, and co-author of *The Systems Work of Social Change: How to Harness Connection, Context, and Power to Cultivate Deep and Enduring Change*. He currently serves as Director of the Schwab Foundation for Social Entrepreneurship and Head of Social Innovation at the World Economic Forum. Prior to this, he founded and led the Bertha Centre for Social Innovation at the University of Cape Town, where he remains Adjunct Associate Professor. François attained his medical degree from the University of Cape Town, his MBA from the University of Oxford, and his MSc from the London School of Hygiene and Tropical Medicine.

Alessandro Braga is Adjunct Professor at Xenophon College London in the UK and a teaching fellow at the University of Milano-Bicocca in Italy. He conducts research on public value, place and sustainability leadership, and administrative reforms. He has held academic positions in the UK, USA, Italy, Denmark, and Peru. He is the author of articles in international peer-reviewed journals such as *Regional Studies*, *Public Money & Management*, and *Teaching Public Administration*.

Ruth Bränvall holds a PhD from KTH Royal Institute of Technology, where her research focussed on innovation for under-served markets for poor or marginalized consumer groups, especially in emerging markets, often referred to as social innovation. She is CEO and General Partner of Impact Invest Scandinavia, which runs an alternative investment fund focused on improving health and quality of life by providing credits and investments to actors with deep impact and innovative approaches. The organization also provides advisory services relating to ESG and impact monitoring and evaluation to other investors and funders.

Leonora Buckland is Senior Researcher at the ESADE Center for Social Impact. She gained her PhD at the University of Oxford and also has a Masters in International Relations from SAIS Johns Hopkins. Leonora has specialized in social entrepreneurship, impact investing, and impact measurement and management for more than a decade after running a venture philanthropy foundation in the UK. She consults widely on these topics for foundations, NGOs, and impact investors across the world, focusing mainly in Europe and Latin America.

Mario Calderini is Full Professor at Politecnico di Milano, where he teaches Management for Sustainability and Impact. He is the Director of Tiresia, the Politecnico di Milano School of Management's Research Centre for Impact Finance and Innovation. In 2021 he was included in the list of the one hundred most influential academics on political topics in the world. His numerous publications in highly-ranked international journals cover several topics in the field of innovation and impact finance. He has been a member of the G8 Task Force for Social Impact Investment. He is a consultant to the European Commission on finance and social impact entrepreneurship.

Eleanor Carter is a UKRI Future Leaders Fellow at the Blavatnik School of Government, University of Oxford and is also Research Director for the Government Outcomes Lab. Eleanor's research investigates challenges in coordinating complex public service delivery networks and cross-sector partnerships. She is one of Apolitical's 100 Most Influential Academics in Government.

Rafael Chaves-Avila is Senior Professor of Economic Policy at the IUDESCOOP research institute of the University of Valencia, Spain. He was Chairman of CIRIEC's Scientific Committee from 2002 to 2012. He is currently a member of the European Commission Expert group on social economy and social enterprises (GECES) and editor of the Ciriec-España journal of public, social and cooperative economy. Recent work includes *Recent evolution of the social economy in the European Union* (EESC), *Transformative policies for the social and solidarity economy* and *Producing statistics on Social and Solidarity Economy* (UNRISD-UN). His Twitter handle is @Rafael_Chaves_9 and his website is www.uv.es/chavesr.

Veronica Chiodo holds a PhD in Management Engineering and is Junior Assistant Professor at the Department of Management, Economics and Industrial Engineering of Politecnico di Milano. Her PhD research investigated the challenges and financial needs of social enterprises in their scaling. She also works as a consultant with venture capitalists, banks, and microfinance institutions to develop a measurement system able to assess the social impact performance of social enterprises in the screening, due diligence, and monitoring phase.

Luigi Corvo has twelve years of experience as a researcher and Program Manager in the Social Innovation and Impact area of study in the Department of Business and Law at the University of Milan-Bicocca. Luigi is also appointed as Social Innovation Expert for the Social Innovation Fund of the Italian Ministry of Public Administration and in 2021 was appointed as a member of the National Council of the Third Sector by the Ministry of Labor and Social Policies. In 2019 Luigi founded Open Impact, an innovative start-up whose mission is to create an open ecosystem of knowledge and skills on impact.

Francesco Gerli is Assistant Professor at the School of Management of Politecnico di Milano. He gained his PhD at the same institution, where he is affiliated to the research group TIRESIA. Francesco holds a MSc in Economics and Social Sciences from Bocconi University. Currently his research focuses on social-tech innovation, social entrepreneurship, and public actors' organizational capacities for facing sustainability transitions.

Malcolm Hayday joined CAF to explore social finance after spending twenty years in international finance. In 2002 he became founding Chief Executive of Charity Bank, the world's only charity and bank. He is Senior Fellow of the Finance Innovation Lab.

Lisa Hehenberger is Associate Professor in the Department of Strategy and General Management at ESADE Business School and Founding Director of its Center for Social Impact. Lisa has published in the most prestigious academic journals, such as the *Academy of Management Journal*, and is the author of numerous books, policy papers, and practitioner reports. She is actively contributing to building the social impact field through her participation in expert groups set up by the European Commission, the OECD, and the G8 and through advisory board seats in impact funds and foundations.

Kai Hockerts is Professor in Social Entrepreneurship at Copenhagen Business School (CBS). He holds a PhD in Management from the University of St Gallen, and before joining CBS was Adjunct Professor at INSEAD. In his function as Academic Director of Responsible Management Education he is leading the CBS curriculum change initiative, with the goal of anchoring responsible management education across the curriculum. His primary research focus is on corporate sustainability strategies and social entrepreneurship.

Anne-Karen Hueske is a Postdoctoral Researcher in Social Entrepreneurship Education at Copenhagen Business School, Denmark. Her research interests are in sustainability transformation of business, sustainable intrapreneurship, social change makers, and social entrepreneurship. She holds a French–German double degree in business administration and did her PhD on innovation barriers at Technische Universität Dresden (Germany). Before joining Copenhagen Business School, she was founding Managing Director of the interdisciplinary research centre PRISMA—Center for Sustainability Assessment and Policy (Germany). She has consulting experience related to sustainability transformation in business, industry and society.

Marieke Huysentruyt is Associate Professor of Strategy and Business Policy at HEC Paris and academic director of the Inclusive Economy Centre at HEC Paris. Before joining HEC Paris, she was co-founder and co-director of the Oksigen eco-system designed to promote and support social business innovation and social entrepreneurship (comprising i-propeller, Oksigen Lab, and the SI2 fund). She has been a faculty member at the Stockholm School of Economics and London School of Economics, and a visiting scholar at Harvard University and the Sante Fe Institute. Marieke's work informs and brings together the broad fields of competitive strategy, behavioural science, and organizational economics. She teaches and carries out research on the 'S' factor in ESG and the 'social scope' of organizations, especially firm strategies designed to tackle inequalities and promote economic opportunity for all.

Veerle Klijn is a social economy policy expert with experience across government, international networks, and international organizations and as a social entrepreneur. She currently works as Lead Consultant on Social Economy for the Schwab Foundation and World Economic Forum. Prior to this role, Veerle headed the policy department of the European Social Enterprise Network (Euclid Network) and worked for the European Commission. She holds a double-degree Masters in European Governance.

Gorgi Krlev is Associate Professor of Sustainability at ESCP Business School in Paris. He also holds a visiting professorship at Politecnico di Milano and a Visiting Fellow position at University of Oxford's Kellogg College. In his research, he deals with social entrepreneurship, social innovations, and impact. He is particularly interested in how cross-sector collaborations and new-field emergence promote societal transformations and contribute to addressing environmental and social sustainability challenges. His work has won numerous awards, including a best book award from the Academy of Management's (AOM) Public and Nonprofit Division for *Social Innovation: Comparative Perspectives*, the Roman Herzog Institute's 2021 Award for innovative contributions to the social market economy, and the International Society for Third Sector Research's (ISTR) 2022 policy impact award.

Leszek Krol is a research associate at Harvard Business School, affiliated with the Harvard Kennedy School's Social Innovation + Change Initiative. He researches how organizations can sustainably balance social, financial, and

environmental goals and the impacts of more democratic forms of organizational governance. He has a bachelor's degree in philosophy from Harvard University.

António Miguel founded MAZE and is responsible for the Government Performance work and the MSM impact fund as a Managing Partner. He has worked in impact investment for +10 years in the UK, Canada, and Europe. António teaches Impact Investment at NOVA SBE and previously was an analyst at Social Finance UK. He holds a MSc in Business Administration from Católica Business School and has been named a Global Shaper by the World Economic Forum.

Sir Geoff Mulgan is Professor of Collective Intelligence, Public Policy & Social Innovation at University College London (UCL). He was CEO of Nesta, the UK's innovation foundation (2011–2019), and of the Young foundation (2004–2011), and from 1997 to 2004 had roles in UK government, including director of the government's Strategy Unit and head of policy in the Prime Minister's office. Past books include *The Art of Public Strategy* (OUP), *Good and Bad Power* (Penguin), *Big Mind* (Princeton UP), *Social Innovation* (Policy Press), and *Another World is Possible* (Hurst/OUP 2022). His Twitter handle is @geoffmulgan and his website is geoffmulgan.com.

Alex Nicholls is the first tenured Professor in Social Entrepreneurship appointed at the University of Oxford. His research interests range across several key areas within social entrepreneurship and social innovation, including social and impact investment; the nexus of relationships between accounting, accountability, and governance; public and social policy contexts; and Fair Trade. To date he has published more than 100 papers and chapters and six books, several with Oxford University Press, which are the highest-selling and most cited academic books on their subjects in the world. His work has been cited more than 12,000 times. He is editor of the *Journal of Social Entrepreneurship*.

Rocío Nogales-Muriel is Director of the EMES International Research Network and Adjunct Professor of Sociology at the University of Zaragoza, Spain. She currently represents EMES as Observer Member in the UN Task Force for Social and Solidarity Economy and is a member of the boards of Culture Action Europe (CAE), the Smart Ib cooperative, and the Spanish Network of Community Culture Entities and Agents (REACC). She is co-editor of the Routledge Studies on Social Enterprise & Social Innovation series.

Marthe Nyssens is Professor of Social Economy at UCLouvain (Belgium). Her work focuses on the conceptual approaches of the social economy and social enterprise and on the links of these organizations with the state, the market, and civil society in different fields of activity: services to people, integration through economic activity, the commons, and the like. Together with Jacques Defourny she coordinated the International Comparative Social Enterprise Models (ICSEM) Project, which involves some 230 researchers from 55 countries around the world. She was a founding member and is currently vice-president of the EMES International Research Network.

Jarrod Ormiston is Senior Lecturer at the TD School (transdisciplinary innovation) at the University of Technology Sydney (UTS), Australia. His research focuses on working with social enterprises and impact investors to enhance their impact, educating entrepreneurs from marginalized backgrounds, and understanding the role of emotions, time, and place in entrepreneurship. Jarrod has worked as a consultant to the Australian government, the OECD, and the United Nations on entrepreneurship and education. Before his work at UTS, Jarrod worked at Maastricht University, University of Sydney, Deloitte, and in various management roles in the non-profit and education sectors.

Michela Pagani completed her PhD on city leadership at the Open University Business School. She works as an independent researcher.

Giulio Pasi is Member of the Advisory Board of the Bureau of Entrepreneurial Finance at the University of Turin and Professor of Economics at Universidad Loyola in Seville. He has served as Scientific Officer at the European Commission Joint Research Centre, leading work on social innovation, new financial engineering, and the relationships between public policy and new markets or industries, as well as the impact of the digital transformation. An expert in policy analysis, strategic foresight, and future studies, he is the author of around sixty publications and is a globally recognized expert in the field of impact investing. He has been a keynote speaker at high-level events organized—among others—by the OECD, the World Economic Forum, and the Global Steering Group on Impact Investing (former G8 taskforce).

Alessandro Sancino is Associate Professor in Management at the University of Milan-Bicocca. He also serves as Senior Lecturer at The Open University (UK) and Adjunct Professor at the University of Italian Switzerland. He is a member of the Executive Board of PUPOL (Public and Political Leadership Academic Network), a fellow of the RSA (Regional Studies Association), and co-chair of the Study Group on Public Network Policy and Management, EGPA (European Group for Public Administration). His research is focused on cities, democracy, government–citizen relations, public value, and social innovation.

Fulvio Scognamiglio is a PhD candidate at The Open University, whose research focuses on governance, public administration, networks, and sustainability.

Kara Sheppard-Jones is Research Fellow at Harvard Kennedy School's Social Innovation + Change Initiative. She has launched, supported, and expanded a dozen social impact initiatives over the past decade in Canada and the US while also conducting research on social movements, the politics of change, and alternatives to capitalism. She holds a bachelor's degree in political science from Yale University and a Masters in political science from McGill University.

Ángel Soler Guillén is Assistant Professor at the Department of Applied Economics at the Universitat de València. From 1996 to 2019 he worked as a senior research technician at the Valencian Institut of Economic Research (Ivie), where he is currently an associate researcher. His fields of research are the economics of education, human capital, human development, the labour market, gender equality, and social economy. About these subjects, he has published ninety-five books and book chapters, as well as sixteen articles in national and international journals, and has participated in more than 100 research projects.

Alexandra Ubalijoro is Research Assistant at MDRC, a social policy research organization in NYC. Prior to that she worked for Professor Battilana, studying organizational behaviour and entrenched norms. She is interested in the study of social psychology, intergroup relations and hierarchy, and the practical application of policy to improve society. She has a bachelor's degree in psychology from Harvard University.

Eva Varga is an independent consultant with expertise in the development of social enterprise, social finance, and their ecosystems. She has designed and run capacity-building and investment-readiness programmes; managed multi-country ecosystem research projects; and provided policy advice to governments in Central Europe and Latin America. Eva has been a member of various expert groups and an advisor to the European Venture Philanthropy Association (EVPA), the OECD, and the European Commission (EC). She is the author of *A Recipe Book for Social Finance* (2016 and 2019, EC). She is the vice-president of Euclid Network.

Willemine Willems is Assistant Professor Science Communication for Wicked Problems at the Athena Institute, Vrije Universiteit Amsterdam. She has a background in political science, philosophy of science, political philosophy and ethics. In her current research she focuses on science communication as reflexive boundary work, on engaging publics in science in times of crisis, and on the role of science in democracy.

Dominika Wruk is Assistant Professor for Sustainable Entrepreneurship at the University of Mannheim. She has been leading the platforms2share research group, focused on platform cooperatives and funded by the German Ministry for Education and Research, for several years. She led the i-share project consortium, in which she was also responsible for analysing the social, ecological, and economic effects of the sharing economy. She has been a SCANCOR visiting researcher at Stanford University.

INTRODUCTION, OVERVIEW AND THEORETICAL ANCHORS

1
Why should we care about social economy science?

Gorgi Krlev, Dominika Wruk, Giulio Pasi, and Marika Bernhard

Practical and policy relevance

The challenges of sustainable development and the COVID-19 pandemic have increased the visibility of the social economy's contribution to socio-economic development and social cohesion. The concept of the social economy spreads from traditional forms of cooperative or solidarity economy organizations to newly emergent phenomena at the organizational or field level, such as impact investing or technology-based ventures that are harnessing the affordances of artificial intelligence for the promotion of the common good.

This widening conceptual understanding results in a dual function. The social economy has demonstrated its key role as an integral part of the global safety net, which especially in times of crisis provides essential goods and services to the most deprived people. This function is stressed for example in NextGenerationEU, the European Commission's newly developed Recovery Action Plan that prioritizes fair transitions and societal resilience (European Commission, 2022c). The social economy has also been recognized as a driver of societal innovation and in rethinking how organizations may create superior economic and social value by harnessing new ways of engaging jointly. This function is for instance expressed in the activities of the COVID Response Alliance for Social Entrepreneurs of the World Economic Forum (WEF), which aims to promote breakthrough collaboration between diverse actors that share an inclusive and sustainability mindset (Maas Geesteranus, Bonnici, & Bruin, 2021).

Social Economy Science provides a multi-faceted analysis of this dual role.[1]

Social economy as the safe pole of society

As regards its first role, traditionally the social economy has been seen as a way to address market failures or state failures. Welfare organizations, cooperative

---

[1] This chapter picks up on and builds out some of the foundations we have laid in our Stanford Social Innovation Review series on 'Reconceptualizing the Social Economy' (Krlev, Pasi, Wruk, & Bernhard, 2021).

Gorgi Krlev et al., *Why should we care about social economy science?*. In: *Social Economy Science*. Edited by: Gorgi Krlev, Dominika Wruk, Giulio Pasi, and Marika Bernhard, Oxford University Press. © Oxford University Press (2023). DOI: 10.1093/oso/9780192868343.003.0001

enterprises, mutual aid societies, civic associations, and others have, for example, addressed the financial exclusion of vulnerable groups of the population (Périlleux & Nyssens, 2017) or sought to find remedies to inadequate responses to homelessness (Teasdale, 2012). Unfortunately, this role was often not interpreted as a vital contribution to society in itself, but as a derivative and imperfect way of fixing what was broken in society by others. This made the social economy the poor cousin of the market and the state, and it has therefore often been unduly ignored (Rajan, 2020)—in societal debates, in shaping (or failing to shape) new institutions that would support the social economy, or in providing financial support to social economy organizations.

Such acts of neglect happened although the social economy is vital for society, since it is a creator and guardian of social cohesion and solidarity, whereby solidarity is defined in an illustrative way by Genschel and Hemerijck (2018, p. 2) as 'the normative expectation of mutual support among the members of large anonymous groups (the class, the party, the nation) [. . . who] ought to share one another's risks and burdens in order to secure the goals and cohesiveness of the group as a whole'. The current crises have not only reminded us of the importance of solidarity, they have also shifted an unprecedented amount of attention to the social economy as *the* place, in which society may heal from polarization (Gerometta, Haussermann, & Longo, 2005), act swiftly on emergencies (Kornberger, Leixnering, Meyer, & Höllerer, 2018), and renew itself for the long run (Smith & Teasdale, 2012).

However, the new interest in and appreciation of those qualities of the social economy is not the only reason why societal stakeholders are taking careful note of what social economy organizations are doing themselves and what they could push other organizations to do.

Social economy as a source of renewal and change

When it comes to its second role, there is a new focus on the social economy because it promotes a green and social transformation that prioritizes principles of inclusion, equity and responsibility (see e.g., Amanatidou, Tzekou, & Gritzas, 2021; Avelino et al., 2019; Bretos, Bouchard, & Zevi, 2020)—elements that are clearly at the heart of the United Nations' 17 Sustainable Development Goals (SDGs). In this light, the social economy is emerging as an alternative way to think about and organize the economy and society.

The social economy's potential as a role model for transformation can be recognized in a global economic system that is in desperate pursuit of reinventing itself and embracing purpose as its driving force (Mayer & Roche, 2021), while purpose is all that social economy organizations are about. Besides, social entrepreneurial action has assumed appeal beyond being a particular organizational type, namely as a universal method of innovative action aimed at addressing social and environmental problems via unconventional approaches (Tracey & Stott, 2017). One can also see social economy principles surface in the rapid and prosocial shifts in business models that have occurred in response to challenges provoked by COVID-19 (Scheidgen, Gümüsay, Günzel-Jensen, Krlev, & Wolf, 2021), or in the emergence of so-called platform cooperatives that combine values-based action, co-determination, and digitization to create a new, more equitable way of doing business (Mannan & Pek, 2021; Schor & Eddy, 2022). Social economy organizations have furthermore initiated unprecedented collective action, such as that of open social innovation processes (Gegenhuber, 2020).

At the level of organizational fields, social and sustainable finance markets have been growing rapidly in recent years. However, there are critical questions as to whether genuine social value is created and social economy organizations, unlike many others, are fighting to safeguard a version of impact that is about positive contributions to society instead of merely reducing harm (Barman, 2020; Nicholls & Emerson, 2016). As regards organizational forms, social economy organizations promote new principles of organizational structure (such as flat hierarchies and decentralization) and new organizational practices (such as participatory decision-making) as well as pioneer new forms of organizational democracy (Ebrahim, Battilana, & Mair, 2014). Finally, when it comes to addressing unfair societal structures, the social economy is a contestant of social inequalities such as gender discrimination, for instance by providing a space for substantially more female founders than are seen in other areas of entrepreneurship (Euclid Network, 2021).

An unprecedented level of support

All these circumstances taken together have garnered support for the social economy. In Europe, for instance, the new European Social Fund Plus (ESF+), which now incorporates the Employment and Social Innovation (EaSI) Programme of the European Commission, seeks to channel almost €100 billion within five years into areas in which social economy organizations operate (European Commission, 2022a and 2022b). Globally, the OECD launched the Global Action 'Promoting Social and Solidarity Economy Ecosystems', a project that will include more than thirty countries over three years (OECD, 2022; for more on global action concerning the social economy, see Bonnici & Klijn, this volume).

We believe *Social Economy Science* will be a valuable resource for decision makers seeking to support the social economy in its dual role, because the book draws on a wide range of organizational representations and institutional contexts of the social economy. At the organizational level it spreads from social-tech ventures (Calderini et al., this volume), to hybrid purpose organizations (Battilana et al., this volume), to local social entrepreneurs in developing countries (Brännvall, this volume). At the field and societal levels, it takes account of newly emergent impact accounting and measurement practices (Hehenberger & Buckland, this volume), of new organizational fields and industries such as social investment (Nicholls & Ormiston, this volume), or of the modernization of welfare states by moving towards outcomes-based contracting (Carter & Ball, this volume). In all of this, the book does not only provide some 'practical implications' that derive from cutting-edge research and analysis. Instead it develops actionable practical and policy guidance on how to amplify social economy capacities or how to reduce existing barriers that stop it from fully developing its transformative potential.

Research relevance

Calls for a 'societal turn' in organization and management research have been growing substantially louder (Bapuji, Patel, Ertug, & Allen, 2020). Research shall move from being interesting to being important (Tihanyi, 2020). It shall help understand and inform action towards addressing the grand challenges of our times, which range from the climate crisis, to poverty, to inequality (Howard-Grenville et al., 2019). In view of these imperatives, topics related to a widening understanding of the social economy have moved from the periphery, mostly located in the outlets of sub-fields in the social sciences such as non-profit studies or development studies, to the centre of attention in general organization and management research (Haugh, 2021; Hertel, Bacq, & Belz, 2019; Palacios-Marqués, García, Sánchez, & Mari, 2019). This is because social economy organizations have a long, but often ignored track record in effectively dealing with such challenges.

The explanatory power of social economy research

Social economy organizations and those involved with them are now being studied as blueprints for new ways of organizing, for instance when it comes to reconciling multiple logics within an organization, especially when logics are competing with each other and seemingly incompatible (Besharov & Smith, 2014), or when paradox arises as organizations need to shift between logics or reconcile them in original ways (Smith & Besharov, 2017). Besides, researchers have highlighted that organizations of the social economy are more likely than others to apply a systems-oriented perspective to social problems, which enables them to come up with more effective solutions to those problems (Mair & Seelos, 2021; Seelos & Mair, 2017). Social economy organizations have also been recognized for their connective function, not only in bridging gaps between organizations from different sectors, but also between organizations and target groups (Krlev, Anheier, & Mildenberger, 2019), or for being major re-shapers of normative institutions in society, which change how we conceive of and deal with problems (Purtik & Arenas, 2017).

Some forms of the social economy, such as sharing organizations with a strong civic and self-organized character redefine the borders between private and communal resources and establish new, or rather reinvigorate old, social practices of sharing, renting, joint usage, or co-working (Wruk, Oberg, Klutt, & Maurer, 2019; Muñoz & Cohen, 2018). They represent a counter-weight to commercialized forms of 'sharing' in the gig economy (Henry et al., 2021). In a similar vein, the circular economy has been supporting the spread of practices of reuse and recycling (Geissdoerfer, Savaget,

Bocken, & Hultink, 2017; Lüdeke-Freund, Gold, & Bocken, 2018). These principles, which may come in industrialized forms when applied by corporates, are however often strongest when organizations or even movements, such as those of ecovillages or transition towns, seek to promote socio-ecological transitions of unprecedented magnitude and radicalness (Loorbach, Wittmayer, Avelino, Wirth, & Frantzeskaki, 2020).

So, the social economy can provide a lens which not only increases our knowledge about new organizational practices, but also helps us better understand broader or more generalizable transformations in the economy and society (Frantzeskaki et al., 2016). What is more, the social economy appears to be *the* research context where we find answers on how to best address complex social challenges.

Unfortunately, we still do not sufficiently understand how the multitude of activities, and the imperative of change on different levels that the social economy carries, interconnect conceptually and how they can be better integrated and supported practically (Krlev, Mildenberger, & Anheier, 2020).

Open puzzles and an approach to solve them

More generally speaking, while we know that social economy organizations necessitate and simultaneously drive change in existing legal and regulatory frameworks and other institutional conditions (van Wijk, Zietsma, Dorado, Bakker, & Martí, 2018), we still lack a good understanding of how organizational actions can be most effectively leveraged to effectuate macro level change (Pel et al., 2020).

More specifically speaking, we for instance know that the social economy's transformative capacity unfolds in collaboration and not in isolated action (Phillips, Alexander, & Lee, 2017). However, we are only beginning to see more attention to how, for example, social economy and social innovation ecosystems would need to look like to unfold this capacity (Audretsch, Eichler, & Schwarz, 2022). We also lack insights into how collaboration may move beyond the level of individual relations of cooperation and to a systemic level (Schaltegger, Beckmann, & Hockerts, 2018; Sharma & Bansal, 2016), or how social economy organizations may level up their change-making and overcome factors that typically limit the process to scale, such as compartmentalization that undermines real collective action (Ometto, Gegenhuber, Winter, & Greenwood, 2018).

We believe *Social Economy Science* will provide answers to these open puzzles through its three main qualities.

First, the book merges a strand of organization theory that is strong in explaining what holds fields together (DiMaggio & Powell, 1991) with transitions theory that helps us understand grand, long-term, and fundamental revolutions and reconfigurations in systems (Geels, 2002). By bringing the two together, we are not only bridging two otherwise largely separated fields of research and research communities, but help amplify our conceptual and methodological repertoire for analysing transformations in and through the social economy.

Second, the book embraces a version and vision of the social sciences that is exploratory and prescriptive rather than merely, and supposedly neutrally, analysing the facts (see especially Mulgan, this volume). If research is to contribute to meeting grand societal challenges, it needs to use the evidence to provide concrete recommendations for action. A unique feature of the book is that *each chapter* does both: provide rigorous empirical analysis, conceptual development, or academic essay-style reasoning *and* a magnitude of prompts on how practice or policy should be improved. This merging of perspectives also helps refine conceptual and practical insights against each other in an iterative way.

Third, the book leaves much room for scholars to take on a normative stance (see for example Hueske, Willems, & Hockerts, this volume). We think this is inevitable, because all of the grand challenges of our times require evaluation (objective assessment) and valuation (judgement) by equal measure to arrive at the *right* decision for a problem, not only the most efficient one. Otherwise social economy actors and researchers alike might become stuck in reductive traps—that is, the conviction that they are addressing a problem, while in fact they are actually perpetuating the problem (Gras, Conger, Jenkins, & Gras, 2019). This may happen because they have not considered the problem in its entirety, have ignored the viewpoint of those affected, or have shied away from actively valuing (that is, normatively taxing) a certain problem to be addressed. Embracing a normative stance can thus provide clearer directions on how elements of the bigger picture fit together.

These three points in combination should provide ample guidance for future research on how to bridge micro and macro divides, how to identify the different ecosystem parts that need to fit together to unleash greater impact and innovation, or how to decipher the factors that enable durable collective action that makes real progress on social and environmental sustainability challenges.

The history of *Social Economy Science*

The legacy of this book goes back to 2019. The following year, 2020, was the year the European Social Economy Summit (EUSES) should have been hosted by the city of Mannheim on occasion of the German presidency of the European Council. In total 1500 participants from all over the world were expected to debate the future of the social economy, which had become an increasing policy priority for the EU. Due to the COVID-19 pandemic the event was postponed to 2021 and moved fully online. While presenting a delay, and maybe leading to a loss of some of the event's relational functions, this also served to boost participant numbers further.

EUSES 2021 can be considered a success judged by the numbers: it was the biggest conference on the social economy to date, with a social media reach of more than 3 million, 3000 conference participants, and more than 600 speakers in sessions of various sizes (City of Mannheim, 2021). The event has also resulted in the Mannheim Declaration on Social Economy, which identifies ten areas that require improvement to better support the social economy (European Social Economy Summit, 2021). These areas span from access to markets, to strengthening networks, to changing regulatory frameworks, to providing more targeted education—all topics to which the chapters in *Social Economy Science* make valuable contributions. While researchers and research played a role in the event, is was primarily driven by and directed at practitioners and policy makers.

Therefore we, that is, the editors of this book, had started planning a small, dedicated research event prior to the main conference based on a prompt by the division head for the subject area at the European Commission at the time. We had initially foreseen a small and short meeting of no more than eighty researchers with an open call for papers. What became of it was a two-day public online event with more than 800 registered participants, from research, practice, and policy, and with leading social economy scholars and practitioners as speakers. Some of the talks and scholarly inputs provided during our Social Economy Science Conference subsequently led to a series on 'Reconceptualizing the Social Economy' with Stanford Social Innovation Review (Krlev, Pasi, Wruk, & Bernhard, 2021), parts of which serve as building blocks for this introduction. The initial inputs by the speakers have now been worked out to full chapters that provide rich analysis, argumentation, and recommendations.

The structure of *Social Economy Science*

The three focus areas of the book relate directly to the social economy's practical relevance as well as three conceptual perspectives to analyse how the social economy promotes change. In the theory chapter, we conceptualize these as three transformation pathways within a 'multi-level model of change in and through the social economy'.

Part I: Innovation for impact

Part I and thus the first transformation pathway focuses on *innovation for impact* types of action by the social economy at the field level, or within particular ecosystems. It shows how new organizational strategies, such as information sharing or the embracement of uncertainty enable more social value creation and innovation (Huysentruyt, this volume), or how such social value and positive impact can be measured in new ways (Hehenberger and Buckland, this volume). It also considers the interface of new technological developments, such as digitization or artificial intelligence, with the social economy (Mulgan, this volume) as well as how the emergence of new organizational fields such as that of social finance and impact investing challenges the existing financial system (Nicholls and Ormiston, this volume).

Part II: Agents of change

Part II and the second transformation pathway build on the diversity of approaches in the social economy and looks at their consequences. It investigates social economy actors as *agents of change* and analyses their spill-over effects to other economic actors and fields. The contributions deal, for example, with how social enterprises contribute to the democratization of work and organizations (Battilana et al., this volume), or show how and why social economy traits may make organizations more resilient to crises (Chaves-Avila and Soler, this volume). The chapters address how social-tech ventures employ emerging technologies to address social exclusion (Calderini et al., this volume), but also how a lack in harnessing local knowledge in developing countries can limit the scaling of positive impact (Branvall, this volume). This part also looks at how the transformative potential of the social economy can be accelerated via a transfer of knowledge from as well as into higher education institutions (Nogales & Nyssens, this volume).

Part III: Partnerships

Part III and the third transformation pathway probe how *partnerships* between the social economy, public administration, and business at the local level could enhance value creation (Sancino et al., this volume). It deals with how elements of organizing can ensure that the target groups of the social economy are involved in better meeting problems and in developing adequate solutions rather than remaining passive recipients of ill-fitting interventions (Hueske, Willems, & Hockerts, this volume). It also turns to the role of social procurement in introducing innovation and impact orientation into the welfare system (Varga & Hayday, this volume), and to the use of relational contracting (Carter & Ball, this volume) as well as new national institutions as vehicles for outcomes-oriented collaboration between private, public and social economy actors (Miguel, this volume).

The mission of *Social Economy Science*

The three parts and transformation pathways are connected through a combination of organizational theory and transitions theory, as established here and developed in more detail in the theory chapter. This helps us put a particular emphasis on systems-oriented analysis within and across complex multi-stakeholder settings. Thereby we do not only seek to advance the social economy research agenda, but also project how the future of the social economy should look like for it to promote transformations of the economy towards sustainability and for it to make society more resilient.

This is why we believe *Social Economy Science* is of interest to academics in a variety of fields such as responsible and social innovation, sustainability management and sustainable finance, sustainable and social entrepreneurship, civil society and nonprofit studies, or transitions studies. We furthermore aim to offer inspiration and guideposts for impact-oriented organizational leaders and policy makers who want to promote coalitions for more effective societal progress on the full range of SDGs.

References

Amanatidou, E., Tzekou, E.-E., & Gritzas, G. (2021). Successful niche building by social innovation in social economy networks and the potential for societal transformation. *Journal of Social Entrepreneurship*, 12, 1–30. https://doi.org/10.1080/19420676.2021.1952478

Audretsch, D. B., Eichler, G. M., & Schwarz, E. J. (2022). Emerging needs of social innovators and social innovation ecosystems. *International Entrepreneurship and Management Journal*, 18(1), 217–254. https://doi.org/10.1007/s11365-021-00789-9

Avelino, F., Wittmayer, J. M., Pel, B., Weaver, P., Dumitru, A., Haxeltine, A., . . . O'Riordan, T. (2019). Transformative social innovation and (dis)empowerment. *Technological Forecasting and Social Change*, 145(3), 195–206. https://doi.org/10.1016/j.techfore.2017.05.002

Bapuji, H., Patel, C., Ertug, G., & Allen, D. G. (2020). Corona Crisis and Inequality: Why Management Research Needs a Societal Turn. *Journal of Management*, 98, 014920632092588. https://doi.org/10.1177/0149206320925881

Barman, E. (2020). Many a slip: the challenge of impact as boundary object in social finance. *Historical Social Research/Historische Sozialforschung*, 45(3), 31–52. https://doi.org/10.2307/26918403

Besharov, M. L., & Smith, W. K. (2014). Multiple institutional logics in organizations: explaining their varied nature and implications. *Academy of Management Review*, 39(3), 364–381. https://doi.org/10.5465/amr.2011.0431

Bretos, I., Bouchard, M. J., & Zevi, A. (2020). Institutional and organizational trajectories in social economy enterprises: resilience, transformation and regeneration. *Annals of Public and Cooperative Economics*, 91(3), 351–358. https://doi.org/10.1111/apce.12279

City of Mannheim (2021). *European Social Economy Summit: #EUSES Magazine*. Available at: https://www.euses2020.eu/wp-content/uploads/2021/12/EUSES-Magazine.pdf

DiMaggio, P., & Powell, W. W. (Eds). (1991). *The New Institutionalism in Organizational Analysis*. Chicago: University of Chicago Press.

Ebrahim, A., Battilana, J., & Mair, J. (2014). The governance of social enterprises: mission drift and accountability challenges in hybrid organizations. *Research in Organizational Behavior*, 34, 81–100. https://doi.org/10.1016/j.riob.2014.09.001

Euclid Network (2021). *The State of Social Enterprise in Europe—European Social Enterprise Monitor 2020–2021*. Available at: https://knowledgecentre.euclidnetwork.eu/download/european-social-enterprise-monitor-report-2020-2021/

European Commission (2022a). *EU Programme for Employment and Social Innovation (EaSI)*. Available at: https://ec.europa.eu/social/main.jsp?catId=1081

European Commission (2022b). *European Social Fund Plus (ESF+)*. Available at: https://ec.europa.eu/social/main.jsp?catId=325&langId=en

European Commission (2022c). *Recovery Plan for Europe*. Available at: https://ec.europa.eu/info/strategy/recovery-plan-europe_en

European Social Economy Summit (2021). *Mannheim Declaration on Social Economy*. Available at: https://www.euses2020.eu/mannheim-declaration/#endorse

Frantzeskaki, N., Dumitru, A., Anguelovski, I., Avelino, F., Bach, M., Best, B., . . . Rauschmayer, F. (2016). Elucidating the changing roles of civil society in urban sustainability transitions. *Current Opinion in Environmental Sustainability*, 22, 41–50. https://doi.org/10.1016/j.cosust.2017.04.008

Geels, F. W. (2002). Technological transitions as evolutionary reconfiguration processes: a multi-level perspective and a case-study. *Research Policy*, 31(8–9), 1257–1274. https://doi.org/10.1016/S0048-7333(02)00062-8

Gegenhuber, T. (2020). Countering coronavirus with open social innovation. *Stanford Social Innovation Review*. Available at: https://ssir.org/articles/entry/countering_coronavirus_with_open_social_innovation

Geissdoerfer, M., Savaget, P., Bocken, N. M.P., & Hultink, E. J. (2017). The Circular Economy - A new sustainability paradigm? *Journal of Cleaner Production*, 143, 757–768. https://doi.org/10.1016/j.jclepro.2016.12.048

Genschel, P., & Hemerijck, A. (2018). *Solidarity in Europe*. European University Institute. Policy Brief. Issue 2018/01. DOI:10.2870/106143

Gerometta, J., Haussermann, H., & Longo, G. (2005). Social innovation and civil society in urban governance: strategies for an inclusive city. *Urban Studies*, 42(11), 2007–2021. https://doi.org/10.1080/00420980500279851

Gras, D., Conger, M., Jenkins, A., & Gras, M. (2019). Wicked problems, reductive tendency, and the formation of (non-)opportunity beliefs. *Journal of Business Venturing*, 105966. https://doi.org/10.1016/j.jbusvent.2019.105966

Haugh, H. M. (2021). Social economy advancement: From voluntary to secure organizational commitments to public benefit. *Journal of Management History*. https://doi.org/10.1108/JMH-06-2020-0035

Henry, M., Schraven, D., Bocken, N., Frenken, K., Hekkert, M., & Kirchherr, J. (2021). The battle of the buzzwords: a comparative review of the circular economy and the sharing economy concepts. *Environmental Innovation and Societal Transitions*, 38(1), 1–21. https://doi.org/10.1016/j.eist.2020.10.008

Hertel, C., Bacq, S., & Belz, F.-M. (2019). It Takes a Village to Sustain a Village: A Social Identity Perspective on Successful Community-Based Enterprise Creation. *Academy of Management Discoveries*, 5(4), 438–464. https://doi.org/10.5465/amd.2018.0153

Howard-Grenville, J., Davis, G. F., Dyllick, T., Miller, C. C., Thau, S., & Tsui, A. S. (2019). Sustainable Development for a Better World: Contributions of Leadership, Management, and Organizations. *Academy of Management Discoveries*, 5(4), 355–366. https://doi.org/10.5465/amd.2019.0275

Kornberger, M., Leixnering, S., Meyer, R. E., & Höllerer, M. A. (2018). Rethinking the sharing economy: the nature and organization of sharing in the 2015 refugee crisis. *Academy of Management Discoveries*, 4(3), 314–335. https://doi.org/10.5465/amd.2016.0138

Krlev, G., Anheier, H. K., & Mildenberger, G. (2019). Results: The comparative analysis. In H. K. Anheier, G. Krlev, & G. Mildenberger (Eds.), *Social innovation: Comparative perspectives* (pp. 257–279). Abingdon, Oxon, New York: Routledge.

Krlev, G., Mildenberger, G., & Anheier, H. K. (2020). Innovation and societal transformation - what changes when the 'social' comes in? *International Review of Applied Economics*, 34(5), 529–540.

Krlev, G., Pasi, G., Wruk, D., & Bernhard, M. (2021). Reconceptualizing the social economy. *Stanford Social Innovation Review*. Available at: https://ssir.org/articles/entry/reconceptualizing_the_social_economy#

Loorbach, D., Wittmayer, J., Avelino, F., Wirth, T. von, & Frantzeskaki, N. (2020). Transformative innovation and translocal diffusion. *Environmental Innovation and Societal Transitions*, 35(5), 251–260. https://doi.org/10.1016/j.eist.2020.01.009

Lüdeke-Freund, F., Gold, S., & Bocken, N. M. P. (2018). A Review and Typology of Circular Economy Business Model Patterns. *Journal of Industrial Ecology*, 23(1), 36–61. https://doi.org/10.1111/jiec.12763

Maas Geesteranus, M., Bonnici, F., & Bruin, C. de (2021). Why 2021 can and should be the year for breakthrough collaboration. Available at: https://www.weforum.org/agenda/2021/01/why-2021-can-and-should-be-the-year-for-breakthrough-collaboration/

Mair, J., & Seelos, C. (2021). Organizations, social problems, and system change: invigorating the third mandate of organizational research. *Organization Theory*, 2(4), 263178772110548. https://doi.org/10.1177/26317877211054858

Mannan, M., & Pek, S. (2021). Solidarity in the sharing economy: the role of platform cooperatives at the base of the pyramid. In I. Qureshi, B. Bhatt, & D. M. Shukla (Eds), *Sharing Economy at the Base of the Pyramid: Opportunities and Challenges* (pp. 249–279). Singapore: Springer.

Mayer, C., & Roche, B. (Eds) (2021). *Putting Purpose into Practice: The Economics of Mutuality*. New York: Oxford University Press.

Muñoz, P., & Cohen, B. (2018). A Compass for Navigating Sharing Economy Business Models. *California Management Review*, 61(1), 114–147. https://doi.org/10.1177/0008125618795490

Nicholls, A., & Emerson, J. (2016). Social finance: capitalizing social impact. In A. Nicholls, R. Paton, & J. Emerson (Eds), *Social Finance* (pp. 1–44). Oxford: Oxford University Press.

OECD (2022). *Social Economy and Innovation*. Available at: https://search.oecd.org/cfe/leed/social-economy/

Ometto, M. P., Gegenhuber, T., Winter, J., & Greenwood, R. (2018). From balancing missions to mission drift: the role of the institutional context, spaces, and compartmentalization in the scaling of social enterprises. *Business & Society*, 4, 000765031875832. https://doi.org/10.1177/0007650318758329

Palacios-Marqués, D., García, M. G., Sánchez, M. M., & Mari, M. P. A. (2019). Social entrepreneurship and organizational performance: A study of the mediating role of distinctive competencies in marketing. *Journal of Business Research*, 101, 426–432. https://doi.org/10.1016/j.jbusres.2019.02.004

Pel, B., Haxeltine, A., Avelino, F., Dumitru, A., Kemp, R., Bauler, T., . . . Jørgensen, M. S. (2020). Towards a theory of transformative social innovation: A relational framework and 12 propositions. *Research Policy*, 49(8), 104080. https://doi.org/10.1016/j.respol.2020.104080

Périlleux, A., & Nyssens, M. (2017). Understanding cooperative finance as a new common. *Annals of Public and Cooperative Economics*, 88(2), 155–177. https://doi.org/10.1111/apce.12160

Phillips, W., Alexander, E. A., & Lee, H. (2017). Going it alone won't work! The relational imperative for social innovation in social enterprises. *Journal of Business Ethics*, 156, 315–331. https://doi.org/10.1007/s10551-017-3608-1

Purtik, H., & Arenas, D. (2017). Embedding Social Innovation: Shaping Societal Norms and Behaviors Throughout the Innovation Process. *Business & Society*, 14(2), 000765031772652. https://doi.org/10.1177/0007650317726523

Rajan, R. (2020). *The Third Pillar: How Markets and the State Leave the Community Behind* (revised and updated). New York: Penguin Books.

Schaltegger, S., Beckmann, M., & Hockerts, K. (2018). Collaborative entrepreneurship for sustainability: creating solutions in light of the UN sustainable development goals. *International Journal of Entrepreneurial Venturing*, 10(2), 131. https://doi.org/10.1504/IJEV.2018.092709

Scheidgen, K., Gümüsay, A. A., Günzel-Jensen, F., Krlev, G., & Wolf, M. (2021). Crises and entrepreneurial opportunities: digital social innovation in response to physical distancing. *Journal of Business Venturing Insights*, 15, e00222. https://doi.org/10.1016/j.jbvi.2020.e00222

Schor, J. B., & Eddy, S. (2022). The just and democratic platform? Possibilities of platform cooperativism. In D. S. Allen, Y. Benkler, R. Henderson, J. Simons, & L. Downey (Eds), *A Political Economy of Justice* (pp. 263–292). Chicago: University of Chicago Press.

Seelos, C., & Mair, J. (2017). *Innovation and Scaling for Impact: How Effective Social Enterprises Do It*. Stanford: Stanford University Press.

Sharma, G., & Bansal, P. (2016). Partners for good: how business and NGOs engage the commercial–social paradox. *Organization Studies*, 38(3–4), 341–364. https://doi.org/10.1177/0170840616683739

Smith, G., & Teasdale, S. (2012). Associative democracy and the social economy: exploring the regulatory challenge. *Economy and Society*, 41(2), 151–176. https://doi.org/10.1080/03085147.2012.661627

Smith, W. K., & Besharov, M. L. (2017). Bowing before dual gods: how structured flexibility sustains organizational hybridity. *Administrative Science Quarterly*, 1–44. https://doi.org/10.1177/0001839217750826

Teasdale, S. (2012). Negotiating tensions: how do social enterprises in the homelessness field balance social and commercial considerations? *Housing Studies*, 27(4), 514–532. https://doi.org/10.1080/02673037.2012.677015

Tihanyi, L. (2020). From "That's Interesting" to "That's Important". *Academy of Management Journal*, 63(2), 329–331. https://doi.org/10.5465/amj.2020.4002

Tracey, P., & Stott, N. (2017). Social innovation: a window on alternative ways of organizing and innovating. *Innovation: Organization & Management*, 19(1), 51–60. https://doi.org/10.1080/14479338.2016.1268924

van Wijk, J., Zietsma, C., Dorado, S., Bakker, F. G. A. de, & Martí, I. (2018). Social Innovation: Integrating Micro, Meso, and Macro Level Insights From Institutional Theory. *Business & Society*, 58(5), 887–918. https://doi.org/10.1177/0007650318789104

Wruk, D., Oberg, A., Klutt, J., & Maurer, I. (2019). The Presentation of Self as Good and Right: How Value Propositions and Business Model Features are Linked in the Sharing Economy. *Journal of Business Ethics*, 159(4), 997–1021. https://doi.org/10.1007/s10551-019-04209-5

2

Public policies to advance the social economy

François Bonnici and Veerle Klijn

Public recognition of the social economy

> *Established in the peri-urban townships in South Africa, Silulo Technologies operates IT training centres and provides job opportunities for unemployed youth across the country in cities, and smaller secondary towns. Having started as a business selling refurbished computers from the boot of a car, Silulo now has more than 40 stores, 16 franchises, and 250 employees around the country. In the past eight years, 60,000 students have completed the six-month IT training, after which more than 50 per cent found regular employment. A profitable business making a social impact, Silulo has helped to lift thousands of families out of poverty.*

This type of enterprise does not exist in South Africa alone but is an example of the social economy which is prevalent around the world. Organizations in the social economy put social and environmental concerns at the heart of their business model, prioritizing social impact over profit maximization (Organization for Economic Cooperation and Development, 2020). They carry out activities in the interests of their members and beneficiaries ('collective interest') or society at large ('general interest') and are governed accordingly (European Commission, 2020). The social economy is composed of a highly heterogeneous set of private actors, including associations, co-operatives, foundations, not-for-profit organizations, voluntary groups, and social enterprises. They exist across all industries, working in for example education, health care, and welfare, but also in technology and waste management (Mair, Wong, Moloi-Motsepe, & Bonnici, 2022).

Should this economy be of interest to the state and governments around the world? In the wake of the COVID-19 pandemic and in the face of multiple, interrelated global challenges such as growing inequality and climate change, political interest in the social economy is gaining momentum. The social economy has rapidly grown in numbers in both developed and emerging economies. In Europe there are now more than 2.8 million social businesses, accounting for 6.3 per cent of employment

François Bonnici and Veerle Klijn, *Public policies to advance the social economy*. In: *Social Economy Science*. Edited by: Gorgi Krlev, Dominika Wruk, Giulio Pasi, and Marika Bernhard, Oxford University Press. © Oxford University Press (2023).
DOI: 10.1093/oso/9780192868343.003.0002

(European Economic and Social Committee, 2017). A United Nations (UN) report (2017) estimates that globally 7 per cent of GDP is made up of the social economy.

Increasingly, governments are turning to the social economy as traditional approaches of fiscal and monetary stimulus seem no longer to suffice in building inclusive and decent economies. A record number of countries, including Vietnam (Central Institute of Economic Management, 2012), France (Law No. 2014-856), South Korea (Kwang Taek, 2010; Act No. 8217, 2017), and Tunisia (International Labour Organization, 2020) are enabling the growth of the social economy by setting up supportive legal frameworks in areas such as procurement, licensing and even tax reductions. The French law, for example, promotes the use of social clauses in public procurement, making them obligatory for municipalities and regions whose annual public procurement exceeds EUR 100 million.

Intergovernmental organizations are also recognizing the contribution of the social economy and encouraging national governments to support the sector. In 2023, for the first time, the United Nations General Assembly adopted a resolution recognizing the contribution of the social and solidarity economy to sustainable development. This came after the European Commission's (2021) Social Economy Action Plan; the OECD's (2022) recommendation on the social and solidarity economy and on social innovation; the ILO's (2022a) resolution on the social and solidarity economy, and on decent work; the African Union's (Patterson, Gombahi, & Kouadio, 2022) ten-year strategy on the social and solidarity economy; and the World Economic Forum (2022) report called 'Unlocking the Social Economy'.

This chapter outlines how the social economy has developed over time; its unique contribution; how it manifests across different parts of the world; why public policy is needed; how public policies are advancing the social economy; and advocates for further research to advance informed and evidence-based policy making in the social economy.

Historical roots of the social economy

While the social economy has recently received a lot of public interest, civic-minded organizations have been driving social progress for centuries. The historical roots of the social economy can be traced back to traditional systems and practices. Origins of the social economy are found in, for example, the spirit of *ubuntu* (humanity) in Eastern, Central, and Southern Africa; in principles of *hui* (reciprocity) in China; and in *sarvodaya* (uplifting of all) in India (Borzaga & Galera, 2014; International Labour Organization, 2022b). Mutual associations and cooperatives have been prevalent in many ancient societies. The corporate form spread through Europe later on and was adopted by municipalities, towns, and universities for political, religious, educational, and civic purposes (Davoudi, McKenna, & Olegario, 2018).

The focus on social purpose of organizations only occurred in the nineteenth century, when market economies started prioritizing the benefits of owners rather than society. This is also when the social economy as we know it today started developing as a counterpoint to uphold values and virtues and to prioritize public and community value over private value. The social economy has its roots in workers' associations emerging in the context of industrialization (Borzaga & Defourny, 2004). These associations addressed needs such as the living and working conditions of vulnerable social groups. In France, for example, the first association of jewellery workers was founded in 1834. In the United Kingdom of Great Britain and Northern Ireland, the first consumer co-operative was established in 1844 by the Rochdale Pioneers, a group of weavers working in the cotton mills in Rochdale (ILO, 2022b). However, the evolution of the workers' movement towards social legislation in the early twentieth century left the social economy losing some of its structure and socio-economic organization.

It was in the 1980s that the social economy started to gain real momentum in the wake of economic crises. Co-operatives, mutuals, and associations created a source of employment through self-management (Nyssens, 1997). A more recent form of social economy is the emergence of social enterprise and social entrepreneurship. These models appeared in the mid-1990s in response to the challenges related to the state versus market dualism (Andersen, Hulgard, & Laville, 2022). Current interest in the social economy is spurred also by citizens that are questioning their economic choices, paying more attention to the origin and manufacturing process, demanding products which are produced sustainably and ethically. This affects their behaviour not only as a consumer, but also as an employee, saver, entrepreneur, or volunteer (Mertens, 2020).

Figure 2.1 shows that over time and given different institutional contexts, the social economy has developed into a diverse set of organizations. While actors in the social economy show a great diversity in terms of legal forms, size, outreach, and sectors, as the figure highlights, they share common principles, practices, and ambitions. Actors in the social economy place social and environmental concerns at the centre of economic activity, putting purpose before profit.

Unique contribution of the social economy

The social economy has emerged as a significant and increasingly recognized economic actor, one that has proven resilient over time and during crises. In times of multiple and interrelated challenges, social economy organizations strengthen resilient communities and help manage major transitions (on social economy resilience see also Chaves-Avila & Soler-Guillen, this volume).

Social economy enterprises play an important role in addressing market and state failures (Noya & Clarence, 2007). They offer social services across communities, especially at a time when government budgets are stressed and subject to cutbacks. Social economy enterprises are successful in reaching out to vulnerable groups and re-integrating them into society. This is because they are locally anchored, and their core purpose is socially driven. Moreover, the social economy can save future

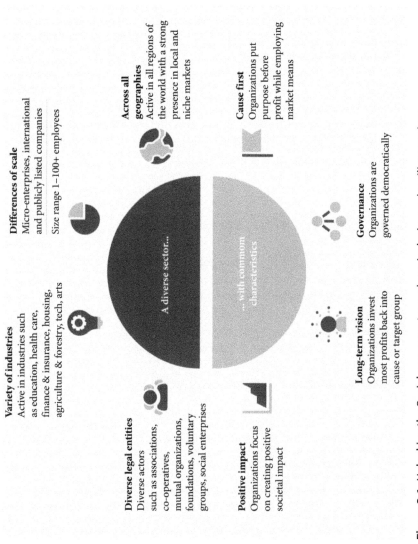

Variety of industries
Active in industries such as education, health care, finance & insurance, housing, agriculture & forestry, tech, arts

Differences of scale
Micro-enterprises, international and publicly listed companies

Size range 1–100+ employees

Across all geographies
Active in all regions of the world with a strong presence in local and niche markets

Cause first
Organizations put purpose before profit while employing market means

Diverse legal entities
Diverse actors such as associations, co-operatives, mutual organizations, foundations, voluntary groups, social enterprises

Positive impact
Organizations focus on creating positive societal impact

Long-term vision
Organizations invest most profits back into cause or target group

Governance
Organizations are governed democratically

A diverse sector...

... with common characteristics

Figure 2.1 Unlocking the Social economy, towards an inclusive and resilient society
Source: World Economic Forum (2022)

costs in public expenses, for example in healthcare by preventing diseases or in unemployment benefits through work integration trajectories (OECD, 2020).

Beyond addressing market and state failures, innovations in the social economy help transform societies to be more inclusive and resilient (Mulgan, 2019). Specific business models in the social economy, such as social enterprise, boost entrepreneurship and drive social innovation. Combining doing good with doing business, social enterprises explore different business models and unlock new sectors (Anheier, Krlev, & Mildenberger, 2019). Also, social economy organizations have by and large demonstrated a remarkable resilience and capacity as employers to maintain and create jobs in times of crises where the government and the market failed. During the Global Financial Crisis, employment in the social economy grew in countries such as Italy and Belgium, while employment in the public and private sectors decreased sharply (11.5% growth in Belgium and 20.1% growth in Italian social co-operatives) (OECD, 2020). By successfully demonstrating alternative ways of conducting economic activities, social economy enterprises inspire other economic actors to mainstream these practices.

A regional overview of the social economy

The social economy is present in every region around the world, but its size and maturity vary greatly between countries, as do the policies that govern and enable it. Confronted with different challenges and policy contexts, the social economy has developed differently across geopolitical regions (ILO, 2017a). The following paragraphs provide an overview of the social economy across these different regions and highlight public policies and legislation that are in place to support it.

Africa

The social economy has a rich history in African countries, where principles of mutual social support and solidarity have been applied for centuries. From the first decade of the twenty-first century references were made to the concept of 'social and solidarity economy', initially in French-speaking North and West Africa and then in the rest of the continent (Borzaga & Galera, 2014). Recently, the concept of social enterprise has begun to attract interest. Table 2.1 provides illustrative examples of the size of the social economy in Africa.

Increasingly recognizing the social economy as a driver of socio-economic progress, in the past decade multiple countries in Africa have adopted laws and policies to promote this type of economic activity (Table 2.1). Cabo Verde, Cameroon, Djibouti, Ghana, Mali, Senegal, and Tunisia have developed legal and institutional frameworks, while Morocco and South Africa are still in the process of developing them (ILO, 2022b).

Table 2.1 Social economy and policy actions in Africa

Size of social economy	Policy actions
• In 2019, the social and solidarity economy in South Africa accounted for 4–6% of total jobs (ILO, 2021a). • Tunisia has around 358 agricultural cooperatives, 3,000 producers' associations, 48 mutual benefit organizations, 289 microfinance institutions, and around 21,000 associations. It represents 1% of the country's GDP and 0.6% of its labour force. In 2020, there were an estimated 33,000 social enterprises in the country (ILO, 2019). • A 2020 study estimates that in Côte d'Ivoire, Egypt, Ethiopia, Ghana, Kenya, Morocco, Nigeria, Rwanda, Senegal, South Africa, Tunisia, and Uganda, social enterprises could provide about 5.5 million direct jobs in social enterprises in 2030. Among these countries, Nigeria has the highest number of social enterprises (1.2 million), while Rwanda has the lowest (4,000) (Barran et al., 2020).	• Tunisia adopted a bill on the social and solidarity economy in 2020. It amongst others creates tailored financing lines for the sector (Law N°2020-30, 30 June 2020). https://www.ilo.org/wcmsp5/groups/public/---ed_emp/---emp_ent/---coop/documents/legaldocument/wcms_750308.pdf • Cameroon prepared a National Programme for the Development of the Social Economy (PNDES) in 2020 and adopted a framework law which defines the standards, principles, and forms of social economy units and establishes structures and instruments that advance their development (Law No. 2019/004). • The ILO, the Government of Flanders, and the National Economic Development Department of South Africa are developing a social economy policy to create access to decent jobs and promote social inclusion and environmental sustainability (ILO, 2017b).

At the regional level, the African Union adopted a 10-year strategy on the Social and Solidarity Economy (2023–2033). It provides a comprehensive policy framework for actions to legitimise, support and expand the social and solidarity economy (Patterson, Gombahi, & Kouadio, 2022).

Americas

In the Americas, solidarity-based practices date back to a period before the establishment of the modern states. Nowadays, the social economy is referred to in the region also as the 'solidarity economy', the 'popular economy', the 'social sector', or the 'impact sector'. Actors that have prominence include producer cooperatives, fair trade organizations, associations, B-corps, social finance institutions, and community-based initiatives such as quilombos. Table 2.2 provides illustrative examples of the size of the social economy in the Americas.

Governments across the Americas are increasingly adopting dedicated social economy policies and/or mainstreaming the social economy into public policy frameworks (Table 2.2). Brazil, Colombia, Ecuador, Honduras, Mexico, and Uruguay have adopted legal and institutional frameworks, while the Dominican Republic is currently developing one (ILO, 2022b).

Table 2.2 Social economy and policy actions in the Americas

Size of social economy	Policy actions
The following examples illustrate the size of the social economy:	
• The Canadian province of Quebec has 11,000 SSE units, employing 220,000 persons and generating a turnover of 47.8 billion Canadian dollars (Chantier de l'économie sociale, 2022) • Costa Rica has more than 6,600 SSE units with integrated development associations (2,850) and solidarity associations (1,467) being the most prominent. The national cooperative census of 2012 indicated that 21 per cent of Costa Ricans were members of cooperatives, the majority of them in the sectors of finance and insurance, commerce, industry and agriculture (Ministry of Labour and Social Security of Costa Rica, 2020)	• Colombia was one of the first countries in Latin America to adopt a framework law on the solidarity economy in 1998. (Law 454, 1998). • Costa Rica has adopted a public policy and action plan on the social and solidarity economy for 2021–25 and established a National Chamber of the Social Solidarity Economy (Public Policy on the Social and Solidarity Economy, 2020). • In the USA, 38 states have passed benefit corporation (B Corp) legislation, allowing entrepreneurs to consider the interests of their stakeholders in addition to profit (Benefit company bar association, 2022).

Arab states

While solidarity with the less privileged is common in the Arab states, the term social economy is not often used. The most widespread term in Arabic is jamʿiyat (associations), which include community-based self-help and charity groups that provide social services in support of poor families. Social enterprises, established largely by young people, have emerged in the region in the past decade. Table 2.3 provides illustrative examples of the size of the social economy in the Arab states.

Governments of the Arab states have not developed dedicated legal frameworks or policies for the social economy. A few countries are currently developing policy and legal frameworks on specific social economy actors, such as co-operatives and social enterprises. These countries include the Occupied Palestinian Territory, Lebanon, Jordan, Saudi Arabia, and the United Arab Emirates (ILO, 2022b).

Asia and the Pacific

The strength of the social economy in the Asia and the Pacific region can be traced back to the principles of solidarity, reciprocity, and mutuality that are deeply rooted in the region's diverse cultures and traditions. Examples include the principles of hui (reciprocity) in China, sarvodaya (uplifting of all) in India, and gotong royong (working together) in Indonesia. In the region, the social economy is also referred

Table 2.3 Social economy and policy actions in Arab states

Size of social economy	Policy actions
The following examples illustrate the size of the social economy:	
• In Jordan, a total of 1,592 co-operatives were registered in 2018 with a total membership of 142,000 persons, 79 creating around 20,000 direct job opportunities (Jordanian National Commission for Women, 2017). Social enterprises are mainly registered under the umbrella of not-for-profit organizations (Oxfam, 2018). • In 2018, the 70 Kuwaiti consumer co-operatives, which operate around 3,000 outlets, controlled 65 per cent of the food and beverage market in the country (Oxford Business Group, 2018).	• There are no dedicated policies or legal frameworks in place at a national level for the social economy in the Arab states.

to as the 'impact economy' and 'inclusive economy'. Third sector organizations and social enterprises are particularly prevalent in Asia and the Pacific. Table 2.4 offers some illustrative examples of the size of the social economy in Asia and the Pacific.

Multiple countries in Asia and the Pacific have adopted policy frameworks in support of the social economy, or in support of particular actors in the social economy such as social enterprises (see Table 2.4). Governments which have developed laws include Cambodia, Singapore, China, Thailand, South Korea, Japan, Malaysia, Indonesia, and the Philippines (ILO, 2022b).

At the regional level, economic ministers from the Association of Southeast Asian Nations (ASEAN) endorsed the 'Guidelines for the Promotion of Inclusive Business in ASEAN', making ASEAN the first region in the world to endorse such a set of guidelines to promote inclusive business (United Nations Research Institute for Social Development, 2018).

Europe and Central Asia

Europe has a strong history of social economy. Its roots can be traced back to the Industrial Revolution and the need to address the living and working conditions of vulnerable groups. Different terms are used in the region, including 'social and solidarity economy', 'social enterprise', 'impact economy', and 'social innovation'. Prominent social economy actors in Europe are co-operatives, mutuals, associations, social enterprises, and foundations. Table 2.4 provides illustrative examples of the size of the social economy in Europe.

The majority of European countries have developed policies and programmes to support the social economy (Table 2.5). In the past decade alone, sixteen European

Table 2.4 Social economy and policy actions in Asia and the Pacific

Size of the social economy	Policy actions
The following examples illustrate the size of the social economy:	
• In South Korea, the social economy is estimated to be worth 3% of the country's GDP (British Council, 2015).	• South Korea set up the Social Enterprise Promotion Act in 2007, providing social entrepreneurs with access to professional services, technical assistance, rental subsidies, and reduced taxes (Act No. 2817, 2017).
• In China, there were more than 30,000 co-operative enterprises in 2020. In the same year, urban co-operatives employed 690,000 persons (National Bureau of Statistics of China, 2021).	• In 2022 Malaysia launched the Social Entrepreneurship Action Framework 2030, which outlines strategies to support social enterprises' growth and competitivity, by enhancing awareness, reach, and their capacity and competency through provision of training on adaptation of technology and digitalization, access to finance and markets (SEMy2030, 2022).
• In New Zealand, the top 30 co-operatives, mutuals and societies have a total revenue of 42.3billion New Zealand dollars (approximately US$30.5 billion) and a membership of 1.4 million and employ close to 48,500 individuals (International Cooperative Alliance-Asia and the Pacific (2020).	
• In India, the number of co-operatives grew from 316,000 with more than 142 million members in 1984–1985 to 854,000 with more than 290 million members in 2016–17 (National Cooperative Union of India, 2018). The country reports close up to 2 million social enterprises (Bertelsmann Stiftung, 2018).	• The Government of Thailand established a Social Enterprise Office in 2010 and adapted the Social Enterprise Promotion Act in 2019 to facilitate tax relief and incentives for social enterprises (Act B.E. 2562, 2019).

Union Member States have adopted legislation on social enterprise and eleven have created strategies or policies for supporting social enterprise development (European Commission, 2020).

At regional level, the European Commission (EC) has taken several policy initiatives to support the social economy. Building on the Social Business Initiative introduced in 2011 and the Start-up and Scale-up Initiative introduced in 2016, the EC launched an Action Plan for the Social Economy in 2021.

The need for public policy

In the wake of the COVID-19 pandemic exposing significant and systemic gaps in our societal and economic architecture, and in the face of multiple, interrelated global challenges such as growing inequality and climate change, interest in the social economy is gaining momentum. Increasingly, governments are recognizing the social economy in public policies as a driver of a more inclusive and sustainable economy.

While there are examples of robust policies in place around the world to advance the social economy (see Tables 2.1–2.5), in the majority of countries today social

Table 2.5 Social economy and policy actions in Europe and Central Asia

Size of social economy	Policy actions
The following examples illustrate the size of the social economy:	

The following examples illustrate the size of the social economy:

- In 2016, the 28 countries that made up the European Union had more than 2.8 million SE units. In Europe as a whole, SE units are significant employers, for instance in the agriculture, finance, energy, and retail sectors. Including both paid and non-paid employment, they represent a workforce of more than 19.1 million, with more than 82.8 million volunteers, equivalent to 5.5 million full-time workers (European Economic Social Committee, 2017).
- In 2020, the Russian Federation had more than 50,000 co-operatives in the country (Federal State Statistics Service of the Russian Federation, 2020).

- In 1991, the Italian government was the first European country to legally recognize the 'social co-operative' which identifies two types of enterprises. Type A co-operatives provide social and care services while type B co-operatives facilitate work integration for certain categories of disadvantaged groups (Italian Law 381/1991).
- In 2018, the Swedish government launched a new strategy for social enterprise, social entrepreneurship, and social innovation. The strategy aims to strengthen the development of social enterprise so that they can participate in solving societal challenges and contribute to sustainable development (Strategy for Social Enterprise, 2018).

economy enterprises operate in a policy vacuum. The social economy is often not politically recognized, not well regulated, not incentivized, and not financially supported. And given the unique character of social economy enterprises—putting social and environmental impact before profit maximization—existing legal forms and company legislation are not well fit for purpose.

As a result, the social economy faces multiple barriers which prevent it from growing and scaling its impact. The European Social Enterprise Monitor, a cross-country quantitative study, finds that the top five most influential barriers are: lack of options to finance the organization once started; overly complex public financing; lack of patient capital; lack of public support schemes; and a weak lobby for social entrepreneurship (Dupain et al., 2021). Even in European countries nearly 70 per cent of social enterprises rate public support for their work as non-existent or very low.

Worldwide, social economy enterprises are faced with limited visibility, lack of supportive legal and regulatory frameworks, lack of verification and standards, inadequate financial resources and access to markets (World Economic Forum, 2022). Representative organizations of the social economy, such as Social Enterprise World Forum and Catalyst 2030, call on governments to design appropriate legislation and implement (funding) programmes to take away these barriers (Catalyst 2030, 2021).

Public support is instrumental in enabling the social economy to drive progress. While limited data is available, countries where governments have adopted supportive policy measures appear to see more social economic activity. The Thomson

Reuters Foundation runs an opinion poll on 'The best countries to be a social entrepreneur'. From its sample of respondents in more than forty countries, it identifies six key areas which are critical for social entrepreneurs to thrive, ranking government support as the number one key area. Countries which have supportive government policies in place are considered among the best countries to be a social entrepreneur.

This is not surprising, as all sectors of industry and the economy have only grown with government investment, infrastructure, incentives, and supportive policies. It is widely accepted, for example, that entrepreneurship is more prevalent in an environment where there is strong government understanding and support (Henrekson & Johansson, 2009; Stam et al., 2012; Acs et al., 2014). Government policies have the power to influence and encourage entrepreneurial activities in areas that are perceived to be neglected, problematic, suffering from market failures or in need of new solutions (Audretsch et al., 2007; Minniti, 2008). The role of the state is thus critical in order to grow the social economy. The next section outlines some of the most significant policy levers which governments can utilize to further strengthen the social economy.

Policy levers to advance the social economy

International organizations and institutions such as the OECD, ILO, and European Commission have produced extensive resources on policy actions that support the social economy, based on examples from countries around the world (OECD, 2017; ILO, 2022a). There has been some positive evolution over the past couple of years, which at least in some countries has led to a clearer vision of what social economy organizations can do, for instance in relation to promoting social innovation or other socio-economic goals (Krlev, Einarsson, Wijkström, & Mildenberger, 2020). Policy levers vary from designing enabling legal frameworks to supporting the production of data on the social economy. The most significant levers and concrete examples of individual policy actions that have already been taken by some national governments are briefly described below.

Designing enabling legal and institutional frameworks

Governments can design legal and regulatory frameworks in collaboration with social economy actors to improve the visibility and recognition of the sector. Dedicated legal forms for social economy organizations can subsequently serve as a reference and basis for targeted public support schemes, such as public procurement and potential tax benefits. Given that the social economy cuts across many economic and social sectors, the institutional framework that governs the social economy is ideally coordinated across policies and governments departments. Moreover, as business models in the social economy develop and change it is useful to establish regular evaluations of the laws and policies and update them where needed.

> ### Box 2.1 Country example—Mexico
>
> In 2012, Mexico adopted the Social and Solidarity Economy Law which creates the legal basis for the social economy, and its promotion through public policy. The law also established the National Institute of the Social Economy, an administrative body attached to the Ministry of Economy which is tasked with the promotion of the social economy through support programmes.

Supporting access to finance

Access to finance and funding is a critical policy lever for the social economy to grow. The public sector can support access to finance by social economy organizations through several mechanisms. Government can act as an investor and funder itself, financing social economy organizations in compliance with regulations regarding aid to enterprises, to improve the long-term financial sustainability of these entities. Besides this, government can encourage the participation of mainstream financial providers and social investors in financing the social economy. This can be done through offering fiscal incentives, alleviating regulatory barriers, leveraging public funds to de-risk private funding, and developing hybrid mechanisms that blend public and private investment (Krlev et al., 2021).

> ### Box 2.2 Country example—European Union
>
> In 2015 the EC and European Investment Fund (EIF) launched the EaSI Guarantee Instrument. Through this instrument, the EIF offers guarantees and counter-guarantees to financial intermediaries, thereby providing them with a partial credit risk protection for newly originated loans to eligible beneficiaries. Thanks to the risk-sharing mechanism, the EaSI Guarantee Instrument enables selected social enterprise finance providers to provide new loans to expand their outreach to social enterprises, facilitating access to finance for target groups who have difficulties in accessing the conventional credit market. To date, 5,500 social enterprises have received support through this instrument (European Investment Fund, 2022).

Enabling access to public and private markets

Another powerful tool to support the social economy development is ensuring its access to public and private markets. In 2017, public procurement alone made up about 12 per cent of GDP across OECD countries, totalling more than USD 674 billion across the OECD. Through public procurement, the public sector can buy goods and services from social economy actors that deliver social and environmental value (on social procurement see Varga & Hayday, this volume). In this way, public procurement becomes a vehicle to meet social, environmental, and economic objectives, such as the reintegration of the long-term unemployed into labour markets, or social and work integration of people from vulnerable groups (OECD, 2022). Besides public procurement, governments can also encourage the private sector to procure from the social economy through, for example, fiscal incentives.

Box 2.3 Country example—United Kingdom

The Public Services (Social Value) Act of the United kingdom came into force on 31 January 2013. It requires public authorities to have regard to economic, social and environmental well-being in connection with public services contracts. The minimum weighing that should be applied to social value is 10%.

Strengthening skills and business development support

Education, training, mentoring, and business development support are also important policy levers to strengthen the social economy. Governments can leverage public funding instruments to facilitate access to dedicated education and training programmes on the social economy in formal and non-formal education. Particular focus is needed on the accessibility of these programmes, both in urban and in rural areas.

Box 2.4 Country example—South Korea

In 2010, South Korea established the Korea Social Enterprise Promotion Agency to foster and promote social enterprises and co-operatives. It provides a range of services, such as training, marketing support, and others, to strengthen the management capacity.

Supporting the production of data

Finally, governments can contribute to the collection of reliable and comparable statistics on the social economy. Policies need an evidence base, but currently there is a lack of data on the scale, scope, and progress of the social economy. National statistical authorities can develop and implement satellite accounts aimed at establishing the effective contribution of the social economy to economic growth and job creation. Besides this, data collection and production by governments could also help measure the various impacts of the social economy on, for example, social cohesion and reducing income inequality.

Box 2.5 Country example—Brazil

In Brazil, for example, the government created the National Secretariat for Solidarity Economy (SENAES) back in 2003, which was, among others, tasked with conducting a mapping study of the Social and Solidarity Economy. On the basis of this information a data bank called the National Solidarity Economy Information System (SIES) was established, which provides data on geographical distribution, types of organizations, sectoral activities, and so forth (ILO, 2017).

Contextualized and evidence-based policy making

The policies that are needed to advance the social economy differ per country and context, and may evolve over time. While there are a range of policy levers that governments can use, which of these policy tools is most effective to strengthen the social economy is not yet clear and depends on specific contexts.

There is no one-size-fits-all policy solution to support the social economy. The social economy manifests differently across the world and is confronted with different socio-economic challenges. Even the name for this type of economic activity differs per region, ranging from social and solidarity economy in Africa to inclusive business or impact economy in Asia. National governments are therefore encouraged to use context-specific quantitative and qualitative data inputs in designing their policies. The OECD Recommendation on Social and Solidarity Economy and Social Innovation (2022) reflects this by stating that governments should 'develop regular evaluation requirements to improve and update laws and policies to evolve with the needs of social economy organizations and including stakeholder feedback as well as qualitative and quantitative evidence'.

The motivation for evidence-based policy making is not unique to the social economy. While it is well established in medicine and public health, increasingly in other policy areas rigorous attempts are being made to base policy decisions on scientific and empirical evidence. Academic research can provide important empirical facts and advance our understanding of policy effects, both ex ante and ex post (Leuz, 2018). The World Bank (2021) has stated: 'In simple terms, statistics are the evidence on which policies are built. They help identify needs, set goals and monitor progress. Without good statistics, the development process is blind: policy-makers cannot learn from their mistakes and the public cannot hold them accountable.'

The role of future research

A major obstacle to effective policy making is the significant lack of data and research on the social economy and a lack of consensus around which metrics to use. The variables that are currently used to measure the size of the social economy are often standard economic performance variables such as contribution to GDP, revenues/expenditures, and number of jobs (United Nations Research Institute for Social Development, 2021). However, the social economy's contribution goes far beyond economic growth and job creation. As Artis et al. (2015, pp. 62–63) point out, 'social economy statistics has difficulties in expressing the full range of characteristics of this economy . . . Attempts to better capture Social Economy's contribution in areas such as democratizing the economy, lowering economic inequalities and acting as countervailing economic power have been made . . . but are still far from being included in national statistical frameworks.' Aside from a few recent studies, mostly in Europe (see Boxes 2.1–2.6), there has not been any systematic collection of data on the social economy. Also, very few attempts have been made to evaluate the impact of past policy interventions on the social economy. Thus, in most cases policy-makers don't have much information about the size, scope and needs of the social economy to base their decisions on.

Box 2.6 Examples of mapping the social economy

There are some attempts to map (specific actors in) the social economy. A few examples:

- The ILO has financed mapping studies of public policies on social and solidarity economy in several countries (2017).
- The EC has financed mapping studies of social enterprise in Europe (2020).
- The British Council has financed mapping studies of social enterprise in more than 25 different countries across the world (2010–2022).

Academic research can play an important role in contributing to the production of statistics on the social economy and evaluate the effectiveness of policies that are in place to support it. Suggestions for future research include:

1. Improve methodologies for the systematic collection and organization of statistical information on the social economy.
2. Develop variables (indicators) for the assessment of the value and performance of the social economy and visualization of its characteristics.
3. Develop mechanisms of performance and impact comparison between social economy entities and other forms of business.

4. Analyse policy interventions that have been implemented to support the social economy, and determine which of these have been most effective in advancing the social economy.

Conclusions

The COVID-19 pandemic has made it evident that the current global economic system lacks the appropriate tools to tackle societal challenges in a timely, adequate, and equitable way. An era of multiple, interrelated challenges is an opportune time to invest in the social economy, which offers an alternative economic model to help achieve our shared objectives for more inclusive and resilient societies.

Around 2.8 million social economy enterprises in Europe alone, and millions more around the world, are dedicating their time to solving societal challenges while running sustainable enterprises. Like other economic sectors, the social economy creates revenues, jobs, and profits, but in addition it creates social and environmental impact and transforms lives for the better. Innovations from the social economy, which pioneers inclusive and sustainable business models, hold lessons for the rest of the economy.

International organizations are recognizing the potential of the social economy and are establishing regional and global efforts to improve the visibility and support the advancement of the social economy. Increasingly, national governments, states, and cities are enabling the growth of the social economy by setting up supportive legal frameworks and policy actions. These efforts are crucial to unlock the potential of the social economy, which still faces barriers of a lack of legal recognition, inadequate financial resources, and restricted access to markets.

While there are a range of policy levers that national and local governments can use to advance the social economy, which of these policy tools is most effective is not yet clear due to a lack of data and research. Thus, in most cases policy-makers don't have much information about the size, scope, and needs of the social economy to base their decisions on. To allow for more effective policy making, there is a role for academic research in contributing to the production of statistics on the social economy and evaluate the effectiveness of policies that are in place to support it.

Ultimately, this will lead to better public policy that enables the social economy to thrive and play a larger role in creating more inclusive and resilient societies.

References

Acs, Z. J., Autio, E., & Szerb, L. (2014). National systems of entrepreneurship: measurement issues and policy implications. *Research Policy*, 43(3), 476–449.

Act B.E. 2562 (2019). *Social Enterprise Promotion Act Thailand.* Available at: https://www.osep.or.th/en/elementor-2866/

Act No. 8217 (2017). Social Enterprise Promotion Act South Korea. Available at: https://www.ilo.org/dyn/natlex/docs/ELECTRONIC/78610/84122/F-684569511/KOR78610%20Eng%202012.pdf

Andersen, L. L., Hulgard, L., & Laville, J. (2022). *The Social and Solidarity Economy: Roots and Horizons.* Available at: https://www.researchgate.net/publication/356970900_The_Social_and_Solidarity_Economy_Roots_and_Horizons

Anheier, H. K., Krlev, G., & Mildenberger, G. (Eds) (2019). *Social Innovation: Comparative Perspectives.* Abingdon: Routledge.

Audretsch, D., Grilo, I., & Thurik, R. (2007). Explaining entrepreneurship and the role of policy: a framework. In: Thurik, A. R., Audretsch, D. B., & Grilo, I. (Eds.) (2007). *Handbook of research on entrepreneurship policy* (pp. 1–17). Cheltenham: Edward Elgar.

Artis, A., Rousselière, D., & Bouchard, M. (2015), Does the social economy count? How should we measure it? Representations of the social economy through statistical indicators. In Marie J. Bouchard and Damien Rousselière (Eds), *The Weight of the Social Economy: An International Perspective* (pp. 39–68). Brussels: CIRIEC & P.I.E. Peter Lang. https://doi.org/10.3726/978-3-0352-6545-3

Barran, E. et al. (2020). *Social Enterprises as Job Creators in Africa. The Potential of Social Enterprise to Provide Employment Opportunities in 12 African Countries 2020–2030. Study.* Available at: https://www.siemens-stiftung.org/wp-content/uploads/2020/10/studie-socialenterprisesasjobcreatorsinafrica-part1-siemensstiftung.pdf

Benefit Company Bar Association (2022). *US Benefit Corporation Legislation.* Available at: https://benefitcompanybar.org/resources/us-benefit-corporation-legislation/

Bertelsmann Stiftung (2018). *The Indian Social Enterprise Landscape: Innovation for an Inclusive Future.* Available at: https://www.bertelsmann-stiftung.de/en/publications/publication/did/the-indian-social-enterprise-landscape

Borzaga, C., & Defourny, J. (Eds.) (2004), *The Emergence of Social Enterprise.* London: Routledge.

Borzaga, C., & Galera, G. (2014). *The Potential of the Social Economy for Local Development in Africa: An Exploratory Report.* European Parliament. https://euricse.eu/wp-content/uploads/2015/03/EXPO-DEVE_ET2014433787_EN.pdf

British Council (2015). *Think Global, Trade Social.* Available at: https://www.britishcouncil.org/sites/default/files/seuk_british_council_think_global_report.pdf.

Catalyst 2030 (2021). *New Allies: How Governments Can Unlock the Potential of Social Entrepreneurs for the Common Good.* Available at: https://catalyst2030.net/wp-content/uploads/2021_New-Allies_How-governments-can-unlock-the-potential-of-social-entrepreneurs-for-the-common-good_vpublish.pdf

Central Institute of Economic Management (2012). *Social Enterprise in Vietnam: Concept, Context and Policies.* Available at: https://www.britishcouncil.vn/sites/default/files/social-enterprise-in-vietnam-concept-context-policies.pdf

Chantier de l'économie sociale (2022, 20 September). *Discover Social Economy in Quebec.* Available at: https://chantier.qc.ca/?lang=en

Davoudi, L., McKenna, C., & Olegario, R. (2018). The historical role of the corporation in society. *Journal of the British Academy*, 6(s1): 17–47. Available at: https://doi.org/10.5871/jba/006s1.017

Dupain, W., Pilia, O., Wunsch, M., Hoffmann, P., Scharpe, K., Mair, J., Raith, M., & Bosma, N. (2021). *The State of Social Enterprise in Europe: European Social Enterprise Monitor 2020–2021*. Euclid Network. Available at: https://knowledgecentre.euclid network.eu/2021/05/25/european-social-enterprise-monitor-report-2020-2021/

European Commission (2020). *Social Enterprises and Their Ecosystems in Europe. Comparative Synthesis Report*. Authors: Carlo Borzaga, Giulia Galera, Barbara Franchini, Stefania Chiomento, Rocío Nogales and Chiara Carini. Luxembourg: Publications Office of the European Union. https://europa.eu/!Qq64ny

European Commission (2021). *Social Economy Action Plan*. Available at: https://ec.europa.eu/social/main.jsp?catId=1537&langId=en

European Economic Social Committee (2017). *Recent evolutions of the social economy in the European Union*. Available at: https://www.eesc.europa.eu/sites/default/files/files/qe-04-17-875-en-n.pdf

European Investment Fund (2022). *EaSI—Guarantee Financial Instrument: Implementation Update*. Available at: https://www.eif.org/what_we_do/microfinance/easi/easi-implementation-status.pdf

Federal State Statistics Service of the Russian Federation (2020), *Unified interdepartmental statistical information system*. Available at: https://fedstat.ru

Henrekson, M., & Johansson, D. (2009). Competencies and institutions fostering high-growth firms. *Foundations and Trends in Entrepreneurship*, 5(1), 1–80.

International Cooperative Alliance—Asia and the Pacific (2020, 26 February). Second ICA-AP Meeting on Development of Cooperatives in Pacific Islands [blog post]. Available at: https://www.ica.coop/en/newsroom/news/second-ica-ap-meeting-development-cooperatives-pacific-islands

International Labour Organization (2017a). *Public Policies for Social and Solidarity Economy. Assessing Progress in Seven Countries*. Available at: https://www.ilo.org/wcmsp5/groups/public/---ed_emp/---emp_ent/---coop/documents/publication/wcms_582778.pdf

International Labour Organization (2017b). *Development of a Social Economy Policy in South Africa (Government of Flanders & National Economic Development Department of South Africa)*. Available at: https://www.ilo.org/global/topics/cooperatives/projects/WCMS_501549/lang---en/index.htm

International Labour Organization (2019). *Public Policies for the Social and Solidarity Economy and their Role in the Future of Work: The Case of Tunisia*. Available at: https://www.ilo.org/global/topics/cooperatives/publications/WCMS_740732/lang---en/index.htm

International Labour Organization (2020, 24 June). *The Tunisian Parliament Adopts a Bill on the Social and Solidarity Economy*. Available at: https://www.ilo.org/global/topics/cooperatives/news/WCMS_749012/lang---en/index.htm

International Labour Organization (2021a). *South Africa's Social and Solidarity Economy: A Study of Its Characteristics and Conditions.* Available at: https://www.ilo.org/wcmsp5/groups/public/---africa/---ro-abidjan/documents/publication/wcms_840760.pdf

International Labour Organization (2021b). *Strengthening Social and Solidarity Economy Policy in Asia. Spotlight on Malaysia.* Available at: https://www.ilo.org/wcmsp5/groups/public/---ed_emp/---emp_ent/---coop/documents/publication/wcms_822183.pdf

International Labour Organization (2022a). *Resolution Concerning Decent Work and the Social and Solidarity Economy.* ILC.110/Resolution II. https://www.ilo.org/wcmsp5/groups/public/---ed_norm/---relconf/documents/meetingdocument/wcms_848633.pdf

International Labour Organization (2022b). *Decent Work and the Social and Solidarity Economy.* Available at: https://www.ilo.org/wcmsp5/groups/public/---ed_norm/---relconf/documents/meetingdocument/wcms_841023.pdf

Italian Law 381/1991. *Law on Social Cooperatives.* Available at: http://extwprlegs1.fao.org/docs/pdf/ita162602.pdf

Jordanian National Commission for Women (2017). *The Current Status, Structure, and Legislation Framework of Cooperatives in Jordan 2016 (from Gender Perspectives).* Policy paper. Available at: https://www.women.jo/sites/default/files/2020-02/Policy%20Paper%20Towards%20Enhancing%20the%20Role%20of%20Women%20in%20Cooperatives.pdf

Krlev, G., Einarsson, T., Wijkström, F., Heyer, L., & Mildenberger, G. (2020). The policies of social innovation: a cross-national analysis. *Nonprofit and Voluntary Sector Quarterly*, 49(3), 457–478. https://doi.org/10.1177/0899764019866505

Krlev, G., Sauer, S., Scharpe, K., Mildenberger, G., Elsemann, K., & Sauerhammer, M. (2021). *Financing Social Innovation—International Evidence. Centre for Social Investment (CSI).* University of Heidelberg & Social Entrepreneurship Network Deutschland e.V. (SEND).

Kwang Teak, L. (2010). Social Enterprise Promotion Act: the case of South Korea. *Asian Dialogue on Economy.* http://www.socioeco.org/bdf_fiche-document-815_en.html

Law No. 2019/004 of 25 April 2019, *Framework Bill Governing Social Economy in Cameroon.* Available at: https://www.prc.cm/en/multimedia/documents/7473-law-n-2019-004-du-25-04

Law No. 2014-856 (2014). *Law on Social and Solidarity Economy France.* Available at: https://www.oecd-ilibrary.org/docserver/9789264268500-10-en.pdf?expires=1663855260&id=id&accname=guest&checksum=2B7455BDE930CB71B038704E91FBAA10

Leuz, C. (2018). Evidence-based policymaking: promise, challenges and opportunities for accounting and financial markets research. *Accounting and Business Research*, 48(5), 582–608. https://doi.org/10.1080/00014788.2018.1470151

Mair, J., Wong, J., Moloi-Motsepe, P., & Bonnici, F. (2022, 16 September). *5 Ways Governments Can Unlock a More Social Economy.* Available at: https://www.weforum.org/agenda/2022/05/5-ways-governments-unlock-social-economy/

Mertens, S. (2020). L'économie sociale tient le bon rythme. Libre Eco weekend Interview by Vincent Slits, pp. 2–3.

Ministry of Labour and Social Security of Costa Rica (2020). *Política Pública de Economía Social Solidaria 2021–2025.* Available at: https://www.mtss.go.cr/elministerio/despacho/politica_ESS.pdf

Minniti, M. (2008). The role of government policy on entrepreneurial activity: productive, unproductive, or destructive? *Entrepreneurship Theory and Practice*, 32(5), 779–790. https://doi.org/10.1111/j.1540-6520.2008.00255.x

Mulgan, G. (2019). *Social Innovation: How Societies Find the Power to Change.* Bristol: Policy Press.

National Bureau of Statistics of China (2021). *China Statistical Yearbook.* Available at: http://www.stats.gov.cn/tjsj/ndsj/2021/indexeh.htm

National Cooperative Union of India (2018). *Indian Cooperative Movement. A Statistical Profile: Sustainable Development and Growth through Cooperatives.* Available at: https://www.kribhco.net/assets/img/Coorporative/Statistical_Profile_2018.pdf

National Policy for the Promotion of the Social and Solidarity Economy Mali (2014). Available at: https://base.socioeco.org/docs/politique-nationale-de-lc3a9conomie-sociale-et-solidaire.pdf

Noya, A. & Clarence, E. (Eds) (2007). *The Social Economy. Building Inclusive Economies,* OECD. Local Economic and Employment Development (LEED). Paris: OECD Publishing.

Nyssens, M. (1997). Popular economy in the south, third sector in the north: are they signs of a germinating economy of solidarity? *Annals of Public and Cooperative Economics*, 68(2), 171–200.

Organisation for Economic Cooperation and Development (2017). *Boosting Social Enterprise Development. Good Practice Compendium.* Available at: https://www.oecd-ilibrary.org/docserver/9789264268500-10-en.pdf?expires=1660724543&id=id&accname=guest&checksum=884BA463704641545E72542141A83462

Organisation for Economic Cooperation and Development (2020). *Social Economy and the COVID-19 Crisis: Current and Future Roles, OECD Policy Responses to Coronavirus (COVID-19).* Paris: OECD Publishing. Available at: https://doi.org/10.1787/f904b89f-en

Organisation for Economic Cooperation and Development (2022). *Recommendation on Social and Solidarity Economy and Social Innovation.* https://www.oecd.org/cfe/leed/social-economy/social-economy-recommendation/

Oxfam (2018). *MEDUP! Jordan Social Enterprise Study.* Available at: https://o4my.org/wp-content/uploads/2021/03/Jordan-Country-Study_compressed.pdf

Oxford Business Group (2018). *Traditional Retail Segments Show Positive Trends, while Kuwait's E-Commerce Market Undergoes Rapid Expansion.* Available at: https://oxfordbusinessgroup.com/overview/ready-shop-traditional-and-online-retail -segments-show-positive-upwards-trends-coming-year

Patterson, J., Gombahi, F., & Kouadio, M. (2022, 10 May). *L'Economie Sociale et Solidaire: un puissant outil de développement pour l'Afrique* [blog post]. Available at: https://www. ilo.org/global/topics/cooperatives/sse/WCMS_844674/lang—fr/index.htm

Public Policy on the Social and Solidarity Economy Costa Rica (2020). Available at: https://www.mtss.go.cr/elministerio/despacho/politica_ESS.pdf

Stam, E., Bosma, N., Van Witteloostuijn, A., de Jong, J., Bogaert, S., Edwards, N., & Jaspers, F. (2012). *Ambitious Entrepreneurship. A Review of the Academic Literature and New Directions for Public Policy.* Den Haag: Adviesraad voor Wetenschap en Technologie-beleid (AWT).

United Nations (2017). *Cooperatives in Social Development.* Report of the Secretary-General. https://digitallibrary.un.org/record/1298696?ln=en

United Nations Research Institute for Social Development (2018). *Mapping of Intergovernmental Documentation on Social and Solidarity Economy.* Available at: https:// knowledgehub.unsse.org/wp-content/uploads/2020/11/2018-EN-Mapping-of-Inter governmental-Documentation-on-Social-and-Solidarity-Economy-UNTFSSE.pdf

United Nations Research Institute for Social Development (2021). *Producing Statistics on Social and Solidarity Economy—Policy Recommendations and Directions for Future Research.* Available at: https://knowledgehub.unsse.org/wp-content/uploads/ 2021/08/WP-2021-SSE-Stats-Chaves-Avila.pdf

World Economic Forum (2022). *Unlocking the Social Economy, Towards an Inclusive and Resilient Society.* Available at: https://www.weforum.org/reports/unlocking-the-social-economy-towards-an-inclusive-and-resilient-society-davos2022/

3

Social economy

Between common identity and accelerating social change

Gorgi Krlev, Dominika Wruk, Giulio Pasi, and Marika Bernhard

The social economy: An unwieldy phenomenon

The social economy is home to a plethora of meanings and represents an umbrella concept that connects a variety of organizational phenomena. The social economy spans from classical forms of social and solidarity-based organizations (Nogales & Nyssens, this volume), to social-tech start-ups (Calderini, Gerli, Chiodo, & Pasi, this volume), to new forms of collective and participatory intelligence (Mulgan, this volume), to the whole field of social and impact-oriented investment (Nicholls & Ormiston, this volume). This richness in meaning is stimulating for what the social economy can be and achieve—and, in the same way, what social economy science can help scholars understand. However, the richness also presents a challenge to form and preserve a common identity within what we consider an organizational issue field, rather than a clear-cut industry or sector (Oberg, Lefsrud, Meyer, 2021).

At the same time, there is an intense debate on the transformative power of the social economy (Chaves-Avila & Soler, this volume). That debate comprises the social economy's important role in (re-)shaping society and economy in a way that includes the socially excluded, not only as target groups but as co-creators (Hueske, Willems, & Hockerts, this volume) or co-decision makers (Battilana, Krol, Sheppard-Jones, & Ubalijoro, this volume). It also covers how embracing social economy principles in new processes of organizing (Huysentruyt, this volume) or in field governance (Carter & Ball, this volume) may help us better meet societal challenges that are currently under-addressed by commercially driven enterprises or policy. In this regard the social economy is a driver of change, similar to how technological or scientific progress has produced profound social evolutions or revolutions (Geels, 2005b).

Due to their multiplicity and their orientation towards positive change, social economy organizations should be central in the growing body of academic work interested in understanding the characteristics, activities, and outcomes of

Gorgi Krlev et al., *Social economy.* In: *Social Economy Science.* Edited by: Gorgi Krlev, Dominika Wruk, Giulio Pasi, and Marika Bernhard, Oxford University Press. © Oxford University Press (2023). DOI: 10.1093/oso/9780192868343.003.0003

organizational activities that addresses social and environmental sustainability challenges (Hehenberger & Buckland, this volume). They should play important roles in research that investigates recent technological and social developments for promoting the scaling of social innovations (Brännvall, this volume). And they should be prominent in research that investigates how new governance arrangements can foster social value creation at different levels, including new collaborations at the local level (Sancino et al., this volume), shifts in the way public procurement is administered (Varga & Hayday, this volume), or changes in how national institutions are designed in support of worthy social outcomes (Miguel, this volume).

While there is some consensus on the role of the social economy as a mainstay of future social organization, conceptualizations of the social economy remain partial and blurry.

An empirical, phenomenon-grounded reason for the blur is that the social economy is subject to constant change: social enterprises have become an established organizational form and have strongly grown in number and visibility over the past decades (Battilana & Lee, 2014). New types of purpose and impact-oriented innovations (Krlev, Mildenberger, & Anheier, 2020) and prosocial business models as mechanisms to enhance the common good have gained prominence in the wake of the COVID-19 pandemic (Scheidgen, Gümüsay, Günzel-Jensen, Krlev, & Wolf, 2021) or in the face of the growing urgency of counteracting climate change (Gismondi et al., 2016). Networks of diverse stakeholders to facilitate learning and exchange, private–public partnerships, and new forms of collaboration are changing the social economy landscape (Wruk, Oberg, Klutt, & Maurer, 2019). Current issues such as impact measurement (Barman, 2020) or new organizational fields such as impact investing (Hehenberger, Mair, & Metz, 2019) involve new actors in a debate about what the social economy even means and what role it has relative to the mainstream economy and within society.

However, we suggest there is a deeper-seated conceptual reason for why our understanding of the social economy is stymied at present. We argue it is because neither of the theoretical perspectives from above (the institutional theory perspective via DiMaggio & Powell, 1983 and the transitions theory perspective via Geels, 2005b) have established a clear presence in the academic discourse surrounding the social economy, not to mention that the perspectives have never been applied to the social economy in unison.

To address this blind spot, we are combining the conceptual lens of organizational issue fields with that of transitions theory. In what follows, we introduce both theoretical concepts and discuss how they apply in the context of the social economy. We then combine both perspectives in a multi-level model of change in and through the social economy. We propose three interrelated transformation pathways that social economy organizations use to enhance transitions of organizations, fields, and society as a whole. With this chapter we thus contribute to a better understanding of how the social economy navigates between ensuring a certain stability as a field, which enables its visibility and legitimacy, and its broader mission to initiate and promote social-ecological transitions.

Theorizing the social economy

The social economy is not a distinct industry or sector. It is rather an umbrella concept that stresses old and new forms of organizing *for* and *with* society, with the explicit aim of addressing societal challenges. One common denominator is that social economy organizations pursue a societal purpose of contributing to the common good by prioritizing social and ecological goals over economic ones, and have some shared organizational practices (for example, that practices are needs-based, participatory, or problem-oriented).

The challenges the social economy addresses are to be understood in the broadest sense, such as that inherent in the Sustainable Development Goals (SDGs). The SDGs span social and environmental goals just as they promote changes in organizations and in policy, and in particular prioritize connections between societal spheres and stakeholders so that solutions move beyond previous pillarization and isolated approaches to complex social challenges (Rittel & Webber, 1973). Umbrella concepts are subject to criticism, because they are often considered conceptually weak and fuzzy, and because they may mean nothing and everything (Hirsch & Levin, 1999). However, umbrella concepts also come with a number of affordances, most importantly that they can serve as the common ground to connect and cross-fertilize strands of research (and practice) that might otherwise remain detached.

The social economy is located at the crossroads of several organizational research streams. When it comes to organizational types, the social economy covers for example solidarity-based organizations, associations, or other non-profit and nongovernmental organizations (Borzaga & Tortia, 2007); social movement organizations (Lee, Ramus, & Vaccaro, 2018); social businesses (Spieth, Schneider, Clauß, & Eichenberg, 2019); social enterprises (Defourny & Nyssens, 2021); and sustainable start-ups (Kim & Kim, 2021). At the level of organizational fields, the social economy overlaps with parts of the sharing economy or the circular economy (Henry et al., 2021), but also comprises the field of social investment (Nicholls & Daggers, 2017). As regards processes of change within society, the social economy is closely related to, for example, social innovations (Krlev, Anheier, & Mildenberger, 2019a) or to socio-ecological transitions (Pel et al., 2020).

These different perspectives on the social economy are furthermore characterized by transitory boundary areas to other fields of research. For example, public–private partnerships, or strategic corporate social or political responsibility activities (e.g., Scherer, Rasche, Palazzo, & Spicer, 2016), have at least some conceptual points of interlinkage with social economy organizations, and in particular the organizational structures, practices, and systems within which they are operating.

Of course, overlaps and separate research communities and conversations within a subject area exist for almost any field of research. However, the cross-cutting phenomenological character of the social economy makes grasping the field and building a common identity very difficult. This applies to finding commonalities between the various organizational forms that can be subsumed into the social economy. But it applies also, and even more importantly, to the social economy's associated practices, such as co-engagement and participatory processes involving target groups (Noya & Clarence, 2007), the high relevance of community-based and bottom-up social value and impact creation (Lall & Park, 2022), or the development of new social accounting practices to capture such value (Busco & Quattrone, 2018).

Towards a social economy science

When scholars spot limitations, shortcomings, or confusion in a research field, almost by reflex, they tend to propose a new concept, analytical angle, or theoretical approach. Such a reaction may propel the diagnosed challenges rather than help to meet them. We might be criticized for being no exception to this pattern. And yet we believe the characteristics of the social economy we outlined make the phenomenological area different from others, in that it is essentially about overlaps, spill-overs, cross-cutting connections to other spheres of society, or a certain degree of fuzziness in the issues it wrestles with.

What is more, it is exactly because of these qualities that the social economy is an exciting venue for scholarly inquiry, and one that outright demands to be studied as a field that is simultaneously unsettled (see 'Struggles for a common identity in the social economy' below) and unsettling (see 'Societal transformations through the social economy' below). Ultimately, this makes the social economy a pole as well as a jolt for organizations in general—and capitalism overall—to become more social, democratic, and sustainable.

By advocating for a *social economy science*, we thus do not want to create a new and siloed field of research that feels artificial, or that could be perceived as a pointless (re-)branding exercise. Instead, we seek to establish a connecting device across the different perspectives, organizational forms, and practices which we laid out above and which to date rarely connect with each other. We do so in order to unleash what a social economy science perspective can teach us about how to transform the economy and make society more resilient.

The theoretical anchors from which we could pick are almost as manifold as the social economy's forms and practices. This book contains a striking variety of theoretical approaches to studying the social economy. One example is exploratory, prescriptive, and imaginative social science to understand not only what the social economy is, but also what it could be (Mulgan, this volume; also Mulgan, 2020). Another contribution uses post-colonial theory to uncover whether social economy organizations revert, or propel deep-seated structures that cause social inequalities (Brännvall, this volume).

Within all available options we have selected two theoretical anchors: organization theory and transitions theory. Organization theory, in particular a neo-institutional lens, can help us conceptualize the building blocks of stability and a common identity within the social economy, on the one side, whereas transitions theory helps us conceptually unpack the transformative power that lies within social economy organizations and their practices.

The social economy as an organizational issue field: Struggling for a common identity

The organizational field subsumes all organizations that 'constitute a recognized area of institutional life' (DiMaggio & Powell, 1983, p. 148). This includes producers of products and services of a certain type, their suppliers and customers, but also meta-organizations, regulatory bodies and media that contribute to shaping institutions that influence what organizations in the field look like and behave. Introducing this meso level of analysis, between individual organizations on the micro level and economy and society on the macro level, has proven to be valuable for understanding and shaping networks, mechanisms, and outcomes in fields. Organizational fields are characterized by two major elements: field members interact more frequently and faithfully with each other than with other organizations in order to jointly provide a societal product (e.g. healthcare or social care) and they have a common meaning system characterized by a shared set of values, norms, and language (DiMaggio & Powell, 1983; Scott, 2013). Field members engage in a common discourse on shared issues that are relevant for the field (Hoffman, 1999).

The relational and discursive elements have been combined into a broader, more encompassing understanding of what holds organizations together, so-called organizational issue fields, that seek to unpack a potential perpetuation of relational and discursive dynamics (Oberg et al., 2021). In this section, we argue that the organizational issue field concept can be fruitfully applied to the social economy. We define the network of organizations that make the social economy and discuss their common practices. We describe the social economy's shared meaning system and refer to issues and debates currently shaping the field. We thereby emphasize how these definitional elements form a common identity for the social economy that makes it radiate beyond the sum of its organizations.

Networks and meta-organizations

Traditionally, the social economy has been conceptualized as consisting of a set of organizational forms: mutuals, associations, cooperatives, non-profit organizations, (welfare) associations and, more broadly, voluntary or community organizations (Borzaga & Tortia, 2007). More recently, the idea of mission-driven organizations has prevailed that broadens the understanding of which organizational forms can be considered to be part of the social economy (Mair et al., 2012). In particular, social enterprises have been recognized as a relevant new organizational form shaping the social economy within the past decade. The field developing around social enterprises (consisting of, among others, universities offering dedicated programmes for social entrepreneurs; incubators for social start-ups; accelerator grants to support ideas that, rather than pursuing a business case, challenge existing social systems;

foundation programmes to build network structures between social entrepreneurs globally, and so on) 'encroached' on the existing overlapping fields shaping the social economy (see Spicer et al., 2019, who provide a critical assessment of this trend). Social economy organizations providing products and services also have intense relations to organizations that are not part of the social economy. Due to the broad nature of services provided, they are also members of other fields. However, they increasingly also build relations within the social economy to organize their supply chains and to exchange knowledge and experience.

Meta-organizations have evolved that play an important role in strengthening such relations between social economy actors. On the demand or delivery side this includes networks such as Ashoka, the Schwab Foundation, Social Economy Europe, or Euclid Network that not only support entrepreneurs but also seek to shape institutions and policy in favour of advancing unconventional solutions to social problems. On the supply side the European Venture Philanthropy Association (EVPA) and the Global Steering Group for Impact Investing (GSG) fulfil similar functions in the goal to improve resource mobilization in the field. Meta-organizations are acknowledged for spurring mutual awareness and recognition within fields, enhancing visibility and legitimacy of fields in society, and organizing collective action, which is particularly imperative when it comes to addressing social and ecological challenges such as human rights, social inclusion, or climate change (Ahrne & Brunsson, 2011; Berkowitz & Dumez, 2016). These diverse organizational forms perceive themselves as part of a social economy that provides 'alternative' forms of social and economic organization. Central social economy actors (e.g. large welfare organizations and cooperatives, or big foundations) mutually recognize each other and thus form an organizational field of the social economy, although within-field relations are far from free of conflict (Ayob, Teasdale, & Fagan, 2016).

Common organizational practices and missions

What social economy organizations have in common is that they provide socially useful products and services that meet an unsatisfied social need (Krlev, Bund, & Mildenberger, 2014). Oftentimes they thereby fulfil demands of disadvantaged communities thus enhancing their social and economic inclusion (Ebrahim & Rangan, 2014). As such, the social economy has a redistributive, regulatory function on economic life. Products and services provided by social economy actors can also be alternatives to existing ones but are produced in a more socially and ecologically friendly way and thereby contribute to the common good (Carini et al., 2020).

Besides the provision of certain products and despite the large diversity of organizational forms, social economy organizations also share organizational practices such as participatory decision-making. This holds in particular for 'older' forms in the social economy such as cooperatives or community organizations. Aiming at promoting social goals with their activities, social enterprises and other newer forms however tend to emphasize social values internally as well. Participatory decision-making, inclusivity, fair payment, high transparency (e.g., public provision of financial statements), embracing a diverse workforce, and establishing close relationships with suppliers to secure a sustainable supply chain, are some examples or structural elements and organizational practices that characterize various organizational forms in the social economy (e.g., Amin et al., 2002).

Shared purpose and meaning structure

With their offerings and models, social economy organizations aim to pursue a dual objective of achieving both economic (e.g., becoming financially self-sustaining) and social goals. In various countries, dedicated legal forms have been created that were explicitly designed for such organizations (Ebrahim et al., 2014). In other countries where dedicated legal forms are lacking, social movements urge policy to close this gap (for example, the so-called Purpose Economy movement in Germany). Such new legal forms not only show the will to recognize particular challenges of social enterprises and to create legal solutions that fit their needs, but also emphasize shared elements and thus a common identity of organizations of similar forms. This contributes to enhancing the public visibility and legitimacy of social economy organizations.

Another way of emphasizing commonalities between diverse social economy organizations is the proliferation of standards and certificates that ascribe certain characteristics to organizations following these standards. One example is the B Corp Certification that aims at transforming the economic system towards a more sustainable one by promoting social purpose-driven organizations. To become a B Corp certified organization, applicants have to demonstrate high social and environmental performance, establish a governance structure to be accountable to all stakeholders, and commit to a high level of transparency of their social and environmental impact (Gehman, Grimes, & Cao, 2019). Other efforts promote the spread of reporting standards among organizations that account for how social goals such as solidarity and social justice as well as environmental sustainability are achieved.[1] These practices inform a broader quest of what kind of value and impact are material to stakeholders, including the environment (Nicholls, 2018).

While such initiatives contribute to enhancing visibility of the social economy, as many certified organizations or organizations applying these standards are in fact social economy organizations, they may also further blur the formation of a common identity of the social economy, as certification organizations promote their own labels and do not establish connections between initiatives. However, all such initiatives contribute to strengthening the legitimacy of organizations whose purpose it is to achieve social and ecological goals—an objective that an increasing number of organizations across the global economy pursue (Mayer & Roche, 2021) in a similar, but supposedly much less pronounced, way than the social economy.

---

[1] See for example https://www.ecogood.org.

Finally, it is also governments and international bodies that not only shape the institutional infrastructure that guides the decisions and behaviour of social economy actors but also contribute to defining shared characteristics and meanings of social economy organizations. Most recently, the European Commission has published the Social Economy Action Plan that brings forward concrete measures to strengthen social economy organizations (European Commission, 2021). Promoting one plan for diverse organizational forms with a shared overall purpose and meaning structure contributes to forming the very identity of the supported field.

Shared issues and debates

Various issues currently shape debates within and on the social economy and involve new actors that encounter social economy organizations. For instance, the proliferation of new investment principles that can be subsumed under the issue of impact investing have introduced new financial actors to interact with social economy organizations (such as venture philanthropists, impact-first investors, and so on: Hehenberger et al., 2019). This development has made the social economy more visible to (institutional) investors who have traditionally not focused on this sector when making their investment decisions. It has further contributed to shedding light on the shared problem of most social economy actors to gain access to financial resources and the perceived growing need—of both investors and social economy organizations—to change this situation (Hockerts, Hehenberger, Schaltegger, & Farber, 2022; Nicholls & Ormiston, this volume).

Debates and developments related to impact measurement provide another example of how current issues shape the social economy and its identity. New impact measurement standards have amplified the public image of social economy organizations' experience in measuring effects of their activities beyond economic terms and have made practices and methods to measure social and ecological impact more relevant to actors outside the social economy (Lall, 2019). Similarly, but less clearly, debates around a set of technologies typically subsumed under labels such as the 'Fourth Industrial Revolution' or the 'Internet of Things' have opened space for social economy organizations to envision their shared role in shaping the direction of current technological developments, thereby stressing socially inclusive rather than merely technocratic ways of dealing with new technologies (Mulgan, 2018).

Taking stock: The social economy and its struggle for a common identity

Taken together, the networks of diverse but in many ways similar social economy organizations, a shared purpose of these organizations of contributing to the common good, a set of organizational structures and practices, shared meanings and values, and shared issues such as impact measurement or impact-first investment, represent the major building blocks of a common identity within the social economy. While a common identity and boundaries of the social economy might still be blurry, there are diverse efforts on different levels (for example, meta-organizations promoting values, legal recognition through new legal forms, and so on) that foster both the public understanding of what constitutes the social economy and the self-recognition of its members within the field.

The social economy as a driver of institutional change and societal transitions

Institutional theory's focus on the field's composition and outfit within a larger societal context is particularly strong at explaining what holds fields together and grants them stability, or, as we just worked out, a common identity. Institutional theory also does move some way towards establishing a systems perspective of structures, actors, and processes and how they affect the economy and society. However, its treatment of economic and political processes and the dynamic change in social structures and practices that make a system is more limited (Micelotta, Lounsbury, & Greenwood, 2017). Scholars have argued that such a systems perspective, although a classic of the social sciences (see Giddens, 1984; Parsons, 1991), is needed now more than ever to master the complex issues, societal challenges, and problems that characterize contemporary societies (Mair & Seelos, 2021). Transitions theory has a rich legacy of grasping not only systems, but in particular streams of change within and across systems (Westley, McGowan, & Tjörnbo, 2017). It tends to provide us with an image of change spanning multiple levels as well as change that may stretch over long periods of time (Pel et al., 2020).

Multi-level change

The so-called multi-level perspective has become a classic of transitions theory (Geels, 2005a). In this concept, Geels connects three different levels: (1) niches, that is, sources of novelty, or abnormal or unusual practices that exist outside the mainstream; (2) socio-technical regimes, that is, a cohesive set of actors, processes, and structures, supposedly much like the organizational issue fields we just discussed, as well as further elements such as culture or technology; and (3) landscapes, that is, the composition of societies, including regulatory and normative institutions, which consist of and are influenced by the individual regimes. The main point that Geels' and subsequent work makes is that once market or social pressures for a niche solution grow big enough—for example, old technology becomes too slow or too costly or cannot provide the demanded quality any more—niche solutions break through and become the new mainstream. The multi-level perspective has been used to explain and conceptualize the historical transition from sailing boats to steam ships (Geels, 2002), or the modern rise of low-carbon electricity transitions (Geels et al., 2016).

We argue here that social economy organizations do not only pioneer and propel the niche solutions, but also actively work towards being the jolt or disruption to the existing economic or social system that opens a space for their approaches to become mainstream. This is made possible by the 'persistent fragile action' that many social economy organizations pursue (Krlev, 2022b). For example, as Krlev analyses, renewable energy cooperatives have worked tirelessly towards promoting decentralized, green energy since the late 1980s and continued this work until the breakthrough of a political prioritization of renewable energy production in many countries globally. Similar arguments can be made for the vanguards of organic agriculture, which were often organized as regional cooperatives, or early promoters of fair-trade, typically small, associations or social enterprises (Nicholls & Opal, 2005). While previously marginal phenomena, taken seriously only by a small group of converted and ethically motivated customers, these social economy movements and corresponding transitions have led to a redesign of entire industries. However, not only small enterprises or social movements, but also established, large-scale social economy actors such as faith-based organizations, can promote fundamental change across levels. One example is the establishment of hospices as a major new institution within the Western healthcare system that was initiated by those traditional actors (e.g., Bridge, Murtagh, & O'Neill, 2014). Without the active change agency of these actors, there would not have been any external factor enabling the breakthrough of their very own solutions to existing social problems.

Challengers and first movers

Most kinds of societal change processes are characterized by struggles between incumbents and contenders, whereby a new status quo is often marked by a transition to a new steady state (Fligstein & McAdam, 2015). Social economy organizations, in contrast to many other organizations, however, keep the level of contestation constantly high, because they are driven by virtues and values and typically fight for a good cause rather than their competitive advantage (Anheier, 2014). Take the current paradigm shift in organizational performance towards assessing social value creation or social impact, for instance. The current discourse and practice (note the link back to the organizational issue field) is currently dominated by Environmental, Social, and Governance (ESG) criteria, which do not only have their origin in the finance industry but are also primarily promoted by it. The proliferation of weak ESG standards continues, because they are the lowest common denominator for many powerful market actors, although we are well aware of their many limitations (Berg, Koelbel, & Rigobon, 2022). Social economy organizations, by contrast, have always advocated a different understanding of impact, namely one that explicitly stresses active value creation rather than, for example, the avoidance of harm (Barman, 2020). The same applies to impact investing, which—as opposed to, for instance, responsible investment—(Yan, Ferraro, & Almandoz, 2018), favours financing underfunded industries and organizations that may offer limited financial returns and is clearly driven by actors within the social economy ecosystem (Mair & Hehenberger, 2014).

The fact that social economy organizations go where it hurts and enter territory that others avoid, because they may face fewer regulatory restrictions and have broader mandates from stakeholders, makes them vanguards of social change (Anheier, 2014). For example, we have recent evidence that social economy organizations are more likely to take action when other actors are hesitant, for instance when faced with 'moral crises' in situations where organizations are only indirectly affected by the crises and have some discretion on whether to act or not. Krlev (2022a) for instance shows how social economy organizations initiated multi-stakeholder part-nerships in the context of the economic crisis of 2008 and the refugee crisis of 2015. Scheidgen et al. (2021) unpack how values-oriented entrepreneurial action, which worked largely according to social economy principles, was key to developing inno-vative solutions to the challenges caused by COVID-19. These instances underpin that the social economy is likely to play a lead role in driving sustainability transitions within established welfare systems (Frantzeskaki & Wittmayer, 2019).

So, no wonder is the social economy so high on the political agenda of recovery plans for the post-COVID era, such as on international action plans by the Euro-pean Commission, the OECD, the ILO, or the World Economic Forum (for more on international policy activities see Bonnici & Klijn, this volume). However, the social economy's first mover feature also increases its vulnerability up to a point where scholars have called some of its members permanently failing organizations (Seibel, 2022). This is why the social economy may be more dependent than other organizational fields on institutional protection, on close integration with the regu-latory and normative institutions surrounding it, and on collaboration across sector borders.

Boundary spanners and connectors

Social economy organizations typically seek to have impact beyond their service, product, or other core activities. An inherent trait of the social economy is that it almost never operates without also promoting a certain advocacy effort. This can for instance concern the promotion of democratic or participatory principles (Defourny & Nyssens, 2021). So what others—for instance, universities—consider a 'third mis-sion', namely the transfer of practices and knowledge or wider positive influence on social practices, represents a core mission to the social economy. Social econ-omy organizations promote this mission through leading by example as to what organizations can stand for, what they can be, and what they can do. There is increas-ing debate regarding the hybridization of the business world, for instance, whereby hybridization refers to relative shifts in the priority of environmental and social goals relative to commercial goals and skilful management of the paradoxes that might occur when different goal sets clash (Smith & Besharov, 2017). Social enterprises have been known to operate on such principles for decades and therefore serve as beacons of how positive social change can be achieved (Nicholls, 2006). While this does not mean that social economy organizations are free from falling into reduc-tive thinking that propels rather than solves so-called wicked social problems (Gras, Conger, Jenkins, & Gras, 2019), it shows that social economy organizations' activities typically radiate far beyond the boundaries of their own field.

Social economy organizations also push for social change via the processes they engage in and which they drive, such as the one of social innovations. Research has found that social economy organizations are critical for social innovation, especially in the early stages of its evolution, due to a number of organizational traits: they tend to be well embedded locally; they are proximate to target groups; and they know vulnerable, marginalized, or excluded target groups well, have access to them, and understand their needs (Krlev, Anheier, & Mildenberger, 2019b). What is more, they are able to exert a function of connectivity between a wide range of diverse actors and act as brokers of joint action (Bouchard, 2012). Through this capacity social economy organizations are able to draw other actors in and influence them not only in direct interaction but also through joint social innovation processes, which typically do not rest on providing a neat solution to a clear problem, but aim to reconfigure social structures and practices and thereby push for large-scale, systemic transitions (Pel et al., 2020). Boundary-spanning effects may for instance include making other organizations act more entrepreneurially in addressing social problems, whereby social innovations can be seen as a method or process of extra-preneurship (Tracey & Stott, 2017).

Taking stock: The social economy as a force for change

These traits of the social economy taken together suggest it will become ever more important in driving change vertically, that is, across levels, spanning from micro-interactions with target groups to promoting shifts in policy agendas, while also driving change horizontally, that is, producing spill-overs, forging alliances, and pushing for action early on across organizations and organizational fields.

A multi-level model of change in and through the social economy

The two perspectives we have just established are not mutually exclusive, but synergetic. A common identity of the social economy enhances the recognition and visibility of the field and its values, practices, and purpose. An important part of its identity is thereby to initiate and promote change in other fields and thus to serve as a driver of change or a disruptive field (Wruk, Schöllhorn, Oberg, 2020). In combination, institutional theory and transitions theory help us paint the big picture and conceptualize different transformation pathways promoted by the social economy. In this section we bring all the elements together and develop a multi-level model of change in and through the social economy.

Zooming into the social economy

We start with a more detailed conceptualization of the organizational issue field of the social economy. Figure 3.1 zooms in on the organizational issue field level. As described above, the field consists not only of a set of diverse social economy organizations, but also of meta-organizations, universities/research centres, government agencies and regulators, target groups, and so on. These actors collaborate with each other and with organizations outside the social economy—such as traditional businesses—to provide socially useful products and services. In contrast to many other fields, the social economy is characterized by high permeability and inclusiveness. It is also marked by interlinkages to other fields and organizations, for instance as mentioned previously to strategic corporate activities on social or political responsibility. These traits are marked in Figure 3.1 by a fluid shape and a transitory border of the field, which reflects a network or actor-centred perspective on the social economy (dashed line and what it encompasses).

The social economy, however, also moves beyond those relations in that it shapes societal debates on relevant issues such as impact measurement or responsible invest-ment. These issues not only have an influence on social economy organizations themselves and their interaction partners, but may also affect organizations and fields that are not in direct contact with the social economy. The wide boundary areas (shaded circle surrounding the social economy shape) are representative of the issue field perspective on the social economy, which highlights that there can be many spillover effects, especially on the level of discourse, and that borderlines are at best transitory.

Figure 3.1 furthermore introduces three characteristics of the social economy that bridge stability and change in the field and hold it together: (1) value creation in ecosystems; (2) positive social change orientation; (3) principles of inclusion and participation.

Value creation in ecosystems

First, the social economy is dominated by shared value creation in ecosystems. Research on ecosystems has generally seen a surge in attention over the past years. The wider organizational issue field of the social economy mainly derives from a shared mission and meaning and provides an institutional setting for a multitude of actors to operate in. The ecosystem by contrast has a narrower and more func-tional orientation, which derives from shared value creation processes, and may either focus on a local context or on cohesive actor constellations within a global setting, where aspects of meta-organizing and coordinated joint strategies and prac-tices play a major role. Some have suggested that ecosystems are a new and more meaningful level of analysis than industry, exactly because of the qualities just men-tioned (Teece, 2014). However, ecosystems in the classical sense, despite embracing some diversity and multitude in the actors they comprise, are marked by a relatively high actor proximity and similarity. For instance, ecosystems as typically investigated cover value chains that span from suppliers, to firms, to distributors—all of which have contractual relations between each other and work on the same or very similar products or services (Jacobides, Cennamo, & Gawer, 2018).

In contrast to this, we have seen that the social economy is far more fluid and more encompassing, and not only tolerates but rests on the complementary value that is created when social economy organizations, firms, or state actors act together, or at least in mutual dependence. The ecosystem concept has therefore recently been applied to capture the social value creation processes that become possible at the nexus of these actors (Audretsch, Eichler, & Schwarz, 2022), and scholars have stud-ied how ecosystems may manifest in sub-phenomena of our umbrella of the social economy, for instance in the sharing economy (Laamanen, Pfeffer, Rong, & van de

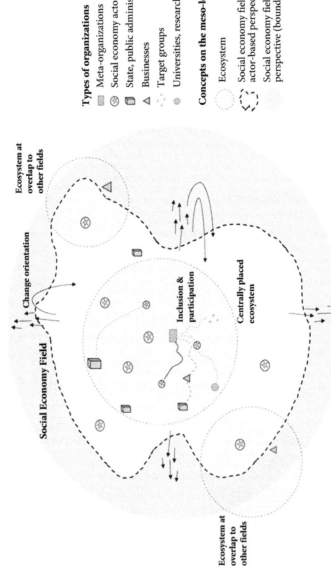

Types of organizations

- ▦ Meta-organizations
- ⊕ Social economy actors
- ▭ State, public administration
- △ Businesses
- ⋰ Target groups
- ● Universities, research, knowledge actors

Concepts on the meso-level

- ◌ Ecosystem
- ⟜ Social economy field - network/ actor-based perspective
- ⟜ Social economy field - issue field perspective (boundary area)

Ecosystem at overlap to other fields

Change orientation

Social Economy Field

Inclusion & participation

Centrally placed ecosystem

Ecosystem at overlap to other fields

Figure 3.1 Organizational issue field of the social economy

Ven, 2018). We argue therefore not only that the social economy can benefit from the ecosystems concept, but also that the social economy is a prime setting to study ecosystems. This is because the organizational population is diverse, multi-faceted, and complex enough to benefit from the multi-layered anchorage of ecosystems and vice versa. With the ecosystem concept, we thereby take an ego-network perspective. The structure and composition of ecosystems that radiate around individual social economy organizations or groups of organizations with similar offerings depend on their value creation processes and are embedded in the wider organizational issue field.

Ecosystems may be centrally placed within the organizational issue field of the social economy. This is for instance the case when social economy organizations focus their value chain activities on the social economy, for example when social economy actors form a new meta-organization that is supposed to represent them as a whole 'to the outside world'. However, more often than not, value chains of social economy organizations involve actors from outside the social economy. As such, ecosystems cut across field borders and contribute to creating field overlaps. One example is social economy organizations in the healthcare sector whose ecosystem includes hospitals, pharmaceutical producers, and other organizations outside of the social economy. Figure 3.1 underpins that many different types of ecosystems exist within the social economy, which may vary by issue areas, geographic areas, regulatory fields, or cross-cutting processes in which actors in an ecosystem are engaged, such as that of social innovation.

Positive social change orientation

Second, both social innovation and other change processes, such as institutional innovation driven by social economy organizations—for instance, the promotion of (social) housing for local communities against dominant trends of privatization (Moulaert & Nussbaumer, 2005)—are representative of the social economy's orientation at effectuating positive social change. This is symbolized in Figure 3.1 by the cloud of arrows heading out from the social economy field. Circular arrows indicate that change processes may affect the realm within the social economy itself. For instance, existing work has evidenced how social enterprises have transformed the more traditional landscape of the social economy, especially in country contexts that are highly regulated (Lindsay & Hems, 2004). At the same time, social economy organizations may also nudge, push, or force other actors into engaging in new types of action. For instance, social movement organizations may directly or indirectly promote social innovation activities in corporates that they are targeting through activism (Carberry, Bharati, Levy, & Chaudhury, 2017).

Many other types of actors have been characterized as engaging in institutional entrepreneurship (Garud, Hardy, & Maguire, 2016), for example not only in disrupting markets with new products, but in creating a market environment that is receptive to new regulative, normative, and cognitive orders (see e.g. Child, Lu, & Tsai, 2007 on the emergence of the environmental protection system in China). However, one might argue that social economy organizations are the prototypical institutional entrepreneurs, since there is hardly any social economy organization that does not carry an advocacy mandate in its mission. Just think about the protected spaces the social economy has built, safeguarded, or promoted when it comes to women's rights or pacifism (Pauly, Verschuere, Rynck, & Voets, 2021), or an inclusive model of health and disability (see e.g., Bauer, Wistow, Hyanek, & Figueroa, 2019). Social economy activities often involve bridging gaps among actors, and acts of political brokerage rather than merely relational brokerage (Stovel & Shaw, 2012); that is, a clear mission to change established institutional practices by means of establishing mutual connections across diverse actors.

Inclusion and participation

Third, principles of inclusion, participation, and interaction characterize the social economy field. Social economy organizations involve partners across sectors, actors within and outside of their ecosystems. These relations and interactions are often a sine qua non for the social economy's change orientation. For example, although, as mentioned before, social economy organizations are often at the vanguard in entering areas from which others shy away, they often require buy-in, support, and even shifts in leadership from other organizations, for instance as social innovations mature and scale (Krlev et al., 2019b), or in situations of crisis when other types of actors may have more resources or power to act (Krlev, 2022a).

The so-called relational imperative, supposedly in marked contrast to more mainstream modes of entrepreneurship, has also been highlighted as an inherent trait of social enterprise, whereby these relations may range from relatively few connections to webs and wide networks (Phillips, Alexander, & Lee, 2017). Interactions may occur with involvement of organizations from all sectors and several fields, but can also be dyadic. Cooperative relations may furthermore be formalized, or they may be based on loose arrangements and sporadic interactions. Such interactions may have a strong participatory character and actively include target groups or other societal stakeholders that are typically not part of an ecosystem. Participation and inclusion are a prerequisite for creating value in social economy ecosystems. Therefore, in Figure 3.1 these principles are indicated as part of the ecosystems, whereby the different qualities of relationships (strong or loose ties) are nuanced by solid or transitory lines.

Zooming out towards the big picture: Three transformation pathways of the social economy

Now, the elements that grant the social economy stability and guarantee its continuous renewal give rise to three transformation pathways that the social economy uses to effectuate change in the wider economy and society. Along these pathways social economy organizations: promote *innovation for impact* (black arrows); act as *agents of change* (light grey arrows); or engage in and through *partnerships* (dotted grey arrows).

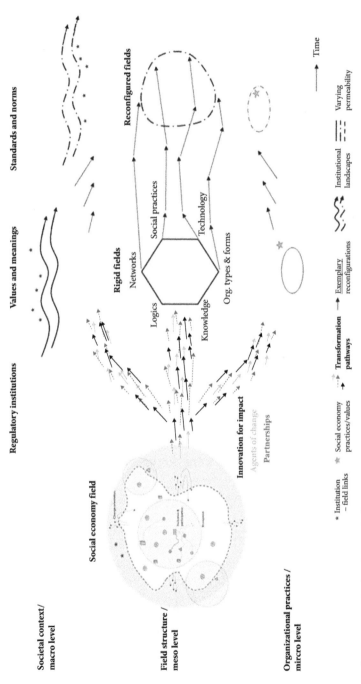

Figure 3.2 Multi-level model of dynamic change in and through the social economy

Each of the pathways can occur and provoke reconfigurations in other organizational environments at three levels of analysis (focus on the middle part of Figure 3.2), namely as regards: (1) their manifested decoupling of organizational practices from social economy values such as solidarity or participation (micro level, oval with excluded star); (2) their rigid field structures (meso level, diamond shape with solid lines); or (3) their regulatory and normative institutions that are at a far distance to the field level (macro level, solid and curved arrows with distant starred institutional links). Figure 3.2 captures the pathways by the three streams of arrows that tackle existing structures in other fields in the form of a trident, which pierces and pushes those established structures towards new reconfigurations. The reconfiguration process is designated in Figure 3.2 by solid black arrows pointing to the right, which mark the effectuated shifts.

Reconfigured fields are then less rigid and more permeable (irregular, rounded shape with dash-dotted lines). Permeability increases for the incorporation of new organizational practices that embed rather than exclude social economy values (enclosed star in oval in the lower part of the figure). It also increases as regards the incorporation of field–institution links, thereby becoming more similar to the close interconnection between the social economy and its regulatory and normative institutions (asterisks in the upper part of the figure located at closer proximity to field). The individual transformation pathways can be characterized as follows.

Specifying the pathways

In the following we only briefly characterize each of the pathways, because they are elaborated in more detail relative to the presentation of contributions to *Social Economy Science* in the next section. Although analytically separating the pathways makes sense to increase precision, as we have also done to structure the contributions to this book, actions along one pathway are often combined with actions on another pathway so that these co-occur. To capture this, Figure 3.2 draws out not separate, but instead multi-pronged streams of arrows.

Innovation for impact

Innovation for impact can be new technologies, new organizational practices or values, and logics manipulating organizational decision-making, fields, or institutions in favour of social and ecological impact. More specifically, social economy organizations may develop standards (e.g., for impact measurement; see Hehenberger & Buckland, this volume), strategies (e.g., for spurring social innovation; see Huysentruyt, this volume), action principles (e.g., designing inclusive digital technologies; see Mulgan, this volume), or decision logics (e.g., investing socially; see Nicholls & Ormiston, this volume).

Agents of change

The role of agents of change assumed by the social economy can be more or less direct. Social economy organizations may act indirectly by serving as prototypes or role models showcasing that alternative business models and practices that are more sustainable work and thereby exert influence on mainstream organizations (e.g., by showing how organizations can become more inclusive and participatory; see Battilana et al., this volume). Or they may prompt evolution and change within the social economy itself by introducing new twists and turns in how it operates (e.g., by harnessing technology more proactively in promoting the common good; see Calderini et al., this volume). They may act directly by sparking the diffusion of alternative ways of organizing within their ecosystems through interactions with and through other actors (e.g., by knowledge transfer via educational institutions; see Nogales & Nyssens, this volume). Or they may contribute to stabilizing systems in turmoil by means of their organizational resilience (e.g., the turmoil caused by COVID-19; see Chaves-Avila & Soler, this volume). Of course, they may also fail to act as agents of change (e.g., when they are ignorant of local stakeholders' needs; see Bränvall, this volume).

Partnerships

Partnerships are the third transformation pathway. Social economy organizations may make target groups and citizens at large their core stakeholders (e.g., by engaging them more actively in their innovation process; see Hueske, Willems, & Hockerts, this volume). They may work at the intersection of and alongside other sectors to advance joint leadership (e.g., in civic leadership constellations within a local context; see Sancino et al., this volume). They may become receiving favoured partners of governments (e.g., through gaining unconditional priority and support within a socially oriented public procurement system; see Varga & Hayday, this volume). Or they may become delivering favoured partners of public administration (e.g., when relational contracting between the social economy and governments stimulates service delivery with worthy social outcomes; see Carter & Ball, this volume). Finally, the social economy may become co-shaper of new institutions together with government (e.g., in designing new institutional infrastructures for social innovation; see Miguel, this volume).

Levels of change

Figure 3.2 furthermore highlights that the change effectuated by the social economy can span from the organizational, to the organizational issue field, to the societal level.

Organizational-level change

At the organizational level, for example, participatory decision-making and shared ownership have spread to actors that have not been associated with the social economy so far. Organizations applying such organizational practices and principles are populating the platform economy (Scholz, 2016), although their visibility and influence within that field are surely very limited at the moment.

Field-level change

With a growing number of adopters within a field over time (moving from bottom to top in Figure 3.2), change occurs at the level of organizational issue fields. So, the jolt of and impetus for change does not come from some external factor that is hard to control, as supposed by the classical multi-level perspective of transitions theory (e.g., market pressures, crises, etc.; see Geels, 2005b), but is proactively created by social economy organizations. A striking example is the unprecedented levels of collective action mobilized by social economy actors such as those witnessed in the large-scale hackathons to address challenges of the COVID-19 pandemic (Bertello, Bogers, & Bernardi, 2021; Gegenhuber, 2020). Such increased interactions with social economy organizations may lead to changes in the positions organizations have in their respective fields, eventually creating more overlaps between the social economy and other fields that may spur further cross-diffusion of practices or values.

Societal-level change

Change also occurs independent of individual fields, on the societal level—especially through changes of regulatory institutions, but also in broader societal standards and norms as well as values and meaning structures shaping the decisions and behaviour of individuals and organizations. The social economy field is marked by a strong embedding of regulatory institutions. Of course, any organizational issue field is interlinked with and influenced by regulatory institutions, but the social economy puts a particularly strong emphasis on shaping laws and regulations. For instance, due to perpetual institutional work (Arenas, Strumińska-Kutra, & Landoni, 2020; Gond & Boxenbaum, 2013; Lowe, Kimmitt, Wilson, Martin, & Gibbon, 2019), social economy organizations are typically proximate to policy and at the same time strive to make it more receptive for the social economy's needs, but in particular its target groups' needs. You could say that the social economy *governs with* regulatory institutions, whereas other fields are often *governed by* regulatory institutions.

Think of the influence of dynamics between the impact investing field, the Impact Management Project, or the International Sustainability Standards Board on ESG criteria and reporting. Although dynamics are hard to disentangle and causality hard to establish, it is because of the constant challenging of ESG standards by more radical social economy groups and advocates that these are being critically discussed. In the future this may lead to an upward movement as regards the meaning of standards, for example when a positive ESG score actually means that positive societal impact is created, which may be codified in regulatory institutions that in consequence effectively sanction green-, white-, or impact-washing (Krlev, 2019).

Characterizing the contributions to *Social Economy Science*

As described above, this book is organized around the three transformation pathways we worked out in our multi-level model of change in and through the social economy. However, there is more to each chapter than being a manifestation of one of the pathways. Table 3.1 provides an overview that demonstrates how the chapters contribute to strengthening the common identity of the social economy's organizational issue field and how the chapters simultaneously emphasize the social economy's role for initiating and promoting social-ecological transitions.

Table 3.1 also displays the range of original theoretical and empirical angles taken by the chapters, which add to the richness of social economy science. While, due to the origins of this book, some chapters have an explicit focus on Europe, many have a more universal character or international focus (especially the global policy chapter by Bonnici & Klijn, this volume, which belongs to the introductory part that sets the scene and connects the contributions). The chapters thereby showcase in an impressive way not only what social economy as a field achieves, but also what studying it can contribute to knowledge in the social sciences.

Part I: Innovation for impact

Huysentruyt applies a behavioural economics perspective in discussing how innovations can be promoted that are driven not by economic goals but by the desire to contribute to the public good. She emphasizes how shaping debates on innovation—for instance, by choosing frames that promote appropriate mental models and prosocial preferences that are embodied by the social economy—can help to raise awareness of the benefits such innovations can bring. She also introduces mechanisms—such as licensing schemes, empowerment of meta-organizations, or building appropriate technological infrastructures—that can be applied to promote innovation in favour of transitions towards a more sustainable future.

Mulgan focuses on technological innovations such as artificial intelligence and applies prescriptive social science to outline how the social economy can embrace such new technologies as part of their models and identity. He suggests that to serve the public good, we need a profound reorientation of (investment) decisions towards applications that stress the inclusiveness of technology. What is more, he shows how new models, programmes, and standards are needed—be they new or updated education programmes or standards for sharing knowledge and data within and beyond the social economy—that embrace social and ecological values more deeply than existing ones.

Nicholls and Ormiston engage in the sociology of markets and deal with new investment practices and principles, how they shape the social economy, and how they initiate change in the finance industry. When investment decisions are increasingly driven by social and ecological aspects, as promoted by social economy actors, this should have implications for most other organizational fields, eventually leading to profound changes of their institutional infrastructures. This is reflected in the multiplicity of drivers stemming from the public and private sector as well as the social economy for diffusing such practices and principles across the financial industries.

Hehenberger and Buckland use an accountability perspective to show how new impact measurement approaches, consisting of a set of processes, indicators, and

Table 3.1 Overview of contributions along the three transformation pathways: innovation for impact, agents of change, partnerships

Transformation pathways	Authors	Original angle	Organizational issue field perspective: What is part of the collective identity?	Transitions perspective: How can change be initiated/promoted?
Innovation for impact	Huysentruyt	Behavioural economics	Innovation for the public good as part of the shared identity of the social economy	Mechanisms and strategies to promote innovation for the public good, which use new and more appropriate frames to shape debates on innovation
	Mulgan	Exploratory and prescriptive social science	Pro-active embracement and shaping of the technological revolution by social economy actors	Participatory action and collective intelligence for just and equitable digitization
	Nicholls & Ormiston	Sociology of markets	Establishing a new market category at the intersection of the social economy and the field of finance	Mobilization of capital with purpose and impact orientation that changes logics of financial markets
	Hehenberger & Buckland	Accountability and evaluation	Impact measurement as shared practice and principle in the social economy	Diffusion of impact measurement approaches into other fields and shaping of societal discourse on managing for impact
Agents of change	Battilana et al.	Democratic organization	Shared and participatory organizational models as characteristic of the social economy	Diffusion of alternative, co-operative, and democratized practices to change the dominant corporate model
	Nogales & Nyssens	Education and knowledge transfer	Networks between higher education institutions and social economy organizations	Transversal knowledge transfer between universities and social economy for greater social value creation
	Chaves-Avila & Soler	Organizational/field resilience	Social economy performance and relationships relative to the mainstream economy	Resilience as an outcome of cooperation-based rather than competition-based organizing
	Calderini et al.	Entrepreneurship	Social-tech ventures (re-)defining new uses of technology	Inclusive and green growth as opposed to the general growth agenda
	Brännvall	Post-colonial theory	Local and non-local interaction in ecosystems for social innovation	Non-participatory dynamics inhibiting the scaling process and thus preventing wider social change

Partnerships	Hueske, Willems, & Hockerts	Citizen engagement in science	Target group participation along the social value creation process of social enterprises (in parallel to citizen participation in science)	More tailored interventions corresponding with the needs of vulnerable or excluded groups
	Sancino et al.	Leadership	Arenas in the local/city context that influence civic leadership and involvement of the social economy in them	Opportunities (or lack of) transversal collaboration and visibility of genuinely civic actors in leadership
	Miguel	Institutional design	Continuity in the identity of Portugal Social Innovation as a new institution (the institution as a durable asset for the social economy)	New institutional outfit and process as a blueprint for the redesign of other institutions
	Varga & Hayday	Public management	Responsible and values-oriented buying practices of the public sector towards the social economy	Impact maximization rather than cost minimization as a governance principle
	Carter & Ball	Contract theory	Contracting as a relational (instead of transactional) device between government, business, and the social economy	More effective service provision and prevention through cross-sectoral collaboration

principles, spread within and beyond the social economy. They emphasize how the impact logic and the tradition of measuring impact shapes the identity of the social economy, and thereby help it gain visibility and legitimacy beyond its own realm. They do not only discuss organic processes of cross-diffusion between fields, but also highlight the role of regulators and how these can contribute to foster such processes through creating a supportive regulatory framework.

Part II: Agents of change

Battilana et al. scrutinize social businesses under the lens of democratic and participatory organizing. They outline the core affordances of hybrid organizational structures and practices or those of co-decision-making by employees relative to the current, substantial societal crises. They then build a bridge to the institutional context and show how, for example, legal shifts or financial strategies that foster such new organizational types may propel change across wider organizational populations.

Nogales and Nyssens analyse the social economy from an education and knowledge exchange perspective. They discuss the possibilities that arise from a two-way transfer of knowledge as well as co-engagement between universities and other knowledge actors with social economy organizations within impact-oriented ecosystems. They also consider how educational activities in universities around social economy practices can level up values-oriented skills for future economy leaders.

Chaves-Avila and Soler investigate social economy resilience in the context of the COVID-19 crisis. Thereby they advance two arguments. First, they highlight the importance of the social economy for the resilience of society by showing how social economy organizations are the first to react to crises. Second, they show that social economy organizations displayed remarkable resilience to the crisis relative to other actors. Thereby social economy organizations represent not only a tool to manage and address change but also a model for how to deal with disruptive change, for others to follow.

Calderini et al. consider a new evolution within the social economy, in which organizations heavily rely on technological innovation to advance social goals: so-called social-tech ventures. Thereby they do not only bridge a formerly perceived divide between the technological and the social; they also offer considerations on the effects this may have, including a wider acceptance and legitimacy of technology, or the emergence of an inclusive as opposed to a smart growth agenda.

Bräanvall studies the social start-ups of Western entrepreneurs in Africa under a post-colonial lens. She highlights how, despite ambitions to the contrary, Western entrepreneurs often fail to consider the local, native perspective or even do not properly involve local actors in the development of solutions that are supposedly meant for them. She outlines how this ignorance may stymie wider transformational effects by hampering the scaling of social innovation.

Part III: Partnerships

Hueske, Willems, and Hockerts draw a striking analogy between participatory processes in the social economy and the public engagement of citizens in science. They
work out how, in particular, what they call orgware—that is, organizational structures
and processes that facilitate engagement throughout the process, from identifying
problems to developing solutions—are necessary to get to an adequate level of representation, voice, and influence by target groups. They thereby define which elements
the organizational issue field would need to possess, but also project the kinds of
transformations that would be possible if target groups had profound opportunities
of involvement rather than being consulted at the very end of the process.

Sancino et al. focus on developing a civic leadership perspective in local settings,
more particularly at the city level. They demonstrate that besides talk and convic-
tions about the superiority of distributed approaches to leadership and collaborative,
multi-stakeholder action, city leadership is clustered in the hands of a small number of leaders, often in formal positions of power. By contrast, the social economy
is not very visible. The authors discuss what this implies for (the lack of) integrated
approaches to local challenges and how the situation could be changed.

Miguel provides a compelling account centred on institutional design. Specifically,
he discusses how the Portugal Social Innovation initiative, which is located at the
intersection between the public, private, and social economy spheres, enables more
effective resource mobilization to social economy organizations. He highlights how
the identity of the initiative had to be established and safeguarded as a durable asset
in order not to lose influence over shifts in the country's political leadership. At the
same time, he outlines how Portugal Social Innovation may serve as a blueprint for
institutional change in other existing institutions—both internally, within the Portuguese public administration, for example, but also in other countries as a new way
of designing market environments in favour of social innovation.

Varga and Hayday start by analysing how established public management practices focus on optimization for lowest costs and expenditures and then contrast this
situation with a newly emergent practice of reversed procurement practices, namely
buying according to social or effectiveness criteria. They show how such new principles can establish a more level playing field between the public sector and the social
economy, but also how such a new governance principle can be used strategically for
maximizing social value creation and impact.

Carter and Ball offer a new version of contract theory, which they label relational
contracting as opposed to transactional contracting. They highlight how the value of
outcomes-based contracts, for example through setting up social impact bonds, radi-
ates beyond the direct benefits generated by those funding partnerships. Contracting
as a relational device instead enables the initiation of diverse actor constellations
around societal challenges so that cross-sectoral combinations of competences and
resources leads to more effective service provision and prevention, especially in the
long run.

Summary: A better grasp over the social economy's traits and societal contributions

Organizational issue fields from institutional theory and social change dynamics from transitions theory are rarely considered in unison, and unfortunately, as a consequence, the different research communities do not speak much to each other. By bringing them together we contribute in two regards. First, our work combines an angle on field stability and common identity by which social economy organizations may fix cracks in society and bridge isolated organizational or issue areas, with a transitions angle that enables us to integrate dynamics across networks of actors, policies, and other forms of influence. Second, due to our previously limited ability to merge these aspects conceptually, the social economy has often been characterized as messy, disorganized, hard to grasp, and therefore potentially powerless compared to other actors and fields. Our conceptual reasoning suggests the opposite is true, and the chapters in *Social Economy Science* shall be testimony to this claim.

References

Ahrne, G., & Brunsson, N. (2011). Organization outside organizations: the significance of partial organization. *Organization*, 18(1), 83–104.

Amin, A., Cameron, A., Hudson, R., & Cameron, A. (2002). *Placing the Social Economy*. London: Routledge.

Anheier, H. K. (2014). *Nonprofit Organizations: Theory, Management, Policy* (2nd ed.). London: Routledge.

Arenas, D., Strumińska-Kutra, M., & Landoni, P. (2020). Walking the tightrope and stirring things up: Exploring the institutional work of sustainable entrepreneurs. *Business Strategy and the Environment*, 29(8), 3055–3071. https://doi.org/10.1002/bse. 2557

Audretsch, D. B., Eichler, G. M., & Schwarz, E. J. (2022). Emerging needs of social innovators and social innovation ecosystems. *International Entrepreneurship and Management Journal*, 18(1), 217–254. https://doi.org/10.1007/s11365-021-00789-9

Ayob, N., Teasdale, S., & Fagan, K. (2016). How social innovation 'came to be': tracing the evolution of a contested concept. *Journal of Social Policy*, 45(4), 635–653. https://doi. org/10.1017/S004727941600009X

Barman, E. (2020). Many a slip: the challenge of impact as boundary object in social finance. *Historical Social Research/Historische Sozialforschung*, 45(3), 31–52. https:// doi.org/10.2307/26918403

Battilana, J., & Lee, M. (2014). Advancing research on hybrid organizing—insights from the study of social enterprises. *The Academy of Management Annals*, 8(1), 397–441. https://doi.org/10.1080/19416520.2014.893615

Bauer, A., Wistow, G., Hyanek, V., & Figueroa, M. (2019). Social innovation in healthcare: the recovery approach. In H. K. Anheier, G. Krlev, & G. Mildenberger (Eds), *Social Innovation: Comparative Perspectives* (pp. 130–148). Abingdon: Routledge.

Berg, F., Koelbel, J. F., & Rigobon, R. (2022). Aggregate confusion: the divergence of ESG rating. *Review of Finance*. Advance online publication. https://doi.org/10.1093/rof/rfac033

Berkowitz, H., & Dumez, H. (2016). The concept of meta-organization: issues for management studies. *European Management Review*, 13(2), 149–156.

Bertello, A., Bogers, M. L. A. M., & Bernardi, P. de (2021). Open innovation in the face of the COVID-19 grand challenge: insights from the Pan-European hackathon 'EUvsVirus'. *R and D Management*, 37(3), 355. https://doi.org/10.1111/radm.12456

Borzaga, C., & Tortia, E. (2007). Social economy organisations in the theory of the firm. In A. Noya & E. Clarence (Eds), *The Social Economy: Building Inclusive Economies* (pp. 23–60). Paris: OECD Publishing.

Bouchard, M. J. (2012). Social innovation, an analytical grid for understanding the social economy: the example of the Québec housing sector. *Service Business*, 6(1), 47–59. https://doi.org/10.1007/s11628-011-0123-9

Bridge, S., Murtagh, B., & O'Neill, K. (2014). *Understanding the Social Economy and the Third Sector* (2nd ed.). New York: Palgrave Macmillan.

Busco, C., & Quattrone, P. (2018). Performing business and social innovation through accounting inscriptions: an introduction. *Accounting, Organizations and Society*, 67, 15–19. https://doi.org/10.1016/j.aos.2018.03.002

Carberry, E. J., Bharati, P., Levy, D. L., & Chaudhury, A. (2017). Social movements as catalysts for corporate social innovation: environmental activism and the adoption of green information systems. *Business & Society*, 2, 000765031770167. https://doi.org/10.1177/0007650317701674

Carini, C., Borzaga, C., Chiomento, S., Franchini, B., Galera, G., & Nogales, R. (2020). *Social Enterprises and Their Ecosystems in Europe: Comparative Synthesis Report*. Available at: https://op.europa.eu/en/publication-detail/-/publication/4985a489-73ed-11ea-a07e-01aa75ed71a1/language-en

Child, J., Lu, Y., & Tsai, T. (2007). Institutional entrepreneurship in building an environmental protection system for the People's Republic of China. *Organization Studies*, 28(7), 1013–1034. https://doi.org/10.1177/0170840607078112

Defourny, J., & Nyssens, M. (Eds) (2021). *Social Enterprise in Western Europe: Theory, Models and Practice* (1st ed.). New York: Routledge.

DiMaggio, P. J., & Powell, W. W. (1983). The iron cage revisited: institutional isomorphism and collective rationality in organizational fields. *American Sociological Review*, 48(2), 147–160. https://doi.org/10.2307/2095101

Ebrahim, A., Battilana, J., & Mair, J. (2014). The governance of social enterprises: mission drift and accountability challenges in hybrid organizations. *Research in Organizational Behavior*, 34, 81–100. https://doi.org/10.1016/j.riob.2014.09.001

Ebrahim, A., & Rangan, V. K. (2014). What impact? A framework for measuring the scale and scope of social performance. *California Management Review*, 56(3), 118–141.

European Commission (2021). *Social Economy Action Plan*. Available at: https://ec. europa.eu/social/main.jsp?catId=1537&langId=en

Fligstein, N., & McAdam, D. (2015). *A Theory of Fields*. Oxford: Oxford University Press.

Frantzeskaki, N., & Wittmayer, J. M. (2019). The next wave of sustainability transitions: elucidating and invigorating transformations in the welfare state. *Technological Forecasting and Social Change*, 145(5), 136–140. https://doi.org/10.1016/j.techfore.2018. 09.023

Garud, R., Hardy, C., & Maguire, S. (2016). Institutional entrepreneurship as embedded agency: an introduction to the special issue. *Organization Studies*, 28(7), 957–969. https://doi.org/10.1177/0170840607078958

Geels, F. W. (2002). Technological transitions as evolutionary reconfiguration processes: a multi-level perspective and a case-study. *Research Policy*, 31(8–9), 1257–1274. https:// doi.org/10.1016/S0048-7333(02)00062-8

Geels, F. W. (2005a). Processes and patterns in transitions and system innovations: refining the co-evolutionary multi-level perspective. *Technological Forecasting and Social Change*, 72(6), 681–696. https://doi.org/10.1016/j.techfore.2004.08.014

Geels, F. W. (2005b). *Technological Transitions and System Innovations: A Co-evolutionary and Socio-technical Analysis*. Cheltenham, UK, Northampton, MA: Edward Elgar.

Geels, F. W., Kern, F., Fuchs, G., Hinderer, N., Kungl, G., Mylan, J., . . . Wassermann, S. (2016). The enactment of socio-technical transition pathways: a reformulated typology and a comparative multi-level analysis of the German and UK low-carbon electricity transitions (1990–2014). *Research Policy*, 45(4), 896–913. https://doi.org/10.1016/ j.respol.2016.01.015

Gegenhuber, T. (2020). Countering coronavirus with open social innovation. *Stanford Social Innovation Review*. Available at: https://ssir.org/articles/entry/countering_ coronavirus_with_open_social_innovation

Gehman, J., Grimes, M. G., & Cao, K. (2019). Why we care about certified B Corporations: from valuing growth to certifying values practices. *Academy of Management Discoveries*, 5(1), 97–101. https://doi.org/10.5465/amd.2018.0074

Giddens, A. (1984). *The Constitution of Society: Introduction of the Theory of Structuration*. Berkeley: University of California Press.

Gismondi, M., Connelly, S., Beckie, M., Markey, S., & Roseland, M. (Eds). (2016). *Scaling Up: The Convergence of Social Economy and Sustainability*. Athabasca University Press.

Gond, J.-P., & Boxenbaum, E. (2013). The glocalization of responsible investment: contextualization work in France and Québec. *Journal of Business Ethics*, 115(4), 707–721. https://doi.org/10.1007/s10551-013-1828-6

Gras, D., Conger, M., Jenkins, A., & Gras, M. (2019). Wicked problems, reductive tendency, and the formation of (non-)opportunity beliefs. *Journal of Business Venturing*, 105966. https://doi.org/10.1016/j.jbusvent.2019.105966

Hehenberger, L., Mair, J., & Metz, A. (2019). The assembly of a field ideology: an idea-centric perspective on systemic power in impact investing. *The Academy of Management Journal*, 62(6), 1672–1704. https://doi.org/10.5465/amj.2017.1402

Henry, M., Schraven, D., Bocken, N., Frenken, K., Hekkert, M., & Kirchherr, J. (2021). The battle of the buzzwords: a comparative review of the circular economy and the sharing economy concepts. *Environmental Innovation and Societal Transitions*, 38(1), 1–21. https://doi.org/10.1016/j.eist.2020.10.008

Hirsch, P. M., & Levin, D. Z. (1999). Umbrella advocates versus validity police: a life-cycle model. *Organization Science*, 10(2), 199–212. https://doi.org/10.1287/orsc.10.2.199

Hockerts, K., Hehenberger, L., Schaltegger, S., & Farber, V. (2022). Defining and conceptualizing impact investing: attractive nuisance or catalyst? *Journal of Business Ethics*, 11(15), 1. https://doi.org/10.1007/s10551-022-05157-3

Hoffman, A. J. (1999). Institutional evolution and change: environmentalism and the U.S. chemical industry. *Academy of Management Journal*, 42(4), 351–371. https://doi.org/10.5465/257008

Jacobides, M. G., Cennamo, C., & Gawer, A. (2018). Towards a theory of ecosystems. *Strategic Management Journal*, 39(8), 2255–2276. https://doi.org/10.1002/smj.2904

Kim, S., & Kim, A. (2021). Going viral or growing like an oak tree? Towards sustainable local development through entrepreneurship. *The Academy of Management Journal*. Advance online publication. https://doi.org/10.5465/amj.2018.0041

Krlev, G. (2019, 18 March). Three elephants in the impact investing room. Available at: https://www.pioneerspost.com/news-views/20190318/three-elephants-the-impact-investing-room

Krlev, G. (2022a). Let's join forces: institutional resilience and multistakeholder partnerships in crises. *Journal of Business Ethics*. Advance online publication. https://doi.org/10.1007/s10551-022-05231-w

Krlev, G. (2022b). The hiding hand, persistent fragile action, and sustainable development. In M. Hölscher, S. Toepler, R. List, & A. Ruser (Eds), *Civil Society: Concepts, Challenges, Contexts* (pp. 101–115). Heidelberg: Springer.

Krlev, G., Anheier, H. K., & Mildenberger, G. (2019a). Introduction: Social innovation—what is it and who makes it? In H. K. Anheier, G. Krlev, & G. Mildenberger (Eds), *Social Innovation: Comparative Perspectives* (pp. 3–35). Abingdon: Routledge.

Krlev, G., Anheier, H. K., & Mildenberger, G. (2019b). Results: the comparative analysis. In H. K. Anheier, G. Krlev, & G. Mildenberger (Eds), *Social Innovation: Comparative Perspectives* (pp. 257–279). Abingdon: Routledge.

Krlev, G., Bund, E., & Mildenberger, G. (2014). Measuring what matters—indicators of social innovativeness on the national level. *Information Systems Management*, 31(3), 200–224. https://doi.org/10.1080/10580530.2014.923265

Krlev, G., Mildenberger, G., & Anheier, H. K. (2020). Innovation and societal transformation—what changes when the 'social' comes in? *International Review of Applied Economics*, 34(5), 529–540.

Mair, J., Battilana, J., & Cardenas, J. (2012). Organizing for Society: A Typology of Social Entrepreneuring Models. *Journal of Business Ethics*, 111(3), 353–373. https://doi.org/10.1007/s10551-012-1414-3

Laamanen, T., Pfeffer, J., Rong, K., & van de Ven, A. (2018). Editors' introduction: business models, ecosystems, and society in the sharing economy. *Academy of Management Discoveries*, 4(3), 213–219. https://doi.org/10.5465/amd.2018.0110

Lall, S. A. (2019). From legitimacy to learning: how impact measurement perceptions and practices evolve in social enterprise–social finance organization relationships. *Voluntas*, 30(3), 562–577. https://doi.org/10.1007/s11266-018-00081-5

Lall, S. A., & Park, J. (2022). How social ventures grow: understanding the role of philanthropic grants in scaling social entrepreneurship. *Business & Society*, 61(1), 3–44. https://doi.org/10.1177/0007650320973434

Lee, M., Ramus, T., & Vaccaro, A. (2018). From protest to product: strategic frame brokerage in a commercial social movement organization. *Academy of Management Journal*, 61(6), 2130–2158. https://doi.org/10.5465/amj.2016.0223

Lindsay, G., & Hems, L. (2004). Sociétés Coopératives d'Intérêt Collectif: the arrival of social enterprise within the French social economy. *Voluntas*, 15(3), 265–286. https://doi.org/10.1023/B:VOLU.0000046281.99367.29

Lowe, T., Kimmitt, J., Wilson, R., Martin, M., & Gibbon, J. (2019). The institutional work of creating and implementing Social Impact Bonds. *Policy & Politics*, 47(2), 353–370. https://doi.org/10.1332/030557318X15333032765154

Mair, J., & Hehenberger, L. (2014). Front-stage and backstage convening: the transition from opposition to mutualistic coexistence in organizational philanthropy. *Academy of Management Journal*, 57(4), 1174–1200. https://doi.org/10.5465/amj.2012.0305

Mair, J., & Seelos, C. (2021). Organizations, social problems, and system change: invigorating the third mandate of organizational research. *Organization Theory*, 2(4), 263178772110548. https://doi.org/10.1177/26317877211054858

Mayer, C., & Roche, B. (Eds). (2021). *Putting Purpose into Practice: The Economics of Mutuality*. New York: Oxford University Press.

Micelotta, E., Lounsbury, M., & Greenwood, R. (2017). Pathways of institutional change: an integrative review and research agenda. *Journal of Management*, 43(6), 1885–1910.

Moulaert, F., & Nussbaumer, J. (2005). Defining the social economy and its governance at the neighbourhood level: a methodological reflection. *Urban Studies*, 42(11), 2071–2088. https://doi.org/10.1080/420980500279752

Mulgan, G. (2018). *Big Mind: How Collective Intelligence Can Change Our World*. Princeton and Oxford: Princeton University Press.

Mulgan, G. (2020). *The Case for Exploratory Social Sciences*. Available at: https://thenew.institute/en/media/the-case-for-exploratory-social-sciences

Nicholls, A. (Ed.) (2006). *Social Entrepreneurship: New Models of Sustainable Social Change*. Oxford: Oxford University Press.

Nicholls, A. (2018). A general theory of social impact accounting: materiality, uncertainty and empowerment. *Journal of Social Entrepreneurship*, 9(2), 132–153. https://doi.org/10.1080/19420676.2018.1452785

Nicholls, A., & Daggers, J. (2017). Academic research into social investment and impact investing: the status quo and future research. In O. M. Lehner (Ed.), *Routledge Handbook of Social and Sustainable Finance* (pp. 68–82). London: Routledge.

Nicholls, A., & Opal, C. (2005). *Fair Trade: Market-driven Ethical Consumption.* London, Thousand Oaks, CA: Sage.

Noya, A., & Clarence, E. (Eds) (2007). *The Social Economy: Building Inclusive Economies.* Paris: OECD Publishing.

Oberg, A., Lefsrud, L., & Meyer, R. E. (2021). Organizational (issue) field perspective on climate change. *Economic Sociology_the European Electronic Newsletter*, 22(3), 21–29.

Parsons, T. (1991). *The Social System* (2nd ed.). London: Routledge. Available at: http://site.ebrary.com/lib/alltitles/docDetail.action?docID=10165022

Pauly, R., Verschuere, B., Rynck, F. de, & Voets, J. (2021). Changing neo-corporatist institutions? Examining the relationship between government and civil society organizations in Belgium. *Public Management Review*, 23(8), 1117–1138. https://doi.org/10.1080/14719037.2020.1722209

Phillips, W., Alexander, E. A., & Lee, H. (2017). Going It Alone Won't Work! The Relational Imperative for Social Innovation in Social Enterprises. *Journal of Business Ethics*. 156, 315–331. https://doi.org/10.1007/s10551-017-3608-1

Pel, B., Haxeltine, A., Avelino, F., Dumitru, A., Kemp, R., Bauler, T., . . . Jørgensen, M. S. (2020). Towards a theory of transformative social innovation: a relational framework and 12 propositions. *Research Policy*, 49(8), 104080. https://doi.org/10.1016/j.respol.2020.104080

Rittel, H. W. J., & Webber, M. M. (1973). Dilemmas in a general theory of planning. *Policy Sciences*, 4(2), 155–169. https://doi.org/10.1007/BF01405730

Scheidgen, K., Gümüsay, A. A., Günzel-Jensen, F., Krlev, G., & Wolf, M. (2021). Crises and entrepreneurial opportunities: digital social innovation in response to physical distancing. *Journal of Business Venturing Insights*, 15, e00222. https://doi.org/10.1016/j.jbvi.2020.e00222

Scherer, A. G., Rasche, A., Palazzo, G., & Spicer, A. (2016). Managing for political corporate social responsibility: new challenges and directions for PCSR 2.0. *Journal of Management Studies*, 53(3), 273–298. https://doi.org/10.1111/joms.12203

Scholz, T. (2016). *Platform Cooperativism—Challenging the Corporate Sharing Economy.* Rosa Luxemburg Stiftung. http://www.academia.edu/download/44556273/scholz_platformcooperativism21.pdf

Scott, W. R. (2013). *Institutions and Organizations: Ideas, Interests, and Identities.* London: Sage.

Seibel, W. (2022). Successful failure: functions and dysfunctions of civil society organizations. In M. Hölscher, S. Toepler, R. List, & A. Ruser (Eds), *Civil Society: Concepts, Challenges, Contexts* (pp. 69–82). Heidelberg: Springer.

Smith, W. K., & Besharov, M. L. (2017). Bowing before dual gods: how structured flexibility sustains organizational hybridity. *Administrative Science Quarterly*, 1–44. https://doi.org/10.1177/0001839217750826

Spicer, J., Kay, T., & Ganz, M. (2019). Social entrepreneurship as field encroachment: how a neoliberal social movement constructed a new field. *Socio-Economic Review*, 17(1), 195–227.

Spieth, P., Schneider, S., Clauß, T., & Eichenberg, D. (2019). Value drivers of social businesses: a business model perspective. *Long Range Planning*, 52(3), 427–444. https://doi.org/10.1016/j.lrp.2018.04.004

Stovel, K., & Shaw, L. (2012). Brokerage. *Annual Review of Sociology*, 38(1), 139–158. https://doi.org/10.1146/annurev-soc-081309-150054

Teece, D. J. (2014). Business ecosystems. In M. Augier & D. Teece (Eds), *The Palgrave Encyclopedia of Strategic Management* (pp. 1–4). London: Palgrave Macmillan. https://doi.org/10.1057/9781137294678.0190

Tracey, P., & Stott, N. (2017). Social innovation: a window on alternative ways of organizing and innovating. *Innovation: Organization & Management*, 19(1), 51–60. https://doi.org/10.1080/14479338.2016.1268924

Westley, F., McGowan, K., & Tjörnbo, O. (Eds) (2017). *The Evolution of Social Innovation: Building Resilience through Transitions*. Cheltenham: Edward Elgar.

Wruk, D., Schöllhorn, T., & Oberg, A. (2020). Is the sharing economy a field? How a disruptive field nurtures sharing economy organizations. In I. Maurer, J. Mair, & A. Oberg, *Theorizing the Sharing Economy: Variety and Trajectories of New Forms of Organizing* (Vol. 66, pp. 131–162). Emerald Publishing Limited.

Wruk, D., Oberg, A., Klutt, J., & Maurer, I. (2019). The presentation of self as good and right: how value propositions and business model features are linked in the sharing economy. *Journal of Business Ethics*, 159(4), 997–1021. https://doi.org/10.1007/s10551-019-04209-5

Yan, S., Ferraro, F., & Almandoz, J. (2018). The rise of socially responsible investment funds: the paradoxical role of the financial logic. *Administrative Science Quarterly*, 13, 000183921877332. https://doi.org/10.1177/000183921877332

PART I

INNOVATION FOR IMPACT

4

The joint search for new approaches with a public good benefit

Four strategies and the role of social economy organizations

Marieke Huysentruyt

Introduction

In a world on fire (global climate crisis), in the grip of a pandemic (health crisis), and experiencing a steep, socially divisive economic downturn (social and economic crisis), compelling ideas and approaches that can effectively create both economic growth and social justice are urgently called for (von der Leyen, 2021; European Pillar of Social Rights, 2017). Recent years have seen a surge of social and political movement—so-called contentious crises (McDonnell & Cobb, 2020)—that expose firms and governments alike to criticism, and advocate social change.[1] There is a unique momentum now to build a twenty-first century economy that stands on moral values, justice, and social considerations (Barney & Rangan, 2019; Bowles & Carlin, 2020; George, Howard-Grenville, Joshi, & Tihanyi, 2016). One potential problem, though, is that decision-makers rarely foresee incentives for citizens, employees, groups of individuals, organizations, or groups of organizations to actually explore, to search in partnership for new ideas and approaches that promote both freedom and the cultivation of solidarity, fairness, reciprocity, and sustainability, and economic prosperity—giving way to the well-known free-riding problem. This raises an important policy question or opportunity: can policies designed to motivate people, communities, or organizations to jointly search for solutions to pressing societal challenges—solutions that benefit us all but are privately costly to discover—to help more effectively build a twenty-first century economy?

Inspired by insights from recent experiments finding strong complementarities between individuals' prosocial orientation, transparency, and incentives to innovate for the public good, this chapter proposes a comprehensive set of strategies

---

[1] Examples include the Yellow Vests (gilets jaunes) protests in France, the Black Lives Matter and #MeToo movements, the Extinction Rebellion movement, the Occupy London movement, and the Arab Spring movement.

Marieke Huysentruyt, *The joint search for new approaches with a public good benefit.* In: *Social Economy Science.*
Edited by: Gorgi Krlev, Dominika Wruk, Giulio Pasi, and Marika Bernhard, Oxford University Press.
© Oxford University Press (2023). DOI: 10.1093/oso/9780192868343.003.0004

available to decision-makers to encourage individuals, communities, or organizations to search together for solutions that speak to today's pressing social problems. Further, for each strategy, this chapter spells out the specific contributions that social economy organizations can make to enhance its effectiveness. Such contributions leverage social economy organizations' ability to recognize and leverage the power of social ties and social relations and to motivate people to contribute to the (local) commons and foster prosociality, among other things.

The remainder of this chapter is organized as follows. First, I succinctly present a theoretical framework from which the four strategies are derived. Second, I present the four strategies one by one, and detail several promising concrete actions for each. Third, I discuss the contributions that social economy organizations can make to improve the success of each strategy: its effectiveness and reach. I conclude with several directions for future research and policymaking.

Theoretical backbone: A dynamic model of joint exploration for the public good

The article entitled 'Exploration in Teams and the Encouragement Effect: Theory and Experimental Evidence' that I co-authored with Emma von Essen and Topi Miettinen, published in *Management Science* (2020), serves as the theoretical backbone of this chapter. The starting point of this article was the following observation: when it comes to innovation, we tend to think of innovation whose value can be readily appropriated by the innovator (through, say, patents or commercialization); innovation that yields predominantly private benefits (think of the private consumption of a latest consumer electronic device) and comes to light in specialized labs inside firms (R&D facilities), universities, or in-between spaces (through R&D partnerships). Innovation where the value created cannot be readily appropriated, that yields predominantly public benefits (positive externalities) and comes to light through voluntary, decentralized search, remains largely undertheorized and overlooked. Yet, precisely the latter type of innovation—what we refer to as innovation for the public good—has a critical role to play in moving us forward beyond the current global health, climate, and economic crises. Such innovation can meaningfully address the problems of poor or declining educational systems, unequal access to affordable health care, imminent environmental challenges, international terrorism, social fragmentation, and chronic offending in low-income, urban neighbourhoods, to name but a few pressing problems.

Examples of exploration or innovation for the public good abound. Innovation for the public good can arise at schools when teachers together search for new pedagogical tools to improve the engagement of students at risk of dropping out of school; in the streets when neighbours spontaneously search for ways to enhance local social cohesion; in industry-specific networks when industry leaders partner to set new international standards; online when tech entrepreneurs search for new ways to match the needs of refugees with citizen initiatives; in a coop when farmers search for crop varieties that enhance biodiversity; or at work when employees improvise to make their peers feel more engaged. These search processes produce knowledge and can yield the kinds of innovation that prior work has also referred to as social innovations, inclusive innovation, or responsible innovation.

In von Essen, Huysentruyt, and Miettinen (2020), we first analyse a two-person, two-stage model of sequential search where both information and pay-off external-ities exist and then test the derived hypotheses in the laboratory. We theoretically show that, even when agents are self-interested and perfectly rational, the infor-mation externality induces an encouragement effect: a positive effect of first-player exploration on the optimality of the second player exploring as well. When agents have other-regarding preferences and imperfectly optimize, the encouragement effect is strongest. The explorative nature of the game raises the expected surplus compared with a pay-off equivalent public goods game. We empirically confirm our main theoretical predictions using a novel experimental paradigm. Please refer to the published article for more details.

By centring on individuals' willingness to explore and comparing behaviour across different regimes varying the public good value of discovery and the degree of uncertainty, our research complements the growing stream of literature in which experiments are used to study the micro-foundations of innovation and their (social) impacts (Ederer & Manso, 2013; Burtch, He, Hong, & Lee, 2022). The article is also closely related to a large literature in behavioural economics that explores the role of other-regarding preferences to team performance outcomes and public good con-tributions (Camerer, 2003; Cappelen et al., 2015, Güth et al., 2007; Levati et al., 2007).

Four main findings of special interest to the present chapter stand out (von Essen et al., 2020). First, the greater the public value of the innovation (or the pay-off externality), the more individuals are willing to explore. Second, other-regarding preferences (and imperfect optimization) increase individuals' propensity to explore. Third, the information externality induces a positive informational encouragement effect: a positive effect of the first-player exploration on the optimality of the second player exploring as well. Fourth, uncertainty raises rather than decreases expected overall contributions to explore. Together, our findings underscore the role of pub-lic value benefits, other-regarding preferences, uncertainty, and learning in the joint search for the public good.

Strategies that enable joint exploration for the public good

The theoretical model introduced in the previous section advances four major factors—individuals' prosocial inclination, the level of uncertainty regarding whether a solution can be found, and the presence and size of informational and pay-off spillovers—that drive individuals' incentives to explore together and search for innovations for the public good. Many of these factors may appear intuitive, but some are surprising and have been overlooked. They are all powerful. They provide a strong theoretical basis for the strategies available to decision-makers who seek to elicit greater contributions to search for the public good and improve the efficacy of such search efforts.

Strategy No. 1: Raise the stakes

The greater the shared, public value of discovery, the more people are willing to explore, just as in the traditional free-riding models. This insight readily points to a first compelling strategy, which is to attempt to amplify the stakes—the actual and/or perceived gains from successful search. Concretely, decision-makers may be well advised to reframe the complex societal problems for which they seek to trigger more innovation in ways that better connect with people, that redress mistaken beliefs about such problems and/or make more salient the intrinsic benefits from exploring in partnership, all of which raise the stakes.

Many societal issues that urgently call for new ideas and approaches are hugely complex and difficult to grasp or connect with. Take climate change, for example. More information about why climate is changing, or even its impacts on polar bears, may satisfy our curiosity but does not necessarily make us more concerned about climate change or more willing to search for climate actions. Climate change is abstract rather than concrete. People often think of climate change as something that happens to faraway people and places. Global warming is often perceived as a niche issue. An important way to encourage people to get activated and search for alternative solutions, therefore, concerns the way we frame societal issues and the public good benefits that exploration yields. To close the psychological distance with which people view environmental and social challenges and elicit climate actions, for example, Hayhoe (2022) suggests we relate climate change to things people care about on a day-to-day level, such as the future of their children, social justice, or outdoor sports.

Issue frames are often chosen inadvertently, even in a setting where intrinsic motivation is known to play an important role, as if they matter little. However, a large and robust literature in the social sciences has demonstrated that seemingly minor changes in the framing—what we communicate about an issue, programme, or challenge—can have surprisingly large behavioural effects (e.g., Durand & Huysentruyt, 2022; Ganguli, Huysentruyt, & Le Coq, 2021). Issue frames and subtle informational cues can affect selection or whose attention we attract as well as subsequent exploration efforts, and thus the quality of exploration outcomes. To illustrate, in a field experiment that I and co-authors conducted in collaboration with one of the United Kingdom's largest support agencies in the field of social entrepreneurship (Ganguli, Huysentruyt, & Le Coq, 2021), we found that an emphasis on the monetary rewards that the agency provides appeals to more money-orientated candidate nascent social entrepreneurs, crowding out their more prosocial counterparts. The selection resulting from the extrinsic monetary incentive cue also led to worse performance at the end of the one-year grant period.[2] In sum: framing matters. Different people have different concerns and priorities, so there is no one framing that is right for all situations. Issue frames, however, influence the efficacy of communication about the issue.

The complexity of many societal issues may also lead us to hold incorrect or unclear mental models of the various systems they involve (Orion, 2002; Kempton, 1986). It is human nature, however, to avoid complexity (Bettinger et al., 2012; Bhargava, Loewenstein, & Sydnor, 2015; Hastings & Weinstein, 2008; Kling et al., 2012), because complexity tends to make us feel uncomfortable. Studies have shown that just simplifying information can affect parents' school choices (Hastings & Weinstein, 2008), individuals' healthcare decisions (Bhargava, Loewenstein, & Sydnor, 2015), individuals' savings decisions (Beshears et al., 2015), utilization of welfare benefits (Bhargava & Manoli, 2015) and individuals' take-up of services offered by corporate social initiatives (Durand & Huysentruyt, 2022). The risk is that the cognitive strain imparted by a societal problem's complexity (or the possible benefits from a solution) creates sufficient negative feelings about it that people will ignore or avoid the opportunity to innovate. This suggests an important role for decision-makers, which is to raise awareness about today's pressing social problems and make salient the impacts of alternative solutions using simple but accurate, actionable, and action-oriented terms.

Finally, decision-makers may be tempted to raise the stakes by introducing a private benefit attached to successful exploration for the public good; say, by offering monetary rewards. However, recall my example of a field experiment about monetary incentives, which showed that this can backfire. Consistent with our own work, Deserrano (2019) shows that financial incentives can crowd out the most pro-socially motivated applicants for a job vacancy at an NGO, and lead to lower performance of the new recruits. Monetary incentives can crowd out moral sentiments or prosocial behaviour (Bowles & Polanía-Reyes, 2012), such as blood giving (Titmuss, 1972) or charitable donations (e.g., Gneezy & Rustichini, 2000; Ariely et al., 2009; for review articles see Gneezy et al., 2011, Bowles & Polania-Reyes, 2012). Decision-makers are therefore well advised to prioritize the use of intrinsic incentives linked to exploration—for example, by triggering image or status concerns, giving people a greater sense of self—and collective efficacy, or making salient the valuable social ties that searching together helps to build.

To sum up, a first promising strategy available to decision-makers is to boost people's expected payoffs from discovery. Concrete actions involve issue reframing, simplifying information, and correcting flawed understandings of pressing societal

---

[2] Guzman, Oh, & Sen (2020) similarly examine the effect of social or money frames on selection of innovative entrepreneurs into a competition and find that women and individuals located in more altruistic cultures were more responsive to the social impact messages than by the money. The power of seemingly minor content cues has been empirically shown in a wide range of consequential decision-making areas, including important career-related decisions (Dal Bó et al., 2013, Ashraf et al., 2020, Desaranno, 2019, Guzman et al., 2020, von Essen et al., 2020) consumer finance (Choi et al., 2017), charity giving (Kessler & Milkman, 2018), organizational public goods (Blasco et al., 2019), academic science (Ganguli et al., 2017) and crowd science (Lyons & Zhang, 2019;

issues, and finally tapping more explicitly into intrinsic motives to elicit individual contributions to joint search efforts for the public good.

Strategy No. 2: Boost information-sharing

In settings where search is distributed and voluntary, it is essential that individuals can share and update information about which solutions are potentially still feasible and about others that have been tested and abandoned during the search process (von Essen et al., 2020). This not only increases motivation to explore (encouragement effect), and thus the amount of search effort expended, at least when there is a high probability of finding a solution, but also increases search efficiency as it helps avoid duplication efforts. A second strategy therefore for decision-makers so as to improve search for the public good revolves around information-sharing: incentivizing greater sharing of information about tried-but-failed solutions.

Prior work on learning communities suggests that, most importantly, trust and a shared passion lead people to band together and exchange knowledge. One way to build trust is to create the opportunity for repeated interactions. Many communities of practice indeed meet regularly—for lunch on Fridays, say—though some communities of practice are connected primarily by email networks (Wenger & Snyder, 2000). It is interesting to note that the large and influential body of work led by Elinor Ostrom would suggest that face-to-face communication is essential to sustain joint exploration efforts over time (Ostrom, 1998, 2002). Whether this still holds true today is an interesting question that warrants further systematic scrutiny. Overall, information-sharing infrastructure ideally foresees incentives to encourage repeated interactions between its contributors.

A recent trend in academic research calling for greater transparency resonates well with the underlying idea of accelerating information-sharing. It seems that the creation of simple online repositories, carefully curated or peer reviewed by high-status individuals, represents a powerful way forward, increasing individual incentives to share valuable lessons learned.[3]

A distinct, but complementary, way for decision-makers to encourage information-sharing and thus accelerate discovery is to attempt to transform or activate dormant knowledge. To see this, consider the notion of recombinant innovation, where old ideas can be reconfigured in new ways to make new ideas (Weitzman, 1998). Since most ideas or parents lie idle, they represent an important source of underutilized information (old ideas). Decision-makers could mandate or strongly incentivize patent-holders to make available their patents or knowledge for social purposes, for instance by granting time-bounded permission to use their knowledge in pre-defined markets for societal value creation. The idea is somewhat reminiscent of government schemes seeking to ensure access and use of generic

[3] For a recent example, see: https://aletheia-platform.netlify.app/

drugs (such as for HIV/AIDS).[4] Relatedly, innovation agencies, public and private alike, could mandate that recipients of innovation grants make available their knowledge, notably to bolster discovery for social goals or present an action plan themselves as to how they plan to accelerate the social impact of their innovations. Government certainly has some clout in implementing such regulation as public funds play an important role in the financing of research (Mazzucato, 2015).

In sum, a second compelling strategy available to decision-makers is to ease and encourage greater information-sharing among people, communities, or organizations. Concrete actions are wide-ranging: they include building new or supporting existing information-sharing initiatives that leverage the power of repeated interactions to build trust and elicit high-quality information-sharing, as well as encouraging the accessibility and use of old or dormant information to accelerate successful discovery.

Strategy No. 3: Promote prosociality

The stronger an individual's other-regarding preferences, the more likely it is that he or she will contribute to a joint search for the public good. This is a powerful insight. Luckily, people's preferences are much more malleable than we tend to believe. Hence, there are a host of actions that decision-makers can undertake to promote or strengthen prosociality.

At the organizational level, a fast-growing recent literature has suggested that purpose-driven organizations are especially well positioned to harness and inculcate greater prosocial motivation among their stakeholders, notably their employees. Henderson (2021) conjectures that this gives purpose-driven organizations a comparative advantage to explore systemic innovation. Purpose can give more meaning to work (Pink, 2011), create a stronger sense of identity (Akerlof & Kranton, 2005), and consequently raise productivity and elicit higher-quality, more creative searches (Burbano, 2016; Bode & Singh, 2018; Besley & Ghatak, 2005). Tsui (2012) makes a strong call for infusing organizations with more compassion, defined as an affective state and a broad class of emotional and behavioural responses that motivate the desire to help when one witnesses suffering. Compassion is closely associated with sympathy, kindness, tenderness, warmth, caring, or love (Goetz, Keltner, & Simon-Thomas, 2010). Perspective-taking, focusing on another's viewpoint and emotions—a fundamental aspect of meaningful communication—has also been found to promote prosociality (Chatruc & Rozo, 2022). Other research, including my own (Andersson et al., 2017), has found that organizations with a more prosocial culture are better attracting prosocial employees. Together, these studies underscore

---

[4] Impact Licensing Initiative (http://www.impactlicensing.org/), a non-profit start-up, has already stepped up to this challenge, and in a variety of social problem areas—ranging from medicine, renewables to mental health—is thinking up new applications, business models, and partnerships that allow technology holders to leverage their technology towards making progress against these problems.

the importance of softer aspects of management, such as prosocial culture, social purpose, compassion, and perspective-taking, to promote prosociality at work. The Pact Law of 22 May 2019 in France is in this respect a good example of how decision-makers can promote softer aspects of management. This law mandates companies in France to clarify their mission, beyond profit maximization.

Organizations can also try to leverage the prosocial interests and preferences of people external to their organization to improve innovation outcomes. Individuals who strongly value prosociality and openness to change are more likely to be able to see systems as malleable and to be able to imagine systemic transformation (Stephan & Huysentruyt, 2020). Targeted search, whereby ideas are sourced from individuals who strongly value self-transcendence and openness to change, has been found to yield more creative ideas for corporate sustainability innovations. This is not trivial as past research has found that corporations using broadcast search processes are not only often overwhelmed by the large number of ideas to evaluate, but that they also tend to select the ideas that are the least innovative or novel relative to their own past experiences (Piezunka & Dahlander, 2015).

At a broader, societal level, recent literature suggests that deliberate efforts to nurture prosocial preferences or attitudes among children can work. Kosse et al. (2020) analyse such one such programme that was tested in Germany, targeted at second-grade children of low socio-economic status families. The programme provides children with a mentor for the duration of one year. Conceptually, the idea of the programme was to extend a child's horizons and to foster the acquisition of new skills and experiences through social interactions between mentor and child. The mentor enriches a child's social environment and serves as a potential prosocial role model. Evaluation of this programme revealed that two years after the programme, children who were assigned to the programme revealed a significant and persistent increase in prosociality.

A third compelling strategy available to decision-makers is thus to boost and/or tap prosociality. Concrete actions involve promoting soft management skills such as purpose, culture, and perspective-taking; supporting open innovation initiatives that target individuals who strongly value prosociality and openness to change; and developing educational programmes that nurture prosociality, especially among young kids.

Strategy No. 4: Embrace an uncertainty mindset

Uncertainty in the production process of joint research for public goods, perhaps surprisingly, raises expected surplus compared to a pay-off equivalent public goods setting without uncertainty. This insight underlies our fourth and final strategy, which is for decision-makers to embrace an 'uncertainty mindset' (Tan, 2020). This may seem somewhat counterintuitive, as our brains are hardwired to see uncertainty as a risk or threat. It is physiologically normal to feel stress when faced with unfamiliar situations. However, recent research has found that embracing uncertainty, rather than denying it, makes teams more effective, innovative, and adaptable—and happier, too. Avoiding the negative feelings or discomfort that uncertainty tends to generate can indeed become a barrier to learning and ultimately performance. Thus, decision-makers are well advised to not only play up the uncertainty characteristic of search processes, but also help individuals embrace uncertainty.

One concrete action to this effect is for decision-makers to talk about the uncertainty that search involves; to be explicit about it, rather than hide it. This should trigger greater search contributions. At the same time, this may also help 'normalize' the idea of confronting or embracing uncertainty. Relatedly, decision-makers may seek to help people be more accepting towards uncertainty. Because acceptance allows us to see the reality of the situation in the present moment, it frees us up to move forward, rather than remaining paralysed (or made ineffective) by uncertainty, fear, or argument. To practise acceptance, we surrender our resistance to a problematic situation and to our emotions about the situation (Neff, 2012).

Practising humility, defined as appreciating the strengths of others, acknowledging one's limitations, and seeking feedback for improvement, also helps to embrace uncertainty. Prior research has found that greater humility among senior executives regarding their organization's efficacy to respond to complex societal challenges alone leads them to adopt complex systems frames and helps them to recognize the value of local constituents' resources and capabilities and become more willing to join meta-organizations and search for solutions in partnership (Valente & Oliver, 2018). Meta-organizations, defined as organizations of collective action made up of autonomous organizations or individuals that are not bound by authority but share a system-level goal (Gulati et al., 2012), in turn show special promise to host joint exploration efforts.

To sum up, a fourth strategy targeted at improving joint exploration is to promote an uncertainty mindset—concretely, to play up the uncertainty that search processes involve, and promote the acceptance of uncertainty and practising humility.

Role of social economy organizations

Social economy organizations, including associations, cooperatives, foundations, mutual organizations, and social enterprises (OECD, 2022), are widely thought to be at the forefront of social innovation. Many attempt to develop innovative solutions to improve the quality of life and wellbeing of individuals and communities while addressing socio-economic and environmental challenges, including those emerging with the COVID-19 pandemic and climate crises. Together, they help us imagine and realize an economy that embraces freedom and the associated norms of reciprocity, altruism, and fairness to enhance growth and wellbeing. Yet, their contributions are often marginalized from political discourse.

Characteristic of social economy organizations is their ability to recognize and leverage the power of social ties, relations, and pressures (often locally) to motivate people to contribute to the (local) commons and foster prosociality, among other things. This section builds on a large and robust literature that has demonstrated the many strengths (and weaknesses) of social economy organizations. What is new is that it identifies the distinct contributions of social economy organizations to ensure the successful elaboration and implementation of the four strategies available to decision-makers to promote joint search for the public good. Below, I discuss the potential for social economy organizations to strengthen the efficacy of each strategy, one by one.

To help raise the stakes more effectively: Many non-profit advocacy organizations, such as Greenpeace and Amnesty International, hold invaluable insight into how to reframe complex societal problems and redress mistaken beliefs about such problems. As they compete against a growing number of social economy organizations in an environment that has become increasingly 'noisy' with information, they are hard pressed to find more effective means to be heard. A recent study evaluating the different frames used by environmental advocacy organizations suggests that an economic frame and a personal frame are most effective to mobilize behavioural support (Zeng, Dai, & Javed, 2019).

Social economy organizations are renowned for putting a lot of emphasis on intrinsic benefits of being (and staying) involved. They typically leverage intrinsic incentives to motivate their staff and limit the use of extrinsic rewards, mindful of the potential crowding-out effects that the latter can produce. They often deliberately pursue the cultivation of moral sentiments to enhance their functioning. At the same time, social economy organizations are also well positioned to alert us to the 'dark sides' of strong intrinsic motivation—they can contribute to the development of burnout, mental health problems, and so on.

In a similar vein, funders of social economy organizations, such as the World Bank, have been testing alternative payment schemes whereby funding is conditional upon social outcomes (for example health outcomes), the underlying idea being that this strengthens people's intrinsic incentives to deliver social goods. Further, social economy organizations may be required to spend the bulk of the funds on organization-level inputs, such as equipment or employee training, not on personal benefits such as wage increases. Together with co-authors, I have studied the impact of performance-based finance in healthcare in the Democratic Republic of Congo and found that such schemes can effectively help improve operating efficiency and reduce stillbirths and neonatal deaths (Fangwa et al., 2022).

In sum, social economy organizations can help decision-makers think up effective ways to play up the public benefits that successful discovery yields and make salient intrinsic rewards, and thus raise the stakes, encouraging greater joint search for the public good.

To encourage people to share information: Many social economy organizations rely on information-sharing mechanisms to achieve their mission, be it to promote recycling (Barnosky, Delmas, & Huysentruyt, 2022) or the adoption of new agricultural technologies (BenYishay & Mobarak, 2019). Consider the example of Yoyo, a French social enterprise focused on making recycling not only more convenient but also more fun (The Yoyo team, 2023). Yoyo has created a network of coaches and sorters in six major cities in France (Paris, Lyon, Bordeaux, Marseille, Reims, and Mulhouse). The system is simple: sorters sign up to the platform, then choose a local Coach, drop by to pick up their first bag, and then start filling it with plastic bottles. Once full, the bags are returned to the Coach, and then Yoyo picks up the bags and delivers them to the nearest recycling centre. Sorters receive points for diverting plastic bottles from landfill, which they can exchange for gifts. Yoyo builds a sense of community by creating social links locally and exploits those links to attract new recruits, sustain commitment over time, and notably spread information. It puts great emphasis on positive reinforcement and steers away from shaming, let alone penalties. Relatedly, many social economy organizations have become increasingly savvy about how to diffuse information widely and cost-effectively. Recent studies have found that seeding simple information with highly central individuals in local networks—'gossipers' in Banerjee et al. (2019)—can lead to greater diffusion than relying on random individuals. In our context of joint search for public good solutions, highly central individuals may also be able to accelerate the spread of information and, if trusted, encourage information-sharing itself.

Many social economy organizations curate online information platforms (with DIY tips and tricks or on parenting skills) as well as communities of practices (for example in global health). Their non-profit status often acts as a credible sign that they do not seek to profit from individuals' willingness to share ideas or shirk on costs in the interest of profits.

At a societal level, social economy organizations are also believed to play an important role in democratizing societies—encouraging people to speak up and express their opinions; representing a plurality of perspectives; enabling individuals to engage in self-determined actions and to challenge existing norms. Whether these practices also lead people to share information in the context of joint search for public good benefits remains unclear. This may well depend on the importance of individualism in the society.

Finally, social economy organizations could also play an active role as licensee—leveraging underexploited knowledge (patents) to better address pressing societal problems. Hybrid social economy organizations, those that mix a charity logic with a commercial one, are likely to garner most trust among businesses (with dormant technology). In my own work with Ute Stephan, I have found that social entrepreneurs are better at identifying the most creative opportunities for sustainable innovation relative to mainstream business entrepreneurs and employees (Stephan & Huysentruyt, 2020). For these reasons, social entrepreneurs, who tend to be very open to change and value self-transcendence, may well be perfect candidates to strike social licensing agreements with.

In sum, with respect to enabling and accelerating information exchange, decision-makers can seek to mobilize the contributions of social economy organizations in three distinct ways. First, decision-makers could try to expand the most successful information-sharing platforms and communities that social economy organizations curate. Second, they could try to adopt lessons learned from social economy organizations in terms of how individuals can be encouraged to freely voice their views and share information, and how such information can be most effectively diffused. Finally, they could seek out social economy organizations as candidate social impact license holders.

To help spread prosociality: Social economy organizations have a rich tradition of leveraging prosocial values (such as compassion and empathy) and prosocial behaviours (such as caring, volunteering, and giving) to serve their social cause and ensure organizational sustainability. These are precisely the values and behaviours that are expected to lead individuals to engage more in joint exploration for the public good.

Many social economy organizations target the wellbeing of children and youth, using, for instance, mentors to elicit greater prosociality. Their practices, when leveraged by schools or even preschools nationwide, have tremendous potential to affect not just student outcomes in the short term, but also wellbeing in the longer run.

However, social economy organizations can also have a more indirect impact on prosociality in society. For example, many social economy organizations partner with for-profit firms, including large multinational companies, through, say, corporate social initiatives (Durand & Huysentruyt, 2022), cross-sectoral collaborations (Bode, Rogan, & Singh, 2019), or market-exchange relationships (such as procurement). Such collaborations can help strengthen the prosocial preferences of the firms' employees, and thus represent another powerful conduit to spread prosocial preferences.

In sum, with respect to strengthening individuals' prosociality, decision-makers can seek to support or scale the activities of social economy organizations committed to spreading prosociality at large and of those with a goal to promote prosociality among children and youth, in particular. Further, decision-makers may wish to encourage the emergence of cross-sectoral collaborations, whereby collaborations with social economy organizations can help raise the prosociality of all actors involved.

To help promote an uncertainty mindset: Many social economy organizations face increasing uncertainty: notably financial uncertainty, but also institutional, policy, and impact uncertainty. Many social economy organizations operate in nascent markets or weak contexts where strong blueprints are missing and thus where uncertainty prevails. These contexts push them to find ways to navigate growing uncertainty, including embracing it as a force for innovation and survival. One particular response is to pursue effectuation decision-making processes, rather than causation pathways. Accordingly, social economy organizations will start with their means (not with their ends), leverage contingencies, set affordable loss, form partnerships, and control the controllable (Sarasvathy, 2001). They take the future as fundamentally unpredictable, yet controllable through human action. Effectuation evokes creative and transformative tactics.

From organizational culture to organizational design, there are many factors at the level of an organization that will influence the extent to which its members are encouraged to explore. For instance, a tolerance for early failure and rewards for long-term success have been shown to be effective in motivating innovation (Ederer & Manso, 2013).

Many social economy organizations act on systemic problems, whereby it is often difficult to disentangle the impacts that they make from those of the many other actors involved. This gives rise to problems of attribution and impact uncertainty. Social economy organizations therefore hold invaluable lessons learned regarding how to cope with impact uncertainty and avoid that this undermines stakeholders' motivation to contribute.

In sum, to encourage people to embrace uncertainty and jointly explore for the public good, decision-makers may seek to promote effectual reasoning, tolerate early failure and reward longer-term success, and make salient the many types of uncertainties, including impact uncertainty, that these search processes involve.

Conclusion

In many domains there is a pressing need for decision-makers, public and private alike, to encourage individuals, communities, or organizations to partner up more and jointly search for solutions that are intrinsically public goods. However, these settings suffer from the free-riding problem when exploration is privately costly and cannot be contracted upon, and benefits are shared and cannot be privately appropriated. In this chapter I have asked what are the most promising strategies available to decision-makers to overcome the free-riding problem and encourage a greater joint search for the public good. I used a theoretical two-person, two-stage exploration model, validated in a controlled laboratory setting, to derive four key strategies. They are: to raise the stakes or the expected gains from successful exploration; to make information-sharing easier and more desirable; to nurture prosociality among people; and to embrace an uncertainty mindset. While there are many ways in which decision-makers can put these strategies into practice, I argue that one promising and cost-effective way is to leverage the unique know-how and capabilities of social economy organizations. Table 4.1 provides a summary overview.

There are two limitations worth highlighting and discussing. The findings in von Essen, Huysentruyt, and Miettinen (2020) suggest that the four strategies to promote innovation for the public good are complementary, that is, that their effects on exploration for the public good reinforce one another. But this remains to be shown in the field. Second, uncertainty can be fractioned into two distinct psychological constructs: risk (known probabilistic outcomes) and ambiguity (unknown probabilistic outcomes). In this chapter I focused on uncertainty as in risk and/or ambiguity; however, in some specific innovation settings, it may be worthwhile to disentangle the two.

The work presented here opens a rich agenda for future research. What is the cost-effectiveness of each strategy, and of specific underlying actions? Might there be an ideal sequencing or ordering of strategies with which to take these strategies to the

Table 4.1 Four strategies to promote joint search for the public good, concrete actions, and contribution of social economy organizations

No	What is the strategy?	What actions would help decision-makers realize the strategy?	What can social economy organizations do to improve success of the strategy?
1	Raise the stakes	Reframe the societal challenge Correct mistaken beliefs about the societal challenge Make more salient the expected public good benefits from successful discovery Strengthen intrinsic incentives to explore	Advise on what are most effective communication frames Advise on how to exploit intrinsic incentives without backfiring
2	Boost information-sharing	Create trusted spaces for people with a shared passion Scale up existing information-sharing platforms Transform dormant knowledge Mandate recipients of innovation grants to make available their findings	Make available and scale up information-sharing platforms that they already curate Advise on how social networks can be used to accelerate the sharing and diffusion of information Generate creative ideas for how dormant knowledge can be reconfigured
3	Promote prosociality	Support the development of purpose-driven organizations Promote softer aspects of management Encourage open innovation initiatives with social entrepreneurs Develop educational programmes that nurture prosociality	Advise on how to nurture prosociality Contribute to narrow search for sustainability challenges launched by businesses Scale up their educational programmes on fostering prosociality
4	Embrace an uncertainty mindset	Talk about uncertainty Promote acceptance of uncertainty Promote self-compassion practice humility	Talk about uncertainty in their fundraising campaigns Advise on how to strengthen uncertainty acceptance Scale up their activities that promote self-compassion and humility

field? What happens when there is uncertainty about the 'state of the world' in which we live—that is, whether a solution to the societal problem can be found with high or low probability: might this change our policy recommendations?

This chapter does not claim that strategies targeting innovation for the public good are the *only* solution to today's climate, health, social-economic, and contentious crises. Nonetheless, it advances that sensible innovation policy design is a key part of the solution to rebuilding an economy that stands on moral values, justice, and social consideration. Social economy organizations have an essential role to play in making these strategies work.

References

Akerlof, G. A., & Kranton, R. E. (2005). Identity and the economics of organizations. *Journal of Economic Perspectives*, 19(1), 9–32.

Andersson, O., Huysentruyt, M., Miettinen, T., & Stephan, U. (2017). Person–organization fit and incentives: a causal test. *Management Science*, 63(1), 73–96.

Ariely, D., Bracha, A., & Meier, S. (2009). Doing good or doing well? Image motivation and monetary incentives in behaving prosocially. *American Economic Review*, 99(1), 544–555.

Ashraf, N., Bandiera, O., Davenport, E., & Lee, S. S. (2020). Losing prosociality in the quest for talent? Sorting, selection, and productivity in the delivery of public services. *American Economic Review*, 110(5), 1355–1394.

Banerjee, A., Chandrasekhar, A. G., Duflo, E., & Jackson, M. O. (2019). Using Gossips to Spread Information: Theory and Evidence from Two Randomized Controlled Trials. *The Review of Economic Studies*, 86(6), 2453–2490. https://doi.org/10.1093/restud/rdz008

Barney, J., & Rangan, S. (2019). Editors' comments: why do we need a special issue on new theoretical perspectives on market-based economic systems? *Academy of Management Review*, 44(1), 1–5.

Barnosky, E., Delmas, M., & Huysentryt, M. (2022). *The Circular Economy: Motivating Recycling Behavior for a More Effective System*, Working Paper.

BenYishay, A., & Mobarak, A. M. (2019). Social learning and incentives for experimentation and communication. *The Review of Economic Studies*, 86(3), 976–1009.

Beshears, J., Choi, J. J., Laibson, D., Madrian, B. C., & Milkman, K. L. (2015). The Effect of Providing Peer Information on Retirement Savings Decisions. *The Journal of Finance*, 70(3), 1161–120. https://doi.org/10.1111/jofi.12258

Besley, T., & Ghatak, M. (2005). Competition and incentives with motivated agents. *American Economic Review*, 93(5), 616–636.

Bettinger, E. P., Long, B. T., Oreopoulos, P., & Sanbonmatsu, L. (2012). The Role of Application Assistance and Information in College Decisions: Results from the H&R Block Fafsa Experiment Quarterly *Journal of Economics*, 127(3), 1205–1242. https://doi.org/10.1093/qje/qjs017

Bhargava, S., & Manoli, D. (2015). Psychological frictions and the incomplete take-up of social benefits: evidence from an IRS field experiment. *American Economic Review*, 105(11), 3489–3529.

Bhargava, S., Loewenstein, G., & Sydnor, J. (2015). Do Individuals Make Sensible Health Insurance Decisions? Evidence from a Menu with Dominated Options. Cambridge, MA: National Bureau of Economic Research.

Blasco, A., Jung, O. S., Lakhani, K. R., & Menietti, M. (2019). Incentives for public goods inside organizations: field experimental evidence. *Journal of Economic Behavior and Organization*, 1(160), 214–229.

Bode, C., & Singh, J. (2018). Taking a hit to save the world? Employee participation in a corporate social initiative. *Strategic Management Journal*, 39(4), 1003–1030.

Bode, C., Rogan, M., & Singh, J. (2019). Sustainable cross-sector collaboration: building a global platform for social impact. *Academy of Management Discoveries*, 5(4), 396–414.

Bowles, S. (2016). *The Moral Economy: Why Good Incentives Are No Substitute for Good Citizens*. New Haven: Yale University Press.

Bowles, S., & Carlin, W. (2020, May). Shrinking capitalism. In *AEA Papers and Proceedings* (Vol. 110, pp. 372–377).

Bowles, S., & Polanía-Reyes, S. (2012). Economic incentives and social preferences: substitutes or complements? *Journal of Economic Literature*, 50(2), 368–425. https://doi.org/10.1257/jel.50.2.368

Burbano, V. C. (2016). Social responsibility messages and worker wage requirements: field experimental evidence from online labor marketplaces. *Organization Science*, 27(4), 1010–1028.

Burtch, G., He, Q., Hong, Y., & Lee, D. (2022). How Do Peer Awards Motivate Creative Content? Experimental Evidence from Reddit. Management Science, 68(5), 3488–3506. https://doi.org/10.1287/mnsc.2021.4040

Camerer, C. (2003). *Behavioral Game Theory: Experiments in Strategic Interaction* Princeton: Princeton University Press.

Cappelen, A.W., Reme, B.-A., Sørensen, E.Ø., & Tungodden, B. (2015). Leadership and incentives. *Management Science*, 62(7), 1944–1953.

Choi, J. J., Haisley, E., Kurkoski, J., & Massey, C. (2017). Small cues change savings choices. *Journal of Economic Behavior & Organization*, 142, 378–395.

Dal Bó, E., Finan, F., & Rossi, M. (2013). Strengthening state capabilities: the role of financial incentives in the call to public service. *Quarterly Journal of Economics*, 128(3), 1169–1218.

Deserranno, E. (2019). Financial incentives as signals: experimental evidence from the recruitment of village promoters in Uganda. *American Economic Journal: Applied Economics*, 11(1), 277–317.

Durand, R., & Huysentruyt, M. (2022). Communication frames and beneficiary engagement in corporate social initiatives: evidence from a randomized controlled trial in France. *Strategic Management Journal*, 43(9), 1823–1853.

Ederer, F., & Manso, G. (2013). Is pay-for-performance detrimental to innovation? *Management Science*, 59(7), 1496–1513.

European Pillar of Social Rights (2017). The European Pillar of Social Rights Action Plan. Retrieved from https://op.europa.eu/webpub/empl/european-pillar-of-social-rights/en/

Fangwa, A., Flammer, C., Huysentruyt, M., & Quélin, B. (2022). *Corporate Governance and Social Impact of Non-Profits: Evidence from a Randomized Program in Healthcare in the Democratic Republic of Congo*, Working Paper.

Ganguli, I., Gaulé, P., Guinan, E., & Lakhani, K. (2017). *Do Scientists Care about Kudos? A Field Experiment on Status Rewards in Academia* Working paper, University of Massachusetts, Amherst.

Ganguli, I., Huysentruyt, M., & Le Coq, C. (2021). How do nascent social entrepreneurs respond to rewards? A field experiment on motivations in a grant competition. *Management Science*, 67(10), 6294–6316.

George, G., Howard-Grenville, J., Joshi, A., & Tihanyi, L. (2016). Understanding and tackling societal grand challenges through management research. *Academy of Management Journal*, 59(6), 1880–1895.

Gneezy, U., & Rustichini, A. (2000). Pay enough or don't pay at all. *Quarterly Journal of Economics*, 115(3), 791–810.

Gneezy, U., Meier, S., & Rey-Biel, P. (2011). When and why incentives (don't) work to modify behaviour. *Journal Ecomonic Perspectives*, 25(4), 191–210.

Goetz, J. L., Keltner, D., & Simon-Thomas, E. (2010). Compassion: an evolutionary analysis and empirical review. *Psychological Bulletin*, 136(3), 351.

Gulati, R., Puranam, P., & Tushman, M. (2012). Meta-organization design: rethinking design in interorganizational and community contexts. *Strategic Management Journal*, 33(6), 571–586.

Güth, W., Levati, M. V., Sutter, M., & Van Der Heijden, E. (2007). Leading by example with and without exclusion power in voluntary contribution experiments. *Journal of Public Economics*, 91(5), 1023–1042.

Guzman G., Oh, J. J., & Sen, A. (2020). What motivates innovative entrepreneurs? Evidence from a global field experiment. *Management Science*. 66(6), 4359–4919, iii–iv.

Hastings, J. S., & Weinstein, J. M. (2008). Information, School Choice, and Academic Achievement: Evidence from Two Experiments. *Quarterly Journal of Economics*, 123(4), 1373–1414. https://doi.org/10.1162/qjec.2008.123.4.1373

Hayhoe, K. (2022). *Saving Us: A Climate Scientist's Case for Hope and Healing in a Divided World*. Humphrey School of Public Affairs' Swain Climate Policy Series, University of Minnesota.

Henderson, R. (2021). Innovation in the 21st century: architectural change, purpose, and the challenges of our time. *Management Science*, 67(9), 5479–5488.

Kempton, W. (1986). Two Theories of Home Heat Control. *Cognitive Science*, 10(1), 75–90. https://doi.org/10.1207/s15516709cog1001_3

Kessler, J. B., & Milkman, K. L. (2018). Identity in charitable giving. *Management Science*, 64, 845–859.

Kling, J. R., Mullainathan, S., Shafir, E., Vermeulen, L. C., & Wrobel, M. V. (2012). Comparison friction: Experimental evidence from medicare drug plans. *Quarterly Journal of Economics*, 127(1), 199–235. https://doi.org/10.1093/qje/qjr055

Kosse, F., Deckers, T., Pinger, P., Schildberg-Hörisch, H., & Falk, A. (2020). The formation of prosociality: causal evidence on the role of social environment. *Journal of Political Economy*, 128(2), 434–467.

Levati, M. V., Sutter, M., & van der Heijden, E. (2007). Leading by Example in a Public Goods Experiment with Heterogeneity and Incomplete Information. *Journal of Conflict Resolution*, 51(5), 793–818. https://doi.org/10.1177/00220027073 02796

Lyons, E., & Zhang, L. (2019). Trade-offs in motivating volunteer effort: experimental evidence on voluntary contributions to science. *PloS one*, 14(11), p.e0224946.

Mazzucato, M. (2015). The green entrepreneurial state. In: Leach M., Newell P., & Scoones I. (Eds.). *The Politics of Green Transformations* (pp. 134–152). London: Routledge.

McDonnell, M.-H., & Cobb, J. A. (2020). Take a Stand or Keep Your Seat: Board Turnover after Social Movement Boycotts. *The Academy of Management Journal*, 63(4), 1028–1053. https://doi.org/10.5465/amj.2017.0890

Neff K. D. (2012). The science of self-compassion. In Germer C., Siegel R. (Eds), *Compassion and wisdom in psychotherapy* (pp. 79–92). New York: Guilford Press.

OECD (2022), *Legal frameworks for the social and solidarity economy: OECD Global Action Promoting Social and Solidarity Economy Ecosystems*, OECD Local Economic and Employment Development (LEED) Papers, No. 2022/04, OECD Publishing, Paris, https://doi.org/10.1787/480a47fd-en

Orion, N. (2002). An Earth systems curriculum development model., In: Mayer, V. J. (Ed.) *Global Science Literacy* (pp. 159–168). Dordrecht: Springer Netherlands.

Ostrom, E. (1998). A behavioral approach to the rational choice theory of collective action: presidential address. *American Political Science Review*, 92(1), 1–22.

Ostrom, E. (2002). Common-pool resources and institutions: toward a revised theory. *Handbook of Agricultural Economics*, 2, 1315–1339.

Piezunka, H., & Dahlander, L. (2019). Idea rejected, tie formed: organizations' feedback on crowdsourced ideas. *Academy of Management Journal*, 62(2), 503–530.

Pink, D. H. (2011). *Drive: The Surprising Truth about What Motivates Us*. London: Penguin.

Rodríguez Chatruc, M., & Rozo, S. V. (2022). Discrimination toward migrants during crises. *Migration Studies*, 10(4), 582–607. https://doi.org/10.1093/migration/mnac027

Sarasvathy, S. D. (2001). Causation and effectuation: toward a theoretical shift from economic inevitability to entrepreneurial contingency. *Academy of Management Review*, 26(2), 243–263.

Stephan, U., & Huysentruyt, M. (2020) *The Distinctive Value of Social Entrepreneurs for Open Sustainable Innovation*. Working paper.

Tan, V. (2020). *Uncertainty mindset: Innovation insights from the frontiers of food*. New York: Columbia University Press.

The Yoyo team (2023). *Connecting Eco Friendly Companies to the Green Minded*. Retrieved from https://yoyo.eco/

Titmuss, R. M. (1972). *The gift relationship: From human blood to social policy*. Bristol: Bristol University Press.

Tsui, A. S. (2012). Presidential address—on compassion in scholarship: Why should we care? *Academy of Management Review*, 38(2), 167–180.

Valente, M., & Oliver, C. (2018). Meta-organization formation and sustainability in Sub-Saharan Africa. *Organization Science*, 29(4), 678–701.

von der Leyen, U. (2021). *2021 State of the Union Address by President von der Leyen*. European Commission: Brussels.

von Essen, E., Huysentruyt, M., & Miettinen, T. (2020). Exploration in teams and the encouragement effect: theory and experimental evidence. *Management Science*, 66(12), 5861–5885.

Weitzman, M. L. (1998). Recombinant Growth. *Quarterly Journal of Economics*, 113(2), 331–360. https://doi.org/10.1162/003355398555595

Wenger, E. C., & Snyder, W. M. (2000). Communities of practice: the organizational frontier. *Harvard Business Review*, 78(1), 139–146.

Zeng, F., Dai, J., & Javed, J. (2019). Frame alignment and environmental advocacy: the influence of NGO strategies on policy outcomes in China. *Environmental Politics*, 28(4), 747–770.

5

The social economy and the Fourth Industrial Revolution

The risks of marginalization and how to avoid them

Geoff Mulgan

Introduction: the challenge of the 4IR

The Fourth Industrial Revolution (4IR) is a broad framework or umbrella term covering not just data and artificial intelligence (AI), but also their links to physical objects: infrastructures, cars, homes, and cities. Some of the writing on it is pure hype. But it also describes important, and very real, trends.

The 4IR presents big challenges to the social economy. A decade ago, there were high hopes that the social economy would play a dominant role in the next phase of the digital economy, and in particular the spread of new platforms. This was the promise of the sharing economy that would allow people to share their time, their goods, and their services more easily. These promises precisely echoed the earlier hopes that the internet would usher in a world of equality and democracy, flattening hierarchies of all kinds. Instead, just as the internet ended up dominated by a small number of global companies, so did the sharing economy field end up dominated by for-profits such as Uber and Airbnb.

I have been closely involved as a funder and investor in many projects—some in civil society, some commercial, and some public sector. I have, for example, seen the struggles to turn 'platform cooperativism' from a promising concept into a plausible option for running services at significant scale. But these alternatives remain marginal and a similar pattern could happen with the next generations of AI. So, it is important to be clear about how the social economy in all its forms can act more strategically to shape the development and application of this family of technologies.

Unfortunately, this task is not helped by the fact that much of the commentary on the 4IR—both enthusiastic and critical—takes a technological determinist view whereby new technologies directly shape society (either generating new wealth or corroding democracy or similar; examples include Zuboff, 2019), rather than recognizing the potential to shape the direction of both R&D and applications, and the co-evolution of technologies and social systems. Instead, I argue for a better combination of policy action and what I call 'exploratory social science'—the deliberate

Geoff Mulgan, *The social economy and the Fourth Industrial Revolution*. In: *Social Economy Science*. Edited by: Gorgi Krlev, Dominika Wruk, Giulio Pasi, and Marika Bernhard, Oxford University Press. © Oxford University Press (2023). DOI: 10.1093/oso/9780192868343.003.0005

mapping out of desirable new social arrangements and governance (Mulgan, 2021).

Understanding the technology: AI and related data as GPTs

Let me start with a brief description of the technologies that are making new options possible. There are many different strands of digital technology relevant to this discussion, including both hardware and software. They include data and the widespread use of data, whether for analysis, customer relationship management, policy, or almost everything else.

There is a long history of research into what are called GPTs, or general purpose technologies. Past examples include the car, electricity, and the telephone. These tend to have transformative effects on many areas of life and the economy. Digital technologies include many potential GPTs. The ability to data well has become essential for many areas of life, from marketing to managing pandemics. Another cluster of relevant technologies is the platforms—of many kinds, whether for selling, for exchange, or for social interactions. Again, these are ubiquitous in daily life: mainly commercial ones such as Facebook and TikTok, but also including non-commercial ones such as Wikipedia. Then there is AI of all kinds, including machine learning (ML), which is embedded in generic tools—accounting, payroll and HR, customers—and in many of the devices we carry around, and is widely seen as a GPT. There are also other variants of AI, including computer vision, robotics and natural language processing, conversational interfaces such as Amazon's Alexa or Microsoft's Cortana, augmented/virtual reality interfaces, and powerful new tools such as ChatGPT that could turn out to represent a leap in the capacity of AI to handle language and meaning. Finally, there is the related umbrella term of 'the Internet of Things', which refers to connections between physical objects and the tools that are used to manage energy, transport, and buildings. This broad family of technologies has the potential to affect almost every aspect of the social economy and civil society: how it organizes, how it connects to citizens, how it learns, and how it manages money.

Ethics and regulation to guide the 4IR

The 4IR—a broad umbrella term for the many technologies mentioned above—was first promoted by the World Economic Forum and has been picked up enthusiastically by business and some governments. Civil society has had relatively little involvement (I use civil society as a broader category than the social economy, including charities, campaigns, and social movements as well as more obviously economic organizations such as social enterprises, mutuals, and coops).

There are the beginnings of a scholarly literature on the possible social impacts of the 4IR but it is often quite thin (Callahan, 2014), and more focused on ethics offering general principles (Floridi et al., 2018) rather than detailed analysis of social impacts. The main focus has been on the various ways in which AI could threaten values—truth, peace, democracy, and so on—through algorithmic warfare or the proliferation of fake news or deep fakes; algorithmic bias built into decision-making tools, particularly in fields such as criminal justice; and potential abuses of facial recognition and other tools. Greater vigilance of this kind is clearly vital as AI becomes more ubiquitous and plays a bigger role in decisions, and the extraordinary philanthropic and commercial funding for centres for AI ethics around the world is welcome.

However, this work has tended to be general rather than particular; it has tended to exclude politics; and, apart from a handful of exceptions (New Technologies and Digitisation, 2020), there continues to be little work on public policy options (so that policymakers in the European Commission and national governments have had to develop the options for themselves). While many of the ethical proposals that have been made are sensible (Floridi & Cowls, 2019) they have been relatively limited in their impact (Horvitz, 2017), often lacking nuance on social implications, let alone strategic options (Taddeo & Floridi, 2018), and tending to generate codes or lists, which in turn have turned out to be hard to implement (Mulgan, 2019). In the wake of GDPR, some moves have been made to enhance the social dimension of technology, with the EU at the forefront of moves to require algorithms to 'explain themselves' and the idea of using counterfactuals (i.e. statements of how things could have been different) to explain algorithmic decisions without having to 'open the black box' (which may be necessary given the huge complexity of some current AI applications). The EU has also moved ahead with comprehensive legislation banning uses of algorithms for facial recognition and social credit, mirrored on the other side of the world by new legislation introduced in China in late 2021.

Promoting technology for good

Most of these moves have presented the technologies of the 4IR as a threat that needs regulation and constraining. On the other hand, there have been some moves to promote more socially oriented AI. Healthcare is probably the most advanced, with AI used for diagnosis, chatbots for patient interactions, covered in many surveys. There are many examples in agriculture—using ML to spot patterns in crops, such as Aerobotics combining drones and AI to spot pests, or the Ethiopia Coffee Exchange providing a range of informational feedback to growers. There is a great deal of AI in education—for curriculum design, assessment, direct online delivery of material customized to individual pupils (Baker et al., 2019)—including specific funding streams (I initiated one of these in the UK, particularly focused on commissioning tools that would make teachers' lives easier). There are some uses of AI in democracy—such as Polis and other tools for orchestrating debate, as used in vTaiwan (an online–offline consultation process which brings together various stakeholders) and elsewhere—and there are some more specialist applications such as refugeesAI, designed to help with resettlement.

Civil society (Mulgan et al., 2018) has become more effective at using already mature digital technologies, though less so in terms of the leading edges. This is apparent in the growing digital social innovation field in Europe, which has connected the growing community of several thousand charities, social enterprises, and grassroots groups using data sharing and interoperability across Europe. There are many good examples of initiatives to raise capacity in civil society, from TechSoup in the US to cibervoluntarias in Spain to CAST in the UK. DataKind helps civil society to make better use of their own and others' data, while Seoul is home to the civil society-focused Big Data Academy. Other examples include the Mobilisation Lab aimed at activists. There are examples on the frontiers of technology such as Open Bionics harnessing the power of robotics to create open-source, affordable, lightweight, modular, adaptive robot hands and prosthetic devices, which can be easily reproduced using off-the-shelf materials and rapid prototyping techniques. Meshpoint produces devices for creating peer-to-peer internet networks in disaster areas and refugee camps, and projects involving blockchain such as Tonic and Provenance, which use the technology to make supply chains more transparent (MeshPoint.One 2022). Globally, chatbots have been used for everything from voter registration to workplace harassment, and Field Ready uses digital fabrication in disaster zones. These are imaginative and promising but still very small-scale.

There are also now a few specialist programmes in this space, such as Google.org's Impact Challenge (https://www.google.org/opportunities/), which backs initiatives applying AI for social good, and the AI for Good platform, which seeks scalable practical applications of AI for global impact. A few of these connect governments and civil society. In North America ambitious projects in Saskatchewan and Allegheny tried to link foundations, NGOs, and government in the use of AI to act preventively in relation to social risks. The moves in the US to create a National Research Cloud—providing computing resources for researchers through a partnership of government, business, and universities—are a good example of more publicly oriented initiatives, though civil society is missing.

The space for these kinds of partnership has potentially grown as there has been more scepticism of programmes led by the big platforms (such as Google's spinout Sidewalk Labs project in Toronto or Replica in Portland).

Philanthropic funding has been crucial for the growth of work on AI ethics, though less effective in engaging with uses of AI in society, and even less effective in addressing how AI tools could be used by philanthropy itself. In general, capacity remains much stronger in the commercial field, so that commercial influence on philanthropic giving is probably more important than programmes initiated by foundations. For example, Facebook enabled giving to charity via its Facebook Messenger Service, Salesforce partnered with United Way in the US to add an advice function to its workplace giving platform based on its AI-powered 'Einstein', and newer firms such as Splunk and Element AI have presented ambitious plans in this area.

Collective intelligence

While huge commercial and military investment has flowed into artificial intelligence there has been much less serious attention to collective intelligence and the role of new tools in harnessing the intelligence of thousands of millions of citizens. This, however, is set to be just as important for the role of civil society and the social economy.

I define collective intelligence as intelligence at scale—mobilizing large numbers of individual brains, and often combining human and machine intelligence (a much lengthier definition and analysis is provided in my book *Big Mind* (Mulgan, 2017)). Our mobile phones collect data on a vast scale, and that is now matched by sensors and the smart chips in our cars, buildings, and trains. Some Chinese cities—such as Hangzhou—are deliberately creating what they call 'city brains' linking up their infrastructures, for example automatically adjusting traffic lights to cope with emergencies.

But some of the best examples combine machine intelligence with human intelligence. Over the past few years many experiments have shown how thousands of people can collaborate online in analysing data or solving problems, and there has been an explosion of new technologies to sense, analyse, and predict. We can see some of the results in things like Wikipedia and its many offshoots, such as Wikihouse, and the spread of citizen science in which millions of people help to spot new stars in the galaxy, observe nature, or analyse tumours. There are new business models such as Duolingo, which mobilizes volunteers to improve its service providing language teaching, and collective intelligence examples in health, where patients band together to design new technologies or share data.

The recent UNDP report on collective intelligence included summaries of many projects combining CI and AI in useful ways (Peach et al., 2021).

The next step is to use these new kinds of collective intelligence to address problems such as climate change or disease. Doing that requires careful design, curation, and orchestration. It is not enough just to mobilize the crowd. Crowds are all too capable of being foolish, prejudiced, and malign. Nor it is enough just to gather lots of data or to hope that brilliant ideas will emerge naturally. Thought requires work and structure—to observe, analyse, create, remember, and judge and to avoid the many pitfalls of delusion and deliberate misinformation. But the emerging field of collective intelligence now offers many methods for communities to organize themselves in new ways. These can be described as 'intelligence assemblies' that combine multiple functions—observation, analysis, memory, creativity, and judgement—and have shown the emerging models in many fields from business (Googlemaps) to ecology (Planetary Skin and Copernicus) to health (AIME to Metasub).

Take air quality as an example. A city using collective intelligence methods will bring together many different kinds of data to understand what is happening to air, and the often complex patterns of particulates. Some of this will come from its own sensors, and some data can be generated by citizens. Artificial intelligence tools can then be trained to predict how it may change, for example because of a shift in the weather or driving patterns.

The next stage then is to mobilize citizens and experts to investigate the options to improve air quality, looking in detail at which roads have the worst levels or which buildings are emitting the most, and what changes would have most impact. The aim is to generate a batch of projects and experiments—some requiring the formal authority of the city, some not—and transparent metrics for assessing success. And finally, cities can open up the process of learning, seeing what is working and what is not and feeding this back into the now formally constituted community of stakeholders, helped by global bodies like the Clean Air Fund and World Resources Institute.

Yet the relative lack of investment is one reason why we have also seen little progress in how intelligently our most important systems work—democracy and politics, business, and the economy. This is apparent in the most everyday aspect of collective intelligence—how we organize meetings. The everyday design of meetings in academia, business, and government draws very little on the science of how to make meetings effective and how they can make the most of the collective intelligence of the people in the room (I wrote about this in a chapter in my book *Big Mind* (Mulgan, 2017). A simple test of this statement is to ask the organizers of meetings—in universities or other institutions—what science, research, or other knowledge they use to guide their design or operation of meetings such as conferences, boards, or seminars. Very few can answer this question). The imbalance can also be seen in too many political systems where leaderships are a lot less smart than the societies they claim to lead. Martin Luther King spoke of 'guided missiles but misguided men' and we are surrounded by institutions packed with individual intelligence that nevertheless often display collective stupidity.

Not all the insights about collective intelligence are new. Many of the examples of successful collective intelligence are quite old—such as the emergence of an international community of scientists in the seventeenth and eighteenth centuries; the Oxford English Dictionary's mobilization of tens of thousands of volunteers in the nineteenth century; or NASA's Apollo programme, which at its height employed more than half a million people in more than 20,000 organizations. But the tools at our disposal now are radically different—and more powerful than ever before.

Strategic considerations for the social economy

This overview shows that the social economy or civil society has sought both to constrain and guide the direction of technological development (through law, regulation, and ethical codes) and to mobilize it to address social needs (see e.g. Anheier et al., 2015; Krlev et al., 2020; OECD, 2010). However, most of these actions have been relatively marginal, whether in terms of funding or impact.

Looking to the decade ahead, the big issue for the social economy is whether it will be just a taker or a shaper of these trends. In a more negative scenario, it will use many

AI products, but these will mainly be provided by commercial firms. There may be massive job destruction, which will undermine other social goals. Meanwhile, social economy actors will continue to lack the capital and expertise to compete with big platforms (repeating the story of the sharing economy in 2010s) as well as lacking access to data—the vital input for ML of all kinds—and will continue to lack the means to influence either the direction of R&D or the broader policy environment. Perhaps too their productivity will continue to fall behind the commercial sector because of slow adoption.

In a more positive scenario these would be reversed: access to capital and capability would allow social enterprises to compete successfully and achieve the economies of scale and scope needed to prevail, while the field will succeed in shaping R&D to focus on social priorities (rather than military or big commercial), including such things as homelessness, refugee integration, and public health. They would help shape a favourable regulatory and policy environment, including rules on privacy, transparency, and open data and they would help to shape specific systems contexts, particularly around climate change and the future of work.

The key question is whether a more strategic approach is possible. Strategy can mean many things, whether for companies, NGOs, or governments. At the level of the European Union it means a concerted attempt to shift the direction of change on many fronts, mobilizing the powers of the European Commission and other actors that can include national, regional, and city governments as well as investors and foundations.

Europe has often tried to act strategically—in relation to climate change, for example, or the creation of the euro or joint defence arrangements. But it has not acted so strategically in relation to the social economy, primarily because this was less of a priority politically.

In the 2020s, if there was a political will to act, a more strategic approach—to be supported by the European Commission, governments, funders, and big NGOs—would have to address each of the following issues:

- Investment in viable models
- Reorienting R&D to social goals
- Developing new models of shared data and knowledge.

Some of these can be organized generically. But their application will also vary by sector. In the next sections I therefore flesh out what that might mean.

Net zero as an example

Achieving serious reductions in carbon emissions is one of the greatest challenges of the century. Civil society has been at the forefront of making the case for change and showing what change means in practice—highlighting the need to transform almost every aspect of society and the economy, including the technical design of energy, transport, and buildings; everyday behaviours (from diets to travel); policies—taxes, subsidies, incentives, regulations—at multiple levels from the local to the national and global. The social economy is heavily involved in this—from recycling to reducing waste, campaigning to change attitudes, or developing new models of ownership for energy.

But its role in the next stages may be limited by many of the factors described above, as decarbonization requires mobilizing many of the key technologies of the 4IR—data, AI, and IoT. There is now a growing literature on AI and net zero (for a serious attempt at mapping the links between AI and the SDGs, using expert consultation, see Rolnick et al., 2019; Victor, 2019; Vinuesa et al., 2020) documenting a huge amount of activity under way attempting to use AI to respond to climate change, from managing electricity networks to inventing new materials. Some is focused on more detailed mapping of climate change itself and extreme weather patterns; other work is on topics such as reducing energy use (e.g. DeepMind's project on Google's own energy use), transport planning, solar geo-engineering, and finance. The range of this work is well captured in various overviews (Rolnick et al., 2019).

Ambitious targets have been set by national governments (e.g. net zero for Norway by 2030 and Finland by 2035), and by companies (e.g. Siemens). But few have coherent strategies for achieving the Paris Agreement targets in ways that make full use of the social economy or of digital technologies.

Progress is being made in reorienting investment flows to green technologies—building on more than three decades of pioneering work. But much less progress has been made on the orchestration of the data, knowledge, and insights needed to achieve far-reaching change in systems of energy, transport, and housing, as well as the best ways to connect in the social economy in all its forms.

A more strategic approach to enable the social economy to play its full part would require some of the following.

Investment in social innovation

Achieving the targets will require much more success in mobilizing communities to play their part in reducing emissions, learning for example from leading ecotowns such as Freiburg and investing in promising new social enterprise models. This would include topics such as reducing food waste or changing eating behaviours, again making use of data and explicit hypothesis testing. About some of the options, including how to boost place-based action, there are useful lessons to be learned here from pan-European competitions and challenges.

R&D and experiment

The second priority is to reorient R&D to encompass the social economy as well as hardware. There are large flows of funding and investment into some aspects of R&D—particularly where this fits into well-established frameworks for product innovation—but there are also major gaps, such as experiments to discover new knowledge about some of the trickier aspects of carbon reduction such as what has been learned with incentive schemes for energy efficiency, or likely job impacts of circular economies. There will be a need for more experimentation around things such as home insulation, community energy, and zero carbon transport, with clear hypotheses to be tested, peer learning between those running similar experiments, and rapid sharing of results (including data). Some governments—such as Finland—are putting in place more systematic methods of linking multiple local experiments around decarbonization with shared data and learning. At a European level the Net Zero Cities programme is promising. Such platforms for connecting experiments will be vital for Europe's cities and towns, and its social economy, ideally with APIs allowing for real-time consolidation of data; shared protocols for the design and assessment of experiments; and shared in-depth evidence analyses and syntheses. This is vital space for NGOs and social enterprises to demonstrate their effectiveness.

Strategic action on shared data and knowledge

Currently, although there are huge amounts of relevant data, relatively little of it is standardized and easily accessible—from benchmarking data within sectors to carbon emissions data. Much of it is proprietary in the hands of large commercial firms—whether digital platforms or energy providers. What is needed is the collection, curation, and sharing of key data on emissions and carbon footprints of supply chains, cities and neighbourhoods, and individuals (which in turn would require new standards for data and active curation) to enable civil society to play a full part. Some work is under way on this—including some dashboards, projects such as Carbon Tracker using satellite data to map coal emissions, and some attempts to shift to 'presumed open' approaches to energy data—but it is fairly fragmented and not integrated with money allocations. There are individual programmes in cities such as Helsinki, Amsterdam, and Copenhagen that are ambitious in scale, with Copenhagen aiming to be carbon neutral by 2025, the first capital city to do so (City of Copenhagen 2020). Their plans are quite detailed in relation to buildings, transport, and energy, but very thin on data, and with little explicit mention of the social economy. There are also major unresolved issues—such as ownership and accessibility of smart meter data, and the probable need for new institutions to act as guardians/curators of this data. Getting a data strategy right may also be key in the long term to shifting company reporting and the behaviour of financial markets and investors (and giving the public more reliable information on whether their pensions and other assets are either helping or hindering carbon reduction).

Similar considerations apply to evidence and shared knowledge: the IPCC orchestrates global knowledge on the diagnosis of climate change but there is less organized evidence about what works—in fields ranging from retrofitting to community energy to food waste. Again, market pressures mean that businesses have strong incentives to learn. But for more systemic or public interest aspects of carbon reduction there is a gap in terms of responsibility and action. Some organizations are attempting more multi-level strategies—such as Climate KIC or C40—but their resources are limited, and C40 took a very long time to evolve into even quite modest knowledge orchestration roles. Even where there is plenty of evaluation and evidence, what's missing is the synthesis in forms that are easily accessible, for example to a municipality or social enterprise. This impedes the adoption of productivity-enhancing innovations.

The role of the social economy in adaptive systems for jobs and skills

Another field which requires a strategic approach is jobs, where again the interface of the issue, the social economy and new digital tools present both big opportunities and big threats. Over the next twenty years many countries face big challenges to future employment—as the combination of automation, artificial intelligence, 4IR, and other trends, such as the shift to a circular economy, threatens existing jobs in key industries, from manufacturing to retail and white-collar roles. For the social economy these challenges are huge—both directly affecting how they organize work, and indirectly through their role in helping people adapt. Again, these require a combination of investment in new models, reorientation of R&D, and the development of new shared institutions and governance models.

Long-term trends and changing skills needs

There have been many forecasts looking ten to twenty years into the future. The dozens of studies (World Bank, Oxford, McKinsey, Nesta, UNCTAD, PWC) use slightly different methods, though most combine expert opinions with ML. They are far from perfect, but most commentators agree that there will be an even higher premium on basic literacy and numeracy in the future—continuing a very long-term trend—but now including some other kinds of literacy such as ability to use the internet. Most agree that there is a high likelihood of automation of many repetitive manual and non-manual tasks, though with some exceptions where perception, manipulation, and creative and social intelligence play a role. So, for example, tasks requiring subtle dexterity have often been thought to be relatively resistant to automation; but there are signs of some progress now in automating difficult tasks in fields such as embroidery, leather work, or machine repair.

Investment and funding

So, as in other fields, a first priority is to ensure flows of funding and capital into promising new methods of supporting people with skills. In most countries it is expected that jobs demand will rise in fields such as care, education, and tourism, partly because of what economists call 'positive elasticities of demand' (people pay more as a share of income for these things as incomes rise) and partly because these are hard to automate. Europe needs to ensure that investment in social economy start-ups and scale-ups enables it to play a full part in these areas of growth, particularly ones involving care, education, food, and leisure, all of which have a prospect of jobs growth in the next few decades.

Adoption

Civil society has generally been slower to adopt new digital technologies than business or the public sector (Gagliardi et al., 2020). So intensive programmes are needed to drive up adoption rates among smaller NGOs and social enterprises, as well as small businesses. Most expect there to be greater demand for digital skills, though this is complex. There is bound to be some more demand for generic awareness of digital technology, understanding of coding, data analysis, and how to use the internet. There is also likely to be growing demand for some very job-specific digital skills in fields such as AI, virtual reality or augmented reality, and analytics. But many digital skills could be in lower demand—as they are superseded by next-generation technology, and often these are the easiest tasks to automate using AI.

Changing training and education

The social economy already plays important roles in training and education—both targeting social exclusion and helping to provide more universal services—but it could be doing much more. It will be helped by support in making the most of data and the AI tools that already help to tailor education to personal needs, assessment tools, and peer support. Again, this requires both capital and competence.

The social economy may also be particularly well placed to support the kinds of generic skills that are becoming more important in the economy—abilities to collaborate, communicate, and create. These are often learned best through doing projects in teams and on real-world problems rather than traditional pedagogy—a spirit that is often more natural for social projects than it is for traditional schools and colleges.

Helping people to navigate change

To guide both supply and demand, Europe needs to mobilize many sources of intelligence to help its labour markets adapt quickly and efficiently. These include data, tacit knowledge, business insights, evidence, and experience from other countries. As with decarbonization, we need to look at creating shared commons of data and knowledge rather than assuming that the market can solve the problem. Individuals often lack the knowledge or motivation to reskill. Employers may see little benefit for them in training employees for new jobs with someone else. Within the public sector there may be complex and fragmented responsibilities; lack of a shared perspective on vulnerabilities and opportunities; misalignment of policy.

However, there are some promising moves. For example, the Swedish Public Employment Service launched Jobtech, a platform that provides access to datasets such as occupation forecasts, current and historical job adverts, and a data-driven dynamic competence map. In France, Bob (an open-source platform that provides jobseekers with personalized career advice, based on data from France's Public Employment Service) provides another good example.

Future variants of these are likely to require comprehensive and curated real-time data on current patterns—the state of jobs demand, what skills are being looked for in jobs, pay levels—ideally in a format easily analysed by geography and sector. There will need to be assessments of job vulnerability, drawing on analysis that breaks jobs down into bundles of competences. These become most useful if they can be shared in easily accessible ways with workers, students, and schoolchildren. There is a parallel need for analysis of emerging opportunities, including growing jobs and potential fields for new jobs—so as to feed into the design of training and other systems, as well as business strategies.

Many countries are grappling with similar issues, sometimes helped by global bodies such as the ILO, WEF, and OECD. Commercial firms are expanding what data is available and how it is used—such as Burning Glass, Faethm, LinkedIn, and others. Policy innovation is happening around mid-career training, new kinds of personal training accounts, and transitional income, with some countries, such as Singapore, putting in place comprehensive programmes. But no country has yet created a really effective shared intelligence—which is a necessary if not sufficient condition for navigating the possible storms ahead. And none has fully engaged the social economy in this more strategic approach to change.

The role of the social economy in the future of care

A third crucial field is care for the elderly, which is another great challenge of the next few decades, given the demographic trends facing Europe and the rest of the world. The weaknesses of many care systems have been revealed by COVID. As a generalization, the sector struggles to make the most of technology, despite the apparent promise of monitoring, robotics, and other technologies for care, and often suffers from low productivity, low pay, and low status.

Although there have been big programmes of investment in assistive technology—including ones funded by the European Commission—these have generally been very disappointing in terms of impact, partly as a result of the R&D models (with far too little user engagement or sense of real needs and experiences), partly because they have been too technology-driven rather than needs-driven, and partly because the social economy has been so little involved.

The key organizations in this field, particularly in the social economy, have struggled to access capital and thus to make the most of new potential tools, including use of data, sensors, and assistive tech. This is another field where there is still very weak organization of data and knowledge as a commons—collective intelligence of 'what works'. An individual care home, for example, will struggle to find useful and useable evidence on the many issues it faces.

Meanwhile, the lack of a social perspective has often inhibited the many programmes in this space focused on technology, underestimating the importance for care of human support, psychology, and relationships, which are often better provided by social organizations.

These issues were brought into the spotlight in many countries during the COVID-19 pandemic as care homes bore the brunt of the crisis in terms of mortality and often had much weaker systems of organization than those found in health. They are not helped by the imbalances of pay which mean that care workers are often among the lowest paid. In the US, for example, some 48 per cent of the lowest paid workers were deemed essential—paradoxically, a much higher percentage than among the highest paid workers (I co-lead the International Public Policy Observatory, which has worked closely with care systems on improving use of evidence and data. See e.g. 'IPPO', 2021).

So in this sector too, a strategic approach would combine flows of capital into new models for providing care; more R&D and experimentation in these models, combining technology and human support; and a restructuring of the ways in which knowledge and data are organized, making them much more a commons.

Some conclusions

These observations on climate change, jobs, and care have some common themes. First, they all highlight the need for a more strategic approach, that combines:

- Investment in viable models
- Reorienting R&D to social goals
- Developing new models of shared data and knowledge.

Second, they all highlight strategic importance of collective intelligence, shared use of knowledge, insight, and data. The full benefits of the next generations of data and technology will only be realized if much of this intelligence is organized as a commons. But in most countries these are still largely balkanized or proprietary, owned by private firms and not available for social impact.

Third, they highlight the need for new kinds of academic engagement—what I call exploratory social science, which means the conscious work of designing options for the future, whether new ways to manage energy, healthcare, or democracy. This work has largely disappeared from universities and it makes it much harder for civil society to play an active role in shaping policy debates, offering pictures of what might be feasible and desirable a generation from now. A huge amount is invested in comparable work around technologies, describing possible futures for smart cities, smart homes, or smart industries. On the social side there is almost nothing (Mulgan, 2022).

These are some of the macro issues. At a more micro level the new methods of collective intelligence could be used more actively to innovate in net zero, jobs, and care, making it easier to understand and solve problems, tapping into a wider network of capabilities. The social economy has been quite slow to grasp the implication of these ideas—though they have been adopted by important initiatives such as the UNDP Accelerator Labs networks (Peach et al., 2021), and recognized by institutions such as the European Parliament and some mayors such as Beppe Sala in Milan. Such ideas are beginning to be implemented on a large scale in some parts of the world (e.g. Taiwan, or India, where the societal platform programmes are a good example of how civil society and government can collaborate in organizing collective intelligence).

These projects ask: what a city would look like that could truly think and act? What if it could be fully aware of all of its citizens' experiences; able to remember and create, and then to act and learn? This might once have been a fantasy. But it is coming closer. Cities can see in new ways—not just through sensors and commercial and other data, but also with citizen-generated data on everything from the prevalence of floods to the quality of food in restaurants. Cities can create in new ways, through open challenges that mobilize public creativity. And they can decide in new ways, as cities like Madrid and Barcelona have done with online platforms that let citizens propose policies and then deliberate.

Yet overall, the huge imbalance between the capabilities of civil society and those of the military, the state, and big business is probably growing, not shrinking. This makes it harder to anticipate, prepare, and respond.

Although science and technology studies has repeatedly emphasized the vital role of 'social shaping' of technology, there is almost no academic literature on the strategic question of how the social economy can play a more active role in this shaping. We need, perhaps, a new field to develop that bridges the retrospective analysis of science and technology studies with a more prospective strategic approach to the shaping of R&D programmes, adoption, experimentation, and the organization of the key enablers of the next few decades, notably data and AI.

References

Anheier, H., Krlev, G., Preuss, S., Mildenberger, G., Einarsson, T., & Flening, E. (2015). *Social Innovation in Policy: EU and Country Level Profiles and Policy Perspectives. A Deliverable of the Project: 'Impact of the Third Sector as Social Innovation' (ITSSOIN), European Commission—7th Framework Programme*. Brussels.

Baker, T., Smith, L., & Anissa, N. (2019). *Educ-AI-tion Rebooted? Exploring the Future of Artificial Intelligence in Schools and Colleges*. Nesta. Available at: https://www.nesta. org.uk/report/education-rebooted/

Callahan, W. A. (2014). Citizen Ai: warrior, jester, and middleman. *The Journal of Asian Studies*, 73(4), 899–920. https://doi.org/10.1017/S0021911814001004

City of Copenhagen (2020). *Carbon Neutral Capital | International.kk.dk*. Available at: https://international.kk.dk/carbon-neutral-capital

Floridi, L., & Cowls, J. (2019). A unified framework of five principles for AI in society. *Harvard Data Science Review*, 1(1). https://hdsr.mitpress.mit.edu/pub/l0jsh9d1/ release/8

Floridi, L., Cowls, J., Beltrametti, M., Chatila, R., Chazerand, P., Dignum, V., Luetge, C., Madelin, R., Pagallo, U., Rossi, F., Schafer, B., Valcke, P., & Vayena, E. (2018). AI4People—an ethical framework for a good AI society: opportunities, risks, principles, and recommendations. *Minds and Machines*, 28(4), 689–707. https://doi.org/10. 1007/s11023-018-9482-5

Horvitz, E. (2017). AI, people, and society. *Science*, 357(6346), 7–7. https://doi.org/10.1126/science.aao2466

IPPO (2021, 1 December). Strategies to support social care workers during COVID-19: a global scan of responses to severe staffing challenges. Available at: https://covidandsociety.com/strategies-social-care-workers-covid-19-global-scan-responses-severe-staffing-challenges/

Krlev, G., Einarsson, T., Wijkström, F., Heyer, L., & Mildenberger, G. (2020). The policies of social innovation: a cross-national analysis. *Nonprofit and Voluntary Sector Quarterly*, 49(3), 457–478. https://doi.org/10.1177/0899764019866505

MeshPoint.One (2022). *Building Blocks of a Smart City*. Available at: https://www.meshpointone.com/

Mulgan, G. (2017). *Big Mind*. Princeton: Princeton University Press.

Mulgan, G. (2019). *AI Ethics and the Limits of Code(s)*. Available at: https://www.nesta.org.uk/blog/ai-ethics-and-limits-codes/

Mulgan, G. (2021). *The Case for Exploratory Social Sciences*. Hamburg: The New Institute.

Mulgan, G. (2022). *Another World Is Possible: How to Reignite Social and Political Imagination*. London: Hurst & Company.

Mulgan, G., Adams, K., & Stokes, M. (2018). *Civil Society and the Fourth Industrial Revolution*. Nesta. Available at: https://www.nesta.org.uk/blog/civil-society-and-fourth-industrial-revolution/

Gagliardi D., Psarra F., Wintjes R., Trendafili K., Pineda Mendoza J., Haaland K., Turkeli S., Giotitsas C., Pazaitis A., & Niglia F. (2020). *New Technologies and Digitisation: Opportunities and Challenges for the Social Economy and Social Economy Enterprises*. Brussels: Publications Office of the European Union.

OECD. (2010). Social entrepreneurship and social innovation. In OECD, *SMEs, Entrepreneurship and Innovation* (pp. 185–217). Paris: OECD. https://doi.org/10.1787/9789264080355-50-en

Peach, K., Berditchevskaia, A., Mulgan, G., Lucarelli, G., & Ebelshaeuser, M. (2021). *Collective Intelligence for Sustainable Development: Getting Smarter Together*.

Rolnick, D., Donti, P. L., Kaack, L. H., Kochanski, K., Lacoste, A., Sankaran, K., Ross, A. S., Milojevic-Dupont, N., Jaques, N., Waldman-Brown, A., Luccioni, A., Maharaj, T., Sherwin, E. D., Mukkavilli, S. K., Kording, K. P., Gomes, C., Ng, A. Y., Hassabis, D., Platt, J. C., … Bengio, Y. (2019). *Tackling Climate Change with Machine Learning*. https://doi.org/10.48550/ARXIV.1906.05433

Taddeo, M., & Floridi, L. (2018). How AI can be a force for good. *Science*, 361(6404), 751–752. https://doi.org/10.1126/science.aat5991

Victor, D. G. (2019, 10 January). How artificial intelligence will affect the future of energy and climate. *Brookings*. Available at: https://www.brookings.edu/research/how-artificial-intelligence-will-affect-the-future-of-energy-and-climate/

Vinuesa, R., Azizpour, H., Leite, I., Balaam, M., Dignum, V., Domisch, S., Felländer, A., Langhans, S. D., Tegmark, M., & Fuso Nerini, F. (2020). The role of artificial intelligence in achieving the Sustainable Development Goals. *Nature Communications*, 11(1), 233. https://doi.org/10.1038/s41467-019-14108-y

Zuboff, S. (2019). *The Age of Surveillance Capitalism: The Fight for a Human Future at the New Frontier of Power*. London: Profile Books.

6
Financial market transformations for investing in social impact

Alex Nicholls and Jarrod Ormiston

Introduction

The social economy in the European Union (EU)[1] represents an important element of the overall economy both in terms of its economic impact (13.6 million jobs, 8% of GDP across the EU)[2] and its wider social impact in terms of innovations designed to address intractable social, community, and environmental issues (Amin, Cameron, & Hudson, 2002). The social economy aims to generate a positive—measurable—social impact together with economic impact. Moreover, the social economy embodies and promotes the fundamental values of social solidarity and civic engagement. In this context, discourses of the social economy also have the potential to change the wider debates concerning the purpose of organizations and the structure and objectives of the economy more generally—such as issues of shareholder priority, equity, and the short-termism of investment—as a form of transformative social innovation (Nicholls & Ziegler, 2019). Today, in the EU, the social economy is of relevance to a range of policy fields, including climate and the environment, education, health, energy, financial stability, technology, and research and innovation.[3] In the COVID-19 and post-COVID-19 world, the social economy offers an alternative economic model—connecting actors from government, not-for-profits, and for-profit organizations—that may provide important insights into how to increase the resilience and heterogeneity of business ecosystems more generally and reduce the risk of exogenous shocks to the economy as a whole.

In the EU context, social enterprise has been framed as a key component of the wider social economy (Borzaga & Defourny, 2004).[4] The EU defines social enterprise as an entrepreneurial organization trading in the social economy whose

---

[1] The social economy in the EU consists of 2.8 million social enterprises, mutual and co-operative associations, and foundations: see https://ec.europa.eu/social/main.jsp?catId=1537&langId=en
[2] See: https://ec.europa.eu/social/main.jsp?catId=1537&langId=en
[3] For example, DG CLIMA Climate and DG ENVIR Environment; DG EAC Education, Youth, Sport and Culture; DG SANTI Health and Food Safety; DG ENER Energy; DG FISMA Financial Stability, Financial Services and Capital Markets Union and DG ECFIN Economics and Financial Affairs; DG CONNECT Communications Content, Networks, and Technology; DG RTD Research and Innovation.
[4] See: https://ec.europa.eu/growth/sectors/proximity-and-social-economy/social-economy-eu/social -enterprises_en

Alex Nicholls and Jarrod Ormiston, *Financial market transformations for investing in social impact*. In: *Social Economy Science*. Edited by: Gorgi Krlev, Dominika Wruk, Giulio Pasi, and Marika Bernhard, Oxford University Press. © Oxford University Press (2023). DOI: 10.1093/oso/9780192868343.003.0006

main objective is to have a social impact rather than make a profit for their owners or shareholders and which uses its profits primarily to achieve social objectives.[5] While the development of innovative tools and entrepreneurial organizations to address social problems is nothing new, historically such ventures have operated outside of the market in the voluntary, charitable, or not-for-profit sectors. Social entrepreneurship emerged as a new field of action in the early 2000s, blending market and non-market approaches (Nicholls, 2007). Social entrepreneurship refers to a broad range of actors, and there is no single legal form for social enterprises in the EU: social enterprises can be work integration co-operatives, private companies limited by guarantee, or not-for-profit organizations such as provident societies, associations, voluntary organizations, charities, or foundations.[6] Social enterprises are driving social change across Europe in the fields such as employment, education, and well-being (Baglioni, 2017). Despite their importance for economy and society, social enterprises face the challenge of acquiring sufficient financial resources to help them in developing their businesses and scaling their impact (Castellas, Ormiston, & Findlay, 2018; Doherty, Haugh, & Lyon, 2014). This chapter explores how the new field of impact investment can contribute to the growth of social enterprises across Europe.

Impact investment has emerged over the past few decades as an alternative approach to investing that intentionally seeks to create social and/or environmental returns alongside financial ones (Nicholls, 2010; Hehenberger, Mair, & Metz, 2019; Höchstädter & Scheck, 2015). Policy-makers have been heavily involved in the development of impact investment markets (Casasnovas, 2022; Casasnovas & Ferraro, 2022; Spiess-Knafl & Achleitner, 2012). In the UK, for example, policy-makers were seen as drivers of the social impact investing market (Casasnovas & Ferraro, 2022). Governments are viewed as playing a critical role by creating an enabling environment for impact investment (Phillips & Johnson 2021). Governments can shape impact investment markets through regulation, direct investment, co-investment, and intermediation (Casesanovas, 2022; Schmidt, 2022).

This chapter focuses on how policy-makers can support impact investment and funding for social economy enterprises across the EU. Hehenberger (2020) recently reviewed the trajectory of EU policy supporting impact investment. Since 2011, the European Commission has launched a series of initiatives to support social enterprises and impact investment in the social economy such as the Social Business Initiative, the Expert Group on Social Entrepreneurship (GECES), the Expert Group on Social Economy and Social Enterprises (also GECES), the European Social Entrepreneurship Fund (EuSEF) regulation, the Programme for Employment and Social Innovation (EaSI), and the European Investment Fund (EIF). The policies have contributed to the legitimization of impact investment across Europe (Hehenberger, 2020). The importance of impact investment in supporting the social

---

[5] See: https://ec.europa.eu/growth/sectors/proximity-and-social-economy/social-economy-eu/social-enterprises_en

[6] See: https://ec.europa.eu/growth/sectors/social-economy/enterprises_en

economy in Europe was strengthened in the Social Economy Action Plan published in 2021.[7] One of the key pillars of the plan focuses on creating an ecosystem for the growth of social enterprises and other social economy enterprises that supports them accessing finance and scaling up. This chapter contributes to this pillar by setting out the landscape of impact finance specifically available to social enterprises and other social economy enterprises. It also makes a series of policy recommendations for the EU impact investment market based on an analysis of relevant policy innovations in the United Kingdom and elsewhere.

Defining impact investment

A fundamental challenge for the ongoing development of the impact investment market relates to the contested nature of its boundaries and terminology. Before the widespread adoption of the term 'impact investment', the market for impact finance was defined as, variously, 'social finance',[8] 'social impact investment',[9] or 'social investment'.[10] This shift from 'social' to 'impact' was driven by two factors: first, a concerted attempt to integrate with the mainstream financial system, for whom 'social' was typically associated with Socially Responsible Investment (SRI) that negatively screened out poorly performing investments against good-governance guidelines rather than actively seeking positive social impact deals/funds; second (as evidenced by the formation of the Impact Management Project),[11] a focus on measuring, managing, and reporting the social and/or environmental impact of investments, potentially as a new 'alpha' of all investments. Casasnovas and Ferraro (2022) highlight these competing terms by contrasting the emergence of 'social investment' in the UK, with a tendency to focus on domestically oriented social economy organizations, and the emergence of 'impact investment' in the US, with a stronger focus on for-profit firms with a social and/or environmental mission. Another significant discourse of impact investment, *contra* the various 'social' definitions, was to reject the assumption of a social–financial trade-off in investments, where an increased social 'return' required an impairment of financial return. Despite these efforts to demarcate and define the impact investment market, contested definitions remain—most notably in terms of 'venture' philanthropy and 'sustainable' investment.

Venture philanthropy (VP) emerged in the USA in the early 2000s, as a consequence of the substantial wealth that accrued to Silicon Valley venture capital and technology billionaires being directed towards a 'new' philanthropy (Moody, 2008; Van Slyke & Newman, 2006). The Roberts Enterprise Development Fund (REDF)—founded by George Roberts, joint founder of the private equity firm KKR—pioneered this new form of philanthropic giving that aligned venture capital principals with

---

[7] See: https://ec.europa.eu/social/main.jsp?catId=1537&langId=en
[8] See, for example: https://www.socialfinance.org.uk
[9] See, for example: https://www.oecd.org/dac/financing-sustainable-development/development-finance-topics/social-impact-investment-initiative.htm
[10] See, for example: https://www.sibgroup.org.uk
[11] See: https://impactmanagementproject.com

grant making.[12] This VP model was based on long-term (multi-iteration) grant making linked to pro-bono venture development support and robust impact metrics, specifically the Social Return on Investment model that attempted to monetize social impact.[13] Subsequent to REDF, a number of other VP organizations emerged, including New Philanthropy Capital[14] in the US and UnLtd[15] in the UK. In 2004, a coalition of European VP organizations came together as the European Venture Philanthropy Association.[16] The EVPA now has more than 270 members from more than thirty countries that connect through events and activities to share best practices and a common vision. Following the same model—and founded by the same entrepreneur, Doug Miller—the Asian Venture Philanthropy Network (AVPN) was established in 2011. By 2020, the AVPN had 615 member organizations in 16 markets across Asia.[17] Finally, in 2019, the Africa Venture Philanthropy Alliance (AVPA) was established.[18] The majority of VP members are now also actively engaging with the notion of impact investment to define their work.

'Sustainable investment' typically uses various types of social or environmental data to help investors make better decisions around asset performance and improve long-term results. More recently such investment has been reframed as Environmental, Social, or Governance (ESG) finance. Within ESG finance there are two categories (discussed further later in the chapter): *positive* ESG finance, which provides direct growth or start-up capital to high-impact projects often aligned with the UN Sustainable Development Goals (SDGs);[19] and *negative* ESG finance, which deploys capital according to a set of screening criteria—'to do no harm'—typically in secondary markets. Sustainable investment does not typically take an 'ethical' stance or represent particular investor values or beliefs.[20] As discussed below, the majority of negative ESG sustainable investment falls outside the scope of impact investment, whereas positive ESG sustainable investment aligns with the concept of impact investment.

SRI[21] extends the ESG principles of negative screening to make more proactive investment choices (sometimes using ESG data) that align with an investor's personal, environmental, or social values and beliefs (Yan, Ferraro, & Almandoz, 2019). Typical categories of SRI are sustainability and clean technology with the strongest sectoral focus being on 'green' finance (Meng, Newth, & Woods, 2022).[22] A distinction between ESG and SRI, for example, would be, in the former, to screen out

---

[12] See: https://redf.org
[13] See: http://www.socialvalueuk.org/resources/sroi-guide/
[14] See: https://www.thinknpc.org
[15] See: https://www.unltd.org.uk
[16] https://evpa.eu.com/about-us/what-is-venture-philanthropy
[17] See: https://avpn.asia/about-us/
[18] See: https://avpa.africa
[19] See: https://sdgs.un.org
[20] See, for example: https://www.rbcwealthmanagement.com/en-eu/insights/the-growth-of-impact-investing-building-wealth-with-positive-outcomes
[21] See, for example, https://www.investopedia.com/terms/s/sri.asp
[22] Bloomberg sized the market for the Green Finance assets under management at $32 trillion in 2019, see further: https://www.bloomberg.com/graphics/2019-green-finance/

tobacco companies from a portfolio and, in the latter, to invest in healthcare that addresses lung disease.[23]

Finally, it is important to note the curious absence of co-operative and mutual finance from discussions of the impact investment market, despite such finance being an analogous, though distinctive, market of capital deployed for social impact (Michie, 2015). This is likely a product of two factors: first, the impact of co-operative and mutual finance is largely internal and a function of its organizational structure as membership organizations designed to address market failures or pattern of monopsony in markets; second, because co-operatives and mutuals are largely absent from mainstream financial markets since they do not issue equity or raise market debt, being instead typically self-funding or relying on retail bank finance. Nevertheless, co-operatives and mutual organizations play a key role in several impact sectors, including housing,[24] agriculture,[25] health,[26] work integration,[27] insurance,[28] and banking.[29] Many of these sectors are substantial. For example in 2017 the global market share of mutual and co-operative insurers stood at 26.7 per cent across more than ninety countries with assets worth $8.9 trillion. This market employs more than 1 million people and serves 960 million people as members or policyholders.[30] Similarly, in 2018 the global co-operative banking sector had assets of EUR 7.4 billion (McKillop et al., 2020).

Consistent with the development of social entrepreneurship, the allocation of money for social good is also nothing new, though the term 'impact investment' only emerged recently. There is a centuries-long—typically faith-based—tradition of providing resources for the community or the poor and more formalized charity and philanthropy goes back almost 200 years (Nicholls, 2010). However, over the past twenty years a new model of finance-for-good has emerged: impact investment. The Global Impact Investment Network (GIIN)[31]—a not-for-profit dedicated to building the infrastructure of the field via convening and research—has defined impact investment as 'investments made with the intention to generate positive, measurable social and environmental impact alongside a financial return'.

---

[23] See, for example: https://www.rbcwealthmanagement.com/en-eu/insights/the-growth-of-impact-investing-building-wealth-with-positive-outcomes
[24] See, for example: https://ldn.coop/wp-content/uploads/2015/01/Financing_Co-operative_and_Mutual_Housing-1.pdf. Also, note Big Society Capital's strategic focus on investment in the social housing sector and housing associations: https://bigsocietycapital.com/how-we work/focus-areas/homes/
[25] See, for example: https://www.agweb.com/opinion/agricultural-cooperatives-around-world
[26] See, for example: https://www.un.org/development/desa/cooperatives/wp-content/uploads/sites/25/2019/03/190326_ihco_EGM-nairobi.pdf
[27] See, for example: https://www.eurofound.europa.eu/publications/report/2019/cooperatives-and-social-enterprises-work-and-employment-in-selected-countries
[28] See, for example: https://www.thenews.coop/136824/sector/banking-and-insurance/co-operative-mutual-insurers-outperform-insurance-sector-market-share-growth/
[29] See, for example: https://economics.rabobank.com/contentassets/95274037ebc548bc99ae02abadf18489/cooperatiestudie-200910_tcm64-94102.pdf
[30] https://www.icmif.org/publications/financial-insights/global-mutual-and-cooperative-market-infographic-2016
[31] Established in 2009, the Global Impact Investment Network (GIIN) is a not-for-profit membership organization with 280 members across 41 countries building industry infrastructure and supporting activities, education, and research that help accelerate the development of the impact investment industry. See further: https://thegiin.org

More recently, the Global Steering Group for Impact Investment (GSGII)[32]—a transnational coalition of thirty-three National Advisory Boards supporting the development of the impact investment field globally—has extended this definition: 'Impact investment optimizes risk, return and impact to benefit people and the planet. It does so by setting specific social and environmental objectives alongside financial ones and measuring their achievement.'

This change of focus reflects a wider agenda to mainstream impact investment by engaging more closely with the language and logics of conventional finance. One of the main distinguishing features is that measuring and reporting impact are central to impact investment (Barman, 2015; Lehner, Nicholls, & Kapplmüller, 2022; Ormiston, 2019; 2022).

Drivers of impact investment

The drivers behind the emergence of impact investment cut across the three sectors within most liberal democracies: the private sector, the public sector, and the social economy.

In the private sector there has been an increasing interest in a range of 'sustainable' or 'responsible' investments. This has been driven by investor preferences, notably of millennials, who will benefit from the largest transfer of inherited wealth in history over the next decade.[33] In addition, institutional investors, such as pension funds and insurance firms, are recalibrating their long-term investment risk models to include social and environmental factors as material for their investment portfolios.[34] Much of this new investment takes the form of 'screened' funds that incorporate ESG factors into their investment selection criteria. Some estimates put the ESG/SRI market at approximately 45 per cent of all assets under management.[35] Attendant on this market has been the development of new measurement and accounting systems such as the UN Principles for Responsible Investment,[36] Global Reporting Initiative, and Social Accounting Standards Board (SASB). However, despite this substantial growth in finance linked to ESG/SRI factors, the market has been widely criticized for having limited—or poorly measured—impact on environmental or social ills, primarily

---

[32] The GSGII was established in August 2015 as the successor to, and incorporating the work of, the Social Impact Investment Taskforce established under the UK's presidency of the G8. The GSGII currently has thirty-two countries plus the EU as members. See further: https://gsgii.org
[33] According to Forbes, millennials will inherit more than $68 trillion from their baby boomer parents by the year 2030. See further: https://www.forbes.com/sites/jackkelly/2019/10/26/millennials-will-become-richest-generation-in-american-history-as-baby-boomers-transfer-over-their-wealth/#3dcc954b6c4b
[34] See, for example: https://www.institutionalassetmanager.co.uk/2020/05/19/285756/esg-will-be-industry-standard-within-five-years-say-institutional-investors
[35] The MSCI Index estimated the total ESG market in 2020 to be $40.5 trillion. See further: https://www.pionline.com/esg/global-esg-data-driven-assets-hit-405-trillion. BCG estimated that total global assets under management were approximately $89 trillion in 2019. See further: https://image-src.bcg.com/Images/BCG-Global-Asset-Management-2020-May-2020-r_tcm23-247209.pdf
[36] See https://www.unpri.org/pri/what-are-the-principles-for-responsible-investment

because many funds simply screen out poorly performing companies rather than targeting new investment in high-impact sectors.[37]

In terms of the public sector, since the 1980s a range of policy innovations based on the theory of New Public Management have innovated public spending regimes around new models of privatization and public–private partnerships (Osborne and Gaebler, 1992; Osborne, 2007). This significant policy shift has created a new market for private providers of public services as well as—more recently—refocusing public spending more generally on effectiveness and efficiency via outcomes-driven spending and contracting models (Warner, 2013). In both cases, significant private capital has moved into the provision of public goods. While being less obviously 'social' than ESG, such capital has helped to grow a sector of social economy organizations.

In terms of the social economy, there has been increased engagement with private capital by the social economy organizations driven by the shortfall of grants and philanthropic capital to match the pressing global, social, and environmental needs. This has also driven social economy organizations to develop new, for-profit, models that engage with private capital.

At the trans-national level, the establishment of the United Nations' SDGs[38] in 2015 required significant financing across its seventeen areas of action. As of 2019, it has been estimated that there will be a shortfall of between $2 trillion and $4 trillion annually—roughly 50 per cent of the total needed—to achieve SDGs by 2030.[39] Impact investing thereby provides an avenue for investors to contribute to the SDG agenda (Castellas & Ormiston, 2018).

Taken together, across all sectors of the global economy, these forces are driving the emergence of impact investment as a tool to finance social economy activity.

The spectrum of impact investment

The following sections of this chapter, on the spectrum of impact investment, global market size, and financial returns, were previously published in a report by the lead author entitled 'Sustainable Finance: A Primer and Recent Developments'.[40] The earlier report was prepared for the Asian Development Bank to inform the report 'Asian Development Outlook 2021: Financing a Green and Inclusive Recovery'.[41]

Considering impact investment as a spectrum highlights that multiple types of capital are brought together in the impact investment market (Moran &

---

[37] See, for example, critiques of ESG ratings systems—https://www.economist.com/finance-and-economics/2019/12/07/climate-change-has-made-esg-a-force-in-investing—as well as warnings over 'greenwashing' funds: https://www.ftadviser.com/investments/2020/07/16/be-critical-of-esg-credentials-to-avoid-greenwashing-funds/

[38] The Sustainable Development Goals (SDGs) were established in 2015 by the United Nations General Assembly as a part of the '2030 Agenda' UN Resolution. The SDGs represent a set of seventeen interlinked goals designed to be a 'blueprint to achieve a better and more sustainable future for all', see further: https://www.un.org/sustainabledevelopment/sustainable-development-goals/

[39] https://www.sustainablegoals.org.uk/filling-the-finance-gap/

[40] See: https://www.adb.org/sites/default/files/institutional-document/691951/ado2021bp-sustainable-finance.pdf

[41] See: https://www.adb.org/publications/asian-development-outlook-2021

Ward-Christie, 2022). The spectrum of impact investment includes all types of private capital that are deployed for social impact, including: grants; foundation assets deployed as Programme-Related Investment (PRI) or Mission-Related Investment (MRI); sub-market and market return investments (though not typically fully risk-adjusted); development finance; and positive ESG. The spectrum reflects both 'broad' and 'core' impact investment.

Figure 6.1 sets out the spectrum of impact finance organized by three categories: impact only; impact first; finance first. These correspond to different expected returns (not typically risk-adjusted). The figure also shows the estimated global market size and estimated returns for each type of capital. Given the absence of any consolidated financial performance data sets on most of the types of finance in the spectrum, the returns have been estimated from publicly available sources and should be seen as indicative.

The following sub-sections unpack the elements of the spectrum of impact investment and outline the available insights on market size and financial returns.

Grants

In terms of grants, the global market can be estimated at $75 billion. This is approximated from 5 per cent of total foundation assets globally—the legal requirement for charitable status in the USA, though not elsewhere.[42] This figure also excludes government grants to social enterprises, although these may be quite substantial sums. For example, the UK government has deployed in excess of £1 billion of public money to support the development of the social enterprise sector and impact investment infrastructure since 2010.[43]

With respect to returns, grant capital is deployed with the assumption of 100 per cent loss. As 100 per cent loss finance, grants play an important role both as start-up risk capital and as concessionary sustainable finance within blended finance structures and deals.

Programme-Related Investment

Programme-Related Investment (PRI) and Mission-Related Investment (MRI) form a part of a foundation's overall invested assets by using endowment capital to generate impact.

---

[42] Calculating the total value of philanthropic assets globally is difficult, since there is no single data set available. This figure is, therefore, an estimate based upon P. Johnson (2018) *Global Philanthropy Report* (Hauser Institute for Civil Society) valuation of global foundation assets at $1.5 trillion, see https://cpl. hks.harvard.edu/files/cpl/files/global_philanthropy_report_final_april_2018.pdf. This is likely to a larger figure in 2020.
[43] This figure includes: the endowment of UnLtd (£100 million); grants from the Futurebuilders (£215 million) and Investment and Contract Readiness (£60 million) Funds; co-investments with Bridges Fund Management (>£20 million); unclaimed bank account assets to the Reclaim Fund (>£850 million) of which Big Society Capital has deployed >£600 million to 2019.

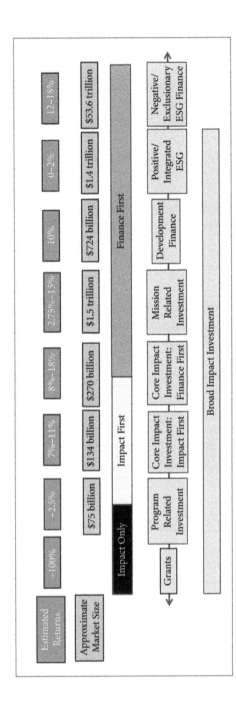

Figure 6.1 Spectrum of impact investment

PRIs typically take the form of debt capital to fund programmatic activities, often in concert with grants, and expect the return of capital only.[44] In the USA, PRIs can be included in the annual 5 per cent allocation of 'grant' capital.

The returns to PRI are estimated to vary between capital preservation and some loss-making. For example, KL Felicitas Foundation—with aims to invest 100 per cent of its assets as impact—reported a –2.5 per cent p.a. loss on its PRIs.[45] Moreover, under the US Internal Review Code for charity tax regulation, PRIs can be included in the minimum 5 per cent of total assets per annum which should be dispersed as grants, suggesting that they are expected to make some level of loss (Brest, 2016).

Core impact investing

Following the definition noted above, in the 2020 annual report, the GIIN estimated the 'core' impact investment market size at $404 billion.[46] However, the survey data will, likely, underestimate the total market size as it is based on a sample of only 290 respondents. In terms of sectors, the GIIN data suggested that the categories of impact investments were evenly spread between energy (16 per cent of all investments), financial services (12 per cent), forestry (910 per cent), food and agriculture (9 per cent), and micro-finance (8 per cent). In terms of instruments, private debt (37 per cent) and publicly traded debt (24 per cent) accounted for more than half of all capital invested, with private equity the third largest at 16 per cent and publicly traded equity the fourth largest at 10 per cent.

Impact investment can be either impact-first or finance-first depending on the structure of the fund/deal and investor expectations; expected returns vary between capital preservation and sub-market return (impact first) and risk-adjusted market returns (finance first).[47] In terms of expected financial returns, foundations, not-for-profit asset managers, and family offices were largely 'impact first' and would accept some sub-market rate investments. On the other hand, pension funds, insurance companies, for-profit asset managers, and development finance institutions were 'finance first' and generally expected risk-adjusted market returns.

In terms of impact investment returns, the GIIN 2020 survey separated out the data into either 'developed market' or 'emerging market' categories and then by

[44] See, for example, UK government guidelines: https://www.gov.uk/government/publications/charities-and-investment-matters-a-guide-for-trustees-cc14/charities-and-investment-matters-a-guide-for-trustees

[45] See: https://www.thinknpc.org/wp-content/uploads/2018/06/In-pursuit-of-deep-impact_NPC_KLF-Digital-1.pdf

[46] The GIIN Annual Impact Investor Survey 2020 included data from 290 impact investors who had deployed $404 billion. See: https://thegiin.org/assets/GIIN%20Annual%20Impact%20Investor%20Survey%202020%20Executive%20Summary.pdf. However, this does not include all impact investors, so is likely an under-estimate for the entire market.

[47] The GIIN Annual Impact Investor Survey 2020 included data from 290 impact investors. In terms of returns, 67% of this sample suggested that their investments achieved risk-adjusted market returns, 18% achieved below risk-adjusted market rate returns (but close to the market rate), and 15% achieved below risk-adjusted market rate returns (closer to capital preservation) see: https://thegiin.org/impact-investment/need-to-know/%23s2

type of finance (as annualized, realized, gross returns).[48] In developed markets, the average actual return with an expected, risk-adjusted, market rate return was 16 per cent from private equity, 13 per cent from real assets, and 8 per cent from private debt. In emerging markets, the average actual return with an expected, risk-adjusted, market rate return was 18 per cent from private equity, 10 per cent from private debt, and 8 per cent from real assets. While these returns look broadly in line with the typical risk-adjusted returns on mainstream private equity[49] and private debt,[50] there remain important empirical questions concerning whether these returns are properly risk-adjusted given the—typically non-financialized—impact risk variable in the overall capital structure.[51] Across the GIIN 2020 survey sample, more than 50 per cent of respondents saw a 'severe' or 'moderate' financial risk in several categories of performance, including business execution and management risk (23%+54%); country and currency risk (18%+40%); macro-economic risk (17%+49%); financing risk (13%+46%); and market demand and competition risk (9%+44%).

In developed markets, the average actual return with an expected below-market rate return was 10 per cent from private equity and 7 per cent from private debt. In emerging markets, the average actual return with an expected below-market rate return was 11 per cent for private equity and 8 per cent for private debt. In both below-market scenarios, real assets did not expect a sub-market return. The GIIN data also suggested that the majority of its sample investors' financial returns were either 'in line with' or 'outperforming' expectations, with only 12 per cent reporting that they were 'underperforming'.

Mission-related investment

MRIs take the form of debt or equity and typically aim to further the foundation's missions and make a competitive financial return (Henriques et al., 2016). The potential market size of MRI investments could, potentially, equal the total assets of all foundations, or roughly $1.5 trillion globally.[52]

---

[48] The median age of inception of the investments in the sample was 2011.
[49] Average returns globally from 2009 to 2019 were 15.3%, see: https://www.marketwatch.com/story/private-equity-returns-have-gone-up-that-may-not-last-2020-06-18
[50] The average return in private debt globally from 1998 to 2016 was between 10% and 15%, see: https://www.ipe.com/research-the-rise-of-private-debt/10012090.article. However, the COVID pandemic will likely severely affect more recent returns, see: https://www.fnlondon.com/articles/private-debt-funds-set-for-worst-performance-since-the-global-financial-crisis-20200807
[51] Interestingly, however, there is some data that suggests that impact finance outperforms the market. This may be for several reasons including: overall better risk management (ESG funds, see: https://www.ft.com/content/733ee6ff-446e-4f8b-86b2-19ef42da3824); exploiting new, growth markets (green finance, see: https://www.bloomberg.com/graphics/2019-green-finance/); lack of correlation with market risk (micro-finance, see: https://www.triodos.co.uk/ethical-investments/microfinance-fund/LU0842307588).
[52] For pioneers in using MRI as 100% of assets see: KL Felicitas Foundation, https://klfelicitasfoundation.org; FB Heron Foundation, https://www.heron.org; T100, https://toniic.com/t100/; and the Ford Foundation's decision to engage in MRI, https://www.marketplace.org/2020/07/02/ford-foundation-darren-walker-charitable-organizations-philanthropy-economy-social-bonds/.

MRIs, as was noted above, typically seek market returns.[53] However, *contra* this assumption, KL Felicitas Foundation's overall endowment—aside from PRIs— returned only 2.75 per cent p.a. as MRI, so this could be seen as indicative of a lower threshold for MRI returns.

Development finance

A further important impact finance sector is development finance.[54] This sector includes multi-national agencies, such as the Asian Development Bank, Inter-American Development Bank, and International Finance Corporation (IFC); regional agencies, such as the European Bank for Reconstruction and Development; and national agencies, such as CDC in the UK. There is no single data set for all development finance, but in 2019 the IFC suggested that the twenty-five Harmonized Indicators for Private Sector Operations signatory DFIs could be seen as impact investors with total assets under management of $742 billion.[55]

Development finance returns can be estimated from some of the larger players in the market. For example, IFC recorded an average return on assets in a range of 0.1 per cent to 1.6 per cent between 2015 and 2019,[56] whereas CDC returned an average 10.3 per cent between 2012 and 2016.[57] Furthermore, an analysis of the equity returns on IFC, European Bank for Regeneration and Development (EBRD), and FMO showed an average of 10 per cent between 2003 and 2015.[58]

ESG

An additional category of impact investment is capital deployed thematically for an ESG purpose. Such ESG finance can be categorized as either positive/integrated or negative/exclusionary. An important distinction between negative and positive ESG finance is in terms of the additionality of impact, which relates to the 'Double Delta' of sustainable finance.[59] The Double Delta analysis distinguishes

---

[53] As a benchmark, the average market returns over ten years to June 2020 were S&P 500 14.7% and Dow Jones Industrial 15.04%: https://www.wealthsimple.com/en-us/learn/average-stock-market-return.
[54] In earlier estimates of the size of the impact investment market, development finance was typically excluded, see, for example, the GIIN Annual Impact Investor Survey 2019: https://thegiin.org/assets/GIIN_2019%20Annual%20Impact%20Investor%20Survey_ExecSumm_webfile.pdf. The 2019 GIIN report estimated the market to be $239 billion, whereas the 2020 report estimated the size to be $404 billion. The large increase appears, at least partly, to be a consequence of the inclusion of some development finance institutions in the 2020 survey sample for the first time.
[55] See: https://www.ifc.org/content/dam/ifc/doc/mgrt/the-promise-of-impact-investing.pdf
[56] See: https://www.ifc.org/wps/wcm/connect/corp_ext_content/ifc_external_corporate_site/annual+report/financials
[57] See: https://www.devex.com/news/financial-returns-likely-to-go-down-over-next-5-years-says-cdc-chair-92943
[58] See: https://publications.iadb.org/en/comparative-study-equity-investing-development-finance-institutions
[59] See: https://www.credit-suisse.com/media/assets/microsite/docs/responsibleinvesting/the-double-delta-of-impact-investing.pdf

between the additionality of impact at the investee/enterprise level and the additionality of impact at the investor/capital level. From this perspective, ESG capital that is invested by buying listed equity or debt in the mainstream markets has no additionality in terms of impact,[60] whereas new investment into new impact enterprises or to grow innovations has double additionality in terms of impact.

In 2018, the global total of assets under management that followed some form of ESG thematic approach amounted to approximately $60 trillion—or more than half of all assets under management.[61] All of the major investment banks now manage ESG funds, as well as many specialist fund managers.[62] Accurate data on the exact size and scope of each category is not publicly available. However, some broad conclusions can be drawn from what is available. The evidence suggests that the vast majority—more than 95 per cent—of ESG finance falls under the negative/exclusionary category that screens investments by a variety of ESG criteria including corporate practices, best-in-class comparators, norms-based analysis against global standards (ILO, UNCEF, OECD), and level of ESG integration in corporate strategy (see Table 6.1).

The data also suggests that the majority of ESG investing is in public equity and fixed income debt—categories that indicate a focus on mainstream businesses that are publicly listed. Following the logic of the Double Delta model noted above, these ESG investments are not materially impactful.[63] In terms of geography, the European ESG market is focused mainly on an exclusionary approach, whereas the US market is focused more on ESG integration.[64]

Table 6.1 ESG finance allocated by theme 2018

Theme	Negative/exclusionary	Positive/integrated
Negative screening	19.8	
ESG integration	17.5	
Corporate engagement	9.8	
Norms-based	4.7	
Best-in-class	1.8	
Sustainability-themed		1.0
Community focus		0.4
TOTAL $ Trillion	**53.6**	**1.4**

Source: Bloomberg[a]
[a] See: https://www.bloomberg.com/graphics/2019-green-finance/

---

[60] While there is a plausible argument that 'active' equity ownership may affect positive impact via changing corporate strategy or policy in listed companies, there is little evidence of this in practice.
[61] See: https://www.bloomberg.com/graphics/2019-green-finance/
[62] See: https://www.bloomberg.com/graphics/2019-green-finance/
[63] See: http://www.gsi-alliance.org/wp-content/uploads/2019/03/GSIR_Review2018.3.28.pdf
[64] See: http://www.gsi-alliance.org/wp-content/uploads/2019/03/GSIR_Review2018.3.28.pdf

Positive/integrated ESG

Positive/integrated ESG investment deploys additional capital to create additional investee impact aligned with the SDGs, most notably as green or social bonds. It is focused on private markets and early stage, high potential impact companies. Therefore, this category of ESG finance fulfils the broad definition of impact investment. However, negative/exclusionary ESG investment deploys capital thematically through a screened investment analysis aiming to 'do no harm' via investments that are typically made in large, publicly listed companies via secondary markets. While negative/exclusionary ESG finance does provide additional capital, it does not create additional impact at the investee level and, as such, it does not fulfil the definition of impact investment. However, in order to capture the full range of sustainable finance deployed for environmental and/or social impact, the spectrum sets of impact investment acknowledge both the positive/integrated and negative/exclusionary ESG categories.

The following sub-sections unpack the positive ESG categories of green bonds and social bonds, as well as the returns on negative ESG investing.

Green bonds

The green bond market has been growing rapidly.[65] In 2019, $257.7 billion of green bonds were issued globally—growth of 51 per cent on the 2018 total of $167.3 billion. Of these, Europe accounted for 45 per cent while the Asia-Pacific market issued 25 per cent, with China the largest Asian issuer.[66] Some estimates suggest that this market could account for up to $1 trillion in new issuances by 2021.[67] In 2019, the largest cumulative issuers of green bonds were the US Federal National Mortgage Association ($22.8 billion); the German Reconstruction Credit Institute ($9.02 billion); the Dutch State Treasury Agency ($6.66 billion); the Republic of France ($6.57 billion); and the Industrial and Commercial Bank of China ($5.85 billion).[68] Moreover, in a 2019 survey of 135 hedge funds in thirteen countries—with assets under management of $6.25 trillion—84 per cent reported 'an increased interest in ESG-orientated funds and strategies over the last 12 months'.[69] All the major global stock exchanges have listings for green bonds as public debt.[70]

The data on the pricing of green bonds remains mixed (Liaw, 2020). Some analysis suggests that the pricing does not typically reflect any sort of risk premium.[71] As such, returns are typically close to conventional bonds, which have been between

---

[65] See: https://www.msci.com/esg-ratings
[66] See: https://www.climatebonds.net/resources/reports/2019-green-bond-market-summary
[67] See: https://expertinvestoreurope.com/green-bonds-forecast-investments-to-break-through-1trn/
[68] See https://expertinvestoreurope.com/green-bonds-forecast-investments-to-break-through-1trn/
[69] See: https://www.cnbc.com/2020/02/14/esg-investing-numbers-suggest-green-investing-mega-trend-is-here.html
[70] See: https://www.forbes.com/sites/brendancoffey/2019/11/12/esg-stocks-are-having-a-fantastic-year/?sh=6fd53e352fbb and https://www.climatebonds.net/green-bond-segments-stock-exchanges
[71] See: https://blogs.cfainstitute.org/investor/2019/10/08/green-bonds-vs-traditional-bonds

zero and 2 per cent over the past five years.[72] For example, in 2020 Barclays issued a £400m, six-year green bond to support climate-related products and initiatives, with an annual yield of 1.70 per cent.[73]

Social bonds

Social bonds are also emerging as a new market for positive/integrated ESG finance. The first social bond was issued by the Instituto de Credito in Spain in 2015. It focused on offering sub-market loans to small and medium-sized organizations in deprived areas with the aim of accelerating economic growth and creating local jobs. The three-year social bond raised EUR 1 billion from a range of international investors. This was followed by a second EUR 1 billion Spanish social bond—also in 2015—issued by Kutxabank to provide affordable housing in the Basque country.[74] In 2017, the IFC launched a Social Bond Program that offered investors an opportunity to allocate social bond investments focused on the SDGs with a triple-A rated credit risk. Finance from the bonds focused on supporting banking for women and inclusive business programmes, which benefit under-served populations in emerging markets, including women and low-income communities with limited access to essential services such as basic infrastructure and finance. By 2020 the IFC had issued thirty-nine social bonds, raising $3.1 billion.[75]

In 2020 the SDG Impact project, within the UNDP, launched a set of SDG Impact Standards for SDG Bonds.[76] These standards contained six standards under four topic areas: strategic intent and impact goal setting; impact measurement and management; transparency and comparability; and context and governance. By 2020, total issuance had reached $33.1 billion, up from $6.2 billion in 2019. This accounted for 28 per cent of the total sustainable finance bond market.[77]

While the available data is more limited for social bonds, they seem to follow a similar pricing profile to green bonds without any risk premium. For example, in 2020, Assura issued a £300 million, ten-year social bond with an annual yield of 1.5 per cent.[78]

[72] See, for example: https://www.climatebonds.net/files/reports/cbi_gb_pricing_2h2018_08052019.pdf
[73] See: https://home.barclays/news/press-releases/2020/10/barclays-raises-p400m-through-second—green-bond—issue-/
[74] See: https://www.gbm.hsbc.com/-/media/gbm/reports/insights/social-bonds.pdf
[75] See: https://www.ifc.org/wps/wcm/connect/corp_ext_content/ifc_external_corporate_site/about+ifc_new/investor+relations/ir-products/socialbonds
[76] See: https://sdgimpact.undp.org/assets/SDG-Impact-Standards-for-Bonds_First-Public-Consultation-Draft.pdf
[77] See: https://cib.bnpparibas.com/sustain/capital-markets-and-covid-19-have-social-bonds-come-of-age-_a-3-3503.html
[78] See: https://www.investegate.co.uk/assura-plc/rns/pricing-of—300m-social-bond/20200908161950 3846Y/

Negative ESG investing

In terms of the returns on negative/exclusionary ESG finance, the available data suggests that the top performing stocks had a return of 12–16 per cent in 2018–2019.[79] This compares to 29 per cent growth in the S&P 500 for the same period.[80] However, Barclays' analysis of the ESG performance of its funds between 2013 and 2020 showed rough parity between ESG and non-ESG equity returns, averaging approximately 18 per cent annual growth.[81]

Learning from policy innovation in the UK

Maduro et al. (2018) provided an extensive overview of the social impact investment landscape in the EU and noted that the UK has the most developed market infrastructure. Over the past decade, the UK government has been a global pioneer in terms of policy innovation for impact investment, launching several key policy innovations to support the growth of the market (Nicholls & Teasdale, 2017; Nicholls & Teasdale, 2020).

In 2010, the UK Cabinet Office published a strategy to grow the social investment market.[82] Subsequent to this, in 2013, the Cabinet Office established a Social Impact Investment Task Force (SITF).[83] Established by the UK government in 2013 and coordinated by the Cabinet Office, the SITF was given the remit to grow the impact investment market globally. Members of the Taskforce included representatives from the UK, Canada, the EU, France, Germany, Italy, Japan, USA, and Australia, as well as several development finance institutions. The SITF established a range of topic-specific working groups to agree key principles and approaches, provide relevant examples and draft papers to produce recommendations for policy-makers. Working groups were set up in the areas of impact measurement, asset allocation, international development and impact investment, and mission alignment. In addition to the working groups, the taskforce oversaw the preparation of a report on the global social investment market by the Organisation for Economic Co-operation and Development (OECD). The OECD published its report in 2015.[84]

The SITF members also each developed a national advisory board (NAB) to examine ways of accelerating the growth of the impact investment market in their own country/region. These boards brought together leaders of organizations active in impact investment, philanthropic foundations, social enterprises, and mainstream

[79] See: https://www.ftadviser.com/investments/2019/10/10/esg-investing-provides-strong-returns/
[80] See: https://markets.businessinsider.com/news/stocks/sp-500-2019-annual-return-for-year-best-since-2013-2019-12-1028790061?
[81] See: https://www.investmentbank.barclays.com/our-insights/3-point-perspective/esg-funds-looking-beyond-the-label.html?cid=paidsearch-
[82] See: https://assets.publishing.service.gov.uk/government/uploads/system/uploads/attachment_data/file/61185/404970_SocialInvestmentMarket_acc.pdf
[83] See: https://www.gov.uk/government/groups/social-impact-investment-taskforce#members-of-the-taskforce
[84] See: https://www.oecd.org/sti/social-impact-investment-9789264233430-en.htm

investment organizations. Each NAB produced an annual report, including policy recommendations. In 2015, the SITF was superseded by the GSGII (discussed earlier). In addition to deploying public finance as start-up capital for the sector (noted earlier), the UK government used a range of other policy levers to support the market. These included regulation, legislation, fiscal policy, and public spending innovations such as Social Impact Bonds.

Regulation

With respect to regulation, in 2005 the UK government launched the first new legal form of incorporation for more than 100 years, specifically aimed at social enterprises: the Community Interest Company (CIC). By mid-2020, more than 19,000 organizations had registered as CICs.[85] To be eligible to register as a CIC, an organization must already be a Company Limited by Guarantee (CLG); a Company Limited by Shares (CLS); or a Co-operative, Mutual, or Industrial and Provident Society (a form of mutual company). Registered charities are excluded. The policy objective of the CIC model was to facilitate more investment into social enterprises as a recognized legal entity that would ensure an impact focus. In addition, every CIC is required to file an annual report to the Regulator setting out some details of their social impact. A number of legal requirements are built into the CIC model: an asset lock, that does not allow for a CIC to be bought out to realize an asset such as property; a dividend payment cap (for CLSs) of 35 per cent of net annual profits; a performance-related interest loan cap of 20 per cent of outstanding debt (for CLGs).[86] These requirements were designed to discourage organizations that took a finance-first rather than impact-first approach registering as CICs. In addition, any investment in a CIC attracts Social Investment Tax Relief (discussed later in the chapter). Despite these factors, it still remains unclear how much new capital has actually been raised by CICs.[87]

In terms of building the supply side, an important policy innovation in terms of regulation was the Public Services (Social Value) Act.[88] Introduced by the UK government in 2013, this Act aimed to grow the social enterprise sector by increasing the scope for access to public sector contracts. The Act required all public sector commissioners to *consider* social value when evaluating tender applications for contracts above £111,676 (central government) and £172,514 (for other bodies). However,

---

[85] See: https://communityinterestcompanies.blog.gov.uk/2020/09/09/annual-report-2019-to-2020-community-interest-companies/

[86] See: https://www.isonharrison.co.uk/blog/how-could-a-community-interest-company-meet-your-enterprise-needs/

[87] For example, see the rather nebulous comment 'A solid number of CICs are already receiving social investment and this market has grown significantly': https://www.accountingweb.co.uk/business/finance-strategy/community-interest-companies-funding-for-growth/

[88] See: https://www.gov.uk/government/publications/social-value-act-information-and-resources/social-value-act-information-and-resources

takeup has been limited. By 2015, only 11 per cent of local authorities had applied the Act in their commissioning process and only 27 per cent of those which tendered for contracts were chosen on their superior social value criterion.

Legislation

With respect to legislation, the UK government has introduced two Acts aimed at developing the impact investment market both in terms of the supply side and the demand side. In terms of a supply-side measure, in 2005 the UK government set up a Commission on Unclaimed Assets, tasked with exploring how unclaimed assets in dormant bank accounts—specified as having had no transactions for fifteen years or more—could be reclaimed to benefit society. Following the recommendations of the Commission, in 2008, as a supply-side measure, the government introduced the Dormant Bank and Building Society Accounts Act.[89] The act specified that retail bank account assets that were dormant—again, defined as being without any transactions for fifteen years or more—should be transferred to a new, non-statutory body, the Reclaim Fund, for 'good causes'.[90] The Reclaim Fund was administered by the Co-operative Banking Group as a 100 per cent shareholder; it released funds via the National Lottery Community Fund to each of the four administrative areas of the UK.[91] Participation by banks and building societies was voluntary. Nevertheless, twenty-two did agree to release their dormant assets annually, including the four big high street banks—HSBC, Lloyds, Barclays, and the Royal Bank of Scotland. By 2020, £1.35 billion in dormant bank account assets had been transferred from 118,000 accounts; only £93 million had been reclaimed by customers, or roughly 7 per cent. From these dormant assets, the Reclaim Fund allocated £745 million to the National Lottery Community Fund to disburse.[92] In 2015, the UK government launched a Commission on Dormant Assets to explore other sources of dormant assets from pension and insurance funds and investment and wealth management portfolios. The Commission reported back in 2017 and suggested that a further £1.6 billion of unclaimed assets could be accessed.[93] However, as of 2020, none of its recommendations have been implemented.[94]

Of the various 'good causes' to which dormant assets have been directed, the most significant is Big Society Capital (BSC). In 2008, when the Dormant Bank and

[89] See: https://www.legislation.gov.uk/ukpga/2008/31/contents
[90] See: https://www.reclaimfund.co.uk/about-us/. By 2020, 15,000 'good causes' had been funded across the UK.
[91] See: https://www.reclaimfund.co.uk
[92] See: https://fr.zone-secure.net/-/Reclaim_Fund_Annual_Report_and_Accounts_2019/-/#_page=1&page=1
[93] £715 million from investments and wealth management; £550 million from the pensions and insurance sectors; £150 million from securities; £140 million from banks and building societies. See: https://www.gov.uk/government/news/2-billion-boost-set-to-transform-charity-and-voluntary-sector-funding
[94] See: https://assets.publishing.service.gov.uk/government/uploads/system/uploads/attachment_data/file/727189/Tackling_dormant_assets_-_recommendations_to_benefit_investors_and_society__1_.pdf

Building Society Accounts Act passed, one of its three specified purposes focused on creating a 'Social Investment Wholesaler' with the objective of building the supply of capital to impact investment funds by co-investment with other asset managers, while not making direct investments itself. In 2011, as part of the 'Merlin Agreement' that specified the terms of the financial bail-out between the UK government and the major UK high street banks, a commitment was included that the four largest banks should each contribute £50 million in equity into the 'Big Society Bank'. The combination of unclaimed assets and the Merlin Banks' equity capitalized BSC. In 2012, BSC was launched as the world's first wholesale impact investment intermediary.[95] By 2019, BSC had signed £2 billion in commitments with other investors, of which £1.3 billion had been drawn down. In these deals, BSC mobilized £626 million of dormant assets to achieve greater than 3x leverage of its assets.[96] Following an initial phase of opportunistic co-investment, BSC now focuses on three categories of impact: early interventions in health and education; place-based investment, focused on areas of deprivation; homes and social housing.

In terms of building the demand side, in 2015 BSC created the Access Foundation in collaboration with the National Lottery Community Fund and the UK government's Cabinet Office (responsibilities now transferred to the Department for Culture, Media and Sport, DCMS). The Access Foundation's objectives were to support charities and social enterprises in England 'to become more financially resilient and self-reliant, so that they can sustain or increase their impact'.[97] Specifically, the aim was to drive the economic development of charities and social enterprises such that they could diversify their income base and become investment-ready to access impact investment and providing a pipeline of potential deals for a BSC co-invested fund. The Access Foundation's capital structure consists of a £60 million endowment from DCMS and £45 of 'blended growth' capital split equally between BSC and the National Lottery Community Fund.[98] This combination of endowment and blended capital allows the Access Foundation to combine grants with sub-market loans in various deal structures to address a capital gap in terms of investment readiness in the social sector. At the same time, it aims to create new investment opportunities for the funds with which BSC co-invests. The Access Foundation developed three programmes to address its objectives:[99]

- *The Growth Fund*: launched in 2015 as a co-investment fund, the £45m Growth Fund offered a range of grants and small-scale unsecured loans to charities and social enterprises to bridge a gap in the market for small-ticket, sub-market finance. By 2018 it had co-invested with sixteen other funds (with fifteen social investors) totalling £50m in capital allocated to 250 small social organizations

[95] See: https://bigsocietycapital.com
[96] See: https://bigsocietycapital.com/investment-numbers/
[97] See: https://access-socialinvestment.org.uk/us/what-we-do/
[98] See: https://access-socialinvestment.org.uk/us/the-story-so-far/
[99] See: https://access-socialinvestment.org.uk/us/the-story-so-far/

(<50-% with turnover >£250k) with an average investment size of £64k. This contrasts with the median investment size of c. £250k.

- *The Reach Fund*: launched in 2016, the Social Investment Business was selected to run the Reach Fund to build investment capacity in social enterprises. By 2018, more than 220 grants totalling more than £3m had been made. The median turnover of the grantees was >£100k. Seventy of those grantees went on to raise investment to a total value of more than £17m.
- *The Impact Management Programme*: Launched in 2017, and delivered in partnership with New Philanthropy Capital, the programme provided £1.8m of grants to build impact management skills and capacity in charities and social enterprises who are seeking impact investment or new government contract opportunities.

In addition to these core programmes and in collaboration with BSC, the Access Foundation also developed the Good Finance website[100] in 2016 as a resource to provide advice and examples to help social enterprises access finance. In the first three years the website was used by 74,000 users who engaged with eighty investors and advisors. In 2017, the Access Foundation also created the Connect Fund—in partnership with the Barrow Cadbury Trust—as another initiative to build the impact investment infrastructure. By 2019, the Connect Fund had supported more than fifty projects around the UK with capacity building, data sharing, building networks, developing standards and templates, and sharing market information. Finally, in 2018, the Access Foundation launched the Enterprise Development Programme (EDP), to support early stage social enterprises as a twelve-month pilot scheme. The EDP worked with the Social Investment Business to manage two grant products—feasibility grants and larger enterprise development grants—and with the School for Social Entrepreneurs to manage social enterprise learning in two cohorts of experiential programmes for leaders working on homelessness and youth training. During the pilot phase, ninety-two grants were made, totalling £1.25m.

Fiscal policy

With respect to fiscal policy, in 2014 the UK government introduced Social Investment Tax Relief (SITR).[101] The new tax relief was specified in three ways: income tax relief of 30 per cent on annual investments of up to £1 million with a carry back relief to the tax year preceding the year of investment; deferral that matched the investment to capital gains made in the three years prior to, or one year following, the date of the investment; exemption of gains on subscribing for shares realized on their disposal (which will not be subject to tax providing that a claim for income tax relief

---

[100] See: https://www.goodfinance.org.uk
[101] See: https://www.gov.uk/guidance/venture-capital-schemes-apply-to-use-social-investment-tax-relief

is made three years after the date of the investment). In terms of the requirements to apply for SITR, investments must be made into a specified set of organizations—charities, CICs, Community Benefit Societies (with an asset lock of fewer than 500 employees and less than £15m in assets), and Social Impact Bonds (as agreed by the Department for Culture, Media and Sport—discussed further presently)—up to a maximum, per organization, of £1.5 million over the life of the organization. For the individual investee, the maximum investment is capped at £1 million per year. The take up of SITR has been surprisingly modest—by 2016/17 only £5.1million of investment had been subject to the tax relief, against a UK Treasury projection of £83.3 million.[102] This is perhaps because of a lack of infrastructure—as of 2018, there were only four SITR funds available to investors.

Public spending innovation: Social Impact Bonds

In the context of this broad range of UK government support for the impact investment market, perhaps the most innovative initiative has been the development of Social Impact Bonds (SIBs) (Edmiston & Nicholls, 2018).[103] SIBs are not, in fact, bonds of any sort. Rather, they are a form of contingent future liability contract—or, more simply, a payment-by-results contract[104]—between an investor, an outcomes payer, and a service provider, where the returns to the investor are directly linked to clear measures of social impact. In 2010, the UK launched the world's first SIB focused on reducing re-offending by ex-prisoners at Peterborough Prison (Nicholls & Tomkinson, 2015). The Peterborough SIB was broadly considered to be a success and the UK government committed to develop a number of further SIBs. By 2020, the UK had seventy-six SIBs in development or under way, mobilizing £44.7 million. Moreover, SIBs are now a global phenomenon. In 2020 the global total of impact bonds was 195 mobilizing £441 million in twenty-six countries.[105] The UK continues to dominate the SIB market, but a range of other countries have also launched several SIBs, including the US (31), Kenya (13), the Netherlands (13), and Australia (9). Across the EU (excluding the UK), there are forty-eight SIBs. In terms of sectoral focus, the largest sectors for impact bonds are employment and training (32%), homelessness (17%), health (16%), and child and family welfare (15%). The outcomes-based investment model has also been applied to other impact

---

[102] See: https://www.sibgroup.org.uk/sites/default/files/files/What%20A%20Relief%20-%20SITR%20research%20report.pdf

[103] See: https://www.socialfinance.org.uk/what-we-do/social-impact-bonds; https://www.gov.uk/guidance/social-impact-bonds; https://golab.bsg.ox.ac.uk/the-basics/impact-bonds/; https://www.brookings.edu/series/impact-bonds/

[104] In the US these are typically known as 'pay for success' contracts. See: https://www.air.org/resource/pay-success-social-impact-bonds/

[105] Data varies slightly, but there are three important impact bond resources. See: https://sibdatabase.socialfinance.org.uk; https://golab.bsg.ox.ac.uk/knowledge-bank/indigo-data-and-visualisation/impact-bond-dataset-v2/; https://www.brookings.edu/series/impact-bonds/

areas, including international development,[106] the environment,[107] conservation,[108] and humanitarian aid.[109]

In principle the SIB model can be applied to any intervention that satisfies three conditions: the outcome is measurable and can be given an agreed financial value; there is an outcomes payer; there are investors. This has made impact bonds very attractive to the impact investment community since they seem to offer an elegant model by which to 'price' impacts in the market, build robust outcomes data, and offer the potential of reaching substantial scale. Furthermore, and perhaps more significantly, the outcomes logic of impact bonds seems to be having an important effect in public services commissioning more generally, particularly in healthcare and pharmacology.[110] For example, in the UK in 2015, payment-by-results contracts accounted for more than £15 billion of public spending.[111]

The state of impact investment in the European Union

In the EU context, various institutions have supported the development of impact investment, including the European Commission (EC), the European Investment Bank (EIB), and the EIF. The European Union NAB is a joint initiative of the EC, the EIB, and the EIF, headquartered in Luxembourg. The objective of the NAB is to mobilize more than EUR 1 billion, with EUR 370 million already committed by the EIF.[112]

The EIF has focused on what is calls 'social' impact investment into projects working on social cohesion. EIF is the only impact investment wholesaler developing a pan-EU strategy. In 2020 EIF managed $1.1 billion currently invested in micro-finance and social enterprise.[113] The fund has provided support to develop the intermediary space to address a market failure in the access to finance for social enterprises. Specifically, the EIF developed a Social Impact Accelerator (SIA)[114] and the EFSI Equity Instrument.[115]

The SIA is a fund-of-funds wholesaler managed by EIF and invests in other social impact funds which target social enterprises across Europe. The SIA closed in 2015 at EUR 271m across nineteen funds with 3.5x leverage. The SIA brought together

---

[106] See: https://qualityeducationindiadib.com

[107] See: https://www.goldmansachs.com/media-relations/press-releases/current/dc-water-environmental-impact-bond-fact-sheet.pdf

[108] See: https://www.ft.com/content/2f8bf9e6-a790-11e9-984c-fac8325aaa04

[109] See: https://www.icrc.org/en/document/worlds-first-humanitarian-impact-bond-launched-transform-financing-aid-conflict-hit

[110] See, for example: https://golab.bsg.ox.ac.uk/toolkit/technical-guidance/awarding-outcomes-based-contracts/; http://www.pmlive.com/pharma_news/greater_manchester_backs_move_to_outcome-based_payment_1279006

[111] See: https://www.nao.org.uk/report/outcome-based-payment-schemes-governments-use-of-payment-by-results/

[112] https://gsgii.org/nabs/european-union/

[113] https://gsgii.org/reports/country-profile-european-union/

[114] https://www.eif.org/what_we_do/equity/sia/index.htm

[115] https://www.eif.org/what_we_do/equity/efsi/index.htm

resources from the EIB Group and external investors, including Credit Cooperatif, Deutsche Bank, the Finnish group SITRA, and the Bulgarian Development Bank (BDB).

The EFSI Equity Instrument was a joint venture between the European Commission and the EIF to fund further innovations in the fields of artificial intelligence, blockchain, space technology, impact investment, and blue economy. Within this, and in common with the SIA, the EFSI Equity Instrument focused on supporting the intermediary sector to provide more capital to social enterprises. Across the EU there is also a significant green finance sector with a sustainability and climate focus.[116]

The EIF is also responsible for managing the EaSI programme, which was launched in 2014. Within the EaSI there are three impact investment initiatives: the EaSI Guarantee ($446.1 million); the EaSI Capacity Building Investment Window (EUR 16 million); and the EaSI Funded (Debt) Instrument (EUR 220 million). Each aims to increase the flow of capital to social enterprise by building the intermediary sector and de-risking impact investments. As of 2015, fifteen EU countries had enacted some form of regulation that specifically targets social enterprises.[117]

The EBRD is another institution catalysing the growth of the impact investment markets. In 2015, the EBRD committed to allocate 40 per cent of its annual investment (by 2020) into a Green Economy Transition (GET) via direct green investment, technical support, policy advocacy, and concessional co-investment.[118] By 2019 the EBRD had issued EUR 5.2 billion in ninety-two green bonds, including a $700 million, five-year Climate Resilience Bond. In 2020 the EBRD issued a new set of GET objectives for 2021–2025.

Despite this wide range of initiatives, the Maduro et al. (2018) overview of the social impact investment landscape in the EU demonstrated that the landscape of social impact investment is highly heterogenous across the region. Similarly, the Expert Group on Social Entrepreneurship (GECES, 2018) noted the importance of improving access to finance for social enterprises in Europe, highlighting the need for increased public investment in capacity building for investment readiness and supporting the development of impact investment infrastructure and co-investment as catalytic capital in blended models with private finance. These observations suggest that a more coherent overall policy agenda from the European Commission would be beneficial for future market development and growth across the EU.

Policy recommendations for the EU context

The market for impact investment is growing in the EU and providing increasing capital to social enterprises for both start-up and growth. However, the market remains incomplete, fragmented, and inefficient. Policy can play a central role in developing

---

[116] See, for example, https://impact-investment.eu/en/
[117] https://gsgii.org/reports/country-profile-european-union/
[118] See: https://www.ebrd.com/what-we-do/get.html

the market. There is clearly a value in developing specific policy agendas across the EU to grow the impact investment market in the region. Reflecting on similar policy innovations in the UK, these opportunities can exploit a range of policy interventions, including direct investment, co-investment, regulation, fiscal policy, legal forms, and knowledge management. These would identity and address gaps in the existing market infrastructure in terms of the supply side, the demand side, and intermediation (see Table 6.2).

Increasing the supply side of impact investment

- **Develop public procurement social value legislation:** In 2019, the European Commission reported that there are a range of examples of public procurement policies in place across twelve countries in the EU that support social enterprise access to public contracts and include 'social clauses' in contracts, reserved contracts, exclusion contracts, and social labels.[119] In addition, in 2018 the EIB established a set of framework guidelines for procurement that included a recommendation that tenders should be 'encouraged to contribute to the protection of the environment, human well-being, human rights, gender equality, combating climate change and promotion of sustainable development'.[120] These initiatives could be further developed as a consistent pan-European policy to increase the incentives for outcomes-based commissioning and payment-by-results contracts following the regulatory model set out in the UK Public Service (Social Value) Act. By implementing such a policy at EU level, issues around national state aid should be avoidable.
- **(Co)-invest in impact bonds and outcomes funds:** Consistent with this policy agenda, the EU could deploy capital directly and indirectly (by co-investment) to develop impact bond investment and outcomes payment funds to leverage other types of capital into social and environmental impacts around its broader policy agendas concerning the climate crisis, economic development, and the resilience of social infrastructure. Where such funds develop a robust—and market-contingent—connection between impact and financial value (returns), they would also increase both the efficiency and effectiveness of the allocation of public capital.
- **Co-create evergreen impact funds:** EU direct investment could also provide capital to co-create 'evergreen' social and environmental funds that roll over capital to avoid the traditional limited-life structures with arbitrary exit timelines of conventional funds. Evergreen funds typically offer more flexibility for fund managers and social enterprises with multiple liquidity events throughout the fund's life. However, they can prove hard to raise in the

---

[119] See: https://op.europa.eu/en/publication-detail/-/publication/3498035f-5137-11ea-aece-01aa75 ed71a1

[120] See: https://www.eib.org/attachments/strategies/guide_to_procurement_en.pdf at p. 9.

mainstream market, given their complexity and relative novelty. De-risking and proving such funds with public capital could leverage mainstream capital into impact.[121]

- **Create tax incentives for impact investment:** In terms of fiscal policy, tax incentives for impact investment are already in place in two EU countries: in France, with investment into SCICs; and in Italy, with investment into government specified social enterprises. Such policies could be extended to the EU as a whole, with some provision to local market contexts.

Building the demand side of impact investment

- **Create a common EU social enterprise form of incorporation:** Currently, sixteen EU countries have some form of legislation that recognizes and regulates social enterprise activity—including both new legal forms and transversal legal status that cuts across existing organizational forms of incorporation dependent on pre-defined social criteria.[122] The majority of these recognize the social cooperative type of organization that has played an important role in the social economy for many years. In terms of this form of legislation, the EU could move further towards establishing a common legal form of incorporation for social enterprises such as the CIC in the UK or the Benefit Corporation in the US. Such an approach would allow impact investors better to identify legitimate social enterprises in the market for capital, thus decreasing the transaction costs of finding potential investees.

- **Provide capacity-building grants to social enterprises and support capacity-building infrastructure**: Another market failure in the current impact investment landscape is the relative lack of investment-ready social enterprises. The EU can play a catalytic role to address this issue by direct investment in capacity building in the investee sector. This would allow social enterprises to move away from a reliance on grants towards accessing investment. In addition, this would help drive innovation and scalability in the best-performing social enterprises. This policy could follow existing examples such as the UK Investment and Contract Readiness Fund, discussed previously.

- **Build networks of best practice in investment readiness:** Linked to direct investment, the EU could also build networks of investment readiness expertise—leveraging, for example, the EVPA and EU NABs—to share best practice and models.

---

[121] For example: I(x) Investments represent a permanently capitalized holding company. I(x) was founded by Warren Buffett's grandson, Howard W. Buffett. I(x) Investments makes equity investments with longer timelines than standard investment funds to seed other equity investments: https://ixnetzero.com/

[122] https://ec.europa.eu/social/BlobServlet? docId=12987&langId=en

Building impact investment intermediaries

- **Establish dormant accounts legislation:** Supporting the creation of an impact investment wholesale bank could represent an important policy innovation in terms of building the intermediary infrastructure. In 2016 a question was raised in the European Parliament concerning legislation to release dormant bank accounts to capitalize such wholesalers (following the example of BSC in the UK and an initiative in Switzerland),[123] but as yet no policy has been established.
- **Expand non-financial disclosures and co-create a 'Bloomberg' for Impact platform:** The lack of a robust reporting and disclosure framework for the social impact of capital represents another significant obstacle to the development of an efficient impact investment market. EU policy has made progress in terms of potential regulation around company-level non-financial and environmental disclosure.[124] The next step would be to develop a similar approach to impact disclosure likely linked to current work by the SDG Impact project,[125] the IFC,[126] and the IMP.[127] Such disclosure would also generate the impact performance data sets that are currently lacking in the market. EU investment in a 'Bloomberg' platform for impact data would be a transformational contribution towards reducing information asymmetries, increasing market efficiency, and growing the flows of capital to the social enterprises that deliver the most impact.
- **Invest in impact data technologies:** Investment in impact technology represents another important opportunity to build the intermediary infrastructure. The EU could deploy grant and investment capital to support the development of lean data technologies, big data collection, and AI algorithmic data analysis focused on environmental and social impact.[128] Such action would not only support other regulatory strategies to improve disclosure and the availability of impact data, but also create employment and contribute to the development of the European technology sector.

Future research opportunities

These policy recommendations for the EU context also indicate fruitful avenues for future research opportunities.

---

[123] See: https://www.europarl.europa.eu/Doceo/document/E-8-2016-004628_EN.html
[124] See: https://ec.europa.eu/info/business-economy-euro/company-reporting-and-auditing/company-reporting/non-financial-reporting_en
[125] See: https://sdgimpact.undp.org
[126] See: https://www.impactprinciples.org/9-principles
[127] See: https://impactmanagementproject.com
[128] See, for example: https://www.60decibels.com

Table 6.2 Policy innovations for the European Union impact investment market

	Supply side	Demand side	Intermediation
Direct investment	Impact bond outcomes funds	Capacity-building grants	Impact data technologies
Co-investment	Impact bond co-investment funds Co-investment in impact evergreen funds	Capacity-building infrastructure	Co-create a 'Bloomberg' for impact platform
Regulation	Public procurement Social value legislation		Dormant accounts legislation Expand non-financial disclosure
Fiscal policy	Impact investment tax relief		
Legal forms		Single EU social enterprise form of incorporation	
Knowledge management		Build networks of best practice in investment readiness	

Research on direct and co-investment

Social economy researchers should explore the effectiveness of capacity of building programmes for social economy organizations. Insights on the effectiveness of these programmes will provide insights on how to connect social economy organizations with the impact investment market. Building on the growing research on SIBs (Edmiston & Nicholls, 2018; Fraser, Tan, Lagarde, & Mays, 2018; Ormiston, Moran, Castellas, & Tomkinson, 2020), future research could identify a broader range of impact domains where impact bonds and outcomes-based commissioning could be implemented. Research could also explore the role of catalytic capital deployed by governments to generate additional private capital into impact investment markets (Ormiston, Charlton, Donald, & Seymour, 2015). Finally, research should also explore how the beneficiaries in impact investment and social economy action can be embedded in the design and implementation of impact investment products (Casasnovas & Jones, 2022).

Research on regulation and fiscal policy

Future research should explore the relationship between social procurement policies and impact investment to understand whether building public markets for social economy organizations increases impact investment capital. Exploring this link would contribute to growing work on the impact of social procurement policy for social economy organizations (Cutcher, Ormiston, & Gardner, 2020; Denny-Smith, Williams, & Loosemore, 2020; Furneaux & Barraket, 2014). Building on the work of Katelouzou and Micheler (2022) future research could also explore the effectiveness of impact investment tax relief in incentivizing more capital across the impact investment spectrum.

Research on investment readiness

Future research should explore the investment readiness of a wide range of social economy organizations across the spectrum of impact investment. Previous research has only explored investment readiness for a limited range of investment products (Hazenberg, Seddon, & Denny, 2015). Understanding the investment readiness of social economy organizations across the spectrum will provide insights on how to support social economy organizations to take advantage of the increasing appetite of impact investors.

Conclusions

This chapter has set out the range of impact capital available to support the development of social entrepreneurship globally and in the EU context. The spectrum of impact investment ranges from grants to ESG finance and offers returns from 100 per cent loss to market or above market returns. Taken as a whole, this capital is equivalent to more than half of all assets under management globally. In terms of available capital, the spectrum is dominated by the two types of ESG capital noted previously. However, even if negative/exclusionary ESG capital is excluded, the total market size remains substantial at roughly $22 trillion. While the core impact investment sector (as defined by the GIIN) is growing, it remains a small proportion of the whole at roughly $400 billion. Going forward, two key opportunities for the future growth of impact investment will be accessing foundation assets and negative/exclusionary ESG finance.

In the case of foundation assets, there is a huge opportunity to leverage more capital for impact. Generally speaking, foundation assets are not invested for impact. For example, historically, the Rockefeller Foundation has invested only approximately $68 million (or 1.8 per cent of its total endowment) in MRIs focused on renewables, clean energy and technology, and sustainable forestry. Moreover, only $85 million (or 2.2 per cent) of the endowment is invested in negative/exclusionary ESG.[129] This leaves roughly 96 per cent of assets invested in the mainstream (non-impact) markets. In a response to this in-balance between the impact focus of foundation assets and grant making, in 2017, the Ford Foundation made a strategic decision to commit $1 billion of its endowment to MRIs.[130] However, this was still only 8 per cent of its total endowment of $12.4 billion. Total foundation assets are estimated to be $1.5 trillion (see above). Assuming the same MRI investment as the Rockefeller Foundation, this

---

[129] See: https://www.rockefellerfoundation.org/wp-content/uploads/Rockefeller-Foundation-Social-Investing-Guidelines.pdf.pdf

[130] https://www.fordfoundation.org/the-latest/news/ford-foundation-commits-1-billion-from-endowment-to-mission-related-investments/

would mean that 96 per cent of these assets—or an additional $1.44 billion—could be made available for impact finance as MRIs going forward.

In terms of ESG finance, since more than 95 per cent (or roughly $53.5 trillion) of this finance falls under the negative/exclusionary category that does not conform to the Double Delta model, there is an important opportunity to leverage this capital into positive/integrated ESG investment. For example, if 50 per cent of this investment were directed towards providing additional capital to fund the SDGs, then the current shortfall would disappear.[131]

As has been set out in this report, innovative policy has played an important role in developing the impact investment market to date. Going forward, EU policy-makers can use regulation pro-actively to scale and shape this market, better to address the social and environmental issues that currently need such urgent attention.

References

Amin, A., Cameron, A., & Hudson, R. (2002). *Placing the Social Economy*. Abingdon: Routledge.

Baglioni, S. (2017). A remedy for all sins? Introducing a special issue on social enterprises and welfare regimes in Europe. *Voluntas: International Journal of Voluntary and Nonprofit Organizations*, 28(6), 2325–2338.

Barman, E. (2015). Of principle and principal: value plurality in the market of impact investing. *Valuation Studies*, 3(1), 9–44.

Borzaga, C., & Defourny, J. (Eds). (2004). *The Emergence of Social Enterprise* (Vol. 4). London: Psychology Press.

Brest, P. (2016). Investing for impact with program-related investments. *Stanford Social Innovation Review*, 14, 19–27.

Casasnovas, G. (2022). When states build markets: policy support as a double-edged sword in the UK social investment market. *Organization Studies*, 44(2), 1–24.

Casasnovas, G., & Ferraro, F. (2022). Speciation in nascent markets: collective learning through cultural and material scaffolding. *Organization Studies*, 43(6), 829–860.

Casasnovas, G., & Jones, J. (2022). Who has a seat at the table in impact investing? Addressing inequality by giving voice. *Journal of Business Ethics*, 179(4), 1–19.

Castellas, E. I., & Ormiston, J. (2018). Impact investment and the Sustainable Development Goals: embedding field-level frames in organisational practice. In: Holt, D., Al-Dajani, H., Apostolopoulos, N., Jones, P., & Newbery, R. (Eds.). *Entrepreneurship and the Sustainable Development Goals* (Vol. 8, pp. 87–101). Bingley: Emerald Publishing Limited.

Castellas, E. I-P., Ormiston, J., & Findlay, S. (2018). Financing social entrepreneurship: The role of impact investment in shaping social enterprise in Australia. *Social Enterprise Journal*, 14(2), 130–155.

---

[131] See: https://www.bloomberg.com/graphics/2019-green-finance/

Cutcher, L., Ormiston, J., & Gardner, C. (2020). 'Double-taxing' Indigenous business: exploring the effects of political discourse on the transfer of public procurement policy. *Public Management Review*, 22(9), 1398–1422.

Denny-Smith, G., Williams, M., & Loosemore, M. (2020). Assessing the impact of social procurement policies for Indigenous people. *Construction Management and Economics*, 38(12), 1139–1157.

Doherty, B., Haugh, H., & Lyon, F. (2014). Social enterprises as hybrid organizations: a review and research agenda. *International Journal of Management Reviews*, 16(4), 417–436.

Edmiston, D., & Nicholls, A. (2018). Social Impact Bonds: the role of private capital in outcome-based commissioning. *Journal of Social Policy*, 47(1), 57–76.

Fraser, A., Tan, S., Lagarde, M., & Mays, N. (2018). Narratives of promise, narratives of caution: a review of the literature on Social Impact Bonds. *Social Policy & Administration*, 52(1), 4–28.

Furneaux, C., & Barraket, J. (2014). Purchasing social good (s): a definition and typology of social procurement. *Public Money & Management*, 34(4), 265–272.

GECES (The Expert Group on Social Entrepreneurship) (2018). *Social Enterprises and the Social Economy Going Forward: A Call for Action from the Commission Expert Group on Social Entrepreneurship*. European Commission.

Hazenberg, R., Seddon, F., & Denny, S. (2015). Intermediary perceptions of investment readiness in the UK social investment market. *VOLUNTAS: International Journal of Voluntary and Nonprofit Organizations*, 26(3), 846–871.

Hehenberger, L. (2020). How to mainstream impact investing in Europe. *Stanford Social Innovation Review*. https://doi.org/10.48558/Q6PN-5S75

Hehenberger, L., Mair, J., & Metz, A. (2019). The assembly of a field ideology: an idea-centric perspective on systemic power in impact investing. *Academy of Management Journal*, 62(6), 1672–1704.

Henriques, R., Nath, A., Cote-Ackah, C., & Rosqueta, K. (2016). Program Related Investments. *The Center for High Impact Philanthropy*. Retrieved from: https://www.impact.upenn.edu/wp-content/uploads/2016/04/160415PRIFINALAH-print.pdf.

Höchstädter, A. K., & Scheck, B. (2015). What's in a name: an analysis of impact investing understandings by academics and practitioners. *Journal of Business Ethics*, 132(2), 449–475.

Katelouzou, D., & Micheler, E. (2022). Investor capitalism, sustainable investment and the role of tax relief. *European Business Organization Law Review*, 23(1), 217–239.

Lehner, O. M., Nicholls, A., & Kapplmüller, S. B. (2022). Arenas of contestation: a Senian social justice perspective on the nature of materiality in impact measurement. *Journal of Business Ethics*, 179(15), 1–19.

Liaw, K. T. (2020). Survey of green bond pricing and investment performance. *Journal of Risk and Financial Management*, 13(9), 193.

Maduro, M., Pasi, G., & Misuraca, G. (2018). *Social Impact Investment in the EU. Financing Strategies and Outcomes Oriented Approaches for Social Policy Innovation: Narratives, Experiences, and Recommendations*. JRC Science for Policy Report.

McKillop, D., French, D., Quinn, B., Sobiech, A. L., & Wilson, J. O. (2020). Cooperative financial institutions: a review of the literature. *International Review of Financial Analysis*, 71: 101520.

Meng, T., Newth, J., & Woods, C. (2022). Ethical sensemaking in impact investing: reasons and motives in the Chinese renewable energy sector. *Journal of Business Ethics*, 179, 1091–1117.

Michie, J. (2015). Co-operative and mutual finance. In Alex Nicholls, Rob Paton, and Jed Emerson (Eds), *Social Finance* (pp. 133–155). Oxford: Oxford University Press.

Moody, M. (2008). 'Building a culture': the construction and evolution of venture philanthropy as a new organizational field. *Nonprofit and Voluntary Sector Quarterly*, 37(2), 324–352.

Moran, M., & Ward-Christie, L. (2022). Blended social impact investment transactions: why are they so complex? *Journal of Business Ethics*, 179, 1011–1031.

Nicholls, A. (2007). *Social Entrepreneurship: New Models of Sustainable Social Change.* Oxford: Oxford University Press.

Nicholls, A. (2010). The institutionalization of social investment: the interplay of investment logics and investor rationalities. *Journal of Social Entrepreneurship*, 1(1), 70–100.

Nicholls, A., & Teasdale, S. (2017). Neoliberalism by stealth? Exploring continuity and change within the UK social enterprise policy paradigm. *Policy and Politics*, 45(3), 323–341.

Nicholls, A., & Teasdale, S. (2020). Dynamic persistence in UK policy making: the evolution of social investment ideas and policy instruments. *Public Management Review*, 23(6), 802–817.

Nicholls, A. & Tomkinson, E. (2015). The Peterborough Social Impact Bond. In *Social Finance*, edited by Alex Nicholls, Rob Paton, & Jed Emerson (pp. 282–310). Oxford: Oxford University Press.

Nicholls, A. & Ziegler, R. (Eds). (2019). *Creating Economic Space for Social Innovation.* Oxford University Press.

Ormiston, J. (2019). Blending practice worlds: impact assessment as a transdisciplinary practice. *Business Ethics: A European Review*, 28(4), 423–440.

Ormiston, J. (2022). Competing discourses of impact measurement: insights from the field of impact investment. In Hazenberg, R., & Paterson-Young, C. (Eds.). *Social Impact Measurement for a Sustainable Future* (pp. 101–128). Cham: Springer International Publishing.

Ormiston, J., Charlton, K., Donald, M. S., & Seymour, R. G. (2015). Overcoming the challenges of impact investing: insights from leading investors. *Journal of Social Entrepreneurship*, 6(3), 352–378.

Ormiston, J., Moran, M., Castellas, E. I., & Tomkinson, E. (2020). Everybody wins? A discourse analysis of competing stakeholder expectations in Social Impact Bonds. *Public Money & Management*, 40(3), 237–246.

Osborne, D. (2007, June). Reinventing government: what a difference a strategy makes. In *7th Global Forum on Reinventing Government: Building Trust in Government* (pp. 26–27).

Osborne, D., & Gaebler, T. (1992). *Reinventing Government: How the Entrepreneurial Spirit Is Transforming Government.* Reading, MA: Addison Wesley Public Comp.

Phillips, S. D., & Johnson, B. (2021). Inching to impact: the demand side of social impact investing. *Journal of Business Ethics,* 168(3), 615–629.

Schmidt, R. (2023). Are business ethics effective? A market failures approach to impact investing. *Journal of Business Ethics,* 184, 505–524.

Spiess-Knafl, W., & Achleitner, A.-K. (2012). Financing of Social Entrepreneurship. In C. K. Volkmann, K. O. Tokarski, & K. Ernst (Eds.), *Social Entrepreneurship and Social Business* (pp. 157–173). Wiesbaden: Gabler Verlag.

Van Slyke, D. M., & Newman, H. K. (2006). Venture philanthropy and social entrepreneurship in community redevelopment. *Nonprofit Management and Leadership,* 16(3), 345–368.

Warner, M. E. (2013). Private finance for public goods: Social Impact Bonds. *Journal of Economic Policy Reform,* 16(4), 303–319.

Yan, S., Ferraro, F., & Almandoz, J. (2019). The rise of socially responsible investment funds: the paradoxical role of the financial logic. *Administrative Science Quarterly,* 64(2), 466–501.

7

How impact measurement fosters the social economy

From measurement of impact to learning and management for impact

Lisa Hehenberger and Leonora Buckland

Impact measurement as a key enabler of the social economy ecosystem

This chapter aims to provide a clear view on the topic of impact measurement for the social economy in Europe, including a description of the state of the art and identification of present and future challenges and opportunities. We will also advance some provocative but scientifically grounded recommendations as to which policy measures could help in addressing the identified challenges and capitalizing on the opportunities.

The social impact of a social economy organization can be considered as 'the social effect (change), both long-term and short-term, achieved for its target population as a result of its activity undertaken—taking into account both positive and negative changes, and adjusting for alternative attribution, deadweight, displacement and drop-off' (Clifford et al., 2015:7).[1] Impact measurement is thus the measurement of *social change* achieved for the *targeted population* attributed to the *activities* of the social economy actor during a *specific period of time*. The change might be both positive and negative and it may be necessary to consider unintended consequences of one's actions.

Impact measurement is not just a technical tool to determine whether a specific intervention has had an impact on its target population. Social economy actors, including co-operatives, mutual societies, non-profit associations, foundations, and social enterprises,[2] increasingly recognize the importance of better understanding their impact so that they can use data derived from the impact measurement process

---

[1] More specifically, social impact is adjusted for the effects achieved by others (alternative attribution), for effects that would have happened anyway (deadweight), for negative consequences (displacement), and for effects declining over time (drop-off). GECES report: Proposed approaches to social impact measurement. https://op.europa.eu/en/publication-detail/-/publication/0c0b5d38-4ac8-43d1-a7af-32f7b6fcf1cc.

[2] https://ec.europa.eu/growth/sectors/social-economy_en

Lisa Hehenberger and Leonora Buckland, *How impact measurement fosters the social economy*. In: *Social Economy Science*. Edited by: Gorgi Krlev, Dominika Wruk, Giulio Pasi, and Marika Bernhard, Oxford University Press. © Oxford University Press (2023). DOI: 10.1093/oso/9780192868343.003.0007

to learn and improve their activities and systems (Lall, 2019). In theory, social impact measurement should be a powerful tool to improve the European social economy. It can help individual organizations set realistic objectives; monitor, learn from, and improve their activities; prioritize decisions; and access funding (Nicholls, 2007). As an illustration, a survey of 1000 charities and social enterprises in the UK by New Philanthropy Capital (Ní Ógain et al., 2013) showed that a majority measured impact as requested by their funders, but the main benefit for the charities and social enterprises was that it helped them improve their services. Similarly, Lall (2019) finds that social enterprises first use impact measurement to signal legitimacy to funders but gradually come to see it as a tool for organizational learning. When impact measurement becomes integrated in the core functioning of a social economy actor, it should ultimately help this actor work towards achieving a greater impact, and identify potential negative outcomes, or assess the risk of no impact being achieved. Through increased transparency, impact measurement may also channel increased resources to address societal problems.

Collectively, social impact measurement can help organizations working on similar social issues or in similar geographic areas better understand the aggregate impacts of their work and collaborate to achieve greater change. And at a European level, agreed-upon standards, common indicators, and benchmarks can allow policymakers to evaluate the impact of the social economy on society, advocate for more public funding of social economy organizations, and help donors and investors direct their resources to the interventions that have the most impact.

Impact measurement is not without its challenges. Critics of impact measurement have alerted to the risks of channelling resources to interventions that are easy to measure, but potentially have a low impact (Hehenberger & Harling, 2015). Long-term effects of interventions involving multiple stakeholders and addressing complex challenges are more difficult to measure and might therefore be overlooked. In addition, if impact measurement is seen as imposed from above rather than driven and undertaken by the social economy actor, it can lead to negative behaviours such as 'gaming' the impact indicators and cherry-picking service users most likely to help accomplish targets. Although such arguments are certainly valid, we would like to claim that complex societal and/or environmental issues may need measurement and calculation to incentivize action.

A clear example of where better measurement can incentivize action is climate change. Academic research on multivocality (Ferraro, Etzion, & Gehman, 2015) has shown that a concept such as climate change is able to rally support from multiple stakeholders by its very ambiguity, allowing different types of actors to analyse the concept from their own perspective and with their own evaluative framework. However, the support often stops at the level of advocacy. For action to proceed, there is a need to clearly demarcate the scope of activity for a particular actor, assigning accountability, to define the objectives of the activity and to integrate those objectives into current management systems. Being able to measure and calculate impact allows social economy actors to manage their organizations towards greater impact. The tools and calculations developed for this purpose not only can serve current social economy actors but will be crucial in moving the entire economy in a more social and environmental direction. Integrating impact into accounting systems is an important step towards accounting for what economists have previously considered 'externalities' (Hehenberger & Harling, 2018). Promising work in this direction is currently under way at Harvard Business School to develop impact-weighted accounts.[3] Efforts to account for social impact have the potential to alter financial markets, corporate activity, and public administration from within, transforming our understanding of both the 'social' and the classical economies and facilitating the urgent task of 'building back better' in the aftermath of the COVID pandemic.

What does impact measurement mean and what does it involve—the basics

Impact measurement involves several dimensions, including the impact measurement *process*, the *indicators* adopted, and *principles* for reporting, transparency, and disclosure. Several organizations and networks have undertaken efforts to standardize and harmonize these dimensions.

Impact management process

An example of an attempt to describe the *impact measurement process* for social economy actors is the one recommended in the EU's GECES[4] report, which built on research conducted by the European Venture Philanthropy Association (Hehenberger, Harling, & Scholten, 2013). The process included 'identifying clearly the social impact sought, the stakeholders impacted, a "theory of change" for social impact, putting in place a precise and transparent procedure for measuring and reporting on inputs, outputs, outcomes and for assessing thereby the impact actually achieved, followed by a "learning" step to improve impacts and refine the process' (Clifford et al., 2015:24). The impact logic chain outlined in Figure 7.1 shows more clearly the difference between inputs, outputs, outcomes, and impact using a concrete example. While inputs and outputs can be somewhat easy to measure, outcomes and impact are much harder to evaluate and often require more resources and skills. While outcomes can be described as the effects on a target population, we define impact as the attribution to changes in outcome, or in other words, attributable outcome. On that note, it is important that Social Purpose Organizations (SPOs) do not simply imagine broad, unattainable impacts (e.g., to end poverty) which their measurements cannot come close to understanding their contribution towards.

---

[3] https://www.hbs.edu/impact-weighted-accounts/the-opportunity/Pages/default.aspx
[4] GECES is the European Commission's Expert Group on Social Economy and Social Enterprise. For more information see: https://single-market-economy.ec.europa.eu/sectors/proximity-and-social-economy/social-economy-eu/social-enterprises/expert-groups_en.

Figure 7.1 Impact logic chain

SPO's Planned Work		SPO's Intended Results		
1. Inputs	2. Activities	3. Outputs	4. Outcomes	5. Impact
Resources (capital, human) invested in the activity	Concrete actions of the SPO	Tangible products from the activity	Changes resulting from the activity	Outcomes adjusted for what would have happened anyway, actions of others & for unintended consequences
€, number of people etc.	Development & Implementation of programs, building new infrastructure etc.	Number of people reached, items sold, etc.	Effects on target population e.g. increased access to education	Attribution to changes in outcome. Take account of alternative programs e.g. open air classes
€50k invested, 5 people working on project	Land bought, school designed & built	New school built with 32 places	Students with increased access to education: 8	Students with access to education not including those with alternatives: 2

Source: Elaborated by EVPA from Rockefeller Foundation Double Bottom Line Project in Hehenberger, Harling & Scholten, 2013

The generic impact measurement process recommended in the EU's GECES report is still valid today, although the level of sophistication with regard to the tools and best practices employed to perform each step has improved. Furthermore, the term impact management has gained traction over the past few years as field actors have recognized the need to move beyond technical tools and frameworks to integrating impact in management systems. Impact management can be defined as the systems, processes, culture, and capabilities related to impact measurement (Hehenberger et al., 2020). The concept builds on existing fields, such as that of monitoring and evaluation, which has been widening to incorporate learning. What is innovative about impact management is the emphasis on a more dynamic and organization-wide attempt to determine impact, with an emphasis on the 'how' and 'for what purpose' as well as the 'what'. The specifics of this integration will depend on the type of actor, as will be discussed later in the chapter).

Indicators

Some argue that the lack of a standardized set of *indicators* across similar interventions in the social economy as a whole is limiting (Bengo et al., 2016). However, similar social economy actors working on similar social or environmental issues are starting to find common ground. Although it is impossible to define overarching, common impact *indicators* for all social interventions, it is possible to develop standardized indicators to measure similar interventions. *Taxonomies* have developed over the years that allow actors who are involved in similar interventions, for instance the integration of disadvantaged communities in the workforce, to clearly define measurable outputs and outcomes. For example, in social impact investment, the IRIS taxonomy[5] has emerged as a standard. However, it is still difficult to compare and benchmark the results of social impact measurements, even for similar actors. Whereas the implementation of the process can be verified or even audited, the resulting data is difficult to compare and we seem to be far away from auditing social 'accounts'.

Principles

The *principles* for reporting, transparency, and disclosure include the importance of openly explaining how the process of impact measurement was implemented and reporting actual impact results, with appropriate evidence. The concept of *proportionality* is important to consider here. Impact measurement should ultimately be useful for the social economy actor to better understand the impact it is having. The resources implemented to measure impact need to be proportionate to the size of

---

[5] https://iris.thegiin.org/

the intervention, by which we mean the set of activities that lead to a social or environmental impact. The level of evidence required as underpinning for the impact measurement may increase for more advanced actors and for larger interventions. At ESADE we have led the ESADE-BBK Community of Practice on impact measurement and management, involving more than fifty European foundations.[6] Our discussions have highlighted the need for increased transparency and data sharing among social economy actors with the objective of improved scrutiny and accountability, but also shared learning and to enable funders to compare and benchmark interventions for optimal resource allocation (Hehenberger et al., 2022). A related topic is that of social auditing and external verification of social impact which is increasingly debated and put forward as a way to ensure social economy actors are not 'marking their own homework', although there are voices that fear creating a parallel and expensive accounting system to the private sector which may not deliver better impact for the sector.

The state of play with European social economy actors and social impact measurement

Social economy actors widely discuss, consider, and implement social impact measurement and it is evident that these actors are facing and responding to a stronger climate for rigorous evidence concerning the social and environmental impact of their services and activities. Key drivers of this wave of social impact measurement include public sector procurement and accountability mechanisms which ask for social value to be described and evidenced as part of a tender or contracting process. Also important is a funder-led focus on concrete measurement indicators related to projects or organizations financed and an overdue, growing scrutiny of social economy organizations from citizens themselves. However, the starting points, motivations, and situations of each of the main social economy players are distinct and there is a diversity and plethora of individual contexts and narratives accompanying this broad framing, as will be outlined later in the chapter. The widely recognized plurality of the social economy creates a range of barriers and enablers regarding social impact measurement. Nevertheless, a unifying insight from practitioner-led research is how far the theory and discourse of social impact measurement is divorced from the reality on the ground, whatever the social economy actor. This divergence is particularly acute for smaller and less well-resourced social economy actors, as well as in certain geographies where the social impact measurement wave is weaker. In a recent cross-country comparison of evaluation in eight different European countries (Denmark, Estonia, France, Germany, Italy, Poland, Spain, and the United Kingdom), this gap between desired production and actual practice regarding impact data is clear, with up to 45 per cent of expert respondents claiming that impact evaluations

---

[6] https://www.esade.edu/en/faculty-and-research/research/knowledge-units/center-social-impact/research/community-practice

are carried out only 'occasionally'. Evaluation is conducted most frequently where evaluation is also more rigorous methodologically, specifically in Denmark, Poland, and the United Kingdom among the selected countries (KPMG, 2018).

Operating foundations, non-profit organizations, and social action associations

The group of non-market actors which makes up by far the largest part of the social economy in Europe, employing more than 66 per cent of those in the social sector (Monzón & Chaves, 2017), has, in general, been somewhat resistant to jump fully aboard the train of social and environmental impact measurement. Approaches have been patchy and inconsistent and have generated data of dubious quality which cannot be easily compared (Harlock, 2013). Many operating foundations and non-profits are not yet conducting social impact measurements of their activities and may not buy into the prevailing logic and motivation regarding why they ought to spend precious resources on it. Different reporting requirements and a diverse group of accountability needs of various stakeholders (general public, private donors, government contracts, etc.) without commonly agreed social impact measurement frameworks potentially create confusion, duplication, and excess work. For some organizations this represents an imposed bureaucratic burden rather than an enhancing, strategic, and central part of their activities.

Impact assessment 'by the gut', or with anecdotal data, is still surprisingly prevalent. There is a general lack of awareness of the important differences between monitoring, evaluation, and learning and a shortage relative to the need of relevant impact management skills and capabilities within the sector. Many operating foundations, non-profit organizations, and social action associations may be performing a basic type of monitoring related to assessing outputs, that is, the concrete and short-term results of their activities, and perhaps also assessing the quality of their service delivery. However, more rigorous evidence and evaluations which dive into the subtler, longer-term changes in the lives of users/beneficiaries and communities (i.e. the longer-term outcomes) and properly consult and include stakeholder and beneficiary voices are quite rare, although growing. Social impact measurement by such non-market actors is therefore primarily output-led rather than outcome-led, often not answering the most important questions about how the people or planet are affected over time. While output-led data is valuable, particularly in monitoring and basic organizational performance management, it does not enable a deeper understanding of change, which is the fundamentally important concept embedded in 'impact'.

This landscape overview is slowly shifting over time, and it is clear that larger operating foundations and non-profits understand the urgency and necessity of improving in this key area, in particular if they want to attract funds and partner with the public sector. The past decade has seen precipitous growth in social impact evaluations, particularly related to international development (Cameron et al., 2016), which requires an increase in the number of social impact professionals. Indeed, many European social economy actors are becoming increasingly sophisticated as creators and consumers of social impact measurement, for example working with universities on rigorous, external, independent evaluations.

There are interlinked barriers affecting the ability of these social economy actors to advance in social impact measurement, the greatest being financial resources. Conducting a social impact assessment, in the strict sense of the term, involves observing and analysing the changes produced by activities and determining the effects that are directly and solely attributable to the action of those activities. Using this approach is sometimes complicated, even impossible, without significant resources and a scientific base. In a perpetually resource-constrained environment, which has only become more acute during the COVID crisis, some organizations decide that there is not enough investment to spare on monitoring, evaluation, and learning, which can be relatively costly, with such spend needing to be traded off crucially with delivery of frontline services. In many instances, donors and public sector commissioners are demanding impact measurement but are still unwilling to pay for it, which creates a vicious cycle of low-quality evidence. Another key barrier is simple overwhelm about the different options and methodologies that exist to conduct social impact measurement (there are hundreds of different impact measurement tools and methodologies) coupled with different stakeholder impact reporting needs (Harlock & Metcalf, 2016). Finally, there is still some cultural resistance to the idea of *counting* '*what cannot be counted*' and whether in fact social impact measurement is imposing a managerial framework on the social economy field where it doesn't fit (Zimmer & Pahl, 2016). This is a valid and important criticism by social economy actors which must be explored and to which space must be given. However, the social economy must not lose sight of the fact that what is not valued will not have value within the system.

Social enterprises

Although impact measurement among social enterprises is a relatively nascent field, a range of different approaches and frameworks have been suggested for a sector which needs to manage the demands of both donors and investors, as well as balancing financial with social returns (Bengo et al., 2016). As a fast-growing and innovative part of the social economy, social impact measurement is fairly widely accepted, prioritized, and implemented by social entrepreneurs, with around 60 per cent of social enterprises measuring impact regularly according to the 2020–2021 European Social Entrepreneurship Monitor (Dupain et al., 2021) Since many social enterprises seek funds from social and impact investors who have put social impact measurement (and management) in the spotlight, they are generally more open and oriented to conversations about Key Performance Indicators (KPIs) and social output and outcome measures. However, there is still a wide variety of understanding and practices related to social impact measurement in different national contexts. The lack of better practices and stronger frameworks for measuring impacts is recognized to impede the performance of the sector as well as its growth and scale (Wilkinson, 2015).

On the ground, particularly for earlier-stage social entrepreneurs, few are following a rigorous, professionalized approach to impact assessment—for example, Social

Return on Investment, pre/post survey of users/beneficiaries, or formal Theory of Change with indicators (Molecke & Pinkse, 2020). While such social entrepreneurs recognize the importance of impact measurement and management for funder accountability, they have reframed the question 'how much impact?', which more formal impact measurement ultimately tries to get at, as 'is there impact?' (Molecke & Pinkse, 2020). In this way they avoid a rigorous analysis or impact evaluation, rather relying on pre-existing operational output-level data to signal impact and provide the impression of quantitative data analysis (Molecke & Pinkse, 2020). It is expected that over time funders may provide more resources for a greater rigour of evaluation or that social entrepreneurs themselves may invest since they believe it is essential for their growth and scaling, and for organizational learning (Lall, 2019).

Donors including social and impact investors

Philanthropy is on the rise globally, with European foundations spending nearly EUR 60 billion in 2015 and with more than 147,000 charitable foundations in the twenty-four European nations that the Donors and Foundations Networks of Europe (DAFNE) represents (McGill, 2016). European grant-makers are at the beginning of their journey to embrace and catalyse social impact measurement. For many, impact measurement is a challenge. In France, 34 per cent of foundations stated that they had difficulties evaluating their projects or programmes and in Belgium only half were asking for social impact reporting from their grantees (Mernier & Xhauflair, 2017). However, leading grant-making foundations are starting to occupy the role they need to occupy as capacity-builders and enhancers of these practices among their partners (grantees, investees) (Hehenberger et al., 2020). In general, transparency and accountability dynamics are not natural characteristics of the donor sector (particularly private foundations) with few pressures, apart from those which are self-generated, to properly report on their impact. This results in an often opaque and mysterious world with limited possibilities for public scrutiny of impact. While there is not widespread data about the social impact measurement practices of grant-makers in Europe (as opposed to the US, where this data is more routinely collected), it is clear that among the largest, leading grant-making foundations there is a growing impact orientation—to prioritize understanding their own impact as well as funding capacity building and social impact measurement of their grantees and investees. Many grant-makers are afraid of imposing a significant reporting burden and establishing more transactional relationships with their grantees—they are conscious of balancing demands for accountability and transparency from their boards with a desire for trusting, learning partnerships where social impact metrics should not be the central focus. We have seen this clearly among the fifty foundations involved in the ESADE-BBK Community of Practice (Hehenberger et al., 2022), although these philanthropists are perhaps the frontrunners of the impact management wave and there are many smaller, less resourced foundations who are not part of this 'coalition of the willing' and are latecomers to these newer philosophies.

Impact investors

The impact investment field has focused significantly on impact measurement in order to differentiate it from the wider investment field and has been behind a move towards more standardization of approaches. Impact investors were at first keen to implement the Social Return on Investment (SROI) approach as it resonated with how they traditionally thought about return on investment and it allowed for monetization of impact. SROI is defined as a form of adjusted cost–benefit analysis that takes into account, in a more holistic way, different types of impacts. However, as impact investors have become more sophisticated in their understanding of impact, they have also realized that any framework is as good as the data and assumptions that feed into it. Impact investors who are serious about impact (and not just investment) need to work harder on measuring impact and collecting and reporting impact data (Hehenberger & Harling, 2018). The EVPA guide (Hehenberger et al, 2013) tried to make sense of the myriad of frameworks and tools to develop best practice recommendations valid at the level of the impact investor and the social enterprise. As mentioned above, the EU's GECES report built heavily on those recommendations in terms of a defined process of measuring impact, and the G8 taskforce on social impact investment further defined guidelines (Social Impact Investment Taskforce, 2014). Since then, several interesting developments have moved the sector forward.

Impact investors now follow a fairly standardized approach of measuring and managing impact. In terms of indicators, the IRIS taxonomy, promoted by the Global Impact Investment Network, has become a standard in the sector, although increasingly impact investors are also developing their strategies to target specific SDGs. However, the indicators associated with the SDGs tend to be macro-level and more difficult to apply for individual organizations. Therefore, impact investors use the SDGs as aspirational and visionary targets that they work towards more generally as part of their investment strategy. The Impact Management Project (https://impactfrontiers.org/norms/investment-classification/), a multi-stakeholder initiative for impact investors to work towards common standards and categories, is helpful as it decomposes the somewhat lofty concept of impact into more specific dimensions of *what, who, how much, contribution*, and *risk*. These initiatives are helping impact investors integrate impact into the investment process in an increasingly standardized manner. The Operating Principles for Impact Management (https://www.impactprinciples.org) further provide concrete recommendations for how this integration should be executed in an impact investment fund with further scrutiny recommended through public disclosure and independent verification. Figure 7.2 summarizes how impact can be integrated in the impact investment process. The impact-investing investment process can be considered as involving the steps of deal screening, due diligence, deal structuring, investment management, exit and evaluation, and post-exit follow-up, each with what we consider particular appropriate impact measurement tools, methodologies, or frameworks outlined in the Figure below the step. The Impact Management Platform (https://impactmanagementplatform.org/) groups together the main tools and initiatives employed by impact investors.

The Impact Investing Investment Process

Investment Strategy	Deal Screening	Due Diligence	Deal Structuring	Investment Management	Exit	Evaluation & Post-exit Follow-up
Decide on the **impact objectives** – *the impact thesis* - of the impact investor, according to its *Theory of Change* and aligned with **target SDGs**. This will guide the investment process.	**Screen deals according to the impact thesis** of the impact investor – should help impact investor achieve its impact goals.	Conduct due diligence developing specific questions related to the **IMP dimensions**: *What, Who, How much, Contribution and Risk*	Develop impact objectives for investee to achieve during investment period. Define **KPIs to measure** – use standardized indicators where possible, e.g. IRIS. Define NFS.	Monitor progress **towards impact objectives** at regular intervals (more often for outputs, less frequently for outcomes). Suggest improvements if necessary.	Conduct exits considering the effect on **sustained impact**.	Evaluate **degree of achievement of impact objectives**. Include data in **impact report** of impact investor. Include **learnings to improve impact management** of fund.

IMPACT MANAGEMENT PROJECT

IRIS

INVESTING FOR IMPACT

evpa

EUROPEAN VENTURE PHILANTHROPY ASSOCIATION

Figure 7.2 Integrating impact in the investment process

In recent years, evidence points to a growing trend and pressure to report on impact and ESG in the financial sector, as evidenced by the Sustainable Finance Disclosure Regulation (SFDR) in the EU. The SFDR is designed to help institutional asset owners and retail clients understand, compare, and monitor the sustainability characteristics of investment funds by standardizing sustainability disclosures. The Impact Finance Taskforce is an industry-led Taskforce invited by the G7 Presidency to provide concrete recommendations on how to mobilize private capital for the SDGs. It notably launched a report that included strong support for the International Financial Reporting Standards Foundation's International Sustainability Standards Board's (IFRS-ISSB) efforts to create a global reporting 'baseline' on impact related to enterprise value.[7] These efforts indicate that sustainability and impact reporting in the financial sector will become increasingly harmonized. This provides an opportunity to mobilize further capital to initiatives that have social impact, but these need to fit within the parameters of investors' investment strategies.

Co-operatives

Little is known about co-operatives' socio-economic impact as there is a scarcity of measurement and reporting by co-operatives themselves and limited comprehensive datasets on their outcomes (Benos et al., 2018). Scholarly work has favoured using appraisal tools common to market actors, but these do not speak to the dual nature of the co-operative, with its distinct business and membership objectives. Social enterprises might provide better inspiration for the co-operative sector. EU-funded research has illustrated useful social impact measurement methodologies for co-operatives, such as the cost–benefit analysis which was applied to Italian work integration co-operatives in Trento, with data collected over six years.[8] It is unclear whether such methodologies have been mainstreamed in the sector. The World Co-operative Monitor project aims to provide visibility to the movement by monitoring and demonstrating the impact of large co-operatives, from both an economic and a social perspective, but there is no overarching impact measurement framework for the co-operative sector. Nor is transparent, aggregate social impact data collected (World Co-operative Monitor, 2019).

Bright spots and state of the art approaches for social impact measurement in the social economy

There are many exciting opportunities which shine a light on a brighter future regarding social impact measurement by the social economy. First we discuss the important topic of standardization, for which there has been some progress across the social

---

[7] The ISSB will sit alongside and work in close cooperation with the IASB, ensuring connectivity and compatibility between the IFRS Accounting Standard, the ISSB's standards, and the IFRS Sustainability Disclosure Standards. https://www.ifrs.org/
[8] https://www.euricse.eu/projects/analysis-of-the-social-impact-of-social-enterprises-and-social-cooperatives-on-work-integration/

economy, although clearly there are opportunities for further development. Then we move to discuss other bright spots, some which are related to cross-sectoral collaboration on impact measurement and cross-pollination between different sectors facilitated by the growing role of data and technology. Other bright spots we outline touch on 'softer' mindset shifts, to embrace more power-sharing between different actors, which is relevant to the development in Europe of impact measurement approaches that embrace equity, diversity, and inclusion and more accountability to the communities they seek to serve.

Standardization and the state of social impact measurement tools and methodologies

One of the widely recognized barriers to social impact measurement by the social economy is arguably the lack of standards, in particular clear metrics and indicators to determine social impact across diverse social issue areas. We define standards as an approach which actors sign up to or adopt and for which a body is responsible for developing and monitoring adherence towards. Standards in the Environmental, Social, and Governance (ESG) arena have been a critical way of creating a common language and set of criteria among diverse actors, and there is an appetite from some in the social economy to create a more coherent set of standards for the social economy (and/or impact economy). There has been a plethora of initiatives to find an appropriate social value accounting mechanism, which could lead the social economy to be able to value and compare social impact. For policy-makers the benefits of such a standard metric are clear, as they may finally be able to define and communicate the value of the social economy as well as to determine the relative utility of different social interventions. Indeed, the motivation for such initiatives has been to unlock innovation, clarify which interventions are effective, and increase the likelihood of public and private sector funding of social activities and innovation. Yet initiatives such as SROI (explained previously) and Social Impact Accounting, which initially gained traction, have been subject to significant criticism (Vik, 2017). A higher or lower SROI may not necessarily reflect greater or lesser social impact and singularly focusing on SROI may lead to a one-dimensional portrayal of the organization's activities (Gibbon & Dey, 2011). Although social economy players may still seek to aggregate their impact across different social issue areas, there is growing acceptance that a synthetic unit of social impact analysis could be impossible (Clifford et al., 2015).

Other routes towards greater standardization have been experimented with, including process-based frameworks and the development of dashboards and scorecards (Bengo et al., 2016). A key focus, particularly within the social enterprise and impact investment sectors, has been on a convergence of process-based frameworks with a greater emphasis on embedding key impact management principles. The convergence between different frameworks in the impact-investing sector could be an example and an inspiration for the social economy in general. The Impact Management Project, for example, has brought together more than 2000 practitioners and provides a forum for building global consensus on how to measure, manage, and report impacts on sustainability. It is an approach that has quietly but surely led to a growing acceptance by a wide variety of stakeholders about what 'impact' means and how it can be measured. Such collaborative, multi-stakeholder initiatives to develop meaningful impact measurement frameworks could be the way forward for the whole social economy.

The more recent UN SDG Impact Standards also offer an opportunity to align different sectors' understanding and reporting of impact based on the SDG goals and indicators. Most recently, SDG Impact published the *UNDP SDG Impact Standards for Enterprises* (SDG Impact, Version 1.0, 2021) to provide a common language and a clear system to fully integrate the SDGs into all business and investment decision-making processes. These are destined for social economy, private sector, and public sector actors. They bridge the Impact Management Project's (IMP) Five Dimensions of Impact and ABC Impact Classifications with sustainable reporting frameworks, thus integrating a more social economy perspective with the corporate sustainability reporting. Ultimately these SDG Impact Standards hope to enable investors to push for greater harmonization, analysts to be able to benchmark and compare across enterprises, and policy-makers to align regulations with standards. There are four SDG standards, one for each theme (as shown in Figure 7.3, these are strategy, management approach, transparency, and governance), and a set of associated indicators.

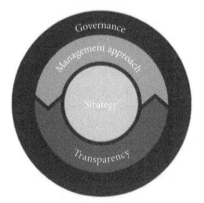

Standard 1 (Strategy): Embedding foundational elements into purpose and strategy

Standard 2 (Management Approach): Integrating foundational elements into operations and management approach

Standard 3 (Transparency): Disclosing how foundational elements are integrated into purpose, strategy, management approach and governance, and reporting on performance

Standard 4 (Governance): Reinforcing commitment to foundational elements through governance practices

Figure 7.3 SDG impact standards

Shared measurement approaches

This is where players from different sectors jointly agree on an approach for measuring change within an entire system (for example, the education system in a certain territory). This is different from standards, which are normally not sectoral-specific. COVID has highlighted the inter-connectedness and even greater importance of systems thinking in social innovation and social change. Such shared measurement approaches feel more purposeful and meaningful, with more data collected from a range of social economy and public and private sector actors and a sense of players collectively being able to move the social impact needle and the whole being greater than the sum of the parts. Shared approaches require social economy actors to focus less on how impact can be attributed to the work of a specific actor and to focus more on how actors together can contribute collectively to addressing societal challenges. In theory the idea of collective impact is interesting for organizations whose asset owners, including grant-making foundations, are less worried about financial returns. The lack of attribution may be an issue for certain types of social economy actors who compete for scarce resources and need to demonstrate results at organizational level. For example, impact investors are interested in claiming the impact of the organizations they invest in so that they can show positive impact performance. While there are many collective impact initiatives in the US, there are only a few in Europe—most notably in Denmark and the UK— but interest in them is growing. One of the five pillars of the collective impact approach is shared measurement, where all participants agree on the ways success will be measured and reported, with a short list of common indicators identified and used for learning and improvement (Preskill et al., 2014). Although formalized collective impact structures are currently rare in Europe, COVID has accelerated the desire for social economy actors to work together both on delivering and evidencing impact. As more such shared measurement approaches are tested within Europe, greater evidence could be generated for specific social issue areas. The challenge will be to develop a set of meaningful indicators generated from such bottom-up, multi-stakeholder collaborations which are broad enough to have relevance for the whole system and deep enough to be actionable for individual actors within that system.

Social Impact Bonds (SIBs), which are public–private partnerships that fund effective social services through performance-based contracts, are another example of collaboration on social impact measurement by players from different sectors (public, private, social economy) (see also Carter & Ball, this volume). By March 2022 there have been 220 SIBs globally contracted in thirty-seven countries across six sectors, representing more than $462 million in upfront investment in social services committed.[9] Several European countries have large markets for impact bonds, in particular the United Kingdom but also the Netherlands and Portugal. The European Investment Bank launched a EUR 10m fund with BNP Paribas for co-investment into SIBs in the UK. While this was criticized for the costly nature of the transaction, in particular the social impact verification procedures commonly provided by a third-party social impact measurement service provider (Roy et al., 2018), SIBs have led to interesting dialogues between sectors about social impact measurement. The centrepiece of any SIB is the definition of measurable, explicit outcome metrics at the outset of a project, against which delivery is evaluated. Agreeing these outcomes and goals entails a negotiation and dialogue between the different stakeholders. Methodological rigour for evaluations has tended to be relatively high, although there are concerns about the validity and viability of some baseline data used (Edmiston & Nicholls, 2018). SIBs that have an experimental design embedded that compares the

---

[9] https://www.brookings.edu/research/social-and-development-impactbonds-by-the-numbers/

performance of an intervention group with that of a control group are particularly important for the evidence base (drawn either from historical data or from individuals that do not receive a social service, that is, a 'living control group'). In this sense, such evaluations have the benefit of achieving what is not possible for most social economy organizations: a 'true' understanding of impact generated by the service provided which separates out other possible contributing factors, and thus addresses the issue of attribution. SIBs are therefore increasing the supply of evidence for certain interventions, which can then be used by other social economy actors in the same social issue area in other geographies. A positive 'side-effect' of the need for upfront data to develop a SIB is that policy-makers and commissioners might think more holistically about social issues, potentially inspiring more data-driven policies. For example, when the city of Barcelona started developing a SIB for children in care, they collected data that allowed them to see what hadn't worked in the past, and where they should invest their resources. Academic studies have highlighted the risks of SIBs bringing with them financialization logics, including metrics and measurement processes that may circumvent the state and position social policy delivery in the custody of the market (McHugh et al., 2013; Nicholls & Teasdale, 2017; Warner, 2013). While not without their critics, SIBs have generated significant interest from financial actors (even in mainstream finance) and have proven how far outcome-based measurement of complex social problems is possible when enough financial resources are provided to do it in a meaningful, rigorous way.

Data and technology

The social economy is recognized to be lagging behind when it comes to digitization and data (Fruchterman, 2016). Harnessing big data might be the great missed opportunity of the past decade, but there is hope that the social economy is opening up to the possibilities that it offers. There are significant opportunities for the use of *big data* to improve social impact measurement practices. It provides access to a wide new range of data sources, can increase sample sizes and the probability of inclusion of vulnerable groups, and can help to develop longitudinal data sets. Yet, take-up by the evaluation community of big data has been slow, primarily due to cultural and language differences between evaluation and data science. Data scientists are not yet commonly employed by the social economy (York & Bamberger, 2020). Moreover, there are barriers to the use of such big datasets in social impact measurement, particularly those that are being provided by governments—for example, the quality of the data, and the fact that data governance standards may not have been set and useful data might be inaccessible or buried in administrative systems from which it is costly to extract and make sense of (Desouza & Smith, 2014).

However, there are promising initiatives concerning big data. Causality is a main challenge that development economists have addressed through experimental designs, with randomized control trials being the gold standard (Duflo et al., 2007). For example, in the UK, *data labs* have emerged which allow social economy actors to set up quasi-randomized control trials by using large-scale administrative data to find a control group. The most advanced case is justice data related to prisoners and re-offending which allowed many social economy actors to test the effectiveness of their interventions and ultimately to be able to compare between different interventions. Emerging findings are interesting: for example, that the average impact (when positive) is much lower than in 'usual' impact studies and that education-based interventions seemed to be delivering the greatest impact (Piazza, Corry, Noble, & Bagwell, 2019). Other data labs using government administrative data in health, employment, and education are being considered in the UK. Such data labs could be replicated within other national European contexts. There are also open-source data initiatives emerging to help gather and aggregate the fragmented information on funding and to start to build outcome-level open-source databases, particularly in the impact-investing field. European examples of funder-led data-sharing collaboratives include 360 Giving in the UK (https://www.threesixtygiving. org), through which nearly 150 funders now publish their grants data, with more than £32 billion of grants data accessible to be compared and analysed. In Portugal, the Calouste Gulbenkian Foundation partnered with the Portuguese government to create One Value (https://onevalue.gov.pt/page/1), a free-access website that gathers and systematizes information about public investment in several priority response areas (social protection, education, health, employment, and justice).

Another important data initiative related to the social enterprise sector is Lean Data now called 60 Decibels by Acumen (https://acumen.org/lean-data/), which leverages mobile technology to communicate directly with customers and beneficiaries collecting impact data efficiently and at a low cost. With such cost-effective, large-scale data collection techniques, social economy actors can more easily get in touch with their beneficiaries and find out how their lives have changed after interventions.

Shifting social economy power dynamics through more stakeholder-led social impact measurement processes

Social impact measurement touches on key themes of trust and transparency. Increasingly, funders (whether grant-makers, social investors, or even public sector commissioners) are aware that top-down approaches ultimately will bear little fruit if the social economy actors do not see their value. The social economy actor must own and find useful the whole social impact measurement process and they (in conjunction with the end beneficiary) need to have decision rights in what impact is considered meaningful, what data is collected, and how it is collected. Power has been a silent, unexplored terrain in impact measurement but it is now emerging as a crucial element of the equation (Kelly, 2018). Funders need to go beyond merely consulting with stakeholders and move relations to a partnership-led dynamic between funder/commissioner and the social value creator in which power is more actively shared and distributed. It is only when this happens that the impact measurement process can become more honest, authentic, and valuable—unlike current circumstances, in which social economy actors can feel under undue pressure to perform to impact targets which may not have enough relevance to them and which could stifle social innovation and flexibility, as well as risking core values of the social economy (a risk highlighted during COVID). Even social impact accounting methodologies such as SROI, which can seem alien to certain social economy actors, can have the potential to be meaningful if performed in a way that empowers stakeholders in the social impact measurement process (Nicholls, 2018).

A related and important consideration is how far diversity and inclusion approaches need to be embedded within the social impact measurement process, to ensure that voice is given to beneficiaries and communities traditionally not heard. Including their voices in the very *design* of such processes may be necessary to avoid unconscious systemic biases that it is difficult to later remove or correct.

Inspiration and cross-pollination with impact transparency movements in other sectors

There has been a long history of the corporate and financial sectors experimenting with social auditing approaches, in order to capture and account for social and environmental impacts within sustainability reporting. In recent years the scope of the social audit has been expanding to include greater integration of the social accounting processes, which involve a detailed preparation and accounting of social metrics, targets, and milestones. There are some key characteristics of social audits used by corporates: multi-perspective (that is, including different stakeholders); comparative (that is, the organization can see how it is evolving over time and in comparison with others working in a similar field); regular, comprehensive, and verified (that is, by an independent third party). There are different social audit tools used by corporates but the best known is the Global Reporting Initiative (https://www.globalreporting. org), which has developed the most widely used sustainability reporting standards. However, while progress has been made, many investors and corporates still reiterate the need for more consistent and comparable sustainability reporting at the global level due to the continued presence of different sustainability reporting frameworks, standards, and metrics, each seeking to produce specific products for their own stakeholders.[10] The recent merger between the Sustainable Accounting Standards Board and the Climate Disclosure Standards Board to form the International Financial Reporting Standards Foundation's International Sustainability Standards Board (IFRS-ISSB) aims to further harmonize these efforts.[11] Observers still remain sceptical about the credibility and rigour behind sustainability reporting, with the key risk of impact-washing, which is where claims are made about the impact brought about by an investment, product, or service which are not clearly evidenced.

Due to the growth of sustainable and ESG investing globally, the search for clearer, comparable, and global environmental and social impact data is more urgent than ever. We expect to see significant cross-pollination between the social economy and the financial and corporate sectors on the subject of how to understand and report, especially on social impact. There is likely to be more fluidity between sectors, also exemplified by the growth of the hybrid organizational form—Benefit Corporations

---

[10] For example: Taskforce on Climate-related Financial Disclosures (TCFD), Global Reporting Initiative (GRI) reporting standards, Sustainability Accounting Standards Board (SASB) reporting standards.
[11] https://www.ifrs.org/news-and-events/news/2021/11/ifrs-foundation-announces-issb-consolidation-with-cdsb-vrf-publication-of-prototypes/

(B-Corps)—of which there are more than 4,800 worldwide. B-Corps have incorporated a clear societal purpose into their missions, intending to achieve a positive social impact as they internalize their social and environmental effects. The certification process for B-Corps can serve again as inspiration for market actors within the social economy. Accredited B-Corps are companies that have accepted voluntary third-party social participation and environmental audits conducted by B Lab, a non-profit company. The B-Corp certification process covers five impact areas: environment, workers, communities, customers, and business model, with the possibility of creating standardized, benchmarked impact data for participants and investors, and with an overall assessment rating for each B-Corp (out of 200).

Moving from proving impact to learning and improving impact

The preceding sections have illustrated the current state of play in the European social economy concerning social impact measurement, as well as key opportunities and possibilities which we find to be present, although unevenly distributed across actors and regions. While there are bright spots and excellent practices, much of the social economy is in the grip of a vicious cycle as illustrated in Figure 7.4(a) below. The key original issue is a lack of resources and capabilities regarding impact measurement which creates an evidence base with limited rigour, and which is at the 'output' rather than the 'outcome' level so it is hard to judge whether meaningful change has occurred. On top of some cultural resistance by over-stretched social economy actors and a KPI approach of funders/commissioners which actors do not feel captures what they achieve, a 'proving impact' model prevails, where data is generated purely for fundraising or compliance purposes, there is a loss of data sharing or comparability resulting in time being spent ticking boxes, but with limited learning alongside it. There is a missed opportunity to develop an evidence base of the impact of different interventions which can be used across the social economy.

We believe that one of the keys to moving towards a more virtuous circle, as outlined in Figure 7.4(b), is for the central focus to move from a technocratic, compliance-oriented mindset to a learning mindset—that is, from 'proving impact' to 'improving impact'. For this to happen, social impact measurement needs to be framed as a holistic, organization-wide process (impact management) rather than as a siloed, technical exercise. Moreover, it is essential that this impact management process is properly empowering for stakeholders and beneficiaries and is part of a multi-stakeholder, collaborative, partnership approach by funders and commissioners, where social economy actors accept and are not afraid to account for impact risk and negative impact. As the quality and relevance of impact data, evaluation, and reporting increase for social economy actors, this will naturally lead to enhanced collaboration and data sharing, which should result in more innovation, exploration, and flexibility concerning interventions. There is also likely to be a greater

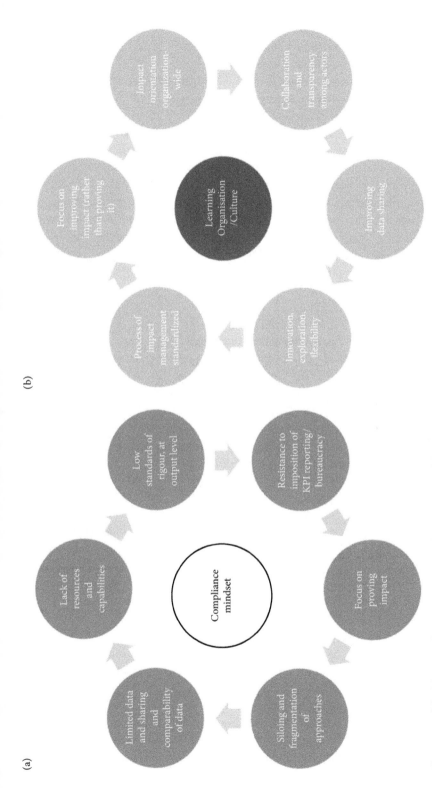

Figure 7.4 (a) Vicious circle: proving impact; (b) Virtuous circle: improving impact

standardization of the impact management process as actors work more closely across the social economy, thus increasing their knowledge-sharing and reducing fragmentation and over-customization.

Developing a learning culture is not an overnight proposition for many social economy actors and requires several steps and considerations, as well as changes in behaviour of funders/commissioners, as evidenced in Lall (2019). A learning organization needs to be reflected in leadership, governance, and culture, but also in learning structures and processes. Ideally, social economy actors have defined roles and responsibilities for capturing, distilling, applying, and sharing knowledge internally and externally, with specific processes that are part of daily workflows. Such learning structures are currently lacking. A large-scale study of learning in the non-profit sector illustrated that only 40 per cent believe that their existing processes are effective for encouraging learning, and only half created incentives around learning (Taylor Newberry Consulting, 2018). There are important, inter-linked themes that organizations must consider on these impact management learning journeys, with a recognition that culture change will take time (Hehenberger et al, 2020):

- *Designing an impact management approach*: this covers the 'what', 'where', 'when', and 'how' of impact management including, for example, designing which tools are used, how impact data is collected from whom and validated, and how stakeholders can be included in the process. These are the essential first steps in any impact management strategy.
- *Resourcing and organizing for impact management*: this is about ensuring that the organization is budgeting sufficiently for impact management and creating an appropriate organization-wide framework.
- *Embedding impact management through organizational culture*: enabling the shift from a compliance mindset to an impact mindset where learning and honest reflection are prioritized.
- *Building capacity*: ensuring that the right impact management skills and capabilities exist within the organization or are hired externally, as required.
- *Collaborating, sharing knowledge, and being transparent*: pooling impact data, developing shared measurement approaches and sharing learning in an open-source way.

While this important re-framing of impact management and learning takes place, the work can still continue in terms of developing robust standards and indicators for the social economy. These top-down approaches (developing common standards and metrics which speak to the complexity of impacts involved and the inherent particularities of the social economy) and bottom-up approaches (learning cultures within social economy organizations) are ultimately mutually reinforcing and need to be considered as connected, distinct parts of the puzzle of improving social economy impact measurement and management.

The role of the European Union in fostering impact measurement and management as a key pillar of the evolving social economy

In the aftermath of the Covid-19 pandemic and under the current escalating humanitarian and financial crisis triggered by Russia's invasion of Ukraine, it is important to reflect on what we want Europe to look like in the future. As put forward in this chapter, the role of impact measurement stretches beyond enabling social economy actors to manage towards greater impact. Integrating the different dimensions of impact measurement *and* management into policies and systems will be key to catalyse the action required to achieve the intended impact of those policies. The recommendations put forward are especially relevant for the execution of the *European Action Plan for Social Economy*, published in December 2021, but also need to be taken into account for other policies mentioned in what follows.

Europe is at the forefront of developing policies to promote a just and sustainable socio-economic development. Ursula von der Leyen, President of the European Commission (von der Leyen, 2021), has emphasized the social dimension as a core European priority. In December 2019 the European Commission announced the European Green Deal, approved by the European Parliament in 2020, through which Europe marked its ambition to become the first climate-neutral continent by 2050. As part of the European Green Deal, in January 2020, the Commission presented its first reflections on building a strong social Europe by designing a Just Transition mechanism. It provides targeted funding to generate the necessary investment in the most affected regions through fundamental restructuring of the economy, structural changes in business models and new skill requirements. InvestEU,[12] one of the funds of the Multiannual Financial Framework (MFF) 2021–2027, will among other areas target social enterprises and microfinance, and bring together under one umbrella a range of European financial instruments. InvestEU introduces a minimum climate action target as well as sustainability-proofing of investments, in order to verify that investments maximize benefits and minimize any adverse impacts in terms of climate, environmental, and social considerations. The Commission's 2018 Action Plan on Financing Sustainable Growth (European Commission, 2018) introduced an EU taxonomy (or classification system) of what is considered to be 'sustainable' and 'green'. The Taxonomy Regulation was approved by the European Parliament and Council in June 2020. The Regulation required the Commission to publish a report by the end of 2021 on how the taxonomy could be extended to cover social objectives and the social economy is currently under development. Additionally, the European Pillar of Social Rights plays a key role in ensuring that the transitions of climate neutrality, digitalization, and demographic change are socially fair and just for all. The social economy, including its actors, practices, and tools, will be a pivotal lever in

---

[12] In 2018, EVPA organized a webinar and wrote a policy brief on the Multiannual Financial Framework 2021–2027, InvestEU and ESF+. Both are available here.

achieving a just transition, not just through the implementation of its activities, but also through its experience of measuring and managing impact.

The European Action Plan for Social Economy seeks to enhance social innovation, support the development of the social economy, and boost its social and economic transformative power. It builds on significant work completed since the 2011 publication of the Social Business Initiative (SBI), an action plan to support the development of social enterprises, social economy and social innovation, as well as the Start-up and Scale-up initiative. The SBI led to important developments such as the set-up of the Expert Group on Social Entrepreneurship (GECES 2011–2018) and the subsequent one on Social Economy and Social Enterprises (GECES 2018–2024)[13] that brings together private actors in order to assist the European Commission with advice on the roll-out of, and research on, social economy policies. GECES developed a European methodology on social impact measurement in 2015 to be applied across the European social economy. The methodology, as introduced above, was consequential as it was explicitly included in the European Social Entrepreneurship Fund (EuSEF) Regulation and in the criteria used by the Programme for Employment and Social Innovation (EaSI), which made more than EUR 86 million available in grants, investment and guarantees in 2014–2020 to social enterprises who could demonstrate they had a 'measurable social impact'. The European Action Plan for Social Economy stresses the importance of social impact measurement to 'enable the social economy to communicate its impact and access impact-driven finance more easily' (European Commission, 2021).

Recommendations for policy-makers

For these policies to channel funding to the social economy, the sector needs to be able to show that the public sector gets its 'money's worth'. Pan-European policies do not always trickle down effectively at national or regional level, and some countries have developed more rapidly than others. Investment strategies and policies must take into consideration the different stages of maturity. As identified in this chapter, the main barriers associated to social impact measurement that social economy actors face include a lack of financial and human capital dedicated to impact measurement, a lack of transparency and data sharing, siloed approaches, and a generalized focus on proving rather than improving impact.

In the European Action Plan for Social Economy, the European Commission commits to mapping existing practices, launching trainings, and developing 'simple standard methodologies' for social impact measurement. These measures mainly address the challenges we identified related to the lack of financial and human capital dedicated to impact measurement. We propose the following concrete recommendations for policy-makers to implement these ambitions:

---

[13] For more information on the GECES, visit the dedicated European Commission webpage.

- *Identify and promote best practices on impact measurement and management for different types of social economy actors.* The European networks and associations that support social economy subsectors (e.g., foundations, co-operatives, social enterprises, etc.) could lead this effort with EU funding. Such best practices could include, for example, how social economy actors can focus more on learning; how to embed diversity and inclusion in impact management; and the development of a partnership, power-sharing, impact management approach by funders and commissioners.
- *Support the training and certification of social impact professionals.* There is a need to increase both the number and quality of dedicated social impact professionals. Policy-makers should recognize this need and develop concrete actions to alleviate it. Such actions could include the establishment of specific academies/training institutions and an official certification as social impact evaluator at European and/or Member State level.
- *Support the capacity building of social economy actors in implementing impact measurement and management.* Grants could be provided for social economy staff to attend specialized trainings offered by certified educational institutions and for the social economy actor to hire trained social impact professionals.
- *Promote a clear, simple impact management process for social economy actors.* Currently there is a gap between the theory of impact measurement and practice among social economy actors, related to a lack of clarity and proliferation of different social impact measurement tools and methodologies. A stronger, shared process for social economy actors could enable greater clarity and simplification. This could be similar to the Operating Principles for Impact Management for impact investors which provide a framework for investors to ensure that impact considerations are purposefully integrated throughout the investment life cycle.

Furthermore, to promote data sharing and transparency and to avoid siloed approaches, we recommend the following actions:

- *Fund research that provides scientific evidence around impact.* Scientific evidence on impact is costly and time-consuming and may be prohibitive for smaller social economy actors. Initiatives such as the Abdul Latif Jameel Poverty Action Lab (JPAL) in the US that develop randomized control trials to show the cause and effect of social interventions need major funding from public and private institutions. The evidence gained from such research needs to be shared broadly in the public domain.
- *Catalyse and support open data initiatives relating to social impact.* The social impact economy is lagging the private sector in terms of digitization. The opportunities of data mining and data science to increase social impact are immense. Sponsorship could be provided to national and EU-wide data sharing and open data initiatives relating to social impact metrics and measurement and EU-wide

data labs could be developed on specific social impact issues. Grants should be provided to support the involvement of data scientists within the social economy.

- *Encourage transparency and reporting on social impact metrics.* Clearer guidelines should be developed around impact reporting, building on the success of international multi-stakeholder initiatives such as the IMP and the SDG Impact Standards. Social economy actors should be rewarded for sharing data by greater access to funding and public procurement contracts.

- *Enable monetization of impact related to public funding.* Public sector funders need data to understand if they are allocating public money in the most efficient manner, and are subject to public scrutiny. Initiatives such as unit cost databases (UCD) that are being implemented in the UK and Portugal[14] could be worth further exploration.[15]

Finally, to shift the focus from *proving to improving impact*, we recommend to:

- *Promote the philosophy of learning and learning organizations among social economy actors*, for example sponsoring national-level and EU-wide social impact learning conferences and exchanges. There needs to be a change in the language and discourse around social impact measurement, from accountability as an end in itself towards learning journeys that encompass both success and failure and which enable innovation, flexibility, and exploration relating to social impact creation.

Conclusion

As evidenced in this chapter, social impact measurement has made important headway in recent years in the European social economy. Although there are still sceptics, increasingly social economy actors are embracing social impact measurement as at minimum inevitable, and in the best of cases relevant and useful. Social issues are complex and multifaceted, requiring thoughtful approaches to understand both the depth and scale of the problem to design interventions that actually generate change. Therefore, a future research agenda on impact measurement requires attention to both understanding the problem in depth, and testing how and to what extent solutions actually generate change—rather than assuming that a particular way of organizing (Wry & Haugh, 2018) will automatically achieve the intended effect. A main take-away from this chapter is that social economy actors should move their focus from producing reports to please funders to generating data that truly captures the reality of the beneficiaries of their programmes. Only by understanding

---

[14] https://evpa.eu.com/knowledge-centre/publications/unit-cost-databases
[15] UCDs gather a set of estimated unitary costs in areas such as health, education, housing, and social services and are particularly relevant when delivering public services through outcome-based mechanisms, as the estimated costs can be used as references to price outcomes.

how interventions change the lives of the target population will social economy actors know if they are successful. This type of data should have the power to convince potential funders that it is worthwhile to invest. For such a shift to happen, we need to generate a climate of transparency and trust where social economy actors are allowed to experiment and make mistakes. Public and private funders who are serious about achieving impact need to be ready to take on risk by investing in innovative interventions that can produce novel solutions to our societal problems. There is significant potential for the European Action Plan for Social Economy to further catalyse the positive trends and bright spots in social impact measurement highlighted. This increased EU-wide funding and attention could help to address the current gap between theory and practice that we have also illustrated, allowing social impact measurement to be a key enabler of a thriving European social economy.

References

ESADE Center for Social Impact. https://www.esade.edu/itemsweb/wi/ECSI/Publications/Taking_Pulse_European_Foundations_report.pdf

Bengo, I., Azzone, G., & Calderini, M. (2016). Indicators and metrics for social business: a review of current approaches, *Journal of Social Entrepreneurship*, 7(1), 1–24. https://doi.org/10.1080/19420676.2015.1049286

Benos, T., Kalogeras, N., Wetzels, M., de Ruyter, K., & Pennings, J. M. E. (2018). Harnessing a 'currency matrix' for performance measurement in cooperatives: a multi-phased study, *Sustainability*, 10, 4536. https://doi.org/10.3390/su10124536

Cameron, D. B., Mishra, A., & Brown, A. N. (2016). The growth of impact evaluation for international development: how much have we learned? *Journal of Development Effectiveness*, 8(1): 1–21. https://doi.org/10.1080/19439342.2015.1034156

Clifford, J., Hehenberger, L., Fantini, M., Grabenwarter, U., Ratti, M., & Valcarcel, M. (2015). Proposed approaches to social impact measurement. Brussels; Luxembourg: *European Commission.* https://op.europa.eu/en/publication-detail/-/publication/0c0b5d38-4ac8-43d1-a7af-32f7b6fcf1cc

Desouza, K. C., & Smith, K.L. (2014). Big data for social innovation. *Stanford Social Innovation Review.* https://ssir.org/articles/entry/big_data_for_social_innovation

Duflo, E., Glennerster, R., & Kremer, M. (2007). Using randomization in development economics research: A toolkit. *Handbook of Development Economics*, 4, 3895–3962.

Dupain, W., Pilia, O., Wunsch, M., Hoffmann, P., Scharpe, K., Mair, J., Raith, M., & Bosma, N. (2021). The state of social enterprise in Europe—European Social Enterprise Monitor 2020–2021. Euclid Network. https://knowledgecentre.euclidnetwork.eu/download/european-social-enterprise-monitor-report-2020-2021/

Edmiston, D., & Nicholls, A. (2018). Social Impact Bonds: the role of private capital in outcomes-based commissioning, *Journal of Social Policy*, 47(1): 57–76. https://www.researchgate.net/publication/316283593_Social_Impact_Bonds_The_Role_of_Private_Capital_in_Outcome-Based_Commissioning

European Commission (2018). Action Plan: financing sustainable growth https://ec.europa.eu/info/publications/sustainable-finance-renewed-strategy_en

European Commission (2021). Building an economy that works for people: an action plan for the social economy. https://ec.europa.eu/social/main.jsp?langId=en&catId=89&newsId=10117&furtherNews=yes#navItem-1

Ferraro, F., Etzion, D., & Gehman, J. (2015). Tackling grand challenges pragmatically: robust action revisited. *Organization Studies*, 36(3), 363–390. https://doi.org/10.1177%2F0170840614563742

Fruchterman, J. (2016). Using data for action and impact. Stanford Social Innovation Review. https://ssir.org/articles/entry/using_data_for_action_and_for_impact

Gibbon, J., & Dey, C. (2011). Developments in Social Impact Measurement in the third sector: scaling up or dumbing down? *Social and Environmental Accountability Journal*, 31(1), 63–72. https://doi.org/10.1080/0969160X.2011.556399

Harlock, J. (2013). Impact measurement practice in the UK third sector: a review of emerging evidence. *Third Sector Research Centre Working Paper 106*, University of Birmingham. http://epapers.bham.ac.uk/1800/1/WP106_Impact_measurement_practice_in_the_UK_third_sector_-_Harlock%2C_July_2013.pdf

Harlock, J., & Metcalf, L.J. (2016). Measuring impact: prospects and challenges for third sector organisations. *Voluntary Sector Review*, 7(1), 101–108. https://doi.org/10.1332/204080516X14534734765005

Hehenberger, L., Buckland, L., & Gold, D. (2020). From measurement of impact to management for impact: European Foundation learning journeys. *ESADE Entrepreneurship Institute*. https://www.esade.edu/en/faculty-and-research/research/knowledge-units/center-social-impact/research/from-measurement

Hehenberger, L., Buckland, L., Reijnders, L., & Gold, D. (2022). Taking the Pulse of the European Foundation Sector—Moving from Proving Impact to Improving Impact. Barcelona: ESADE Center for Social Impact.

Hehenberger, L., & Harling, A. (2015). What are the challenges to measuring the social impact of social enterprises? In Noya, A., *Policy Brief on Social Impact Measurement for Social Enterprises* (pp. 14–17). Paris: Organisation for Economic Co-operation and Development (OECD). https://www.oecd.org/social/PB-SIM-Web_FINAL.pdf

Hehenberger, L., & Harling, A.-M. (2018). Moving Toward "Impact-Adjusted" Financial Returns. *American Journal of Evaluation*, 39(3), 408-412. https://doi.org/10.1177/1098214018778899

Hehenberger, L., Harling, A., & Scholten, P. (2013). A practical guide to measuring and managing impact. *European Venture Philanthropy Association* (EVPA). https://evpa.eu.com/knowledge-centre/publications/measuring-and-managing-impact-a-practical-guide

Kelly, P. (2018). An activity theory study of data, knowledge, and power in the design of an international development NGO impact evaluation. *Information Systems Journal*, 28. https://doi.org/10.1111/isj.12187

KPMG (2018). The future of welfare. https://assets.kpmg/content/dam/kpmg/it/pdf/2018/07/KPMG-The-Future-of-Welfare.pdf

Lall, S. A. (2019). From legitimacy to learning: how impact measurement perceptions and practices evolve in social enterprise–social finance organization relationships. *Voluntas*, 30(3), 562–577. https://doi.org/10.1007/s11266-018-00081-5

McGill, L. T. (2016). Number of registered Public Benefit Foundations in Europe exceeds 147,000. Foundation Center. https://philea.issuelab.org/resource/number-of-registered-public-benefit-foundations-in-europe-exceeds-147-000.html

McHugh, N.A., Sinclair, S., Roy, M., Huckfield, L., & Donaldson, C. (2013). Social Impact Bonds: a wolf in sheep's clothing? *Journal of Poverty and Social Justice*, 21(3), 247–257. https://doi.org/10.1332/204674313X13812372137921

Mernier, A., & Xhauflair, V. (2017). Les fondations en Belgique. *Fédération Belge des Fondations Philanthropiques.* https://www.lesfondations.be/fr/file/file/15/inline/Les%20Fondations%20en%20Belgique.pdf

Molecke, G., & Pinkse, J. (2020). Justifying social impact as a form of impression management: legitimacy judgements of social enterprises' impact accounts. *British Journal of Management*, 10, 42. https://doi.org/10.1111/1467-8551.12397

Monzón, J-L, & Chaves, R. (2017). Recent evolutions in the social economy in the European Union. *CIRIEC, European Economic and Social Committee.* https://www.eesc.europa.eu/sites/default/files/files/qe-04-17-875-en-n.pdf

Ní Ógáin, E., Lumley, T., Pritchard, David. (2013). Making an impact: impact measurement among charities and social enterprises in the UK. *New Philanthropy Capital.* https://www.thinknpc.org/wp-content/uploads/2018/07/Making-an-impact.pdf

Nicholls, A. (2007). *What is the future of social enterprise in ethical markets.* London: Office of The Third Sector.

Nicholls, A. (2018). A general theory of social impact accounting: materiality, uncertainty and empowerment. *Journal of Social Entrepreneurship*, 9(2), 132–153. https://doi.org/10.1080/19420676.2018.1452785

Nicholls, A., & Teasdale, S. (2017). Neoliberalism by stealth? Exploring continuity and change within the UK social enterprise policy paradigm. *Policy & Politics*, 45(3): 323–341. https://doi.org/10.1332/030557316X14775864546490

Piazza, R., Corry, D., Noble, J., & Bagwell, S. (2019). 'Data labs, a new approach to impact evaluation'. *New Philanthropy Capital.* https://www.thinknpc.org/resource-hub/data-labs-update/

Preskill, H., Parkhurst, M., & Splansky Juster, J. (2014). *Guide to Evaluating Collective Impact.* FSG Reimagining Social Change. Retrieved from https://www.fsg.org/resource/guide-evaluating-collective-impact/

Roy, M., McHugh, N., & Sinclair, S. (2018). A critical reflection on social impact bonds. *Stanford Social Innovation Review.* https://ssir.org/articles/entry/a_critical_reflection_on_social_impact_bonds#

Social Impact Investment Taskforce (2014). *Measuring Impact—Subject Paper of the Impact Measurement Working Group.* http://gsgii.org/wp-content/uploads/2017/07/Measuring-Impact-WG-paper-FINAL.pdf

Taylor Newberry Consulting (2018). *Achieving Greater Impact by Starting with Learning.* https://theonn.ca/wp-content/uploads/2018/09/Achieving-Greater-Impact-by-Starting-with-Learning-September-2018.pdf

Vik, P. (2017). What's so social about Social Return on Investment? A critique of quantitative social accounting approaches drawing on experiences of international microfinance. *Social and Environmental Accountability Journal*, 37(1), 6–17. https://doi.org/10.1080/0969160X.2016.1263967

von der Leyen, U. (2021). *2021 State of the Union Address by President von der Leyen.* European Commission: Brussels.

Warner, M. E. (2013). Private finance for public goods: Social Impact Bonds. *Journal of Economic Policy Reform*, 16(4), 303–319. https://doi.org/10.1080/17487870.2013.835727

Wilkinson, C. (2015). A map of social enterprises and their eco-systems in Europe, Synthesis Report. *European Commission*, https://www.euricse.eu/projects/a-map-of-social-enterprises-and-their-eco-system-in-europe/

World Co-operative Monitor. (2019). Exploring the cooperative economy. https://monitor.coop/sites/default/files/publication-files/wcm2019-final-1671449250.pdf

Wry, T., & Haugh, H. (2018). Brace for impact: uniting our diverse voices through a social impact frame. *Journal of Business Venturing*, 33(5), 566–574. https://doi.org/10.1016/j.jbusvent.2018.04.010

York, P., & Bamberger, M. (2020). Measuring results and impact in the age of big data: the nexus of evaluation, analytics and digital technology. *Rockefeller Foundation.* https://www.rockefellerfoundation.org/report/measuring-results-and-impact-in-the-age-of-big-data-the-nexus-of-evaluation-analytics-and-digital-technology/

Zimmer, A., & Pahl, B. (2016). Learning from Europe: report on third sector enabling and disabling factors, TSI Comparative Report No. 1, Seventh Framework Programme (grant agreement 613034), *European Union*. Brussels: Third Sector Impact. http://thirdsectorimpact.eu/site/assets/uploads/documentations/comparative-report-learning-europe/TSI-comparative-report-No.-1.pdf

PART II

AGENTS OF CHANGE

8
Beyond a niche approach

Could social business become the norm?

Julie Battilana, Leszek Krol, Kara Sheppard-Jones,
and Alexandra Ubalijoro

Introduction

The public health crisis spurred by the COVID-19 pandemic has been anything but isolated: it has revealed and deepened both economic and social crises characterized by rising inequalities, unfolding against the backdrop of an increasingly severe environmental crisis. Research across the natural and social sciences underscores the role of corporations in not only contributing to these crises but deepening them (Amis et al., 2020). The exclusive focus on profit maximization that has been the dominant mantra in the corporate world over the past decades has been associated with environmental destruction and rising inequalities (Armour & Gordon, 2014; Lazonick & O'Sullivan, 2000; Stout, 2012). These inequalities have, in turn, endangered democracies and their stability, as exemplified by the rise of far-right and authoritarian leaders who have gained influence around the globe (Levitsky & Ziblatt, 2018), and who often deny the existence of the climate crisis (Lockwood, 2018; Schaller & Carius, 2019).

This multidimensional crisis threatens our collective safety and longevity on Earth, our only home. It also threatens the gains that movements of the past have made to expand rights and opportunities and it threatens the democracies past generations have fought to create and strengthen in order to share power and prevent atrocities (Freedom House, 2022). Research across the social and natural sciences underscores the danger of the status quo (Brown, 2019; IPCC, 2022; Stiglitz, 2012). These crises make clear that our social and economic systems must change.

In this context, there is an imperative to examine how alternative forms of organizing—ones that diverge from the dominant corporate model focused solely on profit maximization—can help confront this multidimensional crisis. As we consider the critical question of how to reimagine our economic system, there is much to learn from the social economy, which has long been home to diverse types of organizations that diverge from the dominant corporate model (Battilana, 2015). It has been a venue for experimental and innovative organizational models that pursue collective wellbeing rather than solely profit maximization. Among the plethora of

Julie Battilana et al., *Beyond a niche approach*. In: *Social Economy Science*. Edited by: Gorgi Krlev, Dominika Wruk, Giulio Pasi, and Marika Bernhard, Oxford University Press. © Oxford University Press (2023). DOI: 10.1093/oso/9780192868343.003.0008

social economy organizations ranging from foundations to civic associations and co-operatives, some are hybrid organizations that pursue social and environmental goals alongside financial ones, thereby combining aspects of typical for-profits and not-for-profit organizations (Battilana, 2018; Battilana & Lee, 2014; Besharov & Smith, 2014). Such social businesses, also often referred to as social enterprises (Dacin et al., 2011; Dees, 2001; Mair, 2010; Mair & Martí, 2006), are not new. Some have existed for decades or longer, and they provide a useful vantage point from which to reimagine the corporate model. As such, in contrast to the neoliberal refrain that the social sector should learn from the business world, we suggest that there is much that the mainstream business world can—and must—learn from alternative models of organizing that have developed in the social economy. Innovations stemming from the social economy can help reimagine corporations and spur change in the broader economy.

Yet, over the past decades, the social economy has tended to evolve in parallel with the rest of the economy, seemingly implying that some businesses could legitimately focus solely on maximizing profit and returns to shareholders, while more socially minded entrepreneurs, business leaders, and workers could make the decision to join the social economy. This separation between the market economy and the social economy has enabled social businesses to establish their legitimacy as alternative forms of organizing in the social economy, partially insulated from the market pressures of profit maximization at the expense of all else. But this dichotomy has also prevented the social economy from moving beyond its niche.

Today we find ourselves at a crossroads. On the one hand, the status quo might persist: the social economy could continue to evolve in parallel with the rest of the economy, resulting in a social economy that remains niche. This scenario presents two significant risks. The first risk is to social businesses, as remaining niche may ultimately threaten their survival. If social businesses remain a minority in a world driven solely by profit maximization, they will have continued difficulty accessing necessary resources because of their lack of alignment with dominant organizational forms (DiMaggio & Powell, 1983; Meyer & Rowan, 1977), and so will struggle to survive. The second risk is one for all of us as a society: if the sole pursuit of profit maximization remains the driving force of the business world, then inequalities will continue to increase and we will continue to destroy our natural ecosystems at a speed that endangers not only other species but also our own (Battilana, 2022). Alternatively, some of the organizational models pioneered within the social economy, such as the hybrid models adopted by social businesses, could permeate into the broader economy. This permeation of social business models would contribute to changing the way business is done, enabling the pursuit of social and environmental goals alongside financial ones to become the norm.

Because of the risks associated with the status quo, we argue for the need not only to examine the factors that will enable the social economy to thrive in the years to come, but also to explore how alternative models of organizing stemming from the social economy, specifically the category of social businesses, can help recast the corporate model. Accordingly, in this chapter, instead of endorsing the well-established mantra that social economy organizations should turn to businesses to learn how to operate more effectively, we explore what social businesses can teach us about the transition to a corporate model and economic system no longer exclusively focused on profit maximization, but rather organized around the pursuit of social and environmental goals alongside financial ones. As calls for corporations to transform themselves abound (Henderson, 2020; Gulati, 2022; Kaplan, 2019; Serafeim, 2022), we propose that what we have learned from social businesses can serve as a roadmap not only to change corporations themselves, but also to reform the institutional context in which they operate to better support both social businesses and companies that may try to emulate them. In doing so, this chapter draws the contours of an institutional environment that rewires incentive structures and norms so businesses are guided by, and held accountable for, their social and environmental impacts in addition to their financial goals.

Diverging paths: the double movement of business and the social economy

Though today the social economy exists largely in parallel to the dominant market economy, these two spheres have not always been so separate. Instead, this dichotomy is the result of well-documented historical trends. We turn first to the evolution of business norms towards the sole pursuit of profit maximization. Second, we trace the history of the development and growth of the social economy, sometimes entwined with and at other times separated from the dominant market economy.

The rise of an exclusively profit-focused corporate model

The ubiquity of the shareholder value maximization paradigm in the past decades belies the fact that an emphasis on increasing profit and share price above all else was not always the dominant capitalist model. For instance, a 1932 article in the *Harvard Law Review* argued that corporations should incorporate social goals alongside financial ones (Dodd, 1932). In fact, for much of the first part of the twentieth century, corporate leaders held that corporations needed to serve not only their equity shareholders, but also their 'customers, creditors, employees, suppliers, and the broader society' (Stout, 2013, p. 2004). This is not to say that this awareness prevented corporations from exploiting workers (federal labour protections were only won in the 1930s in the United States, for example), fighting unions, enforcing racist Jim Crow laws, discriminating against women, or damaging the environment; in many cases, they reproduced the dominant power hierarchies and social exclusions of the times. It merely suggests that the idea of a corporation's responsibility to society, above and beyond maximizing profits, was not nearly so alien in the early twentieth century as it has been over the past decades.

Emphasis on service to society at large was reflected by early professional managers, who developed a wide lens regarding whom corporations were meant to serve (Khurana, 2007). But this led to the so-called agency cost problem for the owners and shareholders of companies. The agency cost problem refers to the risk that the interests of investors and shareholders (i.e., 'principals') may not be aligned completely with the interests of company leadership, managers, and executives (i.e., 'agents') (Jensen & Meckling, 1976). Around the same time, economists created and refined principles that would be used to justify 'shareholder primacy' by positing that the sole purpose of corporations was to make money (see Friedman, 1970). Adopting this new model of shareholder primacy was viewed as a way to mitigate the agency cost problem.

The articulation of the agency cost problem and the development of the concept of shareholder primacy buttressed a change that would permeate throughout the global economic system, deepening the divergence between the social economy and the market economy. This trend, combined with doubts raised about the then-dominant model of management that looked beyond just shareholders (see Stout, 2013; Khurana, 2007), created a new class of assertive investors, who in turn embraced shareholder primacy and supported its spread. The primary objective of successful executives was increasingly framed, both in companies and at institutions of higher learning, as an effort to exclusively create financial value for shareholders without regard for anything else. New managers exposed to this model as their default ideal of corporate governance reinforced shareholder primacy in the companies they joined (Smith & Rönnegard, 2014), including not only corporations based in the United States but also companies around the world (Canals, 2012). The World Bank and International Monetary Fund also routinely recommended the United States' model of corporate governance, including a focus on shareholder value maximization, to developing countries (Singh et al., 2005) and the structural adjustment programmes they imposed also induced a shift towards this corporate governance model (Reed, 2002). These pathways helped shareholder primacy permeate much of the international financial market.

The global dominance of shareholder value maximization as a business imperative has had important social and environmental consequences. CEO compensation has soared, often tied to stock prices, while workers' real wages have stagnated. For example, in the United States, while CEO compensation grew by 1,460 percent between 1978 and 2021, wages for average workers increased by only 18.1 percent during the same period (Bivens & Kandra, 2022). In many cases, emphasis on profit maximization has also prompted the use of layoffs, precarious scheduling, and understaffing, which have been detrimental to workers' physical and mental health and their economic security (Kalleberg, 2011; Kelly & Moen, 2020; Pfeffer, 2018; Schneider & Harknett, 2019; Wood, 2020).

The focus on shareholder value maximization has also accelerated the world towards 'climate catastrophe' (UN News, 2022), as corporations have made lofty commitments but continue to prioritize profits over people and the planet. Research by Wright and Nyberg (2017) has revealed the difficulty that the pursuit of profit maximization presents for a reorganization of business practices around environmental goals. In their longitudinal study of major Australian corporations, they find that even those who had initially made strong climate commitments ultimately exhibited 'a regressive pattern toward traditional business concerns over time' because of 'market imperatives' (Wright & Nyberg, 2017, p. 1655). The norms and practices of business as usual have contributed to today's multidimensional crisis, underscoring the need for a new model that meets individual and collective needs, sustainably. One ecosystem has aimed to do just that: the social economy. Its long and vibrant history reveals hundreds of years of innovations, as humans have built alternative systems, with different operating logics, values, norms, and incentives.

The development of the social economy

In parallel to the dominant market economy, the social economy has charted its own path as the ecosystem that houses non-profit organizations as well as co-operatives, associations, foundations, and private forms of social enterprise (Defourny & Nyssens, 2008). Though the boundaries between the dominant market economy and the social economy may have been more porous in the past, the social economy has its own rich history. Dating back to the nineteenth century, amid the dire social conditions of the European industrial revolution, ideas about the welfare of workers and communities emerged and quickly gained traction across the continent. Faced with precarity and hardship, the new industrial working class turned to each other, building networks of solidarity to meet their needs: from mutual aid funds to insure against illness or accidents, and food banks and consumer co-operatives to buy and trade food, clothes, and other essential goods, to worker co-operatives to regain control over the means of production (Moulaert & Ailenei, 2005). Throughout the nineteenth and twentieth centuries, innovative organizational forms were institutionalized in the social economy in order to respond to the needs of people and communities (Moulaert & Ailenei, 2005). The concept of 'social enterprise' (sometimes used synonymously with 'social business') was initially developed in the early 1980s (Defourny & Nyssens, 2010; Spreckley, 1981), and first took root as a distinct legal form in Italy in the 1990s. These organizations, oriented towards meeting previously unmet local needs while providing stable sources of work and income for marginalized populations, were legally recognized by the country's parliament as 'social cooperatives' in 1991 (Defourny & Nyssens, 2008).

The social economy has grown considerably in recent decades; a 2017 report commissioned by the European Economic and Social Committee estimated that the social economy in Europe alone represents 13.6 million paid jobs and almost 83 million volunteers spread over 2.3 million enterprises (Monzón & Chaves, 2017). In other regions, two reports estimate that there are between half a million and one million social enterprises in Southeast Asia (British Council et al., 2021), and that social enterprises are responsible for between 28 and 41 million jobs in Sub-Saharan Africa (Richardson et al. 2020; for a recent summary of global data, see: World

Economic Forum, 2022). Many countries around the world have joined the movement, adopting their own legal recognition of social enterprises, which we explore in the following sections.

Though social enterprises have a long history of balancing social and environmental goals alongside financial sustainability, the category remains fluid. The EMES European research network, composed of established university research centres and individual researchers, has developed criteria that are not intended as prescriptive but rather aim to delimit the 'ideal type' of social enterprise (Defourny & Nyssens, 2008). They develop several indicators across their evaluative criteria, including: (i) An explicit aim to benefit the community (moving beyond mere profit maximization) (ii) launched by a group of citizens responding to a need they face (iii) with democratic decision-making for organizational members, rather than decision-making based on capital ownership, and with (iv) stakeholder participation and (v) limited profit maximization and distribution unless it furthers the social aims of the organization. The EMES indicators, though not prescriptive or unanimous, nonetheless highlight the growing consensus that European social enterprises are characterized by a commitment to democratic decision-making, and to service to their members and to their communities (Defourny & Develtere, 2000). Broadly, these organizations, which are also at times referred to in the literature as social businesses (Santos et al., 2015), diverge from dominant organizational forms in both the social and business sectors. As such, they are hybrid organizations with social, environmental, and financial goals each at the heart of their operations (Battilana & Lee, 2014).

For the purpose of reimagining the corporate model, the field of research that has studied these social businesses, a subset of social economy organizations, is especially pertinent. Indeed, the existential imperative we face to shift away from a model of shareholder value maximization towards a system of production and exchange of goods and services that centres collective welfare and environmental sustainability makes social businesses worthy of study. Whereas the dominant corporate model is driven by shareholder value maximization and short-term profit generation, the social economy, including social businesses, centres on shared values of care, support, and solidarity (Amin et al., 2002). When faced with difficult economic decisions, a traditional firm might lay off thousands of workers to maintain profit growth and pay out dividends to shareholders, as exemplified during the COVID-19 pandemic (Useem, 2020). By contrast, a social business might open the decision to all their stakeholders; in fact, worker participation in strategic decision-making has been associated with the minimization of negative social effects such as layoffs and unemployment (Gregorič & Rapp, 2019). By disentangling their operations from the obligation to fulfil shareholder value maximization, social businesses show that an alternative model is possible.

Although they have generated great hopes as alternative forms of organizing, social businesses face their own set of unique challenges. Research (e.g., Battilana & Dorado, 2010; Battilana et al., 2017; Battilana, 2018) has documented and examined the hybrid nature of these organizations, which diverge from dominant organizational forms in both the social and business sectors. Straddling categories as they do is not easy. Far from it. When organizations fall between established categories, it is harder for them to be regarded as legitimate (Hsu et al., 2009; Ruef & Patterson, 2009; Zuckerman, 1999). But research on social businesses also highlights activities these organizations can engage in to mitigate the challenges they face. We turn to these challenges, and their mitigants, in the following section.

Organizational-level challenges and mitigants available to social businesses

Constantly having to adjudicate between competing social, environmental, and financial goals requires social businesses to regularly make tradeoffs. Some scholars have argued that these tradeoffs do not exist, yet both qualitative and quantitative research reveal that they do, and that social businesses constantly face them (Battilana et al., 2022). Admittedly, certain organizational configurations, such as limitations on profit generation and redistribution, may exert less financial pressure on an organization. Nevertheless, the necessity of financial sustainability for all social businesses exerts some financial pressure, leading to tradeoffs. These, in turn, generate unique challenges for social businesses, including challenges related to access to tangible resources as well as intangible identity tensions (Battilana, 2018).

Research in organization studies has enabled us to learn a great deal about the practices in which social businesses can engage to deal with these tradeoffs. But, as we will see, engaging in these practices is neither easy nor sufficient to overcome all the challenges these organizations face. We will begin this section by briefly sketching the challenges social businesses currently experience, then we will address what we have learned about how these organizations can alleviate these challenges.

Challenges facing social businesses

Social businesses face challenges relating to the allocation of funding and talent, internally and externally. On the internal front, in their study of work integration social enterprises (WISEs) in France, Battilana et al. (2015) found that tensions arise between social workers—who help the long-term unemployed people that WISEs hire to build skills and re-enter the job market—and production managers—who oversee worker productivity—about how much time employees should spend on the production line versus receiving mentorship and support. Externally, while the recent trend of impact investing has helped meet some of the funding needs of social businesses (Bugg-Levine & Emerson, 2011; Höchstädter & Scheck, 2015), qualitative and quantitative research (e.g., Battilana et al., 2017; Cobb et al., 2016; Lee, 2014; Spiess-Knafl & Scheck, 2019) indicates that social businesses still struggle to find funding. Additionally, because of the predominance of other organizational forms, it is difficult for social businesses to find employees who have the requisite experience in both the business and the social sectors. Employees that come from either sector may require different training, education, and organizational processes to allow them to identify with and successfully integrate the social business (Bacq et al., 2020; Battilana & Pache, 2018; Besharov, 2014).

Social businesses also face challenges related to organizational identity. The pursuit of joint financial and social objectives (Daudigeos & Valiorgue, 2018; Grenier & Bernardini-Perinciolo, 2015) creates identity tensions, because social businesses have to reconcile values (Besharov, 2014; Chandler, 2014; Glynn, 2000) often perceived as conflicting or competing (Château Terrisse, 2012; Poldner et al., 2017). This tension is compounded when different organizational members are found to be speaking 'different languages', one with an emphasis on social goals and the other with an emphasis on financial ones (Dean & McMullen, 2007). This tension can also create emotional distress for those working in social businesses (Ashforth et al., 2014; Bacq et al., 2020).

In the context of the broader market, it is worth noting that, until recently, there were few legal structures tailored to social businesses. And while some legal structures have been created that try to better fit their needs, unfamiliarity with and uncertainty about these new legal structures make utilizing them difficult. For instance, Marquis (2020) finds that legal concerns about transparency requirements for US benefit corporations have impeded uptake of this new legal form. Additionally, the legitimacy of social businesses is frequently an issue in the eyes of external partners, as partners from the for-profit and not-for-profit sectors approach social businesses with differing expectations and might be disappointed when social businesses do not meet those expectations (Aurini, 2006; Hsu, 2006; Hsu et al., 2009; Lallemand-Stempak, 2017; Pache & Santos, 2013).

How social businesses can mitigate the challenges they face

Research has also helped identify practices in which social businesses can engage to effectively pursue and sustain multiple objectives (for reviews see Battilana, 2018; Doherty et al., 2014; Smith et al., 2013). Here, we highlight four sets of organizational practices that help mitigate the challenges social businesses face: setting and monitoring organizational goals, structuring organizational activities, selecting and socializing organizational members, and practising dual-minded leadership (Battilana et al., 2019). Though these practices are not sufficient to ensure that social businesses can break out of their niche, they remain important as intermediary measures on the path to broader changes to the institutional context.

Setting and monitoring organizational goals
While organizations of all types pursue multiple goals (Cyert & March, 1963; Gavetti et al., 2007; March & Simon, 1958; Simon, 1947), social businesses are unique in how opposed their social versus their financial goals may be perceived to be (Battilana, 2018). Multiple goals can be made salient for organizational members

by institutionalizing multiple aims in an organization's mission, bylaws, and policies (Ashforth & Reingen, 2014), and implementing success metrics for social, environmental, and financial goals can help prevent 'mission drift' (Smith & Besharov, 2019). Ambiguities around the causes and effects of social and environmental problems can make developing social performance metrics difficult (Ebrahim, 2019), but research has highlighted that progress can nonetheless be made by negotiating shared reference points with relevant stakeholders, which enables collaborative social and environmental metric development (Nason et al., 2018). Social businesses can also adopt social and environmental performance metrics developed by third party organizations, which include (among others) B Labs (Gehman & Grimes, 2017), the Global Reporting Initiative (Global Reporting Initiative, 2020), and the Sustainability Accounting Standards Board (Battilana & Norris, 2014), which merged with the International Integrated Reporting Council to form the Value Reporting Foundation in 2021.

Structuring organizational activities

The second set of practices, which centres on organizational activities, includes assessing whether activities are integrated—combining social, environmental, and financial impacts into one activity—or differentiated, with separate activities for social, environmental, and financial impacts respectively (see Galbraith, 1977; Lawrence & Lorsch, 1967; Mintzberg, 1979 for seminal work on organizational design and see Battilana & Lee, 2014; Battilana et al., 2017 for reviews of the application of this tradition to hybrid organizations). While integrated and differentiated organizations may approach the problem of coordination differently, ensuring that all goals are represented throughout the organization can help maintain a social business' hybrid purpose. Designated spaces of negotiation, in which organizational members representing the social, environmental, and financial components of an organization's activities meet to balance tradeoffs, can also help hybrid organizations like social businesses maintain their hybridity (Battilana et al., 2015).

Selecting and socializing organizational members

Third, strategies surrounding the selection and socialization of organizational members present another way in which social businesses can work to alleviate the challenges that come with their dual nature. Research has found that hiring 'pluralist managers', who support social, environmental, and financial values, helps maintain hybridity (Besharov, 2014). Other social businesses employ workers who are oriented towards either the social/environmental or financial aspects of the business' mission, sometimes by necessity given divisions in the broader economy and education trajectories. Such workers may require more intentional socialization to enable them to understand and value both social and environmental goals (Bacq et al., 2020). Finally, some social enterprises focus on hiring 'blank slates', candidates without experience in either social/environmental or financial contexts, for entry-level positions, making the hybrid model their first work experience (Battilana & Dorado, 2010).

Regardless of which strategy is pursued, socialization is critical for teaching and rein-forcing certain values and behaviours in organizational members (Ashforth & Mael, 1989; Van Maanen & Schein, 1979), both in formal systems for training and reward-ing organizational members and in the informal processes through which members interact day-to-day (Ashforth et al., 2007; Feldman, 1976; Jones, 1986; Saks & Ash-forth, 1997). In the context of social businesses, effective socialization of members reinforces social, environmental, and financial goals.

Practising dual-minded leadership

The fourth and final set of practices emphasizes practising dual-minded leader-ship, which manifests at the management level when organizational leaders 'affirm, embody, and protect' the organization's financial, social, and environmental val-ues and address tensions proactively (Battilana et al., 2019, p. 132). Dual-minded leaders in hybrid organizations do not attempt to avoid the inevitable appearance of financial/social/environmental tradeoffs, but instead work to identify outcomes that ensure the company as a whole maintains its focus on all aspects of its mission. Beyond top executives, board members can also help ensure an organization does not drift from its hybrid purpose. Intentional selection of board members with both business and social/environmental expertise can support an organization's focus on multiple goals, though it may also lead to increased conflict (Battilana et al., 2019). This conflict may be overcome through appeal to a chairperson or executive director who can encourage both types of goals, and/or through a model of collegial gover-nance, in which governance actors individually champion environmental, financial, and social goals respectively, while collectively adhering to the company's multiple values (Bacq et al., 2020).

These various interventions have been found to help social businesses mitigate the challenges they face. But such internal strategies will not suffice to break social busi-nesses out of their niche, enable them to thrive, and make them the norm. To access vital resources, organizations must be viewed as legitimate. This need to be legit-imized impels organizations to comply with dominant norms, even though doing so may not be the best way to operate—neither for themselves nor for the stakeholders they serve (DiMaggio & Powell, 1983; Meyer & Rowan, 1977). To recast the corpo-rate model, then, it is critical to change the institutional context in which businesses operate. In the next section, we identify three key levers for changing the institutional context: legal forms, sustainability metrics, and financial and fiscal strategies. Build-ing on existing research, we argue that these three levers will prove instrumental in facilitating businesses' transition from solely pursuing financial goals to pursuing—and being held accountable for—social and environmental goals alongside financial ones.

Reshaping the institutional environment

There is only so much that social businesses can do to survive in an environ-ment that is not designed to support them. The institutional context in which these organizations operate has a significant impact on their success, both through its potential to lessen the intensity of the financial/social/environmental tradeoffs they face and by supporting the creation of new social businesses (Battilana et al., 2022). What we have learned from research on social businesses is not only what such organizations can do internally to try to mitigate the tensions they face, but also how the institutional context in which they operate plays a consequential role in shaping their emergence, resilience, and survival. For instance, we noted in the previous section the use of legal forms to help reduce and work through internal tensions. Yet, there remain important gaps in information, access, and coherence that act as barriers to the widespread adoption of such legal forms. Similarly, though individual organizations lean on metrics to set and evaluate their hybrid goals, the plurality of reporting systems, and their voluntary nature, inhibit broader accountability. At present, the status quo is still largely set up to support dominant organizational forms, leaving social economy organizations such as social businesses the task of navigating a system not designed for them. To make social businesses the new norm in the business world requires creating an institutional context that favours their development and success and encourages typical companies' transition towards more sustainable ways of organizing aligned with social businesses. In particular, in this chapter, we emphasize three levers that can facilitate this shift. These are:

(1) Legal structures
(2) Accountability metrics
(3) Financial and fiscal strategies

In the following sections, we consider existing advances in these three domains, their benefits and drawbacks, and potential for the future (for a summary see Table 8.1).

Lever 1: Legal structures

The range of legal forms available to entrepreneurs as they choose how to incorporate their organizations can play a determining role in how they structure their activities, influencing critical organizational decisions such as revenue structure, ownership and governance mechanisms, and sourcing and supply chain. If legal forms that have become associated with profit maximization remain the most available, widely known, and accessible forms, then exclusive focus on profit will continue to prevail, with all the devastating consequences outlined above. If, however, new legal forms are recognized, are made accessible, and become mainstream, organizations will be able to choose from among many forms and select one that truly suits their mission. This may also facilitate the adoption of laws that both incentivize and reward organizations which, by virtue of their legal status, bind themselves by law to integrating social and environmental considerations into their strategies and operations alongside financial considerations.

Table 8.1 Three levers for reshaping the institutional context in which social businesses operate

Legal structures	*Existing forms:* Hybrid legal forms (e.g., community interest companies in the UK, benefit corporations in the US, *Società Benefit* in Italy, *Sociétés à mission* in France) offer legal legitimacy to social businesses that bind themselves by law to pursuing social and environmental goals in addition to financial ones. Democratic legal forms, such as co-operatives and co-determination models, give workers' interests, priorities, and concerns space in organizational decision-making. *Increasing recognition and enhancing forms:* While legal structures that account for multiple purposes have recently been developed, there is still barriers in recognition and legitimacy faced by companies that forego the traditional focus on profit maximization. More work can be done to incentivize companies to take up such forms, and existing forms can also be compared, integrated, and improved with emphasis on creating frameworks that enable forms to meet the needs of disparate contexts.
Accountability metrics	*Current metrics:* A variety of sustainability metrics (GRI, CDP, CDSB, SASB, and many more) have been developed in the past two decades to standardize the measurement of corporate environmental and social impacts. A number of these standard-setting bodies are now in the process of merging and aligning. *Toward convergence:* As various standard-setting bodies begin to merge and consolidate, it is critical that, before being endorsed and/or mandated by public authorities, standards be democratically debated and legitimated, be tailored to the context in which they are implemented, and include a mechanism for updating standards as time goes on.
Financial and fiscal strategies	*Social business funding streams:* Impact investor funding, community-based funding (crowdfunding and community control), and government funding (grants, funds, and Social Impact Bonds) have offered social businesses tailored funding sources. *Future policy innovations:* Informed by a careful and democratic convergence of standards and a clarification of legal forms, governments could adapt a company's fiscal treatment based on their social and environmental impacts, not only their financial standing. By rewarding positive impacts and penalizing negative ones, such a policy could help shift corporate behaviour and drive real change.

Hybrid legal forms

New legal forms have emerged around the world as a result of experimentation and innovation in the social economy. Among the first of these new legal forms developed over the past twenty years was the community interest company (CIC) in the United Kingdom, which has two noteworthy features that offer a potential remedy to the risk of deviating from or abandoning one's social mission. The first is that CICs are subject to a Community Interest Test applied regularly by an oversight body, the CIC Regulator, to ensure that their operations continue to benefit society (Cross, 2004). The second is an asset lock, which ensures that a CIC's assets are legally protected and retained for community benefit in perpetuity, even in the event that the CIC is sold, ceases operations, or attempts to convert to another legal form (Triponel & Agapitova, 2017). Similarly, in South Korea, social enterprises can take the form of social co-operatives, a legally protected form of organization that requires that its members meet specific criteria set by the Korea Social Enterprise Promotion Agency. As a requirement, these enterprises must provide national job-creation services, social services, local community contributions, or a combination of these. In addition, similarly to the British model, they are subject to an asset lock provision dictating the use of their resources in the event of dissolution (Triponel & Agapitova, 2017). Both models represent examples of how structural accountability mechanisms can be put in place to ensure companies and their leaders stay true to their mission and are held responsible for adhering to them. It is also worth noting, however, that the South Korean legal form, which was partially inspired by the UK model, has been criticized by some for not being adequately adapted to a new national context (Park et al., 2017), highlighting the need to adapt these legal forms based on the local context with the involvement of stakeholders on the ground.

Meanwhile, in the United States, a popular legal form for social businesses is the benefit corporation,[1] a model championed by B Lab, the developer of the B Corp certification (Marquis, 2020; McDonnell, 2016). The benefit corporation was designed to alleviate the concerns of socially minded entrepreneurs that they might be legally exposed to claims by their shareholders should they decide to prioritize goals other than maximizing shareholders' financial returns. The benefit corporation form explicitly requires consideration of the needs of stakeholders beyond just shareholders. Some have argued that this legal form does not go far enough, however, as shareholders can unilaterally discard the social purpose of a benefit corporation by voting to reincorporate or by amending its articles of incorporation to alter its legal form (Reiser & Dean, 2017).[2]

In 2016 Italy became the first European state to mimic the US benefit corporation legislation, with the creation of the *Società Benefit*, a hybrid corporate form that allows profit-seeking companies to declare a social and environmental purpose, which the company's directors are responsible for protecting (Nigri et al., 2020). In turn, in 2019 France passed the PACTE law, which, among other changes, revised the French civil code to allow any new or existing French company, regardless of its legal form, to become a *société à mission* without changing its underlying legal form or status (Bercy Infos, 2022). To become a *société à mission,* a company must include a motive ('*raison d'être*') in their articles of association that highlights the organization's social and environmental objectives. To maintain its status, every two years the *société à mission* must undergo a verification process by an independent third party

---

[1] The two main legal forms for social businesses in the United States are the Public Benefit Corporation for those incorporating in the state of Delaware and California's Social Purpose Corporation. Given the prevalence of incorporation in Delaware, the Public Benefit Corporation is most widely known.
[2] Whether, by whom, and under what conditions the social purpose of a corporation can be changed is a question currently being debated. Currently, in Delaware, the threshold to vote on a change in incorporation status is 50 percent of the Board. Is that threshold too low? Should benefit corporations not be able to change their status at all? Should other stakeholders have a say? These are critical questions up for debate.

organization. However, *société à mission* represents a voluntary designation that a company can adopt, and the only consequence for a company found not to be working toward its stated social or environmental goals is that it will be forced to drop the designation (Bercy Infos, 2022). Nonetheless, its implementation comes as a further step in France's commitment to non-financial corporate goals in its economy.

While these legal forms represent one way in which organizations can legally constitute themselves, they are far from the only way. Legal forms that centre on full participation of workers in decision-making also make up an important part of the social economy.

Legal forms ensuring full participation of workers in decision-making

A long tradition of scholarship underscores the risk that typical hierarchical organizations may succumb to market pressure and deviate from their social/environmental goals in the quest for organizational survival and efficiency (Selznick, 1949; Weber, 1946). Meanwhile, research on hybrid organizations and co-operatives suggests that organizations with democratic decision-making processes may be better at avoiding mission drift and balancing their multiple objectives (Battilana et al., 2018). Leaning on the strength of political democracy at mending diverse values and viewpoints, they suggest that democratic decision-making provides spaces of negotiation where productive tensions between social, environmental, and financial imperatives can surface and be deliberated. This insight shines light on the role that democratic ways of organizing could play in accelerating the shift from the single-minded pursuit of profit to a balanced pursuit of multiple objectives.

Co-operatives have a long and rich history of workplace democracy around the world. Their legal form centres on democratic decision-making in which all members are allowed to vote on critical strategic measures, regardless of capital ownership and contribution (Fici, 2013). Beyond co-operatives, though, legal requirements for board-level employee representation are another conduit for democratic decision-making. These requirements also have a long history, particularly in Europe. In Germany, for instance, a system of codetermination in work has antecedents dating back well into the nineteenth century, and the first German law on codetermination was passed in 1920 (Zahn, 2015). This system legally requires that workers in companies over a certain size comprise either one third or one half of the total membership of a company's board.[3] This second condition, required for corporations of 2,000 or more employees, is a quasi-parity model. This means that, while the number of seats on German boards is evenly divided between shareholders and employees, in the event of a tie the tiebreaking vote is cast by the chairman of the board, who is appointed solely by shareholders (Addison, 2009). Worker board representatives are selected by work councils, which represent workers in negotiations with management and coordinate with national unions.

---

[3] A third model, establishing true parity between workers and shareholders, was implemented in 1953 for specific German industries, namely coal and steel (Addison, 2009). These same two industries drove the formation of the European Coal and Steel Community, an antecedent of the modern European Union.

Germany is not unique in having adopted codetermination laws. Other European Union countries, such as Sweden and Austria, have also implemented similar laws (Munkholm, 2018). Though more research into the benefits and drawbacks of the codetermination model is needed, as is the case for many of the models we discuss, a meta-analysis of codetermination studies has found no significant difference in productivity or performance between organizations with and without codetermination (Addison, 2009). Additionally, German firms that adhere to codetermination are less likely to lay off workers in times of social and economic crises (Gregorič & Rapp, 2019; Kim et al., 2018), which lends initial evidence to the idea that codetermination enables the interests of workers, not only shareholders, to guide decision-making.

Toward a unified framework?

Despite the plethora of legal forms extant around the world, no widely adopted unifying framework has yet emerged. Those who wish to adopt a hybrid legal form may face barriers, notably a lack of awareness of each form's existence, benefits, and implications, as well as varying legal treatment across countries, which add to the complexity of navigating these alternative legal forms (Aguirre, 2021; Bohinc & Schwartz, 2021; Reiser, 2011, 2013). The European Union has made some strides in providing a more uniform legal structure for social businesses through the development and adoption of European Cooperative Society (SCE) regulation in 2003. This legal structure, aimed specifically at co-operatives, provides organizations that meet certain criteria the ability to operate within the entire European Economic Community without the need to establish subsidiaries in each individual nation. A report by the European Commission, however, found that uptake has been limited, in part due to minimum capital requirements and the form's legal complexity and setup costs.

On the research front, the European Commission's multi-year mapping exercise has catalogued various models of social enterprise within Europe (e.g., Hulgård & Chodorkoff, 2019; for a comparative synthesis, see Borzaga et al., 2020). In a further move towards standardization, the European Union's Social Business Initiative established an operationalized definition of social enterprises in 2011. Then in April 2022, in collaboration with the European Union, the Organization for Economic Cooperation and Development published a guidance manual (OECD, 2022) for policy-makers to better assess the rationale and tools needed to develop unified legal frameworks for social enterprises. This development represents a step forward in the process of providing social businesses with better legal recognition, but more work is needed to help improve the legal structures available to them. One question facing the international community is whether a unified legal framework for social businesses should be created, and, if so, what should be included in it. A unified framework could help overcome the current informational, bureaucratic, and financial barriers to adopting new legal forms while providing these organizations with increased legitimacy, and would also open the door to governments rewarding or incentivizing organizations that adopt these legal forms. This raises the next crucial point: to regulate rewards and/or incentives for businesses to adopt socially and environmentally beneficial models, social and environmental metrics will prove critical.

Lever 2: Accountability metrics

While in theory commendable, the many recent public announcements of the intentions of corporations to pursue goals beyond shareholder value maximization have proved insufficient to drive real change. For instance, a 2019 announcement by the Business Roundtable, an organization of which the CEOs of most major US corporations are members, indicated that corporations should consider the interests of not only their shareholders, but also their customers, employees, and society at large (Business Roundtable, 2019). Yet a recent analysis (see Wry et al., 2021) found that corporations that signed the Business Roundtable statement were actually 20 per cent more likely than corporations that did not sign it to fire their employees at the start of the COVID-19 pandemic. Signatories were also less likely to donate to relief efforts, to offer customer discounts, and to shift production to pandemic-related goods than non-signatories.

In contrast to announcements of good intentions, research has proven the importance of accountability metrics in influencing corporate behaviour (Dobbin et al., 2015; Marquis, 2020). For instance, in 1973, in an effort to bring consistency and comparability to the financial reporting process, the Securities Exchange Commission (SEC) established that the Financial Accounting Standards Board (FASB), a private body, would set the accounting standards for public companies (SEC, 1973, 2003). While many organizations are working to develop metrics for social and environmental behaviour, there is not yet a unified and officially sanctioned set of standards in the social and environmental arenas, leaving the door open to 'impact washing' and 'green washing' (impact washing's environmental equivalent). We turn to some of the many organizations currently developing social and environmental metrics in the following section.

Multiple measurement systems

The past decades have seen a rise in recognition that current metrics for evaluating businesses, predicated solely on financial returns, do not capture the true impacts and costs of businesses to society. One of the first organizations that aimed to systematically capture the environmental and social impacts of businesses, the Global Reporting Initiative (GRI), was founded in 1997 partially as a response to public outcry following the Exxon Valdez oil spill (Global Reporting Initiative, 2020). In 2000, the GRI released the first global framework for sustainability reporting. In the years that followed, several other organizations that aimed to more comprehensively account for business impacts were founded, including the CDP (formerly the Carbon Disclosure Project) in 2002, the Climate Disclosure Standards Board (CDSB) in 2007, the International Integrated Reporting Council (IIRC) in 2010, and the Sustainability Accounting Standards Board (SASB) in 2011, among many others.

However, feedback from a variety of stakeholders in the past decade revealed that the heterogeneity of reporting standards was creating confusion both for companies earnestly attempting to report on their sustainability performance, and for investors or other stakeholders aiming to hold companies accountable for their performance on these dimensions. As a response to this confusion, in September 2020, the GRI, CDP, CDSB, IIRC, and SASB released a joint statement of intent announcing a shared vision for a comprehensive corporate sustainability reporting system (CDP et al., 2020a). In December 2020, they released a joint prototype of climate-related financial disclosure (CDP et al., 2020b). The GRI and SASB subsequently collaborated on a report explaining how to effectively utilize both GRI and SASB standards in sustainability reporting (GRI & SASB, 2021). These efforts to work more closely together have spurred a wave of consolidation in the sustainability metrics space. In June 2021, SASB and the IIRC merged to form the Value Reporting Foundation (Value Reporting Framework, 2021). The Value Reporting Foundation in turn was consolidated with the CDSB into the International Sustainability Standards Board under the International Financial Reporting Standards (IFRS) Foundation in August 2022 (Integrated Reporting, 2022).

While this move toward greater alignment in the industry is promising, substantive issues remain. Of particular importance is the fact that the mere existence of metrics, even if they are well aligned, is not enough to ensure that companies actually change their behaviour to align with their stated social, environmental, and financial goals (Rogers, 2019). One major criticism of existing metrics is that they allow corporations to conflate their sustainability measurement with making efforts to actually become more sustainable (Milne & Gray, 2012; see also Barkemeyer et al., 2015; Flower, 2015). Reinforcing this point, one study found that companies using the GRI framework engaged in several legitimizing strategies when they reported negative sustainability outcomes, many of which were symbolic as opposed to substantive (Hahn & Lülfs, 2014). The same study notes that, because of the GRI's voluntary nature, there are limited ways for the GRI to increase reporting on negative aspects of companies' sustainability performance, but speculates that mandatory regulation might be able to do so.

The European Union is taking a first step in this direction. In 2021, the European Commission endorsed a proposal for a comprehensive collection of measures aimed at directing resources towards sustainable enterprise in Europe called the Corporate Sustainability Reporting Directive (CSRD) (European Commission, 2021a). The CSRD will expand on the 2014 Non-Financial Reporting Directive, which required companies with more than 500 employees to report on a predefined list of non-financial issues, such as environmental impact and respect for human rights (European Commission, 2022). Entering into force in January 2023, the CSRD requires all large companies and all companies listed on EU regulated markets (except listed microcompanies) to report on non-financial metrics for financial years beginning in 2024 (European Commission, 2021b). The directive suggests that the ultimate language adopted for these metrics should be developed through consultation with a number of key stakeholders, including technical advice from the European Financial Reporting Advisory Group and with an opinion required from the European Securities and Markets Authority. However, the CSRD remains a tool for reporting, and does not require companies to take action to change their practices if they are found to be socially and environmentally harmful. Further government action, then, is likely needed to ensure that organizations take substantive steps to improve their social and environmental impacts, as opposed to merely citing the measures themselves as a sign of progress.

The political work of convergence

Developing and maintaining a convergent set of sustainability standards is not merely a technical process. It entails important political decisions, as we as a society must decide what we value and hence what to measure. So far, many organizations have set standards that are guided by their own principles and methodologies. But these choices have critical implications for all of us collectively. For instance, many standard-setting organizations focus on environmental sustainability. This issue is a critical one, and indeed more must be done to avert the worst impacts of climate change and environmental degradation. However, this focus alone is not enough to ensure that both humans and the planet are placed at the heart of our economic system: what of worker sustainability and wellbeing? Do we wish to measure a corporation's impact on social cohesion and inequality? What about the number of jobs created compared to those laid off? And should we require corporations to report how they use profit—whether it is redistributed widely, reinvested in better services, or paid out to shareholders? The progress on the environmental dimensions is critical, and must continue, but progress on social metric development is still lagging. The #MeToo movement, followed by the murder of George Floyd and massive Black Lives Matter protests around the world, certainly accelerated talk of diversity, equity, and inclusion, though research underscores the importance of moving beyond one-off trainings and reorganizing the very distribution of resources and power in organizations (Dobbin & Kalev, 2018; Kalev et al., 2006). The 'Great Resignation' and high-profile unionization efforts have also put worker power, and power sharing, on the agenda, as scholars and researchers put forth mechanisms for giving workers, who can be seen as 'labour investors', formal governance power (Ferreras, 2017).

These are important questions with important collective ramifications. Their answers will guide the contours of our new economic system. The exercise of setting sustainability standards is thus not merely technical, but profoundly political. It requires deliberation and exchange as members of society decide together the standards to which companies should be held accountable. Hence, we must ensure that the bodies tasked with creating and updating sustainability standards as they evolve over time enable power sharing by including workers, environmental groups, affected communities, and other key stakeholders. If these standards are developed behind closed doors, or with mere consultation but without shared decision-making power, they risk perpetuating forms of exclusion and bias that result from existing power hierarchies (Battilana & Casciaro, 2021).

Also key in this process will be ensuring that minimum thresholds for organizational performance are established, such that exceptional performance on one metric does not enable a company to skirt its obligations on other fronts. For instance, a company that performs exceptionally well in its work to limit carbon emissions should not be given licence to underpay or disempower its workers and still receive high marks as a result, and vice versa. Instead, standard-setting bodies, which must themselves represent diverse stakeholders, should ensure that organizations meet standards that enhance environmental sustainability as well as human sustainability for their workers, local communities, and other stakeholders. Leveraging the need for funding may well be one way to incentivize the adoption of ambitious social and environmental targets.

Lever 3: Financial and fiscal strategies

Entrepreneurs, business leaders, and workers need capital to start and grow organizations in the social economy as they do in the traditional economy. The availability of designated funds, tailored to the realities of social businesses, as well as the stipulations associated with these funds can influence how an organization develops and whether it thrives. We survey some of the options available to social businesses, and identify areas for improvement and further research, in what follows.

Impact investor funding

One area that has received much attention in recent years is the emergent impact investing sector, which was estimated at approximately $715 billion in 2020. Coined in 2007 by the Rockefeller Foundation, the term 'impact investing' is distinguished from its predecessor 'socially responsible investing' (SRI) in that while SRI focuses on avoiding the provision of financial support to organizations that harm society or the environment, impact investing focuses on providing funding to organizations creating a positive impact, not merely avoiding negative ones (Marquis, 2020). Both practitioners and academics have converged on similar definitions of impact investing, though important discrepancies remain, including the eligibility of investees according to their organizational or financial structures (Höchstädter & Scheck, 2015).

Yet despite the remarkable growth of the impact investing market, the most frequently cited issue in the Global Impact Investing Network (GIIN)'s 2020 annual survey was the (lack of) availability of appropriate capital across the risk/return spectrum. Additionally, as the impact investing market matures, so too do concerns among practitioners about the potential for 'impact washing' (i.e. deceptive practices by which companies falsely claim their investments have a positive social impact). Concerns about impact washing were the most cited challenge that surveyed impact investors expect to face in the coming years (GIIN, 2020). Establishing a unified baseline of transparency for funders and organizations to adhere to could help alleviate these concerns, while also helping ensure organizations are held responsible for their stated versus achieved social and environmental goals.

Community funding

Small-scale investing is another method for funding certain organizations in the social economy. The history of collecting many small donations in order to support a larger effort is obviously not a new one; Joseph Pulitzer employed just such a campaign in support of the Statue of Liberty more than 130 years ago (Fleming & Sorenson, 2016). Crowdfunding has come to prominence more recently because of platform technology's ability to disintermediate between traditional financial institutions and small-scale funders. Several crowdfunding platforms have emerged with a focus on serving organizations with social or environmental aims; some of these platforms are themselves organized as social businesses (Renko et al., 2019). Research on the subject, however, has yet to reach a consensus about the link between crowdfunding and social or environmental goals. Some researchers have found that crowdfunding projects experience more success when they embrace a 'sustainability orientation' by highlighting social and/or environmental goals (Calic & Mosakowski, 2016), while others have found that social ventures perform best in a crowdfunding context when they highlight either their economic or their social benefits, but not both (Moss et al., 2018). Other research has found that traditional 'commercial entrepreneurs' on average raise much more capital than social entrepreneurs, though this average is somewhat skewed due to the inclusion of a small number of very successful commercial campaigns (Parhankangas & Renko, 2017). Despite disagreement in the literature, crowdfunding is still broadly viewed as a promising alternative to traditional sources of funding for organizations in the social economy (Farhoud et al., 2021; Lehner, 2013). The advent of sustainability-focused crowdfunding platforms in particular raises the possibility of crowdfunding as a funding mechanism to mitigate the challenges that social businesses face in raising capital from more traditional sources.

However, crowdfunding is not without its challenges, and more research on the effectiveness of crowdfunding platforms at providing social businesses with regular, sustainable funding is needed. Also worthy of further exploration are community funding options, which would enable members of local communities to directly pool resources to finance organizations that support positive social or environmental outcomes for their community. Such efforts for funding would help share power beyond large institutional investors to potentially local stakeholders who would both be supporters of and affected by a proposed initiative. While to date academic literature on community funding initiatives appears limited, a number of promising organizations have emerged in this space that are worthy of further study, including for instance the organizations that constitute the Seed Commons in the United States, which describes itself as 'a national network of locally rooted, non-extractive loan funds that brings the power of big finance under community control' (Seed Commons, 2021). Increased research attention to community funding may help uncover more critical insights that will prove important in ensuring community-oriented social businesses receive the funding needed to not only survive, but thrive.

State funding

The state certainly also has a critical role to play in funding social enterprises. In terms of directly supporting the financial needs of social businesses, international governmental support could build off examples like the European Union Social

Entrepreneurship Funds (EuSEF) framework[4] or the EUR 200 million microfinance and social entrepreneurship fund launched by the European Union, the European Investment Bank, and the European Investment Fund in late 2019.

In addition to direct funding, governments have also recently explored 'pay for success' models such as Social Impact Bonds (SIBs), through which a private investor partners with a not-for-profit to support the provision of a social service. If certain predefined outcomes are achieved, the external investor is entitled to a reimbursement from the government in addition to some return (Fraser et al., 2018). While the development of this funding model has been met with much interest and enthusiasm (Arena et al., 2016), recent research has highlighted a number of challenges, including that SIBs may represent a dissipation of government responsibility (McHugh et al. 2013), a financialization of the not-for-profit and public sectors (Cooper et al., 2016), and may increase emphasis on the most easily quantifiable social problems and on target beneficiaries most likely to succeed (Edmiston & Nicholls, 2017; Fraser et al., 2018; Warner, 2013).

Fiscal policy

Finally, legal forms, sustainability metrics, and funding converge around an important potential lever: fiscal policy. A recent example of fiscal policy being used to undergird prosocial impacts has been the adoption of climate-oriented policies, including carbon taxes and emissions trading schemes, in countries across the world. In Australia, for instance, a carbon tax that went into effect in 2012 reduced CO_2 emissions by between 11 and 17 million tons in the following two years (O'Gorman & Jotzo, 2014), the largest fall in greenhouse gas emissions for the nation in twenty-four years (Hannam, 2014). Unfortunately, the example of Australia also serves as a cautionary tale that highlights that such policies require political work to gain durable support. Only two years after it was implemented, Australia became 'the first country in the world to abolish a functioning carbon pricing scheme' (Dayton, 2014, p. 362). Critics condemned the GDP losses and rising electricity costs that resulted from the tax (Robson, 2014). Retroactive studies have examined the ultimate failure of this policy, including through the lens of elected political officials (Ike, 2020), and through the lens of public acceptance (Hammerle et al., 2021), both of which highlight the reality that such a change is political and cannot be viewed from a merely technical perspective.

So, fiscal policy can be used to incentivize the move towards and growth of social businesses, but careful attention must be paid to the political dimensions of such change. Informed by a careful and democratic convergence of standards, governments may adopt a progressive corporate taxation scheme which takes into account not just the financial standing of a company, but also its positive or negative social and environmental impacts. Just as companies are currently taxed based on their profits, so too could their fiscal treatment vary as a function of their social and

---

[4] See Regulation (EU) No 346/2013 of the European Parliament and of the Council of 17 April 2013 on European social entrepreneurship funds.

environmental impacts. Implementing such a policy would require clear legal forms and consistent social and environmental reporting standards, emphasizing that these three levers for change should be pursued in concert with one another. Prototypes of such a system might be tested on a smaller scale, with research on their effectiveness informing wider implementation. By incentivizing positive impacts and/or penalizing negative impacts, such a policy would help address legitimate concerns that participation in sustainability measurement does not drive real change.

Conclusion

Today, the world faces a set of severe and interlocking crises, which include the ongoing public health challenges related to the COVID-19 pandemic, social and economic inequality, rising authoritarianism, and environmental degradation. Calls to reform our social and economic systems abound, and social businesses that are designed to put social and environmental concerns at their core alongside financial ones can be part of the answer to those calls. This alternative model of organizing may prove useful in devising an antidote to the excesses of the corporate system that has been dominant over the past decades.

But social businesses also face unique challenges that stem in part from an institutional context that favours shareholder primacy. As discussed, they cannot overcome these challenges on their own. While research has helped identify practices they can adopt to lessen the intensity of the financial/social/environmental tradeoffs they experience as they pursue multiple objectives (Battilana et al., 2022), these practices are not sufficient to ensure the success and growth of the social business sector.

Instead, the institutional context in which organizations operate must change so as to better support existing social businesses and incentivize a shift away from the dominant corporate model. We have discussed three potential levers that might drive change in the institutional context. First, creating accessible new legal structures can build the legitimacy of social businesses and help the pursuit of social and environmental goals permeate the corporate world. Second, converging on a comprehensive—and ambitious—measurement system can help ensure that companies disclose not only their financial standing, but also their social and environmental impacts. This is a key tool for holding them accountable for their actions and behaviours, helping to prevent green washing or impact washing. Finally, ensuring tailored funding is available to social businesses can serve to sustain and scale their impact. Importantly, when combined, clear legal structures and a unified measurement framework can equip policy-makers to reward companies that contribute to collective and climate welfare and penalize those that damage society and the planet. Though these specific suggestions are not exhaustive, legal forms that structure an organization's obligations, ambitious measurements that hold companies accountable for more, funding that is channelled to organizations that contribute to a healthy environment and fair society, and fiscal policy that rewards (or penalizes) them based on their respective benefits and costs to society can help lay the foundations of a new economic system.

Given the diversity of social enterprise models, which treat profit generation, governance, ownership, and other organizational components differently, further research is necessary to tease apart the consequences, benefits, and challenges of each organizational form. Though no one model has yet emerged as the single alternative to the profit-maximizing firm, the plurality of models represents fertile ground for empirical research linking organizational form with costs and benefits to society. This line of inquiry may also inform further research on the effectiveness of coercive versus incentive-based policy-making in shifting corporate business models and behaviour. Finally, the emergent research and experimentation on degrowth, a socially sustainable and equitable reduction of society's energy and resource use, and the quest for alternatives to growth-based development (Kallis et al., 2018) is also likely to intersect with this research agenda, especially with regards to metric development.

As the past decades have revealed, neoliberal logic has permeated throughout not merely the economic but also the social and public spheres. Hence, in closing, a disclaimer is necessary: the aim of this chapter—explaining how social business logic could permeate the corporate sector—is not a call for social business to permeate the social or public sectors. As the COVID-19 pandemic has demonstrated, certain sectors serve society better when protected from market forces (Stiglitz, 2021). To address the multidimensional crises we face, this chapter does not argue for not-for-profits to adopt more business practices—a common refrain of the past decades. Instead, this chapter argues for the opposite: it is urgent that the logic and practices of the social economy permeate into the business world, paving the way for an alternative to neoliberal capitalism. This shift represents nothing short of reimagining the value and purpose of business in society.

Together, we have within our power the ability to help facilitate these critical changes, many of which are already being explored or have been adopted in part in different countries. But time is of the essence. We can decide to learn from the multidimensional crisis we are facing or continue with business as usual at our own and our planet's peril. It is up to us, as workers, as consumers, and as citizens, to rise to this challenge to build a more just, equitable, and sustainable tomorrow.

References

Addison, J. (2009). *The Economics of Codetermination: Lessons from the German Experience*. New York: Palgrave Macmillan US. https://doi.org/10.1057/9780230104242

Aguirre, E. (2021). Beyond profit. *U.C. Davis Law Review*, 54(4), 2077–2148.

Amin, A., Cameron, A., & Hudson, R. (2002). *Placing the Social Economy*. Abingdon: Routledge. https://doi.org/10.4324/9780203166123

Amis, J. M., Mair, J., & Munir, K. A. (2020). The organizational reproduction of inequality. *The Academy of Management Annals*, 14(1), 195–230. https://doi.org/10.5465/annals.2017.0033

Arena, M., Bengo, I., Calderini, M., & Chiodo, V. (2016). Social Impact Bonds: block-buster or flash in a pan? *International Journal of Public Administration*, 39(12), 927–939. https://doi.org/10.1080/01900692.2015.1057852

Armour, J., & Gordon, J. N. (2014). Systemic harms and shareholder value. *Journal of Legal Analysis*, 6(1), 35–85. https://doi.org/10.1093/jla/lau004

Ashforth, B. E. & Mael, F. (1989). Social identity theory and the organization. *Academy of Management Review*, 14(1), 20–39. https://doi.org/10.5465/AMR.1989.4278999

Ashforth, B. E. & Reingen, P. H. (2014). Functions of dysfunction: managing the dynamics of an organizational duality in a natural food cooperative. *Administrative Science Quarterly*, 59(3), 474–516. https://doi.org/10.1177/0001839214537811

Ashforth, B. E., Rogers, K. M., Pratt, M. G., & Pradies, C. (2014). Ambivalence in organizations: a multilevel approach. *Organization Science*, 25(5), 1453–1478. https://doi.org/10.1287/orsc.2014.0909

Ashforth, B. E., Sluss, D. M., & Saks, A. (2007). Socialization tactics, proactive behavior, and newcomer learning: integrating socialization models. *Journal of Vocational Behavior*, 70(3), 447–462. https://doi.org/10.1016/j.jvb.2007.02.001

Aurini, J. (2006). Crafting legitimation projects: an institutional analysis of private education businesses. *Sociological Forum*, 21(1), 83–111. https://doi.org/10.1007/s11206-006-9004-8

Bacq, S., Battilana, J., & Bovais, H. (2020). *The Role of Collegial Governance in Sustaining the Organizational Pursuit of Hybrid Goals.* Working Paper.

Barkemeyer, R., Preuss, L., & Lee, L. (2015). On the effectiveness of private transnational governance regimes—evaluating corporate sustainability reporting according to the Global Reporting Initiative. *Journal of World Business: JWB*, 50(2), 312–325. https://doi.org/10.1016/j.jwb.2014.10.008

Battilana, J. (2015). Recasting the corporate model: what can be learned from social enterprises. In S. Rangan (Ed.), *Performance and Progress: Essays on Capitalism, Business, and Society* (pp. 435–461). Oxford Scholarship Online. https://doi.org/10.1093/acprof:oso/9780198744283.001.0001

Battilana, J. (2018). Cracking the organizational challenge of pursuing joint social and financial goals: social enterprise as a laboratory to understand hybrid organizing. *M@n@gement*, 21(4), 1278–1305. https://doi.org/10.15122/isbn.978-2-406-09248-3.p.0053

Battilana, J. (2022). Introduction: for a fairer, more democratic, greener society. In I. Ferreras, J. Battilana, & D. Méda (Eds). *Democratize Work: The Case for Reorganizing the Economy* (pp. 1–16). Chicago: University of Chicago Press. https://doi.org/10.7208/chicago/9780226819631.001.0001

Battilana, J., Besharov, M., & Mitzinneck, B. (2017). On hybrids and hybrid organizing: a review and roadmap for future research. In R. Greenwood, C. Oliver, T. B. Lawrence, & R. E. Meyer (Eds), *The SAGE Handbook of Organizational Institutionalism* (2nd ed., pp. 128–162). Thousand Oaks: SAGE Publications. https://doi.org/10.4135/9781526415066

Battilana, J., & Casciaro, T. (2021). *Power, for All: How It Really Works and Why It's Everyone's Business*. New York: Simon and Schuster.

Battilana, J., & Dorado, S. (2010). Building sustainable hybrid organizations: the case of commercial microfinance organizations. *Academy of Management Journal*, 53, 1419–1440. https://doi.org/10.5465/AMJ.2010.57318391

Battilana, J., Fuerstein, M., & Lee, M. (2018). New prospects for organizational democracy? How the joint pursuit of social and financial goals challenges traditional organizational designs. In S. Rangan (Ed.), *Capitalism beyond Mutuality? Perspectives Integrating Philosophy and Social Science* (pp. 256–288). Oxford: Oxford University Publishing. https://doi.org/10.1093/oso/9780198825067.001.0001

Battilana, J., Kimsey, M., Paetzold, F., & Zogbi, P. (2017). *Vox Capital: Pioneering Impact Investing in Brazil*. Harvard Business School Case 417–451 (Revised January 2018). Harvard Business School Publishing.

Battilana, J., & Lee, M. (2014) Advancing research on hybrid organizing: insights from the study of social enterprises. *The Academy of Management Annals*, 8(1), 397–441. https://doi.org/10.1080/19416520.2014.893615

Battilana, J., & Norris, M. (2014). *The Sustainability Accounting Standards Board*. Harvard Business School Case 414–478 (Revised January 2015). Harvard Business School Publishing.

Battilana, J., Obloj, T., Pache, A-C., & Sengul, M. (2022). Beyond shareholder value maximization: accounting for financial/social tradeoffs in dual-purpose companies. *Academy of Management Review*, 47(2), 237–258. https://doi.org/10.5465/amr.2019.0386

Battilana, J., & Pache, A. C. (2018, 26 January). Les entreprises doivent s'engager dans une transformation profonde, *Le Monde*. https://www.lemonde.fr/idees/article/2018/01/26/des-organisations-tournees-vers-la-maximisation-du-profit-ne-changeront-pas-du-jour-au-lendemain_5247835_3232.html

Battilana, J., Pache, A.-C., Sengul, M., & Kimsey, M. (2019). The dual-purpose playbook. *Harvard Business Review*, 97(2), 124–133. https://hbr.org/2019/03/the-dual-purpose-playbook

Battilana, J., Sengul, M., Pache, A.-C., & Model, J. (2015). Harnessing productive tensions in hybrid organizations: the case of work integration social enterprises. *Academy of Management Journal*, 58(6), 1658–1685. https://doi.org/10.5465/amj.2013.0903

Bercy Infos (2022). *Comment devenir une société à mission?* Ministère de l'Économie, des Finances et de la Souveraineté industrielle et numérique. https://www.economie.gouv.fr/entreprises/societe-mission

Besharov, M. L. (2014). The relational ecology of identification: how organizational identification emerges when individuals hold divergent values. *Academy of Management Journal*, 57(5), 1485–1512. https://doi.org/10.5465/amj.2011.0761

Besharov M. L., & Smith, W. K. (2014). Multiple institutional logics in organizations: explaining their varied nature and implications. *Academy of Management Review*, 39(3), 364–381. https://doi.org/10.5465/amr.2011.0431

Bivens, J., & Kandra, J. (2022, 4 October). CEO pay has skyrocketed 1,460% since 1978: CEOs were paid 399 times as much as a typical worker in 2021. Economic Policy Institute. https://www.epi.org/publication/ceo-pay-in-2021/

Bohinc, R., & Schwartz, J. (2021). Social enterprise law: a theoretical and comparative perspective. *Ohio State Business Law Journal*, 15(1), 1–28.

Borzaga, C., Galera, G., Franchini, B., Chiomento, S., Nogales, R., & Carini, C. (2020). *Social Enterprises and Their Ecosystems in Europe. Comparative Synthesis Report.* European Commission, Publications Office of the European Union. https://europa.eu/!Qq64ny

British Council, United Nations Economic and Social Commission for Asia and the Pacific, & Social Enterprise UK (2021). *The State of Social Enterprise in South East Asia.* https://www.britishcouncil.org/sites/default/files/the_state_of_social_enterprise_in_south_east_asia_0.pdf

Brown, W. (2019). *In the Ruins of Neoliberalism: The Rise of Antidemocratic Politics in the West.* New York: Columbia University Press. https://doi.org/10.7312/brow19384

Bugg-Levine, A. & Emerson, J. (2011). *Impact Investing: Transforming How We Make Money while Making a Difference.* Hoboken, NJ: Jossey-Bass.

Business Roundtable (2019). *Our Commitment.* https://opportunity.businessroundtable.org/ourcommitment/

Calic, G., & Mosakowski, E. (2016). Kicking off social entrepreneurship: how a sustainability orientation influences crowdfunding success. *Journal of Management Studies*, 53(5), 738–767. https://doi.org/10.1111/joms.12201

Canals, J. (2012). *Leadership Development in a Global World* (IESE Business Collection). London: Palgrave Macmillan UK. https://doi.org/10.1057/9781137283320

CDP, Climate Disclosure Standards Board, Global Reporting Initiative, International Integrated Reporting Council, and Sustainability Accounting Standards Board (2020a). *Statement of Intent to Work Together towards Comprehensive Corporate Reporting.* https://29kjwb3armds2g3gi4lq2sx1-wpengine.netdna-ssl.com/wp-content/uploads/Statement-of-Intent-to-Work-Together-Towards-Comprehensive-Corporate-Reporting.pdf

CDP, Climate Disclosure Standards Board, Global Reporting Initiative, International Integrated Reporting Council, and Sustainability Accounting Standards Board (2020b). *Reporting on Enterprise Value Illustrated with a Prototype Climate-related Financial Disclosure Standard.* https://29kjwb3armds2g3gi4lq2sx1-wpengine.netdna-ssl.com/wp-content/uploads/Reporting-on-enterprise-value_climate-prototype_Dec20.pdf

Chandler, D. (2014). Morals, markets, and values-based businesses. *Academy of Management Review*, 39(3), 396–406. https://doi.org/10.5465/amr.2013.0320

Château Terrisse, P. (2012). Le dispositif de gestion des organisations hybrides, régulateur de logiques institutionnelles hétérogènes? Le cas du capital-risque solidaire. *Management & Avenir*, 54(4), 145–167. https://doi.org/10.3917/mav.054.0145

Cobb, J. A., Wry, T., & Zhao, E. Y. (2016). Funding financial inclusion: institutional logics and the contextual contingency of funding for microfinance organizations. *Academy of Management Journal*, 59(6), 2103–2131. https://doi.org/10.5465/amj.2015.0715

Cooper, C., Graham, C., & Himick, D. (2016). Social impact bonds: the securitization of the homeless. *Accounting, Organizations and Society*, 55, 63–82. https://doi.org/10.1016/j.aos.2016.10.003

Cross, S. R. (2004). The community interest company: more confusion in the quest for limited liability. *Northern Ireland Legal Quarterly*, 55(3), 302. https://doi.org/10.53386/nilq.v55i3.775

Cyert, R. M., & March, J. G. (1963). *A Behavioral Theory of the Firm*. Hoboken, New Jersey: Prentice-Hall.

Dacin, M. T., Dacin, P. A., & Tracey, P. (2011). Social entrepreneurship: a critique and future directions. *Organization Science*, 22(5), 1203–1213. https://doi.org/10.1287/orsc.1100.0620

Daudigeos, T., & Valiorgue, B. (2018). On objects and material devices in the organisational responses to institutional pluralism: insights from economies of worth. *Management International*, 22(3), 121–128. https://doi.org/10.7202/1060898ar

Dayton, L. (2014, July 18). Australia scraps carbon tax: becomes first country in the world to turn back on tool to curtail emissions. *Science Insider*. https://www.science.org/content/article/australia-scraps-carbon-tax

Dean, T. J., & McMullen, J. S. (2007). Toward a theory of sustainable entrepreneurship: reducing environmental degradation through entrepreneurial action. *Journal of Business Venturing*, 22(1), 50–76. https://doi.org/10.1016/j.jbusvent.2005.09.003

Dees, J. G. (2001) *The Meaning of 'Social Entrepreneurship'.* Draft Paper. http://www.fuqua.duke.edu/centers/case/documents/dees_SE.pdf

Defourny, J., & Develtere, P. (2000). The social economy: the worldwide making of a third sector. In J. Defourny, P. Develtere, B. Fonteneau, S. Adam, & S. Anthony Stilitz (Eds), *Social Economy: North and South* (pp. 17–48). Leuven: Centre d'économie sociale de l'Université de Liège.

Defourny, J., & Nyssens, M. (2008). Social enterprise in Europe: recent trends and developments. *Social Enterprise Journal*, 4(3), 202–228. https://doi.org/10.1108/17508610810922703

Defourny, J., & Nyssens, M. (2010). Conceptions of social enterprise and social entrepreneurship in Europe and the United States: convergences and divergences. *Journal of Social Entrepreneurship*, 1(1), 32–53. https://doi.org/10.1080/19420670903442053

DiMaggio, P. J., & Powell, W. W. (1983). The iron cage revisited: institutional isomorphism and collective rationality in organizational fields. *American Sociological Review*, 48(2), 147–160. https://doi.org/10.2307/2095101

Dobbin, F., & Kalev, A. (2018). Why doesn't diversity training work? The challenge for industry and academia. *Anthropology Now*, 10(2), 48–55. https://doi.org/10.1080/19428200.2018.1493182

Dobbin, F., Schrage, D., & Kalev, A. (2015). Rage against the iron cage: the varied effects of bureaucratic personnel reforms on diversity. *American Sociological Review*, 80(5), 1014–1044. https://doi.org/10.1177/0003122415596416

Dodd, E. M. (1932). For whom are corporate managers trustees? *Harvard Law Review*, 45(7), 1145–1163.

Doherty, B., Haugh, H., & Lyon, F. (2014). Social enterprises as hybrid organizations: a review and research agenda. *International Journal of Management Reviews*, 16(4), 417–436. https://doi.org/10.1111/ijmr.12028

Ebrahim, A. (2019). *Measuring Social Change: Performance and Accountability in a Complex World*. Palo Alto: Stanford University Press. https://doi.org/10.1515/9781503609211

Edmiston, D., & Nicholls, A. (2017). Social Impact Bonds: the role of private capital in outcome-based commissioning. *Journal of Social Policy*, 47(1), 57–76. https://doi.org/10.1017/S0047279417000125

European Commission (2021a). *Questions and Answers: Corporate Sustainability Reporting Directive Proposal*. European Commission. https://ec.europa.eu/commission/presscorner/detail/en/qanda_21_1806

European Commission (2021b). *Proposal for a Directive of the European Parliament and of the Council amending Directive 2013/34/EU, Directive 2004/109/EC, Directive 2006/43/EC and Regulation (EU) No 537/2014, as regards corporate sustainability reporting*. European Commission. https://eur-lex.europa.eu/legal-content/EN/TXT/?uri=CELEX:52021PC0189

European Commission (2022). *Corporate Sustainability Reporting—EU Rules Require Large Companies to Publish Regular Reports on the Social and Environmental Impacts of Their Activities*. European Commission. https://ec.europa.eu/info/business-economy-euro/company-reporting-and-auditing/company-reporting/corporate-sustainability-reporting_en

Farhoud, M., Shah, S., Stenholm, P., Kibler, E., Renko, M., & Terjesen, S. (2021). Social enterprise crowdfunding in an acute crisis. *Journal of Business Venturing Insights*, 15, 1–6. https://doi.org/10.1016/j.jbvi.2020.e00211

Feldman, D. C. (1976). A contingency theory of socialization. *Administrative Science Quarterly*, 21(3), 433–452. https://doi.org/10.4324/9781315247533-11

Ferreras, I. (2017). *Firms as Political Entities: Saving Democracy through Economic Bicameralism*. Cambridge: Cambridge University Press. https://doi.org/10.1017/9781108235495

Ferreras, I., Battilana, J., & Méda, D. (2022). *Democratize Work: The Case for Reorganizing the Economy* (M. Richmond Mouillot, Trans.). Chicago: University of Chicago Press. https://doi.org/10.7208/chicago/9780226819631.001.0001

Fici, A. (2013). Cooperative identity and the law. *European Business Law Review*, 24(1), 37–64.

Fleming, L., & Sorenson, O. (2016). Financing by and for the masses: an introduction to the special issue on crowdfunding. *California Management Review*, 58(2), 5–19. https://doi.org/10.1525/cmr.2016.58.2.5

Flower, J. (2015). The International Integrated Reporting Council: a story of failure. *Critical Perspectives on Accounting*, 27, 1–17. https://doi.org/10.1016/j.cpa.2014.07.002

Fraser, A., Tan, S., Lagarde, M., & Mays, N. (2018). Narratives of promise, narratives of caution: a review of the literature on Social Impact Bonds. *Social Policy & Administration*, 52(1), 4–28. https://doi.org/10.1111/spol.12260

Freedom House (2022). *Freedom in the World 2022.* https://freedomhouse.org/sites/default/files/2022-02/FIW_2022_PDF_Booklet_Digital_Final_Web.pdf

Friedman, M. (1970, 13 September). The social responsibility of business is to increase its profits. *New York Times Magazine*, 122–126. https://www.nytimes.com/1970/09/13/archives/a-friedman-doctrine-the-social-responsibility-of-business-is-to.html

Galbraith, J. R. (1977). *Organization Design.* Boston: Addison-Wesley.

Gavetti, G., Levinthal, D., & Ocasio, W. (2007). Perspective—Neo-Carnegie: the Carnegie School's past, present, and reconstructing for the future. *Organization Science*, 18(3), 523–526. https://doi.org/10.1287/orsc.1070.0277

Gehman, J. & Grimes, M. (2017). Hidden badge of honor: how contextual distinctiveness affects category promotion among certified B corporations. *Academy of Management Journal*, 60(6), 2294–2320. https://doi.org/10.5465/amj.2015.0416

Global Impact Investing Network (2020). *Annual Impact Investor Survey 2020* (10th ed.). https://thegiin.org/assets/GIIN%20Annual%20Impact%20Investor%20Survey%202020.pdf

Global Reporting Initiative (2020). *Our Mission and History.* https://www.globalreporting.org/about-gri/mission-history/

Glynn, M. A. (2000). When cymbals become symbols: conflict over organizational identity within a symphony orchestra. *Organization Science*, 11(3), 285–298. https://doi.org/10.1287/orsc.11.3.285.12496

Gregorič, A., & Rapp, M. S. (2019). Board-level employee representation (BLER) and firms' responses to crisis. *Industrial Relations*, 58(3), 376–422. https://doi.org/10.1111/irel.12241

Grenier, C., & Bernardini-Perinciolo, J. (2015). Le manager hybride, acteur-passeur et acteur-clôture aux frontières institutionnelles. *Revue française de gestion*, 5, 125–138. https://doi.org/10.3166/rfg.250.125-138

GRI, & SASB (2021). *A Practical Guide to Sustainability Reporting Using GRI and SASB Standards.* https://www.sasb.org/knowledge-hub/practical-guide-to-sustainability-reporting-using-gri-and-sasb-standards/

Gulati, R. (2022). *Deep Purpose: The Heart and Soul of High-Performance Companies.* New York: HarperCollins.

Hahn, R., & Lülfs, R. (2014). Legitimizing negative aspects in GRI-oriented sustainability reporting: a qualitative analysis of corporate disclosure strategies. *Journal of Business Ethics*, 123, 401–420. https://doi.org/10.1007/s10551-013-1801-4

Hammerle, M., Best, R., & Crosby, P. (2021). Public acceptance of carbon taxes in Australia. *Energy Economics*, 101, 1–12. https://doi.org/10.1016/j.eneco.2021.105420

Hannam, P. (2014, 13 June). Fall in greenhouse gas emissions biggest in 24 years. *Sydney Morning Herald*. https://www.smh.com.au/environment/climate-change/fall-in-greenhouse-gas-emissions-biggest-in-24-years-20140613-zs7be.html

Henderson, R. (2020). *Reimagining Capitalism in a World on Fire*. New York: PublicAffairs.

Höchstädter, A. K., & Scheck, B. (2015). What's in a name: an analysis of impact investing understandings by academics and practitioners. *Journal of Business Ethics*, 132(2), 449–475. https://doi.org/10.1007/s10551-014-2327-0

Hsu, G. (2006). Jacks of all trades and masters of none: audiences' reactions to spanning genres in feature film production. *Administrative Science Quarterly*, 51(3), 420–450. https://doi.org/10.2189/asqu.51.3.420

Hsu, G., Koçak, Ö., & Hannan, M. T. (2009). Multiple category memberships in markets: an integrative theory and two empirical tests. *American Sociological Review*, 74(1), 150–169. https://doi.org/10.1177/000312240907400108

Hulgård, L., & Chodorkoff, L. (2019). *Social Enterprises and Their Ecosystems in Europe. Country Report: Denmark*. Publications Office of the European Union. https://ec.europa.eu/social/BlobServlet?docId=21200&langId=en

Ike, V. (2020). The impact of veto players on incremental and drastic policy making: Australia's carbon tax policy and its repeal. *Politics and Policy*, 48(2), 232–264. https://doi.org/10.1111/polp.12346

Integrated Reporting (2022, 1 August). IFRS Foundation completes consolidation with Value Reporting Foundation. Retrieved from: https://www.integratedreporting.org/news/ifrs-foundation-completes-consolidation-with-value-reporting-foundation/.

IPCC (2022). Climate change 2022: impacts, adaptation, and vulnerability. In H.-O. Pörtner, D. C. Roberts, M. Tignor, E. S. Poloczanska, K. Mintenbeck, A. Alegría, M. Craig, S. Langsdorf, S. Löschke, V. Möller, A. Okem, & B. Rama (Eds), *Contribution of Working Group II to the Sixth Assessment Report of the Intergovernmental Panel on Climate Change*. Cambridge: Cambridge University Press. https://www.ipcc.ch/report/sixth-assessment-report-working-group-ii/

Jensen, M. C., & Meckling, W. (1976). Theory of the firm: managerial behavior, agency costs and ownership structure. *Journal of Financial Economics*, 3, 305–360. https://doi.org/10.1016/0304-405X(76)90026-X

Jones, G. R. (1986). Socialization tactics, self-efficacy, and newcomers' adjustments to organizations. *Academy of Management Journal*, 29(2), 262–279. https://doi-org.ezp-prod1.hul.harvard.edu/10.2307/256188

Kalev, A., Dobbin, F., & Kelly, E. (2006). Best practices or best guesses? Assessing the efficacy of corporate affirmative action and diversity policies. *American Sociological Review*, 71(4), 589–617. https://doi.org/10.1177/000312240607100404

Kalleberg, A. L. (2011). *Good Jobs, Bad Jobs: The Rise of Polarized and Precarious Employment Systems in the United States, 1970s–2000s*. New York: Russell Sage Foundation.

Kallis, G., Kostakis, V., Lange, S., Muraca, B., Paulson, S., & Schmelzer, M. (2018). Research on degrowth. *Annual Review of Environment and Resources*, 43(1), 291–316. https://doi.org/10.1146/annurev-environ-102017-025941

Kaplan, S. (2019). *The 360° Corporation: From Stakeholder Trade-offs to Transformation.* Palo Alto: Stanford Business Books. https://doi.org/10.1515/9781503610439

Kelly, E. L., & Moen, P. (2020). *Overload: How Good Jobs Went Bad and What We Can Do about It.* Princeton: Princeton University Press. https://press.princeton.edu/books/hardcover/9780691179179/overload

Khurana, R. (2007). *From Higher Aims to Hired Hands: The Social Transformation of American Business Schools and the Unfulfilled Promise of Management as a Profession.* Princeton: Princeton University Press. https://doi.org/10.1515/9781400830862

Kim, E. H., Maug, E., & Schneider, C. (2018). Labor representation in governance as an insurance mechanism. *Review of Finance*, 22(4), 1251–1289. https://doi.org/10.1093/rof/rfy012

Lallemand-Stempak, N. (2017). Rethinking hybrids' challenges: the case of French mutual insurance companies. *M@n@gement*, 20(4), 336–367. https://doi.org/10.3917/mana.204.0336

Lawrence, P. R. & Lorsch, J. W. (1967). *Organization and Environment: Managing Differentiation and Integration.* Boston: Harvard University.

Lazonick, W., & O'Sullivan, M. (2000). Maximizing shareholder value: a new ideology for corporate governance. *Economy and Society*, 29(1), 13–35. https://doi.org/10.1080/030851400360541

Lee, M. (2014). Mission and markets? The viability of hybrid social ventures. *Academy of Management Proceedings*, 2014(1). https://doi.org/10.5465/AMBPP.2014.13958abstract

Lehner, O. M. (2013). Crowdfunding social ventures: a model and research agenda. *Venture Capital*, 15(4), 289–311. https://doi.org/10.1080/13691066.2013.782624

Levitsky, S., & Ziblatt, D. (2018). *How Democracies Die.* New York: Broadway Books.

Lockwood, M. (2018). Right-wing populism and the climate change agenda: exploring the linkages. *Environmental Politics*, 27(4), 712–732. https://doi.org/10.1080/09644016.2018.1458411

Mair, J. (2010). Social entrepreneurship: taking stock and looking ahead. In A. Fayolle & H. Matlay (Eds), *Handbook of Research on Social Entrepreneurship* (pp. 15–28). Cheltenham: Edward Elgar Publishing. https://doi.org/10.4337/9781849804684.00007

Mair, J., & Martí, I. (2006). Social entrepreneurship research: a source of explanation, prediction, and delight. *Journal of World Business*, 41(1), 36–44. https://doi.org/10.1016/j.jwb.2005.09.002

March, J. G., & Simon, H. A. (1958). *Organizations.* Hoboken, New Jersey: Wiley.

Marquis, C. (2020). *Better Business: How the B Corp Movement Is Remaking Capitalism.* New Haven: Yale University Press. https://doi.org/10.12987/9780300256154

McDonnell, B. H. (2016). Benefit corporations and public markets: first experiments and next steps. *Seattle University Law Review*, 40, 717–742.

McHugh, N., Sinclair, S., Roy, M., Huckfield, L., & Donaldson, C. (2013). Social Impact Bonds: a wolf in sheep's clothing? *Journal of Poverty and Social Justice*, 21(3), 247–257. https://doi.org/10.1332/204674313X13812372137921

Meyer, J. W., & Rowan, B. (1977). Institutionalized organizations: formal structure as myth and ceremony. *American Journal of Sociology*, 83(2), 340–363. https://doi.org/10.1086/226550

Milne, M. J., & Gray, R. (2012). W(h)ither ecology? The triple bottom line, the Global Reporting Initiative, and corporate sustainability reporting. *Journal of Business Ethics*, 118(1), 13–29. https://doi.org/10.1007/s10551-012-1543-8

Mintzberg, H. (1979). *The Structuring of Organizations: A Synthesis of the Research.* Hoboken, New Jersey: Prentice-Hall.

Monzón, J. L., & Chaves, R. (2017). *Recent Evolutions of the Social Economy in the European Union.* CES/CSS/12/2016/23406. European and Economic Social Committee. https://www.eesc.europa.eu/sites/default/files/files/qe-04-17-875-en-n.pdf

Moss, T. W., Renko, M., Block, E., & Meyskens, M. (2018). Funding the story of hybrid ventures: crowdfunder lending preferences and linguistic hybridity. *Journal of Business Venturing*, 33(5), 643–659. https://doi.org/10.1016/j.jbusvent.2017.12.004

Moulaert, F., & Ailenei, O. (2005). Social economy, third sector and solidarity relations: a conceptual synthesis from history to present. *Urban Studies*, 42(11), 2037–2053. https://doi.org/10.1080/00420980500279794

Munkholm, N. V. (2018). *Board-level Employee Representation in Europe: An Overview.* European Commission Directorate General for Employment, Social Affairs and Inclusion. https://eu.eventscloud.com/file_uploads/e0bd9a01e363e66c18f92cf50aa88485_Munkholm_Final_EN.pdf

Nason, R. S., Bacq, S., & Gras, D. (2018). A behavioral theory of social performance: social identity and stakeholder expectations. *Academy of Management Review*, 43(2), 259–283. https://doi.org/10.5465/amr.2015.0081

Nigri, G., Del Baldo, M., & Agulini, A. (2020). Governance and accountability models in Italian certified benefit corporations. *Corporate Social Responsibility and Environmental Management*, 27(5), 2368–2380. https://doi.org/10.1002/csr.1949

O'Gorman, M., & Jotzo, F. (2014). *Impact of the Carbon Price on Australia's Electricity Demand, Supply and Emissions.* CCEP Working Paper 1411.

OECD (2022). *Designing Legal Frameworks for Social Enterprises: Practical Guidance for Policy Makers.* Local Economic and Employment Development (LEED). OECD Publishing. https://www.oecd-ilibrary.org/sites/172b60b2-en/index.html?itemId=/content/publication/172b60b2-en

Pache, A.-C., & Santos, F. (2013). Inside the hybrid organization: selective coupling as a response to competing institutional logics. *Academy of Management Journal*, 56(4), 972–1001. https://doi.org/10.5465/amj.2011.0405

Parhankangas, A., & Renko, M. (2017). Linguistic style and crowdfunding success among social and commercial entrepreneurs. *Journal of Business Venturing*, 32(2), 215–236. https://doi.org/10.1016/j.jbusvent.2016.11.001

Park, C., Lee, J., & Wilding, M. (2017). Distorted policy transfer? South Korea's adaptation of UK social enterprise policy. *Policy Studies*, 38(1), 39–58. https://doi.org/10.1080/01442872.2016.1188904

Pfeffer, J. (2018). *Dying for a Paycheck: How Modern Management Harms Employee Health and Company Performance—and What We Can Do About It.* HarperBusiness.

Poldner, K., Shrivastava, P., & Branzei, O. (2017). Embodied multi-discursivity: an aesthetic process approach to sustainable entrepreneurship. *Business and Society*, 56(2), 214–252. https://doi.org/10.1177/0007650315576149

Reed, D. (2002). Corporate governance reforms in developing countries. *Journal of Business Ethics*, 37, 223–247. https://doi.org/10.1023/A:1015239924475

Reiser, D. B. (2011). Benefit corporations: a sustainable form of organization. *Wake Forest Law Review*, 46, 591–625.

Reiser, D. B. (2013). Regulating social enterprise. *UC Davis Business Law Journal*, 14, 231–246.

Reiser, D. B., & Dean, S. A. (2017). Evaluating the current menu of legal forms for social enterprise. In Reiser, D. B., & Dean, S. A. (Eds.). *Social Enterprise Law: Trust, Public Benefit, and Capital Markets* (pp. 52–76). Oxford: Oxford University Press. https://doi.org/10.1093/oso/9780190249786.003.0004

Renko, M., Moss, T. W., & Lloyd, A. (2019). Crowdfunding by non-profit and social ventures. In H. Landström, A. Parhankangas, & C. Mason (Eds), *Handbook of Research on Crowdfunding* (pp. 249–268). Cheltenham: Edward Elgar Publishing. https://doi.org/10.4337/9781788117210.00017.

Richardson, M., Agyeman-Togobo, K., & Catherall, R. (2020). *Global Social Enterprise: Social Enterprise and Job Creation in Sub-Saharan Africa.* British Council. Available at: https://www.britishcouncil.org/sites/default/files/social_enterprise_and_job_creation_in_sub-saharan_africa_final_singlepages.pdf.

Robson, A. (2014). Australia's carbon tax: an economic evaluation. *Economic Affairs*, 34(1), 35–45. https://doi.org/10.1111/ecaf.12061

Rogers, J. (2019, 29 April). The long and winding road to materiality. *Jean-Rogers.com.* Available at: https://www.jeanrogers.com/index.php/2019/04/29/the-long-and-winding-road-to-materiality/.

Ruef, M., & Patterson, K. (2009). Credit and classification: the impact of industry boundaries in nineteenth-century America. *Administrative Science Quarterly*, 54(3), 486–520. https://doi.org/10.2189/asqu.2009.54.3.486

Saks, A. M., & Ashforth, B. E. (1997). Organizational socialization: making sense of the past and present as a prologue for the future. *Journal of Vocational Behavior*, 51(2), 234–279. https://doi.org/10.1006/jvbe.1997.1614

Santos, F., Pache A.-C., & Birkholz, C. (2015). Making hybrids work. *California Management Review*, 57(3), 36–58. https://doi.org/10.1525/cmr.2015.57.3.36

Schaller, S., & Carius, A. (2019). *Convenient Truths: Mapping Climate Agendas of Right-wing Populist Parties in Europe.* Berlin: Adelphi Consult GmbH.

Schneider, D., & Harknett, K. (2019). Consequences of routine work-schedule instability for worker health and well-being. *American Sociological Review*, 84(1), 82–114. https://doi.org/10.1177/0003122418823184

Securities and Exchange Commission (1973, 20 December). *Accounting Series Release no. 150*. 5 Fed. Sec. L. Rep. (CCH) 172, 172. United States Securities and Exchange Commission.

Securities and Exchange Commission (2003, 28 April). *Reaffirming the Status of the FASB as a Designated Private-sector Standards Setter*. Policy Statement/Exchange Act Release Nos. 33-38221; 34-47743; IC-26028; FR-70. United States Securities and Exchange Commission. Available at: https://www.sec.gov/rules/policy/33-8221.htm

Seed Commons. (2021). *About Seed Commons*. Available at: https://seedcommons.org/about-seed-commons/

Selznick, P. (1949). *TVA and the Grass Roots: A Study in the Sociology of Formal Organization*. New York: Harper & Row.

Serafeim, G. (2022). *Purpose and Profit: How Business Can Lift Up the World*. Nashville: HarperCollins Leadership.

Simon, H. A. (1947). *Administrative Behavior*. New York: Macmillan.

Singh, A., Glen, J., Zammit, A., De-Hoyos, R., Singh, A., & Weisse, B. (2005). Shareholder value maximisation, stock market and new technology: should the US corporate model be the universal standard? *International Review of Applied Economics*, 19(4), 419–437. https://doi.org/10.1080/02692170500208533

Smith, C. N., & Rönnegard, D. (2014). Shareholder primacy, corporate social responsibility, and the role of business schools. *Journal of Business Ethics*, 134(3), 463–478. https://doi.org/10.1007/s10551-014-2427-x

Smith, W. K., & Besharov, M. L. (2019). Bowing before dual gods: how structured flexibility sustains organizational hybridity. *Administrative Science Quarterly*, 64(1), 1–44. https://doi.org/10.1177/0001839217750826

Smith, W. K., Gonin, M., & Besharov, M. L. (2013). Managing social-business tensions: a review and research agenda for social enterprise. *Business Ethics Quarterly*, 23(3), 407–442. https://doi.org/10.5840/beq201323327

Spiess-Knafl, W. & Scheck, B. (2019). *Social Enterprise Finance Market Analysis and Recommendations for Delivery Options*. European Commission, Directorate-General for Employment, Social Affairs and Inclusion. Available at: https://ec.europa.eu/social/BlobServlet?docId=22516&langId=en

Spreckley, F. (1981). *Social Audit: A Management Tool for Co-operative Working*. Sully: Beechwood College Limited.

Stiglitz, J. E. (2012). *The Price of Inequality: How Today's Divided Society Endangers Our Future*. New York: W.W. Norton & Company.

Stiglitz, J. E. (2021). The proper role of government in the market economy: the case of the post-COVID recovery. *Journal of Government and Economics*, 1(100004), 1–7. https://doi.org/10.1016/j.jge.2021.100004

Stout, L. A. (2012). *The Shareholder Value Myth: How Putting Shareholders First Harms Investors, Corporations, and the Public*. Oakland: Berrett-Koehler.

Stout, L. A. (2013). The toxic side effects of shareholder primacy. *University of Pennsylvania Law Review*, 161, 2003–2023.

Triponel, A., & Agapitova, N. (2017). *Legal Framework for Social Enterprise: Lessons from a Comparative Study of Italy, Malaysia, South Korea, United Kingdom, and United States.* World Bank. Available at: https://openknowledge.worldbank.org/handle/10986/26397.

UN News (2022, 21 March). UN chief warns against 'sleepwalking to climate catastrophe'. United Nations. Available at: https://news.un.org/en/story/2022/03/1114322.

Useem, J. (2020, 6 August). Beware of corporate promises: when firms issue statements of support for social causes, they don't always follow through. *The Atlantic.* Available at: https://www.theatlantic.com/ideas/archive/2020/08/companies-stand-solidarity-are-licensing-themselves-discriminate/614947/.

Value Reporting Framework. (2021). *IIRC and SASB Form the Value Reporting Foundation, Providing Comprehensive Suite of Tools to Assess, Manage and Communicate Value.* Available at: https://www.integratedreporting.org/news/iirc-and-sasb-form-the-value-reporting-foundation-providing-comprehensive-suite-of-tools-to-assess-manage-and-communicate-value/

Van Maanen, J., & Schein, E. H. (1979). Toward a theory of organizational socialization. *Research in Organizational Behavior*, 1, 209–264. Available at: https://core.ac.uk/download/pdf/4379594.pdf.

Warner, M. E. (2013). Private finance for public goods: Social Impact Bonds. *Journal of Economic Policy Reform*, 16(4), 303–319. https://doi.org/10.1080/17487870.2013.835727

Weber, M. (1946). *Essays in Sociology.* Oxford: Oxford University Press.

Wood, A. (2020). *Despotism on Demand: How Power Operates in the Flexible Workplace.* Ithaca: Cornell University Press. Available at: https://doi.org/10.7591/cornell/9781501748875.001.0001

World Economic Forum (2022). *Unlocking the Social Economy: Towards an Inclusive and Resilient Society.* Available at: https://www3.weforum.org/docs/WEF_Unlocking_the_Social_Economy_2022.pdf.

Wright, C., & Nyberg, D. (2017). An inconvenient truth: how organizations translate climate change into business as usual. *Academy of Management Journal*, 60(5), 1633–1661. https://doi.org/10.5465/amj.2015.0718

Wry, T., Chuah, K., & Useem, M. (2021). *Rigidity and Reversion: Why the Business Roundtable Faltered in the Face of COVID.* Wharton School Working Paper.

Zahn, R. (2015). German codetermination without nationalization, and British nationalization without codetermination: retelling the story. *Historical Studies in Industrial Relations*, 36, 1–27. https://doi.org/10.3828/hsir.2015.36.1

Zuckerman, E. W. (1999). The categorical imperative: securities analysts and the illegitimacy discount. *American Journal of Sociology*, 104(5), 1398–1438. https://doi.org/10.1086/210178

9
Empowering knowledge and training in higher education to leverage social economy action on societal challenges

Rocío Nogales-Muriel and Marthe Nyssens

Introduction

In the public debate in general, and in the scientific debate in particular, various umbrella concepts are used to cover those initiatives different from the for-profit private sector and the public sector—social economy, solidarity economy, social enterprise—which we will here refer to as the 'SE field'. Around the 2000s, social innovation also began to appear as a novel area of scientific inquiry, which can be considered as complementary to SE-related areas. The SE field is regaining momentum at the EU policy level, with the approval of a European Plan for the Social Economy in December 2021 (European Commission, 2021).

The purpose of this chapter is to discuss the role of research and training in higher education to leverage social economy action on societal challenges. How is research on these topics generated and circulated? Who and what are the main actors, sources of funding, and dynamics that support research and education in the SE field? And most importantly, how does this knowledge contribute to the strengthening of social economy ecosystems? The core of our contribution is to analyse how the various SE concepts and recent SE research developed within the various research networks as well as how higher education training initiatives can contribute to the public debate and the development of the SE ecosystem.

We first cast light on the various 'SE notions' and propose to analyse them as relevant analytical resources to enrich the scientific and the public debate. Rather than opposing these concepts to one another, we advocate for a research stance that considers each one of them as a particular 'spotlight' offering a specific analytical potential to shed light on the dynamics of the third sector (Defourny & Nyssens, 2017). We follow by briefly describing the landscape of SE research in the past decades and reflecting on the role of research networks to support SE ecosystems. The next section delves into formal training on SE. By looking at the consolidation paths and lessons learned from some pioneering training initiatives, some reflections emerge on the possible contributions that formal training programmes can

Rocío Nogales-Muriel and Marthe Nyssens, *Empowering knowledge and training in higher education to leverage social economy action on societal challenges*. In: *Social Economy Science*. Edited by: Gorgi Krlev, Dominika Wruk, Giulio Pasi, and Marika Bernhard, Oxford University Press. © Oxford University Press (2023). DOI: 10.1093/oso/9780192868343.003.0009

make to SE ecosystems and society in general. The final section gathers some policy recommendations based on the previous sections.

An increasing interest in third sector research, crystallized around different SE concepts

Since the 1970s, various approaches have shown the existence of a third sector—distinct from the for-profit private sector and the public sector—in our economy: what we call the 'SE field', covering social economy, solidarity economy, and social enterprise. Indeed, although each of these concepts is the subject of specific conceptual debates, they are largely interconnected. The level of acceptance of these approaches has been discussed in different circles. They followed different paths until several circumstances gathered them under similar radars for policy-makers, practitioners and, increasingly, researchers.

Monzón Campos (2016) addresses the question of the evolution of the social economy concept as an object of scientific research at the university level through tracing the genealogy of the term, from its initial appearance in 1830 up until the end of the nineteenth century—when it dies away—and to its subsequent 'revival' in the 1970s. This umbrella concept is still at the heart of the European debate, with the recent approval of the European Social Economy Action Plan. A growing trend of research on social enterprise is observed (Defourny & Nyssens, 2010; Alegre et al., 2017) and is characterized by efforts to set up a common research agenda (Doherty et al., 2014; Persaud & Bayon, 2019). Other initiatives aim to set up research agendas in connected areas, such as the solidarity economy (Laville, 2016) or social innovation (Moulaert & MacCallum, 2019). These concepts did not appear in a chronological way but have all their own history and roots and remain in usage over the years.

The social economy: values, status, and rules

Although there is no single definition of the social economy, it is almost always presented as encompassing two key aspects. On the one hand, the term is used to describe private, non-capitalist categories of organization, with special status and rules: cooperatives, associations, and mutuals—and, with increasing frequency, foundations. On the other hand, the social economy refers to the principles and values which are supposed to inspire certain modes of operation: independent management, aim of serving the organization's members or the community rather than maximizing profit (hence a low return on capital or/and a pre-distribution of surpluses to suppliers or workers and redistribution to customers, plus joint reserves that cannot be shared), member equality, and a democratic decision-making process. When the social economy was first officially recognized in France, it was defined as being composed of cooperatives, mutuals and those associations whose production activities make it possible to assimilate them to these previous types. So, at the time, only the associations that were managing 'infrastructures and related services' were included. Subsequently, however, many more associations were included in the social economy, and they became by far the largest component of the social economy in terms of jobs and number of organizations.

The European Commission (EC) began to show an interest in the social economy in the late 1980s. Prior to the 2000s, a unit was dedicated to the social economy within the Directorate General XXIII, that is, the Enterprise Policy, Trade, Tourism and Social Economy Directorate. Today, the privileged interlocutors of social economy actors within the EC remain DG Employment, Social Affairs and Inclusion (EMPL) and DG Internal Market, Industry, Entrepreneurship and SMEs (GROW), although other DGs and units also work on this theme. Since the end of the 1980s, European social economy conferences have been organized in various EU member states. Since the one held in Paris in 1989, about twenty major conferences on this subject have been held throughout the EU, with an opening to social enterprise during the most recent years. In December 2015, all member states agreed through the conclusions of the EU Council to promote the social economy as a key driver of economic and social development in Europe. This agreement was a crucial milestone as it recognized the unique role of social economy actors in attaining smart, sustainable, and inclusive growth; creating high-quality employment; and promoting social cohesion, social innovation, local and regional development, and environmental protection.[1] The European Social Economy Action Plan, launched in December 2021, aims to support social economy organizations and social enterprises in scaling up their activities and social impact, innovating, and creating jobs. The plan draws on the unique characteristics of social economy organizations to ensure that the green and digital transitions and strengthening communities and improving social resilience. The plan taps into the social economy's economic and job-creation potential, as well as its contribution to a fair and inclusive recovery and the green and digital transitions.

The solidarity economy: re-embedding economics in society

In very concise terms, the solidarity economy may be defined as referring to 'all economic activities subject to a will to act democratically, in which social relations of solidarity have priority over individual interest or material profit' (Laville, 2006: 253). More precisely, the solidarity economy is not defined in terms of legal status; what characterizes solidarity economy activities is rather their twofold—economic and political—dimension.

At the economic level, the solidarity economy stresses reciprocity and mutual commitment among the people who give birth to the initiative (what French authors refer to as the *'impulsion réciprocitaire'*). Activities are then consolidated through mixing different types of resources: the initial reciprocal resources (e.g. the giving

---

[1] https://data.consilium.europa.eu/doc/document/ST-15071-2015-INIT/en/pdf

of voluntary labour) are subsequently replaced by public contributions, linked to redistribution, and by market resources. Due to its insistence on a combination of various economic resources and principles, the solidarity economy approach invites resistance of the growing hegemony of approaches driven by sole market forces.

The political dimension of the solidarity economy, on the other hand, is expressed 'in the construction of public spaces that allow a debate among the stakeholders on the social demands and the purposes being pursued' (Laville, 2006: 253, our translation). Whether this takes the form of protest against or cooperation with the public authorities, the key aspect is that major societal challenges are taken up explicitly by revitalizing democratic debate from within. One major issue, therefore, lies in maintaining autonomous public spaces that are distinct from but complementary to the public spaces instituted and regulated by the public authorities.

On the basis of the complementarities between the 'social economy' and 'solidarity economy' approaches, and since both movements share common roots in the pioneering associationism of the nineteenth century, it appears logical that, more and more frequently, reference should be made to the 'social and solidarity economy' (SSE) and that both notions should be combined rather than opposed. Thus, since the early 2000s, various federations, support structures, educational programmes, and other consultative bodies have deliberately chosen to refer to the 'SSE' field. To name just a few examples, this is the case with the French State Secretariat for the Social and Solidarity Economy, which adopted the term in 2001; with the Regional Chambers of the Social and Solidarity Economy (CRESS—previously Regional Chambers of the Social Economy, or CRES); with the Inter-University Network for the Social and Solidarity Economy (RIUESS); and with the UN Inter-Agency Task Force on Social and Solidarity Economy (UNTFSSE).

Social enterprise

In Europe, the emergence and rise of the concept of social enterprise owes much to the success of social cooperatives, which appeared in Italy in 1991, and to the British government's policy of promoting social enterprise, implemented from 2002 onwards. The social enterprise approach and its analytical potential shed light on certain specific dynamics within social and solidarity economy organizations, as well as beyond the boundaries of the SSE field. The EC adopted such a perspective, to a large extent, with the launch of its 'Social Business Initiative', in October 2011; this initiative aimed at 'building an ecosystem to promote social enterprises at the heart of the social economy and social innovation' (EC, 2011). In the United States, the idea of social enterprise/entrepreneurship covers a wide variety of meanings, associated to different 'schools of thought'. Generally speaking, Anglo-Saxon approaches are divided around two focal points (Defourny & Nyssens, 2010): on the one hand, many insist on commercial activities that serve a social mission ('the earned income school'); on the other hand, others focus on the innovative nature of initiatives launched by multi-talented social entrepreneurs ('the social innovation school').

In Europe, the very first academic study of social enterprise covering several countries and comparing different types of social enterprise dates back to the late 1990s (Borzaga & Defourny, 2001); it was carried out by the EMES network.[2] The EMES approach derives from extensive dialogue among several disciplines (economics, sociology, political science, and management) as well as among the various national traditions and sensitivities present in the European Union. Moreover, guided by a project that was both theoretical and empirical, it preferred from the outset the identification of various indicators over a concise and elegant definition. These indicators have since 2010 been grouped in three subsets, referring respectively to the economic and entrepreneurial dimension, the social dimension, and the governance-related dimension of social enterprise. Particularly worth underlining is the fact that these indicators were never intended to represent a set of conditions that an organization should meet to qualify as a social enterprise; rather than constituting prescriptive criteria, they describe an 'ideal-typical' social enterprise in Weber's terms, that is, an abstract construction or an analytical tool, analogous to a compass, which helps to locate social enterprises ('stars') or groups of social enterprises ('constellations') relative to one another in the 'galaxy' of social enterprises.

However, the comparative analysis of social enterprise types or models still lacked strongly integrated theoretical foundations and, even more, empirical surveys that would enable researchers to statistically test typologies of social enterprise models. The International Comparative Social Enterprise Models (ICSEM) project (2013–2020), carried out within the EMES network, was designed with a view to bridging these gaps. It aimed to document the diversity of social enterprise models as a way (1) to overcome most problems related to the quest for a unifying and encompassing conceptualization of social enterprise; (2) to try to theoretically and empirically build an international typology of social enterprise models; and, consequently, (3) to pave the way for a better understanding of social enterprise dynamics and ecosystems. Some 230 research partners from 55 countries and all regions of the world were involved the ICSEM research community.

In a first, theoretical stage, four social enterprise models, generated by specific institutional trajectories, were identified: a social-business model, a social-cooperative model, an entrepreneurial nonprofit model and a para-public social enterprise model (Defourny & Nyssens, 2017). The existence of three of these four theoretical models (namely the social-business model, the social-cooperative model, and the entrepreneurial nonprofit model) was strongly supported by empirical evidence: indeed, these three models were found in thirty-nine of the forty-three countries covered by the ICSEM survey. Therefore, the collected data showed that, while social enterprises are influenced by institutional factors at the macro level, they

---

[2] This EU-funded research project was carried out from 1996 to 1999. It focused on 'the Emergence of Social Enterprise in Europe'—hence the acronym of the French title, 'EMES', which was subsequently retained by the research network that had carried out the project.

stem from all parts of the economy and can be related to different organizational backgrounds—namely, the nonprofit, the cooperative, and the business sectors—which exist in almost all countries (Defourny & Nyssens, 2021). The existence of the parastatal SE model is not confirmed by the identification of a distinct group of enterprises. However, one should not conclude too quickly that the public sector is absent from the field of social enterprise. In fact, it is found within some clearly identified groups, often involved as a partner in the creation of social enterprises—in particular social-integration enterprises. It is also possible that local researchers, considering a priori social enterprises as inherently private initiatives, did not consider public sector initiatives as potential social enterprises.

Social innovation

Historically, social innovation (see *inter alia* the pioneering work of Chambon et al., 1982) emerged as a specific field before the social economy and social enterprise concepts did. At EU political level, the report from the Bureau of European Policy Advisors (BEPA, 2010) constituted a major milestone in the reflection on social innovation. According to BEPA (2010), social innovations are new ideas (products, services, and models) that simultaneously meet social needs (more effectively than alternatives) and create new social relationships or collaborations. In other words, they are innovations that are not only good for society but also enhance society's capacity to act. The EC subsequently launched several initiatives on this subject: the Social Innovation Europe initiative, which aimed at the development of networks and the exchange of good practices; the publication of a *Guide to Social Innovation* (EC, 2013); and the financing of social innovation through structural funds and research programmes.

Although, within these initiatives, social innovation is far from being limited to the SE field, this type of enterprise is nonetheless highlighted as a central actor in social innovation. For example, the above-mentioned Social Business Initiative aims at 'creating a favorable climate for social enterprises, key stakeholders in the social economy and innovation'.[3] In the field of social enterprise, the 'social innovation' school of thought (Defourny & Nyssens, 2010) specifically puts the emphasis on the profile and behaviour of innovative social entrepreneurs.

The SSE is also increasingly explicitly associated with the dynamics of social innovation, which is a novelty (Bouchard & Levesque, 2017). Indeed, while the social economy has been innovative since the nineteenth century, both organizationally and institutionally and in terms of the purposes it serves, the adoption of social innovation as an unavoidable reference in this field is relatively recent (Klein et al., 2014; Lévesque 2007, 2013; Moulaert et al., 2013; Nogales-Muriel, 2023).

Analysing these debates, several authors (Laville, 2014; Nyssens, 2015; Bouchard & Levesque, 2017) propose to distinguish between a 'weak' and a 'strong' conception

---

[3] http://ec.europa.eu/internal_market/social_business/index_en.htm

of social innovation. In the weak conception of social innovation, market actors seem to define the landscape; social enterprises are characterized by the pursuit of measurable social impacts and the use of managerial methods. For some authors, the social dimension takes its place alongside financial return and risk without challenging the rules of the capitalist system. In this weak conception, the present wave of social entrepreneurship and social innovation might partly act as a process of hierarchization and selection of social challenges according to their amenability to being treated in an entrepreneurial and commercial mode as well as that of a public–private social finance scheme.

Adopting a strong conception of social innovation means not only recognizing that social innovation and SE initiatives produce social impacts by providing goods and services to meet unsatisfied needs, but also acknowledging their institutional dimension, that is, their role in the development and implementation of norms and regulations, both at the level of the organization and beyond. These norms and regulations shape the fundamental equilibrium within our societies, in particular the respective places of the market, the state, and civil society.

Facing these conceptual debates, different positions can be adopted. Some could argue that one concept, with a precise definition and clear boundaries, should emerge. Various tentative definitions have been put forward, but they have often increased the feeling of confusion among researchers, observers, or newcomers in the 'SE field'. Indeed, the lack of a shared understanding and definition of SE is today acknowledged by most researchers, and it even seems reasonable to speak of the 'impossibility of reaching a unified SE definition'. Therefore, there is a fine line between allowing room for diversity and complete fragmentation. This plurality in the body of knowledge reflects the inherent diversity of the SE field itself. This diversity makes academic systematization challenging but necessary. It calls for a more conscious and engaged epistemological stance on the part of researchers after years of research have opened the door to an improved understanding of increasingly complex dynamics and phenomena. Rather than choosing the best concept and the best definition, past and current research allows the development of strong analytical foundations to each of these concepts, allowing space for debate and providing analytical tools to shed light on the complex and multidimensional dynamics of the third sector.

The strong development of SE research: actors and funding

A plurality of actors for a variety of complementary research

A large array of institutional and individual agents are involved in different types of SE research as we show in Figure 9.1.

Universities (and associated centres) are usually involved in research that can be considered as fundamental. Their researchers are concerned with core questions that

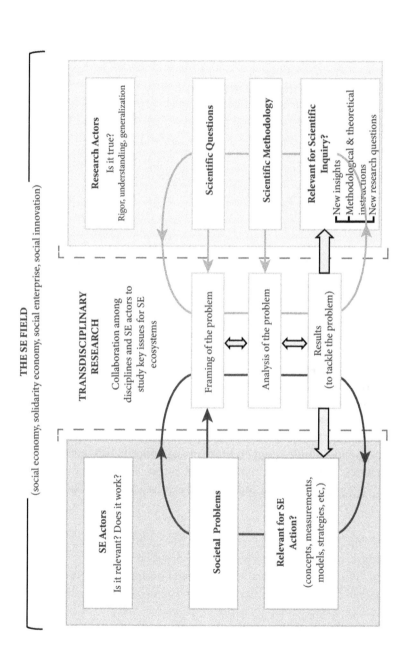

THE SE FIELD
(social economy, solidarity economy, social enterprise, social innovation)

Research Actors
Is it true?
Rigor, understanding, generalization

Scientific Questions

Scientific Methodology

Relevant for Scientific Inquiry?
New insights
Methodological & theoretical instructions
New research questions

TRANSDISCIPLINARY RESEARCH

Collaboration among disciplines and SE actors to study key issues for SE ecosystems

Framing of the problem

Analysis of the problem

Results
(to tackle the problem)

SE Actors
Is it relevant? Does it work?

Societal Problems

Relevant for SE Action?
(concepts, measurements, models, strategies, etc.)

Figure 9.1 Researching the SE field to leverage social economy action on societal challenges
Source: Based on Lang et al. (2012)

point to mechanisms at play within the various fields and models explaining these mechanisms. Indeed, they undertake research primarily to acquire new knowledge of the underlying foundation of phenomena and observable facts. They attempt to explain the mechanisms underlying the dynamics of the SE fields over time. They can also conduct more applied research involving undertaking original investigation in order to acquire new knowledge, although it is directed primarily towards a specific practical aim or objective. The focus is, in this case, on meeting societal demands through the practical use of research and problem solving.

Transdisciplinary research is increasingly considered as a useful approach for codifying weakly theorized concepts, such as has been the case with social economy and related notions mentioned here. There is a growing trend of this kind of research, not only directed at practical issues but also at building new knowledge jointly with social actors. It includes not only academics from different disciplines, but also practitioners and their knowledge and expertise from real-life practice. Knowledge is co-produced through the participation of both scientific and practice-based actors in the research process, promoting both scientific rigour and the practical usability of the results.

In this context, traditional top-down views about knowledge production are being complemented by new trends in horizontal knowledge construction between academia and practitioners' worlds.

The DNA of research led by universities is the systematization of work around central research questions and the mobilization of analytical frameworks to tackle said questions and the scrutiny and criticism that these processes and results may undergo on the part of the whole scientific community, including formal peer review processes at play within the system.

Knowledge mobilization (considered as 'collaborative entanglement': Bennet & Bennett, 2008) between different agents of the ecosystem has paved the way for formal trainings but also for other forms of activities, such as collaborative research, service-learning opportunities, joint problem solving, collective advocacy, resource-sharing structures, seminars and colloquia, and so on. Traditionally, four broad categories of community–campus collaboration can be identified (Nichols et al., 2013: 27):

1. relationships between individual faculty members and community organizations which are not supported by institutional structures;
2. community–campus collaboration supported by centres or institutes;
3. institutional structures organized within and across academic settings to systematically engage community partners in research; and
4. multi-institutional community-based research partnerships operating regionally, nationally, and internationally.

Professional consultants, ranging from specialized individuals to large consulting firms, constitute another category of agents conducting research. They have been increasingly involved in the SE field and the type of investigation they conduct is mostly of an applied nature. However, some of their interventions would not strictly qualify as research. A good guide to what does and what does not constitute a research and experimental development (R&D) activity determines whether the activity is novel, creative, uncertain in its outcome, systematic, and transferable and/or reproducible. These five elements distinguish between what is referred to as contract research or consultancy activity (OECD, 2015).

Think tanks are a specific label of consultancy organization connected to the idea of advocacy based on research. They tend to be active in various fields of SE activity (care, climate change, labour, and so on) and nurture valuable connections with agents from the SE ecosystem.

In the past decades university consulting has also been consolidated in the social sciences, creating an interesting hybrid model for research, with repercussions that are worth taking into account (Perkmann & Walsh, 2008). For instance, Jensen et al. (2010) show how, while consultancy organizations benefit from government-sponsored research through the faculty they hire as consultants, university research projects may indirectly benefit from the consultants' diverse experience and approaches to problem solving. It could be argued that, as Rentocchini et al. (2014) have pointed out, in the SE research field academic consulting is well aligned with academic research agendas, which increases the complementarity between academic research and academic consulting. This could also explain the difficulty to conceive of research on SE that would not have implications (even in the long term) for policy or practice. For instance, researchers are exposed to new contexts of research application and to areas of inquiry relevant for policy and practice 'that can spur insightful ideas for research' (Rentocchini et al., 2014: 72).

Well-established SE organizations, representative bodies, and advocacy organizations also provide valuable sources of data and analysis, albeit usually with sectorial and/or geographic limitations. Some groups of cooperatives, mutuals, and other legal forms have enough capacity to include R&D departments or at least to undertake research systematization efforts. A well-known illustration would be the case of Mondragon, whose industrial group supports research and training through the Mondragon University. Federations and international sectorial bodies also contribute relevant data, analysis, and networking opportunities. An example is provided by the International Cooperative Alliance (ICA), which through its Committee on Cooperative Research aims to bridge academic research and the cooperative world.

Regarding the nature of the issue to be studied, understanding what kind of research is being conducted by each type of actor and what kind of knowledge they produce will help us appreciate to which area of the SE ecosystem the research effort will eventually contribute. They constitute diverse and complementary sources of knowledge to be tapped but their goals, processes, and timeframes need to be clarified *ex ante*. Of course, frontiers between these different types or research are sometimes blurred and these categories proposed here should be considered as ideal-types in the Weberian sense.

In addition to the variety of actors, it is worth noting the wealth of knowledge on SE that exists at different geographic levels: indeed, research initiatives with national and local research scopes co-exist with international research. Research developed by international consortiums has the advantage of gathering researchers from different traditions and with various backgrounds, thus strengthening the comparative perspective, while research focused on particular geographical contexts offers insights on specific developmental trends and factors.

The role of research networks

Research networks and communities have always been a key channel to nurture knowledge. The objectives of sustained collaboration articulation through scientific networks are multiple:

1. To empower the SE research community through the integration of established and emerging researchers and scholars in likeminded and horizontal communities.
2. To ensure the access to a national (if available) and/or international network to early-career researchers, including PhD candidates. In particular, the doctoral path has been recognized as a particularly harsh, lonely, and competitive journey, referred to as a 'valley of sh!t'.[4] Joining the networks provides a unique opportunity to early-stage researchers to improve their academic and social skills while acting as nurturing environments for joint initiatives (seminars and conferences, training schools, publication outlets, opportunities for study visits and co-writing, and so on). Through these support networks future generations of researchers build a sense of community, find inspiring role models, and come up with coping strategies to support the endeavour of pursuing an academic career.
3. To connect different research traditions, epistemologies, and practices, creating a supportive environment for innovative research collaborations, in many cases incorporating multi-disciplinary approaches. Indeed, many SE researchers are aware of the fragmentation in SE research and they engage in networking as a way to overcome such fragmentation as well as isolation. While doing so, they are helping not only to connect scientific communities and traditions but ultimately to consolidate SE as a research field via research communities.
4. To contribute to research agendas at various geographical levels. Indeed, networks function as mutual learning environments where concrete research agendas may emerge from researchers themselves. They could also be channels to foster dialogue with practice and policy stakeholders (Barco Serrano and Nogales-Muriel, 2020). In this sense, it could be argued that international research projects constitute a unique way of networking and nurturing the

---

[4] Beth Patmore, lecture delivered at the 7th EMES International Training School building on the work of The Thesis Whisperer (https://thesiswhisperer.com).

potential of future collaborations, leading to more solid input into research agendas as well as into policy and practice domains.

5. Networks in general tend to play an institutionalization role within the SE field, which includes increasing the field-level receptivity of organizational practices that are less well known among citizens; they also help consolidate the legitimization of plural field-level audiences (Huybrecths & Haugh, 2018).

Without aiming to be exhaustive, Table 9.1 summarizes some of the main networks and communities devoted to SE research.

As we have seen, the emergence and strengthening of research communities both through stable networks at all geographic levels and through scientific events and working and affinity groups constitutes a driver for SE ecosystems. The latter gather semi-stable and informal communities of SE researchers and scholars with a lot of potential for impacting the field around them. The large number of emerging and consolidated networks included in Table 9.1 represents a positive trend for the field even if additional challenges may arise from such evolution.

Table 9.1 Examples of research networks and communities around SE

	International	World regions	National
Scientific networks	• Arnova • EMES International Research Network • ISTR, International Society for Third Sector Research	• ANSES, African Network of Social Entrepreneur-ship Scholars (South Africa) • RILESS, Network of Latin American Researchers on Social and Solidarity Economy (Latin America)	• CIRIEC national chapters in Austria, Belgium, France, Portugal, and Spain • FinSERN(Finland) • IRIS (Italy) • KASES, Korean Association for Social Economy Studies (Korea) • RIUESS, Réseau Inter-universitaire de l'Economie Sociale et Solidaire (France) • SERNOC, Social Entrepreneurship Research Network for the Nordic Countries (Baltic countries)
Networks linking scientific and practice communities	• CIRIEC International • ICA Network	• ICA regional research committees (e.g. the European Board for Cooperative Research)	
Around scientific conferences	• EGOS • ISIRC		

The relevance of research for SE ecosystems

The contribution of research to the recognition and visibility of SE

Some thirty years after the first wave of research on SE in Europe, research on social enterprise and the SSE has recently been recognized as crucial for recognition and visibility by agents of the ecosystem at all levels (EC, 2020a; EESC, 2016). Moreover, research has been explicitly identified in strategic policy documents, such as the Social Business Initiative (EC, 2011) or the recent Social Economy Plan (EC, 2021), and its relevance for practice and policy-making has been confirmed repeatedly.[5]

SE mappings carried out at the EU level contributed to increasing the visibility of the SE ecosystem in this region. The study entitled 'The Social Economy in the European Union' that has been carried out by the EESC since 2008, updated in 2012 and 2016, recognizes the importance of research and training (among other actions) to structure SE in Europe (EESC, 2016). In addition to the first mapping on social enterprise, which had been published in 2014, in January 2020 the EC issued a completely updated version of the Mapping of Social Enterprise Ecosystems, covering twenty-eight member states and seven neighbour countries. The Synthesis Report of this updated mapping explicitly states that, notwithstanding its limitations, 'research has contributed to enhancing the visibility of social enterprises and related phenomena as well as to raising the awareness of citizens and policy-makers about the relevance of such themes for society' (EC, 2020a: 95).

In the context of measuring the contribution of SE to the economies of the EU Member States, national statistical offices could become key allies of academic researchers and representative umbrella organizations in estimating not only the weight of SE but also their evolution over time and in predicting trends for such evolution. Statistical knowledge of SSE was non-existent in most countries in the early 1990s. The publication, in the final years of the twentieth century, of the first data from the Comparative Nonprofit Sector Project initiated by the Johns Hopkins University in the United States was the first milestone. Some countries have a satellite account focused on associations as in Belgium and Portugal, more recently. Despite their recent improvement, statistical data on the social economy often remain poor, scattered, and inconsistent, without temporal follow-up and mostly without international comparability. We are therefore still at the experimentation or prototype stage in this field and not at the stage of producing series under the responsibility of national statistical institutes, even if debates around SE satellites accounts and more generally regarding statistics on SE organizations remain important (Enjolras et al., 2018; UNRISD, 2019).

The contribution of research to the analysis of SE diversity

If we want to advance knowledge and to develop evidence-based policies able to foster the development of a sustainable SE ecosystem, there is a need to acknowledge

---

[5] In addition to the policy documents mentioned in the text, the Experts' Group on Social Entrepreneurship (GECES) issued a Call for Action in 2016 entitled 'Social Enterprises and the Social Economy Going Forward' that also mentioned this aspect. Available at: https://ec.europa.eu/docsroom/documents/24501/attachments/2/translations/en/renditions/native

the huge diversity of SE models in different industries which are key for the development of sustainable societies; and in order to achieve such a goal, it is imperative to link research efforts to the vast diversity of empirical developments in the SE field. This is not to say that field realities have not been carefully observed or analysed to date. On the contrary, a great deal of existing empirical work is extensively used in case study-based teaching. But case studies do not bring much evidence about the wide spectrum of SE families, categories, and models: they are precisely selected to illustrate a specific model or issue in a given context and they do not capture the extensive reality of the field.

There is, therefore, a challenge in achieving a full understanding of the diversity of SE models emerging across Europe and globally, their conditions of emergence and development, and their contribution to the general interest—all of which is necessary to improve our understanding of their contribution to society and of their potential to address major contemporary societal challenges. In this quest for knowledge that would be relevant at the academic, practice, and policy levels, four central questions emerge:

- What are the SE conceptions and models in which SE practices and policies are embedded in each national/regional context?
- What are the innovative contributions of SE conceptions and models in answering new social and ecological needs (health and social care, energy and transport, food supply chains, finance, circular economy, culture, and so on) that are central to the development of more sustainable societies?
- What institutional development (public policies, norms, legal forms, intersectoral partnerships, and so on) can support the scaling up and sustainability of these different SE models?
- What is the potential role of social enterprise in the development of norms and regulations at the level of the system, through their 'institutional work'?

An in-depth understanding of the different models of social enterprise makes it possible to identify future challenges that are anything but trivial. One can understand that the trajectories observed across Western and Eastern Europe can prove quite different, depending on whether the historical contexts have been marked by shrinking or resisting welfare states in the past four or five decades. This diversity is largely highlighted by the results of the ICSEM project and by the rich national contributions collected in two collective works dedicated respectively to Central and Eastern Europe (Defourny & Nyssens, 2021a) and to Western Europe (Defourny & Nyssens, 2021b).

The contribution of research to the policy debate

SE research has shown its capacity to documenting and explaining the functioning of viable collective alternatives aimed at tackling complex social challenges, thus opening the door to designing policy (and other) measures to support them. The urgency of these challenges together with the personal commitment of new generations of researchers to undertake fair and sustainable transitions may explain the intensively applied nature of some of the SE research conducted.

Identifying the synergies between policy-making and research implies both looking at what has been done in the past, and assessing present conditions for collaboration. Two decades of intensive exchanges and collaborations between SE representatives, public servants and policy-makers, and researchers and scholars has paved the way for focused action. If 'research is identified as a key factor for the institutionalization (recognition) of social enterprises, particularly in CEE countries' (EC, 2020a: 95), the focus should now be on learning how this policy–research interaction works (from a critical perspective) and developing actions to support it. The challenge is to better connect researchers and SE stakeholders to enhance shared understanding, with a view to influencing and informing in turn the development of new social, labour, and economic policies and practice interventions that have a proven capacity to foster SE development and thereby contribute to the development of sustainable societies.

The dichotomy between fundamental and applied research could be overcome by adopting the epistemological stance of 'transdisciplinary research' by redefining the contribution of different stakeholders as sources of knowledge. In such perspective, the various agents of SE ecosystems can consider research as an empowering asset, inherent in the ecosystem, sharing the goal of developing methods, tools, and processes to systematize and make that knowledge as available as possible. Notwithstanding power issues inherent in information creation and management, the familiarization of non-academic actors to processes that enhance and support the creation of knowledge about their ecosystem could contribute to rendering created sectorial borders less strict. In such a perspective, different actors belonging to the SE ecosystems could have a role in the production of knowledge strategies such as the incorporation of practice systematization, and documentation in social enterprises could be an example of this empowerment process towards transformative research.

Europe has a proven track record of putting research to the service of consolidation of the SE ecosystem.

Education and training on SE for the next generations

Developing specialized training on SE

As mentioned in the study 'Recent Evolutions of the Social Economy in the European Union' (EESC, 2016), creating a European Higher Education Area specializing in SE constitutes a current challenge that is worth addressing.

SE education and training have existed for a long time in countries with a long tradition of SE practice, and are rapidly developing in countries where the phenomenon is rather new (EC, 2020a). The array of forms that the education and training offer may take is large; it includes initial and continuing training, undergraduate and graduate courses and modules, master's and PhD programmes, MOOCs from Higher

Education Institutions (HEI) as well as training organized by federations of SE enterprises, think tanks, and international organizations, such as the ILO Academy. A promising format, with a long-standing tradition in some Latin American and Mediterranean countries, is the popular university. A recently revamped concept, popular universities provide lifelong learning opportunities across professional (and personal) stages of citizens' lives, without limitations imposed by formal access requirements. These institutions are locally rooted; they collaborate closely with local authorities and receive funding through local bodies, SE organizations, and low participant fees; they target adults but also specific social groups, such as youngsters and women; and they rely on the volunteer work of instructors and administrators (Stromquist & Lozano, 2018).

The low level of inclusion of SE in research agendas until the 2000s, combined with the high relevance of the topic to policy-makers and practitioners, prompted the development of a practice that has become a common trait of pioneering SE programmes developed within HEI before the 2000s: the close contact and steady collaboration with actors of the SE ecosystems. This is confirmed in most of the secondary data sources consulted and corroborated by the synthetic ad hoc survey of MA programs carried out in the context of this chapter in September 2020.

Some illustrations of these categories include: including practitioners as trainers into modules or lectures of training programmes; devoting volunteer or pro-bono time in social enterprises; and having students complete in-placement assignments, final projects, or theses within the organizations and, more recently, through service learning programmes—a method which combines previous features. This is how programmes such as Euricse's Master's Degree in Management of Social Enterprises (Master GIS)[6] or Harvard Business School's Social Enterprise Initiative (SEI)[7] began, respectively in 1995 in Italy and in 1993 in the US.

This close connection with practitioners, which, as mentioned above, was a common traits of pioneering SE programmes, remains today an important feature of most training programmes.

Learning from experience: pioneering MA programmes in Europe

Master (MA) programmes on SE organized by HEI across Europe have been developing for the past two decades mainly led by economics and management faculties and participation of political studies and sociology. They slowly constitute an interesting addition for graduating students seeking a different career path. They also attract professionals already involved in the SE ecosystem. These programmes offer also a promising avenue to encourage early-career researchers to stay in academia as instructors and researchers.

---

[6] https://www.euricse.eu/training/master-programme-in-management-of-social-enterprises/
[7] https://www.hbs.edu/socialenterprise

Our exploratory and limited overview based on secondary data review and an ad hoc exploratory survey points to the emergence of critical tensions after decades of experience and to the need to reach trade-offs to balance different interests. For instance, some MA programmes thrive on attracting international audiences, adopting a comparative perspective and teaching some courses in English, while facing the rootedness of SE practice and experience. While some programmes may attract internal support from their departments and institutions, this support may change over time or become irrelevant if not enough students are attracted.

Given the institutional relevance of MA programmes and the positive impact they have on the potential of motivated citizens (who, after completing such programmes, become active in the field, contributing to the development of SE ecosystems), we conducted an exploratory exercise based on a limited and exploratory sample of fourteen official master's programs in Europe. Such survey was useful to identify some relevant issues; however, we must emphasize the non-representative nature of the selected sample. Moreover, it has to be stressed that the distribution of MA programmes on SE across Europe is highly uneven, with some countries offering dozens of them (France has more than forty) and others having only a very limited offer in this regard (Spain, for example, has only two official university master's programmes on SE). Based on a sample of fourteen programmes across Europe, we advance some reflections upon some characteristics that appear promising in terms of contributing to the future of SE (see Appendix for a listing of the programmes included in this chapter).

Initial sparks, key initiators, evolution, and sustainability over time

The historical evolution of the fourteen programmes reviewed point to a complex institutional journey, which required, for the programmes to be established, the mobilization of a critical mass of influential individuals and collectives, both within the university and outside it. Opportunity windows linked to internal and external factors may emerge when agendas to stimulate university-level education on SE studies converge. In some cases, the opportunity window emerged with the possibility to develop a specialization track within a broader entrepreneurship programme. A decisive factor is usually the participation of a high-ranked university administrator in an event linked to the SE field (conference, seminar, workshop, and so on), which led him to realize that SE was not just a 'fashionable topic'. This example bears testimony to the high impact potential of awareness-raising and networking initiatives in countries with emerging SE communities. Almost all of the cases reviewed began with the alignment of a critical vision, embedded in a first-hand experience, either with the local SE reality or with international research networks supporting this initial spark.

The story of these official programmes confirms the existence of an 'intrapreneurial process' involving the developmental stages described by Austin and Rangan (2019): giving birth, starting an experiment, gaining acceptability, being embraced, and achieving irreversibility. All the stages are characterized by a collective dimension worth highlighting, usually under the leadership of a driven leader or small group of leaders. The leader(s) of the initiative tend(s) to be either an individual with a well-established position in the HEI (although there are exceptions) and s/he draws on the field network developed over years of research, or a group of promoters. In the latter case, the core group of initiators usually brings together academics and practitioners (including umbrella organization representatives) who have identified the need for such a training programme in their immediate context. As already mentioned, interaction with and support from practitioners is a common trait among the surveyed programmes.

Analysis of the development path of the reviewed programmes shows that the initial reluctance of departments and colleagues can be gradually overcome by demonstrating the quality of the programme, by securing the commitment of relevant faculty members, by recruiting a growing number of students, and by documenting connections with the ecosystem, including for the recruitment of students. The support from the field in the form of funding for chairs or jointly organized events is central for building the case for a teaching programme in this area.

As for threats and opportunities for the viability of the programmes, several elements are mentioned. Regarding threats, the issue of decreasing enrolment in some MA programmes poses a key issue for their sustainability. Poor communication and lack of promotional skills of the staff involved were identified as an internal weakness to be tackled as well. Some constructive insights proposed to address the shortage of students enrolled include, first, the possibility of accepting students with no first degree on the topic but who have extensive SE experience through the Validation of Professional Experience (VAE) programme. Second, the option of combining initial and continuing education (for recent bachelor's graduates and professionals) is proposed as a strength, as it allows the emergence of synergies between young and older people. However, despite the real-life context that the mixing of initial and continuing education offers, it is rarely done and it usually remains contested within universities. Third, increasing the marketing and communication capacity of the staff is considered as a positive strategy to attract new students. Lastly, the promotion of other learning formats, more accessible and with a horizontal governance, such as popular universities, was also mentioned. A trend also highlighted by respondents was the fact that traditional business schools at the international level have incorporated in their programmes courses and seminars on SE and sustainability, thus expanding the number of options available to students interested in SE topics.

Programme content

Most programmes reviewed see themselves as not being limited to a single discipline—or, in other words, as being interdisciplinary. In addition to the institutional barriers to the setting up of this kind of programme, the combination of disciplines included in the course curriculum requires to cut across disciplines and departments. Combining courses on economics, ethics, management, sociology, and political science, for example, demands flexibility on the part of trainers so as to identify and develop common teaching areas around SE. Given the specialized nature of these programmes, there seems to be an underlining assumption that a trade-off between the 'core business' (SE) and openness to related themes (sustainability, social impact, social innovation, co-production, and partnerships, philanthropy, CSR, and so on) has to be stricken.

For a programme to be innovative in the European landscape of MA programmes, the connection to research is increasingly crucial. In this sense, a willingness, on the part of the core teaching staff, to translate research expertise into dedicated teaching has to be present from the beginning.

The understanding, among the initiators and trainers of these courses, is that people who enrol in these programmes have a certain awareness level of the challenges facing our societies and of some of the strategies that are emerging to build collective responses to such challenges. Through these programmes, they usually go through a personal journey that includes a reflective and a prospective dimension: they are invited to reflect and act upon the current economic system, its dead-ends, current experiments, and the conditions for a change of scale. This personal journey is supported through an emphasis on group work (in some cases including for the final thesis, which can be completed as a consultancy-based group exercise) combined with individual work. Case studies and study visits are also included in most programmes, allowing for a collective analysis of key challenges and the formulation of proposals for innovative solutions to respond to identified needs. Learning-by-doing methodologies are included as a way of facilitating the assimilation of theoretical contents and the application of hand-in, practical experience, aimed at finding solutions infused by collective intelligence.

Career development prospects

A major advantage of programmes of this kind is that they nurture direct contacts and exchanges with SE agents from the beginning. Creating one's own network through mandatory internships, completing consultancy-type projects based on learn-by-doing methods and sometimes even acquiring hands-on experience in launching social enterprises through incubation programmes constitute unique eye-opening opportunities for the students. This is enriching not only in pedagogical terms but also, more pragmatically, in professional career terms. Students usually graduate from the programme with a thorough preparation to cover managerial positions in the SE ecosystem within SE federations and representative bodies and public and private programmes supporting SE; to collaborate with various agents as external consultants; and/or to launch new social enterprises. A pressing external challenge, however, has to do with the level of wages in SE organizations, and with the fact that only recently has SE begun to be considered as something else than a reduced niche.

International dimension

The participation of an international student body is considered a plus for all the programmes, although some hindering factors have been identified (part-time schedule for those who have limited financial means and cannot work in the host country; lack of funding; visa problems; and so on). Several attempts at creating cross-country master's exist, but their concrete implementation generally appears complex, due mostly to administrative reasons. Several strategies have been developed in response to this limitation: organizing a programme among several HEIs from the same country with an international dimension (e.g. Belgium); completing a double degree among countries (e.g. the University of Valencia allows a combination with certification from the University of Bologna, and vice versa, while others have double and triple certifications with universities in other countries); organizing in-depth hands-on immersion programmes in other countries, with different SE ecosystems (for example, the Danish Master in Social Enterprise Management organizes a study trip to the UK). A promising strategy was developed in Tallinn University through the Estonian 'e-residency system', which offers international participants in the SEMA the possibility to continue using the advanced digital environment available during their training even after completing the degree and returning to their home countries.

The issue of language is of paramount importance for this kind of training; it is also a difficult balance to strike. On the one hand, teaching in English allows for students to have a wider offer in terms of materials and even job placement and mobility globally. However, on the other hand, teaching in local languages enables closer connections with the local SE ecosystem, thus strengthening the impact of the programmes in their own context. A compromise can be found by teaching specific courses in English or encouraging students to participate in international exchanges, ideally organized by the programme itself (seminars, study visits, international examples, and so on).

The contribution of MA programmes to SE ecosystems

After decades of experience, the networking power of these programmes is not to be underestimated. Indeed, newcomers to the SE field through these programmes are integrated into international, national, and local networks that connect social enterprises, the institutions that support them, current students, alumni (many of whom occupy prominent positions within the social economy), and academic researchers. Ultimately, these programs are realizing what a virtuous circle supporting an engaged community around a specific training like this could be.

More specifically, one can distinguish three kinds of contribution that training programmes like the ones reviewed here make to SE ecosystems and their agents: field-related contributions, academia-related contributions, and contributions to the overall recognition of SE ecosystems.

Regarding field-related contributions, MA programmes have proven to enhance the competences of graduates as future SE professionals while allowing social enterprises to improve their self-reflectivity skills. Indeed, knowledge gaps have been recognized as one of the motivations behind the launching of SE training initiatives across Europe (EC, 2020a). Most MA programmes encourage a new entrepreneurial approach to social transformation that overcomes the divide between business competencies, on the one hand, and social competencies, on the other hand, and which focuses on essentially hybrid-model organizations, demanding new skills to succeed. Let us note that the role played by focused assignments and in-place internships that strengthen some of the entrepreneurial functions of the organization while simultaneously providing real-life learning settings to students.

The second way in which the training programmes can consolidate SE ecosystems relates to the possibilities for academic careers they open, through providing positions within the academia to early-career researchers willing to follow a professional path that combines teaching, research, and testing of theoretical findings on the ground.

The last—and possibly most elusive—area of contribution is related to the gaining of in-depth knowledge and recognition of the SE field as a relevant area of academic activity, due to its close relation to the sustainability of societies. SE training programmes point in many cases to questions lying at the core of the profound questioning that HEIs are undergoing in our societies. HEIs indeed became 'crystallized' as institutions with a specific notion of progress at a specific historical moment and with strong ties to their (local) communities, but they are now facing a society fraught with seemingly contradictory notions—globalization versus decarbonization; hyper-connectivity versus social isolation; and so on—or with emerging phenomena (such as the 'working poor') that question their very essence and contribution to societies. In this changing context, it is worth emphasizing the role of power internally and the resistance to change of institutions like universities. Indeed, some academic literature and policy documents dealing with the role of HEIs in studying, teaching, and sparking social transformation tend to overlook crucial issues of power within HEIs' wider institutional settings. The issue of what benefits HEIs may generate from interactions with non-academic stakeholders needs to be taken into account when recommending ways to support SE (Benneworth & Cunha, 2015).

Main lesson for the future: empowering knowledge as a lever for SE ecosystems

The role of HEIs—and particularly of universities—in our societies is currently undergoing a profound transformation (Santos, 2017; Vogt & Weber, 2020). As knowledge-based institutions, HEIs seem to be ideally placed in a context where information and knowledge (and their management) constitute the central asset for societies (Benneworth & Cunha, 2015). HEIs, *qua* centres of knowledge, expertise, and learning, represent a wealth of possibilities for the development of territories and populations. However, traditional strategies for supporting the potential of HEIs to contribute to innovation 'do not maximize the social, environmental and economic impact of university research that is not aimed at commercial potential' (Nichols et al., 2013: 27). Recent proposals to help societies harness the full potential of HEIs include the application of the integrative framework of 'anchor models' or 'whole-institution approach' to this kind of institution (McNeill & Boorman, 2020; Mehling & Kolleck, 2019). As large organizations rooted in a given place, with a purpose tightly connected to that place and requiring a long-term commitment to it, HEIs are 'anchor institutions' that could play a crucial role in 'anchor collaboratives' (McNeill & Boorman, 2020). In this context, the infrastructure, relationships, and operational priorities of HEIs require, therefore, a long-term commitment to that place (Smallbone et al., 2015). As such, HEIs are called to play a unique role in the alignment of collective resources, the facilitation of knowledge, and the empowerment of the next generations of citizens. Through locally based social innovation, HEIs could contribute to tackling global challenges through diverse and locally rooted responses—including SE.

Climate change is most likely the most important challenge, directly affecting everything else; consequently, the 'regional transition paths towards sustainability' (RTPS) approach provides an interesting approach when applied to HEIs. However, HEIs' impact is dependent both on highly engaged 'frontrunners', holding key positions within the institutions, who support change and are able to engage wider university management leadership (Radinger-Peer & Pflitsch, 2017). An interesting question for future research emerges: what are the consequences of combining the anchor model and the RTPS approach in relation to HEIs? The development of a transdisciplinary research type is certainly a privileged way to foster the HEI contribution to the development of sustainable ecosystems.

From a SE ecosystem perspective, the key question of connecting what we *already* know about SE and how can knowledge be developed within SE ecosystems remains. In this perspective, we can formulate some concrete recommendations focused on supporting research activity and training to foster the SE ecosystem.

Regarding research, SE should consolidate as an academic field in itself, drawing from various disciplines and allowing for critical thinking and complementary epistemologies to emerge. The lack of scientific legitimacy of SE studies within academic institutions has resulted in the voices of SE scholars still remaining poorly heard in mainstream research settings such as scientific committees and private and public research funding agencies. In particular, there is an urgent need to empower the next generation of SE researchers. This new breed of scholars shows traits of 'engaged scholarship' (Campbell & Lassiter, 2010) and their lack of legitimacy are making their survival difficult, thus endangering an important part of the SE ecosystem.

Unfortunately, the presence of SE or even hybrid organizational models in research agendas remains insufficient. Therefore, reinforcing the presence of SE-related topics across EU and nationally funded research would contribute to increased fundamental knowledge of SE, improved evidence-based policy supporting SE, and, ultimately, strengthen the consolidation of SE as an academic field with vibrant research communities.

However, not only is an increase in the amount of research conducted required but a new 'outside-the-box' transdisciplinary research is also needed to address current societal, economic, and environmental challenges. Encouraging and funding the setup of new transdisciplinary research using novel methods and combining SE ecosystem agents is encouraged. Likewise, stimulating the creation of stakeholder platforms that enable the access and participation of communities in research processes would add to this innovation. In this context, TIESS (Innovative Territories in Social and Solidarity Economy; in French 'Territoires innovants en économie sociale et solidaire'), in Québec, Canada, provides a unique and interesting example. Conceived as a social economy transfer organization, TIESS fosters co-construction of knowledge by practitioners and researchers, mainly through research partnerships. The funding for this connection between stakeholders and university researchers comes primarily from public authorities, mainly the Canadian Science Policy Centre.[8]

Despite R&D's potentially significant benefit to the public good and contribution to innovation initiatives in general, it is undergoing intensive transformation due to globalization processes and a variety of funding and performance arrangements. R&D activity requires long-term, patient financing. In this context, in addition to sustaining public budgets for SE research, conducting a thorough study on the sources of finance for SE research, their evolution, and future trends, would unleash the power of varied funding sources that could support SE ecosystems. For instance, when it comes to philanthropic support, the example of the Research Forum of the European Foundation Centre (EFC) or the work conducted by the Expert Group on 'Foundations, Venture Philanthropy and Social Investments' of the EC DG for Research and Innovation could be used as relevant examples.

Regarding training, several ideas could be tackled within formal training environments (mostly HEIs) to support the development of SE ecosystems.

Mainstreaming strategies for including SE topics in traditional curricula could include the following ideas: first, to reduce the cognitive gap of trainers regarding SE in general in order to overcome their resistance to the sector; second, to widen the scope of traditional economics and management courses integrating alternative organizational models; third, to incorporate institutional pluralism in basic bachelor's courses across disciplines; fourth, to fine-tune MAs focused on SE and increase support to render them visible; fifth, to close the gap between the academic

[8] For more information on TIESS, visit https://tiess.ca/qui-sommes-nous/le-tiess-en-bref/

and entrepreneurial world in order to allow trainers to base their courses on cases from the real economy, including social enterprises; sixth, to enable other managerial voices to discuss their skills sought in the real economy; and, lastly, to promote pedagogical methodologies based on the potential of collective learning and action (Dekimpe, 2020).

Capacity-building both of researchers and of communities is fundamental (Franco & Tracey, 2019). To increase the potential of knowledge, it requires effective mechanisms or strategies to support knowledge mobilization (or learning). This may take the form of knowledge brokers and knowledge translators that account for different sets of cultures, rhythms, aims, and dynamics at play. These knowledge brokers are intermediary (as organization or person), aiming to develop relationships and networks with, among, and between producers and users of knowledge by providing linkages, knowledge sources, and in some cases knowledge itself. These opportunities for learning across professional, disciplinary, and organizational borders have to be institutionally supported if they are to set the stage for social innovation (Nichols et al., 2013; Franco & Tracey, 2019).

Research has been recognized as a lever for the recovery of Europe from COVID-19: 'Our response to the Covid-19 crisis can either amplify or mitigate the deeper and longer-term crises that our planet is facing. The fundamental systemic change towards sustainability needs to emerge from science-informed design' (EC, 2020b: 3). This must include research on SE as a way not only to support the initiatives that have emerged from citizens to respond to emergencies but also to reframe the way in which cross-sector collaboration occurs in post-disaster contexts. A concluding crucial question for research remains whether (and how) collaboration between HEIs and communities leads to social change and social innovation within territorial systems.

Appendix: Summary information of the MA programmes surveyed

Table 9.2 contains information on the fourteen MA programs included in this exploratory study. Some of them, however, were no longer offered by the time this publication was printed. The URLs and information provided were gathered during the desk review and expert interview process.

Table 9.2 Programmes included in the study

Full name (and acronym)	HEI	Country	Year of launch	URL
MA in Social Economy	Catholic University of Louvain (FOPES) and University of Liege (HEC)	Belgium	2019	https://uclouvain.be/prog-2020-ecso2mc http://www.hec.uliege.be/fr/masters/master-specialisation-en-economie-sociale
MA in Management of Social and Sustainable Enterprises (MESD)	Centre for Social Economy, HEC-University of Liege	Belgium	2011	http://www.hec.uliege.be/index.php/en/masters/master-in-management/management-of-socialy-responsible-sustainable-enterprises
MA in Social Enterprise Management (SEM)	Roskilde University	Denmark	2013	https://ruc.dk/en/master/social-entrepreneurship-and-management-int
Social Entrepreneurship MA study program (SEMA)	Tallinn University	Estonia	2018	https://sema.tlu.ee
MA 2 Human Resource Management, Social and Solidarity Economy track (Master 2 GRH ESS)	University of Aix-Marseille	France	2001	https://formations.univ-amu.fr/ME5BGH-PRBGH5AD.html
MA on Co-operative and Social Enterprise	University College Cork	Ireland	2005	https://www.ucc.ie/en/ckl10
MA in Management of Social Enterprises	University of Trento/Euricse	Italy	1995	www.mastergis.eu
MA in Management for Social Economy	Univ. Bologna/AICCON	Italy	2002 (1997)	https://corsi.unibo.it/2cycle/ManagementSocialEconomy
MA in Economics of Cooperative Firms (MUEC)	Univ Bologna/AICCON/Cooperative umbrella organizations			https://www.aiccon.it/en/formazione/master-universitario-economia-della-cooperazione/

Programme	University	Country	Year	Link
MA in Social Work and Social Economy (SOWOSEC)	Babeş-Bolyai University in Cluj-Napoca	Romania	2009	https://www.ubbcluj.ro/en/programe_academice/masterat/
MA in the Social Economy (Cooperatives and Nonprofit Organizations)	University of Valencia	Spain	2009	https://www.uv.es/uvweb/universidad/es/estudios-postgrado/masteres-oficiales/oferta-masteres-oficiales/master-universitario-economia-social-cooperativas-entidades-no-lucrativas-1285848941532/Titulacio.html?id=1285850876704
MSc Charity Resource Management MSc Charity Resource Management MBA (Co-operative Leadership and Social Entrepreneurship)	Sheffield Hallam University	UK	2009 (*discontinued)	• https://www.shu.ac.uk/courses/business-and-management/pgcert-cooperative-leadership-and-social-entrepreneurship/part-time/2020 • Not available • https://www.shu.ac.uk/courses/business-and-management/pgcert-cooperative-leadership-and-social-entrepreneurship/part-time/2020

Acknowledgements

The authors would like to thank the initiators and coordinators of the university master's programmes surveyed for their precious time and information. We would like to thank in particular Alessandro Caviola and Paolo Fontana (Italy), Benjamin Huybrechts (Belgium), Lars Hulgård and Luise Li Langergaard (CSE-RUC), Giorgia Perra (Italy), Francesca Petrella (France), Carol Power (Ireland), Adina Rebeleanu (Romania), Rory Ridley-Duff (United Kingdom), and Audrone Urmanaviciene and Zsolt Bugarszki (Estonia). In addition, we would like to thank Sophie Adam, and Sarah Waring for her language editing support. Our appreciation also goes to Marie Bouchard for her insightful comments on the manuscript.

References

Alegre, I., Kislenko, S., & Berbegal-Mirabent, J. (2017). Organized chaos: mapping the definitions of social entrepreneurship. *Journal of Social Entrepreneurship*, 8(2), 248–264.

Austin, J., & Rangan, V. K. (2019). Reflections on 25 years of building social enterprise education. *Social Enterprise Journal*, 15(1), 2–21.

Barco Serrano, S., & Nogales Muriel, R. (2020). Social enterprise research from an international perspective: key agents, challenges and opportunities ahead. *Ibero-American Journal of Solidarity Economy and Socio-ecologic Innovation, RIESISE*, 3, December 2020, 7-16.

Bennet, A., & Bennet, D. (2008). *Knowledge Mobilization in the Social Sciences and Humanities: Moving from Research to Action*. Frost, WV: MQI Press.

Benneworth, P., & Cunha, J. (2015). Universities' contributions to social innovation: reflections in theory & practice. *European Journal of Innovation Management*, 18(4), 508–527.

BEPA (Bureau of European Policy Advisers) (2010). *Empowering People, Driving Change: Social Innovation in the European Union*. Luxembourg: European Commission. Available at https://ec.europa.eu/migrant-integration/librarydoc/empowering-people-driving-change-social-innovation-in-the-european-union

Borzaga, C., & Defourny, J. (2001). *The Emergence of Social Enterprise*. London and New York: Routledge.

Bouchard, M. J. & Lévesque, B. (2017). Les innovations sociales et l'économie sociale: nouveaux enjeux de transformation sociale. In J. Defourny & M. Nyssens, *Économie sociale et solidaire. Socio-économie du 3e secteur* (pp. 397–442). Paris and Brussels: De Boeck.

Campbell, E., & Lassiter, L. (2010). From collaborative ethnography to collaborative pedagogy: reflections on the other side of Middletown Project and community-university research partnerships. *Anthropology & Education Quarterly*, 41(4), 370–385.

Chambon, J.-L., & David, A. (1982). *Les Innovations Sociales*. Paris: Presses Universitaires de France.

Defourny, J., & Nyssens, M. (2010). Conceptions of social enterprise and social entrepreneurship in Europe and the United States: convergences and divergences, *Journal of Social Entrepreneurship*, 1(1), 32–53.

Defourny, J., & Nyssens, M. (2017). Fundamentals for an international typology of social enterprise models. *Voluntas*, 28(6), 2469–2497.

Defourny, J., & Nyssens, M. (Dir.). (2021a). *Social Enterprise in Central and Eastern Europe: Theory. Models and Practice*, Abingdon: Routledge.

Defourny, J., & Nyssens, M. (Dir.). (2021b). *Social Enterprise in Western Europe: Theory, Models and Practice*. Abingdon: Routledge.

Defourny, J., Nyssens, M., & Brolis, O. (2021). Testing social enterprise models across the world: evidence from the International Comparative Social Enterprise Models (ICSEM) Project. *Nonprofit and Voluntary Sector Quarterly*, 50(2), 420–440.

Dekimpe, Emilie (2020). *The legitimacy of the cooperative model: A consensus towards the factors that lead to the neglect of the cooperative model in educational institutions.* Louvain School of Management, Université Catholique de Louvain.

Doherty, B., Haugh, H., & Lyon, F. (2014). Social enterprises as hybrid organizations: a review and research agenda. *International Journal of Management Reviews*, 16(4), 417–436.

EC (2013). *Guide to Social Innovation*. Available at: https://ec.europa.eu/eip/ageing/file/759/download_en?token=mNGSe_T7

EC (2020a). *Social Enterprises and Their Ecosystems in Europe. Comparative Synthesis Report.* Authors: C. Borzaga, G. Galera, B. Franchini, S. Chiomento, R. Nogales, & C. Carini. Luxembourg: Publications Office of the European Union. Available at: https://europa.eu/!Qq64ny

EC (2020b). *The Role of Research and Innovation in Support of Europe's Recovery from the COVID19 Crisis*, Policy Brief. Luxembourg: Publications Office of the European Union. Available at: https://ec.europa.eu/info/sites/info/files/research_and_innovation/strategy_on_research_and_innovation/documents/ec_rtd_covid19-recovery.pdf

Enjolras, B., Salamon, L. M., Sivesind, K. H., & Zimmer, A. (2018) *The Third Sector as a Renewable Resource for Europe: Concepts, Impacts, Challenges and Opportunities.* New York: Springer.

European Commission (2011). *Social Business Initiative: Creating a Favourable Climate for Social Enterprises, Key Stakeholders in the Social Economy and Innovation*, SEC(2011) 1278 final. European Commission. Available at: https://ec.europa.eu/transparency/regdoc/rep/1/2011/EN/1-2011-682-EN-F1-1.Pdf

European Commission (2021). *Social Economy Action Plan*. Retrieved from https://ec.europa.eu/social/main.jsp?catId=1537&langId=en

European Economic and Social Committee (2016). *Recent Evolutions of the Social Economy in the European Union.* Authors: J. L. Monzón & R. Chaves, CIRIEC-International. Brussels: EESC. Available at https://www.eesc.europa.eu/sites/default/files/files/qe-04-17-875-en-n.pdf

Franco, I. B., & Tracey, J. (2019). Community capacity-building for sustainable development. *International Journal of Sustainability in Higher Education*, 20(4), 695.

Jensen, R., Thursby, J., & Thursby, M. (2010). University–Industry Spillovers, Government Funding, and Industrial Consulting. NBER Working Papers n. 15732. Available at: https://www.nber.org/papers/w15732

Klein, J.-L., Laville, J.-L., & Moulaert, F. (Eds). (2014). *L'innovation sociale*. Paris: Érès.

Lang, D. J., Wiek, A., Bergmann, M., Stauffacher, M., Martens, P., Moll, P., Swilling, M., & Thomas, C. J. (2012). Transdisciplinary research in sustainability science: practice, principles, and challenges. *Sustainability Science*, 7, 25–43.

Laville, J.-L. (2006). *Economie solidaire*. In J.-L. Laville & A. D. Cattani, *Dictionnaire de l'autre économie* (pp. 23–37). Folio actuel, Paris: Gallimard.

Laville, J.-L. (2014). Innovation sociale, économie sociale et solidaire, entrepreneuriat social, une mise en perspective historique. In J. L. Klein, J. L. Laville, & F. Moulaert (Eds), *L'innovation sociale*. Eres, 45–80.

Laville, J.-L. (Ed.). (2016). *L'économie sociale et solidaire. Pratiques, théories, débats*. Paris, Le Seuil.

Lévesque, B. (2007). Le potentiel d'innovation sociale de l'économie sociale: quelques éléments de problématique. *Économie et Solidarités*, 37, 1, 13–48.

Lévesque, B. (2013). Social innovation in governance and public management systems: toward a new paradigm? In F. Moulaert, D. Maccallum, A. Mehmood, & A. Hamdouch (Eds), *The International Handbook on Social Innovation: Collective Action, Social Learning and Transdisciplinary Research* (pp. 25–39). Cheltenham: Edward Elgar Publishing.

McNeill, J., & Boorman, C. (2020). Universities and place-based social innovation: anchor models as integrative frameworks. Delivered at the International Social Innovation Research Conference (ISIRC) 2020.

Mehling, S., & Kolleck, N. (2019). Cross-sector collaboration in higher education institutions (HEIs): a critical analysis of an urban sustainability development program. *Sustainability*, 11, 4982.

Monzón Campos, J. L. (2016). La economía social en la literatura económica y en los hechos. 30 años delCIRIEC-España, *Revista de Economía Pública, Social y Cooperativa*, No. 88/2016 (pp. 287–307). Valencia: CIRIEC-Spain.

Moulaert, F., & MacCallum, D. (2019). *Advanced Introduction to Social Innovation*. Cheltenham: Edward Elgar Publishing.

Moulaert, F., Maccallum, D., Mehmood, A., & Hamdouch, A. (Eds). (2013). *The International Handbook on Social Innovation: Collective Action, Social Learning and Transdisciplinary Research*. Cheltenham: Edward Elgar Publishing.

Nichols, N., Phipps, D. J., Provençal, J., & Hewitt, A. (2013). Knowledge mobilization, collaboration, and social innovation: leveraging investments in higher education. *Canadian Journal of Nonprofit and Social Economy Research/Revue canadienne de recherche sur les OBSL et l'économie sociale, ANSERJ*, 4(1), Spring/Printemps, 25–42.

Nogales-Muriel, R. (2023). *Social Innovation, Social Enterprises and the Cultural Economy. Cultural and Artistic Social Enterprises in Practice.* London and New York: Routledge.

Nyssens, M. (2015). Innovation sociale et entreprise sociale: quels dialogues possibles? Une perspective européenne. In J.-L. Klein (Ed.), *La transformation sociale pas l'innovation sociale (Innovation Sociale)* (pp. 335–348). Presses de l'Université du Québec.

OECD (2015). *Concepts and definitions for identifying R&D. In Frascati Manual 2015: Guidelines for Collecting and Reporting Data on Research and Experimental Development.* Paris: OECD Publishing. Available at: https://doi.org/10.1787/9789264 239012-4-en

Perkmann, M., & Walsh, K. (2008). Engaging the scholar: three types of academic consulting and their impact on universities and industry. *Research Policy,* 37, 1884–1891.

Persaud, A., & Bayon, M. (2019). A review and analysis of the thematic structure of social entrepreneurship research: 1990–2018, *International Review of Entrepreneurship,* 17(4), 495–528.

Radinger-Peer, V., & Pflitsch, G. (2017). The role of higher education institutions in regional transition paths towards sustainability. *Review of Regional Research,* 37, 161–187. Available at: https://link.springer.com/article/10.1007/s10037-017-0116-9

Rentocchini, F., Manjarrés-Henrìquez, L., D'Este, P., & R. Grimaldi (2014). The relationship between academic consulting and research performance: evidence from five Spanish universities. *International Journal of Industrial Organization,* 32(1), 70–83.

Santos, B. de S. (2017). *Decolonising the University: The Challenge of Deep Cognitive Justice.* Cambridge Scholars Publishing.

Smallbone, D., Kitching, J., & Blackburn, R. (2015). *Anchor Institutions and Small Firms in the UK: A Review of the Literature on Anchor Institutions and Their Role in Developing Management and Leadership Skills in Small Firms.* Technical Report, UK Commission for Employment and Skills.

Stromquist, N. P., & Lozano, G. (2018). Popular universities: their hidden functions and contributions. In M. Milana, S. Webb, J. Holford, R. Waller, & P. Jarvis (Eds), *International Handbook on Adult and Lifelong Education and Learning,* London: Palgrave.

UNSRID (2019). *Opportunities and Challenges of Statistics on SSE.* Available at: https://knowledgehub.unsse.org/project-opportunities-and-challenges-of-statistics-on-sse/

Vogt, M., & Weber, C. (2020). The role of universities in a sustainable society: why value-free research is neither possible nor desirable. *Sustainability,* 12, 2811; https://doi.org/10.3390/su12072811

10

Social economy resilience facing the COVID-19 crisis

Facts and prospects

Rafael Chaves-Avila and Ángel Soler Guillén

Introduction

We began the year 2020 by reflecting on and trying to provide answers to the challenges of our time: the climate and environmental crisis; the growth in inequality and hunger; the challenge of the digital revolution and the Fourth Industrial Revolution, as well as the challenge of governance and global financial stability—and then a new, great crisis burst in with a planetary force that shook and paralysed all countries: the coronavirus pandemic.

Just a few months after the outbreak of this health shock, its effects were already devastating: according to the Johns Hopkins Coronavirus Resource Center (n.d.), by mid-January 2021 the coronavirus pandemic had infected more than 333 million people worldwide and had caused the deaths of 5.6 million people, a scenario comparable to that of the Spanish flu at the beginning of the twentieth century. In the economic sphere, the drops in GDP and the destruction of employment seen during the first few months of the pandemic find similar precedents only in the 1930s.

The COVID-19 crisis highlights the unavoidable threat to humanity posed by recurrent viral pandemics. However, this is not the only external threat it faces. Natural disasters, such as devastating earthquakes, floods, and other catastrophes of nature continue to be menaces, and their threat is growing in a context of global climate change. Other serious threats, this time of human origin, such as wars and armed conflicts, are still alive.

What is undeniable is that the COVID-19 crisis and other pandemics, natural disasters, and armed conflicts are conceived in economics as non-economic external shocks or shocks exogenous to the economic system, which have a hard and widespread impact on countries at the macroeconomic level. It is recognized that this type of external shock has an undoubtedly greater impact than strictly economic recessions. But it is also clear that the institutional framework and the social and economic structure of a country, including the social economy, can aggravate or

Rafael Chaves-Avila and Ángel Soler Guillén, *Social economy resilience facing the COVID-19 crisis*. In: *Social Economy Science*. Edited by: Gorgi Krlev, Dominika Wruk, Giulio Pasi, and Marika Bernhard, Oxford University Press. © Oxford University Press (2023). DOI: 10.1093/oso/9780192868343.003.0010

mitigate the impact of these disasters. Therefore, it is pertinent to analyse shocks and ecosystems from the social resilience perspective.

According to Walker et al. (2004), Keck & Sakdapolrak (2013), and Manca et al. (2017), the concept of resilience refers to a society's ability to adapt to shocks, as well as to take advantage of them as opportunities for economic and social development. They identify three dimensions of an ecosystem's social resilience: its absorption capacity, that is, its capacity to face and react to shocks or persistent structural changes, resisting them; its adaptation capacity, or capacity to adopt a degree of flexibility, making small changes in the system; and finally its transformation capacity, or transformability, which occurs when shocks are of such magnitude that they are no longer manageable and make the existing system unsustainable so that it requires far-reaching changes, including structural transformations. This transformation capacity also introduces the dimension of systemic learning in the sense of the capacity to use shocks as windows of opportunity for the social and economic development of the ecosystem. The concept of resilience includes, in addition to these three capacities, a capacity to maintain the levels of social welfare achieved as well as to continue progressing on a sustainable human development path. Finally, society's resilience function is directly linked to its social and economic structure.

The aim of this chapter is to analyse the resilience role of the social economy in the face of the Covid-19 crisis. The hypothesis used is that this crisis has given the social economy an extraordinary opportunity to show its true capacity to address market and state failures and, above all, to demonstrate its important contribution to social and economic resilience. The main theoretical arguments on the systemic role of the social economy are reviewed and empirical evidence is provided based, on the one hand, on a meta-analysis of a series of studies that have recently been carried out both in Spain and in other European countries, and, on the other hand, on our own statistical work.

The chapter starts with the concept and socio-economic functions of the social economy, based on the main references in the literature. The resilience functions of the social economy and the theory of the emergency management cycle are then presented. Based on empirical information, the impact on health and the emergency situation generated by the COVID-19 pandemic are addressed and then the response of the social economy in this critical context is analysed. The following section examines the impact of the health emergency and, in particular, the impact of government action to address it, including measures of social containment and disengagement on the economy, the world of work, and the social economy. It highlights that, although the crisis has had negative effects on the social economy, they have been significantly lower in the social economy than in the rest of the economy, thus revealing its greater capacity for resilience. The response of the social economy to mitigate the economic and employment impact of the COVID-19 crisis is discussed below. The chapter then examines the new context created by the COVID-19 crisis, its constraints, and emerging needs and opportunities. Finally, it sets out conclusions and proposals for addressing the new challenges and benefits of the systemic functions of the social economy.

The social economy and its socio-economic functions in societies

The Social Economy (SE) also called the social and solidarity economy, is a broad field in the economies between the public and the private for-profit sectors. With deep roots dating back to the nineteenth century and long work in the scientific field, the definition of the SE has been institutionalized at the international level (Monzón & Chaves, 2017) by institutions such as the United Nations through the International Labour Organization, the European Commission, and the European Economic and Social Committee. The recent International Labour Organization (ILO) Resolution (2022) states:

> The social and solidarity economy encompasses enterprises, organizations and other entities that are engaged in economic, social, and environmental activities to serve the collective and/or general interest, which are based on the principles of voluntary cooperation and mutual aid, democratic and/or participatory governance, autonomy and independence, and the primacy of people and social purpose over capital in the distribution and use of surpluses and/or profits as well as assets . . . According to national circumstances, the SSE includes cooperatives, associations, mutual societies, foundations, social enterprises, self-help groups and other entities operating in accordance with the values and principles of the social and solidarity economy.[1]

The worth of the social economy. Many scholars agree that the social economy generates social and economic impact, at micro, meso, and macro levels (Bouchard, 2010; Chaves & Monzón, 2012; Chaves et al., 2013; Itçaina & Richez-Battesti, 2018). This positive impact has been particularly evidenced in different areas, such as job creation, public welfare, citizen empowerment, local development, promotion of social values, social capital, and improved social service delivery. In this context, several theories have provided arguments that have highlighted certain properties of the social economy, and agree on its overall positive impact. In this sense, a set of theories argue that the SE plays macroeconomic functions in modern economies. The theory of the participatory economy (Weitzman, 1984; Kruse, 1994) argues that enterprises based on employee participation in profits have the potential to increase both macroeconomic performance, by achieving lower unemployment levels and thus mitigating economic cycles, and microeconomic performance, by increasing productivity and quality. The institutional failures approach (Hansmann, 1981; Hansmann & Weisbrod, 1975) is based on the failures of the private for-profit businesses and governments and stresses the greater economic capacity of the non-profit sector to supply certain public and private goods. Finally, the socio-economic approach defends the social economy system's regulatory function by providing new responses

---

[1] ILO (2022): Resolution concerning decent work and the social and solidarity economy, 10 June 2022. (https://www.ilo.org/ilc/ILCSessions/110/reports/texts-adopted/WCMS_848633/lang—en/index.htm)

and social innovation through innovation in products, processes, and forms of organization, and by encouraging participation and control by workers and users (Chaves & Demoustier, 2013). To sum up, this literature highlights two systemic functions of the social economy: reparative and transformative. The first addresses the failures and issues of economies that require responses to achieve greater wellbeing, and the second reveals the innovative capacity of the social economy to explore new avenues and to change the system.

These functions of the social economy are particularly crucial in crisis contexts and link to the concept of resilience seen above and its three dimensions: that of resisting shocks so that the negative impacts of the crisis are significantly lower in the social economy than in the rest of the economy; to recover more quickly from the crisis and, once the crisis is over, to find a fairer and more sustainable way of development; and finally of reducing the risks and vulnerabilities of the system.

The social economy resilience function in contexts of shocks

In order to have a precise understanding of the resilience function of the social economy in crisis contexts, the theory of the emergency management cycle (Wisner & Adams, 2002) is considered. According to this theory, the management of external shocks (catastrophes or crises) has five phases: mitigation, preparedness, response, recovery/reconstruction, and development.[2]

The mitigation phase aims to prevent potential disasters and emergencies. It involves actions aimed at preventing these disasters and reducing the probability of their occurrence. These envisage that the disaster is reasonably possible and will have an appreciable impact. The preparedness phase aims to design programmes and actions to reduce the disaster's impact once it has occurred, especially in terms of health and human lives. Both phases precede the emergence of the emergency situation. The response phase aims to respond, during the course of the emergency, with concrete actions that protect health and lives and minimize economic damage. The recovery phase aims at developing reconstruction actions to restore the pre-disaster situation, both socially and economically.

Disasters have direct and indirect, transitory and/or permanent effects. Direct effects are those related to loss of life and health and damage to physical infrastructure. Indirect effects occur on economic activity, in terms of damage to business structures and in the form of impacts on production and trade. Indirect effects are generally transitory, with economic activity recovering to its pre-crisis level.

The context of reconstruction is an *opportunity to introduce far-reaching reforms* by laying the foundations for a new model of social and economic development for a country that is considered to be better than the existing model. The change of model generally meets with resistance, and such a context alters this resistance.

---

[2] United Nations, International Strategy for Disaster Reduction (http://www.un-spider.org).

The country's social and institutional structures, among them social economy cooperatives and non-profit entities, play an important role in dealing with external disasters or shocks: these are key factors in coping with shock, adapting, and recovering from it. The impact of disasters has been found to be less in socio-economic systems with democratic, more egalitarian, and better resourced institutions and public policies, where there are more incentives to develop adequate prevention and effective and immediate response systems. Inadequate social and institutional systems can, on the contrary, amplify the effects of the disaster.

Many research studies, such as the ILO Report (Parnell, 2001), Simo and Bies (2007), Rao and Greve (2018), and Paarlbertg et al. (2020), have examined territories' community resilience to disasters and provided empirical evidence. They agree that systems with higher levels of social cohesion, greater social capital, greater capacity for social mobilization, and more co-operatives and social economy organizations better respond to and manage crises and pandemics. Rao and Greve (2018), for example, reveal that the greater the civic capacity, social infrastructure, and social capital that existed in a community before the disaster, the lesser the impact of mortality from a pandemic outbreak. The ILO Report (Parnell, 2001) shows that the abundance of social economy entities constitutes a breeding ground for sociability, resilience, and recovery from crises. To sum up, social and institutional structures are critical factors in mitigating crises and supporting recovery.

Co-operatives and social economy entities develop important resilience functions in the five phases of the disaster management cycle, which are inherent to the systemic functions of the social economy explained before. Assuming the disaster management cycle perspective as a general framework, the above mentioned ILO Report is the main reference point on the contribution that social economy is able to make in terms of resilience (Parnell, 2001).[3]

In the preparedness and mitigation phases, co-operatives and social economy entities can participate in the prevention and design of actions against disaster threats. They can also organize effective socio-health and economic assistance. They also contribute to improving the capacity of political promotion of the populations potentially affected by the disasters, since they are organized in co-operatives, so that they have a better representation and capacity of interlocution both in the formulation of prevention policies and, above all, in reconstruction and recovery.

During the emergency phase, they provide essential services to the population, maintaining the jobs and livelihoods of the population affected by the crisis. Indeed, in the COVID-19 pandemic, two properties of the social economy proved particularly valuable. The first was its ability to maintain jobs and economic activity compared to other organizations; that is, although the crisis has negative effects on the social economy, these impacts are lower in the social economy than in the rest of the economy, revealing the greater resilience of the social economy. In other words, if the economy as a whole had behaved like social economy enterprises, the overall impact of the COVID crisis would have been significantly lower. The second

---

[3] This ILO Report (Parnell, 2001) documents each of these contributions in detail with numerous cases and studies from around the world.

property of the social economy is its support for local supply chains, strengthening local economies—a property particularly valued in the context of problems in the functioning of global supply chains.

They also reduce the *vulnerability of population groups* most likely to be negatively affected by disasters. Co-operatives and social economy entities also increase the collective capacity of communities to face crises, acting on behalf of the affected populations with one voice. Finally, the psychological dimension is also important: in times of crisis, people are often overcome by a sense of despair, which is aggravated when they feel totally dependent and reliant on outside help. Self-help initiatives, such as co-operatives and social economy initiatives, combat this feeling of helplessness. The very act of cooperation and the feeling of solidarity it engenders, together with the replacement of external dependency, are important parts of the recovery process.

In the recovery phase, co-operatives and social economy entities support the relatively rapid economic and employment reintegration of the crisis-affected population into their usual living patterns through the provision of services and the creation and maintenance of jobs and livelihoods. They also can directly assist in the reconstruction process and can contribute to financing rehousing programmes for social groups devastated by the crisis.

In the recovery and reconstruction phase, co-operatives can be key allies of public policies of reconstruction and development whose objectives go beyond restoration of damage or return to the status quo before the crisis, but propose a medium- and long-term development model. Therefore, co-operatives and social economy entities are key agents that promote and catalyse socio-economic transformation in times of crisis. Indeed, structural changes in the system are difficult and require organizations capable of challenging existing economic power structures. Social economy entities often become the only credible organizations capable of seriously playing that role by achieving peaceful change. Therefore, recovery and reconstruction policies must rely on co-operatives and social economy entities, supporting them decisively, if they want to make a deep change in the development model.

To recover from the crisis with sustainable and fair development, and as they are schools of democracy, co-operatives and social economy entities contribute to promoting or restoring democracy, which is often an important part of crisis response programmes. They contribute to forming citizens better prepared to play their role in a modern democratic state. For the cooperation process to work, the people involved must act together using democratic forms of organization. This experience, in turn, helps people build the political stability essential for sustainable development.

The emergency situation resulting from the COVID-19 crisis and the state of alarm, and the social economy responses

The COVID-19 health shock demanded mitigation and effective and immediate response from the health, social, and economic systems.

An emergency situation will bring about new social, health, and economic needs (Center for Disease Control and Prevention, 2007). These are: (1) health needs—more health facilities (hospital beds), more respirators, more pharmaceuticals, more testing for infection, more personal protective equipment (masks, gloves, gowns, etc.), more health workers, more people to track infection, more laboratories and research to develop vaccines; (2) social service needs—attention to the most vulnerable groups (the elderly, the homeless, the disabled, etc.), from personal care to shopping and household chores; (3) maintenance needs for essential services such as water, telecommunications, energy, and rubbish collection; (4) food supply needs; (5) needs for income maintenance and financial support to paralysed companies; and (6) needs to adapt social and labour relations to the new context, in the form of teleworking and telecommunications.

As in war economy situations, since the beginning of the state of alarm in March 2020, the most affected European countries, such as Spain, have reoriented their economies by prioritizing satisfaction of the aforementioned needs. In Spain, the COVID-19 crisis has highlighted the failures of the private market and governments to respond satisfactorily to these new demands. Government failures are mainly attributed to a lack of structural investment in the public health system, while private market failures are due to an economic model based on industrial offshoring and a high dependence on international supply chains (De Vet et al., 2021). With the breakdown of international supply chains during the pandemic, serious problems have emerged in the health production cluster.

The social economy has played a decisive role in the collective effort in the face of the pandemic emergency phase (Organisation for Economic Co-operation and Development [OECD], 2020a). It has been a powerful agent for identifying urgent needs arising from the COVID-19 crisis and to provide effective and innovative responses.

The social economy's response to the COVID-19 emergency situation

As expected, the social economy, co-operatives, NGOs, and volunteers have deployed an impressive response to the health emergency resulting from COVID-19. The Social Economy Europe Open Letter to the European Commission, the European Parliament and the European Council entitled 'An unprecedented crisis requiring an unprecedented response from the EU to restore economic and social progress' (Pedreño, 2020) specified the multidimensional contribution of the European social economy to the crisis. It indicated that:

> The Social Economy is contributing by 1) providing health care for all, and producing and distributing pharmaceutical products, 2) providing social services, especially for the most vulnerable groups such as the elderly, migrants and refugees or the homeless, 3) producing and distributing food through agri-food and consumer cooperatives, 4) ensuring the provision of other basic services such

as energy, water, telecommunications, cleaning and recycling, 5) guaranteeing financial support and technical assistance to Social Economy enterprises and the real economy through cooperative and ethical banks, micro-credit institutions and credit unions, 6) being an important industrial agent in strategic industrial sectors, including the production of socio-health materials and bioservices, and 7) promoting teleworking and implementing strategies to ensure that jobs and economic activity are maintained during and after the pandemic. (Pedreño, 2020)

This deployment of human and material resources of the social economy has been documented in multiple reports, databases, and websites around Europe.

In Spain, social economy organizations have been particularly active in the face of the pandemic. The responses have been broad and diversified, ranging from an unprecedented increase in the activity of voluntary organizations to rapid responses to urgent health needs and responses adapted to the issues of the different sectors. Indeed, according to the Observatory on Volunteering, volunteering has tripled during the pandemic, reaching 4.5 million volunteers, of whom more than 1.5 million work in social action organizations. At the same time, around 500 social economy entities affiliated with the Spanish Social Economy Umbrella CEPES have acted in the face of the COVID-19 pandemic, providing medicalization services for facilities and relocation of infrastructures, redirecting their production to manufacture protective materials and clothing (masks, respirators, 3D, etc.), producing cleaning and disinfection products, providing health, social, and welfare services, and maintaining distribution and supermarket services, essential electricity and water supply services, and other solidarity initiatives.[5] They have continued to maintain their education, teaching, and training services, and where possible, given the restrictions and social distancing, culture and leisure.

An example of the rapid response of the social economy to the problems of supply of health and protection material was the initiative of the Mondragon co-operative group, which, through the Gipuzkoa co-operative Bexen Medical, acquired industrial machinery in the first weeks of the state of alert to mass-produce surgical masks in a context of shortages in the country. Subsequently, other co-operatives in the group, such as Onnera, Mondragon Assembly, Cikautxo, and Fagor electrónica, reoriented their production, adapting it to the new health demands arising from the emergency situation (masks, respirators, protective visors, among others). Finally, in the financial sphere, various co-operative credit entities provided support, deferring deadlines or facilitating access to credit. Another example is the Fons Cooperatiu per l'Emergència Social i Sanitària, an innovative crowdfunding fund promoted by various entities such as the Fundació Roca Galés, the Xarxa d'Economia Solidària, and the Grup ECOS, among others, and the Federación de Cooperativas de Trabajo Asociado, which has also made a significant financial contribution. This fund, managed by the Coop57 Foundation, aims to give financial support to initiatives of the Catalan social economy, which provide a response to the health, social, and economic emergency caused by the COVID-19 crisis.

At the European level, the European Commission maintains a website called 'Social Economy Community'. It has set up an information and exchange space entitled 'Social economy in the fight against coronavirus'. It has a database of hundreds of initiatives and actions developed by the European social economy that provide services in response to the situation of the pandemic, ranging from volunteering to services for the elderly, technological solutions and on-line courses, and food services.

At the international level, of particular interest is the International Labour Organization (ILO, 2020a) website entitled 'Cooperatives and wider SSE enterprises

Table 10.1 Responses of the cooperatives and social economy to the COVID-19 crisis

Responses in labour field	Measures aimed at improving safety and working conditions in the workplace
	Measures aimed at modulating work organization, such as the extension of teleworking and the recommendation to stay home on paid leave for vulnerable workers
Support with services to people	Health sector cooperatives have set up support funds and distributed protective equipment to their members, to workers in essential enterprises and to front-line health workers
	Cooperatives in basic services (energy, water, telecommunications, cleaning, financial) have reduced costs for their members in terms of late charges and special payment arrangements
Responses in the supply chain	Supply chain stabilization measures, protecting small farmers' food production and maintaining the supply of goods through consumer cooperatives for the growing demands of consumers who spend more time at home
Responses in innovation and adaptation of production	Industrial production cooperatives have redirected their production towards essential goods such as hand disinfectants and face masks and distributed them to high-risk populations, including frontline workers such as healthcare workers
Responses in adequacy of access to information and telework	Cooperatives and their representative organizations have adapted their information systems, developed online resource platforms, videoconferencing, telematics member meetings, and so on
Financial responses	Fundraising campaigns and reorientation of existing funds for the recovery phase after the pandemic
Responses to inadequacy for emergency action by governments	The social economy has carried out actions of political incidence on governments and international organizations in order to change the current development paradigm and strengthen the multilateral system and solidarity networks
	They have called on governments to include cooperatives and other social economy entities in emergency and reconstruction plans, including their representation in the emergency working groups and committees and the creation of specific funds

Source: ILO, 2020a

respond to Covid-19 disruptions, and government measures are being put in place.
Table 10.1 summarizes the responses of the social economy to the COVID-19 crisis.[4]
    Finally, the OECD (2020a) report also contains multiple cases of social economy
responses deployed in OECD member countries.

Economic and labour impact of the COVID-19 crisis

During the early part of the COVID-19 crisis, government measures to combat the
coronavirus, in particular confinement and, to a lesser extent, social distancing, liter-
ally paralysed the bulk of the economy, except for its essential services. Pérez and
Maudos (2020) estimate that a 50 per cent halt in overall economic activity for
one month generates a 4 per cent contraction in annual GDP. Because of economic
interrelationships, an economic standstill has several consequences. The first derives
from the confinement itself, which paralyses non-essential sectors due to government restrictions such as restrictions on mobility, and social distancing, which in
turn directly affect the reduction in activity, the level of employment, and the level of
income of the affected population. Second, it affects demand, which cannot be exercised due to mobility and distancing or due to the reduction in income and contracts.
Third, the stagnation of sectors generates shortages in other sectors, interrupting
the value chain, which is particularly serious where international supplies are concerned. Fourth, it generates uncertainty and worsens the expectations of consumers
and investors, who reduce their purchases of durable goods and the level of investment. The COVID-19 crisis therefore generated a supply shock but also a contraction
in demand (Pérez & Maudos, 2020).
    The impact on GDP is a way to synthetically demonstrate the depth of the crisis,
which has not been seen since the 1930s and 1940s. According to Eurostat (2022), as
a result of the measures adopted by governments in the fight against the virus, especially confinement in the spring of 2020 due to COVID-19, the average fall in GDP
of European Union countries was 11.3 per cent during the second quarter of 2020
(Figure 10.1), the main period of the confinement. The impact on GDP was harder
on countries such as the United Kingdom and Spain (Panel A), which presented
reductions of 18.8 per cent and 17.7 per cent respectively, while in the United States
the reduction was less, that is, 8.9 per cent. In Panel B of Figure 10.1 we can observe
that among the selected countries, in the third trimester of 2021 only Spain had still
not reached a level of income corresponding to the first trimester of 2020.
    The *impact on employment* was also strong. For Spain, various bodies, such as the
International Monetary Fund (IMF), the European Commission, the Bank of Spain,
and the Spanish government, predicted significant job losses due to the restrictive
measures and distancing that had to be applied. The estimates were correct, since

---

[4] The ILO (2020a) report details dozens of examples of responses by cooperatives and the social economy to the emergency, mainly from their second and third tier structures. We invite the reader to look
at it.

(a) Quarter-on-quarter variation rate of GDP. II quarter of 2020

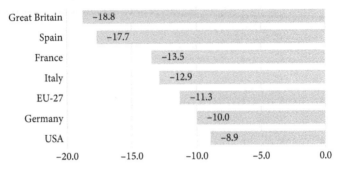

(b) GDP at market prices. III quarter of 2021. (I quarter of 2020= 100)

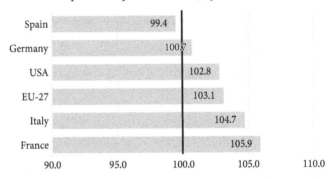

Figure 10.1 Impact on GDP of the Covid-19 pandemic: Selection of countries. (a) quarter-on-quarter variation rate of GDP. II quarter of 2020; (b) GDP at market prices. III quarter of 2021 (I quarter of 2020 = 100)

Source: Eurostat (2022), INE (2021, 2022) and own elaboration

on the one hand the jobless rate in Spain increased, from 13.8 per cent in the fourth trimester of 2019 to 16.3 per cent in the third trimester of 2020, and continued to be reduced from then on up to the fourth trimester of 2021. On the other hand, those affiliates to the social security system decreased from 19.3 million workers in December to 18.4 million in April of 2020, after which the number began to increase. In addition to the loss of jobs and increased unemployment, 3.4 million salaried workers accepted temporary employment arrangements (ERTE[5]) and 1.1 million self-employed workers requested loans due to a standstill in job offers, representing 24.6 per cent of those contributing to social security claimant numbers in April of 2020.

---

[5] ERTE, the Spanish temporary unemployment scheme, is a special administrative labour procedure that allows companies to temporarily lay off workers or reduce working hours; workers are entitled to unemployment benefits, while the company must continue to pay social security contributions. Once the measure is terminated, the workers return to their jobs according to their previous contractual conditions.

The COVID-19 crisis revealed an uneven impact in terms of branches of activity and types of company according to their economic and financial situation. Their greater or lesser adaptation to the new conditions imposed by the new crisis context,[6] specifically those linked to the consideration of essential services, proximity in their supply and consumption, and the possibility of using new digital technologies (teleworking, online commerce, etc.), will condition their level of economic and employment impact in the short and medium term. Those sectors and companies with the greatest barriers in digitalization or in a situation of business vulnerability due to high indebtedness and liquidity problems will probably have greater difficulties.

Various studies have analysed the heterogeneous impact of this crisis by branches of activity (Collado & Rodriguez, 2020). Pérez and Maudos (2020) identify three groups of sectors according to the level of impact, both economic and employment-wise: (a) low: agriculture, some manufacturing (e.g. agri-food industry), energy, some service branches (e.g. telecommunications), and public services; (b) medium: various branches of manufacturing and services (e.g. financial, consultancy, and other computer-related activities, information services); (c) high: commerce, tourism, hotels and restaurants, transport, culture and entertainment, professional services, construction, and so on.

During spring 2020, the impact of the COVID-19 crisis on employment by branches of activity was mixed. In Spain, the variation in the number of social security affiliates and the number of people in ERTE status is revealing. According to the Bank of Spain's Report 2019, some branches of the services sector were more affected by the crisis, such as the arts, leisure and entertainment, hotels and restaurants (accommodation and food service activities), other services activities, wholesale and retail sales, education, and administrative services (Banco de España, 2020). Industry and the construction sector suffered an intermediate-level fall, while the primary sector, health and social services activities, the financial and insurance sector, and the water supply, sanitation, and waste sectors were barely affected (see also Figure 10.2). Two of the sectors most affected by the COVID-19 crisis have been tourism (Pitarch, 2020) and culture and the creative industries (Abeledo et al., 2020). These are precisely some of the branches of activity where the social economy is relatively more present. Figure 10.2 shows also that these branches of activity reveal difficulty in recovering: in October 2021, eighteen months after the lockdown, they continued to show a negative impact on employment.

In the other OECD countries, the branches of activities whose employment levels have been affected by the pandemic coincide with the analysis for Spain (OECD, 2021).

Government measures concerning the labour market have been adopted in all OECD countries to dampen the effect of the pandemic on employment. Among those countries with a greater percentage of salaried workers which created programmes of

---

[6] Later in the chapter we will discuss the new Covid-19 context, its uneven impact among economic sectors, and implications for the future.

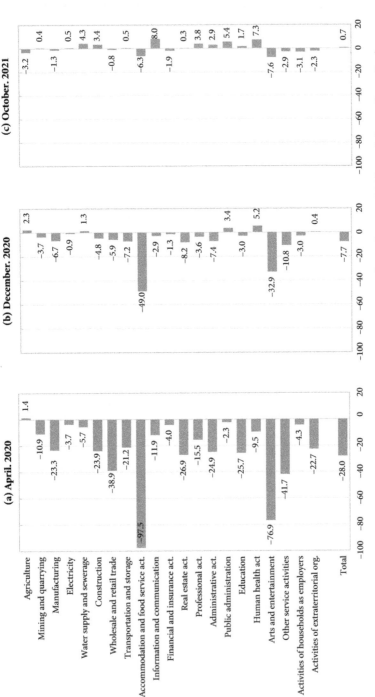

Figure 10.2 Estimated impact of the Covid-19 pandemic on employment compared to February 2020 by activity sections. Spain

Note: The figures of termination of activity by branch of activity have been estimated adopting the hypothesis that sectoral distribution is the same as that of the ERTEs and that, therefore, the sectoral impact of Covid-19 operated in a similar manner with regard to salaried and autonomous workers

Source: Seguridad Social (2022a, 2022b, 2022c) and own elaboration

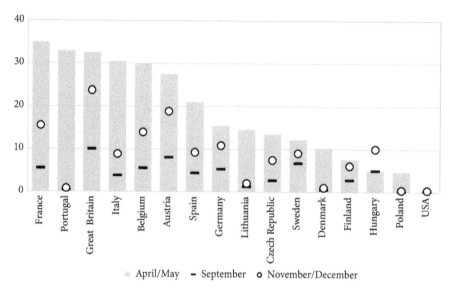

Figure 10.3 Participation in job retention schemes. Share of dependent employees. 2020

Source: OECD (2021)

employment protection at the beginning of the pandemic, we can cite (Figure 10.3) France, Portugal, Great Britain, Italy, and Belgium, with values superior to 30 per cent. In September 2020, with improved figures with regard to contagion extending through to the summer, the percentage of workers seeking aid to maintain their jobs was greatly reduced. In winter these figures increased once again, as the data concerning contagion and hospitalizations worsened.

The need for governments to implement plans to maintain employment has been different for the different sectors of the economy, in addition to being reduced since confinement began. In the case of Spain, Figure 10.4 shows that in the hospitality sector, 97 per cent of affiliates availed themselves of such measures in April 2020, and in December of the same year, 40 per cent continued to need help. In October of 2021 this figure was reduced to 7 per cent, hospitality continued to need the most help from the public sector. Sectors involving artistic and recreational activities, other services, and the sale and repair of motor vehicles formed a second group with important needs for assistance.

One of the causes already stated with regard to the need to receive help to maintain jobs is tied to the possibility of teleworking in a context of restrictions, among others mobility. A main challenge for the economy and companies is that of digitalization and, in particular, the extension of teleworking caused by conditions of social distancing due to the problem of contagion. Eurostat (2022) revealed that in 2018 the percentage of employed people between 15 and 64 years of age who were working remotely in Spain was 7.5 per cent, compared to the EU average of 13.5 per cent—quite different from countries such as Sweden, Finland, or the Netherlands,

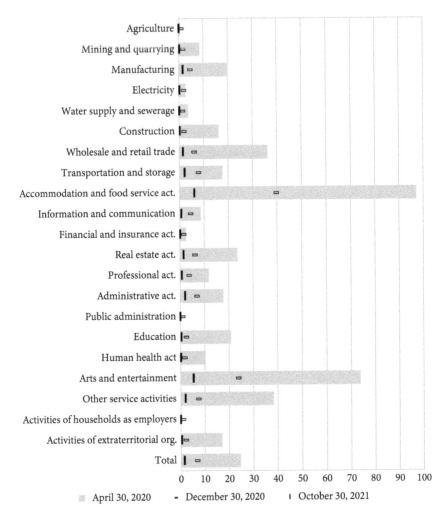

Figure 10.4 Percentage of affiliates in ERTE or with benefit for cessation of activity (Job Retention Schemes) according to activity sections. 2020 and 2021
Source: Seguridad Social (2022a, 2022b, 2022c) and own elaboration

which were above 30 per cent. The imperative of teleworking has forced the spread of this working practice during the pandemic. A Bank of Spain (Anghel et al., 2020) study conducted in April 2020 estimated that the percentage of potential home-based workers could reach 30.6 per cent. Figure 10.5 shows, in the case of Spain, the potential for telework—at 30.6 per cent in total and reaching 60 per cent in sectors such as information and communication, real estate, financial and insurance activities, and professional and education activities—and how the COVID-19 crisis has improved the use of teleworking.

The ILO produced a report on 'Covid-19 and the World of Work' which addressed the impact of the crisis on employment (ILO, 2020b). The OECD also published

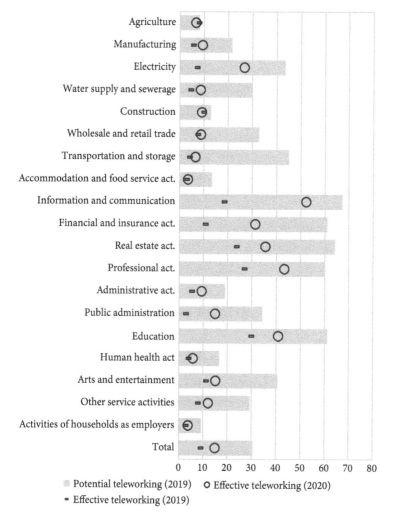

Figure 10.5 Percentage of employed persons by potential and effective digital work according to activity sections. 2019 and 2020

Source: Banco de España (Anghel et al., 2020), INE (2021) and own elaboration

its annual Employment Outlook dedicated to 'Job security and the Covid-19 crisis' (OECD, 2020b). Similarly, the United States Bureau of Labor Statistics provided revealing data on the reality of teleworking by branch of economic activity, worker income levels, institutional sectors (public, private, and non-profit), and labour categories, among others.[7] It reveals significant differences: telework is more predominant among people with higher levels of education; those in professional-type occupations; managers and salespeople; those in the financial, professional, and

---

[7] See: https://www.bls.gov/news.release/brs1.htm

information services sectors; those in the manufacturing industry; those in the non-profit sector (as opposed to the for-profit public and private sector); full-time workers; and workers with higher salaries. In contrast, most workers in manufacturing, retail, leisure, construction, and transport can hardly work from home.

Impact on inequality and uncertainty. Last but not least, the crisis has also had an impact in terms of increased inequality. As indicated in the Bank of Spain's 2019 Report cited above, most of the adjustment in job destruction has fallen on temporary workers, who have accounted for 77.2 per cent of the reduction in social security enrolment since the beginning of the crisis. In addition, the COVID-19 crisis has had 'a greater impact on the most vulnerable groups, which is expected to lead to a further deterioration in inequality levels' (Banco de España, 2020). The ILO's 2020 report on the COVID-19 crisis indicates that social and territorial inequalities are producing a differentiated impact with respect to the crisis, accentuating inequalities. No less relevant is the intensification of uncertainty among people, businesses, and workers.

The resilience of the social economy to the impact of the COVID-19 crisis

The major impact of the COVID-19 crisis on the economy, and on the world of work in general, analysed in the previous section has also been felt in the field of the social economy, but the impact has been of lesser intensity in the latter. The data presented below show that the impact of the COVID-19 crisis, by branch of activity and by legal family of the social economy, has clearly been less in the social economy than in the economy as a whole, and that the social economy has shown a better recovery. In short, these data show that the social economy is more economically resilient as it is defined by OECD (Caldera et al., 2017), that is, in the sense of the capacity of an economy to resist shocks, to reduce vulnerabilities, and to recover quickly.

The Social Economy Europe report (Fiorelli & Gafforio, 2020), a Europe-wide study based on a questionnaire carried out during May 2020 and a sample of 275 entities, revealed that 88 per cent of the European social economy enterprises and entities surveyed stated that the pandemic and confinement severely affected their activity and that it had a strong impact on employment in their entities (71 per cent of respondents). Interestingly, 43 per cent of the entities surveyed considered that they would be able to fully recover from the effects of the crisis in the coming months, while around 40 per cent doubted their full recovery capacity and 15 per cent considered that they would not be able to recover. The unequal impact of the COVID-19 crisis on employment by branches of activity—evident in the rest of the economy, as we have analysed before—is also evident in the social economy. The Social Economy Europe study reveals that the impact in terms of employment has been greater in the sectors of social services, education and training, cleaning, security and other personal services, hotels/restaurants and tourism, administrative and support services activities, repairs and culture, and sports and leisure. The least affected sectors, in this order, are water and energy supply, the manufacturing industry, agriculture, transport, information and communication services, and construction.

The Social Economy Europe report (Fiorelli & Gafforio, 2020), revealed that of the labour restructuring implemented in European social economy entities, 31.5 per cent of entities surveyed implemented temporary unemployment mechanisms, 18 per cent reduced or suspended activities, 14 per cent of entities proceeded to reduce the working hours of part or all of their staff, 12 per cent resorted to dismissal and non-renewal of contracts, and a minority, 7 per cent, introduced or extended tele-working as a way of carrying out work activity. In conclusion, the adjustment pattern was the restructuring of work teams, especially with reductions in working hours, restructuring of functions, lay-offs and wage reductions, and, where possible, an increase in voluntary work. A similar pattern was followed by SE entities during the 2008 financial crisis (Chaves & Zimmer, 2017).

The incidence of labour impact seems to have been lower in social economy entities and enterprises, revealing their greater resilience, as will be shown. This hypothesis can be contrasted with the information in Figure 10.6, which represents the interannual variation rate of hiring in the social economy and in the economy in general. The reduction in hiring that began in February 2020 is reflected less intensely in the social economy and also demonstrates a more rapid recuperation up to March of 2021. The social economy has demonstrated less of an overreaction to the pandemic in terms of employment and a better recuperation, both of which underline its resilience.

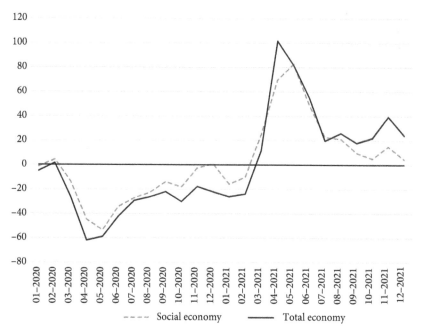

Figure 10.6 Registered contracts. Spain. Interannual variation rate. 2020–2021

Source: Ministerio de Trabajo y Economía Social (2021) and own elaboration

Two other pieces of empirical evidence relative to the greater resilience of labour in the social economy, in this case corresponding to its 'family' of co-operatives and labour societies, have been brought to light by Cancelo et al. (2022). This second study—carried out with data from the second trimester of 2020, when the crisis and confinement were at their peak, consisted of a sectoral shift-share comparative analysis—and revealed that the co-operatives showed an interannual fall in employment of 1.7 per cent, less than that of employment in the general economy. This was counter-checked by separating the 'effects of social economy' and the 'effects by branches of activities'.

The impact of temporary employment arrangements (ERTE) is another way of demonstrating the greater resilience of the social economy in the face of the COVID-19 crisis. In the Valencian Community, according to data from the Conselleria de Economía Sostenible of the Generalitat Valenciana, up to June 2020 65,384 ERTE applications were submitted, affecting 412,714 workers. According to the same source, up to July 2020 the number of force majeure ERTE applications submitted by co-operatives amounted to 300, that is, 0.5 per cent of the total number of applications submitted—a clearly lower incidence in relation to their weight in the Valencian economy, where employment in cooperatives represents 4.4 per cent of private sector salaried employment. This shows the significantly lower impact of ERTE on the co-operative sector and therefore its business and labour resilience. Cancelo et al. (2022), as explained before, demonstrated the differential 'social economy impact' and 'impact by branches of activities'.

Notwithstanding the above, research is needed to provide more evidence of the resilience of the social economy—research that allows for international and regional comparisons and comparisons between branches of activity and legal forms of social economy entities. This research should focus in particular on the key factors that make social economy organizations more resilient institutions. These studies could be linked to those carried out for the rest of the economy and could allow investigation of how a greater space given to the social economy in the shaping of structural policies impacts on resilience, in line with studies developed by the OECD in this regard (OECD & European Union, 2017). Nevertheless, statistical developments are needed in the field of the social economy to make these comparisons.

The new context after the COVID-19 crisis: emerging conditions, needs and opportunities

The post-pandemic context derived from the COVID-19 crisis has created new socio-economic conditions. First, it has promoted digitalization and teleworking, forms of socio-productive relations that lack physical contact; second, it has favoured consumer and labour activities carried out in nearby environments, characterized by reduced socio-economic mobility and with greater accessibility (the so-called last mile solution), to the detriment of activities linked to globalization, disrupting international value chains; third, the new post-pandemic context has spread a health contagion concern, materialized in the imposition of physical distance on both society and the economy, translated into social distance and the use of plastic for its prophylactic suitability against contagion. All of this has encouraged the spread of mistrust, insecurity, uncertainty, and fear of loss of health and life.

The process of digitalization of the economy, a structural trend, has been deepened by the COVID-19 crisis, intensifying the use of teleworking, e-commerce and online teaching. This process will most probably accelerate in the immediate future. Health contagion concerns, the spread of mistrust, and reduction of physical contact are new factors to have emerged with the COVID-19 crisis and may change in the coming years due to the natural sociability of human beings.

This new context has had a positive impact on the companies and people who are better positioned in this new normality; it has harmed those who are adversely positioned. There are new losers and winners, and new forms of inequality are emerging. Indeed, companies, sectors, and jobs that require physical and social contact, such as the hotel and catering industry, small businesses, leisure and tourism, culture, the creative industries, or personal services, known as 'proximity sectors', are being hit hard. Activities linked to international travel, such as international tourism, family and business travel, meetings, and conferences have also been affected. Those activities and jobs that can avoid physical contact by using telework and/or that are able to adapt their tasks to the digital environments of new technologies will see new opportunities for development in this new environment and will be much less affected. This is the case for many service activities, such as some teaching, research, financial, and administrative services. Those people and companies marked by the digital divide—that is, who are unable to use these new technologies or unable to adapt to them—will be progressively displaced and excluded. And this context offers new opportunities for the emergence of new forms of social economy entities, as has historically been the case in periods of crisis and deep transformations. Borzaga et al. (2019) and Dieste (2020) have identified some trends in the social economy linked to digitalization and robotization. Co-operative platforms are an example of emerging forms of social economy entities born in this context.

The COVID-19 crisis has highlighted important government and market failures, mainly in the public health system and with the breakdown of international supply chains during the lockdown period. New economic trends have emerged (Lorenzo, 2020): first, we have seen the strengthening of protectionism and the nationalization of the production of essential products, reducing dependence on international products, markets, and value chains. Second, there has been support for science and national reindustrialization, and third, we have witnessed the valorization of public provision and the production of essential goods and services, such as health, credit, and business rescue.

All of these constraints, needs, opportunities, and emerging trends must be considered by policy-makers when designing recovery and reconstruction policies. Moreover, if these reconstruction policies are to promote a new model of sustainable and just development in the future, they must include measures for institutional change, including ecosystems and institutions that are in line with this new model. The social economy is particularly suited to this context.

There is a wide field for future research in this context. First, it can analyse, with new theories and empirical evidence, the role of co-operatives and social economy organizations in the digital transition, paying special attention to how to avoid generating new vulnerabilities and digital divides. A second field of research concerns theorizing and providing empirical evidence on the capacity of the social economy to produce locally the goods and services demanded by the territory itself, in a logic of proximity and reduction of external vulnerability.

Conclusions and the post-COVID-19 crisis reconstruction phase

The COVID-19 crisis has been and remains one of the most important crises of our time. In addition to its very high socio-health impact, in terms of health and human lives, this crisis is having a deep impact on economies, on the world of work, on inequalities, and on the ways in which people relate to each other. The social economy has also suffered high economic and social impacts of the Covid-19 shock, although with a lesser intensity compared to the general economy.

The social economy has found in the COVID-19 crisis an excellent opportunity to show its true capacity to demonstrate its important contribution to social and economic resilience. It has addressed important market and state failures during the health emergency, responding to the COVID-19 pandemic on multiple fronts where problems or needs have arisen: it has provided social and health services, basic aid, food supplies and prevention equipment, financial support, education and training, awareness raising, community aid organizing, and supply chain reconverting, among others. The social economy has also proven its regulatory macro-function in the economy and world of work.

In the new recovery and reconstruction phase, and also to benefit from the conditions, needs, and opportunities emerging after the COVID-19 pandemic, the potential of the social economy must be exploited. In order to profit from the resilience and adaptive and transformative capacities of the social economy, government should give it a leading space and role in reconstruction and recovery policies. Such policies involving the social economy would not be new, as they have already been tested in recent years. Indeed, a new generation of transformative policies in support of the social economy has been deployed in innovative ways by several national, regional, and local governments in Europe (Chaves & Demoustier, 2013; Utting, 2017; Monzón & Chaves, 2017; Chaves & Monzón, 2018; Chaves & Gallego, 2020). They all start from a high recognition of the systemic functions of the social economy, and then articulate systematic support plans that share some common features: (1) they are based on public–social economy collaboration both in the co-construction (co-design) of policies and in their co-production (implementation); (2) they are conceived from a mainstreaming public policy perspective; and (3) they are complex, systematized, and medium and long-term in terms of their organizational architecture. But more research is needed in order to have greater empirical evidence about the most recent public policies deployed, their instruments, and the evaluation indicators used.

Recent reconstruction policies deployed at national and regional levels, as is the case in Spain, seem to go in this direction (Chaves & Savall, 2020). The European case is also especially significant. The recent approbation of the European Social Economy Action Plan in December 2021 (European Commission, 2021) goes in this direction. Indeed, it recognizes institutionally the social economy and its potential; it establishes the right conditions for the social economy to flourish and opportunities to start up and scale up. Most importantly, it considers the social economy as a key actor for green and digital transitions and for the European social pillar. Finally, it facilitates the institutional and financial framework for state and regional governments to develop broad policies to promote the social economy.

As indicated in UNTFSEE (United Nations Inter-Agency Task Force on Social and Solidarity Economy [UNTFSEE], 2020), making the most of the potential of the social and solidarity economy will depend fundamentally on the willingness of governments to co-design and co-implement public policies and recovery measures within a multi-actor approach, including the social economy itself. This means committing to a new model of social and economic development that is more 'people-centred and planet-sensitive'.

References

Abeledo, R., Bacete, G., Sendra, M., & Álvarez F. (2020). *Impacto de la crisis de la Covid-19 sobre las organizaciones y agentes culturales de la Comunidad Valenciana.* Universitat de València, Econcult.

Anghel, B., Cozzolino, M., & Lacuesta, A. (2020). El teletrabajo en España. Boletín Económico (2/2020). Banco de España. https://repositorio.bde.es/bitstream/123456789/12361/1/be2002-art13.pdf

Banco de España (2020). El impacto de la pandemia en España y la respuesta de la política económica. *Informe Anual 2019* (pp. 117–171). https://repositorio.bde.es/bitstream/123456789/13052/1/InfAnual_2019-Ep4.pdf

Borzaga, C., Salvatori, L., & Bodini, R. (2019). Social and solidarity economy and the future of work. *Journal of Entrepreneurship and Innovation in Emerging Economies,* 5(1), 37–57. https://doi.org/10.1177%2F2393957518815300

Bouchard, M. (Ed.) (2010). *The Worth of the Social Economy: An International Perspective.* Ixelles: P.I.E. Peter Lang.

Caldera, A., de Serres, A., Gori, F., Hermansen, M., & Röhn, O. (2017). *Strengthening Economic Resilience: Insights from the Post-1970 Record of Severe Recessions and Financial Crises.* OECD Economic Policy Papers (20). OECD Publishing. https://doi.org/10.1787/6b748a4b-en

Cancelo, M., Vázquez, E., & Díaz-Vázquez, R. (2022). Impacto de la crisis de la covid-19 en el empleo de las cooperativas y sociedades laborales en España en el año 2020: un análisis shiftshare sectorial. *CIRIEC-España, Revista de Economía Pública, Social y Cooperativa*, 104, 35–64. https://doi.org/10.7203/CIRIEC-E.104.21702

Center for Disease Control and Prevention (2007). *Interim Pre-pandemic Planning Guidance: Community Strategy for Pandemic Influenza Mitigation in the United States—Early, Targeted, Layered Use of Nonpharmaceutical Interventions.* https://www.cdc.gov/flu/pandemic-resources/pdf/community_mitigation-sm.pdf

Chaves, R., & Demoustier, D. (Eds) (2013). *The Emergence of the Social Economy in Public Policy: An International Analysis.* Ixelles: P.I.E. Peter Lang.

Chaves, R., & Gallego, J. R. (2020). Transformative policies for the social and solidarity economy: the new generation of public policies fostering the social economy in order to achieve sustainable development goals—the European and Spanish cases. *Sustainability*, 12(10), 4059. https://doi.org/10.3390/su12104059

Chaves, R., & Monzón, J. L. (2012). Beyond the crisis: the social economy, prop of a new model of sustainable economic development. *Service Business*, 6(1), 5–26. https://doi.org/10.1007/s11628-011-0125-7

Chaves, R., & Monzón, J. L. (2018). La economía social ante los paradigmas económicos emergentes: innovación social, economía colaborativa, economía circular, responsabilidad social empresarial, economía del bien común, empresa social y economía solidaria. *CIRIEC-España, Revista de Economía Pública, Social y Cooperativa*, 93, 5–50. https://doi.org/10.7203/CIRIEC-E.93.12901

Chaves, R., Monzón, J. L., Pérez de Uralde, J. M., & Radrigán, M. (2013). La economía social en clave internacional. Cuantificación, reconocimiento institucional y visibilidad social en Europa, Iberoamérica y Norte de África. *Revista de Estudios Cooperativos*, 112, 122–150. http://www.redalyc.org/articulo.oa?id=36728553006

Chaves, R., & Savall, T. (2020). La política de la Economía Social en la era Covid-19. In I. Bretos & C. Marcuello (Eds), *Informe de la economía social en Aragón 2019: características, dimensión y evolución de la economía social aragonesa* (pp. 136–150). Zaragoza: Universidad de Zaragoza. https://doi.org/10.26754/uz.978-84-122578-1-6

Chaves, R., & Zimmer, A. (Dirs). (2017). *El tercer sector en España y en Europa. Crisis y resilencia.* Universitat de València.

Collado, J., & Rodríguez, M. (2020). Impacto económico en 2020 del covid-19 y de las medidas ejecutadas en España. Generalitat Valenciana; Universitat de València. https://prospectcv2030.com/wp-content/uploads/2020/06/Impacto-COVID19.pdf

Dieste, J. M. (2020). Las plataformas colaborativas como oportunidad para la innovación social. *REVESCO. Revista de Estudios Cooperativos*, 133, e67338. https://doi.org/10.5209/REVE.67338

European Commission (2021). *Building an Economy that Works for People: An Action Plan for the Social Economy.* Publications Office of the European Union. https://data.europa.eu/doi/10.2767/12083

Eurostat (2022). *National Accounts. European Commission.* Retrieved March 2022, from https://ec.europa.eu/eurostat/web/main/data/database

Fiorelli, J., & Gafforio, L. (2020). The impact of Covid-19 on social economy enterprises. Social Economy Europe. https://www.socialeconomy.eu.org/wp-content/uploads/2020/06/SEE-Report-The-impact-of-COVID-19-on-Social-Economy.pdf

Hansmann, H. B. (1981). Reforming nonprofit corporation law. *University of Pennsylvania Law Review,* 129, 497–623. https://heinonline.org/HOL/Page?handle=hein.journals/pnlr129&id=509&collection=journals&index=

Hansmann, H. B., & Weisbrod, B. A. (1975). Defining benefits of public programs: some guidance for policy analysts. *Policy Analysis,* 1(1), 169–196. https://www.jstor.org/stable/42783382

Instituto Nacional de Estadística (2021). Encuesta de Población Activa con variables de submuestra (EPA). Tailor-made microdata mining.

Instituto Nacional de Estadística (2022). Contabilidad Nacional Trimestral de España. Retrieved March 2022, from https://www.ine.es/dyngs/INEbase/es/operacion.htm?c=Estadistica_C&cid=1254736164439&menu=resultados&idp=1254735576581

International Labour Organization (2020a, 24 April). Cooperatives and wider SSE enterprises respond to Covid-19 disruptions, and government measures are being put in place. https://ilo.org/global/topics/cooperatives/news/WCMS_740254/lang—en/index.htm

International Labour Organization (2020b, 29 April). Covid-19 and the world of work (3rd ed.). Updated estimates and analysis. https://www.ilo.org/wcmsp5/groups/public/@dgreports/@dcomm/documents/briefingnote/wcms_743146.pdf

International Labour Organization (2022). Resolution concerning decent work and the social and solidarity economy in International Labour Conference—110th Session, 2022. ILC.110/Resolution II. https://www.ilo.org/wcmsp5/groups/public/—ed_norm/—relconf/documents/meetingdocument/wcms_848633.pdf

Itçaina, X., & Richez-Battesti, N. (Eds). (2018). *Social and Solidarity-based Economy and Territory: From Embeddedness to Co-construction.* Ixelles: P.I.E. Peter Lang.

Johns Hopkins Coronavirus Resource Center (n.d.). COVID-19 Maps. Johns Hopkins University. Retrieved May 2022, from https://coronavirus.jhu.edu/map.html

Keck, M., & Sakdapolrak, P. (2013). What is social resilience? Lessons learned and ways forward. *Erdkunde,* 67(1), 5–19. https://www.jstor.org/stable/23595352

Kruse, D. (1994). Profit sharing and public policy. *Journal of Economic Issues,* 28(2), 439–448. https://doi.org/10.1080/00213624.1994.11505558

Lorenzo, A. (2020, 26 April). Las 30 normalidades que impondrá el coronavirus cuando acaba de la crisis. El Economista. https://www.eleconomista.es/sanidad/noticias/10503829/04/20/Las-30-normalidades-que-impondra-el-coronavirus-cuando-acabe-la-crisis.html

Manca, A. R., Benczur, P., & Giovannini, E. (2017). *Building a Scientific Narrative towards a More Resilient EU Society, Part 1: A Conceptual Framework.* Publications Office of the European Union. https://doi.org/10.2760/635528

Ministerio de Trabajo y Economía Social (2021). Servicio de Empleo Público Estatal (SEPE). Tailor-made microdata mining.

Monzón, J. L., & Chaves, R. (Dirs). (2017). *Recent Evolutions of the Social Economy in the European Union*. European Economic and Social Committee. https://www.eesc.europa.eu/sites/default/files/files/qe-04-17-875-en-n.pdf

Organisation for Economic Co-operation and Development (2020a). *Social Economy and the COVID-19 Crisis: Current and Future Roles. OECD Policy Responses to Coronavirus (COVID-19)*. OECD Publishing. https://doi.org/10.1787/f904b89f-en

Organisation for Economic Co-operation and Development (2020b). *OECD Employment Outlook 2020: Worker Security and the COVID-19 Crisis*. OECD Publishing. https://doi.org/10.1787/1686c758-en

Organisation for Economic Co-operation and Development (2021, 10 March). *Supporting Jobs and Companies: A Bridge to the Recovery Phase*. https://www.oecd.org/coronavirus/policy-responses/supporting-jobs-and-companies-a-bridge-to-the-recovery-phase-08962553/#blocknotes-d7e1115

Organisation for Economic Co-operation and Development & European Union (2017). *Boosting Social Enterprise Development: Good Practice Compendium, Local Economic and Employment Development (LEED)*. OECD Publishing. https://doi.org/10.1787/9789264268500-en

Paarlberg, L. E., LePere-Schloop, M., Walk, M., Ai, J., & Ming, Y. (2020). Activating community resilience: the emergence of COVID-19 funds across the United States. *Nonprofit and Voluntary Sector Quarterly*, 49(6), 1119–1128. https://doi.org/10.1177%2F0899764020968155

Parnell, E. (2001). The role of cooperatives and other self-help organizations in crisis resolution and socio-economic recovery. International Labour Organisation, Cooperative Branch; InFocus Programme on Crisis Response and Reconstruction. https://www.ilo.org/wcmsp5/groups/public/—ed_emp/—emp_ent/—coop/documents/publication/wcms_745892.pdf

Pedreño, J. A. (2020, 8 April). *Social Economy Europe Open Letter: Overcoming COVID-19 Time for Solidarity*. Social Economy Europe. https://www.socialeconomy.eu.org/2020/04/08/social-economy-europe-open-letter-overcoming-covid-19-time-for-solidarity/

Pérez, F., & Maudos, J. (Coords), Albert, C., Alcalá, F., Benages, E., Chorén, P., Escribá-Esteve, A., Herrero, C., Mas, M., Mínguez, C., Mollá, S. Pascual, F., Quesada, J., Reig, E., Robledo, J. C., & Zaera, I. (2020). La superación de la crisis del Covid-19 en la Comunitat Valenciana: Una hoja de ruta de la reconstrucción de la economía. Generalitat Valenciana. https://www.ivie.es/wp-content/uploads/2020/05/La-superaci%C3%B3n-de-la-crisis-del-COVID-19-en-la-Comunitat-Valenciana.pdf

Pitarch, M. D. (2020). Turismo y vulnerabilidad territorial: capacidad de resiliencia de los diferentes modelos turísticos frente a la crisis pandémica del coronavirus en España in Spain. In M. R. Simancas, R. Hernández, & N. Padrón (Coords), *Turismo pos-COVID-19. Reflexiones, retos y oportunidades* (pp. 211–223). Universidad de La Laguna. https://doi.org/10.25145/b.Turismopos-COVID-19.2020

Rao, H., & Greve, H. R. (2018). Disasters and community resilience: Spanish flu and the formation of retail cooperatives in Norway. *Academy of Management Journal*, 61(1), 5–25. https://doi.org/10.5465/amj.2016.0054

Seguridad Social. (2022a). Afiliados en ERTE. Ministerio de Inclusión, Seguridad Social y Migraciones. Retrieved March, from https://www.seg-social.es/wps/portal/wss/internet/EstadisticasPresupuestosEstudios/Estadisticas/EST8/22bfb5ae-8eba-4c44-a258-93a26194e11b

Seguridad Social (2022b). Afiliados último día del mes por provincias y secciones de actividad. Ministerio de Inclusión, Seguridad Social y Migraciones. Retrieved March, from https://www.seg-social.es/wps/portal/wss/internet/EstadisticasPresupuestosEstudios/Estadisticas/EST8/EST10/EST305/EST309

Seguridad Social (2022c). Cese de actividad de trabajadores autónomos. Ministerio de Inclusión, Seguridad Social y Migraciones. Retrieved March, from https://www.seg-social.es/wps/portal/wss/internet/EstadisticasPresupuestosEstudios/Estadisticas/EST45/2562

Simo, G., & Bies, A. L. (2007). The role of nonprofits in disaster response: an expanded model of cross-sector collaboration. *Public Administration Review*, 67, 125–142. https://www.jstor.org/stable/4624690

Seguridad Social (s.d.). Afiliados en ERTE. Ministerio de Inclusión, Seguridad Social y Migraciones. Retrieved March 2022a, from https://www.seg-social.es/wps/portal/wss/internet/EstadisticasPresupuestosEstudios/Estadisticas/EST8/22bfb5ae-8eba-4c44-a258-93a26194e11b

United Nations Inter-Agency Task Force on Social and Solidarity Economy (2020). What Role for the Social and Solidarity Economy in the Post COVID-19 Crisis Recovery? International Labour Organization. https://www.ilo.org/global/topics/cooperatives/publications/WCMS_748794/lang—en/index.htm

Utting, P. (2017). *Public Policies for Social and Solidarity Economy: Assessing Progress in Seven Countries*. International Labour Organization. https://www.ilo.org/wcmsp5/groups/public/—ed_emp/—emp_ent/—coop/documents/publication/wcms_582778.pdf

De Vet, J. M., Nigohosyan, D., Núñez, J., Gross, A.K., Kuehl, S., & Flickenschild, M. (2021). Impacts of the COVID-19 pandemic on EU industries. European Parliament's Committee on Industry, Research and Energy. https://www.europarl.europa.eu/RegData/etudes/STUD/2021/662903/IPOL_STU(2021)662903_EN.pdf

Walker, B., Holling, C. S., Carpenter, S. R., & Kinzig, A. (2004). Resilience, adaptability and transformability in social–ecological systems. *Ecology and Society*, 9(2). https://www.jstor.org/stable/26267673

Weitzman, M. L. (1984). The case for a share economy. *Challenge*, 27(5), 34–40. https://doi.org/10.1080/05775132.1984.11470960

Wisner, B., & Adams, J. (Eds). (2002). *Environmental Health in Emergencies and Disasters: A Practical Guide*. World Health Organization. https://apps.who.int/iris/handle/10665/42561

11

(Un)Successful scaling of social innovation

The role of local social economy actors in promoting
development in emerging markets

Ruth Brännvall

Introduction

Within the field of social innovation and social entrepreneurship, there have been
few examples in the literature of organizations that have been successful in creating and delivering innovative services at a larger scale. Previous examples include
mainly non-profit organizations. Less attention has been given to commercially orientated social entrepreneurs, who wish to deliver economic returns alongside social
impact, especially ventures in developing and emerging economies (Saebi et al., 2018;
Gupta et al., 2020). Innovation in emerging markets is often supported by foreign
entrepreneurs and companies from Europe and the US, bringing new technologies
and knowledge. This chapter presents findings from two illustrative case studies that
focus on the challenges and opportunities for scaling social ventures in collaboration
with local non-profit community-based organizations. This includes the question of
how the social innovators adapt to the local markets, especially for the involvement
of end-users in the innovation process.

Prior research has shown that the ability to design services which support all parties in the processes of value creation and include the customer in creating the experience becomes a source of competitive advantage for the firm (Casadesus-Masanell
& Feng, 2013). Value is determined not only through the products and services themselves, but by the value they co-create with their customers. The research I present
in this chapter provides a complementary perspective to many studies that focus
on external factors to explain the challenges of value creation and scaling. Numerous articles and book chapters have been written about social entrepreneurs' drivers
and motivations for scaling, which list almost exclusively positive attributes. Several
scholars attribute to social innovators abilities to envisage, engage, enable and enact
transformational change (Thompson, Alvy, & Lees, 2000). They are even likely to be
'happy, extroverted, open to experiences' (Koe Hwee Nga & Shamuganathan, 2010).

Ruth Brännvall, *(Un)Successful scaling of social innovation*. In: *Social Economy Science*. Edited by: Gorgi Krlev, Dominika
Wruk, Giulio Pasi, and Marika Bernhard, Oxford University Press. © Oxford University Press (2023).
DOI: 10.1093/oso/9780192868343.003.0011

By adopting a critical view on how these companies and entrepreneurs operate, a more nuanced and more practical perspective can hopefully be presented. Second, social enterprises are highly influenced by their contextual settings (Gupta et al, 2020). For studies in developing and emerging markets, I have therefore chosen to use a post-colonial lens to support this critical and contextual analysis. I will elaborate on the choice of post-colonial theories in the method section of the chapter.

Since 2010 I have studied twenty commercially orientated social entrepreneurs in developing and emerging economies, based on sampling and methods described in my thesis (Brännvall, 2018). The initial research focused on characteristics and motives for the entrepreneurs and ventures. For two of these ventures, I then continued with the development of detailed case studies that provide insights into (1) the use of digital technology in agriculture and (2) innovation in the field of menstrual hygiene products. Bearing in mind the spatial limitations of a single book chapter, more attention will be given here to the latter case. There is generally a great lack of innovation and research in this field that concerns women worldwide (Bobel, 2020). The innovation need is more emphasized in low and middle-income countries due to the obvious constraints on resources and poorer infrastructure for sanitation and waste management. But so-called period poverty has also been brought to our attention by activists in wealthier economies, such as with the 'Free Period Scotland' campaign that led to Scotland becoming the first country in the world where local authorities provide period products for free.[1] Social activists point out the high cost such products have over a lifetime, also for women in other under-served market segments globally. On the positive side, this is a field of innovation in which there are many examples of cross-over and collaborations between private (social) ventures and other actors in the social economy (e.g. Athumani, 2017; WoMena, 2019; Tellier et al., 2020).

By 'social economy', I here refer to the co-operatives, local non-profit organizations, and social enterprises involved in social innovation. Education and training are the focus of local non-profit organizations. Social enterprises (mostly founded by foreign entrepreneurs) are responsible for innovation and commercialization. Non-profits in emerging markets often point out a number of factors that affect the uptake or non-use of a proposed menstrual product, and the social ventures respond mainly by solving one part of the equation—affordability. This is proving to be insufficient.

Background: Why are social innovation and scaling so difficult in the African context?

The companies in the case studies, which I will describe in more detail in what follows, were founded by young entrepreneurs from Europe. They set up operations in different locations in Africa and received international donor money, as well as private funding through programmes aimed at stimulating innovation for the poorest

---

[1] See: https://www.bbc.com/news/uk-scotland-scotland-politics-51629880

in the global South. Such foreign initiatives are typical for African businesses that include advanced technical research and development, or advanced manufacturing, and also for social ventures and enterprises. Innovation activities and adoption of technologies are high among SMEs in Africa (Amankwah-Amoah et al., 2018) but Africa, Latin America, and Oceania are not the originators and developers of such technologies. These regions are consumers of innovation and may add incremental differentiators (Bradley et al., 2012; Radwan, 2018; Bidwell, 2021).

The growth of digital platforms in Africa has been fast in recent years, with more than 365 platforms whose users are mainly attracted to online shopping and freelance services, according to the South African based research organization Insight2Impact (Hunter, 2020). Most of these businesses originated in South Africa, followed by Nigeria, Kenya, and Ghana, according to Insights2Impact, but the data does not reveal to what extent the intellectual property rights of the technologies that these platforms utilize also originated in Africa. In all, ten of the platforms in this sample originated in Asia and sixty-two in Europe or the US. The first-mover advantage that foreign platforms have is clear also here; they have on average three times more users than the local platforms, and among companies that have ceased to operate, 90 per cent originated in Africa (Hunter, 2020).

The foreign-led technology focus in Africa has knock-on effects in the lack of skilled workers in technology, sales, and management. Some argue that the presence of technology in Africa has not contributed to growth that affects inequality and poverty, despite strong growth in availability and adoption (Adejumo et al., 2020). Foreign entrepreneurs may have a technical advantage as they set up their companies in emerging markets, but the lack of skilled workers will then become a barrier to scaling for them as well, as my research showed (Brännvall, 2018). It may play a part in explaining why social enterprises scale in India but struggle in other emerging markets. Technology transferred from one market to another, and in particular from a developed market context into a more resource-constrained market, can only happen when both hard and soft components of the technology (and understanding of the technology) are transferred (Amankwah-Amoah et al., 2018).

Challenges in agriculture (need for public–private collaboration for innovation)

The actors involved in agriculture innovation are numerous and represent a broad and heterogeneous set of actors representing civil society, academia, and the public and private sectors in emerging markets as well as developed economies (Grovermann et al., 2019). Researchers have pointed out areas in need of further innovation, such as systemic approaches to service delivery, process facilitation, and knowledge brokering (Leeuwis & Arts, 2011; Daane, 2010; Swanson & Rajalahti, 2010). Funding has followed suit (Alarcon, 2018; Munthali et al., 2018). A challenge in the field of agri-related innovation may however be that young people are abandoning farming, and particular small-scale farming, in pursuit of careers and/or migration into cities.

On the other hand, the young people who stay in or enter the agricultural sector may be more likely today to see themselves as entrepreneurs (Zmija et al., 2020). The enormous uptake of ICT service and innovation in mobile-based message applications and information services encourages the creation of virtual communities for problem solving and entrepreneurship, such as the 'Youth Agripreneur' initiative by the International Institute of Tropical Agriculture in Nigeria, which targets young people in the agricultural sector.

Munthali et al. (2018) have described three new ICT platforms for agricultural extension in Ghana: one public ('E-extension'), one private ('SmartEx'), and one developed by academics ('Plantwise'). The public and private platforms both aim at coordinating actors among stakeholders in the value chain, many of them being part of the social economy (co-operatives; community-based service delivery organizations). A weakness of both platforms is, however, the profiling of farmers, their needs and demands, and operational attributes, such as production and credit history. Agriculture is a common theme also in research relating to the social economy (e.g. Fonte, 2017; Nasioulas, 2012; Julia & Server, 2003)—understandably so, as climate change will hit emerging markets hard and Southeast Asia is predicted to be the most hard-hit region. In a world that is 2°C warmer, heat-related work productivity loss would amount to more than two months (Shuang et al., 2019).

Challenges in women's hygiene products (high social entrepreneurial activity, low levels of innovation)

Women's health, on the other hand, does not attract the same level of innovation activity and interest from researchers or funders. At a global level, international aid specifically supporting gender equality and women's empowerment remained at 5 per cent of the total OECD countries' donations by 2019, and the subcategory of health receives approximately 0.3 per cent of this annually (OECD, 2019). Gender equality here refers to activities that aim at reducing social, economic, or political inequalities between men and women, girls and boys. Even when focusing on an area that concerns almost all women—products for menstrual hygiene—it is easy to see that menstrual products in the global market have been the same since the 1960s. Incremental innovation may have improved materials and choice, but there are still only three product categories in the mass market (sanitary pads, tampons and menstrual cups). The field is dominated, both in terms of innovation, production, and sales, by a few large multinational corporations. Development and testing have to a great extent been undertaken by medical practitioners (Vostral, 2020). For example, a search of the grant database of the Swedish development and innovation agency Vinnova shows that among 17,249 funded projects in the history of the agency, one single project relates to menstrual products (Vinnova, 2020). The dominance of very few has stifled innovation in the past, especially failing those consumers and users that live in emerging countries. Digital applications that track the menstrual period have on the other hand exploded, dominated by European and American developers, partly as a consumer trend to monitor our bodies and their performance, including fertility (Goode, 2013; Epstein et al., 2017).

The topic of products to manage menstruation is equally hard to find in the academic literature. Studies mainly relate to absenteeism and how schoolgirls in impoverished countries handle menses (Schoep et al., 2018; Hennegan et al., 2019). Many of these studies show a link between the lack of options in handling menstruation and reasons why girls and female students miss school. A meta-study published in the Lancet in 2019 on the use of menstrual cups supports the findings from the interviews undertaken in my own research. In all studies, the use of a menstrual cup (studies included 199 different producers available in 99 countries) required that the user familiarize themselves with the product over several months to use it as intended. The long-term impact study carried out by WoMena in Uganda (2019) also noticed that education and introduction to a menstrual cup took up to six months before the user adopted the product. This may explain the slow uptake of menstrual cups. Although the life cycle of ten years for most cups does mean that a menstrual cup is the most affordable product category in any market today, it is far from a preferred choice.

A handbook on critical menstruation studies, probably the first publication to collect such a large number of academic studies on the topic, 'reveals, complicates and unpacks inequalities across biological, social, cultural and historical dimensions' (Preface of Bobel et al., 2020) but includes just one article on the development of menstrual products, which is a historic review (Vostral, 2020). The missing demographic group in the research is adult working women. The few studies that exist on the effects of menstruation, mainly carried out in high-income countries, point to considerable impact on productivity loss, which in part is explained by the physical experience of menstruation which causes pain and concentration difficulties (Schoep et al., 2018). These studies do not discuss what role different types of sanitation products play in the level of absenteeism in the workplace. A systematic review and metasynthesis of studies done in a total of thirty-five countries concluded that many studies highlighted inadequate access to comfortable, easy-to-use menstrual products as 'problematic' and experiences of how women in the workplace handle menstruation as under-researched. Affordability and accessibility are two major factors for absenteeism among schoolgirls and probably also for productivity loss in low-income countries. The lifetime cost of using products of mainstream brands is estimated to be circa EUR 5000, according to the activist organization Bloody Good Period,[2] which was started by social entrepreneur Gabby Edlin to highlight 'period poverty' among asylum seekers. This, alongside personal experiences of poverty and lack of choice, is the main motive for the entrepreneurs included in our research, foreign as well as local. The standard products also have a large environmental impact, as all products contain plastics, which most often end up in landfill, and are very often individually wrapped in even more plastic. As just noted, the product category with the lowest environmental footprint and the lowest cost of ownership is the menstrual cup, but it comes with many usability issues.

---

[2] https://www.bloodygoodperiod.com/

Another reason to highlight entrepreneurship and the need for innovation for improved access to sanitation and health, in relation to future policies in social economy, is the enormous need for change when it comes to economic participation for women. In many emerging economies, co-operatives and grassroots organizations are important actors of change. In Morocco, for example, co-operatives have become the most viable form of organization capable of including rural populations into economic value chains, in particular in the production of argan oil (Dossa, 2014). At the same time, previous studies have shown that successful co-operatives sometimes need to abandon some basic co-operation principles and adopt a more commercial orientation to attract resources to the organization to enable growth (ibid). The topic of social enterprises and their collaborative efforts to engage different types of stakeholders in innovation and co-creation processes has been explored by some in the literature (Branzei et al., 2018; De Silva et al., 2021; Nascimento et al., 2021), but with few conclusions that are useful to practitioners when it comes to growth and scaling. How can partnerships and alliances be developed that manage the fine balancing act of satisfying both commercial and impact objectives? Some have argued they cannot be combined, among them most notably Muhammad Yunus (Yunus & Weber, 2010). The studies in Morocco cited above, on the other hand, show that, for example, the shift from equal to non-equal dividend distribution based on share of ownership (effectively introducing preference share structures to co-operatives) did help the growth and scaling of the co-operatives, contrary to Yunus' firm argument.

The challenges of multi-territory scaling

Social enterprises and social innovation are succeeding to scale at the local and national levels, in particular in India (see e.g. Ramani & Mukherjee, 2013; Sundaramurthy et al., 2013), but few innovations seem to translate into multiple markets, even within sectors that seem to have similar needs and structures.

The situation is particularly challenging in Africa. The innovation of mobile money transfer in Kenya, for example, which seemed to have the potential to scale across the continent, failed to do so, as it requires similar and favourable industrial and institutional conditions which are underdeveloped in most African countries (Amankwah-Amoah et al., 2018). Less well published and known than the African mobile payment innovation is the E-Choupal service for grain procurement that is deployed through 6100 kiosks in 35,000 villages in India, reaching more than four million farmers (ICT Agri Business, 2022). E-Choupal was created by the company ITC, which is a large Indian multi-business corporation, aiming at lowering the cost of procurement of agricultural products by eliminating costs (actors) in the value chain that do not add value. In the very fragmented Indian market, the proposition to farmers is the choice of where and when to sell their crops, rather than being dependent on the intermediary who made their margins from the information asymmetry. In addition to market prices, which many organizations offer farmers these days, E-Choupal facilitates loans, access to insurance products, and updates on weather forecasts. The physical internet kiosks are also managed by farmers. This model shows that market actors and market mechanisms can be used to promote economic growth among all citizens, and the market itself does not necessarily have to be very unfriendly to the poor and the vulnerable, as stated by scholars such as Haq in his *Reflections on Human Development* (1995).

Looking more at the theoretical level and beyond these particular examples, Zeyen and Beckmann (2019) point out the difference between scaling and growth in an enterprise. Growth and expansion in traditional business ventures is measured mainly by the organizational parameters in number of jobs created, geographical reach, and increase in turnover and profitability. Social innovation, though, can expand beyond an enterprise as the focus is on achieving a social mission, which can include other organizations that help to deliver this mission with or without formal links to the 'original' business venture. The decoupling of growth and scaling can be useful when understanding what strategies are appropriate and available to social ventures and social enterprises. Zeyen and Beckmann summarize three types of scaling: dissemination, affiliation, and branching. They put franchising into the category of affiliation, whereas case studies have shown that hybrid franchise models can also be a way for the originating organization to branch out (Naatu & Alon, 2019).

Growth and scaling are particularly challenging in rural areas with scattered populations. Some enterprises, such as EzyAgric[3] in Uganda and Farm Shop[4] in Kenya, which aim at integrating the value chains in agriculture have demonstrated that it is possible by way of engaging end-users and organizing them into the value chain. These enterprises offer market information and knowledge to the different actors in the value chain, and in particular to the smallholder farmer. McKague et al.'s (2021) study of Farm Shop, an organization that helps solve last-mile distribution problems for agriculture products in Kenya, demonstrates that the organization became stronger when it chose to use a model based on partnerships (franchise) to run its stores, rather than operating them on their own. Farm Store has managed to crack the critical question of how to operate with constant uncertainty about supply and demand by investing heavily in data collection and testing what data is essential to identify the right business model for itself and its franchise partners.

Taking a post-colonial perspective

A critical approach is useful when studying the challenges of scaling a social venture, as it is concerned with situating the material and historical context to the development of (management) ideas and practices (Willmott, 2008; Gupta et al., 2020). In studies of management, some scholars adopt a critical post-colonial perspective (e.g. Kunda, 1992; Nkomo, 1992; Westwood, 2001; Prasad, 2009; Priyadharshini, 2003, Moulettes, 2009) wherein grand discourses on organization, management, and

---

[3] https://ezyagric.com
[4] https://farmshop.co.ke

corporate culture are analyzed. I had started to notice in my early interviews that the founders of the case-study companies expressed views, ideas, and interpretations about the local context that originated in the West, rather than from local knowledge and expertise. Within the field of critical management studies, a few scholars look at organizations that operate in former colonies from this critical perspective, including Banerjee and Duflo (2007) and Karnani (2007a, 2007b). They question the role of business in reducing poverty, as do Arora and Romijn (2011), who argue that business often maintains an unequal power relationship as it targets the so-called Base of Pyramid market segments. The increasing role of advanced knowledge and technology 'favours equally highly educated people and often damages the less qualified' (Milanović, 2016: 54).

Research method

The research setting

To address the research questions, I draw on two case studies that are located in separate and very different sectors in Ghana and Kenya: information services for the agriculture sector, and products for menstrual hygiene. Both of the case companies that I analyse were founded by one or more women of European origin. The new services and products proposed by the social ventures in the research would all have a broad appeal in many developing economies, and this is what they have in common: innovations for increased agricultural output and food security for smallholder farmers in light of climate change, and innovations that strengthen womens' economic participation.

Target groups in both case studies are the poorest, as they potentially stand most to gain in the adoption of these products, and therefore a key part of these ventures' operations is partnerships with actors in the social economy. Although comparisons may be very difficult to make between these very different areas of innovation and economic activity, it may be relevant to note that the level of innovation, as measured by the number of actors engaged in innovation, level of output, and resources invested, is vastly different.

The cases

In my research, I observed and interviewed the founders, end-users, and partners of the two start-ups mentioned above over a five-year period (2012–2017) in order to improve the understanding of the process of end-user inclusion in the innovation process. These two companies were initially part of a population of twenty start-ups which had received grants and/or awards from the Swedish government or the EU for innovation in how they address poor and marginalized groups as customers, employees, or partners. The companies were of different national origins and operated in any sector. I selected the specific two case studies from this larger set of start-ups by doing a theoretical sampling (Eisenhardt & Graebner, 2007) where I set the following key criteria:

1. Innovative or new product or service for under-served market segments

   'Underserved' is here defined as a customer segment, which has no prior or very limited choice and access to similar products and is most often characterized by low purchasing power. Underserved is therefore a term that should not only be associated with developing economies, but with any disadvantaged community.

   (Porter & Kramer, 2011)

2. The product has potential to be productivity-enhancing for users; for example, it may improve chances of economic inclusion in society.
3. The entrepreneur has an intention of bringing a product to market that can benefit society at large.

The criterion of social impact is included in part as an identifier of those organizations that have an interest in under-served segments, and in part these criteria connect the entrepreneurs' own beliefs in increased emancipation and inclusiveness of users, which align with the central idea of this research. The cases show similarities to complement each other (Voss et al., 2002), but have diversifying factors (geography of operation, country of entrepreneur origin, and sectors) to try to ensure that these will be theoretically useful cases (Eisenhardt, 1989a; Flyvbjerg, 2006), as I wish to extend emergent theory.

The first contact with all companies was made in my practitioner context, as CEO of Impact Invest,[5] where I introduced the question about participating in this research study after I had identified the criteria of which type of company to study. I therefore had some background knowledge and pre-understanding of the companies and the interviewees before starting the empirical data collection.

The company focusing on menstrual hygiene closed its operations in Kenya in mid-2014 and continued operating from Europe, and my last formal interview with the co-founder was conducted in August 2014, but I continued with expert interviews for the case. I have also participated in work meetings where the end-user research and information have been discussed with each company. In these meetings, I have made participatory observations about what questions are discussed, what is articulated about end-users, and how the members of these meetings suggest learning more about users. The interviews with the founders have been complemented by journals that I asked the entrepreneurs to use in the first year, as well as interviews with customers, users, and stakeholders to which the entrepreneurs have referred me.

---

[5] www.impactinvest.se/?lang=en

The second case study was complemented by additional exploratory research in Eastern Africa, especially in Uganda, which brought novel products or approaches for menstruation management to the market.

Small organizations that develop one or possibly two products provide a relatively simple unit of analysis. In all the coaching sessions I have with entrepreneurs as a practitioner, I tend to come back to the question of what motivated the entrepreneur to start their business. By this, I have been trying to understand how well the entrepreneur understands their end-user and the market context. Many social innovators depend on their ability to influence change over a whole system, not just in individual services (Mulgan, 2015). Yet, I had noted that some entrepreneurs engage the potential target group in their market research, but most seem to wait until a first version of a product or service is ready before they engage with end-users. So these were the core concerns that my questions and analysis sought to address. In order to get at these issues, which are often hidden behind positive narratives, I applied the critical studies approach introduced earlier in the data analysis. More specifically, I employed the lens of post-colonial studies in analysing my data.

Deconstruction and development of narratives

As the Western science tradition often looks for the optimum, 'right' answer (Kapoor, 2011), who gets to decide what is the right solution for people in under-served markets? How are organizations developing the right capabilities to innovate if there is no discussion about who contributes with different competencies? As explained previously, I have added post-colonial theory as an analytical lens and I am 'blending' the use of theories from different fields in order to analyse these aspects.

Deconstruction is a method used in social science to analyse the empirical material to identify what different narratives exist in the material. This approach is grounded in the works of the post-structuralist philosopher Jacques Derrida, who used it as a technique for language analysis in literature criticism and philosophy. He was interested in exposing what ideologies and assumptions are hidden in a text, and in examining contradictions that reveal the difference between what we want to say and the words we use to express ourselves. (But he also pointed out that deconstruction should not be considered a method in itself (Beardsworth, 1996).) Derrida's approach in the deconstruction of a text was to first focus on what is suppressed by identifying 'hierarchical oppositions'. Hierarchies of thought and language are everywhere (Tsoukas & Hatch, 2001). For example: A is the rule and B is the exception; A is normal and B is abnormal; A is simple and B is complex; A is natural and B is artificial/abnormal. When deconstruction is used to analyse a text, the purpose is to show what it excluded or neglected and what ideals the text is based on. In close-reading every word of a text in 'the context of what is taken for granted assumptions' (Kilduff, 1993: 16), the reader is trying to discover patterns in a text; for example, searching for binary oppositions. Post-colonial criticism is focusing on exposing the norms of the 'white, male, heterosexual and rational' (Bertens, 1995: 7): who then become excluded or neglected (women, people of colour, non-heterosexuals, children and so forth)? The term used for such excluded or ignored collective groups is 'the Other'. An example of deconstruction, with a post-colonial lens, is the reading of a text many years apart and see how it changes meaning over time. The comic book *Tintin in Congo*, which was first published in 1931, has been subject to debate many times about racist stereotypes in children's literature.[6] The author admitted that the first version had portrayed the Congolese as stupid, childish and lazy and acknowledged that his work was influenced by the colonial ideas of that time. He consequently made some alterations of illustrations and wording.

An example of using deconstruction in the context of this chapter can be to exchange the words that describe 'the Other' when (white) entrepreneurs speak about people in emerging and developing markets to 'people from Gothenburg' to see whether it changes anything about how the text reads and how we interpret it. The original quote by one entrepreneur in this study: 'There are quite a lot of people around here who don't care much, who does not seem to think about the future', when describing a local community in Western Africa, may not raise as much of an eyebrow than it would if we exchanged the words 'people around here': 'There are quite a lot of people here in Gothenburg who don't care much . . .'.

Or (another quote): 'There are mountains of condoms in Kenya', versus 'There are mountains of condoms in Gothenburg'. This is an effective way of exposing generalization and stereotypes in the analysis of interviews and literature.

I used the above deconstruction method to exchange certain words during the data analysis to their binary opposite (or closest equivalent). I aimed to understand what influenced the assumptions expressed by the entrepreneurs and their behaviour. I used theories of power and post-colonial deconstruction to identify and explain the internal factors that determine the entrepreneur's attitudes and actions in the relationships with end-users. In the last phase, I also looked for influencing factors in the external context. In doing so, I wanted to ensure that the analysis of the entrepreneurs themselves was not done in isolation, but to recognize that the entrepreneurs operate within an environment where their powers are limited and changing due to different circumstances.

Findings

The 'conservative' users in agricultural and hygiene innovation

The first case company produces subscription-based business intelligence for weather-sensitive industries in the tropical belt countries of West Africa. Their first business proposition has been to provide smallholder farmers with accurate two-day weather forecast and warning alerts, which the farmer receives by a text message

---

[6] https://www.theguardian.com/law/2012/may/14/effort-ban-tintin-congo-fails

on their mobile phone. With the help of such daily accurate weather forecasts, the farmer gets decision support regarding the use of limited resources such as water, fertilizers, and pesticides. The company mainly sells the seasonal subscription in bulk to farmers' co-operative organizations and input suppliers, and any other company that deals with individual farmers on a large scale. The company also intends to market the service directly to farmers through a marketing and distribution agreement with the largest mobile operator in the country, so that any farmer can sign up for the weather service directly from their own mobile phone.

The company remains the only commercial provider of weather forecasts specifically developed for the tropical region of Africa. In her journal as well as in interviews, the founder sometimes commented that farmers are not willing to change. I asked her how she had arrived at the conclusion that they are conservative.

> Through talking with them quite a lot . . . I guess. I have been out in the field and there is a certain resistance against new methods, generally speaking.

Is that generally speaking, or in relation to the service offered?

> No, it is generally so. Then we also know that there are a number of traditional methods for making forecasts and we usually spend an hour during our training discussing the different forecasting methods, pretty often there is a scientific explanation.

She comments in her journal that 'some field officers believe more in God than in our forecasts'. She often came back in the interviews to the point of farmers being conservative, but also said they were appreciative of her and the team coming 'all the way', bringing science and new technology.

> I went back to the [farmer] organization and said that it is questionable that those who are supposed to train the farmers on our product holds this view, since it means there is a lack of trust [in the product]. The organization responded that they would intensify the training in that region and we have modified the training to deepen their knowledge about weather and forecasting so that they in a way are 'certified' to carry out training for our product.

It is challenging to provide a weather forecast for several days through the limited interface of a few messages on a mobile phone. Using symbols at first, in order to also include illiterate users, the company struggled to find the right approach, as many interpretations were possible. When a German nonprofit organization suggested that simple words in English or French should be used for the forecasts instead of pictures and symbols, the company changed the user interface to pure text. End-users understood these messages better.

The second case-study company initially articulated themselves as a social business with the mission of providing a sustainable, affordable menstrual health solution to women and girls worldwide. It has since modified its mission to the provision of 'a healthier, more sustainable, cost-effective and eco-friendly alternative to pads and tampons'. The company made slight changes to the design of a menstrual cup, with the objective of delivering a better product at a lower cost. Its strategy to reaching its customers relied on two main approaches.

The first, and preferred, way was to introduce this product in ordinary retail outlets such as shopping malls and pharmaceutical stores. The company aimed at a low-income to middle-class market that could afford to purchase the product without any subsidies. The retail strategy was also important to signal that this product was a commercial product for the middle class, also when targeting the poorest people. One feedback from the first surveys that the company did together with a local non-profit organization was that girls would not want to use a product 'that was developed for the poor'. What girls really wanted to buy were sanitary pads sold by one of the largest international brands.

The second approach was to collaborate with non-profit organizations and provide a heavily subsidized product to those girls and women who would not have the means to buy the product in a retail store. One of the co-founders commented:

> Introducing an unknown product onto the market takes time. We have been told by some friends who work with solar lamps that it took ten years for solar lamps and solar panels to become accepted and it takes approximately seven different occasions for a customer to hear about a product before consciously noticing it.

Just like the weather company, this company also claims to be 'user-driven' and have an inclusive innovation approach. As an example of such practices, the company developed different sizes of the cup, as this was the 'most common feedback' and also because the founders 'really, really believe in the product'. Feedback had been collected in surveys and interviews that the company had carried out in several districts and for different demographic groups during the pilot phase, and ad-hoc following the commercial launch.

Among the enterprises that focus on menstrual management, many have a primarily educational purpose, but some wish to bring new products to the market. Most social enterprises that focus on menstruation are based in East Africa and are made up of a mix of actors in the social economy and individual social enterprises that are relatively young. The needs of users are hidden and not much spoken of, which in many previous studies has been interpreted as the result of taboos in communities surrounding the topic of menstruation and the female body.

The research findings demonstrate that such 'taboos' do not persist everywhere, contrary to the findings of many previous studies. For example, young girls in Nairobi spoke openly and vocally about their bodies, menstruation, and sexuality, as did girls in the rural town of Kisumu, albeit that some also told stories of staying at home from school while menstruating. Second, the silence surrounding the subject may be just as common in developed economies (Shuang et al., 2019). The link between words such as 'taboos' and 'developing countries' that is prevalent in past published research is a strong stereotype that risks degrading end-users into passive actors in the innovation process.

The case study of the menstrual company shows that since innovation is focused on affordability, its local competitors mainly concentrates on producing reusable textile pads or disposable pads made of plant-based, locally sourced materials. In one instance the affordability aspect led to one enterprise abandoning its own production of pads and instead starting to teach girls, as well as boys, how to make pads. The enterprises that are commercially orientated are exploring new manufacturing methods to use different types of plant-based fibres. The technological development among the African ventures is domestic and the ventures quote a very limited number of partners in the ideation and development phases.

In addition to the case analyses, a colleague at Makere University in Uganda and I did some research to contextualize our cases. We identified three enterprises, out of twelve organizations with operations in Eastern Africa, as interesting complements to our two primary cases that sell their own products in markets other than the originating country. Two of these enterprises were founded by foreigners and one by a local entrepreneur. They all produce sanitary pads by different manual methods. The local entrepreneur has managed to expand with exports to other markets in Africa. (It is perhaps interesting to note that in Uganda we note a mix of men and women in these ventures, whereas we only observed female founders in enterprises founded elsewhere).

Several of the ventures in this research were founded in 2017. The previous year, a candidate for president of Uganda placed the issue of a lack of menstrual products on the agenda and there was a public debate about the lack of funding and resources that led to funding initiatives (Athumani, 2017) as well as entrepreneurial initiatives. The reason why we find so many social enterprises and nonprofits focusing on menstrual hygiene in Uganda specifically may be linked to several international organizations initiating and funding research and development initiatives in Eastern Africa. Among our respondents, several had received funding from UNFPA, UNHCR, bilateral donors, local grants, and some private donors, which had supported the scaling of those organizations that are now well established. In the product category of menstrual products, where cultural aspects are important for the adoption of new products, there are opportunities for partnerships where commercially orientated social enterprises collaborate with actors in the social economy not only for distribution, but also to ensure end-user inclusion in the innovation process.

One of the very few companies that have developed patented solutions in this field, according to the Google Patents and Justia databases, is the American social enterprise Be Girl Inc, which has set up operations in Mozambique, Kenya, and Colombia. They have been awarded several patents for undergarments intended to prevent leakages and staining and to allow women and girls to use any sort of absorbent material for their bleeding.

The role of actors in the social economy for scaling social innovations

In both case studies, the meteorological company and the venture selling a menstrual cup, the founders aimed at integrated growth and scaling. The products were priced at a level that were deemed affordable to the poorest. Over time, both ventures struggled to grow at the same pace as they scaled their social innovations. Both ventures gained their first users through pilots and free-to-use trials, funded mainly by international aid funding and some private philanthropic capital. With large sums of money to fund these pilots and launches, thousands of users were offered the new services.

In the case of the meteorological service, farmers were offered a paid subscription after the trial. Retention rates were high and more than half of users continued subscribing to the service, although on an irregular basis as the micro-payments that were deducted each day from the users' pre-paid mobile accounts often failed due to lack of credit. Each new region and market to which the company expanded required partnerships with farmer associations to promote the service, in the same way that during pilots, and with generous donor funding and private investments, the scaling of the innovation spread to five different countries with a mix of free and paid subscriptions. This was key in order to gain trust, get a 'licence to operate', and scale in these countries. Over time, the entrepreneurs started to realize that they did not always have the means to interpret feedback from end-users, as illustrated by this quote regarding a customer who did not want to sign up for the weather service:

> Do they say 'no' because they do not want the service, or because they do not understand the service?

Some local partners became important actors that also provided the company with feedback on how the service was perceived in terms of accuracy over time and to evaluate whether the service influenced farmers' behaviour (Brännvall, 2016). In an impact study where the venture received support from Yale University to interview users, it turned out that among the farmers who saw the highest increase in yields, as a result of getting access to more precise weather information, there was an overrepresentation of women farmers. But despite examples of successful partnerships that could deliver several benefits to the enterprises, the entrepreneurs mainly perceived these partnerships as useful for distribution and education of end-users.

In the case of the menstrual cup, growth proved a major challenge due to the barrier to adoption (negative customer perception of the cup) and the constant need to educate users. The partners for education of the target groups were more inclined to give away menstrual products than to sell them, which cannibalized potential revenues, as the social enterprise's main go-to market strategy was to sell the cups through retail channels.

Yet, in both case studies, founders still held on to a degree of cultural power advantage over the way to do business, which is manifest in different ways:

I think the brand just needs to be communicated better.

We had a [local] business person as a shareholder in the first year and he was not to be trusted. He cheated us.

With the knowledge about how the market works, compared to in the beginning, I think I am a lot more pragmatic now. And more realistic about how long things take and what you can do and what you cannot do. In the beginning when we got a new contact with an NGO, we were so excited and spent [lots of resources] and 90 per cent of the time nothing happened . . . It is also that the Scandinavian way of efficiency, it is just not like that here.

The interviews and observations during the case studies showed that when entrepreneurs are 'outsiders' to the markets they wish to serve, they hold generalizations and stereotypes of end-users, often limiting and undervaluing their feedback. This offered an important reason for why those ventures did not grow or alternatively were slow to launch new services, as users' requests were not acted upon. One of the foreign entrepreneurs, in the most recent research, pointed out that their products have been designed according to a 'human-centric approach', which to them means that they include end-users' view in the design process and test the acceptance of products in target groups. They use local partners for education (which they too see as an essential part of their business venture) and for data collection with organizations in education and sexual and reproductive health.

Responding to the lack of managerial capacity

Previous publications cited earlier, as well as the data from both case studies, have pointed to the problem of recruiting local people into management positions as a barrier to growth and scaling. The weather forecasting company tried to overcome this by creating virtual teams, to bring in senior business competence from Europe and the US who worked mainly remotely. Although bringing well-needed capacity to the venture, the obvious risk is the disconnect between management and contextual understanding. This problem may in part be constructed, as the foreign entrepreneurs bring a Western idea of how an enterprise should be organized and operated. There are more variations in the formations among local social entrepreneurs; for example, limited private companies versus cooperatives, where the level of democratic decision processes varies, and possibly also the motives and values of the founders. The forms and legal structures of social enterprises, social ventures, and social businesses are evolving and boundaries blurring. Our most recent research among enterprises focused on menstrual hygiene shows a mix of legal forms of incorporations (NGOs or private limited companies) that cannot be distinguished by business idea, social mission, or operations.

Francesconi (2019) proposed that managerial capacity in rural Africa is available for technical development and innovation, but education in management subjects is missing—in particular marketing and industrial economics (understanding pricing, cost structures, product specializations, options for growth, etc.). The interviews we have done in the field of menstrual hygiene show similar types of activities, processes, and collaboration as in Anderson's and Lent's study (2017). We see signs of attempts to organize a value chain—research and production, marketing, and sales and education—but less advanced in comparison to the number of actors involved in the value chain and the technical content, including financial and time-critical components of the services offered by the agricultural enterprises.

Discussion

Both organizations claimed to have a user-centred approach, but my analysis shows that this was not really the case; further, there was not much room for increasing the intensity of collaborations with local partners, which would have helped the organizations to better identify and serve the needs of users and thereby scale their operations. The post-colonial lens was helpful to reach this conclusion as it showed and explained that foreign founders of these organizations were more embedded in and driven by their home countries' cultures. The deconstruction method helped me reveal generalizations and stereotyping of end-users on the part of the foreign entrepreneurs. End-users' influence on the product development, beyond the very first pilots, was limited, and entrepreneurs valued and sought their feedback less over time. Partners in the social economy were critical to extend the reach of both ventures' operations, but had little involvement in the innovation process after the initial projects. The origin of community-based actors also mattered, as illustrated by the example of the German nonprofit organization whose suggestions were implemented by the weather forecasting company while feedback from native community-based organizations carried less weight. In both case studies, local partners were mainly seen as distribution channels. Importantly, this helped explain why one of the ventures did not grow beyond its first years of operation and decided to shut down its local office in Kenya.

The first venture was slow to launch new services, in part due to foreign investors' strong preference for exponential growth of the user base and 'key performance indicators' focused on quantitative metrics. Creativity and good ideas are often based on intuition for 'what could work' and a very reiterative process of trial and error. There are certain elements in the innovation process that need to encourage as much free thinking and new types of input as possible (McKeown, 2014). To increase the chances of successful innovation that leads to new kinds of products that address inequality and economic empowerment, it is very likely that social innovation would benefit from having a much broader set of actors engaged in the process. Complex problems need more perspectives on 'what could work'. Had the ventures engaged local partners to a greater extent also to support capturing of user data and analysis, they may have been able to reap the same long-term value from this as in the case of Farm Shop (which has a stronger co-operative approach and works with local partners more intensely), with better margins and extended reach to serve under-served populations. The research question which results from examining the questions of social innovation and scaling in the African context, and from a critical perspective, is: How can social ventures collaborate better with local partners for the purpose of innovation? Equally, how can actors in the social economy then collaborate with commercially orientated entrepreneurs and companies and not fall into the traditional pattern of undervaluation of what they could contribute in terms of innovation?

Different actors have appeared to support the scaling of enterprises in the second field, such as the initiative by Duke University and UNICEF to accelerate solutions for better menstrual health. More radical thinking is needed, though, when it comes to proposed solutions and more advanced technologies to expand available product categories for different needs and preferences. Several of the enterprises interviewed in Uganda mention having only one laboratory or one incubator as a partner to produce their first prototypes (typically one that was geographically close). We see no evidence that they have attempted to attract advanced technical expertise, or carefully studied where competition fails. We asked the question 'How is your product different?' The most common response referred to price and to minor product features, such as choice of colour and size. It rarely focused on the needs of users or the local populations. The differences that the interviewees mentioned, however, are too small to be perceived as attractive for customers, and this shows in poor sales volumes and very limited or slow growth.

Conclusion

Whereas other fields of innovation in emerging economies have relied on technology transfer, it should also be possible to encourage technology transfer from advanced manufacturers and research laboratories in Europe and elsewhere to develop new materials and to drastically re-think the design of menstrual products. It is a greatly underinvested field of innovation and research. This research shows that an increasing number of entrepreneurs and other actors in the social economy are focusing on the area of women's health and menstrual hygiene. These actors however do not have the innovation capabilities to bring radically better physical products to under-served people. One reason may be that digital solutions are in general preferred by impact investors today over physical product development and distribution. From an investor's perspective, digital solutions seem to scale faster. But this leaves questions about meaningful change over time when the funded solutions are disconnected from aspects of end-users' needs and desires.

Time and time again, end-user research in the field of menstrual hygiene shows that access to water and proper sanitation is essential to be able to use any type of menstrual products while participating in studies and work. Next, innovation and product development to solve 'period poverty' in different geographies is greatly needed, as well as a focus on working women's needs, to complement the previous main research focus of schoolgirls and young women.

In the field of agricultural innovation, the current literature and the case study of the weather forecast company demonstrate that better involvement in the innovation and design processes of users are needed, with an awareness that stereotyping of people in under-served markets risks filtering of information and rejection of bottom-up ideas. A critical perspective can be helpful to allow for openness and empathy in design and innovation processes. Foreign founders (and supporters) should consider 'sanitizing' themselves of a priori assumptions and stereotypes. Future research may investigate the correlation of diversity in management teams with scaling and profitability in social ventures, and explore ways of overcoming the lack of senior local management that ventures claim to be a main obstacle to growth of their operations in Africa.

Annex 1

List of organizations in East Africa included in the research of menstrual products:

Makit
Founded by a Danish team, the company designed a menstrual cup, 'Ruby Cup', produced in China. The company sells its products online in Europe and operates a 'buy one, give one' model which allows distribution in Eastern Africa.

Technology 4 Tomorrow
The organization produces several products, including the MakaPad, a disposable pad made from papyrus fibre. Founded by a Ugandan national.

EcoSmart
Produces disposable pads from sugarcane fibres. Founded by a Ugandan team.

Shuya
A Chinese company that has opened up operations in Uganda, where they promote sanitary napkins.

She for She
Produces reusable menstrual pads from already used textiles in an upcycling process. Founded by a Ugandan team.

Center for Transformative Parenting and Research
Teaches children and youth how to make your own sanitary pads. Ugandan NGO.

Kasole Secrets Company Ltd
Kasole Secrets produces the Glory Sanitary Napkin, a disposable pad engineered with ultra-absorbent and naturally antibacterial and hypoallergenic bamboo fibre, produced in China with plans to open a factory in Tanzania. Founded by a Tanzanian woman.

Femme International
Femme International seeks to make quality, reusable menstrual products available, accessible, and affordable in local markets, and along the last mile throughout East

Africa. They do not produce their own products, but distribute for example the Ruby Cup by Makit. The company was started by a Canadian, their HQ is in Canada, and they have an office in Tanzania. Education programmes are run in Kenya and Tanzania.

SaCoDé (short for Santé Communauté Développement)
SaCoDé is an NGO engaged in different community development projects. One of their focus areas is women's health. They produce a reusable sanitary pad branded Agateka, which means Dignity in Kirundi, which is designed with special straps that allow it to be worn with or without underwear. The organization is based in Burundi.

AfriPads
Reusable menstrual pads and other associated products. Founded by a Canadian couple, based in Uganda.

Xsabo Foundation
German–Ugandan consultancy group Xsabo runs a CSR initiative to teach women, girls, and boys to make disposable sanitary pads from plant-based fibres.

BanaPads (company no longer in operation)
Disposable sanitary pads made out of banana fibre. Started by a male Ugandan social entrepreneur.

References

Adejumo, O., et al. (2020). Technology-driven growth and inclusive growth: implications for sustainable development in Africa. *Technology in Society*, 63, 101373.
Alarcon, S., & Arias, P. (2018). The public funding of innovation in agri-food businesses. *Spanish Journal of Agricultural Research*, 16(4),
Amankwah-Amoah, J., et al. (2018). Contemporary challenges and opportunities of doing business in Africa: the emerging roles and effects of technologies. *Technological Forecasting & Social Change*, 131, 171–174.
Anderson, A., & Lent, M. (2017). Enterprising the rural: creating a social value chain. *Journal of Rural Studies*, 70, 96–103.
Arora, S., & Romijn, H. (2011). The empty rhetoric of poverty reduction at the base of the pyramid. *Organization*, 19(4), 481–505.
Athumani, H. (7 April 2017). Ugandan girls make reusable sanitary pads to stay in school. *VOA News*. https://www.voanews.com/archive/ugandan-girls-make-reusable-sanitary-pads-stay-school
Banerjee, A., & Duflo, E. (2007). The economic lives of the poor. *Journal of Economic Perspectives*, 21(1), 141–167.
Beardsworth, Richard (1996). *Derrida & the Political*. Abingdon: Routledge.
Bertens, Hans (1995). *The Idea of the Postmodern: A History*. Routledge.

Bidwell, N. J. (2021). Decolonising in the gaps: community networks and the identity of African innovation. In H. S. Dunn et al. (Eds), *Re-imagining Communication in Africa and the Caribbean* (pp. 97–115). London: Palgrave Macmillan.

Bobel, C. et al. (2020). *Introduction: Menstrualtion as a Lens—Menstruation as Opportunity. The Palgrave Handbook of Critical Menstruation Studies.* Palgrave Macmillan.

Bradley, S., et al. (2012). Capital is not enough: innovation in developing economies. *Journal of Management Studies.* 49 (4), 684–717.

Brännvall, R. (2016). Enabling user-inclusive innovation in African agriculture. *ICT Update*, 83, 8.

Brännvall, R. (2018). *'They are so damn grateful.' A Longitudinal Study of How Post-colonial Attitudes Influence the Innovation Process in Social Ventures.* PhD thesis, The Royal Institute of Technology (KTH)

Branzei, O., et al. (2018). Going pro-social: extending the individual–venture nexus to the collective level. *Journal of Business Venturing*, 33(5), 551–565.

British Council (2018). Activist to entrepreneur. The role of social entrepreneurs in supporting women's empowerment in Ghana.

Bruner, J. S. (1986). Value presuppositions of developmental theory. *Psychology Press.*

Casadesus-Masanell, R., & Feng, Z. (2013). Business model innovation and competitive imitation: the case of sponsor-based business models. *Strategic Management Journal*, 34(4), 464–482.

Daane, J. (2010). Enhancing performance of agricultural innovation systems. Rural Development News, 76–82.

De Silva, M., et al. (2021). Business model innovation by international social purpose organizations: the role of dynamic capabilities. *Journal of Business Research*, 125(3), 733–749.

Dossa, Z. (2014). *The Potential of Social Economy for Local Development in Africa: An Exploratory Report.* European Union, Directorate-General for External Policies of the Union, Policy Department. https://www.euricse.eu/wp-content/uploads/2015/03/EXPO-DEVE_ET2014433787_EN.pdf

Eisenhardt, K., & Graebner, M. (2007). Theory building from cases: opportunities and challenges. *Academy of Management Journal*, 50(1)

Eisenhardt, K M. (1989a). Building theories from case study research. *Academy of Management Review*, 14(4), 532–550.

Epstein, D., et al. (2017). Examining menstrual tracking to inform the design of personal informatics tools. In *Proceedings of the 2017 CHI Conference on Human Factors in Computing Systems*, 6876–6888.

Flyvbjerg, B. (2006). Five misunderstandings about case-study research. *Qualitative Inquiry*, 12(2), 219–245.

Fonte, M., & Cucco, I. (2017). Cooperatives and alternative food networks in Italy. The long road towards a social economy in agriculture. *Journal of Rural Studies*, 53, 291–302.

Francesconi, N. (2019). Building the managerial capacity in agricultural cooperatives in Africa. *Annals of Public and Cooperative* Economics. https://sites.google.com/site/edcooperatives/publications?authuser=0

Goode, L. (2013). Max Levchin's Glow Fertility App: The Full D11 Session. *All Things Digital.* Available at: https://allthingsd.com/20130529/max-levchins-glow-fertility-app-the-full-session-video/

Grovermann, C., et al. (2019) Eco-efficiency and agricultural innovation systems in developing countries: evidence from macro-level analysis. *PLoS ONE*, 14(4), e0214115.

Gupta, P., et al. (2020) Social entrepreneurship research: a review and future research agenda. *Journal of Business Research*, 113, 209–229.

Haq, M. (1995). *Reflections on Human Development.* Oxford: Oxford University Press.

Hennegan, J. et al. (2019). Women's and girls experiences of menstruation in low- and middle income countries: A systematic review and qualitative metasynthesis. *Plos Medicine*, 16(5): e1002803. https://doi.org/10.1371/journal.pmed.1002803

Hunter, R., et al. (2020), African digital platforms and the future of financial services. An eight country overview. *Focus Note, Insight2Impact.* Available at: https://cenfri.org/wp-content/uploads/ADP-Focus-Note-2019.pdf

ICT Agri Business (2022). E-Choupal. https://www.itcabd.com/e-choupal.aspx

Julia, J. F., & Server, R. J. (2003). Social economy companies in the Spanish agricultural sector: delimitation and situation in the context of the European Union. *Annals of Public and Cooperative Economics*, 74(3), 465–488.

Kapoor, R. (2011). Is there a postnormal time? From the illusion of normality to the design for a new normality. *Futures*, 43(2), 216–220. https://doi.org/10.1016/j.futures.2010.10.012

Karnani, A. (2007a). Doing well by doing good—case study: 'Fair and Lovely' whitening cream. *Strategic Management Journal*, 28, 1351–1357.

Karubanga et al. (2017). How farmer videos trigger social learning to enhance innovation among smallholder rice farmers in Uganda. *Cogent Food & Agriculture*, 3, 1368105.

Kilduff, M. (1993). Deconstructing organizations. *Academy of Management Review*, 18(1), 13–31.

Koe Hwee Nga, J., & Shamuganathan, G. (2010). The influence of personality traits and demographic factors on social entrepreneurship start up intentions. *Journal of Business Ethics*, 95, 259–282.

Kunda, G. (1992). *Engineering Culture: Control and Commitment in a High-Tech Corporation.* Philadelphia: Temple University Press.

Leeuwis, C., & Aarts, N. (2011). Rethinking communication in innovation processes: creating space for change in complex systems. *Journal of Agricultural Education and Extension*, 17, 21–36.

McKague, K., Jiwa, F., Harji, K., & Ezezika, O. (2021). Scaling social franchises: Lessons learned from Farm Shop. *Agriculture & Food Security*, 10(1), 299. https://doi.org/10.1186/s40066-021-00313-w

Mckeown, M. (2014). *The Innovation Book: How to Manage Ideas and Execution for Outstanding Results.* London: Pearson UK.

Milanovic, B. (2016). *Global Inequality: A New Approach for the Age of Globalization.* Boston: Harvard University Press.

Moulettes, A. (2009). *The Discursive Construction, Reproduction and Continuance of National Cultures: A Critical Study of the Cross-cultural Management Discourse.* PhD thesis. Lund: Lund Institute of Economic Research.

Mulgan, G. (2015). The study of social innovation: theory, practice and progress. In Nicholls, A. et al. (Eds). *New Frontiers in Social Innovation Research.* London: Palgrave Macmillan.

Munthali, N., et al. (2018). Innovation intermediation in a digital age: comparing public and private new-ICT platforms for agricultural extension in Ghana. NJAS—Wageningen *Journal of Life Sciences,* 86–87, 64–76.

Naatu, F., & Alon, I. (2019). Social franchising: a bibliometric and theoretical review. *Journal of Promotion Management,* 25(5), 738–764.

Nascimento, L.d.S., et al. (2021). Coopetition in social entrepreneurship: a strategy for social value devolution, *International Journal of Emerging Markets.* https://doi.org/10.1108/IJOEM-09-2020-1062

Nasioulas, I. (2012). Social cooperatives in Greece: introducing new forms of social economy and entrepreneurship. *International Review of Social Research,* 2(2), 141–161.

Nkomo, S. (1992). The emperor has no clothes: rewriting 'race in organizations'. *Academy of Management Review,* 17, 487–513.

OECD (2019). *Aid in Support of Gender Equality and Women's Empowerment.* https://www.oecd.org/dac/financing-sustainable-development/development-finance-topics/Aid-to-gender-equality-donor-charts-2019.pdf

Porter, M. E., & Kramer, M. (2011). Creating shared value. *Harvard Business Review,* 89(1–2), 62–77.

Prasad, A. (2009). Contesting hegemony through genealogy: Foucault and cross cultural management research. *International Journal of Cross Cultural Management,* 9(3), 359–369.

Priyadharshini, E. (2003), Reading the rhetoric of otherness in the discourse of business and economics: towards a postdisciplinary practice. In Prasad, A. (Ed.), *Postcolonial Theory and Organisational Analysis.* London: Palgrave Macmillan.

Radwan, A. (2018). Science and innovation policies in North African countries: exploring challenges and opportunities. *Entrepreneurship and Sustainability Issues,* 6(1), 268–282/

Ramani, S., & Mukherjee, V. (2013), Can breakthrough innovations serve the poor (bop) and create reputational (CSR) value? Indian case studies. *Technovation,* 34, 295–305.

Saebi, T., et al. (2018). Social entrepreneurship research: past achievements and future promises. *Journal of Management,* 45(1), 70–95.

Schoep, M., et al. (2018). Productivity loss due to menstruation-related symptoms: a nationwide cross-sectional survey among 32 748 women, *BMJ Open* 2019;9, e026186

Shuang, Y., et al. (2019). Loss of work productivity in a warming word: differences between developed and developing countries. *Journal of Cleaner Production*, 208, 219–1225.

Sundaramurthy, C. et al. (2013). Social value creation: a qualitative study of Indian social entrepreneurs, *Journal of Developmental Entrepreneurship*, 18(2), 1–20.

Swanson, B. E. and Rajalahti, R. (2010), Strengthening Agricultural Extension and Advisory Systems: Procedures for Assessing, Transforming, and Evaluating Extension Systems. *ARD Discussion Paper 44.*

Tellier, M., et al. (2020). *Practice Note: Menstrual Health Management in Humanitarian Settings.* The Palgrave Handbook of Critical Menstruation Studies. London: Palgrave MacMillan

Thompson, J., Alvy, G., & Lees, A. (2000). Social entrepreneurship: a new look at the people and the potential. *Management Decision*, 38, 328–338.

Tsoukas, M., & Hatch, J. O. (2001). Complex thinking, complex practice: the case for a narrative approach to organizational complexity. *Human Relations*, 54(8), 979–1013

Vinnova (2020). Project database. https://www.vinnova.se/sa-framjar-vi-innovation/projekt/

Voss, C., et al. (2002). Case research in operations management. *International Journal of Operations & Production Management*, 22, 195–219.

Vostral, S. (2020). Of mice and (wo)men: tampons, menstruation, and testing. In Bobel, C. et al. (Eds). *The Palgrave Handbook of Critical Menstruation Studies* (pp. 673–686). Palgrave Macmillan.

Westwood, R. I. (2001). Appropriating the other in the discourse of comparative management. In Westwood and Lindtead (Eds), *The Language of Organizations* (pp. 241–262). Thousand Oaks: Sage.

Willmott, H. (2008). Critical management and global justice. *Organization*, 15(6), 927–931.

WoMena (2019). Menstrual cup interventions follow-up study, Uganda https://womena.dk/wp-content/uploads/2019/04/Menstrual-Cup-Interventions-Follow-up-Study-Report-March-2019_FINAL-V0.2.pdf

Yunus, M., & Weber, M. (2010). *Building Social Business: The New Kind of Capitalism that Serves Humanity's Most Pressing Needs.*

Zeyen, A., & Beckmann, M. (2019). *Social Entrepreneurship and Business Ethics.* Abingdon: Routledge.

Zmija, K., et al. (2020). Small farming and generational renewal in the context of food security challenges. *Global Food Security*, 26, 100412.

12

The centrality of social-tech entrepreneurship in an inclusive growth agenda

Mario Calderini, Veronica Chiodo, Francesco Gerli, and Giulio Pasi

Introduction, parameters, and objectives

The outbreak of the COVID-19 pandemic in early 2020, growing social and territorial inequalities, and the acceleration of climate change are only a few of the disruptive events that characterize recent decades. Scholars continue to debate whether these dramatic phenomena should be seen as game-changers that have triggered new socio-economic paths or accelerators of well-established socio-economic trends. Regardless, our societies entered the 'next normal', and, as Sneader and Singhal (2020) put it, 'in this unprecedented new reality, we will witness a dramatic restructuring of the economic and social order in which business and society have traditionally operated'.

Given this common understanding, it is reasonable to expect thorough reflection on which actors, under which conditions, could contribute to exploring viable paths for the 'next normal'.

This chapter seeks to advance a grounded argument for a general rethinking of social entrepreneurship, its role in the global long-term recovery strategy, and its utility for shaping a new, inclusive EU growth agenda. Alongside this more argumentative effort, the reflections presented will also shed light on some of the most relevant aspects to consider in advancing the proposed rethinking to ensure its comprehensiveness and consistency, and, ultimately, the full deployment of its potential.

Social entrepreneurship is a key part of the social economy. However, defining social entrepreneurship is complicated because the concept is systemic and contested, with indistinct boundaries (Nogales-Muriel & Nyssens, this volume), and the epistemological and ideological perspectives of the authors trying to define it affect the nature of social entrepreneurship. Moreover, social entrepreneurship has a context and location-based identity: the form of a social enterprise depends upon its regulative, welfare, policy, competition, and cultural context (Defourny & Nyssens, 2017).

Mario Calderini et al., *The centrality of social-tech entrepreneurship in an inclusive growth agenda.* In: *Social Economy Science.* Edited by: Gorgi Krlev, Dominika Wruk, Giulio Pasi, and Marika Bernhard, Oxford University Press. © Oxford University Press (2023). DOI: 10.1093/oso/9780192868343.003.0012

Johnson (2000) defines social entrepreneurship 'as an emerging and innovative approach for dealing with societal needs' (p. 1), providing a broad characterization that nonetheless emphasizes social entrepreneurship's intrinsic 'directionality' towards solving needs, problems, and challenges. This broad conceptualization is also coherent with the common 'result-oriented' approach to the topic in the Anglosphere. Meanwhile, Austin et al. (2006) define social entrepreneurship as 'social value-creating activity that occurs within or across the non-profit, business, or government sectors' (p. 2), focusing on the socially positive outcomes that are generated by social entrepreneurship rather than on the specific organizational attributes of social enterprises, mainly the specific legal organizational forms that are adopted. Within these results-oriented conceptualizations, several authors have stressed that social entrepreneurship must be accountable for the societal outcomes and impacts that it generates (Rawhouser et al., 2019; Van Rijn et al., 2021), employing impact evaluation methodologies to prove these impacts.

Conversely, numerous scholars have identified social entrepreneurship by not only its intentional and accountable creation of social value but also the adoption of an 'entrepreneurial approach' or an 'entrepreneurial method' and spirit (Certo & Miller, 2008; Dees, 2007; Peredo & McLean, 2006; Sarasvathy & Venkataraman, 2011; Sinkovics et al., 2014), which concretely distinguishes social enterprises from charity organizations. These scholars stress social entrepreneurship's orientation towards social value creation and entrepreneurial nature and consider it inherently market-driven. Specifically, Bacq and Jansen (2011, p. 388) define social entrepreneurship as the organizational 'process of identifying, evaluating and exploiting opportunities aimed at social value creation employing commercial, market-based activities and of the use of a wide range of resources'.

Simultaneously, Achleitner et al. (2013) underscore the risk of market-based contexts excessively diluting the social value creation mission of social entrepreneurship, stressing that the term 'social entrepreneurship' should generally refer to 'untapped' markets that are inherently linked to wicked problems, precluding or impeding the entry of purely commercial forms of entrepreneurship. Social entrepreneurship organizations can be identified by their capacity to assume an additional degree of risk compared to the risk that is deemed reasonable for an organization that is motivated solely by market returns. In other words, social enterprises operate to satisfy needs and contexts that other commercial market entrepreneurs exclude.

The connections between resolving 'wicked' societal problems, generating social value, and the entrepreneurial and market orientation have led scholars to adopt a Schumpeterian perspective on social entrepreneurship (see Chell et al., 2010; Tapsell & Woods, 2010). Swedberg (2006) defines social entrepreneurship as 'a form of dynamic behaviour in one of the non-economic areas of society' (p. 33). Social entrepreneurship organizations have been characterized as candidate innovators due to their capacity to organize resources for novel solutions to societal and economic challenges (Chell et al., 2010; Tapsell & Woods, 2010; Ghazinoory et al., 2020).

By organizing scarce resources, social entrepreneurial organizations can innovate frugally (Mishra, 2021), offering economic affordability and low complexity: they provide accessible solutions in contexts where institutional voids persist. Moreover, social entrepreneurship has been recognized as representing an entrepreneurial opportunity locus for inclusive innovation that offers re-distributional effects to include marginalized groups in innovation processes (Tello-Rozas, 2016; George et al., 2012).

This discussion also reveals the description of social entrepreneurship as an entrepreneurial actor that shares, de facto, all of the attributes of responsible innovation (as identified by Stilgoe et al., 2013), an observation also made by Lubberink et al. (2018) and Lubberink et al. (2019). Thereby, responsible innovation builds strongly on the element of good and participatory governance (Voegtlin & Scherer, 2017; see Hueske, Willems, & Hockerts, this volume, on participation in social entrepreneurship). Social entrepreneurship organizations thus create 'socio-ethical value' by engaging stakeholders in their innovative activities and unleashing bottom-up systemic change via innovation.

Ultimately, we see that social entrepreneurship has been defined according to many attributes and characterizations. Although we recognize that each approach is inherently valid, we propose a novel characterization incorporating three main concurrent elements to re-draft the boundaries of what social entrepreneurship can do:

1. Directionality: Social entrepreneurship collects entrepreneurial forms that intentionally offer solutions to wicked societal challenges, directing their core business efforts towards services and products to either soften the social costs and consequences of inequalities or overcome structural barriers, thus solving some of the most pressing social issues affecting the population in a given context or worldwide.
2. Societal accountability: Social entrepreneurship features a reflexive element. Social entrepreneurship organizations directly engage with their beneficiaries to offer products and services. Through this direct engagement and the development of appropriate systems for measuring social impact, these organizations are held accountable for their social value.
3. A Schumpeterian-market orientation: Social entrepreneurial organizations demonstrate a natural market orientation based on their capacity for the innovative recombination of resources in disadvantaged contexts. Through this capacity, social enterprises also introduce market mechanisms into 'untapped' markets in which purely commercial forms of entrepreneurship do not operate. They creatively innovate, permitting them to be framed as socially Schumpeterian innovative actors.

Within our definition, we explore how social entrepreneurship can play a role in the context of greater societal transformations and how social entrepreneurs can use technology in new ways to enable inclusive growth.

Field convergence and the role of technology

We recognize that social entrepreneurship is going through a deep transformation. This started well before the pandemic crisis under the pressure of different forces, including emerging societal challenges, shifting consumer preferences towards sustainability-oriented products and services, political advocacy in favour of more inclusive societies, the crisis of traditional welfare systems, and new technological opportunities (Desa & Kotha, 2006a; Ismail et al., 2012; Desa & Basu, 2013; Arena et al., 2018, Scilitoe et al., 2020). Altogether, these pressures are pushing social entrepreneurship towards an evolution that will involve both novel and existing entrepreneurial forms.

Consumer attention to sustainability is encouraging substantial mainstream entrepreneurship to develop advanced corporate social responsibility practices and to accelerate the creation of 'a fourth sector' (Friis, 2009; Rubio-Mozos et al., 2019) rather than the more traditional and established third sector. This fourth sector seeks to encompass the social economy and social entrepreneurship by merging market and profit objectives to respond to environmental and societal needs.

Considering the broader picture, a general convergence of purely commercial entities, on one hand, and purpose-driven actors such as social enterprises, on the other, must be acknowledged.

For instance, some high-growth (innovative) enterprises show increasing attention to social and environmental challenges, sometimes integrating advanced mechanisms of social responsibility in their core functioning, undertaking elaborate social accounting exercises, and even stretching their business models to maximize intentional positive externalities (Markman et al., 2019; Rajesh et al., 2022). Simultaneously, as mentioned above, some social enterprises are evolving into very interesting organizational hybrids, intentionally pursuing profit and measurable social impact objectives (Figure 12.1) and often characterized by a consistent degree of knowledge or technology intensity and a tendency to drift from labour-intensive to capital-intensive entrepreneurial models (Calderini et al., 2021; Arena et al., 2018).

The underlying awareness driving this convergence is that the complexity and the interrelated character of societal challenges require collective effort from private and public actors to be solved. Neither the market nor the state can respond to them

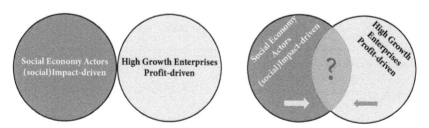

Figure 12.1 Convergence between evolving impact-driven social economy actors and high-growth profit-driven enterprises

alone. This recalls the development of novel and experimental partnerships involving social enterprises and civil society more directly (Mazzucato, 2021; Venturi & Zandonai, 2022). Moreover, the recent acceleration in organizations' digitalization processes (Meige & Schmitt, 2015) calls into question the capacity of the entire social economy to 'entrepreneurially' exploit this technological availability. It specifically addresses social enterprises' capacity to combine technologies into unique social business models that offer novel responses to societal challenges (Scilitoe et al., 2020). Such technological evolution is impossible without the availability of sufficient capital to enable enterprises to adopt technological innovations within their social business models.

This is why the evolution in social entrepreneurship entails hybridizing missions and objectives (Battilana & Lee, 2014; Doherty et al., 2014), managerial structure, financialization, and growing technological intensity.

While this fascinating convergence begs further exploration, the latter aspect is within the remit of this chapter, as it is likely to represent a breakthrough in the future evolution of social innovation and entrepreneurship.

In turn, novel technological and knowledge intensity will probably play key roles in the other transforming areas of social business models, that is, in the evolution of managerial practices and stronger financialization.

Nowadays, the commoditization of technologies, particularly in the digital and software domain, makes a difference. With the expression 'commoditization of technology' (Meige & Schmitt, 2015; Forbes & Schaefer, 2017) we refer to the decreasing adoption costs and increasing ease of use and user-friendliness that characterize the rapid recent development in low- and medium-tech applications that might be relevant for social innovation and social entrepreneurship, such as do-it-yourself manufacts that can be easily reproduced and 'commodified' by 3D printers (Petersen et al., 2017).

In this chapter, we discuss four reasons why, in light of recent technological developments, the relationship between social entrepreneurship and technology should be revisited and why we need a new generation of technology and innovation studies dedicated to social entrepreneurial organizations, reconsidering appropriately designed technology transfer practices and policies (see Table 12.1).

By discussing these four reasons, we aim to provide a systemic understanding of the technological development of social entrepreneurship. 'Systemic' refers to a lens

Table 12.1 The four systemic reasons for the centrality of socialtech entrepreneurship

Reason 1	Technology adoption and the capacity for increased resilience and responsiveness to grand challenges
Reason 2	The endogenous transformation and hybridization enabled by technological intensiveness in social business models
Reason 3	The capacity to improve the societal legitimacy of innovation and technology, mitigating unintended consequences
Reason 4	The relevance of social tech entrepreneurship within a concrete inclusive growth policy agenda

enabling us to analyse the evolution in organizational and social entrepreneurial models in constant relation to much broader socio-economic and policy scenario transformations. We contend that a systemic, in-depth view of the technological evolution in social entrepreneurship may reveal potential co-evolutions (Geels, 2014) in other institutions, organizations, policies, and growth models that are enabled by the nature of the transformation of social entrepreneurship.

Reason 1: Technology adoption in social entrepreneurship, resilience, and responses to grand challenges

The first systemic reason for the centrality of social-tech entrepreneurship is related to the adaptation of social entrepreneurship models and their technological development to the complexity of contemporary societal challenges. The pandemic has revealed the huge potential of different forms of social entrepreneurship to address social problems (La Piana, 2020), as well as some fragilities and limitations in delivering robust, resilient, large-scale solutions.[1]

We can claim that during the pandemic, social enterprises have experienced two divergent, extreme situations: they have been directly exposed to the crisis on the frontlines, experiencing high costs, responsibilities, and risks. They have, in parallel, been pushed to react and innovate to meet the emergency. Parts of the social economy appear to have been more resilient to the crisis than other organizations (Chaves-Avila & Soler, this volume), while other parts were paralysed and unable to perform normal activities and deliver their usual services[2] due to the nature of their activities. Both situations have generated unique consequences. Many social enterprises have seen their social business models, operations, financial stability, and social innovative models severely compromised and, sometimes, shattered.

It is, therefore, legitimate to ask whether the earlier adoption of digital technologies coupled with a more structured financial situation would have offered more resilience and, specifically, permitted social entrepreneurs to deliver more scalable, robust, structural solutions to dramatic emerging problems.

Technology as a response to crises

In the depths of the COVID-19 crisis, many social enterprises' adoption of digital platforms enabled coupling creativity with greater and faster responsiveness to emerging needs (La Piana, 2020). Moreover, digital platforms allowed the

---

[1] See also: 'Social entrepreneurs are first responders to the COVID-19 crisis. This is why they need support', World Economic Forum, https://www.weforum.org/agenda/2020/09/social-entrepreneurs-are-first-responders-to-the-covid-19-crisis/

[2] On the Italian case, see, among others: 'Terso settore a rischio, aiutateci ad aiutare', Quotidiano Sanità, www.quotidianosanita.it; 'Coronavirus—Aggiornamenti e disposizioni per il Terzo Settore', Forum Terzo Settore.

aggregation of the supply and demand for services and goods and unleashed novel, resilient forms of 'platform-based mutualism' and 'cooperative social welfare' (Miedes Ugarte et al., 2020). This was, for instance, true for welfare platforms activated by the Italian co-operative group CGM[3] (Martinelli et al., 2019). Coop-Circuits is another relevant case: it is a French booking and order management 'co-operative platform' developed under a free licence that allows the purchase and sale of artisanal, local, organic, and ethical products through short circuits. While traditional delivery players were quickly saturated during COVID-19, CoopCircuits enabled the rapid bottom-up emergence of local food distribution points on short circuits. With this tool, producers and networks of neighbours could set up tailor-made short-circuit supply solutions within specific territories.

Moreover, as Gagliardi et al. (2020) highlighted, the application of distributed ledger technologies, such as blockchain technologies, had the potential to improve the governance and accountability of social enterprises during the pandemic by facilitating participation and making the consultation of members and beneficiaries more secure and traceable.

The COVID-19 crisis emphasized the relevance of telemedicine and e-care systems. Many social enterprises are involved in healthcare and social assistance (Gagliardi et al., 2020). These enterprises typically operate in proximity to people in need, but they are increasingly asked to operate in 'decentralized areas' or remotely as well; this encompasses the rediscovered 'proximity potential' of the adoption of novel technologies in care-oriented social business models (Blasioli & Hassini, 2021).

Overall, as Venturi and Zandonai (2022) outlined, many original experiences emerged during the pandemic in the social entrepreneurial field. In addition to the proliferation of platforms, there were the novel interactions between fab-labs and social service providers, such as the ISINNOVA case of 3D-printed life-saving valves in Milan (Corsini et al., 2021) or novel partnerships between app developers and social enterprises such as the 'Del+Del' app developed by the Italian TICE co-operative to fight the isolation of elderly citizens.[4]

Together, these trends reveal the systemic potential of interaction between social entrepreneurship and patterns of technological development. This potential is not limited to the pandemic context but accelerates an existing trend in responsiveness to societal challenges.

Longer-term consequences

The value of merging technology with social entrepreneurial action is not restricted to the crisis context. As an example of the growth of impact-oriented, platform-based social enterprises, the Italian enterprise HumusJob has utility beyond the COVID-19

---

[3] See: 'Nasce biellawelfare: la prima piattaforma per i servizi a domicilio ai tempi del Coronavirus', Gruppo Cooperativo CGM.
[4] See: 'Coop. Tice: dalla Fondazione Tim 100mila euro una app contro la solitudine degli anziani', www.legacoopemiliaovest.it.

crisis. HumusJob is a successful start-up and digital platform that supports the agricultural industry in disadvantaged areas of Italy, enabling the hiring of labourers on a fair contractual basis via platform technology and a certification mechanism to address the illegal recruitment of migrants.

Thus, we recognize that a stronger, technology-intensive form of social entrepreneurship, possibly a different entrepreneurial genre altogether, is essential not only for prompt responses to urgent, demanding societal problems but more generally to represent the kind of organization that is best suited to lead in the creation of a new model of growth entailed by the complexity and persistence of contemporary societal challenges.

However, today, we have a limited understanding of the nature of the technology adoption process in social enterprises and social economy organizations more generally: we understand technology transfer practices and processes in this field even less (Vila Seoaen et al., 2013; Gerli et al., 2020).

This calls for further studies about the intertwining of social entrepreneurship's identity and resources and its capacity to adopt certain emerging and innovative technologies. This capacity is likely a function of the specific knowledge that social enterprises possess and the complementarity of novel technologies with that prior embedded knowledge (Cattani, 2005; Nooteboom et al., 2007).

Technology adoption by social entrepreneurship organizations is not solely a matter of organizational capabilities, resources, and knowledge, but also one of interorganizational relationships and ecosystems. As Gerli et al. (2021) claimed, the specific nature of social entrepreneurship is suited to drive an overall rethinking of the ecosystemic models aimed at the technological development of every kind of entrepreneurship.

The relevance of cognitive rather than physical proximity in enabling the technological advancement of social entrepreneurship and the open and demand-oriented nature of the innovations that social enterprises pursue (Gerli et al., 2021; Venturi & Zandonai, 2022) calls for an overall evolution of current models of innovation ecosystems towards more open, user-driven configurations.

For example, clusters—a widespread, ecosystemic innovation policy and conceptual tool (European Commission, 2021)—may be encouraged to evolve towards living lab configurations by applying the lessons of social entrepreneurship. New living lab models are more open, flexible, and user-oriented, as well as co-creative, in nature than traditional cluster models (Carros et al., 2020). Clusters may be reimagined as tools to aggregate localized and place-based societal needs rather than concentrated supportive services.

The open, societal need-oriented nature of social entrepreneurship can enable an evolution in the conceptualization of technology and innovation diffusion models as well (Sahin, 2006), evolving from a linear market-oriented approach towards a generalization paradigm (Wigboldus et al., 2016). The generalization perspective entails a greater and more multifaceted view of the routes and combinations of market and non-market dynamics leading to the societal diffusion of innovations, which can be technical, organizational, or societal. Two experimental examples that fit into such a perspective are the Get-It-Twice and 'Polisocial' projects launched by the largest Italian technical university, Politecnico di Milano, to diffuse and transfer research, knowledge, and technologies through active citizenship, civil society organizations, and territorial networks of social enterprises.[5] Such projects reveal that novel models of technology and innovation diffusion embed both institutionalized technology transfer processes and more informal, participatory, and citizenship-oriented models of innovation diffusion from universities and research centres to society (Goransson, 2017). These models ask technology and knowledge transfer organizations to develop new capabilities to fulfil the novel roles that are open to social-minded actors and present novel experimental research agendas.

Reason 2: The endogenous transformation enabled by technology and hybridity

The second reason for social-tech centrality is related to technology's role as an agent of endogenous transformation in social entrepreneurial models.

Technology and its adoption might change the model of social entrepreneurship and engender an evolution of social entrepreneurial business models towards more radically hybrid archetypes that do not limit profit production ex ante but do not represent profit as the organization's final objective. Social-tech ventures are a good example of this business model evolution. They are start-ups that use technology to develop new products and services that fulfil a social aim (Desa & Kotha, 2006a; Kamariah et al., 2012), for example, by offering loans and financial advice to the 'unbankables' through big data analysis and monitoring or by using a platform to make donors' and investors' payments conditional on verified societal impacts via blockchain-based infrastructure. However, their distinctive feature, compared to more mainstream high-tech start-ups, is that these ventures specifically aim to 'develop and deploy technology driven solutions to address social needs in a financially sustainable manner' (Desa & Kotha, 2006b, p. 159).

New tech-based business and governance models

A clear example of this evolution may refer to social enterprises that used to involve people with autism in standardized and often low-skilled recreational and professionalization activities in the form of social co-operatives or charitable organizations. These enterprises may evolve towards a model where, via appropriate programming software, people with autism can become involved in technology and knowledge-intensive activities. These activities can also be less standardized and more personalized, remunerative, and focused on the specific character of each person's autism. This wordy description suits the case of the social business Specialisterne,

---

[5] See   https://www.som.polimi.it/get-it-twice-la-call-per-innovare-i-sistemi-di-welfare-e-sanita-lomb ardi/ and https://www.yukionlus.org/project/gift-politecnico-milano/?lang=en, respectively.

an organization that is currently active in twenty-three countries and focuses on the high-skilled job placement and training of people on the autism spectrum.

Overall, two elements should be highlighted to underline the centrality of technology in shaping this fundamental transformation from low- and no-tech social entrepreneurship to social-tech ventures. The first is the shift from labour intensity to higher capital intensity that is the obvious consequence of technology adoption. The shift towards capital-intensive models motivates an emergent appetite for capital and financial resources and opens up relevant managerial and governance issues (Arena et al., 2018). Technology adoption creates novel managerial issues, requiring novel resources and capabilities that range from human resources to the complexity of intellectual property management.

Additionally, at the governance level, the technology-induced appetite for capital will bring in new investors with expectations of financial returns alongside social impact objectives. The appearance of this type of investor and stakeholder is likely to perturb the equilibrium between social and economic objectives and introduces new potential sources of mission drift. We therefore argue that the adoption of technology exposes social enterprises to higher risks of mission drift that are worthy of empirical investigation.

Technology as a means for scaling

Meanwhile, a second crucial transformation related to technology adoption is linked to the scaling-up potential of technology and its relationship with social business model sustainability.

Social enterprises typically have thin economic sustainability margins, when they exist at all (Santos et al., 2015). Technology usually enables scaling up and may improve organizations' operational efficiency. Larger volumes of activity and the related scale economies, together with efficiency gains, may reduce unit costs (Scilitoe et al., 2020).

Although we can debate whether the efficiency gains that technology enables should be entirely internalized by social enterprises and not shared with their beneficiaries, when the thin sustainability margins that characterize social enterprises are multiplied by larger volumes, a more robust and economically sustainable social business model can result.

Thus, technology adoption may enable the scaling of societal impacts and improve the financial sustainability of social business models.

In the field of health and social services, technology can enable greater personalization of interventions without decoupling from scaling those interventions (which are often pursued by social co-operatives). For example, the adoption of Care-bidet technology, an automatic toileting system, offers dignity and independence for people with reduced mobility. At the same time, it increases the customizability, diversification, and 'in-depth' scaling of caregiving in relation to the patient. The automatic toilet system allows caregivers to concentrate their working time on the more relational and non-standardized aspects of care work. Also, the adoption of such technology pushes caregivers' social co-operatives towards stronger capital intensiveness to permit technological investment.

The intertwining of technology, e-services, and the social economy can also inspire more technology-intensive 'community-centred' models of care. As discussed, within these models, technology does not substitute for the relational and participatory components characterizing the services offered by the social economy. Rather, technology replaces the most replicable parts of social and care work, enabling scaling alongside more personalized human-based work.

Technology drives hybridization

Thus, by combining the new tech-induced need for capital and tech-enabled economic sustainability and investment readiness, the appetite for and appeal of financial capital are simultaneously created, as shown in the exponential growth of specialized investors operating in the impact–finance segment (GIIN, 2020EVPA, 2020).

This latter consideration suggests that new social tech entrepreneurship can play a crucial role in a hybrid, impact-oriented value chain, bridging the demand for innovative solutions to social problems with impact investors who are willing to provide specialized financial resources to social entrepreneurs that can deliver innovative solutions to such problems.

The academic debate has not yet theorized how social and economic value creation are intertwined and coupled with the more intensive use of technologies in social entrepreneurial organizations that share specific values and identities (Toschi & Grassi, 2021). The literature has identified the hybrid organizing and twofold social–commercial purpose of social entrepreneurs as sources of managerial tensions, ethical challenges, and potential mission drift (Battilana & Dorado, 2010; Smith et al., 2013; André & Pache, 2016). This tendency may be reinforced by the 'appetite of capital' characterizing more technology-intensive models (Arena et al., 2018). Conversely, another stance has recently emerged arguing that the managerial challenges raised by social enterprises' hybrid nature are not a problem but rather can be turned into opportunities to innovate and change (Mongelli, Rullani, Ramus, & Rimac, 2019; Shepherd, Williams, & Zhao, 2019). This may occur even more thanks to the availability of innovative technologies because technologies can catalyse the mobilized financial capital towards opportunities for innovating the responses to societal needs by preserving the social impact-oriented intentionality of impact investment (Bengo et al., 2021).

A relevant further line of research concerns investigating the relationship between the different levels of hybridity characterizing different social entrepreneurial models and their interplay with the adoption of technological innovations. We wonder if and how technologies represent a key factor in shaping the synergy between social and economic value creation in hybrids.

Finally, the tech-enabled scalability potential of social enterprises and their new, structurally systemic role leads us to our third systemic argument.

Reason 3: Social tech entrepreneurship, transformations in innovation policies, and the societal legitimacy of innovation

The third reason for social-tech centrality is related to the potential role of social entrepreneurship not only to provide better solutions to social problems but also to mitigate the unintended effects of patterns of technological innovation and maximize their positive effects on society and individuals.

Recognizing the systemic potential of social-tech entrepreneurship in the context of the evolution of mission-oriented innovation policies towards the broader approach of transformative innovation for grand challenges reveals novel perspectives and research agendas.

Figure 12.2 synthetically describes the theorized coevolutionary dynamic between the technological evolution of social entrepreneurship organizations and the transformative characterization of innovation policies towards a holistic, grand challenges-oriented perspective. This perspective is obtained by addressing technologically evolving social enterprises with appropriate innovation policies. The coevolutionary perspective explains the shift from a traditional innovation-fuelled economic growth model to a transformative innovation-fuelled inclusive growth model.

Transformative innovation policies seek to inspire systemic change that is suitable to respond to grand societal and environmental challenges by leveraging a holistic conceptualization of innovative activities (Borràs & Edquist, 2019; Schot & Steinmueller, 2018; Diercks et al., 2019). They blend societal, technological, and market-oriented aspects with proactive orientations towards solving socio-environmental problems (Fagerberg, 2018; Diercks et al., 2019). In addition, these policies display inclusiveness towards demand-side actors (Schot & Steinmueller, 2018; Diercks et al., 2019; Edler & Boon, 2018) and a

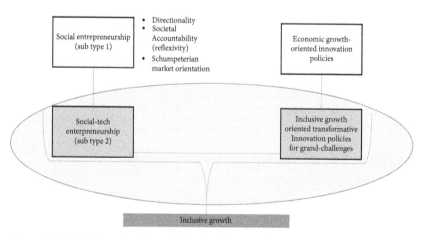

Figure 12.2 The theorized coevolutionary dynamic between social entrepreneurship and innovation policies

component of experimentation and reflexivity towards societal impacts (Schot & Steinmueller, 2016).

Technologically evolving social enterprises may represent appropriate addressee actors for this new generation of innovation policies as they share the main socio-technical attributes that are required by transformative innovation (Calderini et al., 2023). As explained in this chapter social enterprises can have specific marginalized groups as beneficiaries or consumers of innovation and involve marginalized groups and stakeholders in their operations and governance (Bock, 2016; Pinch & Sunley, 2016). Moreover, social enterprises can be geographically inclusive, responding to the social needs of communities and reaching abandoned and marginalized territories (Steiner & Teasdale, 2019). This broad characterization of social and geographic inclusiveness aligns with the trans-local nature of transformative innovations (Loorbach et al., 2020) with place-based origins, scaling geographically and societally (Calderini et al., 2023).

Furthermore, social enterprises are increasingly reflexive organizations that broadly adopt tools for societal and environmental accountability to their stakeholders (Rawhouser et al., 2019). Lastly, transformative social enterprises can build internal and external networks testifying to their capacity to systemically experiment with new collaborations and generate local system changes (Choi, 2015; Choi & Chang, 2019).

During the ongoing technological development of social enterprises (Arena et al., 2018; Monroe-White & Zook, 2018; Turker & Ozmen, 2021), these elements can constitute entrepreneurial building blocks for spreading the knowledge and transferring the benefit of innovations to a vast public, improving the societal legitimacy of science, technology, and innovation in this way.

A good example of the transformative and 'mitigating' potential characterization of social tech entrepreneurship is the French co-operative Atelier Paysan. The Atelier is based on the idea "of granting technical and technological sovereignty to farmers working in marginalized areas of the country" (Calderini et al., 2023, p. 4). The social cooperative provides farmers with an open-source resource platform for self-developing "appropriate" farming tools. Appropriate technologies are robust, cost-effective machinery that requires minimal maintenance, rendering it manageable by the specific communities for which it is intended. These technologies reintegrate elements and methodologies from the past into novel contexts, effectively merging conventional "place-based" expertise with novel technological solutions, thereby enhancing appropriateness (Franco et al., 2020).

Reason 4: Social-tech entrepreneurship and inclusive growth

The previous discussion leads us to the fourth reason for social-tech centrality, which is closely linked to the third. It is focused on the potential of social-tech entrepreneurship to counteract inequalities from a Rawlsian perspective and, overall, deploy a more inclusive model of growth in the context of contemporary economies.

Much expectation has been placed over the past twenty years on the 'knowledge economy' (Godin, 2006), an economic paradigm that is characterized by the centrality of intangibles, knowledge, and technology, which is directly based on the production, distribution, and use of knowledge and information. Typically, it is characterized by the increasing role of creativity, imagination, and persistent innovation in the value creation process (OECD, 1996). Generally, the knowledge economy has been assumed to be able to spur growth and prosperity equitably and inclusively. Consequently, the prevailing innovation policy approach was moulded isomorphically around myths and legends about Silicon Valley (Irwin et al., 2021; Breznitz, 2021), with limited consideration of the idiosyncratic and specific features and enabling factors that would have made such policy innovations successful in Europe.

As an example of this isomorphic trend, recall the science park and incubator hype; the obsession with venture capital and its support on the supply side instead of concentrating on more relevant demand-side, capacity-building issues; and the obstinate faith in science-dominant models of innovation (Breznitz, 2021). We might add the overestimation of the role of universities in technology transfer, the unreasonable reduction of tech transfer to a mere collection of spin-offs and intellectual property rights management issues, and the inexplicable denial of the role and potential of demand-side policies and their consequent under-exploitation (Corsi et al., 2020; Breznitz, 2021; Flanagan et al., 2022).

In this isomorphic policy context, ever more empirical evidence (Compagnucci & Cusinato, 2014; Rodriguez-Pose, 2018) reveals that the 'knowledge economy' in Europe has fallen short of expectations, debatably in terms of absolute growth performance but certainly in terms of the equitable distribution of opportunities. A high density of knowledge and wealth has accumulated in select areas and segments of society. Most geographic areas, communities, and social segments have been left behind or excluded from the knowledge economy. This has resulted in significant discontent—that is, incidentally, one of the sources of the wave of populism, anger, and anti-politics that we are witnessing (Rodriguez-Poses, 2018). This latter is not merely a crucial equity and social justice issue but may impose a glass ceiling on Europe's growth prospects.

The knowledge-based economy model is leading to the creation of narrow 'insular vanguards' (Unger, 2019) that confine and restrict the effects of the knowledge economy.

Therefore, inaugurating a new generation not only of directional and transformative but also of place-based, inclusive, innovation-driven development policies that are driven by a more inclusive idea of growth and enable the shift from 'insular' to 'inclusive' vanguards is crucial.

Finally, in the broad context of the insularity of vanguards, another important element should be considered when outlining future options for innovation-driven growth.

Globally, although research efforts and expenditures are generally increasing, research productivity is falling. This means that ideas are becoming scarcer, as Gutiérrez and Philippon (2019) and Bloom et al. (2020) suggested, and new efficiency issues are emerging in the exploitation of knowledge and its translation into innovation opportunities.

Even this latter observation questions the sustainability of the science-push innovation model and should lead us to reconsider innovation models that have been developed in contexts and by actors that typically operate in conditions of resource scarcity and coherently address complex trade-offs related to sustainability issues with frugal innovation paradigms (George, 2019). These 'frugal capacities' precisely characterize many social enterprises' approaches to innovation, as already discussed (Tapsell & Woods, 2010; Mishra, 2021).

Conclusions: Drafting a novel policy agenda for European social entrepreneurship

In summary, we believe that the classical narrative of the venture capital-fuelled, science-intensive, technology-push model of innovation-driven growth must be, if not revisited, at least paralleled by an equally important inclusive innovation agenda to jointly pursue growth and counteract inequalities and environmental crises.

At the very centre of such an inclusive innovation agenda, we believe a new entrepreneurial genre should be included within policies for growth.

This genre merges technological innovation into a model characterized by prioritizing societal needs, inclusiveness, societal accountability, and the capacity to act in untapped markets that purely commercial entrepreneurship has not entered.

This entrepreneurial genre is social-tech entrepreneurship, which is a model of enterprise that belongs to the social economy but has major appeal and influence on mainstream for-profit corporate models. We argue that this new entrepreneurial genre, coupled with appropriate financial tools and leveraging opportunities in the markets for social needs (Bonoli, 2005), may offer Europe a tremendous opportunity to bridge research and innovation policies, social cohesion policies, and financial policies.

This strong political dimension cannot be kept separate but should form part of a unique, integrated political agenda. It is a very attractive policy approach that might allow Europe to inaugurate a dual policy portfolio in which growth and solving societal challenges and inequalities are addressed through the same instruments in an integrated agenda. It could be seen as the way to enact a 'Twin Transition':[6] a social and digital transformation.

In light of this prospect, having discussed[7] the four crucial reasons to systemically consider the exchange between technological opportunities and social entrepreneurship, we turn to draw some more political conclusions.

---

[6] See: 'The twin green & digital transition: How sustainable digital technologies could enable a carbon-neutral EU by 2050', www.europa.eu.
[7] See: https://ec.europa.eu/environment/ecoap/about-eco-innovation/policies-matters/green-and-digital-twin-transition-also-spurs-inclusive-eco_en

Moving from an old model ...

The relationship between research, innovation, and growth has traditionally been a cornerstone of economic development policies, encompassing traditional, direct fiscal incentives and subsidies, support for venture capital in direct and indirect forms, and bridging institutions, such as science parks and incubators. The implicit assumption of these policy mixes is that the stock of knowledge is large and valuable and that there are active, lively, knowledge-intensive industrial sectors that are willing and able to exploit this knowledge for innovative performance.

Unfortunately, this hypothesis has sometimes been revealed as fragile wishful thinking, especially when applied to place-based innovation policies, as discussed in previous sections.

There is an urgent need for radically new models of innovation-driven growth that are more compatible with the actual consistency, heterogeneity, and geography of small and medium-sized enterprises (SMEs) in Europe.

This short chapter suggests that the new generation of social-tech entrepreneurship and the cross-fertilization of social innovation models with technological opportunities is a valuable opportunity to develop new approaches and instruments that will drive the evolution of social, industrial, and innovation policy-making. These are not substitutes but complements to novel transformative and grand challenge-oriented policy mixes.

... to a new model

The underlying policy idea is that the value of research and innovation has been traditionally conveyed to society via the industrial system, which has exploited knowledge, translated it into economic value and growth, and, eventually, conveyed it back to society. If industry (or a knowledge-intensive industry) is no longer present in certain areas and segments of Europe, the alternative is to consider social-tech entrepreneurship as a way to convey the untapped value of knowledge directly to society, in the absence of a consistent traditional industrial option leveraging commercial entrepreneurship.

This would imply including social enterprises within the bounds of industrial and innovation policies, as the European Commission has started to do by identifying the 'social and proximity' economy as one of the fourteen industrial ecosystems in the 'New Industrial Strategy for Europe'.[8]

Social-tech enterprises are still very few. For example, the percentage of social innovative start-ups among technological innovative start-ups in the Italian context was about 2.2 per cent in 2020.[9]

Nevertheless, the base of social enterprises is very large in Europe. According to European Commission data, ever more organizations can be regarded as

---

[8] See: https://ec.europa.eu/growth/sectors/proximity-and-social-economy_it
[9] See: Startup e PMI innovative (registroimprese.it)

social enterprises: recent statistics report more than two million enterprises that are active in the social economy (about 10 per cent of European enterprises; European Commission, 2020).[10] Some of these are well equipped in terms of managerial structure and have in-depth knowledge of their markets: they typically serve markets that are enjoying encouraging growth prospects and can respond to people's needs, allowing them to decisively contribute to a genuinely inclusive model of growth. Moreover, these organizations often display a high demand for technological innovation if it is appropriately inducted through timely policy-making.

For example, in the Italian context, research conducted by Deloitte, TechSoup, and Fondazione Italia Sociale in 2021[11] revealed that 96 per cent of social enterprises perceived the necessity of innovating their services and products (mainly through incremental approaches), with technological support. Simultaneously, 61 per cent of organizations faced resistance in enacting technological innovation processes for lack of appropriate skills and financial resources.

Thus, the evolution and cross-fertilization with technological opportunities of even a fraction of this base, turning these organizations from labour-intensive to reskilled tech-intensive enterprises, could result in intriguing numbers that could affect European growth rates.

To specify a very simple, clear policy objective, if we could transform 1 per cent of the estimated two million social enterprises in Europe into social-tech enterprises every year, 20,000 new organizations that would not be, technically speaking, brand new—but could easily be considered new high-tech start-ups—would result. This is not only an interesting number but also a fascinating option in terms of inclusive growth.

The vision, therefore, is of the network of social enterprises in Europe as a diffused and distributed incubator and accelerator. Shifting from a model of physical incubators and science parks as sources of innovative entrepreneurship to a model that leverages social innovation and social entrepreneurship networks would mean shifting from a polarized model to a distributed, inclusive model of innovation and growth.

What, then, should be done to seize this opportunity and inaugurate a new season of policies supporting tech-intensive entrepreneurship's potential by leveraging the hidden virtues of social entrepreneurs?

Required policy measures

We suggest that there are at least five areas of intervention that are worthy of exploration.

(1) Rethinking technology transfer and universities' third mission

---

[10] See: Social economy in the EU| Internal Market, Industry, Entrepreneurship and SMEs (europa.eu)
[11] https://www2.deloitte.com/it/it/pages/private/articles/la-domanda-di-innovazione-del-terzo-settore-deloitte-italy—d.html

The first area entails inaugurating a new generation of technology transfer policies that are specifically dedicated to social enterprises and the third sector in general. This encompasses reconsidering universities' third mission to permit new forms of systemic partnerships. In these partnerships, the valorization of research would not occur solely via an economic and market-based perspective. Instead, we need novel technology transfer models that intertwine with universities' third mission. This type of technology transfer is less market- and more challenge-oriented, to engage new actors, such as social entrepreneurship, the third sector, and civil society organizations, in a more generalized perspective.

(2) Engaging 'open innovation models'

The second area requires us to extend the traditional models of open innovation to include social enterprises through more complex and structured profit–not-for-profit partnerships that enable coevolution among organizations, stimulating innovation and mutual knowledge exchange. Social enterprises can contribute to radical 'open the open innovation' initiatives through their capacity to include marginalized groups and societal challenges in innovative activities (Svirina et al., 2016).

(3) Transforming innovation clusters and ecosystems

The third area demands altering the unit of political action from single organizations to social tech entrepreneurial ecosystems and networks. As the European Commission (2021) has already recognized, addressing social entrepreneurship in innovation, technological, and industrial policy-making can enable the evolution of currently adopted collaborative and ecosystemic policy tools (Gerli et al., 2021; European Commission, 2021). Thus, evolutionary ecosystems are the context in which to experiment with new forms of tech transfer for social enterprises. These processes can occur in novel localized and place-based living labs. In these novel milieus, all actors experiment and experientially learn how to mutually forge new modes of tech and knowledge transfer.

(4) Experimenting with social–functional public procurement and demand-side policies

Fourth, we need to revitalize and renovate demand-side innovation policies, leveraging the huge potential of innovative social procurement to offer early market opportunities to social tech start-ups or social enterprises in evolution. The policy mix between social and functional procurement may be a strong incentive for the innovative technological development of social entrepreneurship. This potential could be reinforced and integrated through designing appropriate technological reskilling patterns for social entrepreneurs.

(5) Supporting integer impact investing

Fifth, the emergent social impact investing industry must be supported to unlock the potential of blended-value, patient capital for social-tech enterprises but also steered to ensure the support it offers is not traded off against social value. This may distort both the constitutive value of social entrepreneurship and the nature of impact investing.

We contend that these policy actions may contribute to making social-tech entrepreneurship a key entrepreneurial protagonist of the evolution towards an inclusive European growth perspective.

References

Achleitner, A. K., Lutz, E., Mayer, J., & Spiess-Knafl, W. (2013). Disentangling gut feeling: assessing the integrity of social entrepreneurs. *Voluntas: International Journal of Voluntary and Nonprofit Organizations*, 24(1), 93–124.

André, K., & Pache, A. C. (2016) From caring entrepreneur to caring enterprise: addressing the ethical challenges of scaling up social enterprises. *Journal of Business Ethics*, 133(4), 659–675.

Arena, M., Bengo, I., Calderini, M., & Chiodo, V. (2018). Unlocking finance for social tech start-ups: is there a new opportunity space? *Technological Forecasting and Social Change*, 127, 154–165.

Austin, J., Stevenson, H., & Wei-Skillern, J. (2006). Social and Commercial Entrepreneurship: Same, Different, or Both? *Entrepreneurship Theory & Practice*, 30(1), 1–22.

Bacq, S., & Janssen, F. (2011). The multiple faces of social entrepreneurship: a review of definitional issues based on geographical and thematic criteria. *Entrepreneurship & Regional Development*, 23(5–6), 373–403.

Battilana, J., & Dorado, S. (2010). Building sustainable hybrid organisations: the case of commercial microfinance organisations. *Academy of Management Journal*, 53(6), 1419–1440. https://doi.org/10.5465/amj.2010.57318391.

Battilana, J., & Lee, M. (2014). Advancing research on hybrid organizing: insights from the study of social enterprises. *Academy of Management Annals*, 8(1), 397–441.

Bengo, I., Borrello, A., & Chiodo, V. (2021). Preserving the integrity of social impact investing: towards a distinctive implementation strategy. *Sustainability*, 13(5), 2852.

Bhatti, Y. A., & Ventresca, M. (2013). How can 'frugal innovation' be conceptualized?. Available at: SSRN 2203552.

Blasioli, E., & Hassini, E. (2021). E-Health technological ecosystems: advanced solutions to support informal caregivers and vulnerable populations during the COVID-19 outbreak. *Telemedicine and e-Health*. 28(2): 138–149.

Bloom, N., Jones, C. I., Van Reenen, J., & Webb, M. (2020). Are ideas getting harder to find? *American Economic Review*, 110(4), 1104–1144.

Bock, B. B. (2016). Rural marginalisation and the role of social innovation; a turn towards nexogenous development and rural reconnection. *Sociologia Ruralis*, 56(4), 552–573.

Bonoli, G. (2005). The politics of the new social policies: providing coverage against new social risks in mature welfare states. *Policy & Politics*, 33(3), 431–449.

Borrás, S., & Edquist, C. (2019). *Holistic Innovation Policy: Theoretical Foundations, Policy Problems, and Instrument Choices.* Oxford: Oxford University Press.

Breznitz, D. (2021). *Innovation in Real Places: Strategies for Prosperity in an Unforgiving World.* New York: Oxford University Press, USA.

Calderini, M., Fia, M., & Gerli, F. (2023). Organizing for transformative innovation policies: The role of social enterprises. Theoretical insights and evidence from Italy. *Research Policy*, 52(7), 104818.

Calderini, M., Chiodo, V., Gerli, F. and Pasi, G. (2021). Social-tech entrepreneurs: building blocks of a new social economy, *Stanford Social Innovation Review*. Retrieved from: https://ssir.org/articles/entry/social_tech_entrepreneurs_building_blocks_of_a_new_social_economy

Carros, F., Meurer, J., Löffler, D., Unbehaun, D., Matthies, S., Koch, I., . . . Wulf, V. (2020). *Exploring Human-Robot Interaction with the Elderly: Results from a Ten-Week Case Study in a Care Home.* In: CHI '20, Proceedings of the 2020 CHI Conference on Human Factors in Computing Systems (pp. 1–12). New York, NY, USA: Association for Computing Machinery. https://doi.org/10.1145/3313831.3376402

Cattani, G. (2005). Preadaptation, firm heterogeneity, and technological performance: a study on the evolution of fiber optics, 1970–1995. *Organization Science*, 16(6), 563–580.

Certo, T., & Miller, T. (2008). Social entrepreneurship: key issues and concepts. *Business Horizons*, 51(4), 267–271.

Chell, E., Nicolopoulou, K., & Karataş-Özkan, M. (2010). Social entrepreneurship and enterprise: international and innovation perspectives. *Entrepreneurship & Regional Development*, 22(6), 485–493.

Choi, Y. (2015). How partnerships affect the social performance of Korean social enterprises. *Journal of Social Entrepreneurship*, 6(3), 257–277.

Choi, Y., & Chang, S. (2019). Resource acquisition partnership of nascent social enterprise for sustainability. *International Journal of Entrepreneurship*, 23(2), 1–8.

Compagnucci, F., & Cusinato, C. (2014). The knowledge economy: a new source of regional divergence? *Revue d'Économie Régionale & Urbaine*, 2, 365–393.

Corsi, A., Pagani, R. N., & Kovaleski, J. L. (2020). Technology transfer for sustainable development: social impacts depicted and some other answers to a few questions. *Journal of Cleaner Production*, 245, 118522.

Corsini, L., Dammicco, V., & Moultrie, J. (2021). Frugal innovation in a crisis: the digital fabrication maker response to COVID-19. *R&D Management*, 51(2), 195–210.

Dees, J. G. (2007). Taking social entrepreneurship seriously. *Society*, 44(3), 24–31.

Defourny, J., & Nyssens, M. (2017). Fundamentals for an international typology of social enterprise models. *VOLUNTAS: International Journal of Voluntary and Nonprofit Organizations*, 28(6), 2469–2497.

Desa, G., & Basu, S. (2013). Optimization or bricolage? Overcoming resource constraints in global social entrepreneurship. *Strategic Entrepreneurship Journal*, 7(1), 26–49.

Desa, G., & Kotha, S. (2006a). Ownership, mission and environment: an exploratory analysis into the evolution of a technology social venture. In: Mair, J., Robinson, J., & Hockerts, K. (Eds.). *Social Entrepreneurship* (pp. 155–179). London: Palgrave Macmillan.

Desa, G., & Kotha, S. (2006b). Technology social ventures and innovation: understanding the innovation process at Benetech. In F. Perrini (Ed.), *New Social Entrepreneurship: What Awaits Social Entrepreneurial Ventures?* (pp. 237–259). Northampton, MA: Edward Elgar Publishers.

Diercks, G., Larsen, H., & Steward, F. (2019). Transformative innovation policy: addressing variety in an emerging policy paradigm. *Research Policy*, 48(4), 880–894.

Doherty, B., Haugh, H., & Lyon, F. (2014). Social enterprises as hybrid organizations: A review and research agenda. *International Journal of Management Reviews*, 16(4), 417–436.

Edler, J., & Boon, W. P. (2018). 'The next generation of innovation policy: directionality and the role of demand-oriented instruments'—Introduction to the special section. *Science and Public Policy*, 45(4), 433–434.

European Commission (2020). *Social Enterprises and Their Ecosystems in Europe*. Office of Employment, Social Affairs and Inclusion. https://ec.europa.eu/social/main.jsp?catId=738&langId=en&pubId=8274

European Commission (2021). *Clusters of Social and Ecological Innovation in the European Union*. Brussels: European Commission.

EVPA. (2020). *The 2020 Investing for Impact Survey: A Snapshot of European Investors for Impact*. Brussels: EVPA Knowledge Center.

Fagerberg, J. (2018). Mobilizing innovation for sustainability transitions: a comment on transformative innovation policy. *Research Policy*, 47(9), 1568–1576.

Flanagan, K., Uyarra, E., & Wanzenböck, I. (2022). Towards a problem-oriented regional industrial policy: possibilities for public intervention in framing, valuation and market formation. *Regional Studies*, 57(6), 1–13.

Forbes, H., & Schaefer, D. (2017). Social product development: the democratization of design, manufacture and innovation. *Procedia CIRP*, 60, 404–409.

Franco, W., Barbera, F., Bartolucci, L., Felizia, T., & Focanti, F. (2020). Developing intermediate machines for high-land agriculture. *Development Engineering*, 5, 100050.

Friis, A. (2009). *The Emerging Fourth Sector* (Master's thesis).

Gagliardi, D., Psarra, F., Wintjes, R., Trendafili, K., Pineda Mendoza, J., Haaland, K., Turkeli, S., Giotitsas, C., Pazaitis, A., & Niglia, F. (2020). New technologies and digitisation: Opportunities and challenges for the social economy and social enterprises—executive summary. European Commission, Executive Agency for SMEs. https://doi.org/10.2826/486344

Geels, F. W. (2014). Reconceptualising the co-evolution of firms-in-industries and their environments: developing an inter-disciplinary Triple Embeddedness Framework. *Research Policy*, 43(2), 261–277.

George, G. (2019). *Handbook of Inclusive Innovation: The Role of Organizations, Markets and Communities in Social Innovation.* Cheltenham: Edward Elgar Publishing.

George, G., A. M. McGahan, & J. Prabhu. 2012. Innovation for inclusive growth: towards a theoretical framework and a research agenda. *Journal of Management Studies,* 49(4), 661–683.

Gerli, F., Calderini, M., & Chiodo, V. (2021). An ecosystemic model for the technological development of social entrepreneurship: exploring clusters of social innovation. *European Planning Studies,* 30(10), 1–23.

Gerli, F., Chiodo, V., & Bengo, I. (2020). Technology transfer for social entrepreneurship: designing problem-oriented innovation ecosystems. *Sustainability,* 13(1), 20.

Ghazinoory, S., Nasri, S., Ameri, F., Montazer, G. A., & Shayan, A. (2020). Why do we need 'Problem-oriented Innovation System (PIS)' for solving macro-level societal problems?. *Technological Forecasting and Social Change,* 150, 119749.

GIIN (2020). Annual Impact Investor Survey 2020. Retrieved from: https://thegiin.org/assets/GIIN%20Annual%20Impact%20Investor%20Survey%202020.pdf

Godin, B. (2006). The knowledge-based economy: conceptual framework or buzzword? *The Journal of Technology Transfer,* 31(1), 17–30.

Göransson, B. (2017). Role of universities for inclusive development and social innovation: Experiences from Sweden. In: Brundenius, C., Göransson, B., & Carvalho de Mello, J. M. (Eds.). *Universities, inclusive development and social innovation* (pp. 349–367). Cham: Springer.

Grassi, E., & Toschi, L. (2021). A systematic literature review of technology social ventures: state of the art and directions for future research at the micro-, meso-and macro-level. *Journal of Social Entrepreneurship,* 21(4), 1–33.

Gutiérrez, G., & Philippon, T. (2019, May). Fading stars. *AEA Papers and Proceedings,* 109, 312–316.

Irwin, A., Vedel, J. B., & Vikkelsø, S. (2021). Isomorphic difference: familiarity and distinctiveness in national research and innovation policies. *Research Policy,* 50(4), 104220.

Ismail, K., Sohel, M. H., & Ayuniza, U. N. (2012). Technology social venture: a new genre of social entrepreneurship? *Procedia-Social and Behavioral Sciences,* 40, 429–434.

Johnson, S. (2000). Social entrepreneurship literature review. *New Academy Review,* 2, 1–17.

Kamariah, I., Mir, H. S., & Umee, N., A. (2012). Technology social ventures: A new genre of social entrepreneurship? *Procedia - Social and Behavioral Sciences,* 40, 429–434.

La Piana, D. (2020) COVID-19's impact on nonprofits' revenues, digitization, and mergers. *Stanford Social Innovation Review.* Retrieved from: https://ssir.org/articles/entry/covid_19s_impact_on_nonprofits_revenues_digitization_and_mergers#

Loorbach, D., Wittmayer, J., Avelino, F., von Wirth, T., & Frantzeskaki, N. (2020). Transformative innovation and translocal diffusion. *Environmental Innovation and Societal Transitions,* 35, 251–260.

Lubberink, R., Blok, V., van Ophem, J., & Omta, O. (2019). Responsible innovation by social entrepreneurs: an exploratory study of values integration in innovations. *Journal of Responsible Innovation*, 6(2), 179–210.

Lubberink, R., Blok, V., van Ophem, J., van der Velde, G., & Omta, O. (2018). Innovation for society: towards a typology of developing innovations by social entrepreneurs. *Journal of Social Entrepreneurship*, 9(1), 52–78.

Markman, G. D., Waldron, T. L., Gianiodis, P. T., & Espina, M. I. (2019). E pluribus unum: impact entrepreneurship as a solution to grand challenges. *Academy of Management Perspectives*, 33(4), 371–382.

Martinelli, F. (2019). *Platform cooperativism in Italy and in Europe*. Liège (Belgium): CIRIEC International, Université de Liège.

Mazzucato, M. (2021). *Mission Economy: A Moonshot Guide to Changing Capitalism*. London: Penguin UK.

Meige, A., & Schmitt, J. (2015). *Innovation intelligence. Commoditization. Digitalization. Acceleration. Major Pressure on Innovation Drivers*. Lulu.com.

Miedes-Ugarte, B., Flores-Ruiz, D., & Wanner, P. (2020). Managing tourist destinations according to the principles of the social economy: the case of the Les Oiseaux de Passage cooperative platform. *Sustainability*, 12(12), 4837.

Mishra, O. (2021). Principles of frugal innovation and its application by social entrepreneurs in times of adversity: an inductive single-case approach. *Journal of Entrepreneurship in Emerging Economies*, 13(4), 547–574.

Mongelli, L., Rullani, F., Ramus, T., & Rimac, T. (2019). The bright side of hybridity: exploring how social enterprises manage and leverage their hybrid nature. *Journal of Business Ethics*, 159(2), 301–305.

Monroe-White, T., & Zook, S. (2018). Social Enterprise Innovation: A Quantitative Analysis of Global Patterns. *Voluntas*, 29(3), 496–510. https://doi.org/10.1007/s11266-018-9987-9

Nogales-Muriel, R., & Nyssens, M. (2021). Research to build resilient social economy ecosystems in Europe. *Stanford Social Innovation Review*. Retrieved from: https://ssir.org/articles/entry/research_to_build_resilient_social_economy_ecosystems_in_europe

Nooteboom, B., Van Haverbeke, W., Duysters, G., Gilsing, V., & Van den Oord, A. (2007). Optimal cognitive distance and absorptive capacity. *Research Policy*, 36(7), 1016–1034.

OECD (1996). *The Knowledge-based Economy Organisation*. OECD Publishing.

Peredo, A. M., & McLean, M. (2006). Social entrepreneurship: a critical review of the concept. *Journal of World Business*, 41(1), 56–65.

Petersen, E. E., Kidd, R. W., & Pearce, J. M. (2017). Impact of DIY home manufacturing with 3D printing on the toy and game market. *Technologies*, 5(3), 45.

Pinch, S., & Sunley, P. (2016). Do urban social enterprises benefit from agglomeration? Evidence from four UK cities. *Regional Studies*, 50(8), 1290–1301.

Rajesh, R., Rajeev, A., & Rajendran, C. (2022). Corporate social performances of firms in select developed economies: a comparative study. *Socio-Economic Planning Sciences*, 81, 101194.

Rawhouser, H., Cummings, M., & Newbert, S. L. (2019). Social impact measurement: current approaches and future directions for social entrepreneurship research. *Entrepreneurship Theory and Practice*, 43(1), 82–115.

Rodríguez-Pose, A. (2018). The revenge of the places that don't matter (and what to do about it). *Cambridge Journal of Regions, Economy and Society*, 11(1), 189–209.

Rubio-Mozos, E., García-Muiña, F. E., & Fuentes-Moraleda, L. (2019). Rethinking 21st-century businesses: an approach to fourth sector SMEs in their transition to a sustainable model committed to SDGs. *Sustainability*, 11(20), 5569.

Sahin, I. (2006). Detailed Review of Rogers' Diffusion of Innovations Theory and Educational Technology-Related Studies Based on Rogers' Theory. *The Turkish Online Journal of Educational Technology*, 5, 14–23.

Schot, J., & Steinmueller, W. E. (2016). *Framing Innovation Policy for Transformative Change: Innovation Policy 3.0*. University of Sussex: Science Policy Research Unit (SPRU).

Santos, F., Pache, A. C., & Birkholz, C. (2015). Making hybrids work: aligning business models and organizational design for social enterprises. *California Management Review*, 57(3), 36–58.

Sarasvathy, S. D., & Venkataraman, S. (2011). Entrepreneurship as method: open questions for an entrepreneurial future. *Entrepreneurship Theory and Practice*, 35(1), 113–135.

Schot, J., & Steinmueller, W. E. (2018). Three frames for innovation policy: R&D, systems of innovation and transformative change. *Research Policy*, 47(9), 1554–1567.

Shepherd, D. A., Trenton A. W., & Zhao, E. Y. (2019). A framework for exploring the degree of hybridity in social entrepreneurship. *Academy of Management Perspectives*, 33(4), 491–512.

Sinkovics, N., Sinkovics, R. R., & Yamin, M. (2014). The role of social value creation in business model formulation at the bottom of the pyramid–implications for MNEs? *International Business Review*, 23(4), 692–707.

Smith, W. K., Gonin, M., & Besharov, M. L. (2013). Managing social-business tensions: a review and research agenda for social enterprise. *Business Ethics Quarterly*, 23(3), 407–442. https://doi.org/10.5840/beq201323327.

Sneader K., & Singhal, S. (2020). Beyond coronavirus: the path to the next normal. McKinsey. https://www.mckinsey.com/industries/healthcare-systems-and-services/our-insights/beyond-coronavirus-the-path-to-the-next-normal?

Steiner, A., & Teasdale, S. (2019). Unlocking the potential of rural social enterprise. *Journal of Rural Studies*, 70, 144–154.

Stilgoe, J., Owen, R., & Macnaghten, P. (2013). Developing a framework for responsible innovation. *Research Policy*, 42(9), 1568–1580.

Svirina, A., Zabbarova, A., & Oganisjana, K. (2016). Implementing open innovation concept in social business. *Journal of Open Innovation: Technology, Market, and Complexity*, 2(4), 20.

Swedberg, R. (2006). *Social Entrepreneurship: The View of the Young Schumpeter* (Vol. 3). Edward Elgar Publishing.

Tapsell, P., & Woods, C. (2010). Social entrepreneurship and innovation: self-organization in an indigenous context. *Entrepreneurship & Regional Development*, 22(6), 535–556.

Tello-Rozas, S. (2016). Inclusive innovations through social and solidarity economy initiatives: a process analysis of a Peruvian case study. *VOLUNTAS: International Journal of Voluntary and Nonprofit Organizations*, 27(1), 61–85.

Turker, D., & Ozmen, Y. S. (2021). How do social entrepreneurs develop technological innovation? *Social Enterprise Journal*, 17(1), 63–93. https://doi.org/10.1108/SEJ-05-2020-0034

Unger, R. M. (2019). *The Knowledge Economy*. New York: Verso Books.

Van Rijn, M., Raab, J., Roosma, F., & Achterberg, P. (2021). To prove and improve: an empirical study on why social entrepreneurs measure their social impact. *Journal of Social Entrepreneurship*, 1–23. https://doi.org/10.1080/19420676.2021.1975797.

Venturi, P., & Zandonai, F. (2022). *Neomutualismo: Ridisegnare dal basso competitività e welfare*. EGEA spa.

Vila Seoane, M. F., Guagliano, L. M., Galante, O., & Arciénaga Morales, A. A. (2013). Transferencia de tecnologías a una cooperativa en Argentina: Un estudio de casos. *Journal of Technology Management & Innovation*, 8, 18–18.

Voegtlin, C., & Scherer, A. G. (2017). Responsible innovation and the innovation of responsibility: governing sustainable development in a globalized world. *Journal of Business Ethics*, 143(2), 227–243. https://doi.org/10.1007/s10551-015-2769-z.

Wigboldus, S., Klerkx, L., Leeuwis, C., Schut, M., Muilerman, S., & Jochemsen, H. (2016). Systemic perspectives on scaling agricultural innovations: a review. *Agronomy for Sustainable Development*, 36(3), 1–20.

PART III
PARTNERSHIPS

13
Why and how to engage beneficiaries as co-(social) entrepreneurs?

Considering hardware, software, and orgware for citizen engagement

Anne-Karen Hueske, Willemine Willems, and Kai Hockerts

Motivation

Social entrepreneurs are important actors of the social economy, because they engage in commercial activities with the intention to create societal impact (Mair & Noboa, 2006). The European school of thought on social entrepreneurship emphasizes the process of social innovation, namely the organization of decision-making as a participatory process to nurture democracy in the local community (Defourny & Nyssens, 2013, 2017).

The normative argument to nurture local democracy through engaging in participatory practices is complemented by instrumental and substantial arguments raised by social innovation and social entrepreneurship research that engagement leads to more societal impact of the business model (Cea & Rimington, 2017; Defourny & Nyssens, 2013). Research shows how engaging with stakeholders enables social enterprises to acquire essential resources (Bacq & Eddleston, 2018; Desa & Basu, 2013; di Domenico et al., 2010).

Innovation barrier research in turn informs us that innovation, especially radical innovation, can be hampered by a variety of challenges related to the attitudes and abilities of the organizational members, organizational factors, and external stakeholders (Hueske & Guenther, 2015). For instance, suppliers or customers might be reluctant to innovate due to lack of preparedness (e.g., Bala et al., 2008; Hueske et al., 2015; Lam & Mackenzie, 2005; Zutshi & Sohal, 2004). Engaging stakeholders can help to overcome challenges and implement social innovation Hueske & Guenther, 2021; Montgomery et al., 2012).

Engagement processes add the diverse perspectives of the crowd and can provide better results than consulting experts (Cea & Rimington, 2017). An example is the German #WirVsVirus hackathon. It involved 26,581 participants that were invited to address one out of forty-two broad challenges that were derived from 1,990

Anne-Karen Hueske, Willemine Willems and Kai Hockerts, *Why and how to engage beneficiaries as co-(social) entrepreneurs?*. In: *Social Economy Science*. Edited by: Gorgi Krlev, Dominika Wruk, Giulio Pasi, and Marika Bernhard, Oxford University Press.

problem statements on issues caused by the COVID-19 pandemic. Collectively the participants, who were mobilized by civil society organizations in cooperation with government ministries, generated 1,494 project ideas (Gegenhuber, 2020). Previous research shows that the empowerment of various stakeholder groups increases the innovativeness compared to focusing on one stakeholder group (Defourny & Nyssens, 2013). Social entrepreneurship research claims that involving beneficiaries results for example in better framing of solutions and thereby leads to more acceptance by the stakeholders as the context is better understood, the responses to societal challenges are more tailored to the context and more acceptable for the beneficiaries (Cea & Rimington, 2017; Knight & Kingston, 2021). A counter-example proving this point is the wasting of charity money for developing glasses which were not accepted by poor children because of their design, even though they could have improved the children's eyesight. A supporting example is a user survey designed with children in foster care to provide them with a protected space in which to provide genuine feedback on their experiences.

Those arguments in favour of engagement in social enterprises are juxtaposed with claims that engagement is often not achieved despite great ambitions (Cea & Rimington, 2017; Twersky et al., 2013). Reviewing the literature, we could rarely identify research on engagement in social entrepreneurship; what research there is, is mainly published in practitioner-oriented outlets such as *Harvard Business Review, Stanford Social Innovation Review,* or *Foundation Review* (e.g., Nolan et al., 2019; Twersky et al., 2013; Twersky & Reichheld, 2019).

Considering the advantages of engagement in social entrepreneurship, we aim to inspire research by reviewing it through the lenses of another field of research. Cea and Rimmington (2017) departed their analysis of engagement practices by comparing for-profit and for-impact organizations. They point out that beneficiaries are in a weak position compared to commercial customers of for-profit organizations, who can exert buying power, whereas beneficiaries are likely to accept suboptimal solutions because of a lack of alternatives. Considering the hybrid nature of social enterprises, we will draw on citizen engagement in science and technology as it is motivated by similar normative, instrumental, and substantial arguments as engagement in social enterprises.

Citizen engagement in science and technology facilitates a two-way, instead of a one-way communication process in which citizens would be granted the opportunity to contribute to research agendas and research practices (Grand et al., 2015; Verhoeff & Kupper, 2014). Citizen engagement also claims participation and democracy as central values (Priest, 2018) from the normative perspective. Furthermore, the instrumental and substantial argument is made that engagement increases acceptance (Felt, 2015) and leads to more socially robust solutions (Gibbons, 1999) that are a better fit with future social contexts (Nowotny, 2003).

The parallels outlined in Table 13.1 motivate us to explore how citizen engagement in science and technology can inform greater and more targeted engagement in social entrepreneurship. Research on citizen engagement in science developed along the following stages. First, research on citizen engagement in science focused on hardware, that is, the (technical) tools, and methods of engagement. Next, research

Table 13.1 Comparing reasons for engagement in social enterprises and in science

	Stakeholder engagement, especially beneficiary engagement, in social enterprises	Citizen engagement in science
Normative reasons	Engagement to nurture local democracies and to increase the common good orientation of social enterprise activities	Participation and democracy as central values of scientific and technological progress
Instrumental and substantial reasons	• Greater acceptance, because beneficiaries could genuinely express their needs and co-engage in developing solutions to social problems • More holistic framing of solutions, including aspects that only those affected by a problem can know about • Greater societal impact through transfer and other types of scaling and diffusion	• Greater acceptance because citizens could voice their concerns or bring in ideas • More creative, robust, and user-centred solutions

widened its focus to shed light on the necessary 'software'; that is, researchers made considerations on the mindset that was needed for an effective use of the hardware. Finally, research acknowledged that aspects of organization, such as organizational structures and practices to promote the citizen engagement process, were becoming more important. In other words, it turned to the necessary 'orgware'. We use this evolution and its different elements as orientation to develop counterparts that are applicable to social enterprises.

The chapter is composed as follows. First, we introduce citizen engagement in science and technology and in doing so distinguish between the relevance of hardware, software, and orgware. Next, we explore these three elements for engagement in social entrepreneurship. Finally, we derive a variety of interesting questions for future research that emerge from our conceptual work that seeks to connect the two fields of research.

Citizen engagement in science and technology

Engaging citizens in science and technology[1] finds its roots in the evolving field of science communication. In its basic form, science communication as a field is concerned with shaping and facilitating the interaction between science and society. How such

---

[1] From here onwards we will use the word 'science' when we refer to both scientific practices and practices of technological innovation. From studies done in the field of science and technology, we know that a strict distinction between science as a practice of creating knowledge and technology as a practice of applying such knowledge is not tenable. Whereas scientific researchers are often involved in inventing artifacts (for example in the fields of nanotechnology and synthetic biology), inventors often create knowledge

interaction should be shaped, and what its focus should be, evolved throughout the second half of the twentieth century (Verhoeff & Kupper, 2014). At first, science communicators were concerned with restoring trust between science and society by increasing the public's understanding of science. With such a 'diffusionist concept' of science communication, a so-called deficit model is assumed. Within this model, science communicators are concerned with how to shape and improve processes of transmitting knowledge from science, as a producer of reliable knowledge, to citizens lacking scientific literacy, and who were believed to be easily misled by misrepresentations of scientific insights in the media. The underlying belief of the model is that trust in science will naturally grow when people gain knowledge and understanding of its methods and practices (Bucchi, 2008).

Later controversies about genetic modification of crops and nuclear energy, however, showed that more knowledge and understanding of scientific knowledge does not naturally lead to more trust (Verhoeff & Kupper, 2014). Instead of creating trust through transmitting knowledge, science communicators increasingly believe that the only effective way to improve the relation between science and society is by involving citizens in scientific and technological practices. This directed science communicators to become interested in organizing interactions in which citizens can contribute to the practice and decision-making of science itself (Davies, 2022). Citizen dialogues and other communication formats that allow citizens to share their views, concerns, and values emerged as a research focus of science communication—not only with the purpose of restoring trust, but also motivated by the realization that 'science affects everyone's lives' (Durant et al., 1989, p. 11) and that therefore everyone should be involved.

Citizen engagement in science as a concept refers to this two-way rather than one-way communication process in which citizens are granted the opportunity to contribute to research agendas and research practices (Grand et al., 2015; Verhoeff & Kupper, 2014). As such, citizen engagement can be seen as 'democratic science communication' (Davies, 2022), because it serves not promotional purposes of transmitting knowledge about science but 'the interests of democracy and its citizens by enabling informed decisions about science-related interests' (Priest, 2018, p. 57).

The above-described transition in the field of science communication from the *public understanding of science* to *citizen engagement with science* unfolded in line and in dialogue with a broader movement aiming to open science to citizens and societal actors. Engagement became an important value in institutional contexts such as in science governance bodies and large research institutes (Irwin, 2014). Since the 1990s the European Commission and national funding organizations have set up funding strands aimed at stimulating citizen engagement in science, such as the 'Science with and for Society' and 'Responsible Research and Innovation' programmes (Schuijer et al., 2022). Initiatives aiming to organize citizen and societal engagement

when developing technologies (steam engine and the science of thermodynamics) (Sismondo, 2007). It is as important to consider the social and ethical implications of technology as it is to consider those of science, for the same reasons. In the context of this chapter, it is thus unnecessary to make an analytical distinction between the two.

in a diverse range of sciences and technologies, such as nanotechnology (Davies et al., 2009; Heltzel et al., 2022), synthetic biology (Betten et al., 2018), climate geo-engineering (Bellamy & Lezaun, 2017), health-related research (den Ouden-dammer et al., 2019); and smart city technologies (Fraaije, 2022) have been financed within these funding programmes. The call for aligning science to societal needs and concerns through processes of societal engagement has been prominent ever since (Stilgoe et al., 2013).

In the following sections, we will discuss the broad and diverse body of literature that describes, reflects on, and critiques such practices of engaging citizens in science, structured around its evolution of interests, which moved from the 'hardware' of engagement to its 'software' and 'orgware'.

Hardware

Much of the citizen engagement literature focuses on the so-called 'hardware' of engagement, that is, 'the methods' and tools used in citizen engagement projects 'that can give the public a voice in science policy and decision-making' (Wilsdon et al., 2005, p. 19). This research focus has yielded a rich variety of formats, procedures, and toolboxes, offering diverse sources for those who intend to organize activities aimed at engaging citizens with science and technology and improving the interactions between researchers and the public during such events. Examples of hardware are focus groups (Kupper et al., 2007), citizen juries (Rowe & Frewer, 2005), and various formats of dialogue (Zorn et al., 2012), as well as other ways of setting up an activity designed to gain involvement of participants, or to improve or broaden contributions by spurring creativity and imagination. Articles that focus on hardware discuss, for example, the different design principles of a specific method (Macnaghten, 2021), they develop frameworks or typologies that can help determine what purpose certain citizen engagement formats or designs can achieve (Arnstein, 1969; Pytlik, Zillig, & Tomkins, 2011; Shirk et al., 2012) or they report on how a creative method potentially creates more depth and connection (Nabuurs et al., n.d.).

Software

Despite the rich diversity of available methods, formats, and tools, and ideas about how these can be improved, a research focus on 'hardware' is not sufficient to ensure citizen engagement that adheres to the democratic ideals of equality and empowerment. Often, citizens are invited to initiatives that are called dialogue or citizen engagement, but the space for their contribution is limited because, for example, the problem–solution frame is set beforehand. Take for instance the genetically modified organism debate in the 1990s organized by the Dutch government. Citizens were invited to participate in a nationwide debate about genetic modified organisms, but the government demanded that the discussion be about the conditions under which 'citizens find it acceptable to have GM [genetically modified] products grown or sold in the Netherlands' (Hagendijk & Irwin, 2006, p. 178). The question whether the use of such technology is acceptable to begin with was thus avoided.

Wilsdon et al. (2005, p. 19) therefore urged citizen engagement scholars to broaden their focus on what they call the 'software' of engagement, that is, 'the codes, values and norms that govern scientific practice, but which are far harder to access and change'. Focusing on software, they argue, helps to bring into view how mindsets and cultures hamper or facilitate meaningful engagement. In the literature, diverse software issues are discussed. One of these is related to the above-mentioned example of the Dutch genetic modified organism debate. Even though some science (policy) organizations publicly commit to involving citizens, the initiatives in which citizens are engaged are still shaped by the belief that the citizens' lack of scientific literacy makes it unlikely they have anything of value to offer for science (deficit model) (Bucchi & Neresini, 2007; Powell et al., 2011; Shanley et al., 2022; Wynne, 2006). As a solution, such events often start with an explanation of the science or technology at stake. Such an approach—often well intended, to remove the knowledge inequality—makes it rather difficult for participants to step out of the techno-scientific framing of the issue in the remainder of the interaction. This is problematic not only because it creates a power imbalance, but also because within a techno-scientific framing of issues, some of the concerns that are particularly important in citizens' daily lives are easily rejected as irrelevant, private, or irrational.

Similarly, it makes it difficult for participants to raise such issues, because within such a framing they may feel their arguments must comply with certain standards of so-called rationality. A typical example of an argument that is quickly dismissed within such a dynamic is the 'naturalness of food'. While this is a key concern for many people in their daily lives, within a techno-scientific framing of engagement events about genetically modified crops, for example, it becomes all too easy to set it aside as a 'private—and invalid—preference that requires no further debate' (Swierstra & te Molder, 2012, p. 1050). Such invisible rules (software) are rarely explicitly mentioned, but nevertheless shape the content of interactions to a large extent, resulting in a failure to take deeply felt concerns, and thus important affective responses, into account (Davies, 2014).

Another important software issue of meaningful citizen engagement is the *timing* of engagement. Many authors have emphasized that timing is essential to enable the citizens to have an impact on practices of science (Braun & Koenninger, 2018). Regardless of how they are designed, engagement events often take place at the end of the science, technology, and innovation trajectory (Barben et al., 2007; Guston, 2014; O'Riordan & Haran, 2009). This brings the advantage that by then it may be clear what citizens need to engage with and what public values are at stake. However, it limits the possible input citizens can have beyond the device's user-friendliness, or the colour of its interface. Therefore, many scholars call for 'upstream engagement' (Pidgeon & Rogers-Hayden, 2007; Wilsdon & Willis, 2004) or early engagement (Schuurbiers et al., 2013), for example in the laboratory phase of new technologies, which would enable identifying and anticipating the societal impacts, and collectively building a vision of the future (Sutcliffe, 2011) at a point when there is still a chance to steer the direction of such innovations.

The third software-related issue is its lack of *inclusivity*. There is a common understanding that the democratization of science does not merely entail voting practices, but rather is a continuous conversation with the public. What then becomes of concern is who should be involved in this conversation and how they can be included. Critics have pointed out that often engagement practices merely reach specific target groups such as end-users, patients, or consumers instead of the broad range of citizens that is required (Kupper et al., 2015; Stilgoe et al., 2014). Inclusive engagement is not merely about making sure participants are representative of the demographic groups (gender, age, education, and ethnicity), but also about attaining a diversity in attitudes towards science technology and innovation (Boulianne, 2018). Typically, citizen engagement events are attended by citizens who are interested in science, and not by people who fundamentally question or oppose the innovation at stake. Specifically targeting such groups is something that is rarely done in practice (Lubberink et al., 2017). Some scholars argue for reaching out to groups that are harder to engage—the so-called silent voices, the 'seldom heard'—or, for example, to vulnerable ethnic minority groups, because they tend to be underrepresented in most of these initiatives (Ellard-Gray et al., 2015; Powell et al., 2011). Others have suggested specifically involving so-called unruly publics, that is, participants who are usually disinvited because organizers fear they bring in unexpected and unwanted arguments. Yet, research suggests that such tendencies are evidence of an important underestimation of the contributions such publics have to offer to the discussion about the societal aspects of science (de Saille, 2015; Fraaije, 2022).

Orgware

Focusing on hardware and software alone, however, is still not sufficient to fully understand and improve the complex reality of citizen engagement in science and technology innovation processes. To achieve the changes envisioned by proponents of citizen engagement, the interactions and activities need to be embedded in institutional structures; thus the cultural changes need to happen not only on the individual or group level, but on the institutional level as well (Cohen, 2022; Owen et al., 2021; Schuijer, 2020). Inspired by literature on technological development, we label this aspect of engagement 'orgware': the elements 'constituted by the organizational and institutional conditions that influence' its 'development and application' (Mitcham & Waelbers, 2009, p. 373). In the context of citizen engagement, this denotes the institutional and organizational conditions in which engagement activities are initiated, embedded, and sustained.

An important issue related to the orgware of citizen engagement is the lack of priority and continuity that such activities have in the structures that shape the daily work of researchers. Due to the constant pressure on researchers to facilitate education, publish results of their research work in academic journals, and pursue funding, there is little time left for reaching out to citizens and society (Besley, 2015; Devonshire & Hathway, 2014; Ecklund et al., 2012; Sturzenegger-Varvayanis et al., 2008). Structure and culture provide few incentives for researchers and innovators to engage citizens in the research process. Similarly, with a focus on individual, isolated events, and the often temporary character of appointments of individual researchers, it is a challenge to sustain meaningful practices of engagement. One of the reasons for this is that the personal relations that individual researchers have built with societal organizations or others are necessary for organizing meaningful engagement (Chilvers & Kearnes, 2020). However, these are lost when the appointment of the researcher has come to an end. These issues call for changes that intervene not only in the engagement itself, but also in how scientific research is organized on the level of organizations and institutions.

When doing and learning about citizen engagement it is thus crucial to go beyond viewing and appreciating the hardware and software of individual isolated events— to be aware of 'the *processes and structures* of science governance' that may 'shape, enable, restrict or transform the ways in which participation can be done' (Braun & Koenninger, 2018, p. 685). As described above, beyond the question whether there is space and time for (sustaining) citizen engagement at all, is the question of what kinds of citizen engagement are allowed for by the particularities of the institutional context. To rephrase, orgware of engagement is important for the purpose of embedding the software of engagement in a larger context. The key question is how the desired software of engagement, which pertains to individuals and teams of science communicators, can be fostered by the way institutions are organized and governed. For example, in a study focused on the institutional logics shaping citizen engagement in smart city technologies, Fraaije (2022) found that meaningful engagement was hampered by the lack of skills of the involved city professionals, the dominant narratives on the work floor about what kinds of citizen engagement are valuable, and the strong focus of the city professionals on issues of privacy that are already anchored in the law. Ways of enhancing these practices unveiled by an orgware approach would then entail, among other interventions, fostering narratives on an institutional level that 'emphasize concerns of citizens', 'creating physical spaces' where citizens and innovation teams can interact on a regular basis, encouraging 'management styles' that give space to deal with uncertainty, and finding ways to deal in more reflexive ways with digital laws (2022, p. 153).

Critical integration

Analysing scientific literature on citizen engagement guided by hardware, software, and orgware demonstrates that, beyond methods and tools, the mindset of the innovator and the organizational context need to be considered. Otherwise, the dialogue is reduced to one-way communication, missing meaningful input and contributions from the citizens, and insufficient for engagement. Effective use of software, and especially of orgware, may thereby be able to meet potential weaknesses related to the use of hardware. This is why we focus on how these two elements may be employed in increasing beneficiary engagement in social entrepreneurship.

Engagement in social entrepreneurship through the lenses of software and orgware of citizen engagement

Table 13.2 displays potential parallels between citizen engagement in science and engagement in social entrepreneurship when it comes to the use of software and orgware. We elaborate on these parallels in greater depth in the following sections. It is to be mentioned that our reasoning will show that in a social entrepreneurship context, orgware needs to be adopted beyond the organizational boundaries of the social enterprise. We therefore differentiate an internal and an external orgware perspective, whereby the external perspective comprises funding structures.

Table 13.2 Software and orgware in citizen engagement in science and in social entrepreneurship

	Citizen engagement in science	Social entrepreneurship
Software	• Mindset of researcher to appreciate experiential knowledge and concerns of citizens in good time and in inclusive ways • Culture that nurtures participation and engagement	• Mindset of entrepreneur to develop solutions with beneficiaries, not for beneficiaries • Appreciation for the unique understanding of the problem by those affected by it
Internal orgware	• Relationship and trust building as well as active inclusion of otherwise unheard voices on hopes and fears as regards technology	• Involvement structures and practices during business model ideation to avoid approaches that are missing the point • Inclusive governance: beneficiary engagement in social mission and profit distribution decisions • Procedures to translate beneficiary feedback from engagement and implement it in the organization
External orgware	• Financial support for firmly establishing engagement processes and mechanisms (including relational work) in research institutions	• Investments that prioritize social value creation in line with the expectations of the beneficiaries • Investments that comprehend continuous beneficiary feedback (including critique) as necessary proof of concept

Software

Empowerment of beneficiaries and members, but also wider communities, is the central aim of social enterprises, and leads to trustful relationships (Defourny & Nyssens, 2013; Rothschild, 2018). Research on social entrepreneurship competences emphasizes participation (Biberhofer et al., 2019; di Domenico et al., 2010; Foucrier & Wiek, 2019; Osagie et al., 2016; Wiek et al., 2011). Social entrepreneurs are asked to develop collaborative relations (Miller et al., 2012), and grant more autonomy to staff and volunteers compared to a traditional employer–employee relationship (Lumpkin et al., 2013). All of these aspects are marked by parallels to the software needed for effective citizen engagement in science.

However, this is contrasted by evidence that beneficiaries are often excluded from the decision-making, their input being neglected or ignored (Laidler-Kylander & Stenzel, 2013). For example, Nolan et al. (2019) stress difficulties for social enterprises to obtain representative feedback. Findings point to software-related challenges by social entrepreneurs and also the (impact) investors that may be supporting them that are similar to those mentioned in the context of citizen engagement. These include a feeling of superiority from training and a lack of trust in the expertise of beneficiaries to understand and be able to respond (Cea & Rimington, 2017; Twersky et al., 2013). Furthermore, Cea and Rimington (2017) illustrate with quotes from their interviews that social entrepreneurs are often confident to know the right solution as well as the situation of the beneficiaries so that the entrepreneurs think beneficiary involvement and a proof of concept become superfluous. These findings might have roots in historical patterns in which some are privileged to help and others are recipients of help. Driven by this kind of software, social entrepreneurs feel uncomfortable and called into question by negative feedback from those they try to help, instead of effectively co-engaging with them (Twersky et al., 2013). See Brannvall (this volume) on the negative effects this attitude may have for scaling social innovations.

This kind of mindset describes a software similar to the lack of appreciation for experiential knowledge in the context of citizen engagement, which separates social entrepreneurs from current needs and recent developments as well as from the valuable expertise of beneficiaries (Cea & Rimington, 2017). Acknowledging engagement as a two-way communication process instead (Grand et al., 2015; Verhoeff & Kupper, 2014) draws the attention beyond the social entrepreneur to also scrutinize the mindset of the beneficiary and its engagement experience. Studies show us that the lack of appreciation of the experiential knowledge mindset of the entrepreneurs is complemented by beneficiaries' fear, anxiety, and cynicism (Twersky et al., 2013), accompanied by a lack of resources to participate in engagement, which leads to missing representativeness of beneficiaries and difficulties in obtaining authentic feedback (Nolan et al., 2019). So, the solutions that entrepreneurs develop may be inadequate or ignorant of the deeper roots of a problem, so that they perpetuate rather than address the underlying problems (Gras et al., 2020).

As beneficiaries contribute to the value created by the social enterprises, it is important to understand how they experience the social enterprises (Benjamin, 2021). To establish a respectful relationship, the beneficiaries need to be informed about the engagement process and how the information gained is used (Nolan et al., 2019).

Resources are typically the most often mentioned challenge to innovation (Hueske & Guenther, 2015, 2021). In line with these findings on different innovation processes, Nolan et al. (2019) describe the difficulties for beneficiaries, who might be struggling, with their everyday challenges, to make time for engagement. Therefore, they propose facilitating conditions for beneficiary engagement, such as providing childcare, food, or compensation for the time invested in engagement.

Our discussion shows us that there may be software-related challenges relating to the social entrepreneur or the beneficiary which are hard to overcome. Orgware provides means to address them.

Orgware

Research on citizen engagement has widened its perspectives from hardware to software to consider individuals' mindsets that may influence engagement practices. Mindsets in turn are influenced and governed by their institutional and organizational context, a recognition which led to the consideration of orgware.

However, there are both parallels and differences between citizen engagement and social entrepreneurship in terms of how orgware can help meet deficits in the effective use of software. First, and as a mirror of, for example, crowdsourced innovation projects, co-development of the solution in the form of collective social business model ideation before starting the venture (see e.g. Cea & Rimington, 2017) can ensure good alignment between problems and solutions. Second, and in parallel to transparent assessments of the socio-technical effects of innovations, evaluating beneficiary outcomes before (planned), during (materialized), and after a project (long-term), and translating these results into processes of organizational learning, can help maintain a target group orientation and involvement throughout (Benjamin, 2018; Defourny & Nyssens, 2013; Twersky et al., 2013). In contrast to citizen engagement in science, however, social enterprises possess another ability to increase engagement, namely that of participatory governance structures that make beneficiaries part of all kinds of strategic decisions (Defourny & Nyssens, 2013, 2017).

According to Defourny and Nyssens (2013, 2017), engagement through participatory decision-making processes can be the central purpose of a social enterprise. So, embedding engagement is not an additional activity—like citizen engagement—but can be the raison d'être for social enterprises. Engagement through participation is an essential feature of social enterprises (Kannampuzha & Hockerts, 2019). From an internal perspective on orgware, engagement is enabled through special ownership structures (di Domenico et al., 2010; Lumpkin et al., 2013; Wiek et al., 2011), democratic and participatory management systems, democratic business models, and inclusive, democratic, or cooperative work environments (Foucrier & Wiek, 2019).

From an external perspective, and because constantly upholding engagement is expensive (Nolan et al., 2019; Twersky et al., 2013), engaging beneficiaries for instance in the business model ideation process requires resources, which could be provided by special funding schemes that may be offered by impact investors. Such investors need to be directed at impact and value creation for beneficiaries rather than only seeing the additional resources required to better understand such value creation (for an up-to-date review of the social and impact finance landscape see Nicholls & Ormiston, this volume). The path ahead is still very long. Twersky and Reichheld (2019) claim that 88 per cent of non-profits use beneficiary feedback in the context of their impact measurement practices (for more on impact measurement and management see Hehenberger & Buckland, this volume). However, only 13 per cent use it as the main source and translate it into improvement, due to a lack of resources. Part of enabling engagement practices is to listen to and verify what has been heard from beneficiaries. But the most important part of orgware for engagement is to *develop organizational processes to act upon beneficiary feedback*, and for investors to recognize such feedback as a relevant proof of concept as to whether and how the entrepreneurial model achieves its mission.

Avenues for future research: software, orgware and societal impact

Inspired by citizen engagement research, we viewed engagement in social entrepreneurship through the lenses of hardware, software, and orgware, driven by the argument that engagement leads to more societal impact, and ultimately to direct benefits for those who engage. Figure 13.1 illustrates how we have conceptually discussed and framed the interplay between hardware, software, and orgware. While hardware is crucial for the implementation of engagement practices, and thereby directly related to societal impact, it cannot exist if it is not properly informed by software and embedded in orgware. Software—that is, an open mindset and engagement competencies of those leading social enterprises—is a prerequisite for harnessing the engagement experiences of beneficiaries. Through this, software directly fosters local democracy, which can be interpreted as one key aspect of societal impact or in addition to other societal impacts. At the same time, software shapes the hardware that is eventually put into place and thereby indirectly influences societal impact through another avenue. Orgware in turn is the encompassing context that comprises software as well as hardware, and ensures through internal systems, structures, and processes that these are firmly implemented within the organization and through external arrangements that they are embedded and support at the field or institutional levels. Based on this model, we elaborate directions for future research in the subsections to follow.

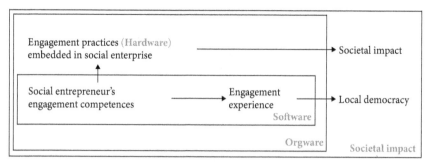

Figure 13.1 Future research needs on the relations between software, orgware, and societal impact

Engagement as societal impact

Previous research has typically investigated societal impact from the social entrepreneur's perspective rather than from that of the beneficiaries (Bacq & Janssen, 2011; Hervieux & Voltan, 2018; Lorenzo-Afable et al., 2020). However, the relationship with beneficiaries is gaining more and more attention (Bonbright, 2014). Increasingly, non-profit organizations are evaluated on how beneficiaries are heard in the organization and how feedback is encouraged and listened to (Benjamin, 2018). Future research should extend the findings by Cea and Rimington (2017) and Twersky et al. (2013) to understand how software, for example the mindset of the social entrepreneur, influences the beneficiary experience of engagement processes. Recognizing the normative claim for empowerment, future studies can triangulate by measuring the beneficiary experience as (1) perceived by the beneficiary versus (2) perceived and intended by the social entrepreneur, and (3) complemented by objective measures for empowerment of beneficiaries.

Interactions between software, orgware, and societal impact

Research on social entrepreneurship competences enlarges the view on software, from only considering the attitudes of individuals to also considering their abilities and knowledge. This stream of research identifies abilities that help enable collaboration (Foucrier & Wiek, 2019; Miller et al., 2012; Wiek et al., 2011) and participation (Biberhofer et al., 2019; di Domenico et al., 2010; Foucrier & Wiek, 2019; Osagie et al., 2016; Wiek et al., 2011). We can extend this line of inquiry by moving from competences to organizational structures and practices, that is, the orgware which might enable 'collective problem-solving procedures' (Redman & Wiek, 2021, p. 6) and which creates truly democratic or cooperative environments (Foucrier & Wiek, 2019). Yet there are many open questions with regard to this nexus of enabling factors for societal impact: what kind of competences and abilities are needed to enable genuine and long-term engagement? How do additional competences and also social enterprises' orgware influence the software of the social entrepreneur? Or how do software and orgware combined influence (enhance or inhibit) the software of beneficiaries? Specifying competences could inform educators of future social entrepreneurs but also impact investors on what kind of software is required and what kind of orgware may help promote the software, or help to formalize and institutionalize it inside and outside the organization.

Social entrepreneurship literature furthermore claims that engagement leads to empowerment (Defourny & Nyssens, 2013, 2017). How does embedding engagement practices in the organization create an equal and trustful relationship? How do co-engagement and mutual interactions influence the mindset of social entrepreneurs and beneficiaries in the long term?

Assessing the impact of engagement

Achieving societal impact is the central aim of social enterprises. Stakeholder involvement is an essential ingredient for societal impact (Bacq & Eddleston, 2018; Battilana, 2021). Stakeholder theory informs us how stakeholders, depending on power, urgency, and legitimacy (Mitchell et al., 1997), influence societal impact (Bailey & Lumpkin, 2021). Empirical evidence shows us that excluding stakeholders and thereby reducing the complex problem, might miss important dimensions (Gras et al., 2020) and can thereby lead to no or even negative societal impact (Hall et al., 2012). Research on beneficiaries of social enterprises in turn emphasizes their influence and effects on the intended impacts and the organizational structures, which may produce such impacts (Benjamin, 2021). But up until now this mostly happens without scholars being able to specify neither quality nor quantity of governance structures that build heavily on engagement. Qualitative studies could identify the process by which engagement practices embedded in orgware may lead to greater or smaller societal impact. Quantitative studies could compare how the societal impact of social enterprises differs depending on the quality of stakeholder engagement. Such studies could use different reference points such as: engagement during sustainable business model ideation, during innovation development, or as part of social enterprises' governance structures.

Engagement and democracy as a central impact

To nurture democracy in the community the social enterprises engage a variety of stakeholders besides beneficiaries, such as customers, employees, volunteers, public authorities, and donors (Defourny & Nyssens, 2017; Low, 2006). This specifies the analysis of the societal impact to empowerment and nurturing of democracy. The challenge thereby is that engagement needs to overcome profound challenges to achieve large-scale societal impact (Bacq & Eddleston, 2018; Montgomery et al., 2012; Sud et al., 2009) such as leveraging their social network to gain support (Alvord et al., 2004) in the form of resources and legitimacy (Desa & Basu, 2013; di Domenico et al., 2010). Yet, we are still very unclear as regards the research question: How do the engagement practices lead to empowerment and increase the local democracy? This could provide a different angle on corporate citizenship—not the corporation as a citizen (e.g., Carroll, 2017) but the social enterprise as nurturer of local democracy.

Negative consequences of engagement

Research shows that the potential benefits of engagement for organizations' innovativeness and their societal impact are counteracted by the fact that including a diversity of actors can make, for example, managing social innovation processes successfully an immense challenge (Krlev et al., 2020). The benefits of stakeholder engagements are contrasted by research that suggests increased participation can decrease the autonomy and the entrepreneurial behaviour of the social enterprise. Therefore, social enterprises are challenged to balance the tradeoff between benefits and challenges of multiple stakeholder involvement related to increased complexity and conflicting demands (Lumpkin et al., 2013). This demands future research to investigate different governance models considering different stakeholders and their impact on the functioning of the business model and its intended societal impact.

Conclusions

Drawing on citizen engagement research to analyse beneficiary engagement by social enterprises, we conclude that effectively implementing engagement methods (hardware) requires competences (software) and embedding engagement in organizational processes and structures (orgware). We extend software from the mindset of entrepreneurs and also consider their engagement competences and the engagement experience of the beneficiaries. We have placed much emphasis on orgware, that is, the organizational embedding of hardware and software; but we have also shown that how engagement is embedded and how this translates into societal impact requires much more empirical work. Regarding societal impact achieved through engagement, more research is needed to specify and quantify the intended societal impact as defined by the mission of the social enterprises and what role local democracy might play therein. We hope to have provided directions for future research on these important social economy issues.

Acknowledgement

This research was carried out within the Horizon 2020 Support for the Research and Innovation Dimension of European Universities project Aurora RI (Grant Agreement number: 1010035804—Aurora RI—H2020-IBA-SwafS-Support-2-2020) and the Erasmus+ university network Aurora Alliance (Grant Agreement number: 101004013—Aurora Alliance—EAC-A02-2019/EAC-A02-2019-1). We thank our colleague Associate Professor Frank Kupper for underlining the importance of orgware and software in citizen engagement. We thank Gorgi Krlev and Dominika Wruk for their constructive and valuable feedback on former versions of this chapter.

References

Alvord, S. H., Brown, L. D., & Letts, C. W. (2004). Social entrepreneurship and societal transformation: an exploratory study. *The Journal of Applied Behavioral Science*, 40(3). https://doi.org/10.1177/0021886304266847

Arnstein, S. R. (1969). A ladder of citizen participation. *Journal of the American Institute of Planners*, 34(4), 216–224.

Bacq, S., & Eddleston, K. A. (2018). A resource-based view of social entrepreneurship: how stewardship culture benefits scale of social impact. *Journal of Business Ethics*, 152(3), 589–611. https://doi.org/10.1007/s10551-016-3317-1

Bacq, S., & Janssen, F. (2011). The multiple faces of social entrepreneurship: a review of definitional issues based on geographical and thematic criteria. *Entrepreneurship & Regional Development*, 23(5–6), 373–403. https://doi.org/10.1080/08985626.2011.577242

Bailey, R. C., & Lumpkin, G. T. (2021). Enacting positive social change: a civic wealth creation stakeholder engagement framework. *Entrepreneurship Theory and Practice*. https://doi.org/10.1177/10422587211049745

Bala, A., Muñoz, P., Rieradevall, J., & Ysern, P. (2008). Experiences with greening suppliers: the Universitat Autònoma de Barcelona. *Journal of Cleaner Production*, 16(15). https://doi.org/10.1016/j.jclepro.2008.04.015

Barben, D., Fisher, E., Selin, C., & Guston, D. (2007). Anticipatory governance of nanotechnology:f oresight, engagement and integration. In E. Hackett, O. Amsterdamska, M. Lynch, & J. Wajcman (Eds), *The Handbook of Science and Technology Studies* (3rd ed., pp. 979–1001). Boston: The MIT Press.

Battilana, J. (2021). For social business to become the norm, we need to build a social business infrastructure. *Stanford Social Innovation Review*. Retrieved from: https://ssir.org/articles/entry/for_social_business_to_become_the_norm_we_need_to_build_a_social_business_infrastructure

Bellamy, R., & Lezaun, J. (2017). Crafting a public for geoengineering. *Public Understanding of Science*, 26(4), 402–417. https://doi.org/10.1177/0963662515600965

Benjamin, L. M. (2018). *Client Authority in Nonprofit Human Service Organizations*. https://doi.org/10.1007/978-3-319-77416-9_9

Benjamin, L. M. (2021). Bringing beneficiaries more centrally into nonprofit management education and research. *Nonprofit and Voluntary Sector Quarterly*, 50(1), 5–26. https://doi.org/10.1177/0899764020918662

Besley, J. C. (2015). What do scientists think about the public and does it matter to their online engagement? *Science and Public Policy*, 42(2), 201–214. https://doi.org/10.1093/scipol/scu042

Betten, A. W., Rerimassie, V., Broerse, J. E. W., Stemerding, D., & Kupper, F. (2018). Constructing future scenarios as a tool to foster responsible research and innovation among future synthetic biologists. *Life Sciences, Society and Policy*, 14(1). https://doi.org/10.1186/s40504-018-0082-1

Biberhofer, P., Lintner, C., Bernhardt, J., & Rieckmann, M. (2019). Facilitating work performance of sustainability-driven entrepreneurs through higher education: the relevance of competencies, values, worldviews and opportunities. *The International Journal of Entrepreneurship and Innovation*, 20(1). https://doi.org/10.1177/1465750318755881

Bonbright, D. (2014). The health and human services sector constituents voice. In M. Mortell & T. Hansen-Turton (Eds), *Making Strategy Count in the Health and Human Services Sector: Lessons learned from 20 Organizations and Chief Strategy Officers* (pp. 255–274). New York: Springer Publishing Company.

Boulianne, S. (2018). *Beyond the Usual Suspects: Representation in Deliberative Exercises.* Athabasca, Alberta: Athabasca University Press.

Braun, K., & Koenninger, S. (2018). From experiments to ecosystems? Reviewing public participation, scientific governance and the systemic turn. *Public Understanding of Science*, 27(6), 674–689.

Bucchi, M. (2008). Of deficits, deviations and dialogues: theories of public communication of science. In M. Bucchi & B. Trench (Eds), *The Handbook of Public Communication of Science and Technology* (pp. 71–90). Abingdon: Routledge.

Bucchi, M., & Neresini, F. (2008). Science and Public Participation. In E. J. Hackett (Ed.), *The handbook of science and technology studies* (pp. 955–1001). Cambridge, Mass: MIT Press.

Carroll, A. B. (2017). The four faces of corporate citizenship. In: Gunningham, N. (Ed.) (2009). *Corporate Environmental Responsibility* (pp. 100–101). Florence: Taylor and Francis.

Cea, J., & Rimington, J. (2017). Designing with the beneficiary. *Innovations: Technology, Governance, Globalization*, 11(3–4), 98–111. https://doi.org/10.1162/inov_a_00259

Chilvers, J., & Kearnes, M. (2020). Remaking participation in science and democracy. *Science Technology and Human Values*, 45(3), 347–380. https://doi.org/10.1177/0162243919850885

Cohen, J. (2022). Institutionalizing public engagement in research and innovation: Toward the construction of institutional entrepreneurial collectives. *Science and Public Policy*, 1–13. https://doi.org/10.1093/scipol/scac018

Davies, S., Macnaghten, P., & Kearnes, M. (2009). *Reconfiguring Responsibility. Deepening Debate on Nanotechnology.* Durham: Durham University.

Davies, S. R. (2014). Knowing and loving: public engagement beyond discourse. In *Science & Technology Studies*, 3(3), 90–110.

Davies, S. R. (2022). Science communication at a time of crisis: emergency, democracy, and persuasion. *Sustainability (Switzerland)*, 14(9). https://doi.org/10.3390/su14095103

de Saille, S. (2015). Dis-inviting the unruly public. *Science as Culture*, 24(1), 99–107. https://doi.org/10.1080/09505431.2014.986323

Defourny, J., & Nyssens, M. (2013). Social innovation, social economy and social enterprise: what can the European debate tell us? In Moulaert, F., MacCallum, D., & Mehmood, A. (Eds.) *The international handbook on social innovation: collective action, social learning and transdisciplinary research* (pp. 40–52). Cheltenham: Edward Elgar.

Defourny, J., & Nyssens, M. (2017). Fundamentals for an international typology of social enterprise models. *VOLUNTAS: International Journal of Voluntary and Nonprofit Organizations*, 28(6), 2469–2497. https://doi.org/10.1007/s11266-017-9884-7

Desa, G., & Basu, S. (2013). Optimization or bricolage? Overcoming resource constraints in global social entrepreneurship. *Strategic Entrepreneurship Journal*, 7(1), 26–49. https://doi.org/10.1002/sej.1150

Devonshire, I. M., & Hathway, G. J. (2014). Overcoming the barriers to greater public engagement. *PLoS Biology*, 12(1). https://doi.org/10.1371/journal.pbio.1001761

Di Domenico, M., Haugh, H., & Tracey, P. (2010). Social bricolage: theorizing social value creation in social enterprises. *Entrepreneurship: Theory and Practice*, 34(4), 681–703. https://doi.org/10.1111/j.1540-6520.2010.00370.x

Durant, J. R., Evans, G. A., & Thomas, G. P. (1989). The public understanding of science. *Nature*, 340, 12–14.

Ecklund, E. H., James, S. A., & Lincoln, A. E. (2012). How academic biologists and physicists view science outreach. *PLoS ONE*, 7(5). https://doi.org/10.1371/journal.pone.0036240

Ellard-Gray, A., Jeffrey, N. K., Choubak, M., & Crann, S. E. (2015). Finding the hidden participant. *International Journal of Qualitative Methods*, 14(5), 160940691562142. https://doi.org/10.1177/1609406915621420

Felt, U. (2015). Keeping technologies out: sociotechnical imaginaries and the formation of Austria's technopolitical identity. In S. Jasanoff & S. H. Kim (Eds), *Dreamscapes of Modernity: Sociotechnical Imaginaries and the Fabrication of Power* (pp. 80–103). Chicago: The University of Chicago Press.

Foucrier, T., & Wiek, A. (2019). A process-oriented framework of competencies for sustainability entrepreneurship. *Sustainability (Switzerland)*, 11(24). https://doi.org/10.3390/su11247250

Fraaije, A. (2022). *Can art save the city? Lessons from action research on art-based citizen engagement towards responsible innovation in 'smart city' Amsterdam*. Amsterdam: VU University Amsterdam.

Gegenhuber, T. (2020). Countering coronavirus with open social innovation. *Stanford Social Innovation Review*. Retrieved from: https://ssir.org/articles/entry/countering_coronavirus_with_open_social_innovation

Gibbons, M. (1999). Science's new social contract with society. *Nature*, 402, C81–C84.

Grand, A., Davies, G., Holliman, R., & Adams, A. (2015). Mapping public engagement with research in a UK university. *PLoS ONE*, 10(4). https://doi.org/10.1371/journal.pone.0121874

Gras, D., Conger, M., Jenkins, A., & Gras, M. (2020). Wicked problems, reductive tendency, and the formation of (non-)opportunity beliefs. *Journal of Business Venturing*, 35(3). https://doi.org/10.1016/j.jbusvent.2019.105966

Guston, D. H. (2014). Understanding 'anticipatory governance'. *Social Studies of Science*, 44(2), 218–242. https://doi.org/10.1177/0306312713508669

Hagendijk, R., & Irwin, A. (2006). Public deliberation and governance: engaging with science and technology in contemporary Europe. *Minerva*, 44(2), 167–184. https://doi.org/10.1007/s11024-006-0012-x

Hall, J., Matos, S., Sheehan, L., & Silvestre, B. (2012). Entrepreneurship and innovation at the base of the pyramid: a recipe for inclusive growth or social exclusion? *Journal of Management Studies*, 49(4), 785–812. https://doi.org/10.1111/j.1467-6486.2012.01044.x

Heltzel, A., Schuijer, J. W., Willems, W. L., Kupper, F., & Broerse, J. E. W. (2022). 'There is nothing nano-specific here': a reconstruction of the different understandings of responsiveness in responsible nanotechnology innovation. *Journal of Responsible Innovation*. https://doi.org/10.1080/23299460.2022.2040779

Hervieux, C., & Voltan, A. (2018). Framing social problems in social entrepreneurship. *Journal of Business Ethics*, 151(2). https://doi.org/10.1007/s10551-016-3252-1

Hueske, A. K., Endrikat, J., & Guenther, E. (2015). External environment, the innovating organization, and its individuals: a multilevel model for identifying innovation barriers accounting for social uncertainties. *Journal of Engineering and Technology Management - JET-M*, 35, 45–70. https://doi.org/10.1016/j.jengtecman.2014.10.001

Hueske, A.-K., & Guenther, E. (2015). What hampers innovation? External stakeholders, the organization, groups and individuals: a systematic review of empirical barrier research. *Management Review Quarterly*, 65(2), 113–148. https://doi.org/10.1007/s11301-014-0109-5

Hueske, A.-K., & Guenther, E. (2021). Multilevel barrier and driver analysis to improve sustainability implementation strategies: towards sustainable operations in institutions of higher education. In *Journal of Cleaner Production*, 291, 125899.

Irwin, A. (2014). From deficit to democracy (re-visited). *Public Understanding of Science*, 23(1), 71–76. https://doi.org/10.1177/0963662513510646

Kannampuzha, M., & Hockerts, K. (2019). Organizational social entrepreneurship: scale development and validation. *Social Enterprise Journal*, 15(3), 290–319. https://doi.org/10.1108/SEJ-06-2018-0047

Knight, R. L., & Kingston, K. L. (2021). Valuing beneficiary voice: involving children living in out-of-home care in programme evaluation. *Evaluation Journal of Australasia*, 21(2), 69–84. https://doi.org/10.1177/1035719X21999110

Krlev, G., Mildenberger, G., & Anheier, H. K. (2020). Innovation and societal transformation—what changes when the 'social' comes in? *International Review of Applied Economics*, 34(5), 529–540. https://doi.org/10.1080/02692171.2020.1820247

Kupper, F., Klaassen, P., Rijnen, M., Vermeulen, S., & Broerse, J. (2015). *Report on the quality criteria of Good Practice Standards in RRI*. Amsterdam: Athena Institute, VU University Amsterdam. Retrieved from: https://rri-tools.eu/documents/10184/107098/D1.3_QualityCriteriaGoodPracticeStandards.pdf/ca4efe26-6fb2-4990-8dde-fe3b4aed1676

Kupper, F., Krijgsman, L., Bout, H., & Buning, T. de C. (2007). The value lab: exploring moral frameworks in the deliberation of values in the animal biotechnology debate. *Science and Public Policy*, 34(9), 657–670. https://doi.org/10.3152/030234207X264944

Laidler-Kylander, N., & Stenzel, J. S. (2013). *The Brand IDEA: Managing Nonprofit Brands with Integrity, Democracy, and Affinity*. Hoboken: Wiley.

Lam, D. M., & Mackenzie, C. (2005). Human and organizational factors affecting telemedicine utilization within U.S. military forces in Europe. In *Telemedicine Journal and e-Health*, 11(1). https://doi.org/10.1089/tmj.2005.11.70

Lorenzo-Afable, D., Lips-Wiersma, M., & Singh, S. (2020). 'Social' value creation as care: the perspective of beneficiaries in social entrepreneurship. *Social Enterprise Journal*, 16(3), 339–360. https://doi.org/10.1108/SEJ-11-2019-0082

Low, C. (2006). A framework for the governance of social enterprise. *International Journal of Social Economics*, 33(5/6), 376–385. https://doi.org/10.1108/03068290610660652

Lubberink, R., Blok, V., Ophem, J. van, & Omta, O. (2017). Lessons for responsible innovation in the business context: a systematic literature review of responsible, social and sustainable innovation practices. *Sustainability (Switzerland)*, 9(5). MDPI. https://doi.org/10.3390/su9050721

Lumpkin, G. T., Moss, T. W., Gras, D. M., Kato, S., & Amezcua, A. S. (2013). Entrepreneurial processes in social contexts: how are they different, if at all? *Small Business Economics*, 40(3), 761–783. https://doi.org/10.1007/s11187-011-9399-3

Macnaghten, P. (2021). Towards an anticipatory public engagement methodology: deliberative experiments in the assembly of possible worlds using focus groups. *Qualitative Research*, 21(1), 3–19. https://doi.org/10.1177/1468794120919096

Mair, J., & Noboa, E. (2006). Social entrepreneurship: how intentions to create a social venture are formed. In *Social Entrepreneurship* (pp. 121–135). Basingstoke, Hampshire: Palgrave Macmillan UK. https://doi.org/10.1057/9780230625655_8

Miller, T. L., Wesley II, C. L., & Williams, D. E. (2012). Educating the minds of caring hearts: comparing the views of practitioners and educators on the importance of social entrepreneurship competencies. *Academy of Management Learning and Education*, 11(3), 349–370. https://doi.org/10.5465/amle.2011.0017

Mitcham, C., & Waelbers, K. (2009). Technology and ethics: overview. In J. Olsen, S. Pedersen, & V. Hendricks (Eds), *A Companion to the Philosophy of Technology* (1st ed., 367–383). Oxford: Blackwell Publishing Ltd.

Mitchell, R. K., Agle, B. R., & Wood, D. J. (1997). Toward a theory of stakeholder identification and salience: defining the principle of who and what really counts. *The Academy of Management Review*, 22(4). https://doi.org/10.2307/259247

Montgomery, A. W., Dacin, P. A., & Dacin, M. T. (2012). Collective social entrepreneurship: collaboratively shaping social good. *Journal of Business Ethics*, 111(3), 375–388. https://doi.org/10.1007/s10551-012-1501-5

Nabuurs, J., Heltzel, A., Willems, W., & Kupper, F. (2023). Crafting the Future of the Artificial Womb. Speculative design as a tool for public engagement with emerging technologies. *Futures*, 151(1), 103184. https://doi.org/10.1016/j.futures.2023.103184

Nolan, C., Howard, K. A., Gulley, K. D., & Gonzalez, E. (2019). More than listening: harnessing the power of feedback to drive collaborative learning. *The Foundation Review*, 11(2). https://doi.org/10.9707/1944-5660.1470

Nowotny, H. (2003). Dilemma of expertise: democratising expertise and socially robust knowledge. *Science and Public Policy*, 30, 151–156. http://www.society-in-science.ethz.ch/index.html.

O'Riordan, K., & Haran, J. (2009). From reproduction to research: sourcing eggs, IVF and cloning in the UK. *Feminist Theory*, 10(2), 191–210. https://doi.org/10.1177/1464700109104924

Osagie, E. R., Wesselink, R., Blok, V., Lans, T., & Mulder, M. (2016). Individual competencies for corporate social responsibility: a literature and practice perspective. *Journal of Business Ethics*, 135(2), 233–252. https://doi.org/10.1007/s10551-014-2469-0

den Oudendammer, W. M., Noordhoek, J., Abma-Schouten, R. Y., van Houtum, L., Broerse, J. E. W., & Dedding, C. W. M. (2019). Patient participation in research funding: an overview of when, why and how amongst Dutch health funds. *Research Involvement and Engagement*, 5(1). https://doi.org/10.1186/s40900-019-0163-1

Owen, R., Pansera, M., Macnaghten, P., & Randles, S. (2021). Organisational institutionalisation of responsible innovation. *Research Policy*, 50(1). https://doi.org/10.1016/j.respol.2020.104132

Pidgeon, N., & Rogers-Hayden, T. (2007). Opening up nanotechnology dialogue with the publics: risk communication or 'upstream engagement'? *Health, Risk and Society*, 9(2), 191–210. https://doi.org/10.1080/13698570701306906

Powell, M., Colin, M., Kleinman, D. L., Delborne, J., & Anderson, A. (2011). Imagining ordinary citizens? Conceptualized and actual participants for deliberations on emerging technologies. *Science as Culture*, 20(1), 37–70. https://doi.org/10.1080/09505430903567741

Priest, S. (2018). Communicating climate change and other evidence-based controversies. In S. Priest, J. Goodwin, & M. Dahlstrom (Eds), *Ethics and Practice in Science Communication* (pp. 55–73). Chicago: University of Chicago Press.

Pytlik Zillig, L. M., & Tomkins, A. (2011). Public engagement for informing science and technology policy: what do we know, what do we need to know, and how will we get there? *Review of Policy Research*, 28(2), 197–217. https://doi.org/10.1111/j.1541

Redman, A., & Wiek, A. (2021). Competencies for advancing transformations towards sustainability. *Frontiers in Education*, 6. https://doi.org/10.3389/feduc.2021.785163

Rothschild, J. (2018). Creating Participatory Democratic Decision-Making in Local Organizations. In: Cnaan, R. A., & Milofsky, C. (Eds.) (2018). *Handbook of Community Movements and Local Organizations in the 21st Century* (pp. 127–140). Cham: Springer International Publishing. https://doi.org/10.1007/978-3-319-77416-9_8

Rowe, G., & Frewer, L. J. (2005). A typology of public engagement mechanisms. *Science Technology and Human Values*, 30(2), 251–290. https://doi.org/10.1177/0162243904271724

Schuijer, J. (2020). *Wading through the Mud. Reflections on Shaping RRI in Practice*. Vrije Universiteit Amsterdam.

Schuijer, J. W., van der Meij, M. G., Broerse, J. E. W., & Kupper, F. (2022). Participation brokers in the making: intermediaries taking up and embedding a new role at the science-society interface. *Journal of Science Communication*, 21(1). https://doi.org/10.22323/2.21010201

Schuurbiers, D., Doorn, N., van de Poel, I., & Gorman, M. E. (2013). Mandates and methods for early engagement. In N. Doorn, D. Schuurbiers, I. van de Poel, & M. E. Gorman (Eds), *Early Engagement and New Technologies: Opening Up the Laboratory* (Vol. 16, pp. 3–14). Dordrecht: Springer Science & Business Media.

Shanley, D., Cohen, J. B., Surber, N., & Stack, S. (2022). Looking beyond the 'horizon' of RRI: Moving from discomforts to commitments as early career researchers. *Journal of Responsible Innovation*, 9(1), 124–132. https://doi.org/10.1080/23299460.2022.2049506

Shirk, J. L., Ballard, H. L., Wilderman, C. C., Phillips, T., Wiggins, A., Jordan, R., McCallie, E., Minarchek, M., Lewenstein, B. V., Krasny, M. E., & Bonney, R. (2012). Public participation in scientific research: a framework for deliberate design. *Ecology and Society*, 17(2), 29–48.

Sismondo, S. (2007). *An Introduction to Science and Technology Studies*. Hoboken: Wiley.

Stilgoe, J., Lock, S. J., & Wilsdon, J. (2014). Why should we promote public engagement with science? *Public Understanding of Science*, 23(1), 4–15. https://doi.org/10.1177/0963662513518154

Stilgoe, J., Owen, R., & Macnaghten, P. (2013). Developing a framework for responsible innovation. *Research Policy*, 42(9), 1568–1580. https://doi.org/10.1016/j.respol.2013.05.008

Sturzenegger-Varvayanis, S., Eosco, G., Ball, S., Lee, K., Halpern, M., & Lewenstein, B. (2008). *How university scientists view science communication to the public*. Ithaca, New York: Cornell University, Department of Communication.

Sud, M., VanSandt, C. v., & Baugous, A. M. (2009). Social entrepreneurship: the role of institutions. *Journal of Business Ethics*, 85(S1), 201–216. https://doi.org/10.1007/s10551-008-9939-1

Sutcliffe, H. (2011). *A report on Responsible Research and Innovation*. Report prepared for DG Research and Innovation: European Commission.

Swierstra, T., & te Molder, H. (2012). Risk and soft impacts. In Sabine Roeser, Rafaela Hillerbrand, Per Sandin, & Martin Peterson (Eds), *Handbook of Risk Theory: Epistemology, Decision Theory, Ethics, and Social Implications of Risk* (pp. 1049–1067). Dordrecht: Springer.

Twersky, F., Buchanan, P., & Threlfall, V. (2013). Listening to those who matter most, the beneficiaries. *Stanford Social Innovation Review*, 11(2). Retrieved from: https://ssir. org/articles/entry/listening_to_those_who_matter_most_the_beneficiaries

Twersky, F., & Reichheld, F. (2019). *Why Customer Feedback Tools Are Vital for Nonprofits. Harvard Business Review.* Retrieved from: https://hbr.org/2019/02/why-customer-feedback-tools-are-vital-for-nonprofits#:~:text=Recent%20analysis%20of %20one%20of,in%20doing%20their%20jobs%20better.

Verhoeff, R., & Kupper, F. (2014). Wetenschap in dialoog. In F. van Dam, L. de Bakker, & A. Dijkstra (Eds), *Wetenschapscommunicatie. Een kennisbasis* (pp. 85–110). Amsterdam: Boom Uitgevers.

Wiek, A., Withycombe, L., & Redman, C. L. (2011). Key competencies in sustainability: A reference framework for academic program development. *Sustainability Science*, 6(2), 203–218. https://doi.org/10.1007/s11625-011-0132-6

Wilsdon, J., & Willis, R. (2004). *See-through Science: Why Public Engagement Needs to Move Upstream.* London: Demos.

Wilsdon, James, Stilgoe, Jack, Wynne, Brian, & Demos. (2005). *The Public Value of Science: Or How to Ensure that Science Really Matters.* London: Demos.

Wynne, B. (2006). Public engagement as a means of restoring public trust in science— hitting the notes, but missing the music? *Community Genetics*, 9(3), 211–220. https:// doi.org/10.1159/000092659

Zorn, T. E., Roper, J., Weaver, C. K., & Rigby, C. (2012). Influence in science dialogue: individual attitude changes as a result of dialogue between laypersons and scientists. *Public Understanding of Science*, 21(7), 848–864. https://doi.org/10.1177/ 0963662510386292

Zutshi, A., & Sohal, A. S. (2004). Environmental management system adoption by Australasian organisations: Part 1: reasons, benefits and impediments. *Technovation*, 24(4). https://doi.org/10.1016/S0166-4972(02)00053-6

14
Civic leadership for a transformative social economy

A comparison of city leadership constellations in Italy and the UK

Alessandro Sancino, Michela Pagani, Luigi Corvo, Alessandro Braga, and Fulvio Scognamiglio

Introduction

The concept of social economy comprises multiple actors engaging in processes of value (co)creation ultimately related to addressing human welfare needs and the common good while promoting economic, societal, and environmental value (Krlev et al., 2021). It is now well recognized that the social economy is a driver of societal innovation and institutional resilience, and can generate superior economic value, blended with environmental and social value (e.g. Krlev, 2022; Bengo et al., 2022).

Much has been written about partnerships among the social economy, citizens, the for-profit sector, and the public sector (Bryson, Crosby, & Stone, 2015). However, we know less about *how* such partnerships can enhance public, social, and shared value (e.g., Andrews & Entwistle, 2010; Cabral et al., 2019; Sancino, 2016). Hueske, Willems, and Hockerts (this volume) have dealt with how processes of citizen engagement may improve the legitimacy of social economy activities, in particular their innovations, and how these can be more tailored to the needs of target groups. Carter and Ball (this volume) have clearly highlighted the role of cross-sectoral partnerships, and in particular of formal relational contracting between the social economy and the public sector, as a way to develop a modern function of public procurement for tackling long-standing and entrenched social challenges. We take a middle position in reference to these contributions, in several regards.

First, in this chapter, we focus on the role of civic leadership as an open, either formal or informal agency that can serve the same purpose of promoting coalitions for progress on social challenges. We use the terms of civic leadership to provide a strong local or regional component of distributed leadership for a given place-based geographical context, while, as we explain later, we consider city leadership as the system of city leaders where city leaders are identified from a positional and reputational

Alessandro Sancino et al., *Civic leadership for a transformative social economy*. In: *Social Economy Science*. Edited by: Gorgi Krlev, Dominika Wruk, Giulio Pasi, and Marika Bernhard, Oxford University Press. © Oxford University Press (2023). DOI: 10.1093/oso/9780192868343.003.0014

perspective. So, city leadership may overlap with civic leadership, but it might also refer to other endeavours too. Second, we consider the public, private, and community/social spheres in combination and look at networks within these spheres as well as connections among them. Third, we adopt a place-based perspective that takes special account of such constellations at the local level.

Specifically, we present an explorative study conducted in two mid-sized cities, one in Italy (Padua) and one in the UK (Peterborough), which aimed at identifying what we call city leaders in inclusive local development. By city leaders, we mean those actors that make things happen at the local level and that have a reputational recognition in one or more of the four main domains of urban governance, namely: political/democratic; public services; business environment; community/social domain. The theoretical consideration and intellectual curiosity behind this study were the following: based on previous research, we are aware that we need multi-stakeholder partnerships and coalitions of civic-minded leaders—but who are city leaders? And how could they be engaged in such collaborative governance arrangements? As we show in the next sections, understanding who city leaders are is not a trivial question.

The chapter proceeds as follows. The next section presents the theoretical framework, whereby civic leadership is framed not as a position but as a willingness to take positive agency for a given place or local environment. The third section describes the methodology of the research conducted. The fourth section highlights the findings. The fifth and final section provides reflections on what this means for the role of the social economy in civic and local leadership as well as partnerships.

What is civic leadership and why does it matter for the social economy?

Civic leadership is a form of leadership that starts from a position and role as an active citizen (in the sense of those taking on stewardship for communal issues), attached to a place (both emotionally and/or physically), that from there can originate leadership dynamics directed at making certain things happen. Some examples of civic leadership are individual citizens who organize groups to clean up cities or organize events, but also (social) entrepreneurs and/or organizations who produce social and shared value, public service professionals who solve collective problems, and people working in any role in public institutions who develop processes aimed at public value generation. We usually look at leadership thinking that it is only about formal leaders in positions of power, and consider it mainly in terms of success in business and/or politics, but leadership today is a more complex and distributed phenomenon, precisely because power is multi-dimensional, dispersed across various actors and segments of society, and contextual according to the instances at stake (Battilana & Casciaro, 2021). To provide a concrete example, civic leadership is not just about the formal institutional and political leadership functions in a place, and may be exercised by any individual and/or organizational actor pertaining to any sector as long as the intention and effects of those leadership interventions are aimed at generating public, social, and/or shared value for a given place (Sancino, 2016). Research on leadership in and of places has bloomed recently (Beer et al., 2019; Collinge, Gibney, & Mabey, 2010; Grint & Holt, 2011; Jackson, 2019; Rapoport et al., 2019; Ropo, Sauer, & Salovaara, 2013), with the aim of delving into the mutual influence of place and leadership and the various forms that place-based leadership can take.

Place is 'a meaningful site that combines location, locale, and sense of place' (Agnew, 1987) and a combination of 'materiality, meaning and practice' (Cresswell, 2014) which provides a unique configuration of social relations and culture. Place and the feelings of attachment people have to their place are important resources for those seeking to engage in civic leadership processes (Hambleton, 2019). Two elements are widely acknowledged in this respect. First, civic leadership is exercised by both formal and informal leaders, who may belong to any sphere (or sector) of the governance system (Ayres, 2014; Beer et al., 2019; Budd et al., 2017; Hambleton, 2014; Sotarauta, 2016; Sotarauta & Beer, 2017). Second, collective action and collaboration among these leaders are essential for implementing an effective place-based leadership (Jackson, 2019), in line with the recent rise and spread of studies and theories on cross-sector collaboration (Crosby & Bryson, 2005), collective leadership (Ospina, 2017), and multi-actor governance (Bryson et al., 2017; Craps et al., 2019).

Different approaches to conceptualize civic leadership

Several scholars have identified different domains (or realms or arenas) from which civic leadership originates and is co-exercised. In particular, three frameworks should be taken into consideration: the Public Leadership framework developed by 't Hart (2014; 't Hart & Tummers, 2019); the New Civic Leadership Framework, developed by Hambleton (2015); and the City Leadership Framework, developed by Budd and Sancino (Budd & Sancino, 2016; Budd et al., 2017).

Table 14.1 below summarizes and compares the domains identified in each framework.

As can be noticed, all frameworks give an important role to political leadership and managerial/professional/administrative leadership (that is, the leadership of the public sector and public service delivery). The main difference among the three frameworks lies in the recognition of the leadership by society, namely the leadership that emerges outside government. In fact, the public leadership framework ('t Hart, 2014; 't Hart & Tummers, 2019) puts this domain of leadership under the broad term of civic leadership, whereas the other two frameworks differentiate it into two or three different arenas, using different terminology to identify the same sub-group of city leaders (i.e., community leadership and civic leadership). In this chapter we refer to civic leadership in its expansive meaning; in other words, we consider civic leadership as making a difference for a given place moving from the assumption that this endeavour may be undertaken from political/democratic arenas, from public services arenas, from business arenas, and from social/community arenas—that is, from

Table 14.1 Three perspectives on domains that define leadership with relevance to collaboration at the local level

Public leadership ('t Hart, 2014; 't Hart & Tummers, 2019)	New civic leadership (Hambleton, 2014, 2015)	City leadership (Budd & Sancino, 2016; Budd et al., 2017)
3 spheres: 1. Political leadership 2. Administrative leadership 3. Civic leadership	5 realms: 1. Political leadership 2. Managerial/ Professional leadership 3. Community leadership 4. Business leadership 5. Trade union leadership	4 arenas: 1. Political leadership 2. Managerial leadership 3. Business leadership 4. Civic leadership

any relational setting where city governance unfolds, as long as at the centre of those leadership interventions there is the intention of improving place-based conditions and generating public, social, and/or shared value in a given place. Thus, readapting from the work of Budd and Sancino, we consider civic leadership as comprising four main governance arenas:

- the political/democratic arena, which deals with the democratic processes and institutional decision-making affecting a city and its citizens;
- the managerial/public services arena, which deals with the public services designed and delivered within a city (e.g., housing, healthcare, education, regeneration, leisure, etc.);
- the business arena, which deals with the processes of (co-)creation of value provided by the private sector;
- the community/social arena, which deals with all the processes provided by the community, the social economy, and all actors operating outside the traditional realms of the public and private sectors.

We use this framework to better understand what governance arenas in different cities look like, who is leading in them, and how separation and collaboration between arenas may matter. In this, we take particular account of the role of the social economy in potentially leading and partnering across arenas.

Box 1 The origins of city leadership in the academic debate

The idea of a plurality of actors who influence (and hence lead) the city and its community has a long history. Hunter (1953) was one of the first to ask 'who runs the

continued

Box 1 Continued

---

community?' by examining the leadership of a US city through the power structures of its community. Rosen (1954, p. 950) excellently summarized the central argument: If the problems which confront individuals and groups in a community are to be dealt with democratically and effectively, can this be done when the citizens are not even aware of who the real leaders of the community are and how they are selected? In this respect, Hunter found that forty out of the half-billion citizens of the investigated city were top city leaders who 'have a virtual monopoly of big decision-making for the entire community' (Smith, 1954). Also, most of these leaders were businessmen and the decision-making processes among these leaders were generally hidden and unknown to the public.

A similar research purpose was at the basis of Dahl's work *Who Governs?* (2005, first published in 1961). Indeed, like Hunter, Dahl investigated the power structure of a US city, finding that city leadership was actually exercised by elected politicians as well as by other types of actors, in particular entrepreneurs and businessmen. This latter point was also supported by Yager (1963), who distinguished four other potential sources of city leadership:

1. Economic groups, which provided the greatest political leadership;
2. The press;
3. Minorities, because of 'the control they can exercise in close elections';
4. Mugwumps, namely 'independent, political, citizen-action groups'.

Summing up, it is clear that city leadership has been understood as a pluralistic and cross-sector form of leadership since the very beginning of its investigation.

Analytic strategy for identifying leaders

According to the literature, the identification of city leaders may result from four main complementary approaches:

- a positional approach, which identifies leaders according to their formal position or office (Bonjean & Olson, 1964);
- an intrapersonal approach, which identifies leaders according to the self-evaluation of leaders themselves (Epitropaki et al., 2017);
- a reputational approach, which identifies leaders according to the evaluation of others, such as followers, the team, and/or the group (Bonjean & Olson, 1964; Epitropaki et al., 2017);
- a decisional approach, which identifies leaders according to leaders' actions during decision-making processes (Bonjean & Olson, 1964).

For example, Hunter (1953) applied a positional approach, Dahl (2005) a decisional one, and Rapoport et al. (2019) a reputational one from an expert's standpoint.

In this study, our identification of city leaders was based on a combination of the positional and the reputational approaches to leadership (Bonjean & Olson, 1964; Epitropaki et al., 2017). This means that city leaders were identified first according to the formal position they hold and then according to other participants' evaluation. In particular, city leaders were considered both as leaders and as followers of other leaders (e.g., Kellerman, 2012; Uhl-Bien et al., 2014), and this follower–leader relationship was at the basis of the data collection, analysis, and visualization.

Methodology

This study is based on a multi-site (e.g., Bishop, 2012) mixed-methods (e.g., Creswell & Plano Clark, 2017; Johnson & Onwuegbuzie, 2004; Stentz et al., 2012) research design conducted in two comparable cities, one in Italy (Padova, Padua in English) and one in the United Kingdom (Peterborough).

Research setting

A city is considered in this study as a human settlement characterized by a certain size in population and/or density, and by specific governmental, socio-economic, and cultural attributes. In this respect, each city is potentially both a unique and a typical case (Bryman, 2011; Yin, 2009). This means that each city is potentially both an extreme case (namely, a very different case from others) and an average case (namely, a case that is very similar to others), depending on the focus of the analysis and the researcher's perspective. Accordingly, an 'area of homogeneity' was delineated, namely, a population of cities that shares sufficient similar background characteristics and from which specific cities could then be purposively identified. In particular, the following criteria were considered to select the two investigated cities.

National context
Cities are embedded in the national context in which they are located even if engaged in multi-level governance dynamics (e.g., Acuto, 2016). In fact, the national context remains a key parameter in comparative analysis, albeit it 'can both influence and at the same time be irrelevant in shaping city leadership patterns' (Budd et al., 2017, p. 332). To further develop this idea of both significance and insignificance of the national context over city leadership, the countries were selected by building on the results of previous work on city leadership (Budd et al., 2017; Budd & Sancino, 2016). The chosen countries were Italy and the UK.

City dimension

There is a tendency to focus city-based studies on large cities (e.g., New York, London, etc.), despite growing recognition of the crucial yet vulnerable role played by medium-sized ones. They are likely to be intermediary cities, namely 'cities that generally play a primary role in connecting important rural and urban areas to basic facilities and services' (Roberts et al, 2016, p. 134), and hence to contribute strongly to regional and national wellbeing (Serrano-López et al., 2019). On the other hand, their vulnerabilities 'are being underestimated compared to those of megacities for four reasons: limited data, political power, personnel and resources' (Birkmann et al., 2016, p. 606). Accepting the call to focus more on this type of city (Birkmann et al., 2016; Eurotowns, 2019), we based our investigation on two medium-sized cities. Drawing upon the four leading classifications of medium-sized cities (Dijkstra & Poelman, 2012; Eurotowns, 2019; OECD, 2020; Roberts et al., 2016), we decided to focus on cities with a population of around 200,000 inhabitants.

Political continuity and minimization of bias

Data for this study were collected mainly in 2018–2019. For data quality reasons we selected cities where no local political elections were planned in 2018 due to the end of councillors' terms. Preference was given to cities to which we had no special accessibility and of which we had no prior knowledge (either theoretical or field knowledge). As a result of this procedure, Padua (Italy) and Peterborough (UK) were selected as research sites. For more information about the cities of Padua and Peterborough please see the Appendix.

Research strategy

Participants in the study were city leaders or key city actors who were selected by combining two sampling techniques based on two leader identification approaches (see Pagani et al., 2021). First, an extensive online desk analysis (e.g., Hewson et al., 2016) based on a positional approach to leader identification (Bonjean & Olson, 1964) was used to select potential participants. In other words, formal city leaders were identified, namely those who formally hold a top management position or who are commonly recognized as leaders (e.g., the leader of the council or the mayor, the deputy mayor, top managers at the town hall and of public organizations, CEOs of businesses and voluntary-sector organizations). Second, participants' responses were used to identify and recruit further potential participants, in line with a snowball sampling strategy based on a reputational approach to leader identification (Bonjean & Olson, 1964; Epitropaki et al., 2017). Moreover, we attempted to involve city leaders belonging to all four governance arenas characterizing our framework, to guarantee a multi-perspective examination of city leadership. As a result of the sampling process, sixty-six participants contributed to

Table 14.2 Number of participants classified per city
governance arenas and city

City governance arena	Padua (Italy)	Peterborough (UK)
Political leaders	15	6
Managerial leaders	8	7
Business leaders	2	7
Community/social leaders	12	9
Total	**37**	**29**

the study—thirty-seven in Padua (Italy) and twenty-nine in Peterborough (UK)—as
shown in Table 14.2.

Data collection, data analysis, and data visualization

Data were collected through an online questionnaire and semi-structured interviews and triangulated with focus groups. More specifically, participants (i.e. city
leaders) have been asked to name at least three important leaders in each of the four
governance arenas which are part of our framework. The questions asked were:
 In your opinion, who are the most important

1. political leaders in your city today?
2. managerial leaders in your city today?
3. business leaders in your city today?
4. leaders of civil society in your city today?

Participants were provided with the definition of each governance arena as above
reported and they had the possibility to answer in any way they wanted (i.e., giving names, formal positions, organizations, groups, etc.); the only request was that
they were sufficiently specific and clear that the named leaders could have been easily identified and, possibly, involved in the study. This generated a whole variety of
answers, according to participants' perceptions and conceptualizations of leadership
and leaders.
 A qualitative approach to Social Network Analysis (SNA) (Hollstein, 2014) and
network visualization (e.g., Withall, Phillips, & Parish, 2007) was taken to explore
data and to identify city leaders. This means that we applied SNA to identify leaders
(actors or nodes, according to SNA's terminology) and not to investigate the more
common network characteristics (e.g., density, centrality, and so on: Borgatti, Brass,
& Labianca, 2009; Scott & Carrington, 2014), as this would have gone beyond the
purpose of our study and would not allow the in-depth richness of analysis that was

required to understand not only leadership positions, but also roles and interlinkages between arenas.

More specifically, we began the analysis process by tidying up and preparing the datasets (one for each city) to be imported in Gephi, the network visualization software (Bastian, Heymann, & Jacomy, 2009), for the analysis and graphical representation of data. In particular, first, we integrated the datasets with missing details, where participants had provided insufficient information to identify the named city leaders. Second, we aggregated city leaders according to the available details to limit the dispersion of replies. In other words, in line with multi-level network analysis (Lazega & Snijders, 2015), when different participants named the same leader in different ways (e.g., a) Gillian Beasley; b) CEO of Peterborough City Council; c) Gillian Beasley, CEO of Peterborough City Council—PCC), we aggregated all similar nodes under a unique appellation which could appropriately define the node (e.g., in the previous example, Gillian Beasley, CEO of PCC). This enabled us to reduce the number of network nodes and produced a more effective network analysis and visualization. Then, we classified each identified city leader according to their governance arena. This was one of the most challenging steps because different people might have different perceptions of the functions played by some city leaders. Finally, an ID was assigned to each identified city leader, as required by Gephi.

At this point, we drew the network to support our analysis and reply to our research question (Grandjean, 2015). Every city leader identified by the participants became a specific node in the network visualization and the size of each node resulted from the number of times it was named by different participants. In other words, the larger nodes in the network were the ones mentioned more often by participants. We decided how to display and colour the nodes (i.e., city leaders) according to two elements: first, the governance arena to which they belong; second, their categorization, in order to group together similar ones (e.g., all councillors are grouped together). These groupings are shown with dashed circles around the similar nodes, whereas dotted circles enclose the nodes which represent the same organization (e.g., the organization and its CEO). Groupings of nodes within a governance arena in Figures 14.1 and 14.2 were made to ease readability and comparisons.

Once the network visualization was completed, to focus on the key city leaders of the two investigated cities, we took into consideration only the ones who were named by at least three participants, hiding all other elements of the network. In very general terms, it can be said that to be considered someone's leader it is necessary to have at least one follower, but in terms of influence and capability to mobilize a city and its community, the one-follower criterion is highly questionable and would provide a very dispersed picture of city leadership. The three-mention threshold which we applied for data analysis and visualization seemed reasonable and enabled a better analysis, providing a variegated account of city leadership, but also allowing a focus on city leaders recognized as such by a group of participants.

Finally, the qualitative material collected at the end of the questionnaire or during the interviews was examined, to go deeper into the analysis.

Focus groups

Two focus groups were organized, one in each city, to validate preliminary findings and expand the data collected throughout the study. All participants who expressed their interest (and hence consent) were invited to these initiatives, which in the end counted eight participants in Padua (Italy) and nine in Peterborough (UK).

Discussions during these initiatives were supported by handouts summarizing and representing the preliminary findings that emerged in both cities and hence allowing participants to compare them. More specifically, after a very brief explanation of the network visualization of the identified city leaders, participants were asked to take a minute to look at the representation and:

- raise any questions about Figures 14.1 and 14.2, in order for us to understand if they were easily understandable;
- discuss the network visualizations, especially about the classification of nodes within each city governance arena;
- express their opinion on the representativeness of the network visualizations of the city they were part of.

The qualitative material that emerged from these initiatives was directly integrated with the data and material collected during the online questionnaires and interviews, and it was used to improve the graphical representations and the formulation of findings.

Findings

The overall analysis was conducted using a dataset of 518 entries for Padua (Italy) and 426 for Peterborough (UK), provided respectively by 37 participants in Padua and 29 in Peterborough. Entries represent the participants' leader–follower relationships, or ties using SNA terminology. However, given the decision to focus only on leaders named by at least three participants (as explained in the Methodology section), in total fifty-two city leaders were identified in Padua (see Figure 14.1) and forty-four in Peterborough (see Figure 14.2). The differences in data across the two cities are summarized in Table 14.3.

Looking at Figures 14.1 and 14.2 and at Table 14.3, it can be noticed that the numbers of identified city leaders are very similar. This enabled us to conduct a good comparison between the two cities, despite the expected contextual differences. Before delving into the findings of each governance arena, an important difference between the two cities can already be noticed by focusing on the top three city leaders who received most mentions by participants. Whereas in Padua the central role given to political leaders is evident (two out of the three top city leaders are political leaders, or PL), in Peterborough the situation is more balanced, with one managerial leader, one political leader, and one business leader.

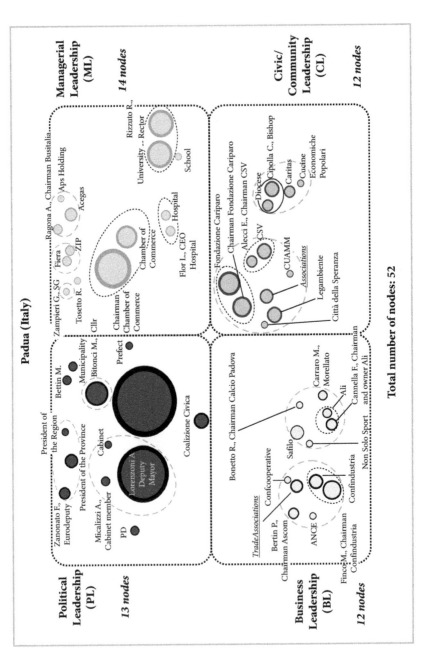

Figure 14.1 The city leader network of Padua (Italy)

Padua (Italy)

Managerial Leadership (ML)

14 nodes

Civic/ Community Leadership (CL)

12 nodes

Ragona A., Chairman Busitalia
Zampieri G., SG
Aps Holding
Acegas
Fiera
ZIP
Tosetto R.
Rizzuto R., Rector
University – Rector
School

President of the Region
Bettin M.
Municipality
Bitonci M.,
Cllr
Chairman Chamber of Commerce
Chamber of Commerce
Prefect
Flor L., CEO Hospital
Hospital

Fondazione Cariparo
Chairman Fondazione Cariparo
Alecci E., Chairman CSV
Cipolla C., Bishop
CSV
Diocese
Caritas
Cucine Economiche Popolari
CUAMM
Associations
Legambiente
Città della Speranza

Zanonato F., Eurodeputy
President of the Province
Micalizzi A., Cabinet member
Cabinet
PD
Lorenzoni A Deputy Mayor
Coalizione Civica

Bonetto R., Chairman Calcio Padova
Carraro M., Morellato
Ali
Cannella F., Chairman and owner Ali
Safilo
Non Solo Sport
Trade Associations
Bertin P., Chairman Ascom
Confcooperative
ANCE
Finco M., Chairman Confindustria
Confindustria

Political Leadership (PL)

13 nodes

Business Leadership (BL)

12 nodes

Total number of nodes: 52

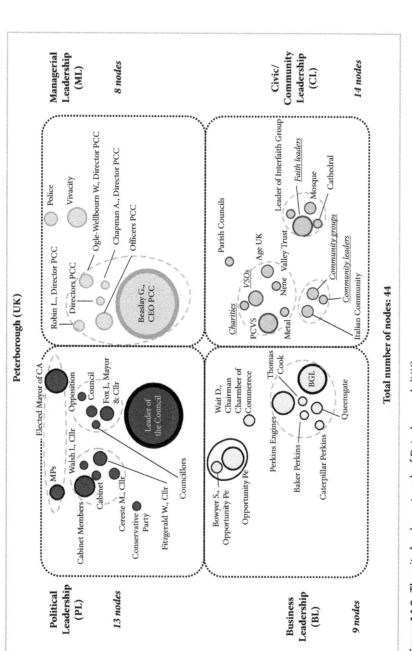

Peterborough (UK)

Political Leadership (PL) — 13 nodes

- MPs
- Elected Mayor of CA
- Walsh L., Cllr
- Opposition
- Cabinet Members
- Cabinet
- Council
- Fox I., Mayor & Cllr
- Cereste M., Cllr
- Conservative Party
- Fitzgerald W., Cllr
- Leader of the Council
- Councillors

Managerial Leadership (ML) — 8 nodes

- Police
- Vivacity
- Robin L., Director PCC
- Ogle-Wellbourn W., Director PCC
- Chapman A., Director PCC
- Directors PCC
- Officers PCC
- Beaslay G., CEO PCC

Business Leadership (BL) — 9 nodes

- Wait D., Chairman Chamber of Commerce
- Bower S., Opportunity Pe
- Opportunity Pe
- Perkins Engines
- Baker Perkins
- Caterpillar Perkins
- Thomas Cook
- BGL
- Queensgate

Civic/Community Leadership (CL) — 14 nodes

- Parish Councils
- Leader of Interfaith Group
- *Faith leaders*
- Mosque
- Cathedral
- Age UK
- Nene Valley Trust
- *VSOs*
- *Community groups*
- *Community leaders*
- *Charities*
- PCVS
- Metal
- Italian Community

Total number of nodes: 44

Figure 14.2 The city leader network of Peterborough (UK)

Table 14.3 Differences in city leaders' identification between the two cities

	Padua (Italy)	Peterborough (UK)
No of entries (participants' leader–follower relationships/ties)	518	426
No of nodes in potential CLN (all participants' replies)	204	200
No of nodes in CLN (with more than 3 mentions)	52	44
Top three city leaders	Mayor (PL; 32 mentions); Deputy Mayor (PL; 26 mentions); Chairman of Chamber of Commerce (ML, 18 mentions).	CEO Peterborough City Council—PCC (ML, 24 mentions); Leader of the council (PL, 22 mentions); BGL Group—financial services company (BL, 10 mentions).

Legend: PL = Political Leader; ML = Managerial Leader; BL = Business Leader

Political leaders

In both cities, the analysis focused on thirteen political leaders, mentioned at least three times. As was expected, the identification of the political leaders in the two cities depends on the context in which they enact their role, and hence are obviously different. However, interesting similarities between the two cities can be observed, as Table 14.4 shows.

The dominant political role is recognized in both contexts as being in the hands of the political figureheads of the cities: the mayor (in Padua) and the leader of the council (in Peterborough). The main differences between the two is that the former is directly elected by citizens, whereas the second is elected by councillors. What is surprising is the dominant political role given to the deputy mayor of Padua, who was mentioned almost as many times as the mayor. One interviewee (Pa33_ML) commented that they represent 'two souls of the same political coalition', and hence both have a strong influence.

As regards Peterborough, the second influential PL—mentioned by eight participants and hence far less than the first one—is the elected mayor of the combined authority. According to the UK Local Government Association, a combined authority (CA) is a legal body set up using national legislation that enables a group of two or more councils to collaborate and take collective decisions across council boundaries. It is established by the Parliament; it is locally owned and requires both the initiative and the support of the councils involved.

Table 14.4 Comparison of types of political leaders identified in the two cities

Type of political leader	Padua	Peterborough
Dominant role	Mayor + Deputy Mayor	Leader of the Council
Cabinet	✓	✓
Council	✓	✓
Representatives of higher levels of government	✓	✓
Party with political majority	✓	✓

As one interviewee commented:

The most important political leader in Peterborough is not in Peterborough. It's the Mayor, it's the Combined Authority Mayor . . . The political leadership has shifted to wherever his offices are at the moment . . . And you can walk down the street and not one person you ask would know that position even exists. Let alone who the occupier of the position is.

(Pe20-BL)

Another interviewee noted: 'He is very influential as he can get things done . . . he has a lot of money to allocate to projects' (Pe19-CL). However, his influence is not always seen positively, given the fact that the elected mayor of the combined authority represents the region and therefore a higher level of government and a larger territory, which also includes Cambridge. For example, one interviewee reported: 'The Metro Mayor has pulled the centre of gravity to Cambridge and we are just the periphery' (Pe2o-BL). Another interviewee remarked that politicians in the region, who influence Peterborough because it is located in the region, 'play a part in that, but is not foremost in their thought' (Pe27-BL).

An interesting difference between the two cities concerns the role of city councillors. In Padua this role is represented by only one actor (Massimo Bitonci, former mayor and leader of the local division of the Northern League), and in Peterborough by four actors.

A surprising finding is the identification of Massimo Bettin, the mayor's spokesman, as a PL of Padua.

Finally, it is also important to remark that, whereas in Italy there is only one established political governance model that can be operated, UK's local governments can decide which local government structure and political governance model to adopt. Therefore, whereas there are some similarities between the two investigated cities because of the similar governance model (both based on a Cabinet executive), more differences could be observed between Peterborough and other English cities that, for example, operate on a committee governance model.

Managerial leaders

The analysis focused on fourteen managerial leaders in Padua and eight in Peterborough. In contrast to the findings related to the political/democratic arena, the identified managerial leaders of the two investigated cities are very disparate (see Table 14.5).

Two main types of managerial leaders have been identified in both cities, namely public services providers and managers working for the council/municipality, but with a very different degree of influence in each city. Public services providers in the Italian case are represented by three organizations with different functions (i.e., transport and multi-utility), whereas in the English case only one public service provider was recognized as a leader, namely Vivacity, a not-for-profit organization that manages several culture and leisure facilities on behalf of Peterborough City Council. Conversely, with regard to managers working for the council/municipality, whereas in Padua this aspect of managerial leadership is perceived as having a very limited leadership role, in Peterborough its influence and importance within the managerial/public services arena is strongly visible in the network visualization, especially given the dominance of one actor: the CEO of Peterborough City Council (PCC), Gillian Beasley. She was recognized as a leader by almost all participants (24 out of 29). As an interviewee commented:

> The person who manages the city, the most powerful one, without doubt, is the Chief Executive. And her name is Gillian Beasley. She is very good . . . she doesn't just manage the council, she manages the community . . . She is a political actor as well, although not elected.
>
> (Pe11-PL)

Table 14.5 Comparison of types of managerial leaders identified in the two cities

Type of ML	Padua (Italy)	Peterborough (UK)
Dominant role	Chamber of Commerce + University	PCC CEO, Gillian Beasley
Chamber of Commerce	✓	
University	✓	
Hospital	✓	
Public corporations	✓	
Public Services Providers (PSP)	✓	✓
Municipality/City Council	✓	✓
Police		✓

Another interviewee said:

> You may have come across Gillian Beasley, that is, the Chief Executive of the City
> Council; she has been here a long time and I think Gillian is very impressive and
> I think a lot of the things that we should take pride [in are] testimony [to] the
> visionary leadership that comes from the managerial class in the city.
>
> (Pe20-BL)

Similarly, another interviewee described her as 'probably one of the best city council
CEOs in the country' (Pe24-PL).

All other types of managerial leaders identified by participants are considered
as such in one city but not in the other. In particular, two of them require brief
comment: the Chamber of Commerce and the university. In Italy, both these organizations and their figureheads were recognized as highly influential. In the UK, the
former is considered as a business organization and not a public sector one, and, in
fact, participants identified it as a business leader. Peterborough does not have a university and this is considered a big limitation of the city, especially in comparison to
its neighbour Cambridge.

Business leaders

The analysis focused on twelve business leaders in Padua and nine in Peterborough.
In both cities the business leadership arena is quite dispersed, as shown in Table 14.6.

The more influential actors (the biggest nodes in Figure 14.1 and 14.2) received,
respectively, nine (in Padua) and ten (in Peterborough) mentions, hence much fewer
mentions than some political and managerial leaders. In fact, even though in both
cities businesses have been recognized as influential, participants struggled, for several reasons, to identify specific ones which play a city leadership role. Participants
were more inclined to recognize as business leaders the umbrella organizations that
represent and are the voices of businesses of the local area.

The identification of these organizations seems to strongly depend on the local
context. In Padua trade associations play this representative role and are perceived
as hugely influential, in line with the national context, where these organizations are

Table 14.6 Comparison of types of business leaders identified in the two cities

Type of ML	Padua	Peterborough
Dominant role	//	//
Trade associations	✓	
Businesses	✓	✓
Opportunity Peterborough (economic development company fully owned by Peterborough city council)		✓
Chamber of Commerce		✓

largely involved in policy decision-making. In contrast, in the English city, Opportunity Peterborough exercises this key role. During the focus group in Peterborough, there was a brief discussion of the identified business leaders within the city. What stood out is that business leaders are probably not aware of or not interested in their civic leadership role. For example, one participant pointed out:

> Look at the names that have been mentioned under the private sector. Most of those are absent in the leadership discussion in the city. So, the fact that they are mentioned is significant. When is the last time everybody met, apart from Queensgate, Thomas Cook, Perkins, Perkins . . . they're cited as important leaders in the city, but I don't see them.
>
> (PeFG7-BL)

Another participant noticed:

> Businesses rock up here because it is a good place to be based, because they can get cheap office accommodation and cheap housing for the work force, cheaper than in some other places around, but they don't sort of invest in the broader sense in the city and in the community.
>
> (PeFG6-BL)

This BL approach to civic leadership was discussed also during the focus group in Padua. The following conversation was had:

> PaFG3-CL: perhaps because there is a tendency to not participate in the civic life of the city, they're too busy on their personal things or there is no willingness to expose themselves.
>
> PaFG6-ML: I think some sectors of society tend to self-reference and hence they tend to avoid facing projects like this, which put in discussion a system of relationships which is taken for granted or overlooked.
>
> PaFG7-ML: Well, the economic sector in Veneto is poorly participative in these initiatives. Entrepreneurs are focused on activities, outcomes, and these research projects are treated with scepticism because either they bring profit to the company or they are ignored.
>
> PaFG1-PL: Maybe the business sector considers research as something of little relevance. I almost feel like there is contempt for research as considered . . .
>
> PaFG1-PL + PaFG3-CL: . . . a waste of time.

Community/social leaders

The analysis focused on twelve civil society leaders in Padua and fourteen in Peterborough. Similarly to business, in both cities the community/social arena is dispersed and lacks a dominant leader (see also Pagani et al., 2021 on this). In fact, the most-named actors received, respectively, eleven (in Padua) and seven (in Peterborough) mentions, much fewer than were received by some political or managerial leaders. Also, despite the widely recognized important role played within and for the city, especially for the delivery of public services and as a voice for the community (Pagani et al., 2021), in both cities participants struggled to name specific civil society leaders, emphasizing the complexity and variegated nature of this leadership arena:

Pa27-ML: There are no key leaders, but a lot of leaders.
Pe25-PL: It's a very diverse, very confusing picture. And it's completely normal. But of course, if you ask me if I can name a few, it's quite difficult. My answer would be 'it depends'.

This suggests two different things. First, civil society actors might lack visibility despite their vital role in driving, for example, cohesion, solidarity, and care services in the city. They thus continue to operate largely under the radar and are not able to unfold a more encompassing transformational function. Second, the social economy might be community-grounded rather than individually grounded. This makes it much harder to name persons whom the consulted experts likely associate most with the word 'leader', despite our focus on leadership that takes account of actors across entire organizations. Grasping the social economy is furthermore complicated by its diversity, which emerges from the different types of leaders identified, which represent three very distinct spheres of society, as better described in a recently published paper (Pagani et al., 2021):

- the third or voluntary sector sphere, which includes all third sector and voluntary sector organizations, and charities. An exemplary quote well illustrates this sphere: 'You need the voluntary sector to deliver so many things because actually you as a city can't afford to deliver these things, so you need to stimulate and finance the voluntary sector to be out and deliver many services that you can't' (Pe11-PL);
- the faith sphere which includes all faith leaders and faith-based organizations;
- the community sphere, which includes community groups and associations, the neighbourhood, local authority/councillors, parish councils, and some people with no specified affiliation or role.

This nicely illustrates the multiplicity that the social economy comprises, which all chapters of this book demonstrate. However, and interestingly, whereas the first two spheres and leaders are observable in both cities, the latter is recognized only in Peterborough—likely because of the very ethnically diverse character of the city. So, we see that the social economy in Padua seems more formalized, whereas it is more grounded in civil society in Peterborough. This may be another source of variation in how strongly and clearly the social economy is recognized as exercising civic leaders and as partners and collaborators of actors in the other arenas: see Table 14.7 below.

Table 14.7 Comparison of types of civic/community leaders identified in the two cities

Type of ML	Padua	Peterborough
Dominant role	//	//
Third sector	✓	✓
Community groups		✓
Faith leaders and organizations	✓	✓

In the first two spheres, two further interesting elements emerge from comparison of the two cities. First, in both cities, a central actor within the civil/civic sphere is the umbrella organization for voluntary sector organizations, namely the Service Centre for Volunteering in Padua and the Peterborough Council for Voluntary Services in Peterborough. Second, the identified faith leaders clearly represent the different cultural and historical context of the two cities. Specifically, whereas in Padua there is a predominance of the Catholic Church, in Peterborough faith leadership is characterized by having different faiths within the city (in fact, participants mainly named faith leaders in general).

Emerging patterns of city leadership and implications for the social economy

Summing up, two main differences emerge from the findings. The first difference relates to where managerial leadership is perceived to be exercised: whereas in Padua it is identified outside of the municipality, mainly in the Chamber of Commerce and the university, in Peterborough it predominantly lies within the City Hall and, more specifically, in the hands of the CEO of the City Council.

The second difference is concerned with social/community leaders. In Peterborough participants recognized community leaders as relevant for their role in representing different publics, while in Padua a key role was assigned to social/community leaders mainly because of their contribution to sustaining public services, with a particularly important role assigned to a local philanthropic foundation. Consequently, and in the attempt to generalize these patterns to some other areas, it is relevant to point out two general risks, namely that some social economy actors might be invisible to city leadership dynamics if not engaged in formal governance processes (Sancino et al., 2021) and that in turn social economy dynamics might be manufactured ad hoc by more powerful actors (e.g., a philanthropic foundation and/or umbrella organizations) active in this field, with associated risks, but also potentially opportunities (Brandsen et al., 2017).

However, what is surprising is that, despite the differences between the two cities stemming from contextual factors, some interestingly similar patterns also emerged from the findings.

The first dimension are the different ways in which city leadership is perceived. The city leaders from the political/democratic and public services/managerial arenas were clearly identified by participants, and some dominant leaders were easily distinguished (e.g., the mayor and the Chamber of Commerce in Padua; the leader of the council and the PCC CEO in Peterborough). In contrast, participants struggled to identify city leaders from society, providing a more fragmented and dispersed picture of the business and social/community arenas.

Second, it is surprising how two cities of about 200,000 residents came to similar conclusions about the number of recognized city leaders (52 in Padua and 44 in Peterborough) distributed across the four governance arenas. This is an interesting finding, as it suggests that city leadership is quite clustered and condensed. For the social economy this may suggest that the spots to be taken to be recognized are few, so that those organizations would need to make a better job at becoming visible as important players. It might also suggest that the breadth of networks is limited and that collaboration across a diversity of actors (at least in a visible sense that is considered significant) to date is limited. This would undermine claims of multi-stakeholder involvement or mark a potential for collaborative action that is simply untapped, so that the evidence and the theoretical argumentation that progress against the sustainable development goals rests on partnerships are not acted on. This may be a new distinctive area of action and legitimation for social economy actors that is important to flesh out as one of the implications and contributions of this explorative study.

The social economy can indeed generate economic, social, and environmental value through the work of social enterprises, co-operatives, and innovative non-profit organizations. However, this value is somewhat limited when actors within the social economy are not recognized as pivotal to making a difference in places. The example of Padua is quite evident: without the local foundation, many opportunities for creating value might be missed or not considered by other city leaders. In this sense, it is important to develop a civic leadership within and with social economy actors (Macmillan & McLaren, 2012) in order to promote and spur effective collaborative and interactive governance arenas among all types of city leaders, while softening the borders between sectors (e.g., Sørensen & Torfing, 2019).

Conclusion: What does this mean for the social economy and for future research on collaboration in civic leadership?

In this chapter, we explored who are recognized as the city leaders in two mid-sized cities located in Europe (Padua in Italy and Peterborough in the UK), from a starting point that considered leadership as an open and dispersed function that can be potentially activated by any citizen and/or organizational stakeholder. We started off from the recognition of the importance of collaboration, cross-sectoral partnerships, and collective agency which is place-based as indispensable to address 'the current and future wellbeing of people, places and the planet relies [and] to resolve the grand and interconnected challenges set out in the United Nations Sustainable Development Goals (SDGs)' (Boorman et al. 2023).

Our findings tested our framework about the city as an open platform for agency in four main governance arenas (political/democratic; managerial/public services; business; community/social domain) and revealed that this decentred vision of city leadership works in the eyes of the city leaders who participated in our study. However, it is important to point out that decentring leadership (Ayers et al., 2021) does not mean ignoring the power imbalances among actors and the cognitive bias about this understanding of leadership that still exist. Indeed, not unexpectedly, it was more difficult to identify city leaders in the social/community and in the business arenas. In the former, a relatively fragmented landscape emerged. In the latter, we noticed difficulty understanding the civic leadership role of businesses in both the cities.

Drawing from French (2021), we argue that civic leadership may rely on SDGs and place-based shared outcomes, and other symbolic signals, as organizing instruments where civic leadership becomes the function of purpose making, aligning and committing actors into broad coalitions towards ambitious goals that generate shared benefits for communities of people and for the environment (because of its place-based nature) (By, 2021). Differently from other forms of leadership that depart from hierarchical positions of authority, civic leadership is a form of leadership wherein the power to mobilize is potentially open to everybody and no central authority is necessarily needed—even if it might be needed at same points to scale up positive endeavours or to prevent the destruction of public, social, and/or shared value (Esposito et al., 2021). Thus, civic leadership may also be understood as the informal dynamics that bring together actors in coalitions, using place—in its symbolic and material features—both as a resource and as an outcome for civic leadership. However, it is important to note that at some points it might be desirable for civic leadership coalitions to be formally entrenched in collaborative governance institutional arrangements created ad hoc or embedded in existing institutions within the social economy or the public sector (Ansell & Torfing, 2021). What our results suggest, unfortunately, is that while there is some readiness to engage in civic leadership, there is still much work to do to build connections among civic leadership constellations and to make the social economy more visible.

We believe that opening up our cognitive understanding and cultural legitimation of civic leadership as a vocation, calling everybody to act in support of collective place-based goals, may contribute to favouring a conceptualization of the social economy as an agent for social change (and not just a market or state-failures fixer), which is one of the conceptualizations promoted in Part II of this book (see also Krlev et al., this volume). Actors in the social economy may indeed take the identification of city leaders as a strategic resource to improve the positioning of their unique strategic capability as being the glue of communities (Rees et al., 2022). They may also do so to develop a new strategic capability, namely to convene and to orchestrate in a creative way city leaders for the achievement of common place-based goals. The legitimacy of social economy actors toward this endeavour is generally high and well recognized by many stakeholders.

Social economy actors may also consider civic leadership as an engine for transformative social innovation in creating new type of ecosystems that are not only focused on economic, social, and environmental value creation, but that also might engage in power and democratic games that are required for transforming current institutions and for facilitating transitions of current economic and political models of modern governance towards a more civic economy (Chalmers, 2021). In this sense, further research may investigate at a macro level the specific mechanisms to be enacted by social economy actors to enhance the learning, replicability, and—if and where appropriate—scaling up of civic leadership ecosystems in different places, as well as the institutional arrangements and roles at the meso and micro levels to be played out by social economy actors to effectively activate, facilitate, and institutionalize civic partnerships addressing critical and timely challenges connected to sustainable development pathways.

Appendix 1: Main characteristics of the two investigated cities

Characteristics	Padua	Peterborough
Country	Italy	United Kingdom
Region	Veneto (North-East of Italy)	East of England, Cambridgeshire
Above-city government level	Province	Combined authority
Important nearby cities	Venice (30 km away) Milan (200 km away)	Cambridge (48 km away) London (120 km away)
Area	92.85 km^2	343 km^2
Population	211,316 inhabitants (end of 2019)	202,259 (estimated, 2019)
Density	2,275 inhabitants/km^2	589 inhabitants/km^2
Described as	Artistic and religious city	Heritage and fast-growing city with a very diverse community
Political governance model	Strong mayor, Cabinet and council	Council leader and Cabinet
Last election	June 2017	May 2016
Incumbent political leader	Sergio Giordani, mayor (left-leaning independent)	Cllr John Holdich OBE (Conservative)
Cabinet members	10 (incl. mayor and deputy mayor)	9

(Continued)

(Continued)

Characteristics	Padua	Peterborough
Councillors	32	60
Administrative tradition	Napoleonic/Southern Europe	Anglo-Saxon
Local government	Municipality	City council, unitary authority
Managerial/administrative head of local government	General manager (incumbent: Giovanni Zampieri)	CEO (incumbent: Gillian Beasley)
Other important PAs	CCIAA, local health units, university	Local police force, local health service
Important PCs/PSPs	AcegasApsAmga, APS Holding, Busitalia, DMO, Fondazione Irpea, Interporto, ZIP	Opportunity Peterborough, Vivacity
GDP (2018)	Veneto Region: 9% of Italian GDP Padua Province: 2% of Italian GDP and 20% of Veneto's one	East of England: 9% of UK GDP Peterborough: <1% of UK GDP and 4% of regional one
Active companies (2018)	20,730	6,840
Type of companies	Majority of micro-enterprises	Majority of micro-enterprises
Main sectors	Wholesale and retail trade; real estate; construction; accommodation and food sector	Business service activities; distribution, transport, accommodation and food; manufacturing
Most influential companies	Alì, Gottardo, Safilo, Acciaierie Venete	BGL Group, Coloplast, Perkins Engines
Unemployment rate (2019)	5.7% provincial average 5.6% regional average 10% national average	6.2% in Peterborough 3.3% regional average 3.8% national average
Civil society	European Volunteering Capital 2020	Community-focused
Organizations	2'135 association and social cooperatives (10 every 1,000 inhabitants)	347 general charities (1.8 every 1,000 inhabitants)
Main scope of intervention	Culture and environment, social and sport activities	Hard to delineate
Key organizations	CSV Padua Fondazione Cariparo	PCVS
Urban resilience policies	1. Resilient Padua. Guidelines for the creation of a plan for climate change adaptation (publication) 2. Plan and manage green areas as a means for urban resilience (conference title)	1. Responsibilities under the Civil Contingency Act 2004 2. 'Think Communities' project in collaboration with Cambridgeshire
Focus of urban resilience	Adaptation to climate change Infrastructure resilience	Community resilience

Source: Pagani, 2021

References

Acuto, M. (2016). Give cities a seat at the top table. *Nature News*, 537(7622), 611–613.

Agnew, J. (1987). *Place and Politics*. Boston: Allen and Unwin.

Andrews, R., & Entwistle, T. (2010). Does cross-sectoral partnership deliver? An empirical exploration of public service effectiveness, efficiency, and equity. *Journal of Public Administration Research and Theory*, 20(3), 679–701.

Ansell, C., & Torfing, J. (2021). *Public Governance as Co-creation: A Strategy for Revitalizing the Public Sector and Rejuvenating Democracy*. Cambridge: Cambridge University Press.

Ayres, S. (2014). Place-based leadership: reflections on scale, agency and theory. *Regional Studies, Regional Science*, 1(1), 21–24. https://doi.org/10.1080/21681376.2013.869424

Ayres, S., Bevir, M., & Orr, K. (2021). Editorial: a new research agenda for decentering public leadership. *International Journal of Public Leadership*, 17(3), 209–221.

Bastian, M., Heymann, S., & Jacomy, M. (2009). Gephi: an open source software for exploring and manipulating networks. *Proceedings of the International AAAI Conference on Web and Social Media*, 3(1), 361–362. https://doi.org/10.1609/icwsm.v3i1. 13937 Battilana, J., & Casciaro, T. (2021). *Power, for All: How It Really Works and Why It's Everyone's Business*. New York: Simon and Schuster.

Beer, A., Ayres, S., Clower, T., Faller, F., Sancino, A., & Sotarauta, M. (2019). Place leadership and regional economic development: a framework for cross-regional analysis. *Regional Studies*, 53(2), 171–182. https://doi.org/10.1080/00343404.2018.1447662

Bengo, I., Boni, L., & Sancino, A. (2022). EU financial regulations and social impact measurement practices: a comprehensive framework on finance for sustainable development. *Corporate Social Responsibility and Environmental Management*, 29(4): 809–819.

Bishop, P. (2012). Multi-Site Case Study. In A. J. Mills, G. Durepos, & E. Wiebe (Eds), *Encyclopedia of Case Study Research* (pp. 588–590). SAGE Publications Inc. http://methods.sagepub.com.libezproxy.open.ac.uk/Reference/encyc-of-casestudy-research/n219.xml

Birkmann, J., Welle, T., Solecki, W., Lwasa, S., & Garschagen, M. (2016). Boost resilience of small and mid-sized cities. *Nature*, 537(7622), 605–608. https://doi.org/10.1038/537605a

By, R. T. (2021). Leadership: in pursuit of purpose. *Journal of Change Management*, 21(1), 30–44.

Bonjean, C. M., & Olson, D. M. (1964). Community leadership: directions of research. *Administrative Science Quarterly*, 9(3), 278–300.

Boorman, C., Jackson, B., & Burkett, I. (2023). Harnessing place leadership theory and practice to grow equitable impact towards the SDGs. *Journal of Change Management*, 23 (1), 53-71.

Borgatti, S., Brass, D., & Labianca, G. (2009). Network analysis in the social sciences. *Science*, 323(5916), 892–895. https://doi.org/10.1126/science.1165821

Brandsen, T., Trommel, W., & Verschuere, B. (2017) The state and the reconstruction of civil society. *International Review of Administrative Sciences*, 83(4): 676–693, https://doi.org/10.1177/0020852315592467.

Bryman, A. (2011). Research methods in the study of leadership. In A. Bryman (Ed.), *The Sage handbook of leadership* (pp. 15–28). Los Angeles, Calif.: Sage.

Bryson, J. M., Crosby, B. C., & Stone, M. M. (2015). Designing and implementing cross-sector collaborations: Needed and challenging. *Public Administration Review*, 75(5), 647–663.

Bryson, J., Sancino, A., Benington, J., & Sørensen, E. (2017). Towards a multi-actor theory of public value co-creation. *Public Management Review*, 19(5), 640–654. https://doi.org/10.1080/14719037.2016.1192164

Budd, L., & Sancino, A. (2016). A framework for city leadership in multilevel governance settings: the comparative contexts of Italy and the UK. *Regional Studies, Regional Science*, 3(1), 129–145. https://doi.org/10.1080/21681376.2015.1125306

Budd, L., Sancino, A., Pagani, M., Kristmundsson, Ó., Roncevic, B., & Steiner, M. (2017). Sport as a complex adaptive system for place leadership: comparing five European cities with different administrative and socio-cultural traditions. *Local Economy*, 32(4), 316–335. https://doi.org/10.1177/0269094217709422

Cabral, S., Mahoney, J. T., McGahan, A. M., & Potoski, M. (2019). Value creation and value appropriation in public and nonprofit organizations. *Strategic Management Journal*, 40(4), 465–475.

Chalmers, D. (2021). Social entrepreneurship's solutionism problem. *Journal of Management Studies*, 58(5), 1363–1370.

Collinge, C., Gibney, J., & Mabey, C. (2010). Leadership and place. *Policy Studies*, 31(4), 367–378. https://doi.org/10.1080/01442871003723242

Craps, M., Vermeesch, I., Dewulf, A., Sips, K., Termeer, K., & Bouwen, R. (2019). A relational approach to leadership for multi-actor governance. *Administrative Sciences*, 9(1), 1–12. https://doi.org/10.3390/admsci9010012

Cresswell, T. (2014). *Place: An Introduction.* John Wiley & Sons.

Creswell, J. W., & Clark, V. L. P. (2017). *Designing and Conducting Mixed Methods Research.* Los Angeles, Calif.: Sage Publications.

Crosby, B. C., & Bryson, J. M. (2005). A leadership framework for cross-sector collaboration. *Public Management Review*, 7(2), 177–201. https://doi.org/10.1080/14719030500090519

Dahl, R. A. (2005). *Who Governs?* (2nd ed.). New Haven: Yale University Press.

Dijkstra, L., & Poelman, H. (2012). *Cities in Europe. The New OECD-EC Definition.* Available at: http://ec.europa.eu/regional_policy/sources/docgener/focus/2012_01_city.pdf

Epitropaki, O., Kark, R., Mainemelis, C., & Lord, R. G. (2017). Leadership and followership identity processes: a multilevel review. *The Leadership Quarterly*, 28(1), 104–129. https://doi.org/10.1016/j.leaqua.2016.10.003

Esposito, P., Ricci, P., & Sancino, A. (2021). Leading for social change: waste management in the place of social (ir) responsibility. *Corporate Social Responsibility and Environmental Management*, 28(2), 667–674.

Eurotowns (2019). *Eurotowns Position Paper on Medium-Sized Cities in Cohesion Policy*. https://www.eurotowns.org/wpcontent/uploads/2019/02/Eurotowns_Position_paper_on_Cohesion_Policy.pdf

French, M. (2021), Two experiments with outcomes frameworks. *Stanford Social Innovation Review*, Fall, 57–58.

Grandjean, M. (2015). Gephi Introduction. Retrieved from http://www.martingrandjean.ch/gephi-introduction/

Grint, K., & Holt, C. (2011). Leading questions: if 'Total Place', 'Big Society' and local leadership are the answers: What's the question? *Leadership*, 7(1), 85–98. https://doi.org/10.1177/1742715010393208

Hambleton, R. (2014). *Leading the Inclusive City: Place-based Innovation for a Bounded Planet*. Chicago: University of Chicago Press.

Hambleton, R. (2015). Place-based collaboration: leadership for a changing world. *Administration*, 63(3), 5–25. https://doi.org/10.1515/admin-2015-0018

Hambleton, R. (2019). The new civic leadership: place and the co-creation of public innovation. *Public Money & Management*, 39(4), 271–279.

't Hart, P. (2014). *Understanding Public Leadership*. London: Palgrave.

't Hart, P., & Tummers, L. (2019). *Understanding Public Leadership* (2nd ed.). London: Red Globe Press.

Hewson, C., Vogel, C., & Laurent, D. (2016). *Internet Research Methods*. Los Angeles, Calif.: SAGE Publications Ltd. https://doi.org/10.4135/9781473920804

Hollstein, B. (2014). Qualitative approaches. In J. Scott & P. J. Carrington (Eds), *The SAGE Handbook of Social Network Analysis* (pp. 404–416). London: SAGE Publications Ltd. https://doi.org/10.1016/j.apgeog.2014.12.021

Hunter, F. (1953). *Community Power Structure: A Study of Decision Makers*. Chapel Hill: The University of North Carolina Press.

Jackson, B. (2019). The power of place in public leadership research and development. *International Journal of Public Leadership*, 15(4), 209–223. https://doi.org/10.1108/IJPL-09-2019-0059

Johnson, R. B., & Onwuegbuzie, A. J. (2004). Mixed methods research: a research paradigm whose time has come. *Educational Researcher*, 33(7), 14–26.

Kellerman, B. (2012). Introduction: twenty-first-century leadership—and followership. In *The End of Leadership* (pp. 6–12). New York: Harper Collins.

Krlev, G., Pasi, G., Wruk, D., & Bernhard, M. (2021). Reconceptualizing the social economy. *Stanford Social Innovation Review*. https://ssir.org/articles/entry/reconceptualizing_the_social_economy

Krlev, G. (2022). Let's join forces: institutional resilience and multistakeholder partnerships in crises. *Journal of Business Ethics.* https://doi.org/10.1007/s10551-022-05231-w

Lazega, E., & Snijders, T. A. B. (Eds). (2015). *Multilevel Network Analysis for the Social Sciences. Theory, Methods and Applications.* Cham: Springer.

Macmillan, R. and McLaren, V. (2012). *Third Sector Leadership: The Power of Narrative,* Working Paper 76, Birmingham: University of Birmingham.

OECD. (2020). Urban population by city size (indicator). https://www.oecdilibrary. org/urban-rural-and-regional-development/urban-population-by-citysize/indicator/english_b4332f92-en

Ospina, S. M. (2017). Collective leadership and context in public administration: bridging public leadership research and leadership studies. *Public Administration Review,* 77(2), 275–287. https://doi.org/10.1111/puar.12706.Collective

Pagani, M. (2021). *City Leaders, Relationships and Urban Resilience: A Mixed Methods Exploratory Study of the City Leadership Network of Padua (Italy) and Peterborough (UK).* PhD thesis, The Open University.

Pagani, M., Sancino, A., & Budd, L. (2021) Essential, complex and multi-form: the local leadership of civil society from an Anglo-Italian perspective. *Voluntary Sector Review,* 12 (1), 41–58. https://doi.org/10.1332/204080520X15902277850841

Rapoport, E., Acuto, M., & Grcheva, L. (2019). *Leading Cities: A Global Review of City Leadership.* London: UCL Press.

Rees, J., Sancino, A., Jacklin-Jarvis, C., & Pagani, M. (2022). 'You can't Google everything': the voluntary sector and the leadership of communities of place. *Leadership,* 18(1), 102–119.

Roberts, B. H., Iglesias, B. M., & Llop, J. M. (2016). Intermediary cities: the bexus between the local and the global. In Edgardo Bilsky, Andrea Ciambra, Mathieu Guerin, & Lodvic Terren (Eds), *Co-Creating the Urban Future: The Agenda of Metropolis, Cities and Territories* (pp. 133–220). Barcelona: United Cities and Local Governments.

Ropo, A., Sauer, E., & Salovaara, P. (2013). Embodiment of leadership through material place. *Leadership,* 9(3), 378–395.

Rosen, G. (1954). Community power structure. A study of 'Decision Makers' by Floyd Hunter. *American Journal of Public Health,* July, 950.

Sancino, A. (2016). The meta co-production of community outcomes: towards a citizens' capabilities approach. *Voluntas: International Journal of Voluntary and Nonprofit Organizations,* 27(1), 409–424.

Sancino, A., Garavaglia, C., Sicilia, M., & Braga, A. (2021). New development: Covid-19 and its publics—implications for strategic management and democracy. *Public Money & Management,* 41(5), 404–407.

Scott, J., & Carrington, P. J. (Eds). (2014). *The SAGE Handbook of Social Network Analysis.* London: SAGE Publications Ltd.

Serrano López, A. L., Freire Chaglla, S. A., Espinoza-Figueroa, F. E., Andrade Tenesaca, D. S., & Villafuerte Pucha, M. E. (2019). Modeling of tourist profiles with decision trees in a world heritage city: the case of Cuenca (Ecuador). *Tourism Planning & Development,* 16(5), 473–493.

Smith, L. (1954). Reviewed work(s): community power structure: a study of 'Decision Makers' by Floyd Hunter. *The Journal of Politics,* 16(1), 146–150.

Sotarauta, M. (2016). Place leadership, governance and power. *Administration,* 64(3/4), 45–58. https://doi.org/10.1515/admin-2016-0024

Sotarauta, M., & Beer, A. (2017). Governance, agency and place leadership: lessons from a cross-national analysis. *Regional Studies,* 51(2), 210–223. https://doi.org/10.1080/00343404.2015.1119265

Sørensen, E., & Torfing, J. (2019). Designing institutional platforms and arenas for interactive political leadership. *Public Management Review,* 21(10), 1443–1463.

Stentz, J. E., Clark, V. L. P., & Matkin, G. S. (2012). Applying mixed methods to leadership research: a review of current practices. *The Leadership Quarterly,* 23(6), 1173–1183.

Uhl-bien, M., Riggio, R. E., Lowe, K. B., & Carsten, M. K. (2014). Followership theory: a review and research agenda. *The Leadership Quarterly,* 25(1), 83–104. https://doi.org/10.1016/j.leaqua.2013.11.007

Withall, M., Phillips, I., & Parish, D. (2007). Network visualisation: a review. *IET Communications,* 1(3), 365–372. https://doi.org/10.1049/iet-com

Yager, J. W. (1963). Who runs our town? *National Civic Review,* 52(5), 255–259.

Yin, R. K. (2009). *Case Study Research: Design and Methods* (4th ed.). Thousand Oaks, CA: Sage.

15

Public structural funds as a catalyst for social innovation

The experience of Portugal Social Innovation

António Miguel

Introduction: Mobilizing EU Funds for public policy experimentation in social innovation

The weight of structural public funds in leveraging the sustainability transition is huge. The European Commission channelled around EUR 450 billion across European Union (EU) Member States through its various funding streams in the period 2014–2020. These are particularly important when market environments are challenging and when partnership approaches and principles are the answer to leverage effective social problem solving.

European Structural and Investment Funds (ESIF) include five major funds that are used to promote policy areas at a European level. The five funds that encompass ESIF are (i) the European Regional Development Fund, (ii) the European Social Fund, (iii) the Cohesion Fund, (iv) the European Agricultural Fund for Rural Development, and (v) the European Maritime and Fisheries Fund. These funds are managed by the EU Member States, by means of partnership agreements.

The EU Funds are levers for the growth of social innovation on the continent. With a policy focus on job creation and sustainable and healthy growth, social innovation is a fundamental pillar of European policy because it is defined as new ideas that meet social needs, create social relationships, and form new collaborations.[1] These innovations can be goods, services, or models addressing unmet needs more effectively.

In 2014, Portugal pioneered the use of EU Structural and Investment Funds (Krlev et al., 2022), with a focus on the European Social Fund (ESF), to foster the social investment and social innovation ecosystem in the country. This resulted in the creation of Portugal Social Innovation,[2] a catalyst institution funded by EUR 150 million from EU Funds.

[1] Social innovation definition by the European Commission available at https://single-market-economy.ec.europa.eu/industry/strategy/innovation/social_en

[2] Please visit Portugal Social Innovation website at https://inovacaosocial.portugal2020.pt

António Miguel, *Public structural funds as a catalyst for social innovation*. In: *Social Economy Science*. Edited by: Gorgi Krlev, Dominika Wruk, Giulio Pasi, and Marika Bernhard, Oxford University Press. © Oxford University Press (2023).
DOI: 10.1093/oso/9780192868343.003.0015

The key principles underlying the creation of Portugal Social Innovation are the promotion of social innovation among public services, the growth of social innovation initiatives in the country, and the contribution towards a social investment ecosystem where public, private, and social organizations work together towards addressing social challenges (Barth et al., 2018). Portugal Social Innovation has created four specific social finance instruments that implement policy initiatives across thematic areas such as education, social protection, health, justice, and training and employment, aligned with EU-based policy objectives.

Given its novelty and experimental nature, Portugal Social Innovation has yielded several learnings in the years since its inception. Various satellite initiatives took place alongside Portugal Social Innovation that provide context on the ecosystem growing in the country. In summary, a single initiative on its own would have not created the rich ecosystem that emerged without other relevant initiatives that were taking place simultaneously (EVPA, 2017).

Important learnings include the fact that Portugal Social Innovation did not sit under a specific thematic ministry but rather was under the umbrella of a broad ministry, which promoted collaboration and interconnectedness across thematic areas. An important learning also entails the need for alignment with public policy priorities, to have social innovation financing instruments as policy instruments rather than something with no additionality for public sector leaders.

Positive spillover effects have resulted from having a market champion like Portugal Social Innovation. In this regard it is also important to mention another crucial market champion, the Calouste Gulbenkian Foundation, which has been working on creating an impact investment ecosystem in Portugal, seeking to test and validate the use of new financing instruments for the third sector and support the development of new business models that combine financial return and social impact.[3]

The Calouste Gulbenkian Foundation is an equidistant independent Foundation which operates independently but at arm's length from the main players in the social innovation ecosystem in implementing innovative initiatives such as the One.Value platform. It funded the launch of the first five Social Impact Bonds in the country and became the main private investor in Portugal, supporting the mobilization of other investors.

Learnings made from the experience of Portugal Social Innovation have also highlighted challenges such as bureaucracy, processes, tax incentives, mobilization of capital, capacity-building, and data collection. These are all excellent precedents to inform future replications of a similar initiative in other countries, which can be used to fast-track implementation based on the Portuguese experience.

Recommendations for future replication include making the funding instruments and the process behind them as innovative as the projects they fund, to continuously foster efficiency in public services. On the governance dimension, the responsibilities shared between managing authorities at a national level and intermediary

---

[3] To learn more about the Calouste Gulbenkian Foundation work in social innovation please visit https://gulbenkian.pt/en/initiatives/sustainable-development-programme/new-financing-instruments/

organizations must also ensure that the delegation of powers is allocated efficiently among partners. The positioning of European Structural and Investment Funds must be in accordance with the main bottleneck faced by national ecosystems: as outcome payers, rather than solely as direct investors. Once there are outcome payers, investors and projects will emerge. It is also paramount to create clear pathways between experimentation and internalization, through which public sector entities codify how they test new interventions, learn from evidence, and are equipped and incentivized to internalize proven interventions as a route to scale effective projects and inform public policy at large. In essence, that is the goal of social innovation—once tested and proven, being able to scale and reach as many of those that can benefit from it.

The Portuguese experience with Portugal Social Innovation should be interpreted as a collection of learnings whose sole objective is to help inform a discussion about the use of European Structural and Investment Funds to promote social innovation in Europe. The impact that EU Funds can have on social innovation are immense and represent a strategic advantage that Europe has in comparison to other regions of the globe.

European Structural and Investment Funds adoption for social innovation in Portugal

The European Commission (EC) and European Union (EU) Member States jointly manage ESIF, whose main objectives are to invest in job creation and a sustainable and healthy European economy and environment. The ESIF focus on research and innovation, digital technologies, supporting the low-carbon economy, sustainable management of natural resources, and small businesses.[4]

All ESIF focus areas are intrinsically related to social innovation. The EC defines social innovation as 'new ideas that meet social needs, create social relationships, and form new collaborations. These innovations can be goods, services or models addressing unmet needs more effectively.'[5] There is a strong link between social innovation and job creation. As such, social innovation is present across the five areas of focus that ESIF targets.

Portugal 2020 was the partnership agreement between Portugal and the European Commission for the period between 2014 and 2020. Under this partnership agreement, Portugal received circa EUR 25 billion. The overarching objectives are aligned with EU policy, focused on job creation and sustainable growth. Of the EUR 25 billion, around EUR 2.2 billion was allocated to the thematic programme 'Social Inclusion and Employment'.[6] Most of the funds for the thematic programme 'Social

---

[4] Source: https://ec.europa.eu/info/funding-tenders/funding-opportunities/funding-programmes/overview-funding-programmes/european-structural-and-investment-funds_en
[5] Source: https://ec.europa.eu/growth/industry/policy/innovation/social_en
[6] Source: https://www.portugal2020.pt/

Inclusion and Employment' have their origins in the European Social Fund—one of the five ESIF.[7]

In 2014, Portugal pioneered the use of the ESF towards social innovation and mobilized circa EUR 150 million for the creation of a Mission Unit named Portugal Social Innovation. This amount was part of the EUR 2.2 billion allocated for 'Social Inclusion and Employment'. Portugal Social Innovation is one of the most structured approaches to creating an institution focused on social innovation in Europe (Krlev et al., 2022).

A Mission Unit is an entity that is created for a specific purpose[8]—in this case, to promote social innovation in the country—and while it is funded by public funds (ESF), it has a dedicated management team composed of experts in the specific topic it aims at addressing. Mission Units are created for a pre-defined period with the aim of specializing the financial and non-financial support towards a specific outcome. For context, other Mission Units have been created in Portugal to address topics such as (i) innovation and knowledge, (ii) valorization of inland rural areas, and (iii) fighting wildfires, among many others.

The Portuguese experience with ESIF adoption to social innovation: Portugal Social Innovation

Portugal Social Innovation is a government initiative aimed at promoting social innovation and stimulating the social investment market in Portugal. It mobilized EUR 150 million from the ESF, deployed across four financing instruments.[9] The institutional design of these four instruments is in accordance with the lifecycle of a social enterprise, from inception to growth and scale-up (Quaternaire, 2015).

Launched in December 2014, Portugal Social Innovation is the first initiative of its kind; it uses ESIF and serves as a blueprint for other EU Member States that wish to promote social innovation through a dedicated entity. To better understand Portugal Social Innovation, it is fundamental to be aware of its three-fold objectives:

1. Promote social innovation and social entrepreneurship in Portugal to create new solutions to social problems, which complement traditional responses and solve important social problems.
2. Stimulate the social investment market by creating financing instruments better suited to the specific needs of the social economy sector and those of innovative and social entrepreneurship projects.
3. Empower players in the social innovation and social entrepreneurship ecosystem in Portugal, improving the response levels of social sector organizations and contributing to the economic and financial sustainability thereof.

---

[7] Source: https://www.portugal2020.pt/content/o-que-e-o-portugal-2020
[8] Source: https://dre.pt/web/guest/legislacao-consolidada/-/lc/105825610/202008121355/73383065/diploma/indice
[9] Source: https://inovacaosocial.portugal2020.pt/en/

This three-fold approach demonstrates that Portugal Social Innovation is acting as a market champion not only by enabling social innovation projects to be funded (through transactions) but also by financing market-building activities and building awareness around social innovation. The elements of awareness and capacity-building are relevant from a long-term perspective of the ecosystem in Portugal.

The four financing instruments deployed by Portugal Social Innovation are the following: (i) capacity-building for social investment, (ii) partnerships for impact, (iii) Social Impact Bonds, and (iv) Social Innovation Fund. The rationale for these financing instruments deployed by Portugal Social Innovation is based on the following tenets:

- *Stage focus.* Each financing instrument is based on a specific stage of the lifecycle of a social enterprise.
- *Mobilizer.* All projects need to have at least one public or private co-investor. The financing instruments work as mobilizers of funding from other investors.
- *Policy alignment.* Funded projects are aligned with public policy priorities, as mapped by Portugal Social Innovation.
- *Outcome-oriented.* The focus of financing is on the achievement of outcomes.
- *De-risker.* Portugal Social Innovation is taking more risk than other co-investors, hence improving the risk–return profile of social innovation projects.

Portugal Social Innovation was designed on the basis of an ex ante evaluation which identified the funding gap for social innovation in the country to be within the range of EUR 150 million–EUR 587 million (Quaternaire, 2015). The four financing instruments were designed as levers to mitigate that funding gap, by mobilizing additional capital from both public and private investors.[10]

The ecosystem of initiatives that emerged alongside Portugal Social Innovation to support policy making

Portugal Social Innovation was launched in 2014, started deploying its first funds in 2016, and entered full operation in 2017, by which time it was operating most of its financing instruments. Portugal Social Innovation mobilized European Union Structural and Investment Funds. Around the same period, the EC, through the EaSI Programme, funded the creation of the Portuguese Social Investment Taskforce. This taskforce mobilized more than thirty stakeholders from the public, private, social, and academic sectors to jointly reflect and create a national strategy for social investment (EVPA, 2017).

Published in 2015, the Portuguese strategy for social investment presented five key recommendations, each targeting a specific group of stakeholders. For

---

[10] Source: https://www.compete2020.gov.pt/admin/images/Realatorio_Final_Avaliacao_Instr_Financ_Lote_2.pdf

each recommendation, there was a concrete action plan, with a timeline and an owner. The five recommendations were: (1) strengthen social organizations through capacity-building programmes; (2) introduce financial instruments suited to social organizations and social innovation; (3) promote an outcomes-based culture in public services; (4) set up a knowledge and resource centre for social innovation; and (5) promote specialist intermediaries to facilitate access to capital[11] (Grupo de Trabalho Português para o Investimento de Impacto, 2015).

These recommendations were fully aligned with the work of Portugal Social Innovation and have helped inform the four financing instruments that were adopted to address the specific needs of social enterprises in Portugal, across different stages. This was inspired by the work of the Young Foundation, through which it was defined that the stages of innovation spread outwards from prompts and ideas to scale and growth (Murray et al, 2010).

In 2018, the Portuguese Social Investment Taskforce launched a progress report[12] which monitored the implementation of the recommendations. The main conclusions of this progress report were the following:

- Confirmation that Portugal Social Innovation has played a crucial role in boosting the Portuguese ecosystem since 2014 by inviting all players to benefit from its instruments.
- The importance of developing initiatives that attract more private capital into the sector.
- The need to involve the public sector, both at central and local level, to ensure that outcome-based commissioning can be widely adopted.

In October 2021, Portugal joined a consortium with other countries to create a National Centre of Competences for Social Innovation, as part of the ESF+ Network of Competence Centres for Social Innovation initiative known as Facilitating United Approaches to Social Innovation in Europe (FUSE). In Portugal, this initiative is co-led by three of the most relevant entities related to social investment and social innovation: Portugal Social Innovation, the Calouste Gulbenkian Foundation, and Agência para o Desenvolvimento e Coesão (which is responsible for managing EU Structural and Investment Funds in Portugal).

Within the scope of the National Centre of Competence for Social Innovation, an Advisory Board has been created with the responsibility of revising the national strategy for social investment and updating its recommendations for the period 2022–2030. It includes representatives from across all segments of the ecosystem: public sector entities, social organizations, investors, market champions, civil society organizations, academic institutions, and others.

---

[11] Please see Portuguese Social Investment Taskforce, 2015 report http://taskforce.maze-impact.com/wp-content/uploads/2015/08/EN_Final-report.pdf
[12] Please see Portuguese Social Investment Taskforce, 2018 progress report http://taskforce.maze-impact.com/wp-content/uploads/2018/09/Progress_report_EN_WEB_092018.pdf

As a result, this Advisory Board is assessing the learnings to date from the implementation of Portugal Social Innovation, identifying the key needs of the Portuguese ecosystem, and proposing updated recommendations and action plans to continue growing the social investment market in the coming years.

Financing instruments adopted by Portugal Social Innovation to increase access to finance and promote policy making

The four financing instruments adopted by Portugal Social Innovation are described below.

Capacity-building for social investment

This financing instrument aims at supporting the development of the organizational and management skills of teams from social enterprises that are involved in implementing social innovation initiatives. To address the specific capacity-building needs of social enterprises, a fixed non-repayable amount of up to EUR 50,000 is allocated to fund a capacity-building initiative proposed by the social enterprise.

A capacity-building initiative can include an assessment of needs, which should be carried out before an application is submitted by an independent entity. Initiatives are expected to last for around eighteen months and should include up to five different interventions in the following areas: value creation model, impact study, strategy, partnerships and growth, marketing, communication and fundraising, organization, governance, leadership, and human resources, financial, control and risk management, operations, and IT management.

The funding from Portugal Social Innovation under this instrument may be used to engage with training consultancy services, mentoring, or certified training initiatives.

Partnerships for impact

This instrument aims at financing the creation, implementation, or expansion of social innovation products, through co-financing with social investors, thus encouraging impact philanthropy and contributing to a more stable, efficient, and sustainable financing model. It finances growth initiatives by social innovation projects, starting at EUR 50,000, through a non-repayable grant and up to 70 per cent of its net financing needs. The remaining 30 per cent must be insured by one or more private or public investors.

This financing instrument demands that applications need to be made for a longer-term period, typically three years. Its objective is to multiply the amount of funding provided by philanthropy in the country, by promoting more long-term projects, a focus on capacity-building and incentives for growth of initiatives that have a proven intervention model.

Social Impact Bonds

This instrument aims at financing, against an outcome-based contract, innovative projects committed to achieving social outcomes and efficiency gains in priority public policy areas, such as social protection, employment, healthcare, justice, and education.

Under this programme, Portugal Social Innovation makes available outcomes funding to local and regional authorities in Portugal that are interested in developing Social Impact Bonds. This facility was designed to improve the financial viability of early Social Impact Bonds and incentivize local government commissioners to move towards paying for outcomes. The objective of this programme is to develop innovative solutions that tackle social issues in areas of public policy. By acting as an outcome payer, rather than as an investor, Portugal Social Innovation is removing the bottleneck in Social Impact Bond development: convincing public sector commissioners who are traditionally output-focused to shift their commissioning towards outcomes.

Applications to this instrument are submitted in partnership with the organizations involved: social enterprises (those that are running the project), investors (those who are financing the project), and public authorities (that confirm whether the project is aligned with public policy and the relevance of the expected outcomes).

Social Innovation Fund

The Social Innovation Fund (SIF) is a social investment fund aimed at supporting social enterprises in the consolidation or expansion stage that are seeking significant investment and have the financial sustainability to repay such investments. It encompasses two separate financial instruments.

Debt—With a wholesaler approach, this instrument provides guarantees and counter-guarantees among other favourable conditions to credit institutions allowing them to fund social enterprises at below the market conditions. The terms associated with these loans, namely grace period, loan maturities, interest rates, and putting up collateral, are better than those usually offered by the market, and are more suited to their actual needs.

Equity—This instrument only co-invests with private investors, and it leverages equity and quasi-equity investment, granting co-investors a call option during the first six years of investment.

These four financing instruments were designed to support social enterprises throughout their lifecycle, as visualized in Figure 15.1.

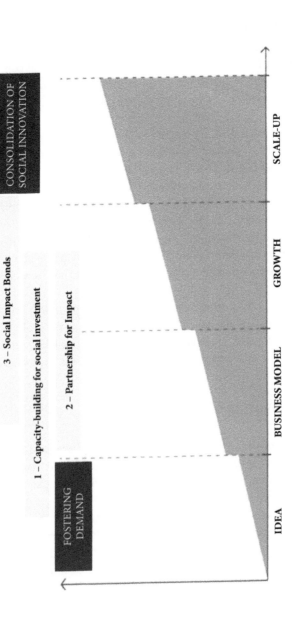

Figure 15.1 The lifecycle of a social enterprise

As of June 2022, Portugal Social Innovation has approved 693 projects, which represent €99 million from European Union funds and €49 million from social investors—private and public. In total, 477 organizations have benefited from funding by Portugal Social Innovation, more than 1.4 million people have been impacted (in a country of ten million), and 841 social investors have funded projects alongside Portugal Social Innovation.

When looking at these figures by instrument, it can be seen that the capacity-building instrument has mobilized EUR 7.4 million for more than 200 organizations, contributing to their skills development and strengthening their ability to deliver impact and raise social investment. Partnerships for Impact, an important match-funding instrument for venture philanthropy, mobilized €101 million in total, of which €79 million came from EU Funds and €32 million from public and private social investors. This instrument reached more than 450 organizations.

Portugal is among the countries in Europe with the most Social Impact Bonds to date—at twenty-two—and has mobilized EUR 11.7 million to pay for outcomes across several social areas. The SIF has supported twelve organizations and mobilized EUR 14.5 million in total, of which EUR 9 million was from EU Funds and €5.5 million from social investors.

In addition, Portugal Social Innovation has reached across the country, having created a network of social incubators and accelerators, partnering with more than thirty organizations in this regard. These organizations include existing incubators from across the country that have embraced social innovation as a new way of promoting their services, as well as new incubators and programmes that have been created from scratch. Impact incubators and accelerators are an emerging trend across Europe (Gianoncelli et al., 2020). In terms of thematic areas supported, projects funded by Portugal Social Innovation range from social inclusion (37 per cent of projects funded) to health (19 per cent), education (15 per cent), and employment (11 per cent). Other thematic areas include justice, digital inclusion, and citizen participation.

Demand has overtaken supply by 1.9x, meaning that for every euro made available in Portugal Social Innovation calls for proposals, EUR 1.9 was sought by social organizations. Finally, it is worth mentioning that the north and centre of Portugal have mobilized more resources from Portugal Social Innovation, at 40 per cent and 35 per cent respectively. In total, these two regions have mobilized one third of the funding available.

Policy learnings based on the first six years of implementation

The pioneering implementation of Portugal Social Innovation since December 2014 has yielded learnings that should inform other EU Member States who want to replicate such an initiative.

Learning No. 1: The positive spillover effect

The creation of Portugal Social Innovation has resulted in several satellite initiatives over the years which have contributed to the overall social innovation ecosystem in Portugal.

For instance, in 2016 a partnership between the Calouste Gulbenkian Foundation, the Portuguese government, Portugal Social Innovation, and MAZE saw the launch of One.Value, a platform that contains over ninety indicators which indicate the unit cost of social issues in the country that were calculated based on public spending[13]. A platform like One.Value allows social enterprises, policy makers, and investors to better value the social outcomes that their projects achieve, hence contributing to a wider conversation about outcome-based commissioning and outcome-based financing (Government Outcomes Lab, 2021).

One.Value is a free and user-friendly knowledge centre that aggregates information about public investment in several social issue areas that are a priority in Portugal. These issue areas include social protection, education, health, employment, and justice. Public investment refers to investment by the Portuguese government. Data made available by One.Value allows a better understanding of the allocation of public investment across social issues in Portugal, as well as fostering the development of innovative interventions that address social issues and incentivize outcome-based commissioning mechanisms.

Portugal has also seen the creation of tax relief for investment in Social Impact Bonds. This tax relief allows private investors to claim a 140 per cent upfront reduction on taxable profit, which is aligned with the tax relief for grants and donations in the country. The aim was to mobilize more private capital towards Social Impact Bonds.

In 2018 another initiative was launched, to promote capacity-building among public sector teams on the theme of outcome-based commissioning. The Outcomes Academy was a joint project between the Calouste Gulbenkian Foundation, Portugal Social Innovation, and MAZE—an impact investment firm—with the aim of fostering the wider adoption of an outcomes-oriented culture within the public sector.

These initiatives were linked to Portugal Social Innovation but are independent from it, demonstrating the positive spillover effect that the creation of a market champion can have in a national ecosystem.

Learning No. 2: The importance of cross-cutting themes

Social innovation was always perceived, from a public policy perspective, as a theme that cuts across various thematic areas—justice, education, social protection, health,

---

[13] Please see more at www.onevalue.gov.pt

among many others (Barth et al., 2018). As a result, the ministerial oversight of Portugal Social Innovation was allocated to an umbrella ministry—the Ministry of Presidency. This has allowed Portugal Social Innovation to launch calls for proposals and to fund social innovation projects across various thematic areas. In addition, it has allowed these projects to address multiple thematic areas in the same project, hence fostering a strong interconnectedness between policy areas.

Learning No. 3: Alignment with public priorities is crucial

Portugal Social Innovation has always aligned with the different ministries and public institutions from across all thematic areas to identify their public policy priorities. This mapping exercise, which preceded any call for proposals, helped ensure that the thematic outcomes that were expected to be achieved by social enterprises were fully aligned with the policy priorities identified by the public sector entity with responsibility for that thematic area (European Commission, 2019). The policy areas, reflected in concrete outcomes, were included in all calls for proposals and made clear to projects applying for funding. For all players in the ecosystem, such data allowed a better understanding of public sector organizations' focuses in terms of resources.

   This close coordination between Portugal Social Innovation and the public entities responsible for public policy across thematic areas is also a corroboration of the importance of having Portugal Social Innovation under the umbrella of a cross-cutting ministry. This has allowed better diagnostics and fostering of projects towards specific areas that are more relevant across public entities.

Challenges identified in the Portuguese social investment ecosystem in the period 2014–2022

The overall dynamics of the Portuguese Social Investment ecosystem, which entailed the cornerstone and anchoring work of Portugal Social Innovation alongside other initiatives such as the Portuguese Social Investment Taskforce, One.Value, and many others, have led to several learnings—already highlighted—but also to various challenges whose identification is important to enable others to fast-track responses.

Challenge 1: heavy bureaucracy linked to the adoption of Portugal Social Innovation financing instruments

Even though Portugal Social Innovation is funding innovative interventions, its funding mechanisms are still based on costs effectively incurred, which creates a set of challenges for the organizations that benefit from this funding. The heavy bureaucratic burden associated with reimbursement processes crowds out projects, which do not apply because they fear they will be unable to meet financial and administrative requirements. Those that do apply and are funded face severe reporting demands; often must absorb expenses which are not deemed eligible for assistance; and experience severe delays in reimbursement, which affects their working capital flows.

One way to mitigate this challenge is through the adoption of other mechanisms that are made available by European Union Structural and Investment Funds, such as simplified cost options and financing not linked to costs. These mechanisms are suitable for all instruments that are outcome-based, such as Social Impact Bonds.

Simplified cost options is a way of reimbursing grants and repayable assistance in which, instead of reimbursing 'real costs', reimbursement occurs according to predefined methods based on inputs, outputs, or results. By its turn, financing not linked to costs is a payment method for grants and repayable assistance in which the reimbursement of expenditure is based on the fulfilment of preestablished conditions or results to be achieved.

Challenge 2: highly geographical concentration of projects funded by Portugal Social Innovation

As stated above, around EUR 1 of every EUR 3 funded by Portugal Social Innovation goes to the regions of the north and centre of Portugal, with smaller amounts going to Algarve, Alentejo, and Lisbon. Therefore, there is a significant geographical concentration of social innovation projects within a small country. This gap is also influenced by the challenges in mobilizing private and public capital in certain regions.

A possible solution for this challenge is the promotion of local and regional partnerships that are leveraged on an online platform where organizations (investees) and investors can be matched according to preference, thematic area, and stage. This should be developed in close partnership with local authorities and municipalities, which play a crucial role in identifying the needs of local communities and projects on the ground.

Challenge 3: low representativeness of social innovation projects among the social economy in Portugal

While 477 organizations have been supported by Portugal Social Innovation since 2014, this is still a relatively small number given the more than 70,000 social economy organizations in the country. Social innovation projects represent less than 1 per cent of the overall social economy, which corroborates the view that there is still a sizeable opportunity to increase the penetration of social innovation in Portugal.

As such, it is fundamental to promote the creation of more social innovation activities, by creating more links with academic institutions—especially universities and higher education institutions—as well as by promoting scholarships for public sector entities to mobilize their employees for training on social innovation with the aim of launching further initiatives within their departments.

Challenge 4: most social organizations in Portugal have capacity-building needs

There is a clear link between the ability of social enterprises to raise finance and their level of skill and competence. In Portugal, a high number of social enterprises have capacity-building needs, as shown by the number of organizations (more than 200) that benefited from the Capacity Building for Social Investment financing instrument promoted by Portugal Social Innovation.

According to mapping done by the University of Aveiro in 2022, most capacity-building needs are in the areas of marketing, communication, fundraising, strategy, and impact management and measurement.

Challenge 5: lack of private capital mobilized for social investment in Portugal

Despite the growth seen in the years since 2014, the social investment ecosystem in Portugal remains reliant on EU Funds, with a significant lower proportion of private capital being mobilized. One of the reasons for this is that the existence of tax incentives for donations and philanthropy in Portugal is competing with social investment—given that there are not tax incentives for the latter, whereby the instrument is a repayable form of finance (except for Social Impact Bonds).

Since Portugal Social Innovation is the entity that certifies projects to be considered Social Innovation and Social Entrepreneurship Initiatives (SISEI), an interesting measure to overcome this challenge would be to extend the tax incentives that are available for Social Economy Organizations to Social Innovation and Social Entrepreneurship Initiatives, with the aim of mobilizing funds for both. These tax incentives, if replicated, can represent up to 140 per cent of the amount invested as being eligible to be deducted upfront on the taxable income of investors in the year that they invested.

Challenge 6: there is no legal framework for social enterprises in Portugal

Even though the social investment market in Portugal has adopted innovative social finance instruments, such evolution has not been accompanied by innovation in legal frameworks. Social organizations remain part of the social economy and are not prone to engage in revenue-generation activities, while private companies solely serve the purpose of profit maximization, with no incentives to focus on wider value creation and social impact.

The lack of a legal framework for social enterprises in Portugal is contributing to the creation of complex legal arrangements whereby social economy organizations are creating private companies fully owned by them (non-profit), hence creating a net of subsidiaries, and increasing transaction costs. This challenge would be mitigated, if not solved, by the creation of a legal framework for social enterprises, as has been adopted in other European countries and the United Kingdom. A denominator that could serve as inspiration for the adoption of a social enterprise framework for Portugal is the one adopted by the EC and its three criteria for a social enterprise:

- Those for whom the social or societal objective of the common good is the reason for the commercial activity, often in the form of a high level of social innovation.
- Those whose profits are mainly reinvested to achieve this social objective.
- Those where the method of organization or the ownership system reflects the enterprise's mission, using democratic or participatory principles or focusing on social justice.

Challenge 7: lack of capacity-building programmes for public sector entities on outcome-based commissioning

If outcome-based commissioning is to be widely adopted within public sector entities at a local and central level, it is fundamental to promote capacity-building initiatives—which double down on the work done by the Outcomes Academy since 2018 in Portugal—to ensure that public sector teams are equipped with the content, tools, and frameworks to implement projects effectively.

Portugal has been leading on the structuring and launching of Social Impact Bonds but has done so in a way that is detached from public sector entities, who are only lightly involved in projects and have no skin in the game when it comes to financial resources. As a result of effective capacity-building, it is expected that public sector entities will become more engaged in the process of defining outcomes, setting targets, and undertaking assessment and monitoring of their implementation for further informing of public policy.

Challenge 8: Lack of a formal pathway that helps innovative social projects to navigate their way from experimentation to wider public provision

The main challenge faced by social innovation projects in Portugal, due to an enormous wave of experimentation promoted by Portugal Social Innovation, is the transition from experimentation into scale and wider provision. Once innovation and experimental projects are proven to work, the fundamental question to address is how they are going to scale and be internalized as public provision, through public policy mechanisms, with the aim of achieving their full potential and reaching as many people as needed.

This topic remains unworked and is one of the main targets that will require more resources and attention for the period until 2030, as Portugal embarks on a new stage of development of its social innovation ecosystem whereby it needs to work on a bipedal velocity—one where it continues to foster innovation and experimentation, and another where it doubles down and scales existing projects that have been proven to work.

Scaling demands different skills when compared to experimenting. Different skills demand capacity-building and sustainability of social innovation projects demands a clear pathway that encompasses ownership within the public sector for the scaling of proven interventions.

Recommendations for future ESIF deployment in social innovation

Every six years, the EC, through the European Structural and Investment Funds, has a golden opportunity to positively influence and stir policy initiatives at Member State level. For most EU countries the multi-annual financing framework, through partnership agreements, represents a sizeable amount of funding, which can make a dent in some thematic areas of relevance for the EU.

Both Member States and the EC have incentives to use ESIF to test and experiment in areas that are common denominators for any leadership. Social innovation is one of them as it is present across all areas of focus for ESIF; namely, job creation and a sustainable growth path for Europe.

As explored in this chapter, Portugal pioneered the use of EU Structural Funds for social innovation by creating the initiative Portugal Social Innovation. This took place in December 2014 and nearly a decade on, several learnings should inform future adoption of ESIF for social innovation. This section is focused on a set of recommendations for the future adoption of ESIF in social innovation, based on the Portuguese experience, with the aim of promoting long-lasting policies.

Recommendation No. 1: Innovation needs to start in the funding process itself, not only on the projects funded

There is no doubt that the first years of implementation have allowed more and better social investment to be deployed into innovative social enterprises in Portugal. The challenge has been that such innovative approach was not adopted to the way that projects are funded.

The clearest example of this challenge could be seen in the Social Impact Bond instrument, through which the ESF plays the role of outcome payer. Typically, an

Impact Bond defines the outcomes that should be achieved, and upon the accomplishment of such outcomes investors are paid based on a pre-defined value for those outcomes.

In the case of Portugal Social Innovation, the Impact Bonds funded through its mechanism are paid if, and only if, outcomes are achieved but there is no value assigned to those outcomes—the payment is based on incurred expenses, just like any other EU-funded project. The fact that outcome payments are in fact reimbursement of expenses creates several obstacles to the growth of an outcomes-based ecosystem:

(i) There is no incentive to complexify the project because the financial incentives are on the activities, not on the outcomes. Hence, investors prefer to fund other types of projects that are not dependent on outcomes.

(ii) Service providers and intermediaries struggle with managing a project that is oriented towards outcomes but whereby most of the resources go into tracking expenses and submitting them to the most granular level of detail.

(iii) No incentives are in place to innovate in terms of service delivery and to undertake performance management with the aim of learning and creating feedback loops to improve the service to beneficiaries.

(iv) Funders do not see a return on their investment, considering the risk they incurred. Funders of Impact Bonds in Portugal have been true pioneers because their focus has been on promoting an outcome-oriented mentality and certainly not due to financial reasons. To simplify, if an investor in an Impact Bond through Portugal Social Innovation invests EUR 100,000, the best-case scenario is that that investor will recover its EUR 100,000 by the end of the project. No return will be paid.

Such a financing approach is not commensurate with the innovative nature of the projects that it is funding, and it is hindering the ability to create a wider and systemic adoption of outcome-based mechanisms.

A way to address this challenge is to promote a larger adoption of the simplified costs methodology. By defining the value of each outcome from the get-go, all partners in an Impact Bond will feel compelled to achieve that outcome in the most efficient way possible. This will foster innovation and collaboration and, if successful, will yield win–win outcomes for all partners.

Please note that while this recommendation is particularly important for outcome-based instruments such as the Social Impact Bond instrument, it also applies to all other instruments deployed by Portugal Social Innovation. A forensic approach to reimbursement of expenses places a disproportionate strain on the social enterprises that are receiving the funding. These social enterprises are typically organizations with some vulnerabilities in terms of management control systems and structure, hence why pressuring them towards a granular expense tracking means that they are not focused on the right things: serving their beneficiaries.

Recommendation No. 2: Consistent delegation of powers to intermediary organizations that manage thematic-specific funds

Portugal Social Innovation is an intermediary organization to whom certain powers were delegated to manage the portion of EU Structural Funds allocated to social innovation in the country. Among the main powers delegated are the responsibility to execute on the strategy, mobilize all relevant stakeholders, deploy the four instruments, select the projects, and monitor them from a 'physical' execution perspective.

It is important to distinguish between 'physical' execution and 'financial' execution. 'Physical' execution refers to all operational activities that were planned at the time of submission of the project. It entails monitoring whether the activities took place and whether the outcomes were met. In this sense, Portugal Social Innovation is responsible to verify the evidence that supports the achievement of outcomes. 'Financial' execution refers to how the project is doing financially as compared to what was initially budgeted. In this sense, it is not Portugal Social Innovation but rather the Managing Authority in charge of this specific area that verifies whether projects are spending and executing in accordance with the budget.

This segregation of powers creates delays in the implementation and management of projects but, most importantly, represents a strong obstacle for dialogue between funded projects and national entities responsible for EU Funds. Too often projects face severe delays in reimbursements due to the siloed nature of verifying the 'physical' execution by Portugal Social Innovation and the 'financial' execution by the Managing Authority within the thematic programme 'Social Inclusion and Employment'.

The recommendation would be to streamline the decision-making process and ensure that the entity that is responsible for specific thematic-based EU funding— in this case, social innovation—is able to retain the full stack of responsibilities and powers to fast-track decisions and engagement with projects that receive funding.

Recommendation No. 3: Position ESIF as outcome payers and not as investors

The main enabler of impact bonds in Portugal (which has nine impact bonds launched since 2015) is the fact that ESIF, such as the ESF, are being used to pay for outcomes rather than to replace the role of the investor. The bottleneck for outcome-based mechanisms is finding who is willing to pay for those outcomes and how much. Portugal has managed to address the question of 'who', by creating Portugal Social Innovation, but not the question of 'how much' as discussed in the first recommendation, related to the payment mechanism of Impact Bonds currently in place.

If Member States want to nourish a culture in public services that is oriented towards outcomes, it is fundamental to inspire local and central government officials by launching pilot projects. One of the ways to launch these is by redirecting some of the EU funding towards outcome-based mechanisms whereby the ESIF define the outcomes and pay for them, once achieved.

One of the learnings from the Portuguese experience is that having EU Funds paying for outcomes alone is not enough. When local and central government officials are not engaged financially in the projects (i.e., don't have financial skin in the game), their engagement is not as high as it could be. For more effective public sector participation, the pool of capital available to pay for outcomes should encompass EU funding but also be complemented by the local/central government budget. This will also contribute towards a smoother transition once the multi-annual financing framework starts to reach its end, as was the case in 2020 with Portugal Social Innovation and its four financing instruments.

Recommendation No. 4: Create a clear route for internalization of projects

One of the main objectives of social innovation is that once innovative interventions are tested and proven to work, they can be internalized as part of public provision, hence improving the quality of services delivered to beneficiaries, at scale. Throughout its four financing instruments, Portugal Social Innovation has supported hundreds of innovative projects, but the question remains: what will happen to them once the Portugal Social Innovation funding is over?

European Structural and Investment Funds mobilized for social innovation should have incentives geared towards not only paying for outcomes (based on the value of those outcomes) but also sustainability of those outcomes, that is, ensuring that they continue over time.

When Impact Bonds are tested, their aim is to complement traditional provision and test if a new intervention could, in conjunction with others, achieve better results for the populations that are being served; when a group of philanthropic organizations funds a group of projects in a specific thematic area, it does not expect to fund that group endlessly, hence corroborating the importance of long-term sustainability of the outcomes.

To design a clear route for internalization, ESIF should incentivize the following:

- Offer a financial premium to managing authorities in countries where tested solutions with proven results are internalized and widely adopted. This premium can come in the form of extra funding made available (as a percentage of total funding) or by foregoing financial penalties in other thematic areas.
- Demand that all social innovation projects have a multidisciplinary governance system that encompasses representatives of the public sector.

- Create educational content through workshops, webinars, and conferences that inspire and convey skills and knowledge for public sector leaders in terms of how innovations can be embedded in public provision and public policy.
- Dedicate a portion of the funding solely to the transition period between the final stages of a project and a potential internalization, to ensure that public sector human resources are well funded and focusing on internalization of innovations does not cannibalize other important tasks.
- Promote learning exchange across EU Member States, to create precedents in common areas of priority, such as employment, healthcare, education, among many others.
- Ensure that all projects that are eligible for further internalization, given their nature and alignment with public policy priorities, are not exclusively funded by EU Funds but also by either/or local and central government entities.

It is important to note that a clear route towards internalization of social innovation projects is likely to positively contribute to the ability of projects in mobilizing more funding, given the fact that several funders are attracted by the possibility of influencing public policy and funding projects that have the potential to be sustainable in the long run.

By adopting these recommendations, the belief is that both Portugal Social Innovation as it enters its next stage of development, and EU Member States willing to replicate its experience, will be able to achieve sustained impact at scale, with the right incentives in place to ensure a lasting systemic adoption of social innovation in public services.

Future research

Portugal Social Innovation is a pioneering initiative and as such has offered many learnings to policy makers across Europe who are keen to adopt policy initiatives that are focused on social innovation. International scoping studies have found it is one of the most holistic approaches to establish support structures for social innovation, which engage public, private, and social economy actors (Krlev et al. 2022). The implementation, instruments, learnings, obstacles, and recommendations have been identified but it is crucial to also point towards the known unknowns, that is, questions to which no answers have yet be provided and that can inform future research.

First and foremost, it is fundamental to bring evidence that catalyst institutions such as Portugal Social Innovation are contributing towards a sustainable and resilient social innovation ecosystem that can go beyond experimentation. So, the initiative is well placed to inform emergent research, for instance surrounding 'financial engineering' that investigates new investment mechanisms which take particular account of new social issues and necessities (Etzion, Kypraios, & Forgues, 2019). Capital has been mobilized to test, experiment, and adopt new financing instruments that promote social innovation but once tested—and those that are proven—the requirement is now focused on growth and scalability. As such, what is the role of European Union Structural and Investment Funds in also promoting the growth and scaling of social innovation initiatives? Purposeful interventions of public actors in institutional design are receiving increasing attention in research (Casasnovas, 2022). The years until 2030 will be a litmus test for Portugal Social Innovation in that regard, and an excellent field to assess many open questions as to how to pursue, steady, and scale such efforts of institutional design successfully.

Another important deep dive is around the topic of impact management and measurement. To what extent can a catalyst institution such as Portugal Social Innovation adopt an all-encompassing approach towards impact management that can suit the various stages of the projects it funds? Addressing this question is particularly challenging when it relates to the field rather than the organizational level, and is thus a real frontier for research (Hockerts et al., 2022; also Nicholls & Ormiston, this volume). An answer to this question could also serve as a blueprint for other similar initiatives that want to promote impact management and measurement across the value chain of projects that they support while ensuring a good fit with the maturity of organizations (see also Hehenberger & Buckland, this volume).

Lastly, there is an unanswered question related to the feeding of structural public policies versus an isolated intervention in social innovation. Portugal Social Innovation has demonstrated that the fact that this is a cross-cutting theme across various ministerial departments supports mobilization in several thematic areas whose social problems cannot be isolated. However, there is a need to promote a more symbiotic approach to create public policies that see social innovation within the remit of each public policy area. Otherwise such efforts risk having mainly a rhetorical function and a lack of material impact or value creation for society (Ayob, Teasedale, & Fagan, 2016). How can similar initiatives ensure that their teams, goals, funding, and policies are not only aligned but a core part of the policy guidelines within each policy area such as employment, healthcare, justice, and others? Answering that question will reveal how social innovation can go from a separate policy area to become a horizontal element that every decision maker adopts in defining their policy priorities.

Conclusions

Public structural funds play an important role in catalysing new markets and ecosystems. Portugal Social Innovation, a catalyst institution that promotes social innovation in Portugal is an archetype example via the mobilization of European Union Structural and Investment Funds.

Over the years since its inception in 2014, Portugal Social Innovation has mobilized around EUR 150 million in funds, a third of which came from private sources, with the aim of funding innovative solutions that effectively address social and environmental challenges.

It has encountered various obstacles, it has amassed an insightful range of learnings, and it has served as a blueprint for other EU Member States that want to replicate its experience. The impact is unequivocal across many dimensions: public policy, access to finance, financial innovation, public governance, building of evidence, and, most importantly, delivering a positive impact in those that benefit from its funding.

This chapter takes stock of this experience and indicates areas for future research, the answers to which will help to inform a better version of what cornerstone initiatives funded by EU Funds can become. Portugal Social Innovation will continue its work in Portugal, as an anchor player in the national ecosystem, which is focused on concrete structural recommendations for the period between 2022 and 2030.

As an evolution from the period 2014–2022, the outlook is oriented towards growth and scaling of all the experiences that have proven effective in the past years. As such, Portugal Social Innovation will continue to be a source of inspiration and leadership for EU Member States working on promoting social innovation at the core of their public policies.

References

Ayob, N., Teasdale, S., & Fagan, K. (2016). How social innovation 'came to be': tracing the evolution of a contested concept. *Journal of Social Policy*, 45(4), 635–653. https://doi.org/10.1017/S004727941600009X

Barth, B., Cruz Ferreira, J., & Miguel, A. (2018) Cross-sector collaboration for better social outcomes. https://www.evpa.ngo/insights/cross-sector-collaboration-better-social-outcomes

Casasnovas, G. (2022). When states build markets: policy support as a double-edged sword in the UK social investment market. *Organization Studies*, 017084062210801. https://doi.org/10.1177/01708406221080133

Etzion, D., Kypraios, E., & Forgues, B. (2019). Employing finance in pursuit of the Sustainable Development Goals: the promise and perils of catastrophe bonds. *Academy of Management Discoveries*, 5(4), 530–554. https://doi.org/10.5465/amd.2018.0137

European Commission (2019). *A Recipe Book for Social Finance: A Practical Guide on Designing and Implementing Initiatives to Develop Social Finance Instruments and Markets*. Authors: E. Varga & M. Hayday (2nd ed.). Luxembourg: Publications Office of the European Union. https://fa-se.de/wp-content/uploads/2019/12/EU-A-recipe-book-for-social-finance-2019-2nd-edition.pdf

EVPA (2017). *National Policy Nexus, Best-Policy-Sharing Initiatives*. Portugal Inovação Social. https://www.evpa.ngo/insights/national-policy-nexus-portugal-inovacao-social

Gianoncelli, A., Gaggiotti, G., Miguel, A., & Charro, I. (2020). *Enablers of Impact—The Role of Incubators and Accelerators in Bridging Investment and Solutions*. EVPA and MAZE https://www.evpa.ngo/insights/enablers-impact

Government Outcomes Lab (2021). *Social Outcomes Contracting in Europe: An Introductory Guide to Social Outcomes Contracting in European Union Member States.* https://advisory.eib.org/publications/attachments/social-outcomes-contracting-in-Europe-10052021.pdf

Grupo de Trabalho Português para o Investimento de Impacto (2015). *Novas abordagens para mobilizar financiamento para a inovação social em Portugal.* http://taskforce.maze-impact.com/

Hockerts, K., Hehenberger, L., Schaltegger, S., & Farber, V. (2022). Defining and Conceptualizing Impact Investing: Attractive Nuisance or Catalyst? *Journal of Business Ethics,* 11(15), 1. https://doi.org/10.1007/s10551-022-05157-3

Krlev, G., Sauer, S., Scharpe, K., Mildenberger, G., Elsemann, K., & Sauerhammer, M. (2022). Financing Social Innovation—International Evidence. Centre for Social Investment (CSI), University of Heidelberg & Social Entrepreneurship Network Deutschland e.V. (SEND). https://www.send-ev.de/wp-content/uploads/2022/01/Financing_Social_Innovation.pdf

Murray, R., Caulier-Grice, J., & Mulgan, G. (2010). *The Open Book of Social Innovation.* Social Innovator Series: Ways to Design, Develop and Grow Social Innovation. https://youngfoundation.org/wp-content/uploads/2012/10/The-Open-Book-of-Social-Innovationg.pdf

Quaternaire (2015). Concurso para a aquisição de serviços com vista à realização das avaliações ex-ante dos instrumentos financeiros dos Programas Operacionais do Portugal 2020 e dos Programas de Desenvolvimento Rural do Continente, dos Açores e da Madeira 2014–2020. https://www.compete2020.gov.pt/admin/images/Realatorio_Final_Avaliacao_Instr_Financ_Lote_2.pdf

16
Social procurement to promote social problem solving

Eva Varga and Malcolm Hayday

Introduction

In the foreword to a recent report about the global state of social enterprise, the director of the Schwab Foundation said that the 'report demonstrates how social enterprise is one of the largest movements of our time'. Social enterprises 'are significant in number and are present in every community around the world'. They 'are essential in the effort to drive more inclusive, sustainable economies and societies' (British Council, 2022, p. 8; cf. also Bonnici & Klijn, this volume).

Over the past few years, governments have become increasingly interested in fostering social economy enterprises in order to address pressing social issues. Social economy can offer innovative thinking and new approaches. Public authorities can use their purchasing decisions to pilot and scale new models, and help grow the social economy at the same time. The public sector has grown into a significant market; approximately 250,000 public authorities spend between 14 and 20 per cent of the European Union's EUR 15 trillion annual GDP on procurement. Procurement is now seen as a policy tool that has the potential to create community benefit and increase the social capital necessary to achieve sustainable transformation. In this chapter we explore what needs to change in the procurement world to harness the potential of this policy tool and of the existing legislative framework to allow new models to be employed for greater impact.

Methodology

Research carried out for this chapter was practice-oriented. In addition to the review of scholarly studies and articles, it prioritized case literature, guides, tools, and the content of online platforms and incorporated the authors' own learnings as practitioners. The authors have more than fifty years' combined experience in social finance and social enterprise and collaborated most recently in the production of two editions of the *Recipe Book for Social Finance* published by the European Union. Desk research was supplemented with information and views obtained directly from

Eva Varga and Malcolm Hayday, *Social procurement to promote social problem solving*. In: *Social Economy Science*. Edited by: Gorgi Krlev, Dominika Wruk, Giulio Pasi, and Marika Bernhard, Oxford University Press. © Oxford University Press (2023). DOI: 10.1093/oso/9780192868343.003.0016

a few European social economy organizations with procurement experience in the form of conversations and interviews. Literature review covers material dated 2012 and after, in order to focus on the impact of recent developments, such as the EU public procurement reform of 2014 or the growing awareness of the importance of the social economy in post-COVID pandemic recovery. Given the roots of this chapter and the established size of the public procurement market in the European Union, we have focused on this geographical area. However, much of the innovation is happening at a regional or even a community level, and in other parts of the world; for example, we have focused on examples in Canada and Australia.

The changing view of procurement

Procurement has been defined as 'the act of obtaining goods and services' (Young, 2020) typically for businesses, but may also refer to the process involved. Public procurement is understood by the European Commission as 'the process by which public authorities, such as government departments or local authorities, purchase works, goods and services from companies' (European Commission, n.d.). Literature also uses two other concepts, purchasing and commissioning, and distinguishes between those and procurement, emphasizing the technical process in purchasing and the focus on people's needs and the corresponding design of appropriate services in commissioning (Furneaux & Barraket, 2014). There is an overlap between the three concepts and some authors consider that 'commissioning encompasses procurement, while procurement in turn encompasses purchasing' (Furneaux & Barraket, 2014, p. 3, quoting Murray, 2009).

In the simplest and traditional understanding, public procurement is a process, which selects the preferred provider(s) of products or services, often in the form of competitive tenders. By outsourcing the production of works and goods and the provisioning of services to other actors, public authorities are able to supplement the capacity of the public sector. Through competitive bidding, the procurement process aims to select the most economical proposal and save public resources.

This simplistic view of public procurement as a transaction or a mechanistic exercise to purchase goods or services is becoming increasingly questioned, as it ignores the potential of procurement to also achieve social and environmental goals. Procurement is now viewed as a policy tool for governments to steer market actors towards desired outcomes, to create and implement certain standards and practices, or to develop innovative solutions, and, in this way, to implement policy objectives. There are initiatives where this is taken even further to show that public procurement has the potential to create community benefit and increase social capital, and this is achieved through collaboration with other stakeholders in the procurement process. Buy Social Canada, for example, advocates for increasing community capital through social purchasing (Buy Social Canada, 2022).

Social procurement is an emerging practice not only in the public sector but also in private markets. It embraces the view that in a new world, competitive bidding and lowest price can no longer be the primary drivers. Markets are evolving, driven by Environmental, Social and Governance (ESG) requirements,[1] the Sustainable Development Goals (SDGs, https://sdgs.un.org/), and the recognition that the world's natural resources are finite. Dynamic partnerships are emerging to generate social and environmental value for customers, communities, and society as a whole.

Socially responsible public procurement

Socially responsible public procurement, here referred to as social procurement, is a relatively new approach to conducting public sector purchases. In the European Commission's view, 'socially responsible public procurement is about achieving positive social outcomes in public contracts' (European Commission, 2021). This is in line with the definition that 'social procurement is the acquisition of a range of assets and services, with the aim of intentionally creating social outcomes (both directly and indirectly)' (Furneaux & Barraket, 2014, p. 8). Governments seek social outcomes in a wide variety of fields: employment and social inclusion of disabled or disadvantaged persons; health services; social and care services; education or cultural areas. Social procurement encourages the use of quality social and environmental criteria instead of the lowest price only, in all or selected phases of the procurement process, from tender documentation through selection, awarding the contract, or monitoring compliance. Social procurement encourages the use of quality social and environmental criteria instead of the lowest price only, in all or selected phases of the procurement process, from tender documentation through selection, awarding the contract, or monitoring compliance. By focusing on social outcomes, social procurement also has the potential to spur innovation in the design and delivery of solutions to social problems.

Social procurement seeks to deliver on a government's social policy goals: (1) by directly ensuring the provision of public services that respond to social needs (in health, social services, or education) through government purchases; (2) by enforcing more socially responsible practices in the economy through obliging economic operators to comply with labour laws and social standards, thus achieving outcomes indirectly; (3) by including private sector and third sector actors in the supply chain (Furneaux & Barraket, 2014).

Past research has identified four types of social procurement in policy documents: (1) procurement of social services from third-sector organizations; (2) procurement of assets or works with social value as a secondary outcome; (3) allocation of works to social enterprises (as opposed to open calls for tender); (4) corporate social responsibility, focusing on compliance with labour and human rights regulations in

---

[1] According to an OECD publication, ESG investments have grown rapidly over the past decade and according to some estimates, professionally managed portfolios that integrate ESG elements exceed \$17.5 trillion globally (Boffo & Patalano, 2020). See Nicholls & Ormiston (this volume) for more about investing in social impact.

public procurement, and on supply chain management in corporate procurement (Furneaux & Barraket, 2014). In the form of collaborative procurement a new type is emerging, which places the emphasis on partnerships and the joint design and delivery of solutions. Such models go beyond the purchaser–contractor-type relationship or the compliance approach suggested by the above typology. Placing the intended social value at the centre, new social procurement is relational rather than transactional, building trust and taking a long-term view.

Social economy and public procurement

Over the past few decades, the social economy has become an important provider of social services and therefore a key stakeholder in public procurement processes in many European countries. In turn, access to public sector markets has become essential for many social economy service providers, as revenue from public sources can be a significant contributor to their sustainability. Trading with the public sector was a main source of income for 33 per cent of the respondents of the 2020–21 European Social Enterprise Monitor (Euclid Network, 2021). In Belgium public contracts have started to replace subsidies and public authorities are becoming increasingly important clients of social enterprises (Nyssens and Huybrechts, 2020). At the same time, there are several countries (e.g., Romania or Hungary) where participation of social economy enterprises in public procurement has remained very limited.

Social economy is an emerging sector with increasing weight and importance in EU economies (CIRIEC, 2017) and with growing relevance for public procurement. Social economy represents about 10 per cent of businesses and employs more than 6 per cent of the total workforce (OECD, 2020). It is based on economic practices that are sustainable and inclusive, responds to social and environmental needs, and uses participatory and democratic governance (OECD, 2020). Social economy enterprises exist in various legal forms (co-operatives, foundations, associations, mutuals, and social enterprises) and are active in a range of sectors from agriculture through social services to culture, banking, and utilities. A large number of social economy enterprises aim to provide employment and livelihoods to people who are excluded from the labour market; work integration social enterprises (WISE) aim specifically at the work integration of disadvantaged people. Social economy enterprises in some EU member states, for example Italy, have become an important part of the welfare landscape by delivering public services in the health and social care fields (Borzaga, 2020).

This diversity across the EU makes it very difficult to accurately assess social economy enterprises and to draw up policy measures for their support that go beyond guidelines (OECD, 2020). CIRIEC introduced a typology of government policies aimed to foster the growth of the social economy: 'soft' policies intend to create a favourable ecosystem for social economy, while 'hard' policies promote the enterprises themselves through supply-side and demand-side measures (CIRIEC, 2018).

Socially responsible public procurement is considered a demand-side measure that increases demand for social economy products and services and is an important mechanism for opening up public markets to social economy organizations. They had advocated for such policy measures at EU and national levels for a long time, which led to public procurement appearing on the EU's social economy agenda in the *Social Business Initiative* policy package in 2011 (European Commission, 2011). When the EU's public procurement reform package was published in 2014, social economy organizations welcomed the new procurement directive (Social Economy Europe, 2018) as a key piece of legislation that would enable them to access public sector markets, generate income, and further their social mission. Only in recent years has it been recognized that social procurement is also about collaboration and partnership for social value creation and community benefit.

European Union: enhancing social value creation through socially responsible public procurement legislation

Public Procurement Directive 2014

The public sector represents a significant market, with 250,000 public authorities spending more than 14 per cent of the EU's GDP annually. To create a level playing field for all businesses across Europe, EU law sets out minimum standards and harmonized procurement rules, which member states are required to transpose into national legislation. One of the main objectives of the 2014 public procurement reform package[2] was to make procurement easier and cheaper for small and medium-sized enterprises (SMEs),[3] while still ensuring best value for money for public purchases and maintaining transparent procedures.

The 2014 directive contains important new provisions for pursuing socially responsible public procurement.[4] It encourages public authorities to move away from the lowest price criterion and aim for the most economically advantageous tender (MEAT) by using the best price–quality ratio (BPQR), which takes into account quality criteria as well as social and environmental considerations.[5] In order to achieve this, the directive introduces a number of instruments that procurement officers can use optionally (see Table 16.1).

The scope of the directive applies to services of general economic interest only, which are basic services carried out in return for payment and are subject to EU internal market, competition and therefore procurement rules. Non-economic services

---

[2] The package contained three directives: Directive 2014/24/EU on public procurement; Directive 2014/25/EU on procurement by entities operating in water, energy, transport, and postal services; and Directive 2014/23/EU on the award of concession contracts.

[3] 'The category of micro, small and medium-sized enterprises (SMEs) is made up of enterprises which employ fewer than 250 persons and which have an annual turnover not exceeding EUR 50 million, and/or an annual balance sheet total not exceeding EUR 43 million' (European Union, 2015).

[4] This paper focuses on 2014/24/EU, the most relevant directive for social economy, but the other two directives contain similar provisions for pursuing socially responsible procurement.

[5] Article 67, Directive 2014/24/EU on public procurement.

Table 16.1 Main social procurement instruments in EU directives

Instrument	Use
Social clauses	May be used in different phases of the process, aiming, for example, at the training and integration of young people in the labour market, gender equality, or accessibility requirements (type 2 or 4). Their use is optional.
Mandatory social clause	Requires economic operators to comply with labour and human rights standards enshrined in EU law, national legislation, or international conventions (type 4).
Reserved contract	Allows public authorities to reserve tender procedures to sheltered workshops and other economic operators whose main aim is the work integration of people with disabilities or other disadvantage, provided that at least 30 per cent of their workforce comes from such beneficiary groups (type 3). Contracts may also be reserved for the procurement of social and health-related services specifically, and awarded to nonprofit organizations or social economy providers for up to a period of three years (type 1 and 3).
'Light regime'	A simplified procurement regime, which may be applied to social, health, educational, and other services, provided that the principles of transparency are observed. The introduction of quality criteria, such as continuity, accessibility, or affordability, rather than price alone is welcome in the procurement of these services. Contracts may be reserved for social economy enterprises.
Innovation partnership	Can be employed to allow public authorities to design innovative solutions jointly with the tenderer, rather than prescribing a solution. This reflects an approach similar to outcomes-based commissioning.
Life-cycle costing methodology	Recommended for calculation of the cost of an asset or service during its entire life-cycle, thus establishing its true cost, not only the cost at the time of awarding the contract.
Other instruments	Preliminary market consultation, certification, and the use of labels are also encouraged by the directive in order to obtain the best price–quality ratio.

such as the police are not subject to internal market rules. Social services of general interest are those that meet the needs of vulnerable citizens, and they can be the most relevant and interesting for social economy enterprises. They include social security, housing, childcare, employment and training services, or social assistance services. Because these can be economic or non-economic in nature, some of them are subject to internal market and procurement rules while others are not (European Commission, 2016).

Social procurement in practice

The EU legislation offers the framework and provisions that support a broader view of social procurement, including pre-market consultation or innovation partnerships. It is the practical implementation of these provisions that can make the difference between successful joint value creation and frustrated procurement attempts.

Public procurement and therefore social procurement in the EU remains within the jurisdiction of the member states and is therefore a national matter. Although the 2014 EU directive had been transposed into national legislation in all member states by 2017, social procurement rules are far from being harmonized across Europe (European Commission, 2018). The directive serves as a guideline, and with the exception of the mandatory provision on compliance with labour laws, it allows for considerable discretion at national level. The result is a great variation in the transposition, interpretation, and implementation of the directive itself, as well as in social procurement practices. There were early discussions about how much this directive can achieve due to most social provisions being optional (Van den Abeele, 2014); the directive has certainly raised awareness of and strengthened the message about social procurement in EU member states. Yet its actual impact will depend on its uptake and implementation in practice.

Buying for Social Impact was a major research and mapping exercise commissioned by the EC in 2018–2020 to gauge progress in legislation and implementation of social procurement at national level across the EU. This action research included fifteen member states and one of its main outputs was a large and diverse collection of procurement case studies (seventy-one cases). The most commonly used social procurement instrument was the reserved contract for the work integration of people with disabilities or disadvantaged workers. Sectoral analysis showed that social procurement was more widespread in the maintenance of public green spaces, cleaning services and social services, while less frequent, but also present, in construction, food processing, catering, and transport services. Social economy organizations were active in a much wider range of industries, yet they did not win public tenders in those (Caimi et al., 2019).

Challenges for socially responsible public procurement

Challenges for successfully achieving social goals through social procurement can be divided in four main groups: (1) challenges relating to the legislative basis; (2) implementation challenges on the side of public authorities; (3) challenges with regard to social value and impact; (4) skills shortcomings on the side of the social economy.

Legislative challenges

In the European Union the legislative challenges relate to the varied transposition of the EU directive in the member states. In certain countries some social procurement articles of the directive have not been transposed into legislation at all and even where they have, their use remains largely optional. There are examples of provisions which have been transposed into national law, yet they apply only to central government procurement, thus missing opportunities at regional and local level. National procurement legislation often leaves quality criteria for social services undeveloped and uses general categories (e.g. staff training) that are not suitable for social services, and, therefore, are easy to ignore (Caimi, 2020). Procurement of social services or innovative solutions is often disconnected from social goals, so commissioners show limited enthusiasm for social considerations.

Implementation challenges

Implementation challenges of social procurement are surmountable even in places where enabling legislation exists. These challenges can be strategic or technical (operational) in nature.

Strategic challenges are about the goals and incentives of public authorities and their commissioners. Social procurement drivers (social goals) are often viewed in conflict with economic drivers (fair competition, lowest price), which leads to procurement officers resorting to the usual practice of selecting the lowest-priced bid. 'In our experience, procurement officers do not want appeals against their award decisions. They fear distorting the competition, so they prefer to keep procurement criteria simple and ignore social considerations.'[6]

Public authorities are often constrained by short-term budgetary concerns as well as the short government life cycle. Historically, in order to retain funds (and control), public authorities often provided public services in-house rather than contracting them out, even if it was to the detriment of service quality. This conditioned their attitude to alternative providers. Public authorities tend to be risk averse and therefore reluctant to try new approaches or invite unknown suppliers to bid, especially if they do not have the tools to evaluate them. Social economy entities are often overlooked simply because public authorities are not familiar with them and their activities. This is confirmed by the fact that only 34 per cent of good practice case studies published in the *Buying for Social Impact* report engaged social economy providers (Tepper et al., 2020). These strategic challenges lead to a misalignment of incentives, which in turn discourages public procurement officers to engage social economy enterprises.

On the operational side, procurement officers are often not aware of the social procurement provisions, so they do not use them (Caimi, 2020). Another obstacle is that the majority of procurement officers still lack the technical skills, knowledge, and even empathy to implement social procurement, be it about the selection of the appropriate procurement phase or the scoring system. An often-cited problem is that the lack of coordination between procurement bodies results in fragmented service provision and low-quality services.[7] And finally, corruption and lack of transparency can distort competition in social procurement or prevent the use of social procurement provisions altogether. These operational challenges are reflected in one of the key findings of the recent *Buying for Social Impact* research, namely, that legislation is necessary, but not sufficient. It must be accompanied by initiatives that

---

[6] Interview with a Hungarian social enterprise.
[7] Interview with a social economy organization in Catalonia.

aid implementation: increase awareness of each other, build trust, improve knowledge, and build capacity among public authorities and economic operators, including social economy enterprises (Caimi, 2020).

Social value challenges

Limited understanding of social value and the lack of outcomes focus are major impediments in the way of procurement to deliver on social objectives. The big questions are what constitutes social value, what social impact should be targeted and over what time horizon, and what the social procurement process should look like. The example of the Welsh government shows one possible way to incorporate social value in procurement (see Box 16.1). In many countries, however, even if social value goals and strategies exist, the communication gap between policy-makers and procurers makes it difficult to translate those strategies into more specific social procurement goals. Procurers often lack beneficiary perspective and focus, and simply buy a service or product using a prescriptive tender from a name they know, rather than concentrating on desired outcomes. 'More abstractly, a government may order a bridge, when what will do the job best is a ferry' (Murray, 2020, p. 15).

Box 16.1 Linking procurement to social value goals

In 2015 the **Welsh government** enacted the **Well-being of Future Generations Act**. Seven well-being goals have been put in place to improve the social, economic, environmental, and cultural well-being of Wales. A subset of national indicators have been set and progress is reported annually (Future Generations Commissioner for Wales, n.d.). In 2021 the Welsh government published its plan for enacting its Wales procurement policy linked directly to the wellbeing goals. The policy commits to long-term sustainable procurement, and intends to clearly show how procurement can support the delivery of the wellbeing objectives. It aligns ways of increasing stakeholder involvement to support innovative and sustainable solutions and promotes value-based procurement. This includes pre-market engagement with supply chains and creating procurement pipelines that allow time to identify sustainable solutions and seek innovation. As part of its commitment the government provides management tools and support to commissioners throughout the tender processes and contract delivery, and is developing a toolkit to support social value and whole-life costing (Welsh Government, 2021).

The practical challenges relating to social value are the lack of experience, capacity, and tools to gather data, evaluate outcomes, and measure impact (Murray, 2020). Even if measurement methods and tools are available, they may be inappropriate, given that social value may be unique in each procurement case depending on the service or product and the stakeholders affected. No matter what methodology is chosen, it will be redundant in the absence of clearly stated social goals (Halloran, 2017). Even where social goals are set and social impact is measured, contract performance may result in different or unintended social outcomes, which makes the final assessment difficult.[8] In the UK, where social value considerations have been encouraged in public service commissioning since the 2013 adoption of the Public Services (Social Value) Act, defining and measuring social value is still identified as the biggest challenge to implementation (Jones et al., 2017).

By not being able to define and measure social value procurement officers risk failing to properly assess whether procurement was successful and distil lessons for the future. They also risk overlooking social washing[9] by companies who might present a false picture of their social and human rights record.

Literature suggests that there is little analysis available on what social value really is obtained by strategic (social) procurement (Halloran, 2017). Research for this chapter confirmed that finding evidence and data for such analysis is difficult. A number of case studies have been written and published from all over Europe about the promotion and use of the EU directive, emphasizing implementation and process-related features or *intended* social impact. However, very little evidence has been published about the actual outcomes and social impact of social procurement.

Skills and capacity challenges in the social economy

The fourth group of challenges relates to the skills and capacities of social economy enterprises. They often find procurement processes to be too complex and overwhelming, and do not have the knowledge, capacity, or the time to participate in the process or draw up a bid. While expert support and consultants may be ready to help, social economy enterprises often cannot afford to buy them. In some cases social economy enterprises are simply not aware of the publication of a procurement tender or their right to bid. Social economy enterprises often lack the skills, methods, and capacity to measure their social impact, thus they are unable to clearly communicate it in tenders. Finally, limited financial and human resource capacity may prevent social economy enterprises from winning larger public sector contracts. Many consider that they hold their resources in trust for the community and are reluctant to bid for contracts whose terms, especially of payment, may put those resources at risk.

---

[8] A case in point is presented by research carried out in the Swedish construction industry, where social clauses on the requirement of internships and employment for migrant workers resulted in short-term solutions for the migrants and additional pressures for the employees of the contractor companies (Troje & Gluch, 2020).

[9] 'Social washing can be defined as a practice aimed at improving a company's reputation through social responsibility initiatives which are not really effective or, in the worst cases, under the guise of social responsibility but with the goal of economic return' (Etica Funds, 2020).

Opportunities for socially responsible public procurement

There are a number of opportunities that can accelerate the use of social considerations in procurement and of new forms of collaboration, and thus benefit social economy organizations. Some of these opportunities open up new markets; others put social enterprises in a better position to win contracts or help public and private purchasers better engage with the social economy and thus achieve better social outcomes.

Increasing urgency to achieve impact

First and foremost, there is increasing urgency to act in order to achieve the SDGs by 2030 and sustainable models and solutions are in high demand. At the same time, the visibility and use of the SDGs as an impact framework has been growing globally as well as locally, in government policy, in corporate practices, and in the social economy. Adherence to the SDGs can help set and articulate social impact goals and select or create appropriate measurement frameworks (Murray, 2020). It has been recognized that SDGs could also help to operationalize policy goals and translate them into more specific (local) social impact goals, or, vice versa, could help aggregate local social value into broader impact. Goal 12, 'Ensure sustainable consumption and production patterns', includes explicit reference to sustainable procurement, but there are a number of other goals which are also relevant for public spending. A tool to operationalize the use of SDGs in the corporate sector exists already, linking the use of development goals to changing corporate procurement. The SDG Action Manager, developed by the B Lab and the UN Global Compact, was designed to assist companies to identify SDGs appropriate for them, set goals and track progress, and understand and share their impact.[10]

Second, the COVID-19 pandemic and crisis can also offer new business opportunities for the social economy in the context of public procurement. While the crisis poses a significant threat to the sustainability and survival of many social economy enterprises due to loss of market revenue or overwhelming service demand, often they are the only actors that are able to step in to replace failing public services. Public authorities have relied on social economy and third sector organizations to ensure the continuity of service provision to vulnerable populations, but going forward they could invite those organizations to participate in collaborative models, and jointly implement innovative solutions that better respond to changing circumstances.[11] The OECD has identified a continuous role of service delivery, crisis mitigation, and innovation of social economy organizations during and after the COVID-19 crisis, emphasizing their resilience, ability to adjust, and innovate. In the long run, policy

---

[10] See: https://unglobalcompact.org/take-action/sdg-action-manager
[11] Interview with a social economy organization in Catalonia.

responses should aim to leverage the social economy's ability to drive systemic change and lead in the transition to a more resilient and sustainable economy (OECD, 2020).

Growing interest of public authorities

First, governments have become increasingly interested in the social economy as a partner in addressing pressing social problems, such as unemployment and social exclusion. They have drawn up social economy strategies and action plans (see examples in Box 16.2), and introduced new legislation to create an enabling environment and to foster the spread and growth of social economy. Over the past few years this been strengthened by a heightened interest in social innovation; public authorities are increasingly driven by better attention to beneficiaries' needs and the search for effective solutions. They are becoming more open to experimentation and pilots, engaging social economy actors as agents of social innovation.

Box 16.2   Social enterprise development strategies

EU Social Economy Action Plan. Growing government interest in social enterprise or social economy development is reflected in strategies at European level that lay out important objectives and policies that aim to foster the development of the sector. The EU's Social Business Initiative (SBI) prioritized access to funding, visibility, and the institutional framework, including public procurement (European Commission, 2011). Ten years after the SBI, the EU published its new Action Plan for the Development of Social Economy. The Plan promises to come up with another comprehensive policy package (Roadmap) for the development of the sector focusing on three areas, very similar to those ten years before: 1. Creating the right policy and legal conditions, including procurement; 2. Opening up opportunities for starting up and scaling; 3. Increasing the recognition of the work and potential of social economy enterprises (European Commission, 2021).

   Social Enterprise Strategy Scotland. Social enterprise development strategies can be found at national level as well. The Social Enterprise Strategy 2016–2026 of the Scottish government has three priorities; stimulating social enterprise, developing stronger organizations, and realizing market opportunity. The third priority includes access to public sector markets and refers to the capacity constraints of social enterprises. It is closely linked with priority 2, which in turn outlines measures to remove those constraints (Scottish Government, 2016).

Second, there is a growing interest of local authorities and cities, in particular, in social procurement, where the proximity to both the social need and the potential providers motivates procurement officers to engage with a range of partners and take social considerations into account (see examples in Box 16.3). Local procurement, with its smaller contract sizes compared to central government tenders, also makes it more feasible for social economy organizations to bid successfully. The majority (76 per cent) of best practice examples published in the *Buying for Social Impact* report (Tepper et al., 2020) are of local procurement cases,[12] carried out by cities or regional governments, suggesting that this is where favourable conditions and future potential exist. Regions and cities are creating their own social outcomes strategies and adopting social impact measurement methods. Some of them draw up social procurement strategies to support the achievement of their social and environmental sustainability goals. As the example of Bologna, Italy shows in Box 16.3, there can be more room for innovation at a local level.

Box 16.3 Cities lead the way—increasing focus on social impact

The city of Wageningen, The Netherlands, has introduced a policy which requires that 5% of the value on all contracts above EUR 50,000 is used by the contractor to employ people who are unemployed or distant from the labour market. The city calls this Social Return on Investment (SROI). Non-compliance can be sanctioned with a fine, which is used by the city for designing new instruments to support job seekers (Tepper et al., 2020).

The municipality of Valladolid, Spain, created a social procurement strategy in 2018 to make public procurement more accessible for SMEs and ensure social and sustainable public procurement. Division of contracts into smaller lots, pre-market consultations, and reserved contracts were used, and the city committed to reserve 8–10% of its total annual procurement to sheltered workshops and WISEs (Tepper et al., 2020).

Social procurement turned upside down
Another approach is exemplified by **Bologna, Italy**, where the logic of public procurement has been turned upside down. The city's leadership encourages citizens to initiate and propose projects with the aim to protect urban commons, and the city to enable and support these. The Bologna Regulation is based on a change in the Italian constitution allowing engaged citizens to claim urban resources as commons and to declare an interest in their management. After an evaluation process, an 'accord' is signed with the city specifying how it will support the initiative with an appropriate mix of resources and specifying a joint 'public–commons' management. The Bologna Regulation sees the city's residents as resourceful, imaginative agents in their own right, attuned to the needs of their community. To date the projects have fallen into three broad categories: living together

continued

---

[12] Based on the 71 cases in Tepper et al. (2020).

Box 16.3 Continued

(collaborative services), growing together (co-ventures), and working together (coproduction). In Bologna dozens of projects have been carried out and 140 other Italian cities have followed suit. Bologna's self-declared ambition is to become a city of collaboration (Scottish Community Alliance, 2022).

Increasing interest in the private sector

The interest in sustainable supply chain management in the corporate sector has been on the rise, presenting a huge opportunity to mainstream social and environmental considerations and offering an enormous market to social enterprises. This interest is no longer rooted in corporate social responsibility alone, but reflects recognition of the fact that social procurement may contribute to a company's competitiveness in the market and its attractiveness to customers and workforce. Recognizing that 'social procurement is a better way to grow', SAP, for example, launched its '5&5 by 25' public initiative to direct 5 per cent of its 'addressable spend' to social enterprises and 5 per cent to diverse businesses by 2025 (Fox-Martin, 2020). 'Buy Social' campaigns that recognize and harness this trend have been launched in several countries to promote social procurement in the private sector (see Box 16.4 for examples).

According to a recent report by Social Enterprise UK on corporate social procurement, the COVID-19 pandemic has seen a 'greater appreciation of the need to align the business interests with those of the communities they operate in' (Social Enterprise UK, 2021, p. 4). The trend is also reinforced by the emergence of ESG investing; companies will have to be accountable to investors who factor social, environmental, and governance criteria into their asset allocation and risk decisions, and want to see sustainable financial returns. The ESG spirit is already present in the procurement context thanks to the social and environmental provisions in procurement regulation. By integrating those considerations into their practices and supply chain, companies may be able to bid more successfully in public tenders.

Box 16.4 Buy Social Corporate Challenge

One of the first initiatives in the world to encourage social procurement among corporations is the Buy Social Corporate Challenge, launched in the UK by Social Enterprise UK in 2016 with support from the government's Department for Digital, Culture, Media & Sport. The objective is that high-profile businesses spend a total of £1 billion purchasing from social enterprises and use their spending to maximize social impact in this way. The initiative was launched in partnership with a few corporations and is an example of long-term thinking around procurement.

Being the umbrella organization for social enterprises, Social Enterprise UK is a well-positioned intermediary to support corporations to find the matching social enterprise suppliers and broker deals for the benefit of both parties. Corporations may receive strategic advisory, training, and communication expertise from the organization. The Challenge had been running for more than five years as of 2022 and has reported £165 million corporate spend with social enterprises, engaging 550 of them as suppliers and creating 2,030 jobs for beneficiaries (Social Enterprise UK, 2021).

Scotland launched its own Buy Social Corporate Challenge in 2021 with support from the Scottish government, offering an online business directory to help match social enterprise suppliers and corporate purchasers (Buy Social Scotland, n.d.). Campaigns in other EU countries are also under preparation with the leadership of social enterprise support organizations and with funding from the European Commission (Lewis, 2022). Enhancing social procurement and supporting the Buy Social feature are among the key elements of the EU's Social Economy Action Plan (European Commission, 2021).

Buy Social has become a global movement with significant progress in Canada. **Buy Social Canada** (https://www.buysocialcanada.com/), itself a social enterprise, is an organization that has been at the forefront of social procurement for more than six years. By building relationships between social suppliers and purchasers, Buy Social Canada is helping to build community capital across Canada. It recognizes that every transaction has an economic, environmental, and social impact. Buy Social Canada also offers social enterprise certification recognized across the country. The certificate allows social enterprises to enter a trusted supplier directory and thus increase their chances to become suppliers. It also gives access to Buy Social Canada's capacity-building support, as well as to networking with purchasers and suppliers. Buy Social Canada also works with public and private purchasers who want to design their own Buy Social Journey and accompanies them through implementation using a partnership model. The variety and interconnected nature of these services demonstrate the Buy Social Canada approach: connect all parties and assist them to make social procurement happen for community benefit.

Governments have started to recognize the benefits of social procurement in the private sector and have been funding Buy Social campaigns, specialist intermediaries and social enterprise supplier databases/platforms in a number of countries. Such efforts can contribute further to the mainstreaming of social and environmental considerations in corporate supply chains and can open up access to private markets for social economy enterprises. Corporate experience offers learnings to public procurement officers in a number of areas: how to set a spending goal linked to social goals; how to identify potential procurement partners; or how to build partnerships.

The emergence of intermediaries

The emergence of intermediaries is an opportunity both for public authorities and interested bidders to make procurement more social and collaborative. Quite often deals simply would not happen without intermediaries. In the Australian public sector market, for example, intermediaries perform a number of functions that facilitate the uptake of social considerations in procurement: they connect purchasers and social economy suppliers; offer training, capacity building, and advisory services to both sides; certify suppliers; assist with social impact measurement; and play an advocacy role in support of social procurement (Barraket, 2019). Intermediaries exist and their functions in procurement are pertinent in EU economies as well,[13] but their numbers and experience vary a great deal among member states. In certain industries, such as construction, internal intermediaries—so-called employment requirement professionals—emerged in order to assist companies to adjust to social clauses on employment and internships (Troje et al., 2019). Intermediaries are often instrumental in corporate social procurement and partnership models as well; they are the initiators and catalysts of supply chain collaborations between companies, social enterprises, and other actors, including public authorities. Box 16.5 illustrates the diversity of forms intermediaries can take and ways in which they can be involved in facilitating social procurement.

Box 16.5 Working with intermediaries

In **Ille et Vilaine, France**, the contracting authority, Département of Ille et Vilaine, engaged a dedicated **Social Clauses Platform** to act as a social clause integration support organization both for the procurers and the bidding companies, and to assist with work integration clauses in a procurement process for sewage services (Tepper et al., 2020).

Partnership for Procurement (P4P) is an initiative funded by the Scottish government to provide interested social enterprises and third sector organizations with guidance on partnership working and collaboration in procurement. In addition to consulting, advice, procurement guides, and toolkits, P4P also offers a platform for a searchable online database of social enterprises and third sector suppliers, Social Enterprise Finder Scotland (https://p4p.org.uk/ready-for-business-register/), useful for both purchasers and potential bidders. It specifically includes a Supported Business search function, which helps public sector commissioners find potential suppliers for reserved contracts according to Scottish regulations.

The Social Value unit in Northern Ireland has been created to assist government departments, their agencies, and arm's-length bodies to maximize the delivery of

---

[13] This is illustrated by many of the 71 good practice case studies in Tepper et al. (2020).

social value through public contracts. Northern Ireland has introduced its equivalent of the Social Value Act; from 1 June 2022, tenders must allocate a minimum of 10 per cent of the total award criteria to social value. A suite of bespoke resources, training modules, and model procurement documentation has been shared on a web portal run by Social Value in order to ensure consistency of approach (Social Value, n.d.).

The **British Columbia Social Procurement Initiative, BCSPI** (https://bcspi.ca/) is a public sector initiative that helps local governments and institutional purchasers use their procurement spending for community benefit. It is a membership model, in which members can take advantage of peer learning, training, and a wide range of resources, such as guides, case studies, tools, and templates. BCSIP takes its members through a member journey from sign-up to training, pilots, policy update, and implementation, including impact measurement of social procurement projects. The initiative offers specific capacity building, training, and support to its members in post-COVID years, so that they can effectively implement social procurement policies for a more resilient recovery. Currently, BCSPI has 30 local governments and organizations among its members; to date it has trained more than 175 people and supported the implementation of more than 100 procurement projects resulting in more than CAN$250 million spent on social procurement.

The emergence of a new type of finance

The emergence and availability of a new type of private finance, namely impact investing, has opened up new areas and ways for social economy enterprises to participate in public service delivery and for public authorities to experiment with innovative solutions. Social Outcomes Contracting (SOC), Social Impact Bonds (SIB), and Outcomes Funds offer new models that target social outcomes and innovation, and share risk in public service delivery using a partnership model. According to the European Investment Advisory Hub (2019) run by the European Investment Bank (EIB), an important player in many SIB and SOC arrangements, 'social outcomes contracting is an innovative form of procuring social services based on outcomes rather than outputs'.[14] SOC strengthens the outcomes orientation of procurement, as the service provider's pay is linked to measurable social impact rather than a prescribed service or product. SIBs are special outcomes-based contracts, where the outcome payer is the government and a third party financier is involved (University of Oxford Government Outcomes Lab, n.d.). Examples of pilot SIBs, such as the Finnish government buying, appear among best practices of socially responsible

---

[14] See also: Advisory Platform for Social Outcomes Contracting, https://eiah.eib.org/about/initiative-social-outcomes-contracting

public procurement (Tepper et al., 2020, pp. 113–116). Outcomes funds go one step further; they are 'a funding mechanism that enables several outcomes-based contracts to be developed and supported in parallel, under a common framework' (University of Oxford Government Outcomes Lab, n.d.). Outcomes funds could be an effective way to commission innovative solutions and help align the interests of stakeholders centring on outcomes (Chapter Social Finance, 2018). See more on SIBs in 16 of this book.

Possible policy measures to respond to challenges and opportunities

We have identified a number of policy measures that have the potential to respond to the above opportunities and address the challenges when rolling out social procurement and engaging social economy enterprises. Table 16.2 illustrates these measures, grouped into four main categories. We believe that measures to improve implementation offer low-hanging fruit and relatively near-term opportunities. Ensuring a social value focus might take more effort, but as it is fundamental, governments and public authorities must start working on it today, in the areas of:

1) commissioning; 2) implementation of social procurement provisions; 3) social economy ecosystems; and 4) future research.

Table 16.2 Policy measures addressing challenges and opportunities

Category	Measures
Focus on social value and outcomes	1. Set social and environmental goals, which lead to strategies that could be the basis of procurement plans 2. Support public authorities (central and local) with guidance, tools and capacity building in setting goals and measuring social impact 3. Pilot outcomes-based commissioning
Improve implementation of social procurement provisions	1. Align interests, offer incentives, and build capacity in public administration 2. Encourage and foster collaboration and partnerships with other actors 3. Support local procurement and innovation 4. Experiment, pilot, and scale successful models through public procurement
Strengthen the social economy ecosystem	1. Use labels or certification 2. Support capacity building for and about social economy enterprises 3. Foster collaboration in ecosystem building
Conduct more research	1. Fund more research about the impact, scaling, and innovation potential of social procurement; gather more data for evidence-based policy making

Address the social value conundrum and encourage outcomes focus in commissioning

The social value challenge must be addressed both by public authorities and bidders in order for social procurement to spread. This includes defining and measuring social value in a consistent way.

What can public authorities do?

First of all, public authorities need to set their social and environmental goals and see a clear role for procurement in achieving them. Based on those goals outcomes strategies can be developed, which can serve as the basis of procurement plans. Central and regional governments can use their social objectives and corresponding strategies to determine the general direction for local authorities. Using the SDGs can lay common ground and offer a comprehensive framework for local and central government to collaborate. An increased outcomes focus instead of a prescriptive purchasing approach would encourage experimentation and pilots, and thus lead to further innovation. The example in Box 16.6 illustrates a consistent legislative and policy approach to integrating social value in procurement.

Box 16.6 Integrating social value in procurement

The **Public Services (Social Value) Act 2012 in the UK** applies to all procurements of services (also in combination with goods) that are subject to the public procurement regulation of 2015. It requires commissioners to consider including social value in all stages of the procurement process (Department for Digital, Culture, Media & Sport, 2018). The Act has been implemented by central government and local authorities alike, reflecting a commitment to outcomes in the commissioning practice at all levels.

Defining and measuring social value has been a challenge for both commissioners and suppliers. A wide range of support and tools have been made available by government, consultants, and other support organizations. One example is the Balanced Scorecard, intended to help commissioners balance economic criteria (lowest cost) and social considerations (Crown Commercial Service, 2016).

Several local authorities have developed their own outcomes strategies and corresponding commissioning frameworks (Kent County Council, 2014), ensuring that social procurement is not just an add-on, but serves broader strategic and policy goals. Research has confirmed that those local authorities that have a defined vision and a clear social value policy are more likely to also find appropriate ways to measure it (Social Enterprise UK, 2021). Unit cost databases price and measure social value and public authorities use them in their cost–benefit analysis

continued

Box 16.6 Continued

and commissioning. The database of the Greater Manchester Combined Authority (GMCA) contains 800 cost estimates in thematic areas such as crime, health, or housing, and is updated regularly (GMCA, n.d.).

The Social Value Act has been revised and evaluated several times, resulting in social value commissioning to be applied by all central government departments. The UK's exit from the EU led to further revisions, but the government intends to keep purpose alignment and social value inherent in procurement legislation. Stakeholders advocate for also retaining collaborative approaches such as the innovation partnerships.[a]

[a] Based on Government Outcomes Lab, University of Oxford, POGO Club online discussion 25 January 2022, available at https://golab.bsg.ox.ac.uk/community/events/transforming-public-procurement/

Second, in addition to the strategic level, central or regional government should also support local authorities with guidance, capacity building, and tools, so that they can operationalize social impact goals and set up systems to monitor and measure outcomes (see example of the Victoria State Government in Australia in Box 16.7). The possibility of creating an SDG Action Manager (https://www.unglobalcompact.org/take-action/sdg-action-manager) type tool for the public sector should be explored, with the purpose of encouraging governments and public authorities to embrace the framework.

Third, where appropriate, public authorities could pilot outcome-based procurement and involve payments by third party funders (e.g. Social Impact Bonds). SIBs demand that players jointly formulate and agree on outcomes, social impact goals, and measurement. SIBs merge two main requirements: providing appropriate finance for impact-driven enterprises *and* funding impact-oriented procurement (social procurement) that engages social economy suppliers. Consistency of approach is fundamental; governments making changes mid-term or at an election can impact social value measurement and the overall evaluation of the success of the project.

Box 16.7 Defining social outcomes and building capacity

In **Australia, the Victoria State Government** has defined social procurement and expressed its commitment in a series of guidance documents. The *Key Concepts* guide contains the social procurement objectives and the corresponding expected outcomes in easy-to-understand language (Victoria State Government, 2018a, 2018b). The government also offers a range of guides and tools to help procurement officers understand social procurement goals and rules and assist in their implementation. These support tools go into details about the phases and technicalities of the procurement process in order to optimize their use. They suggest what type of outcome is achieved best in which phase of the process using which type of supplier. The *Key Concepts* guide suggests that social procurement outcomes can be divided into three categories of key focus areas: suppliers' attributes; social and sustainable[a] business practices; and social and sustainable outcomes. The first category refers to a direct and indirect approach. The direct approach prioritizes purchasing goods and services from social benefit suppliers, which includes social enterprises. The indirect approach means procurement from mainstream suppliers and applying social clauses in the tenders, or requiring mainstream suppliers to include social benefit suppliers as subcontractors. The Victoria State Government has also put a number of tools and a Document Library in the public domain, enlisting guidance notes, case studies, and templates.

[a] Social and sustainable procurement have a separate set of objectives, but are handled together in terms of the key focus areas.

Improve the implementation of social procurement provisions

The social procurement toolkit is sufficiently varied and comprehensive; legislation has provided procurement officers with a wide range of options for inserting social considerations. We suggest that currently there is no need for more legislation, but rather a requirement for further understanding and promotion of the concept of social procurement. Success now depends on whether the right instrument (provision) is used for the right social goal in the right phase of the procurement process and the right providers are engaged. Procurement officers should be supported to get the best combination. This requires that social procurement be viewed as an investment in, for example, social services rather than a procedure to purchase them (Social Finance, 2014); an investment in people, knowledge, and long-term thinking.

What can public authorities do?

Interests and incentives

Most importantly, public authorities should work on aligning the interests of their various departments and at various levels (central versus local). They could set up permanent working groups or thematic task forces centred on specific social issues, whose continuous dialogue would help articulate and align the interests of key actors in public administration. Social procurement strategies could be harmonized with social enterprise development strategies and other government programmes that target social issues of priority. This could also reduce the fragmentation of procurement and service provision.

Second, procurement officers should go beyond short-term thinking motivated by budgets and lowest price. They can use a range of tools, for example life-cycle cost assessment, that could better align social value and economic efficiency by showing the long-term costs and gains of a purchase.

Third, public authorities should build the capacity of commissioners by further training in order to develop their understanding of social procurement rules, legal background, and implications. This could be offered in-house or be purchased from specialized organizations.

Fourth, training and knowledge about social economy enterprises would help increase the willingness of public sector staff to engage and collaborate with them. Such training courses are often available from capacity-building organizations or social enterprise support networks under collaboration schemes with local authorities, or increasingly in the form of university degree programmes on social economy.

Finally, existing procurement tools and guidelines should be shared, translated, or new ones developed. Government procurement portals or knowledge centres could house tools, guides, case studies, and other training material. Procurement resource centres can also be run by intermediary organizations that can work with all parties and often provide training as well.

Collaboration

Public authorities should move towards collaborative, partnership-based procurement, rather than continuing to use the transactional approach. Central and local procurement bodies should be encouraged to collaborate with industry bodies, organizations of procurement professionals, and chambers of commerce, all of whom could give them professional support and training, and play the role of intermediary towards suppliers. Collaboration and joint development of tenders with potential suppliers is an option that is offered in EU procurement rules and commissioners should use them more widely. Innovation partnerships are structured collaborations that could be set up under the 'light regime' for social and health services. Pre-market consultation allows commissioners to better understand what the needs are, as well as what suppliers can offer, before they draw up a tender document. 'Public procurement does not start when the invitation to tender is published' (Murray, 2020).

Procurement officers should work more with intermediaries of the social economy, for example social enterprise networks or community organizations. They offer a number of services and capacities that commissioners lack, and can also assist social economy enterprises. Intermediaries should not just be understood as organizations; electronic databases, online directories, and matching platforms could also help build and mediate relationships.

Localism

Social procurement at local and regional level should receive more attention and focus. Cities and regional public authorities have been the pioneers in introducing social procurement and creating workable solutions. Central governments could collaborate with local public authorities to test new models and disseminate success stories. Various regional and European organizations of local authorities (e.g. the Council of European Municipalities and Regions (CEMR))[15] and financing facilities (e.g. Interreg[16]) could strengthen and fund such collaborative efforts.

Local authorities should be supported to work with their entire toolbox to achieve desired outcomes: public procurement is only one of many tools. Some social services of general interest are not economic in nature; therefore they are not governed by the Public Procurement Directive, so grants or negotiated procedures can be used instead. Procurement processes in their conventional form can be effective when purchasing tried and tested services with pre-defined output indicators from a range of known providers. When public authorities, however, are seeking new solutions for outcomes, and wish to encourage pilots and innovation, they should remain open-minded about all delivery options including the use of grants, negotiated procedures, innovation partnerships, or reverse procurement, as shown in the Bologna example in Box 16.3.

Experimentation

Piloting and experimentation should be encouraged. Public authorities could launch small-sized tenders in social impact areas they would like to learn more about. Pilot procurement would allow them to use social procurement provisions in a flexible manner to learn more about needs, available suppliers, possible models, measurement of results, and final outcomes. Successful pilots could be proposed to scale through public procurement (see Box 16.8). Such pilots need not burden procurement budgets; they could be creatively funded from more flexible sources, such as the European Social Fund or other social innovation facilities.

Box 16.8 Scaling innovation through procurement

Hackney Community Transport in London was founded in 1982 when around 30 local community groups pooled their vehicle resources to provide low-cost minibuses to help their community become more mobile. It is now the core of the wider HCT Group, an award-winning transport social enterprise providing more than 30 million passenger bus trips a year, including London red buses. The contracts with local councils in London, the State of Jersey, and Bristol offered the social enterprise opportunities to scale its innovation. HCT runs public transport for public benefit not private profit, provide jobs for long-term unemployed people, and focus growth in areas of high economic deprivation. HCT has demonstrated to commissioners that the best way to be a sustainable social enterprise is to be an effective enterprise and has grown at an average of 24% a year for 20 years. It offers commissioners a genuine

continued

---

[15] https://www.ccre.org/en/article/introducing_cemr
[16] https://www.interregeurope.eu/about-us/2021-2027/

Box 16.8 Continued

---

partnership aiming to improve services for communities and tackle social exclusion and isolation by community transport. Struck by the COVID-19 pandemic, the social enterprise, however, went out of business in 2022.[a]

[a] See: https://www.route-one.net/news/hct-group-ceases-trading-and-enters-administration/

Strengthen the social economy ecosystem

The third group of measures addresses the challenges and opportunities in procurement indirectly, through strengthening the relevant actors and parts of the social economy ecosystem. While ecosystem building is the joint responsibility of most stakeholders, governments and public authorities play a key role in setting up an institutional and support framework.

What can public authorities do?

First, public authorities could require a label or certificate to verify that bidders meet the social or quality requirements of public procurement. A certification system could directly enhance social procurement in this way. Certification is one of the institutional policies that aim to increase the awareness and recognition of social economy enterprises by government (CIRIEC, 2017) and society as a whole. A social enterprise mark, for example, could address the lack of a specific legal form or law on social economy enterprises. We do not recommend the introduction of a specific legal form of social enterprise for the purpose of public procurement, as such legal forms inevitably exclude many types and forms of social businesses who could be potential suppliers. Instead, a certification by the key characteristics of social enterprise can be a workable and more effective alternative.

Certification schemes can be created and run by government or independent private bodies, whose certificates in turn should be recognized widely (see Box 16.9). Certification can be a successful measure, as long as it is based on market demand and recognition. A label is useless, if it does not bring benefits to enterprises (for example eligibility for or higher scores in public procurement). On the other hand, if certified enterprises do not reach a critical mass and visibility, the label will remain unknown and procurers will be reluctant to take it into account.

Box 16.9 Use of labels

A 2021 white paper published by Public Sector Network in Australia makes the case for using the B Corp certificate[a] in order to create more social value through public procurement. The core of the B Corp certification is the B Impact Assessment, which measures companies in five impact areas: governance, workers, community, environment, and customers. The paper argues that B Corporations offer products and services that governments want to buy, and that the certificate can give confidence to public sector commissioners regarding the environmental and social standards and outcomes of these companies (Public Sector Network, 2021).

In Latvia, the social enterprise legal status allows social enterprises to participate in public procurement with social clauses or reserved contracts. Unfortunately, due to the small number of organizations with social enterprise status, these social clauses have not been widely used (Friedenberga, 2019).

In Estonia, a quality 'label' based on the European Voluntary Quality Framework for social services succeeded to become one of the criteria for the funding of social services. It was developed and implemented jointly by private and public entities using European Social Funds funding (Social Platform, 2015).

[a] B Corp certificates are provided under the auspices of B Lab, a global non-profit organization founded with the belief that business can be used as a force for good. https://www.bcorporation.net/en-us/

Second, public authorities can support social enterprise capacity building. According to CIRIEC's typology of social enterprise development policies, the provision of finance or capacity building are supply-side measures aiming to develop enterprise capacity and increase competitiveness (CIRIEC, 2017). This can be directly relevant to social procurement by addressing the gaps in competencies and financial resources (as mentioned previously in the chapter). Public authorities could also incentivize other stakeholders (e.g. banks, social investment funds for finance, and training organizations or universities for skills) to offer the missing skills or financial resources to social economy enterprises. Funding programmes for social enterprise support organizations or social innovation centres could be relevant mechanisms for offering such incentives.

Third, public policy could also aim to foster collaboration among actors in the ecosystem to improve social economy's chances to successfully participate in public procurement in the long run. Collaboration can take place between any combination of stakeholders with government being an active participant or remaining in the background as a resource provider for the collaborative effort. Collaboration can start by developing a joint understanding of the state of the ecosystem using assessment tools (see Box 16.10).

Box 16.10 Ecosystem assessment

The Better Entrepreneurship Policy Tool (https://betterentrepreneurship.eu/) can be a good first step to gauge the existence or need for ecosystem support policies,

continued

Box 16.10 Continued

---

as well as establish a baseline for public procurement. The tool was developed jointly by the EU and the OECD for the assessment of the social enterprise ecosystem in a territory, using seven dimensions (social entrepreneurship culture, institutional and regulatory frameworks, access to markets and finance, impact, skills, and business development support), and to provide a baseline for policy planning and design. The access to markets dimension includes public sector markets as well, and as such is directly relevant for public procurement.

Future research

Currently, there is only limited written discussion and analysis available about the effectiveness of and social impact delivered by social procurement. Most of the related publications so far have been guides and case studies aimed to help public authorities and commissioners understand, interpret, and implement regulation. Another set of case studies focuses on initiatives and solutions that encourage stakeholders to use social procurement and to collaborate.

In order to move beyond the promotion and education phase, more research and analysis is needed about the impact of social procurement as an effective procurement approach and policy tool on the one hand, and its impact on social economy enterprises (their sustainability and social impact) on the other. This exploration should include the long-term social impact and the unintended consequences of social procurement in order to determine to what extent it delivers social value, and to whom. The perspectives of all stakeholders need to be taken into account: commissioners, beneficiary groups, and their wider communities, as well as suppliers, be they private companies or social economy enterprises.

Pressure to scale successful solutions to social problems is higher than ever. Thus another important research question is whether public procurement is an effective avenue for scaling impact. Can small-scale solutions be successfully scaled? Are the social clauses in procurement effective in mainstreaming social considerations? Outcomes-based public procurement or specific instruments, such as innovation partnerships in social procurement can encourage innovative solutions; so another important question for research is whether they do. And following on from successful innovation, can public procurement be used to scale innovation by social economy enterprises, and do they have the desire or wherewithal to scale?

Evidence and data availability is a challenge. In the past 5–6 years plenty of case studies have showcased good practices in member states that had pioneered the socially responsible approach in procurement, while in other countries very little is available. This points to a need to provide and analyse more data on social procurement cases, particularly the level of engagement and success of social economy enterprises. In addition to data and statistics, there is also a need for qualitative information that explores not only the commissioner's experience, but also those of the social economy enterprises, their clients, and beneficiaries.

Conclusion

Social procurement can promote social problem solving and be a useful lever to increase social and environmental orientation in all types of organizations in the public as well as the private sector. It can work through a wide range of provisions defined by legislation in the EU and around the world (social clauses, reserved contracts, pre-market consultations, and light regimes for social service).

Socially responsible public procurement has the potential to deliver on social goals when it is implemented, when the social goals are clearly set and social value is measured over defined time periods. The most successful procurement cases are those that find the right combination of key elements to achieve their social impact goal. Mastering the technical side of the process is very important for efficiency and transparency, but it is not sufficient without clearly stating the expected social outcomes and impact. There are numerous guides, tools, and templates that can help public procurement officers put the pieces of the puzzle together. In the future more support is necessary in the form of training, skill building, and sharing of good and bad practices in the technical area as well as social value measurement.

Thanks to the special provisions, social procurement has become a policy tool that can also benefit social economy enterprises specifically by allowing them to participate in the provision of goods or services to the public sector, and thus to strengthen their sustainability and further their social mission. This can be done in various forms: directly or by subcontracting with other bidders or in a collaborative procurement setup. Collaboration and partnerships are becoming a central theme. An increasing number of examples demonstrate that joint procurement models can produce more effective outcomes, more innovative solutions, and long-term commitment based on the mutual trust of collaborating partners.

Finally, for social procurement to succeed, it needs to be implemented in the context of and together with other policy measures that help the social economy meet the challenges raised by procurement processes. Building the financial and enterprise capacity of social economy enterprises is essential, so they can successfully bid for and implement public sector contracts. Ecosystem development is important in order to build a culture where social economy enterprises are recognized and have a level playing field to compete or collaborate with other actors. When in harmony with each other, public policies for the development of social economy and socially responsible public procurement can reinforce each other.

References

Barraket, J. (2019). The role of intermediaries in social innovation: the case of social procurement in Australia. *Journal of Social Entrepreneurship*, 11(2), 194–214. https://doi.org/10.1080/19420676.2019.1624272

Boffo, R., and Patalano R. (2020). *ESG Investing: Practices, Progress and Challenges*, OECD Paris. Available at: www.oecd.org/finance/ESG-Investing-Practices-Progress-and-Challenges.pdf

Borzaga C. (2020). *Social Enterprises and Their Ecosystems in Europe. Updated Country Report: Italy*. European Union. https://doi.org/10.2767/173023

British Council, Social Enterprise UK (2022). *More in Common: The Global State of Social Enterprise*. Available at: https://www.britishcouncil.org/sites/default/files/more_in_common_global_state_of_social_enterprise.pdf

Buy Social Canada (2022, 6 January). *Social Procurement Solutions for 2022: Growing the Movement of Community Capital Creators*, retrieved on March 29, 2022: https://www.buysocialcanada.com/posts/update/social-procurement-solutions-for-2022/

Buy Social Scotland (n.d.). *B2B Directory*. Available at: https://www.buysocialscotland.com/business/homepage

Caimi, V. (2020). *Buying for Social Impact*. European Union. https://doi.org/10.2826/694344

Caimi, V., Daniele, D., Martignetti, L. (2019). *Buying for Social Impact: Good practice from around the EU*. European Union. https://doi.org/10.2826/8319

CIRIEC, International Centre of Research and Information on Public, Social and Cooperative Economy (2017). *Recent Evolutions of the Social Economy in the European Union*. European Economic and Social Committee, European Union. https://doi.org/10.2864/255713

CIRIEC, International Centre of Research and Information on Public, Social and Cooperative Economy (2018). *Best Practices in Public Policies regarding the European Social Economy post the Economic Crisis*, Authors: Rafael Chavez Avila and Jose Luis Monzon. European Economic and Social Committee. https://doi.org/10.2864/557903

Crown Commercial Service (2016, 14 October). *Procuring Growth, Balanced Scorecard*. Available at: https://www.gov.uk/government/publications/procurement-policy-note-0916-procuring-for-growth-balanced-scorecard

Department for Digital, Culture, Media & Sport (2018). *The Public Services (Social Value) Act 2012: An Introductory Guide for Commissioners and Policy Makers*. Department for Digital, Culture, Media & Sport (UK). Available at: http://www.gov.uk/dcms

Etica Funds (2020, 3 July). *Social Washing: What Is It and Why Could Covid-19 Be Making It Worse?* Available at: https://www.eticasgr.com/en/storie/insights/social-washing

Euclid Network (May 2021). *European Social Enterprise Monitor Report 2020–2021*. Available at: https://knowledgecentre.euclidnetwork.eu/2021/05/25/european-social-enterprise-monitor-report-2020-2021/

European Commission (2011). *Communication from the Commission to the European Parliament, the Council, the European Economic and Social Committee and the Committee of the Regions. Social Business Initiative: Creating a Favourable Climate for Social Enterprises, Key Stakeholders in the Social Economy and Innovation.* European Commission. Available at: https://eur-lex.europa.eu/legal-content/EN/TXT/?uri=CELEX%3A52011DC0682

European Commission (2016)., *EU Public Procurement reform: Less bureaucracy, higher efficiency. An overview of the new EU procurement and concession rules introduced on 18 April 2016,* European Union, retrieved on March 29, 2022 from https://ec.europa.eu/growth/single-market/public-procurement/legal-rules-and-implementation_en

European Commission (2018). *Public Procurement Guide for Practitioners.* European Union. Available at: https://ec.europa.eu/regional_policy/en/information/publications/guidelines/2018/public-procurement-guidance-for-practitioners-2018

European Commission (2021). *Buying Social: A Guide to Taking Account of Social Considerations in Public Procurement* (2nd ed.). Commission Note, European Union. Available at: https://ec.europa.eu/docsroom/documents/45767

European Commission (n.d.). *Internal Market, Industry, Entrepreneurship and SMEs: Public Procurement.* Retrieved 29 March 2022 from https://single-market-economy.ec.europa.eu/single-market/public-procurement_en

European Investment Advisory Hub (2019, 16 April). *Potential of Scaling Social Outcomes Contracts: Sustainability Bonds with Impact Linked Return,* Draft public report, European Investment Bank. Available at: https://eiah.eib.org/publications/attachments/potential-scaling-social-outcomes-report-en.pdf

European Union (2015). *User Guide to the SME Definition.* European Union. https://doi.org/10.2873/782201

Fox-Martin, A. (2020, 5 October). *Social Procurement: Finding a Better Way to Grow.* SAP News Center. Available at: https://news.sap.com/2020/10/social-procurement-better-way-grow/

Friedenberga, A. (2019). *Ten Years Informally, One Year Formally. How Are Social Enterprises Doing in Latvia?* Peer Country Comments Paper Latvia, Peer Review on Social Economy and Social Enterprise in Legislation and Practice, Slovakia, 20–21 June, 2019. European Union. Available at: https://ec.europa.eu/social/main.jsp?langId=en&catId=1047&furtherNews=yes&newsId=9365

Furneaux, C., & Barraket, J. (2014). Purchasing social good(s): a definition and typology of social procurement. *Public Money and Management, 34*(4), 265–272. https://doi.org/10.1080/09540962.2014.920199

Future Generations Commissioners for Wales (n.d.). *Well-being of Future Generations (Wales) Act 2015.* Available at: https://www.futuregenerations.wales/

Greater Manchester Combined Authority, GMCA (n.d.). Cost Benefit Analysis, retrieved on March 30, 2022 from: https://www.greatermanchester-ca.gov.uk/what-we-do/research/research-cost-benefit-analysis/

Halloran, D. (2017). The Social Value in Social Clauses: Methods of Measuring and Evaluation in Social Procurement. In K. V. Thai (Ed.), *Global Public Procurement Theories and Practices* (pp. 39–58). Cham: Springer International Publishing. https://doi.org/10.1007/978-3-319-49280-3_3

Jones, N., & Yeo, A. (2017). *Community Business and the Social Value Act.* Research Institute Report No. 8, Power to Change.

Kent County Council (2014). *A Commissioning Framework for Kent County Council: Delivering Better Outcomes for Kent Residents through Improved Commissioning.* Kent County Council. Available at: https://www.kent.gov.uk/about-the-council/strategies-and-policies/corporate-policies/commissioning-framework

Lewis, I. (2022, 1 February). 'Buy Social Europe' encourages multinationals to buy from social enterprises. *Impact Investor.* https://impact-investor.com/buy-social-europe-aims-to-encourage-multinationals-to-buy-from-social-enterprises/

Murray, S. (2020). *The Future of Public Spending.* The Economist Intelligence Unit. Available at: https://unops.economist.com/wp-content/uploads/2020/06/Thefutureofpublicspending_responsestocovid19.pdf

Nyssen, M., & Hybrechts, B. (2020), *Social Enterprises and Their Ecosystems in Europe. Country Report, Belgium.* European Union. https://doi.org/10.2767/663183

OECD (2020). *Social Economy and the COVID-19 Crisis: Current and Future Roles.* OECD. Available at: https://www.oecd.org/coronavirus/policy-responses/social-economy-and-the-covid-19-crisis-current-and-future-roles-f904b89f/

Public Sector Network (2021, 29 March). *Creating Social Value for Better Business: Increasing Procurement from Certified B Corporations.* Public Sector Network. Available at: https://publicsectornetwork.co/insight/creating-social-value-through-government-procurement/

Scottish Community Alliance (2022, 7 February). *Bologna Commons,* https://scottishcommunityalliance.org.uk/2022/02/07/bologna-commons/

Scottish Government (2016). *Scotland's Social Enterprise Strategy 2016–2026.* Available at: https://www.gov.scot/publications/scotlands-social-enterprise-strategy-2016-2026/

Social Economy Europe (2018). *The Future of EU Policies for Social Economy: Towards a European Action Plan.* Social Economy Europe. Available at: http://www.socioeco.org/bdf_fiche-document-6381_en.html

Social Enterprise UK (2021). *Buy Social Corporate Challenge, Year 5 Impact Report.* Social Enterprise UK. Available at: https://www.socialenterprise.org.uk/seuk-impact-reports-annual-reviews/buy-social-corporate-challenge-year-5-impact-report/

Social Finance (2014). *Recommendations on Procurement. A report on the issues of public sector procurement and the impact for social investment.* London: The UK National Advisory Board to The Social Impact Investment Taskforce Established under the UK's Presidency of the G8.

Social Finance (2018, 7 February), *Outcomes Fund Note*, Social Finance Outcomes Fund Note. Available at: https://www.socialfinance.org.uk/assets/documents/outcomes-fund-note.pdf

Social Platform (2015). *Public Procurement for Social Progress: A Social Platform Guide to the EU Public Procurement Directive*, Social Platform. Available at: https://www.socialplatform.org/wp-content/uploads/2015/10/Public_procurement_for_social_progress.pdf

Social Value (n.d.), Social Value - Integrating social benefts into public contracts. Available at: https://socialvalueni.org/

Tepper, P., McLennan, A., Hirt, R., Defranceschi, P., Caimi, V., & Elu, A. (2020). *Making Socially Responsible Public Procurement Work. 71 Good Practice Cases*. European Union. https://doi.org/10.2826/844552

Troje, D., & Gluch, P. (2019). Populating the social realm: new roles arising from social procurement. *Construction Management and Economics*. https://doi.org/10.1080/01446193.2019.1597273

Troje, D., & Gluch, P. (2020, 18 June). Beyond policies and social washing: how social procurement unfolds in practice. *Sustainability*. Available at: https://www.researchgate.net/publication/342298124_Beyond_Policies_and_Social_Washing_How_Social_Procurement_Unfolds_in_Practice

University of Oxford Government Outcomes Lab (n.d.). *Impact Bonds*. Available at: https://golab.bsg.ox.ac.uk/the-basics/outcomesfunds/

Van den Abeele, E. (2014), *Integrating Social and Environmental Dimensions in Public Procurement: One Small Step for the Internal Market, One Giant Leap for the EU? Working Paper 2014.8*. European Trade Union Institute. ISSN 1994-4446.

Victoria State Government (2018a). *Victoria's Social Procurement Framework: Buyer Guidance Guide to Evaluation*. The State of Victoria. ISBN 978-1-925551-08-2.

Victoria State Government (2018b). *Victoria's Social Procurement Case Studies and Highlights*. The State of Victoria. ISBN 978-1-925551-06-8.

Welsh Government (March 2021). *Wales Procurement Policy Statement*. Available at: https://gov.wales/wales-procurement-policy-statement

Young, J. (2020). What is Procurement? *Investopedia*. Available at: https://www.investopedia.com/terms/p/procurement.asp

17
Social outcomes contracting

Seeding a more relational approach to contracts between government and the social economy?

Eleanor Carter and Nigel Ball

Introduction: grand challenges and the call for partnership

Grand challenges faced by society are perennial and ever-present in public media discourse: refugee crises, climate-change induced instability, poverty, and poor educational outcomes remain stubbornly persistent in the face of technological, economic, and social progress (George et al., 2016). In the face of such challenges, any expectation that the unilateral action of government can bring about a fix appears naive. There is growing acknowledgement that the necessary resources (i.e., expertise, money, information, community engagement) required to tackle such pernicious challenges are divided among different organizations. Moreover, the necessary means are further fragmented across sectors—public, private, and social. A coming together of resources and know-how is therefore seen to be necessary to respond to such social problems. These co-dependencies thus lead to increasing calls for interaction and cooperation.

Indeed, government partnership with private and social sectors has a long pedigree (Hodge & Greve, 2005). The relevance of social economy actors is key. These are a diffuse and multifarious constellation of entities (without a universally accepted definition) whose purpose is understood to be animated by positive social, societal, or environmental impacts (Krlev et al., 2021). But there is an imperfect history of government engagement with the social sector. Descriptions of the social economy often highlight its *hybrid* characteristics, embodied in organizational forms such as social enterprises (Heins & Bennett, 2016). But the potential of the social economy also comes through its perceived collaborative ethos and ability to bring purposeful cooperation to the heart of cross-sector interactions. In this mode of working, traditional, bureaucratic, and hierarchical modes of control are seen to be less relevant and horizontal relations more salient (Brummel, 2021; Van Ham & Koppenjan, 2001).

Eleanor Carter and Nigel Ball, *Social outcomes contracting*. In: *Social Economy Science*. Edited by: Gorgi Krlev, Dominika Wruk, Giulio Pasi, and Marika Bernhard, Oxford University Press. © Oxford University Press (2023). DOI: 10.1093/oso/9780192868343.003.0017

There has been a trend in many developed economies over the past four decades towards outsourcing many government functions (Alonso et al., 2015). This has led to a more prominent role for social economy actors but has also brought tensions, with observers ruing the lack of mutuality under transactional 'contract culture' (Morris, 1999; Wright, 2022). An appetite to shift from 'contractors for' to 'partners with' the public sector is detected in recent practitioner guides (see e.g. Collaborate Foundation, 2018). Recent trends in practice emphasize how partners' goals are aligned and the importance of maintaining a more equitable relationship between the parties (Ball, 2020). The influential 'collective impact' approach advanced by John Kania and colleagues (2022; 2011) emphasizes that partners should develop a shared agenda, mutually reinforcing activities, and continuous communication. Similar approaches in the private sector have been dubbed 'formal relational' contracts (Frydlinger et al., 2019).

This chapter explores the degree to which 'formal relational contracting', as theorized through scholarly research on private sector contracting, is being witnessed in the social economy. Contracting instruments that aim to make service providers accountable for end results, rather than for compliance to a pre-defined specification, have proved to be a fertile space for experimentation and learning. These so-called payment-by-results contracts are hugely varied in their form and intention, and many reinforce rather than temper transactional attitudes (Carter, 2019). Yet this need not always be the case. The most recent incarnation of such contracts in the social economy is the outcome-based contract, which positions service user *social outcomes* as the objective rather than the service itself. This may provide a route to relational working. We look at the case of a social impact bond, which is a specific form of outcome-based contract, and contrast this with an alliance contract, which relies on an alternative, principle-led form of contractual accountability. We go on to analyse the enablers and barriers to these practices within government and the social economy, where 'business as usual' transactional approaches by government have left citizens with poor social outcomes. We conclude by outlining what is needed to move forward: greater attention in government to contract management (rather than just contract award), and a verifiable commitment to purpose-driven practice among provider organizations.

Understanding the direction of travel: moving away from transactional towards relational?

The limitations of taking a very 'transactional' approach to the buying and selling of goods and services have been widely discussed in the economic literature, especially as they relate to free market exchange. These challenges are particularly pronounced for complex services where it may be difficult to specify upfront exactly what is being bought; for example, where there is a requirement for innovation, or if the need that is to be met is mutable and likely to evolve during contract delivery (Brown et al., 2013). Over time the field of sellers in the market for such goods and services may narrow, as delivery expertise becomes consolidated to a few specialist organizations who in turn come to rely on the custom of a few buyers (Girth et al., 2012; Williamson, 1975).

Studies of such complex contracts in the private sector have revealed that the requirements of traditional transactional contracts lead to frustration on both sides (Frydlinger et al., 2019, 2021). The requirement for a detailed upfront specification becomes less suitable as time goes on, as parties do not have the flexibility required to adapt to changing circumstances and pursue potential improvements. Frictions and shading (cutting quality, withholding cooperation, or 'working to rule' by adhering to the terms of the contract but offering nothing more) may occur, undermining value (Hart & Moore, 2008). In the worst case, there is a 'hold-up' or conflict during the delivery of the contract.

The antidote, according to a pioneering group of scholars and practitioners including David Frydlinger, Kate Vitasek, Jim Bergman, Tim Cummins, and Oliver Hart, is formal relational contracting (Frydlinger et al., 2019, 2021). The framework shown in Figure 17.1 demonstrates why such contracts might better suit the provision of so-called complex goods and services, where innovation and adaptability are essential. The authors identify variability across five dimensions: the focus, the relationship, social norms, risk management, and planning. In Figure 17.1 we augment these dimensions with a consideration of strategic and operational aims to more explicitly link to issues of concern in the social economy (discussed further below). A traditional 'transactional' contract (left-hand portion of Figure 17.1) is arm's-length, uses powers of enforcement as levers of contract compliance, and aims to perfectly anticipate all possible eventualities. A formal relational contract, by contrast, puts the relationship between the parties at the centre. There is an explicit focus on the social norms expected during contract performance, which provides the basis for a constant re-alignment of interests as a way to manage risks to either party, even as circumstances evolve. There is still much debate about how enforceable such contracts are—and therefore whether they truly meet a contract's fundamental requirement to offer parties protection and redress.

So far formal relational contracting has mainly been understood through studies of the private sector, but the ideas may apply in the social economy too. Transactional approaches are inimical to social organizations' ability to forge co-operative relationships and adapt practices as circumstances evolve, due to their tendency to entrench power imbalances and their rigidity. Relational practices, by contrast, seem to align well with the perceived unique value of the social economy, which is purpose-driven and often familiar with the complexity inherent in addressing grand challenges such as poverty and social disadvantage.

Some elements of relational contracting as understood in the private sector can already be distinctively recognized in the social economy, where they are often understood through the lens of 'partnership'. Van Ham and Koppenjan make reference to the longevity or the 'durability' of cooperation and the extent to which partners 'jointly develop products and services and share risks, costs and resources' (Van Ham & Koppenjan, 2001, p. 598). Hodge and Greve (2005, p. 4) foreshadow the 'co-design and commissioning' trend by defining partnerships in terms of the unexpected cross-sectoral synergies they create, as a form of cooperation that 'result[s] in some

	Transactional contract →	← Formal relational contract
Focus	The commercial transaction	The relationship
Relationship	Arm's-length relationship	Partnership
Strategic aims	Deliver commercial contract	Purposeful, guided by shared mission
Operational aims	Buy in particular, bounded skills or capacity	Jointly improve social services, social inclusion or social outcomes
Social norms	Disconnect from social norms	Explicity includes social norms as contractual obligations
Risk management	Use of power and creation of enforceable contractual obligations	Risk avoidance by creation of continuous alignment of interests
Planning	Aims for complete planning, i.e., contract should cover all future contingencies	Creates a balanced, adaptable framework

Figure 17.1 Formal relational contracting in the social economy

Source: Adapted by the authors and informed by Frydlinger et al., 2021 (p. 94) and Scoppetta (2013)

new product or service that no one would have thought of if the public organizations and the private organizations had kept to themselves'. This definition is a clear departure from more typical, transactional modes of contracting between government and non-government actors, towards something more relational (see Brown et al., 2013).

There is often a suspicion that *partnership* is invoked as a shrewd rhetorical device. Critics are concerned that 'partnership' is invoked to add positive overtones to a statement about organizational relationships which might be at least partially unwelcome (privatization), or to make transactional relationships seem more acceptable when on closer inspection most people would not consider them to be a 'partnership' at all. Partnership rhetoric often masks the reality of hierarchically imposed relationships between principals and agents and within supply chains. This zero-sum transactionalism is particularly apparent in high-profile outsourcing failures such as the collapse of post-custody support for prison leavers under the 'Transforming Rehabilitation' programme in the UK (Carter & Ball, 2021).

The evidence suggests three clear features can be used to recognize genuine cross-sector partnership:

(a) Longevity and durability. Partnerships cannot reasonably take place in short-term arrangements.
(b) Emphasis on risk-sharing. Both (or perhaps better put, *all*) parties in a partnership come together on equal terms in the sense that both have to bear parts of the risks involved.
(c) Shared objective. 'True' partners share a joint sense of purpose and have clarity over shared objective and endeavour.

There is concern that conventional cross-sector outsourcing contracts are often deficient in these features and that the benefit of true partnership is stifled.

How then to develop and nurture durable, risk-sharing, purposeful cross-sector partnerships?

It is important to note that the evidence on the effectiveness of cross-sector partnership is often scant or non-existent (Petersen et al., 2018; Rees et al., 2012; Sanderson et al., 2018). The diversity of 'partnership' examples offered in studies and reviews, combined with the lack of detail on their implementation and a paucity of consistent and reliable information on their impact, makes it difficult to assess confidently and comprehensively what works, what does not work, and why. At best, 'the *prevalence of partnerships* in addressing certain types of . . . policy problems suggests that they are *perceived to be helpful* in augmenting existing processes' (Powers, 2017, p. 3, emphasis in original). The perceived value is seen to be particularly the case when private or social economy partners can contribute their specialist knowledge and expertise (for example, NGOs' expertise in supporting specific disadvantaged groups), but applies more generally when 'whole of community' partnerships can work across different policy and programme silos to better integrate services and to coordinate actions that support local economic development. Beyond this, however, 'despite a decade of attempts to evaluate partnership outcomes, the evidence of effectiveness is thin' (Rees et al., 2012, p. 1). It is therefore not possible to draw firm conclusions about what constitutes good practice on the basis of currently available reviews.

Despite the limited research dedicated to the longitudinal study of cross-sectoral partnership arrangements, pragmatic audiences keen to adopt new ways of working may still seek to pursue collaborative cross-sector partnerships. What tips are available for those considering how best to incorporate partnerships into their operations and strategy? In the absence of this information, the risk remains high of 'partnerships being more talk than action, as opposed to genuine collaborative working relationships on the ground' (OECD/IDB/WAPES, 2016, p. 73).

The aim is for partnerships to reach a developed state, capable of integrating the actions and policies of their members in a coherent and organic strategy designed to achieve a common set of objectives. To achieve this, Fadda (cited in Froy & Giguère, 2010, p. 21), suggests there is a need for a set of common goals, and a means of 'producing positive interactions and synergies' that will help to achieve them. For public bodies, who often have disproportionate power in a contracting relationship, this may mean they must 'forsake the simplicity of control for the complexity of influence' (Shergold, 2008 in Powers, 2017, p. 47). Does outcomes-based contracting offer a route to defining common goals? Might it help to place partners on a more equal footing?

Outcomes-based contracting

Outcomes-based contracting is a canopy term beneath which better known phrases such as 'payment-by-results' and 'social outcomes contracting' sit. Under payment-by-results, contracted payment to providers is contingent on the demonstrable achievement of pre-specified output or outcome indicators. For example, an outcomes contract that aims to reduce unemployment may make payment contingent on the number of programme participants who find and sustain a job, rather than—as under more conventional contracting models—paying service providers for inputs or activities such as hiring trainers or delivering training workshops. This outcomes orientation means a precise and closely monitored service specification is not necessary, in theory promising provider flexibility, innovation, and performance improvement.

Such payment-by-results arrangements may *notionally* meet the tripartite definition of partnership set out above, since these contracts do tend to:

(a) be longer-term (i.e., multi-year) contracting arrangements;
(b) share risk, since providers will not be paid unless indicators of success are met, and delivery organizations therefore hold implementation and performance risks;
(c) secure a mutual interest in achieving indicators of success (as embodied in outcome metrics).

However, in reality, much payment-by-results practice is recognized to be a conventional 'lowest-cost-wins' outsourcing exercise and is highly transactional (see Varga & Hayday, this volume). This certainly holds for the most notorious such programme in the UK, a welfare-to-work scheme where large private sector 'prime contractors' were only paid following the achievement of sustained employment outcomes for programme participants (Carter & Whitworth, 2015).

One reason for this shortcoming is that *in practice*, payment-by-results schemes carry a well-known risk of providers opportunistically taking advantage of their knowledge of the on-the-ground situation to increase their revenue under the contract. Such practices have come to be labelled with a curious mix of dairy and motoring metaphors: creaming; parking; churning. Unscrupulous providers might 'cream' the easy cases, 'park' people who are perceived as more challenging to support, and 'churn' the same users through the programme to claim payment repeatedly. Such moral hazard is well established in contract theory and is not unique to payment-by-results (Holmström, 1979), but may be exacerbated by the use of such contracting techniques due to their deliberate lack of detailed service specification and any monitoring thereof. International literature makes clear that the design specificities of programme governance and accountabilities can play a key role in either facilitating or buttressing against these negative provider practices. Scholarship records the crucial but enormously challenging and largely trial-and-error process of programme design that attempts to effectively guard against gaming (Carter & Whitworth, 2015; Finn, 2009; O'Sullivan et al., 2021; Struyven & Steurs, 2005). The design options to manage potential gaming practices are summarized in previous work by Carter and Whitworth (2015). The contracting authority within government might attempt to segment the target population and ask providers to offer different services or payments according to different needs. Or they might attempt to reward progress towards outcomes, not just final outcomes, by offering mid-point 'milestone' payments. Other techniques have included empowering service users themselves to choose between services, and sometimes helping participants to make such choices by providing quality ratings.

Impact bonds and alliance contracts: emerging cases of formal relational contracting in the social economy?

Despite the well-documented setbacks of payment-by-results contracting, emerging evidence from our own research suggests that an outcomes contract allied to a more relational contracting approach might indeed enable the emergence of a true cross-sector partnership that is durable, risk-sharing, and focused on shared goals. One of the more recently developed payment-by-results instruments is the social impact bond, or SIB (also referred to as 'social outcomes contract' or 'pay for success', in reference to the underlying contractual mechanism used). A SIB adds to the traditional bilateral payment-by-results contract by introducing upfront repayable finance provided by a third party, the repayment of which is (at least partially) conditional on achieving specified outcomes (see Carter, 2020 for discussion). A SIB is a three-way relationship between a government commissioner, a service provider, and a social investor. In its most basic form, the commissioner specifies the outcomes to be achieved and paid for; the service provider delivers activities alongside service users to try to achieve these objectives, and social investors provide financing to enable these services to be set up and potentially to bear some of the risk that outcomes are not achieved (see Figure 17.2 and Disley et al., 2016; Fraser, Tan, Lagarde, et al., 2018).

The initial proponents of SIBs optimistically described the model as a 'win-win-win' arrangement wherein socially motivated investors can achieve social and financial returns while service providers receive the necessary funds to scale up existing work and government purchasers only pay for successful programming (Fraser, Tan, Lagarde, et al., 2018). One of the challenges in evaluating and critically appraising the tool is the varied application and justification attached to the experimentation with the SIB model in different national contexts over time (Tan et al., 2021). In part, the varied promises of impact bonds stem from the varied stakeholder perspectives and it is notable that the model is not always investigated through the lens of cross-sector partnership, but may be linked to social enterprise and innovation financing (see Carter & Anastasiu, 2023; Krlev et al., 2022).

Across the world, the adoption of impact bonds has become increasingly common. There are now (at mid-2022) 250 impact bond projects and the model is being used to tackle a range of pernicious social issues including unemployment, poor education outcomes, mental health, poverty reduction, and environmental protection (Government Outcomes Lab, n.d.). Figure 17.3 describes the cumulative adoption of impact bonds across Europe. Over the decade since the introduction of the first impact bond, the tool has been applied with increasing frequency: twenty-five impact

	Payment structure *The degree to which public sector stipulates provider activity*	Intervention risk *The location of risk that chosen intervention does not produce social outcomes as intended*	Market access *Degree to which contract form preferences particular provider types*	Evidence availability *Likely insights on programme performance*
Fee for Service	Activities are highly specified by government and payment is related to fixed processes or outputs	Risk remains with government	Flexible, largely depends on size of contract	Generally limited and dependent on inspection regimes and commissioned evaluation
Payment-by-Results	Payment is linked to the achievement of measurable 'social outcomes' with minimal government prescription of services ('black box' commissioning)	Risk sits with (Prime) providers *(Although may return to Government in the case of large-scale failure)*	Historically, due to Prime contracting structure and turnover stipulations has preferred large, private sector providers	Good understanding of performance against 'paid for' social outcomes; Challenge of getting 'inside' the black box
Social Impact Bond (SIB)	Payment is linked to the achievement of measurable 'social outcomes' though commissioner may specify a particular intervention	Risk sits with dedicated social investors (or may be shared between investors and service providers)	Typically prioritises social economy providers. The use of social investment and/or social Primes may facilitate involvement of smaller charities and social enterprises	Good understanding of performance against 'paid for' social outcomes; Perceived culture of learning and continual improvement. Some SIBs incorporate experimental or quasi-experimental impact evaluations within the payment mechanism (Economy et al., 2022)

Figure 17.2 A simplified illustration of alternative approaches for contracting public service

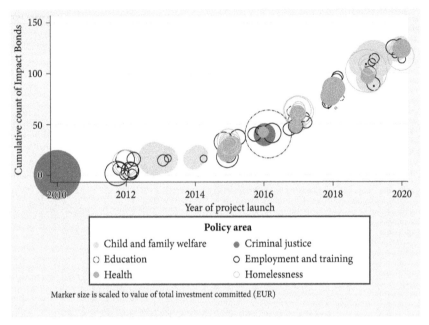

Figure 17.3 Adoption of Impact Bond projects across Europe
Source: Government Outcomes Lab, INDIGO Impact Bond Dataset

bond projects were launched in Europe in 2019. The coloured markers indicate the range of policy areas and show that employment and training and child and family welfare are the two most prevalent issue areas. The first project, launched in 2010, is the widely cited 'One Service' which aimed to reduce re-offending rates for 3,000 people released from Peterborough Prison, to which seventeen impact investors together committed £5 million (c. EUR 5.9 million; Social Finance, 2017).

In this visualization of European impact bonds, the size of the markers is scaled according to the value of the total investment committed to each project and here it is notable that there is little growth in the magnitude of the projects over time, with many still described as pilots. For example, the Spot Evora project (the smallest marker for 2018, with an investment value of EUR 50,000) was launched in Alentejo, Portugal and aims to support sixty young people who are disengaged with school by using motivational mentoring and gamification at school to improve educational outcomes. The largest project by investment size in 2019 is the Kirklees Better Outcomes Partnership and is discussed as a case study below.

Nascent scholarship on the implementation of impact bonds and outcomes-based contracts offers two important reflections. First, there is no typical or standardized arrangement underpinning these technically and operationally complex contracting structures (Arena et al., 2016; Heinrich & Kabourek, 2019); second, these multisector collaboration arrangements are not automatic constructs but need to be produced proactively through institutional work (Lowe et al., 2019). It is this link between institutional work at the inter-organizational level and formal relational contracting that we explore via two novel case studies which each seek to introduce cross-sector *partnership* working. The first case study (Kirklees Better Outcomes Partnership, see Box 17.1) explicitly introduces an outcomes-based contracting arrangement while the second case study (Plymouth Alliance, see Box 17.2) pursues a set of shared principles without an overt outcome-based model.

Box 17.1 Kirklees Better Outcomes Partnership

The Kirklees Better Outcomes Partnership (KBOP) offers an illustration of the promise of a genuine 'partnership' approach. An interim evaluation of the project carried out by our research group, the Government Outcomes Lab in Oxford, describes the challenges associated with the previous contracting arrangements, and a promising new SIB approach which shows emergent signals of more relational working (Rosenbach & Carter, 2021). Prior to the SIB, Kirklees council, in Yorkshire, UK, held 15 contracts with 9 different organizations to deliver services to adults who may need support to live independently. Participants may experience multiple, complex disadvantages, including homelessness or the immediate risk of becoming homeless, mental health or substance misuse issues, or experience of domestic violence or offending. These contracts were a legacy of a government funding programme that began in 2003 and were set up as fee-for-service contracts—in other words, a set of activities was specified, and these specifications are used to monitor delivery. By 2019, a combination of repeated cuts to the funding for this work (the dedicated central government funding for the programme ended in 2010) and a lack of attention to the continued suitability of the contracts had led to persistently poor outcomes for the people accessing these services.

Challenges manifested in four areas. First, the Council team which managed these contracts was severely constrained and limited resources were available for shaping services or for stewarding local delivery organizations to ensure a thriving market to buy from. Second, there was limited performance management and the legacy KPIs were seen to drive some perverse behaviours, such as evidencing throughput and competing for referrals rather than understanding long-term outcomes. Third, there was limited flexibility in the delivery of services, crimping providers' ability to respond with innovative, person-centred approaches. Fourth, there was limited collaboration across provider organizations, meaning service users had to tell their story multiple times with a lack of coordination that discouraged ongoing engagement.

In September 2019, Kirklees council launched a new service that responds to these challenges by remodelling the delivery of services under a single outcomes contract with the involvement of a new coordinating social prime contractor called Kirklees Better Outcomes Partnership. The 5-year outcomes contract enables participants to

continued

Box 17.1 Continued

pursue longer-term outcomes, most notably education, training, and employment (ETE) outcomes. In a pioneering approach, this outcomes contract incorporates learning and adjustment of the outcome measure design (i.e., a flexible rate card) as well as adaptive service delivery. Instead of specifying the length and intensity of 1:1 support to be provided to service users, the service aims to respond to participant aspirations using an asset-based approach. The service aims to facilitate a flexible, person-centred range of outcomes including sustained accommodation; education and qualifications; employment; volunteering; engagement with drug and alcohol services; stability and wellbeing. Instead of fixed fees, payment is linked to the achievement of these outcomes. Instead of being measured on throughput, the service is measured by pre-agreed standardised metrics. A streamlined referral process is enabled by a central intelligence system and by the social prime acting as a central referral hub. The coordination of this process means that participants are no longer sitting on multiple waiting lists. Framing the referral process as an asset-based conversation is intended to overcome known issues with a deficit model.

The shift to a responsive, asset-based approach coupled with an outcomes-focused governance model point towards features of relational contracting. Enhanced flexibility is of great value to the provider organizations who are faced with responding to a range of service user needs that cannot be accurately anticipated at contract launch. An enhanced emphasis on collaboration is anticipated to enable multiple providers to co-ordinate their offer around service users, working together as peers rather than seeking to separately serve the requirements of a remote commissioner.

It is too soon to say whether the new contracting arrangement fully overcomes the known challenges with the legacy services, although early outcomes achievement is promising (Rosenbach, 2022). The research and evaluation work in Kirklees is ongoing. Future analysis seeks to explore known tensions, particularly between the focus on measurable outcome metrics and person-centred practice at the frontline.

Box 17.2 Plymouth Alliance Contract: a principle-led approach to formal relational contracting

A social impact bond is not the only mechanism that might unlock genuine partnership working across sectors, and lead to relational contracting practice. A similar model of bringing multiple providers under a single contract to improve co-ordination has been tried in another UK local authority, Plymouth. Called the

Plymouth Alliance Contract, the council is attempting to address similar challenges to those in Kirklees, to serve a similar population of adults experiencing multiple disadvantage.

Launched in 2019 (the same year as Kirklees Better Outcome Partnership), the contract duration is up to 10 years. Seven providers joined the main contract, with multiple other providers sub-contracted. The CEOs of these providers, alongside three commissioners from the council, make up a 10-member joint decision-making body which controls the £7.7 million annual budget via a principle of unanimity. All the providers, and the council, signed up to a set of 'Alliance Principles' and while these are not strictly enforceable, they provide a reference for the relationships and source of trust-building between the parties (The Plymouth Alliance, n.d.). All members of the alliance commit to working to the following alliance principles:

- to assume collective responsibility for all of the risks involved in providing services under this Agreement;
- to make decisions on a 'Best for People using Services' basis;
- to commit to unanimous, principle and value based-decision making on all key issues;
- to adopt a culture of 'no fault, no blame' between the Alliance Participants and to seek to avoid all disputes and litigation (except in very limited cases of wilful default);
- to adopt open-book accounting and transparency in all matters;
- to appoint and select key roles on a best-person basis; and
- to act in accordance with the Alliance Values and Behaviours at all times.

These can be considered an example of the guiding principles, such as loyalty and equity, advocated by Frydlinger and others as a vessel for formal relational contracting (Frydlinger et al., 2019; Frydlinger & Hart, 2019).

The alliance contract took more than 4 years to negotiate: provider organizations started to collaborate operationally prior to the new contract launching. This led to a strengthening of relationships between provider organizations which provided a basis for the formal alliance contract. In fact, the only organization that has left the alliance since it launched in 2019 was one that joined at the last minute and did not participate in the multi-year relationship-building period, and became uncomfortable with adhering to the financial principles (Ball & Gibson, 2022).

On the surface, the Plymouth Alliance Contract appears to meet the three-part definition of partnership, just as the Kirklees project does, via longevity and durability, emphasis on risk-sharing, and shared objectives. The lengthy set-up period already attests to longevity and durability, as does the 10-year duration

continued

Box 17.2 Continued

of the contract itself. The second part, emphasis on risk-sharing, is present: the seven providers under to the contract share 50% of any budgetary overspend with the council (and within that in proportion to their budget allocation); they also share savings on the same terms. Non-financial risks are shared via the first of the alliance principles. The third part of the definition of shared objectives is perhaps tacit or less prominent, and this is perhaps the most stark point of difference with the Kirklees project. Unlike Kirklees Better Outcomes Partnership, the Plymouth Alliance Contract does not rely on collectively defined, measured outcomes, to which payments are attached, as its principal accountability mechanism. Instead, softer levers were used: a long period of co-design, a long trial period of joint working, and loose 'principles' rather than measurable joint objectives.

Just as with the Kirklees project, it is too soon to say how effective the new approach in Plymouth may be, not just at fixing the issues with the prior arrangement, but at improving outcomes for the people using services.

These two examples illustrate that relational working—in the way it is understood through studies of private sector practice—may be found in multiple contract forms and underpinned by starkly different philosophies. Though the Kirklees project uses a social impact bond structure, SIBs are by no means inherently relational: merely focusing on outcomes through a contract payment mechanism and bringing in a third party to share financial risk are not in themselves sufficient to overcome a tendency towards transactional attitudes in contracting, as the international literature on payment-by-results more broadly attests. This means SIBs could suffer from the same setbacks of creaming and parking earlier described, and lack the relational component to help mitigate this (FitzGerald et al., 2019). The Plymouth project may appear to be less susceptible to these negative provider practices by forgoing payment-by-results, but conversely, may find it lacks sufficient focus on a shared set of objectives, or the means to reliably demonstrate the effectiveness of its approach. There is some evidence to suggest that an explicit focus on measured outcomes can promote a continuous improvement mindset and a learning culture (and ensure sufficient resource is allocated to data for performance improvement) (Fraser, Tan, Kruithof, et al., 2018; Ronicle & Smith, 2020).

In each of the case studies, the pursuit of relational practice is further complicated by the multiplicity of local service delivery organizations involved. Analytically, we must expand beyond conventional bilateral agreements between two parties (i.e., a single 'purchaser' and a single 'provider') to investigate the ways in which multilateral multi-sector ecosystems of service delivery agencies are strategically and operationally aligned in order to deliver holistic, meaningful provision for service users (Whitworth & Carter, 2018).

The barriers and enablers to relational working in cross-sector partnerships

The Kirklees and Plymouth projects both provide an illustration of what relational practice in the social economy can look like, and how it might be supported contractually. Neither was designed by explicitly borrowing design features from formal relational contracts in the private sector, and neither has yet been called a formal relational contract by its proponents. But both illustrate that the three-part definition of partnership (shared purpose, risk-sharing, and longevity) might usefully be refined by making the relational component more prominent.

It is difficult to assess the prevalence of this way of working in practice but the repeated calls for greater partnership working and the perceived frustration among practitioners raise the question of what might catalyse relational working and thus enable purposeful partnerships to be initiated. There are three major considerations for public officials and organizations in the social economy who are attracted to more relational modes of interaction: culture, regulation, and resource.

Cultural considerations

One of the major barriers to relational working within the social economy is that such practices are incompatible with conventional approaches to accountability. Following Jantz et al. (2015, p. 5) accountability is understood as 'a) a system of knowing and evaluating someone's behavior according to some standards and b) as a system of rewards or sanctions that are depending on these evaluations'. Accountability encompasses a system of rules that structure the course of action available to, and chosen by, a set of actors.

Accountability creates the interaction regime that public bodies and social economy must operate within. Just as it is hard to dance to a different tune from the one playing on the loudspeaker, it is hard for organizations and their managers to operate in a way that is at odds with the dominant accountability regime. Though several governance or accountability regimes have been described, Mark Considine and Jenny Lewis (Considine, 2001; Considine & Lewis, 2003) outline four distinctive types—*procedural governance, corporate governance, market governance and network governance*—and suggest that these broadly correspond to developmental phases that have dominated public administration since its post-war origins in the 1940s and 1950s. The traditional notion of hierarchical procedural bureaucracy that emerged in tandem with the post-war welfare state relied on rule-based principles of reliability and procedural fairness. A perceived lack of responsiveness of actors operating under this regime led to the increasing use of performance targets under so-called New Public Management (Hood, 1991). More recently, market-like methods have become prominent in the belief that markets increase efficiency, efficacy, and service responsiveness (though in important ways governments have created artificial 'quasi-markets').

Even as each new approach has come to dominate, prior approaches have left their trace in the public service delivery system. Old-fashioned procedural bureaucracy requires compliance with mandated procedures, which undermines tailoring, adaptation, and flexibility that are the hallmarks of relational practice. What Bevan and Hood (2006) call the 'targets and terror' of New Public Management create a culture of fear that makes the innovation and sharing of power inherent in relational working seem too risky. And the competitive, winner-takes-all approach of the market-like regime reverses any incentives that social economy actors might have to collaborate. None of these dominant accountability regimes therefore seem to create the conditions for the collaborative and trust-based culture that is required to support relational contracting practice.

Other accountability regimes, while less dominant, also leave an imprint on practice. Democratic accountability tends to bear on a system from the top down, as elected representatives seek control as a means to deliver political commitments (Jantz et al., 2015). This puppet-master mindset does not provide a conducive environment for relational approaches. But democratizing accountability from the 'bottom up', by empowering service users through choice (e.g., selection of service provider/and or programme) and voice (feedback and co-production) (Hirschman, 1970), might start to create the imperative for a different way of working, by centring decision-making on service user experience. Despite the long pedigree of such bottom-up approaches, they often remain subordinate in practice.

As shown, these dominant accountability regimes seldom create a culture within government that might fertilize relational working. Perhaps to move forward, relational practice should align itself with innovations in governance. One promising idea is 'network governance', an emerging accountability mechanism that might represent an ideal, but is seldom seen in practice yet (Bovaird & Löffler, 2009). Its intention is that social provision is coordinated across multiple, interdependent providers and agencies using relationships built on trust. The emphasis is on cooperation and co-dependence, with responsibilities shared across an inter-organizational web of public and private actors. This softer and more informal approach, compared to prior accountability types, seems more compatible with relational partnership working. Should it become more widely practised, the two approaches might well evolve hand-in-hand—even if they do not become the dominant mode.

Regulatory considerations

Formal relational contracting in the public sector must fit within a highly regulated public procurement environment. Across the world, public procurement has become rule-bound and procedural in approach. This has been driven by two major considerations: first, efforts to reduce corruption; second, efforts to maximize value for money for the taxpayer by using open competition to drive technical efficiency (in other words, maximizing the amount of a good or service that gets purchased per currency unit spent). Both of these imperatives lead to rules that rely on fair and equitable treatment of all suppliers, and open and transparent competition.

Relational contracting does not sit comfortably with these principles. If a government purchaser decides to cultivate a relationship with a supplier or set of suppliers prior to a contract being signed, it does not look like fair and equal treatment. It could even appear corrupt.

In fact, there are ways to operate relationally and stay within the bounds of procurement regulations. The EU treaty principles specify procedures that allow for co-design and negotiation, such as 'innovation partnerships' and the 'light-touch regime' for social services (Villeneuve-Smith & Blake, 2016). The Bill that follows the UK government's Green Paper on public procurement, which proposed revisions to procurement regulations in the light of the country's exit from the EU, goes even further in allowing procuring authorities to invent their own process (Parliamentary Business, 2022, p. 18). Nonetheless, experts have cautioned that flexible rules do not automatically mean flexible practice—and the dominant accountability regime will still fundamentally drive the behaviour of officials responsible for overseeing procurement processes (Connected Places Catapult, 2022; Sanchez-Graells, 2022). The UK government's own official assessment acknowledges this risk (Cabinet Office, 2022, p. 36).

Resource considerations

At first sight, economic theory would suggest that contracting relationally has lower transaction costs than contracting transactionally, because 'good faith' between the parties takes the place of detailed specifications in protecting against opportunistic behaviour (Williamson, 1975). However, good faith between a government purchaser and a social economy supplier for complex social services does not emerge automatically—it needs to be built, and thus incurs transaction costs, even if these 'costs' are incurred in different ways (Sanderson et al., 2018).

Social impact bonds are expected to attract high transaction costs due to their novelty, relationship complexity, and often lengthy negotiation periods (FitzGerald et al., 2019). It is almost impossible to put a monetary figure on the full costs associated with developing and managing a contract as these are rarely explicitly reported (Disley et al., 2016). Nonetheless, there is a commonly held view that the transaction costs in impact bonds and alliance contracts are 'high' and potentially disproportionate to realized benefits (Gustafsson-Wright & Osborne, 2020; Sanderson et al., 2018).

But counter-intuitively, the high transaction costs may be the key mechanism that brings about productive cross-sector partnerships (compare to Box 17.3). In other words, there may be *transaction benefits* that are unlocked during project delivery by the intensive discussion and negotiation required to set up a relational outcomes-based contract. The additional effort required to develop outcome contracts, such as developing a joint understanding of the social challenge at hand and an agreement on measurable outcome indicators that can be used to assess the success of services, may be integral to underpinning a more collaborative, partnership arrangement between parties. It is possible that the same applies to an alliance contract, but the work is not in agreeing measurable outcome indicators so much as it is in agreeing principles for how to work together operationally (and testing this).

Box 17.3 Creating a space for formal–relational contracting between government and the social economy

What might governments pragmatically do to bring about the required cultural and procedural shifts that will make the emergence of a true partnership approach more likely when the circumstances recommend it? The UK government's £80m Life Chances Fund, launched in 2016 with the principal intention of incentivizing local municipalities to commission using social impact bonds, may offer a useful illustration. The fund contributed up to 50% of the budget for outcomes payments towards 30 projects which launched across England.

Intriguingly, the stated aims of the Life Chances Fund did not include guiding contracting practice towards more purposeful partnerships or relational approaches (Office for Civil Society, 2016), but an observation of how the 31 projects responded to the COVID-19 crisis suggests it may have had this effect. Research conducted by our research group, who are evaluating the fund, found that the governance set-up of social impact bonds gave them resilience that helped them to continue performing as the country entered, and endured, a long national lockdown. Projects were able to adapt to the rapidly changing circumstances and continued to deliver throughout the economic and social disruption (FitzGerald et al., 2021). This resilience was explained by a combination of factors.

With a contract specification centred on desired end outcomes rather than specific activity requirements, providers could adapt their services rapidly as they saw fit, without requiring consultation with massively overstretched government commissioners. Parties to the contracts, which included not just a local government commissioner and a service provider but also the central government department administering the Life Chances Fund and social investment fund managers, agreed between them how to treat payment terms during the pandemic, when the previously agreed payment terms may no longer have been fit for purpose. Of the 31 projects, 10 kept to their original payment terms, while the rest switched temporarily to a different arrangement. No projects resorted to emergency exit clauses that might have freed them from their contractual obligations (known as *force majeure*). While it was harder to understand the human factors behind the decisions that were made, the adaptability of services and flexibility shown around payment terms points towards a relational engagement between the parties.

To what degree this relational practice preceded the crisis, and how much it may have outlasted it, we do not yet know. And neither is it possible to claim that these adaptations were unique to Social Impact Bonds—given the unprecedented nature of the crisis, thousands of organizations had to be flexible and find new ways of relating with their partners. Still, the Life Chances Fund example does point to the value of relational practice when the unexpected happens. It might even point to a way for central governments to incentivize contracting authorities in lower levels of government to consider a new way of contracting. As discussed earlier, the very process of designing and negotiating a new type of contract, which necessarily involved considerable development effort, may have unlocked relational practice.

Conclusion: new tools for new challenges?

An increasing focus on outcomes and the quality of inter-organizational relationships is a good fit with the appetite among public sector and social economy actors who aspire to meaningful partnership. The top-down hierarchy and transactionalism of traditional public administration and New Public Management are increasingly seen as a poor fit for the grand challenges facing society in a 'no-one-wholly-in-charge world' (Bryson et al., 2014, p. 1). The exciting emergent practice that we have discussed in this chapter ignites elements of formal relational contracting seen in the private sector but yet to be coherently introduced in partnerships between governments and actors in the wider social economy. For purposeful partnership and relational practice to take hold, there will need to be a dramatic shift in cultural norms and status quo approaches within both government contracting authorities and the universe of social economy organizations.

On the government side, procurement and contract management will need to be transformed. Officials will need to learn to take risks and venture beyond procedural safety rails. The transactional 'carrot and stick' mindset that often dominates the way government works with other sectors will need to shift to something more equitable. This means governments will need to heavily invest in management capacity, both in terms of skills and person-power. The longstanding neglect of post-award contract and relationship management will need to change too. Relational working is a process of ongoing dialogue and negotiation, throughout the full life cycle of a partnership (Frydlinger et al., 2021). Complex cross-sector partnerships intensify the need for strong government management capacity (Heinrich & Kabourek, 2019).

The new, more collaborative approach is not without risks for governments. The arm's-length approach to cross-sector relationships has helped to mitigate the risk of malfeasance (Brogaard et al., 2020), and efforts to strengthen top-down control and scrutiny have helped to ensure minimum standards are met (Davies et al., 2021). A more elastic approach, if it relies too heavily on trust and personal integrity, risks weakening these safeguards and reversing the progress made on public accountability and raising the floor of practice.

Even if these risks can be managed, change on the government side is not enough. If relational contracting and a focus on social outcomes is to become the norm, then purpose-driven practice will also need to become more common within the non-government service provider landscape. The social economy is partly defined by its social purpose, which equals or surpasses any profit motive. But many service providers are from the private sector. Companies increasingly claim they have 'purpose beyond profit', with the Business Roundtable (2019) of US CEOs recently redefining the purpose of a company to state they must serve all stakeholders and the British Academy (2019) following suit. This commitment will need to become more scrutable if it is to be relied upon in cross-sector partnerships. Otherwise the new, more supple contracting approach will leave too much space for unscrupulous companies to profit unduly—the very 'self-interest seeking with guile' that Williamson cautioned against (Williamson, 1984, p. 198). The risk is real. In the UK, for example, private equity investors have become involved in state-funded children's homes that care for the most vulnerable children in society, and some large providers in this market are 'making materially higher profits, and charging materially higher prices, than we would expect if this market were functioning effectively' (Competition and Markets Authority, 2022).

Contracting experimentation across the social economy poses a fertile but challenging terrain for those researching cross-sector partnership and social programmes. In attending to contracting and managerial reforms, research has often centred on formal structures. Greater scholarly attention is owed to the informal aspects critical to the implementation of relational practice, such as culture, values, and 'craft'. This calls for pioneering multi-disciplinary research that gets beyond the contract on paper to explore the complex relationships and accountabilities binding partners together. For example, how strongly the outcomes focus needs to be embedded in a partnership or contract is not clear—is a shared commitment enough in itself, or should the achievement of outcomes be linked to the financial incentives that emerge in any partnership where funding is involved?

There are important descriptive research objectives to help identify the scope and nature of more 'relational' and 'formal relational' practice. This calls for detailed, observational work, since preliminary empirics on social impact bonds indicate that relational practice is not stable and that when financial pressures and risks are elevated, parties may retreat to the familiarity and predictability of a more transactional approach (French et al., 2022). Evaluative research questions are also key. How might alternative contract types and governance arrangements affect the outcomes and value of cross-sector partnerships? Those pursuing economic analysis, for example, comparing different forms of partnership via cost–benefit or cost-effectiveness analysis, may face challenges with data and methods since tracing the 'impact' associated with alternative contracting arrangements is notoriously challenging. Moreover, understanding the relative 'transaction costs' and 'transaction benefits' calls for granular and standardized disclosure of cost and performance data that is not widely available.

The theoretical underpinnings and emerging case studies point to beguiling benefits for cross-sector partnerships in a more interconnected and complex world.

With greater government investment in improving the quality of partnerships, and a verifiable commitment to purpose from non-government players wishing to enter such partnerships, these benefits could be more widely unlocked. The shift in the dominant accountability regime towards a more collaborative and equitable approach, coupled with the growing importance of the social economy in public service delivery, provides fertile ground for change. With sufficient attention to the risks, there is much to be optimistic about in how actors from across sectors can partner to tackle society's grand challenges.

References

Alonso, J. M., Clifton, J., & Díaz-Fuentes, D. (2015). Did New Public Management matter? An empirical analysis of the outsourcing and decentralization effects on public sector size. *Public Management Review*, 17(5), 643–660. https://doi.org/10.1080/14719037. 2013.822532

Arena, M., Bengo, I., Calderini, M., & Chiodo, V. (2016). Social Impact Bonds: blockbuster or flash in a pan? *International Journal of Public Administration*, 39(12), 927–939. https://doi.org/10.1080/01900692.2015.1057852

Ball, N. (2020). Steadying the swinging pendulum: how might we accommodate competing approaches to public service delivery? In A. Bonner (Ed.), *Local Authorities and the Social Determinants of Health* (pp. 401–420). Bristol: Bristol University Press.

Ball, N., & Gibson, M. (2022). *Partnerships with Principles: Putting Relationships at the Heart of Public Contracts for Better Social Outcomes*. University of Oxford.

Bevan, G., & Hood, C. (2006). What's measured is what matters: targets and gaming in the English public health care system. *Public Administration*, 84(3), 517–538. https:// doi.org/10.1111/j.1467-9299.2006.00600.x

Bovaird, T., & Löffler, E. (2009). *Public Management and Governance* (2nd ed.). Abingdon: Taylor & Francis.

British Academy. (2019, 27 November). The British Academy proposes principles for the age of purposeful business. *The British Academy*. Available at: https://www. thebritishacademy.ac.uk/news/british-academy-proposes-principles-age-purposeful-business/

Brogaard, J., Denes, M., & Duchin, R. (2020). *Political Influence and the Renegotiation of Government Contracts* (SSRN Scholarly Paper No. 2604805). https://doi.org/10.2139/ ssrn.2604805

Brown, T. L., Potoski, M., & Slyke, D. M. V. (2013). *Complex Contracting: Government Purchasing in the Wake of the US Coast Guard's Deepwater Program*. Cambridge: Cambridge University Press.

Brummel, L. (2021). Social accountability between consensus and confrontation: developing a theoretical framework for societal accountability relationships of public sector organizations. *Administration & Society*, 53(7), 1046–1077. https://doi.org/10.1177/ 0095399720988529

Bryson, J. M., Crosby, B. C., & Bloomberg, L. (2014). Public value governance: moving beyond traditional public administration and the New Public Management. *Public Administration Review*, 74(4), 445–456. https://doi.org/10.1111/puar.12238

Business Roundtable (2019, 19 August). Business Roundtable redefines the purpose of a corporation to promote 'an economy that serves all Americans'. *Corporate Governance*. Available at: https://www.businessroundtable.org/business-roundtable-redefines-the-purpose-of-a-corporation-to-promote-an-economy-that-serves-all-americans

Cabinet Office (2022). *Procurement Reform Bill Impact Assessment*. Available at: https://bills.parliament.uk/publications/46429/documents/1767

Carter, E. (2019). More than marketised? Exploring the governance and accountability mechanisms at play in Social Impact Bonds. *Journal of Economic Policy Reform*, 0(0), 1–17. https://doi.org/10.1080/17487870.2019.1575736

Carter, E. (2020). Debate: Would a Social Impact Bond by any other name smell as sweet? Stretching the model and why it might matter. *Public Money & Management*, 40(3), 183–185. https://doi.org/10.1080/09540962.2020.1714288

Carter, E., & Anastasiu, A. (2023). Impact Bonds: Beyond the hype? In *Encyclopedia of Social Innovation*. Cheltenham: Edward Elgar.

Carter, E., & Ball, N. (2021). Spotlighting shared outcomes for social impact programs that work. *Stanford Social Innovation Review*. Available at: https://ssir.org/articles/entry/spotlighting_shared_outcomes_for_social_impact_programs_that_work

Carter, E., & Whitworth, A. (2015). Creaming and parking in quasi-marketised welfare-to-work schemes: designed out of or designed in to the UK work programme? *Journal of Social Policy*, 44(2), 277–296. https://doi.org/10.1017/S0047279414000841

Collaborate Foundation (2018). *The State of Collaboration*. Available at: http://wordpress.collaboratei.com/wp-content/uploads/The-State-of-Collaboration-June-2018.pdf

Competition and Markets Authority (2022). *A Market Study into Children's Social Care in England, Scotland and Wales*CMA. Available at: https://www.gov.uk/government/publications/childrens-social-care-market-study-final-report/final-report

Connected Places Catapult (2022). *Procurement Bill 2022—Initial Assessment*. https://cp.catapult.org.uk/article/procurement-bill-2022-initial-assessment/

Considine, M. (2001). *Enterprising States: The Public Management of Welfare-to-Work*. Cambridge University Press.

Considine, M., & Lewis, J. M. (2003). Bureaucracy, network, or enterprise? Comparing models of governance in Australia, Britain, the Netherlands, and New Zealand. *Public Administration Review*, 63(2), 131–140.

Davies, N., Atkins, G., & Sodhi, S. (2021). *Using Targets to Improve Public Services*. Institute for Government. Available at: https://www.instituteforgovernment.org.uk/publications/targets-public-services

Disley, E., Giacomantonio, C., Kruithof, K., & Sim, M. (2016). *The Payment by Results Social Impact Bond Pilot at HMP Peterborough: Final Process Evaluation Report*. RAND Corporation. https://doi.org/10.7249/RR1212

Economy, C., Carter, E., & Airoldi, M. (2022). Have we 'stretched' social impact bonds too far? An empirical analysis of SIB design in practice. *International Public Management Journal*, 0(0), 1–24. https://doi.org/10.1080/10967494.2022.2077867

Finn, D. (2009). The 'welfare market' and the Flexible New Deal: lessons from other countries. *Local Economy*, 24(1), 38–45. https://doi.org/10.1080/02690940802645471

FitzGerald, C., Carter, E., Dixon, R., & Airoldi, M. (2019). Walking the contractual tightrope: a transaction cost economics perspective on Social Impact Bonds. *Public Money & Management*, 39(7), 458–467. https://doi.org/10.1080/09540962.2019.1583889

FitzGerald, C., Hameed, T., Rosenbach, F., Macdonald, J. R., & Dixon, R. (2021). Resilience in public service partnerships: evidence from the UK Life Chances Fund. *Public Management Review*, 25(4), 1–21. https://doi.org/10.1080/14719037.2021.2015186

Fraser, A., Tan, S., Kruithof, K., Sim, M., Disley, E., Giacomantonio, C., Lagarde, M., & Mays, N. (2018). *Evaluation of the Social Impact Bond Trailblazers in Health and Social Care: Final Report*, 158.

Fraser, A., Tan, S., Lagarde, M., & Mays, N. (2018). Narratives of promise, narratives of caution: a review of the literature on Social Impact Bonds. *Social Policy & Administration*, 52(1), 4–28. https://doi.org/10.1111/spol.12260

French, M., Kimmitt, J., Wilson, R., Jamieson, D., & Lowe, T. (2022). Social Impact Bonds and public service reform: back to the future of New Public Management? *International Public Management Journal*, 0(0), 1–20. https://doi.org/10.1080/10967494.2022.2050859

Froy, F., & Giguère, S. (2010). *Breaking Out of Policy Silos: Doing More with Less*. Available at: https://www.oecd-ilibrary.org/urban-rural-and-regional-development/breaking-out-of-policy-silos_9789264094987-en

Frydlinger, D., Hart, O., & Vitasek, K. (2019, 1 September). A new approach to contracts. *Harvard Business Review*, September–October 2019. Available at: https://hbr.org/2019/09/a-new-approach-to-contracts

Frydlinger, D., & Hart, O. D. (2019). *Overcoming Contractual Incompleteness: The Role of Guiding Principles*. Working Paper No. 26245. National Bureau of Economic Research. DOI: https://doi.org/10.3386/w26245

Frydlinger, D., Vitasek, K., Bergman, J., & Cummins, T. (2021). *Contracting in the New Economy*. London: Palgrave Macmillan.

George, G., Howard-Grenville, J., Joshi, A., & Tihanyi, L. (2016). Understanding and tackling societal grand challenges through management research. *Academy of Management Journal*, 59(6), 1880–1895. https://doi.org/10.5465/amj.2016.4007

Girth, A. M., Hefetz, A., Johnston, J. M., & Warner, M. E. (2012). Outsourcing public service delivery: management responses in noncompetitive markets. *Public Administration Review*, 72(6), 887–900. https://doi.org/10.1111/j.1540-6210.2012.02596.x

Government Outcomes Lab (n.d.). *INDIGO Impact Bond Dataset*. University of Oxford, Blavatnik School of Government. https://doi.org/10.5287/bodleian:6RxneM0xz

Gustafsson-Wright, E., & Osborne, S. (2020). *Do the Benefits Outweigh the Costs Of Impact Bonds?* Brookings. Available at: https://www.brookings.edu/research/do-the-benefits-outweigh-the-costs-of-impact-bonds/

Hart, O., & Moore, J. (2008). Contracts as reference points. *Quaarterly Journal of Economics*, 123(1), 48.

Heinrich, C. J., & Kabourek, S. E. (2019). Pay-for-success development in the United States: feasible or failing to launch? *Public Administration Review*, 79(6), 867–879. DOI: https://doi.org/10.1111/puar.13099

Heins, E., & Bennett, H. (2016). 'Best of both worlds'? A comparison of third sector providers in health care and welfare-to-work markets in Britain. *Social Policy & Administration*, 50(1), 39–58. https://doi.org/10.1111/spol.12126

Hirschman, A. O. (1970). *Exit, Voice, and Loyalty: Responses to Decline in Firms, Organizations, and States.* Boston: Harvard University Press.

Hodge, G., & Greve, C. (2005). *The Challenge of Public–Private Partnerships: Learning from International Experience.* Cheltenham: Edward Elgar Publishing.

Holmström, B. (1979). Moral hazard and observability. *The Bell Journal of Economics*, 10(1), 74–91.

Hood, C. (1991). A public management for all seasons? *Public Administration*, 69(1), 3–19.

Jantz, B., Klenk, T., Larsen, F., & Wiggan, J. (2015). Marketization and varieties of accountability relationships in employment services: comparing Denmark, Germany, and Great Britain. *Administration & Society*, 50(3), 321–345. https://doi.org/10.1177/0095399715581622

Kania, J., & Kramer, M. (2011). Collective impact. *Stanford Social Innovation Review.* Available at: https://ssir.org/articles/entry/collective_impact

Kania, J., Williams, J., Schmitz, P., Brady, S., Kramer, M., & Splansky Juster, J. (2022). Centering equity in collective impact. *Stanford Social Innovation Review*, Winter 2022. https://ssir.org/articles/entry/centering_equity_in_collective_impact#

Krlev, G., Pasi, G., Wruk, D., & Bernhard, M. (2021). Reconceptualizing the social economy. *Stanford Social Innovation Review.* Available at: https://ssir.org/articles/entry/reconceptualizing_the_social_economy

Krlev, G., Sauer, S., Scharpe, K., Mildenberger, G., Elsemann, K., & Sauerhammer, M. (2022). *Financing Social Innovation—International Evidence.* Centre for Social Investment. Available at: https://www.send-ev.de/wp-content/uploads/2022/01/Financing_Social_Innovation.pdf

Lowe, T., Kimmitt, J., Wilson, R., Martin, M., & Gibbon, J. (2019). The institutional work of creating and implementing Social Impact Bonds. *Policy & Politics*, 47(2), 353–370. DOI: https://doi.org/10.1332/030557318X15333032765154

Morris, D. (1999). *Charities and the Contract Culture: Partners or Contractors? Law and Practice in Conflict.* Charity Law Unit, University of Liverpool. Available at: https://www.liverpool.ac.uk/media/livacuk/law/2-research/clpu/clurep1.pdf

O'Sullivan, S., McGann, M., & Considine, M. (2021). *Buying and Selling the Poor*. Sydney: Sydney University Press. https://sydneyuniversitypress.com.au/products/174581

OECD/IDB/WAPES (2016). *The World of Public Employment Services: Challenges, Capacity and Outlook for Public Employment services in the New World of Work*. Organisation for Economic Co-operation and Development. Available at: https://www.oecd-ilibrary.org/employment/the-world-of-public-employment-services_9789264251854-en

Office for Civil Society (2016). *Apply to the Life Chances Fund*. GOV.UK. Available at: https://www.gov.uk/government/publications/life-chances-fund

Parliamentary Business (2022). *Procurement Bill*. https://publications.parliament.uk/pa/bills/lbill/58-03/004/5803004_en_1.html

Petersen, O. H., Hjelmar, U., & Vrangbaek, K. (2018). Is contracting out of public services still the great panacea? A systematic review of studies on economic and quality effects from 2000 to 2014. *Social Policy and Administration*, 52(1), 130–157. https://doi.org/10.1111/spol.12297

Powers, T. (2017). *Partnerships and Contractors in the Delivery of Employment Services and ALMPs: A Literature Review*. Employment Policy Department, EMPLOYMENT Working Paper No. 226. International Labour Office. Available at: https://www.ilo.org/employment/Whatwedo/Publications/working-papers/WCMS_613479/lang—en/index.htm

Rees, J., Mullins, D., & Bovaird, T. (2012). Third sector partnerships for public service delivery: an evidence review. *Third Sector Research Centre*. Working Paper 60. Retrieved from: https://core.ac.uk/download/pdf/15171135.pdf

Ronicle, J., & Smith, K. (2020). *Youth Engagement Fund Evaluation*. Ecorys. Retrieved from: https://assets.publishing.service.gov.uk/government/uploads/system/uploads/attachment_data/file/886650/YEF_Evaluation_Report_.pdf

Rosenbach, F. (2022). *Kirklees Better Outcomes Partnership (KBOP)*. Government Outcomes Lab, Blavatnik School of Government. Available at: https://golab.bsg.ox.ac.uk/knowledge-bank/case-studies/kirklees-better-outcomes-partnership/

Rosenbach, F., & Carter, E. (2021). *Kirklees Integrated Support Service and Better Outcomes Partnership: The First Report from a Longitudinal Evaluation of a Life Chances Fund Impact Bond*. HM Government. Available at: https://assets.publishing.service.gov.uk/government/uploads/system/uploads/attachment_data/file/1003288/Kirklees_Integrated_Support_Service_report.pdf

Sanchez-Graells, A. (2022). Initial comments on the UK's Procurement Bill: a lukewarm assessment. *SSRN Electronic Journal*. https://doi.org/10.2139/ssrn.4114141

Sanderson, M., Allen, P., Gill, R., & Garnett, E. (2018). New models of contracting in the public sector: a review of alliance contracting, prime contracting and outcome-based contracting literature. *Social Policy & Administration*, 52(5), 1060–1083. https://doi.org/10.1111/spol.12322

Scoppetta, A. (2013). *Successful Partnerships in Delivering Public Employment Services.* European Commission, DG Employment, Social Affairs and Inclusion. Available at: https://ec.europa.eu/social/BlobServlet?docId=14096&langId=en

Shergold, P. (2008). Governing through collaboration. In: O'Flynn, J. (Ed.), *Collaborative governance: A new era of public policy in Australia?* (pp. 13-22). Canberra: Australian National University Press.

Social Finance (2017). *World's 1st Social Impact Bond Shown to Cut Reoffending and to Make Impact Investors a Return.* Available at: https://www.socialfinance.org.uk/sites/default/files/news/final-press-release-pb-july-2017.pdf

Struyven, L., & Steurs, G. (2005). Design and redesign of a quasi-market for the reintegration of jobseekers: empirical evidence from Australia and the Netherlands. *Journal of European Social Policy*, 15(3), 211–229. https://doi.org/10.1177/0958928705054083

Tan, S., Fraser, A., McHugh, N., & Warner, M. E. (2021). Widening perspectives on Social Impact Bonds. *Journal of Economic Policy Reform*, 24(1), 1–10. https://doi.org/10.1080/17487870.2019.1568249

The Plymouth Alliance. (n.d.). *Alliance for People with Complex Needs: Principles.* Available at: https://img1.wsimg.com/blobby/go/9f5fcf77-d2f6-4a1f-843d-059bf184ff2f/downloads/Alliance%20Principles.pdf?ver=1656499135782

Van Ham, H., & Koppenjan, J. (2001). Building public–private partnerships: assessing and managing risks in port development. *Public Management Review*, 3(4), 593–616. https://doi.org/10.1080/14616670110070622

Villeneuve-Smith, F., & Blake, J. (2016). *The Art of the Possible in Public Procurement.* Bates Wells & Braithwaite London LLP, HCT Group, E3M. Available at: https://e3m.org.uk/wp-content/uploads/2020/03/the-art-of-the-possible-in-public-procurement-SK-contact-details.pdf

Whitworth, A., & Carter, E. (2018). Rescaling employment support accountability: from negative national neoliberalism to positively integrated city-region ecosystems. *Environment and Planning C: Politics and Space*, 36(2), 274–289. https://doi.org/10.1177/2399654417708788

Williamson, O. (1975). *Markets and Hierarchies: Analysis and Antitrust Implications—A Study in the Economics of Internal Organization.* New York: The Free Press.

Williamson, O. E. (1984). The economics of governance: framework and implications. *Zeitschrift Für Die Gesamte Staatswissenschaft/Journal of Institutional and Theoretical Economics*, 140(1), 195–223.

Wright, C. (2022). Can charities delivering public sector contracts really change the world for the better? *Think NPC*. Available at: https://www.thinknpc.org/blog/chris-wright/

LESSONS LEARNT AND FUTURE AGENDA

18
Conclusions

Where to with Social Economy Science?

Gorgi Krlev, Dominika Wruk, Giulio Pasi, and Marika Bernhard

What have we learnt?

First and foremost, *Social Economy Science* has shown that the social economy has an unjustified reputation as less important, less exciting, or less relevant than other fields when it comes to addressing the big sustainability challenges that societies are facing. In fact, the contributions to the book show quite the contrary—namely, that there might be *more* to learn from the social economy than has previously been acknowledged *and* that the social economy can contribute more to transforming the economy and society to meet sustainability challenges than is typically discussed.

The contributions to the book highlight that the modes by which the social economy promotes change are manifold and that the three transformation pathways (innovation for impact, agents of change, and partnerships), especially when combined, are very powerful in promoting transitions across levels of existing systems. For example, we have seen how social businesses could become role models for new operational principles, logics, and structures in all types of organizations (Battilana et al., this volume). We have also understood how social economy organizations are promoting a vision of impact and its measurement that prioritizes proactive and positive value creation for society. Through it we recognized that this is fundamentally different from when organizations create value for themselves, when fields try to keep societal harm in check, or when actors make only marginal contributions to societal resilience (Hehenberger & Buckland, this volume). Finally, we have also witnessed how purposeful institutional design, which carefully orchestrates governments' agency, private contributions, and the amplification of social economy capacities, can significantly stimulate socially innovative transformations that improve for instance healthcare systems or social service provision (Miguel, this volume).

At the same time, *Social Economy Science* is not naively promoting the social economy as a panacea to all social ills, but also discusses its weaknesses as well as factors that hold it back from unfolding its potential. For example, ignorance towards local knowledge, expertise, and contributions can stymie the diffusion and scaling of innovative solutions to social problems, or it can lead to a poor fit of the supposed solution

Gorgi Krlev et al., *Conclusions*. In: *Social Economy Science*. Edited by: Gorgi Krlev, Dominika Wruk, Giulio Pasi, and Marika Bernhard, Oxford University Press. © Oxford University Press (2023). DOI: 10.1093/oso/9780192868343.003.0018

with the problem (Brännvall, this volume). Also, despite claims and ambitions to the contrary, social economy organizations remain far less assertive and visible in assuming collaborative and civic leadership functions within local contexts than political actors in formal positions of power or businesses elites (Sancino et al., this volume). We can blame other actors for unduly ignoring the social economy or the value of partnerships and collaboration. However, this research suggests that the collective orientation and democratic structure of the social economy might also have drawbacks when it comes to its ability to take on leadership roles.

In the following, we first take stock of the contributions that the chapters of *Social Economy Science* make to different streams of research, especially when considered jointly. In this we relate to elements that grant the social economy stability as well as to the transformation pathways that help it promote change. We then derive an agenda for future research by way of unearthing open research questions relative to the social economy, but also by crafting new research impulses for research beyond the social economy. In a third step, and to remain faithful to the scholar-practitioner and practitioner-scholar character of this book, we give recommendations for policy and practical action on, for, and with the social economy.

Research contributions of *Social Economy Science*

Each chapter to *Social Economy Science* makes a strong contribution to research and practice of its own. Instead of summarizing and giving a recap of those contributions, in the following we try to work out some prominent themes and subjects that emerge when the chapters are considered jointly. In this process, we are guided by our initial theoretical work that established the social economy as an organizational issue field and that derived its three transformation pathways in our multi-level model of dynamic change (Krlev et al., this volume, chapter 3).

Curiously, and in line with our supposition of multi-level effects and the entwinement of the organizational issue field with the pathways, the contributions we highlight below are made by various individual chapters that are spread across parts of the book. Consequently, they also radiate beyond specific transformation pathways we allocated them to. This does not only underpin the integrative character of the book. It also shows that the levels and pathways are in fact to be seen as mutually reinforcing or combinable so as to amplify their impact. By means of the holistic meta-perspective we develop here, we can furthermore derive a future research agenda not only on the social economy, but also beyond it.

Elements that are part of the social economy's organizational issue field

We first turn to elements that we have introduced as essential for the social economy's common identity, its stability, and its standing within the wider economy and society (compare to Krlev et al., this volume). Much as a mirror of the argument above that chapters from different parts of the book can unfold synergies across these parts, the individual elements we discuss below are marked by transitions and interconnections between each other.

Ecosystems

Scholars have only recently noted that social innovation ecosystems, while having similarities with regular entrepreneurial ecosystems, depend on a unique set of systemic support structures, including dedicated support from governments or society at large (Audretsch, Eichler, & Schwarz, 2022). While some of the relevant factors might mobilize naturally in more mainstream entrepreneurial ecosystems, this is much less likely to happen in social economy ecosystems. The reason is that there is mostly not a direct monetary incentive for governments and policy to provide essential support. The social economy and social innovations have a purpose that is different from merely prioritizing social or socio-economic returns. In fact, some social innovations, such as changes in urban cultures and structures towards sustainability, require long-term investments although they do not generate immediate returns (Figueroa, Navratil, Turrini, & Krlev, 2019). Besides, there is typically much less awareness and understanding among the general public of social innovation than of classical types of economic activity, not least because there is not much media attention for social innovation, not to speak of the social economy's role in it (Krlev & Lund, 2020). As a result, dedicated governmental budgets, a long-term socio-political focus, or embrace and engagement of society in social innovation ecosystems—all factors that Audretsch et al. (2022) highlight—are hard to mobilize.

Miguel (this volume) shows how these challenges can be tackled through the mobilization of cross-national (here European) funds, national political ownership, and a truly cross-sectoral engagement in advocacy and the implementation of support in order to create lasting operational structures and processes for social innovation. Nogales and Nyssens (this volume) develop an often neglected aspect, namely that social economy ecosystems would benefit from specific knowledge, expertise, and human capital, which is currently lacking, meaning their evolution is slowed. They also show how two-way knowledge transfers between scientific institutions and the social economy and vice versa, in ways that are fundamentally different to contracted industry research, may accelerate effective social problem solving. Unfortunately, as their research also shows, such types of engagement still represent the exception rather than the rule. *Social Economy Science* thus contributes by highlighting how all these aspects need to be proactively cultivated for strong social innovation and social economy ecosystems to become a reality.

Positive social change orientation

Social economy organizations are recognized as being open, as understanding social problems well (or at least better than other organizations) due to their proximity to vulnerable target groups, and as being perpetual challengers of the status quo when it comes to combating disadvantages for those target groups (Bouchard,

2012; Krlev, Anheier, & Mildenberger, 2019a). Across fields of activity and industries they are developing innovative twists in how to do things differently. For example, they show how to reconcile different goal sets by proactive shifts in organizational strategies (Smith & Besharov, 2017), how non-market problems may be addressed within market settings (Hockerts, 2015), or how market-based solutions can be made more responsive to the needs of vulnerable groups (Quarter, 2015). This makes them appear like the natural leaders of social change within their fields of activity. Hehenberger and Buckland (this volume), for example, show how social economy organizations are putting what some have called the 'impact revolution' (Cohen, 2020) on the public agenda. More specifically, they change how impact is perceived and accounted for.

However, we also see that social economy organizations are facing a lot of push-back and that the impact movement, for instance, is being co-opted by commercial actors, who are watering down standards to established practices of corporate social responsibility instead of proactive social value creation (Barman, 2015). Besides, even on the social economy's home turf, namely community engagement and deep embedding in the local context, social economy organizations do not always succeed in being recognized as leaders (Sancino et al., this volume). As Sancino and colleagues' work shows, not only are leaders of other sectors more visible than those in the social economy, but there are also relatively few interconnections and strong relations between the different leadership arenas in cities. This happens despite the fact that civic, collaborative leadership at the local level, particularly in urban settings (Brandsen, Cattacin, Evers, & Zimmer, 2016; Pradel-Miquel, Cano-Hila, Hila, & García Cabeza, 2020), is supposed to be pivotal for innovation that benefits society (OECD, 2021). *Social Economy Science* thus contributes by sensitizing scholars and decision makers to the fact that a lack of effective responses on how to bridge existing gaps and blind spots risks losing the change orientation (both in terms of network relations and issues to be promoted) that is such a fundamental virtue and characteristic of the social economy field.

Inclusion and participation

The social economy has a long tradition of being portrayed as an inclusive organizational field (Mair, Marti, & Ventresca, 2012), which is populated by organizations that highlight elements of cooperation, co-production, or other processes that bear the co- prefix (Brandsen & Pestoff, 2005; Brandsen, Steen, & Verschuere, 2018). There is an entire school of thought that conceptualizes the social economy and social enterprises based on their principles of democratization and participation (Defourny & Nyssens, 2021; Smith & Teasdale, 2012). In fact, some of the contributions of this book build out and further nuance this image. Chaves-Avila and Soler (this volume), for example, suggest that cooperative forms within the social economy have been particularly resilient in dealing with the COVID-19 crisis—supposedly for this very aspect of embracing participatory and inclusive approaches. Meanwhile, other actors pushed the 'societalization' of the crisis, that is, transferred responsibility for dealing with the crisis from themselves onto the entire society (Brammer, Branicki, &

Linnenluecke, 2020). Battilana et al. (this volume) in turn uncover how, especially when compared to other public and private forms of organization, the elements of cooperation and participation are very present even in market-oriented forms of the social economy, such as social businesses.

However, we also see clear limitations and significant potential for building out this capacity of the social economy. Addressing these limitations may further accelerate renewed interest in how internal and external factors can spur original ownership and governance practices in the social economy (Bretos, Bouchard, & Zevi, 2020). We posit that two factors hold particular potential. First, and in parallel to other processes of engagement in society such as the consultation and inclusion of the public in the development of science and new technology, Hueske, Willems, and Hockerts (this volume) suggest there is much room for improvement when it comes to making citizens co-entrepreneurs or co-innovators of the social economy. A restriction of engagement mechanisms to the very end of the process (in the sense of 'we inform citizens and target groups what we have done for them') only symbolically carries notions of participation and may lead to solutions that are actually not fitting with the problems they should address (Gras, Conger, Jenkins, & Gras, 2019). Second, Bräanvall (this volume) shows how improved local embedding and meaningful inclusion and relationship building, especially when Western entrepreneurs engage in developing countries, are needed to accelerate the scaling of social innovations. *Social Economy Science* thus contributes by flagging that a lack of these qualities may not only lead to poor solution–problem fit, but also hold even very good solutions back from stabilizing and organically growing and diffusing beyond their entrepreneurial stage.

The three transformation pathways

The elements above do not only mark the social economy's organizational issue field, but they also serve as a foundation for the social economy to pursue its three transformation pathways. These in turn may provoke reconfigurations in other fields' composition of ecosystems, their orientation towards positive social change, or their inclination to be inclusive of other actors or to become more participatory (compare to Krlev et al., this volume).

Innovation for impact

A continued conundrum which research in the social sciences has difficulty resolving is how innovative practices at the organizational level lead to change at the level of institutions, especially when those innovations are hard to grasp, complex in nature, locally grown, or relevant to those stakeholders in society that have weak power positions (Pel et al., 2020; van Wijk et al., 2018). This does not apply in the same way to the diffusion of technologies or commercial innovations, where we actually have a good understanding of the process (Rogers, 2003). Commercial innovations tend to break through when older technologies cease to be competitive, when market demand for an innovation is steadily increasing, or when innovations provide so many new affor-dances to other organizations that these start replicating and adopting them in large numbers (Geels, 2005). Many of these mechanisms do not work (as neatly or at all) when it comes to innovations that matter to the social economy, exactly because these innovations exhibit many of the traits mentioned above. So, innovation for impact in the social economy to reach the level of field transformations or change in societal practices or structures may rest on institutional work (Lawrence, Suddaby, & Leca, 2010) or institutional entrepreneurship (Garud, Hardy, & Maguire, 2016), namely, collective work on shaping regulatory and normative institutions that govern society at a very high level.

Nicholls and Ormiston (this volume) show how a gradual levelling up not only by increasing financial volumes, but also by a constant upholding and spread of eth-ical values and principles of materiality to target groups, helps impact investments gain greater influence on the finance industry at large (see also Nicholls, 2018). In contrast to the much softer version of 'investing for society', which is held in respon-sible or sustainable investing (Yan, Ferraro, & Almandoz, 2018), impact investing needs to engage in an active process of challenging established power structures (Hehenberger, Mair, & Metz, 2019). This type of engagement happens equally in other fields of activity, such as sharing platforms or community-oriented models of healthcare that aim to shift agency towards less powerful stakeholders in order to arrive at real transformations (Ziegler & Jacobi, 2020).

Huysentruyt (this volume) in turn develops four novel strategies or modes of action that lie at the level of organizational behaviour, but may alter patterns at the field or institutional level. Those strategies centre, for example, on embrac-ing an uncertainty mindset. Such a mindset has also been promoted for business strategy (Busch, 2020). However, due to the financial and, foremost, social risks involved in embracing such action in the context of social economy missions and target groups, Huysentruyt's suggestions represent a more radical shift than the more business-oriented discussion on uncertainty and serendipity. Huysentruyt's (implicit) argument is that the gap between the multitude of innovative activities pursued by social economy organizations, which by themselves do not easily trans-fer into field or institutional practices, could be bridged by aggregating them to more abstract and high-level action principles to stimulate innovation and ultimately also to leverage impact. *Social Economy Science* thus contributes by showing ways in which innovation and impact can spread across levels, within and beyond the social economy.

Agents of change

Change is under way in many areas of society. A critical role thereby is played by digitalization, artificial intelligence, automation, robotics, and other technological advancements. While these may lead to transformations that can disrupt the world of work (e.g., through making many jobs redundant or replacing workers by machines), or undermine the social fabric of societies (e.g., through racial profiling, human alien-ation, etc.), they also promise affordances when it comes to offering new forms of work through digital platforms, or spurring collective modes of action, or even citizen participation (Mulgan, 2018). Such technologies have already proven to be a major factor in organizing mass mobilization to develop effective solutions for challenges of the COVID-19 crisis (Bertello, Bogers, & Bernardi, 2021; Gegenhuber, Krlev, Scheve, Lührsen, & Thaeter, 2020). They have also enabled entrepreneurial shifts and pivoting in business models for these business models to develop a social component. Scheidgen and colleagues, for example, describe how ventures repurposed an event booking service to improve patient management in medical doctors' waiting rooms (Scheidgen, Gümüsay, Günzel-Jensen, Krlev, & Wolf, 2021). Despite these touchpoints between the social economy and technology, there continues to be a perceived divide between the two fields, although the border between them seems to be crumbling slowly (Krlev, Mildenberger, & Anheier, 2020).

Calderini et al. (this volume) are working on tearing the border down entirely. They illustrate how social economy organizations are using technology to enhance inclusive growth, which matters from a policy perspective and from the perspective of target groups. At the same time, they highlight how the social economy employs technology to fortify its identity, for example by furthering its hybrid character of multiple organizational purposes and diverse goal achievement, and thereby may have a stronger influence on the wider economy as a blueprint for how to address multiple challenges by harnessing technology in socially beneficial ways. In a similar vein, Mulgan (this volume)—at the level of platforms, technological systems, or governance institutions that use cutting-edge technologies in responsible ways (e.g., to connect and pool knowledge on net-zero experimentation in cities)—shows how the social economy can shape technology to be more responsibly employed to serve a greater purpose for society. *Social Economy Science* thus contributes by highlighting that the social economy can be an agent of change in using technology for social value creation as well as in making technology more inclusive.

Partnerships

A research focus on partnerships between actors from different fields of activity or sectors, while growing as an effect of the many crises in the past and present, is well established in organization and management studies and in transition studies (e.g., Bulkeley et al., 2016; Hamann & April, 2013). However, as recently noted, much of this work looks at loose partnerships and forms of interactions, often on generic issues driven by the impetus for good governance or accountability (Krlev, 2022a). This is for example the case when non-profits and non-governmental organizations interact with businesses in pursuit of mutual learning, or improved responsible behaviour and higher societal legitimacy through interactions that serve as checks and balances to the actions of corporations (Weber, Weidner, Kroeger, & Wallace, 2017). Partnerships between the social economy and the public sector also have a very long research tradition. In fact, some welfare states depend on what some scholars have interpreted as social economy organizations being partners that carry out social, health, and welfare service provision backed by a mandate of the state (Hansmann, 1987).

The contributions to our book mark a clear departure from both of these ratio-
nales for partnerships. Carter and Ball (this volume), for example, apply a relational
lens and analyse social outcomes contracting, that is, service provision which prioritizes the maximization of results rather than the minimization of operational costs
in allocating public funds to the social economy. They advance the argument that
such contracts in reality, and when administered cleverly and with care, represent
relational links between state authorities, the social economy, and even for-profit
investors or business partners. They are genuine partnerships rather than standard
service contracts or loose collaborations, because involved parties engage in a process
of mutual interaction, joint encounter, and participatory negotiation—in particular
as regards the agreement and assessment of impact or outcomes criteria (see also
Krlev et al., 2022). Thereby such partnerships become vehicles for initiating cultural change in all involved organizations and their wider fields. Socially responsible
procurement (Varga & Hayday, this volume) can have a similar function. Instead
of transferring responsibility to the social economy for some services, often based
on short-term, renewable contracts, social procurement as a new governance principle would prioritize service provision that is true to social economy values always
and throughout all kinds of buying decisions. This can represent an enormous lever
for lifting the social economy up to a partner at eye-level, rather than a dependent
executioner of pre-defined activities. *Social Economy Science* thus contributes by conceptualizing new ways to amplify partnerships that have positive effects not only at
the relational level of partners, but also when it comes to the outcomes or impacts
that are delivered to society.

Directions for future research

To pick up on the question we posed in our introductory chapter—'Why should
we care about social economy science?'—we offer considerations on open and new
research questions concerning the social economy, which our book encourages. We
also close the loop on our theorizing by means of institutional theory and transitions
theory, by offering wider suggestions for research beyond the social economy, with
a special emphasis on those two theoretical strands.

Future research on the social economy

In our selected research directions within the social economy field, we relate back to
several cross-cutting concepts and subjects covered by our theory chapter: among
others, effectuating change from the perspective of actor networks versus from the
perspective of issue fields; social economy values and the intersection between social
and technology driven processes of innovation; and the aim of achieving large-
scale collaboration between very diverse actors, which only when joining forces will

be able to address the immense social and environmental sustainability challenges society is facing (compare to Krlev et al., this volume).

Appreciating the small and the big, the issue and the network

A lot of the research on sustainability transitions is focused on high-level actors and change processes such as those occurring in welfare systems or entire industries (Frantzeskaki & Wittmayer, 2019). While this is well justified for that research community's interest in large-scale transformations, this existing focus may have unduly bracketed out much smaller kinds of actors and action, namely that of individual social economy organizations. Some social economy organizations are admittedly locally restricted and not able to trespass these boundaries, for instance because locality and local identity are at the heart of their activities (Mensink, Cemova, Ricciuti, & Bauer, 2019). Yet there seems to be a general suspicion that social economy organizations, judged by their size or power positions, are negligibly important when it comes to uprooting systems. At a closer look, however, it is exactly the persistence, radicalness, and fragility of such organizations and actions that makes all the difference (Krlev, 2022b). The lens of organizational issue fields offers an explanation for why that is the case. It suggests that it may not be important that at the network or actor-based level the promoters of change are small, when the issue fields they are pushing are grand. Semantic network analysis can help uncover such issue-based structures and dynamics, in which signals by actors that they promote 'good' values with the 'right' models may be more important than organizational size in order to gain legitimacy within as well as for emerging fields (Wruk, Oberg, Klutt, & Maurer, 2019). Given the right conditions, social economy activities might unfold greater impacts than similar, yet more gradual processes among more powerful actors in policy or business (e.g., Etzion, Gehman, Ferraro, & Avidan, 2017). Or social economy organizations may pull business and public policy along to realize a greater mission and vision (see Krlev, Anheier, & Mildenberger, 2019b).

Important questions are opened up when combining the transitions theory with the organization theory view in this way. For example: What is the effective role of smaller and organizationally less powerful issue work promoted by the social economy, when it is at the same time more agile and supposedly more radical than that of other actors? How can we better understand the ways in which the network level and the issue level in the social economy amplify or stymie each other in granting stability to the field, but also in providing it with a capacity to promote change? What can be the role of social economy organizations in the change process once it enters (and reconfigures) the fields of business and public policy—should social economy organizations move on to confront the next frontier or seek to consolidate the change and safeguard its authenticity and moral standards?

How to design and employ technology in socially beneficial ways?

There is an important debate about the need to humanize new technological developments to avoid effects of disempowerment or social divides (Mansell, 2021).

Curiously, this debate is being held largely without the inclusion of the social economy. This is despite its long experience with upholding and protecting human values, virtues, and ethics, all characteristics that make the social economy a prime setting for humanizing social and economic transactions (Restakis, 2010). We have seen that instances when the social economy gets involved, such as through social tech ventures or in employing technology as a means of engaging the public, are striking, but few. One of the supposed reasons is that, while pushing for positive social change relative to external organizations and fields of activity, social economy organizations seem to show slow uptake or proactive use of digitization (Gagliardi et al., 2020; Bernholz, 2016). Also, as briefly mentioned before, there was a tradition in social economy research of delineating new phenomena such as social innovation from technological innovation as an act of emancipation, that is, to show that, in particular, the process of social innovation rests on different mechanisms than that of technological innovation (Krlev et al., 2020). While this proved true in many regards, with implications for the support of social innovation as also considered in this book, a rather artificial divide might have inhibited more targeted explorations of the intersections of the social economy with modern and future technologies, such as open-source approaches, artificial intelligence, automation, the Internet of Things, big data, data science, and others. The social economy is, by nature, close to relevant subjects of societal debate and research such as the following: digital commons (Alix et al., 2021), through its approaches of cooperative and solidary behaviour; ethics of algorithms (Herzog et al., 2022), through its enacted values of justice, empowerment, and inclusivity; or open data (Fuster Morell & Espelt, 2018), through its ability to mobilize stakeholders, its embracement of openness and accountability, and its orientation at collective benefits. These links should be pursued more in future research.

Our considerations lead to a number of essential questions: How can entirely new social economy models, which are fundamentally designed around technologies, amplify the functions of the social economy and its impacts? How can more proactive involvement of the social economy, and through it potentially of user groups, benefit the development of technologies that are by default inclusive and participatory, and decrease rather than exacerbate social inequalities? How can the social economy increase its capabilities of harnessing new technologies and leading rather than following in the digital transformation?

Sustainable forms of breakthrough collaboration

Scholars broadly agree that collaboration, as opposed to individual action, leads to beneficial social outcomes (Phillips, Alexander, & Lee, 2017). Two reasons are central to this. First, when a broader number of stakeholders is involved in developing solutions to sustainability challenges, this typically increases their legitimacy (Eneqvist et al., 2022; Sørensen & Torfing, 2012). Second, different kinds of expertise, experience, and ideas could help develop novel approaches to problems that have persisted over long periods of time despite efforts to address them (Nidumolu et al., 2014) and lead to innovative actions that increase institutional resilience (Krlev, 2022a). Yet, the obstacles for building lasting collaborations across sectoral borders are very high (Rey-Garcia, Mato-Santiso, & Felgueiras, 2020) and may require the involved actors to promote internal shifts, which are not easy to achieve since they may involve sacrifices in stability and profitability (Bode, Rogan, & Singh, 2019). The difficulty of reaching such a prerequisite is especially high when we presuppose that such internal changes need to happen within every participant of the collaboration. So, so-called breakthrough collaborations, which not only bring an unusual combination of actors together but also enable radically new approaches due to the creativity these deviant combinations might spur (Maas Geesteranus, Bonnici, & Bruin, 2021), might be doomed to remain an empty hope. This holds unless collaborators are able to create system-level synergies and incentives (Mair & Seelos, 2021). For these synergies to occur, however, they require interconnected shifts at several levels, such as the mobilization of different types of financial resources that prioritize social value creation, or a shared understanding of how to manage for and measure impact. In other words, to achieve profound systems change and sustainable breakthrough collaboration as a positive outcome or as a means to positive outcomes (Rayner & Bonnici, 2021), we first require a purposeful redesign of practices at the organizational, field, and societal levels across sectors as well as in the network relations and the issue relations of the social economy.

Prompts for future research derive from these considerations: How can organizational practices, field-level trends, and societal issue areas of different kinds (spanning from logics, to resource mobilization, to decision criteria) be interlocked more effectively to change systems and thereby open spaces for actor collaboration? How can business and policy actors be included in shaping change processes in favour of solidarity and social value (pull forces) rather than being reconfigured by vanguard social economy practices (push factors)? What are the substantive affordances of sustainable—that is long-term, profound, and sustainability-oriented—collaboration, in contrast to more loose and generic forms of collaboration?

Future research beyond the social economy

Our research directions beyond the social economy feed back into the two transversal elements of our conceptual work, namely transitions theory and institutional theory. In relation to these, we highlight two areas of research: learnings from the social economy for studies of multi-level processes of change and transition, and learnings from the social economy for studying complex forms of organizing.

Studying multi-level processes of change and transition

Our proposition to bridge micro, meso, and macro levels of change through combining institutional theory with transitions theory could help social science research grasp processes of change and profound transformation more generally. This is important when set against continued observations from scholars that while we understand the different types and outfits of change processes well, we are much less clear about the mechanisms that may steer such change processes (Bothello &

Salles-Djelic, 2018; Micelotta, Lounsbury, & Greenwood, 2017). We urge researchers to explore how a combination of the two perspectives, as compared to one alone, is more powerful in uncovering mechanisms of effective and profound social change across levels.

The research in this book has, for example, shown how the combination of theoretical lenses helps detect how very small and supposedly unreasonable new practices of social economy organizations, over time, can build up momentum to a level of force that leads to transitions of systems from within. This is fundamentally different from being triggered by outside events and also largely independent from the most powerful actors in a field—in fact, such change may be effectuated explicitly against the agenda of those actors (see also Krlev, 2022b). Building on those findings and analytical approaches should provide important lessons for how organizational practices could diffuse and scale when: a strong economic case is absent (e.g., Vakili & McGahan, 2016 on drug development for rare diseases); technological progress plays a minor role (e.g., Černe, Kaše, & Škerlavaj, 2016 on non-technological innovation); formal and regulatory institutional actors have few incentives for altering rules in a field (e.g., Bapuji, Patel, Ertug, & Allen, 2020 on entrenched social inequalities); or actor agendas do not converge towards a shared goal set (e.g., Grodal & O'Mahony, 2017 on the displacement of ambitious scientific goals).

Our insights on the value of ambitious issue agendas or alternative approaches to organizing change could by equal measure help to extend and challenge existing work on meeting sustainability challenges that stresses structures and processes in which as many stakeholders as possible engage to reach consensus, or that prioritize short-term gains over long-term vision (Gehman, Etzion, & Ferraro, 2022). Despite the ambition that these would prove effective strategies of change, we see in practice that many activities fail to promote profound positive change. Relatedly, existing transitions research has come to move somewhat away from its grounding in the social consequences of technology to include softer aspects of transitions, for instance dimensions of enactment or political processes (see e.g. Geels et al., 2016 on low carbon transitions). Although these accounts take note of the role of social economy organizations in such processes, they fail to appreciate their agents of change role, in particular at the issue level. Overall, that is to say that the micro-foundations of change and the power of alternative approaches of organizing tend to be overlooked (see Sonpar et al., 2009 on micro-foundations of radical change in healthcare). This suggests that more attention should be given, in organization as well as transitions research, to values-oriented forms of organizing, including their granular practices and issue work.

These considerations open up a range of concrete questions for future research: How do mechanisms of change that are non-technological and situated in low power positions drive profound change processes and reconfigurations of systems? How can regulatory institutions systematically sense small-scale, non-mainstream solutions to speed up their process of diffusion and scaling, and proactively shape subsequent institutional change? What is an effective balance between process and structures of wide stakeholder inclusion that aim for reaching consensus versus individual proactivity that may allow seemingly unreasonable approaches to be tested out and visionary agendas to be pursued, which may trigger profound societal change?

Studying complex (new) forms of organizing

New organizational constellations, practices, and interactions are being advocated as key to finding effective responses to complex problems (Gray & Purdy, 2018). We have shown that studying the social economy field can be very helpful in uncovering complexities not only of the problems to be addressed, but also of the solutions to be found (see also Berrone et al., 2016 on community dynamics in addressing grand challenges). Our conceptualization of the social economy as an umbrella concept that can be better understood as an organizational issue field, and all contributions to this book, underpin that there is much to be gained from elevating the status of the social economy in research to better understand how to master complex organizational processes.

For example, scholars have fairly recently evoked collective or impact entrepreneurship approaches, which stress structures and processes of decentralization and bottom-up action, as an important tool in addressing major sustainability challenges (Doh, Tashman, & Benischke, 2019; Markman, Waldron, Gianiodis, & Espina, 2019). There is much to learn from the social economy as to how to establish a common identity and field stability when actors and resources are so dispersed. While this may not matter much for the emergence of innovative ideas and creative action, it will matter for making new action principles, logics, or forms of organizing standard practice. Our focus on decoupling the issues perspective from the actor perspective furthermore helps to amplify emerging work on how individual actors can raise awareness, build coalitions, and raise legitimacy for neglected yet important societal issues (Barberá-Tomás, Castello, Bakker, & Zietsma, 2019).

We believe there is also much to learn from taking the social economy field more seriously for studying so-called new forms of organizing, scholars of which have recently come to consider movements and civic forms of organizing as viable alternatives to dominant modes of action in the capitalist market economy (Kaufmann & Danner-Schröder, 2022). In this it is important to note that new forms of organizing are rarely entirely new, but instead rest on an original combination of old solutions, which may emerge and co-occur in very disparate fields (Puranam, Alexy, & Reitzig, 2014). Among relevant elements of the recombinations that Puranam et al. discuss are transparency, self-selection (or co-determination), intrinsic motivation, and collaboration, all of which at least in part are qualities that may differentiate social economy activities from those of public organizations or mainstream market organizations. Similarly, new forms of internal organizing or restructuring processes in the world of work, such as holacracies or other open forms of organization (Robertson, 2015), have their equivalents in various established forms within the social economy field. And yet there seems little effort whatsoever to transfer findings and implications from the social economy to these new forms of organizing. Instead scholars continue to apply a within-business view to understand these new trends (Bernstein, Bunch, Canner, & Lee, 2016).

Our considerations lead to important new issues for future research, for example: How can social economy practices, structures and processes be harnessed in complex forms of organizing that prioritize collective problem solving and social value creation? How can studying the long tradition of open, collaborative, informal, and bottom-up processes of organizing in the social economy provide directions for the design and enactment of new forms? How can experiences in the social economy with achieving organizational and field stability, mobilizing coalitions, and creating legitimacy for neglected issues inform wider evolutions in the world of work and organizations?

A vision of practice and policy that leverages social economy capacities

A lot of new action is under way concerning the social economy, as Bonnici and Klijn (this volume) outline masterfully in their chapter. So, we believe our work comes at an opportune moment, as profound initiatives are already materializing. However, we have seen that many existing efforts might not be enough, that the social economy is still neglected in many regards, and that it is difficult to find effective answers to some of the challenges the field is facing. Therefore, based on evidence from our book, we develop concrete recommendations for what policy and social economy organizations should do to improve the situation. As the roles of the social economy and policy are often intertwined in these recommendations—in fact, they mostly rest on improving the co-engagement of both sides—we pool our guidance across actors.

Assume leadership and become truly participatory

Almost every organization in the world is now in pursuit of a higher purpose and seeks to generate positive impacts on society. Some do so for substantive reasons, others to satisfy stakeholder demands by means of symbolism and empty claims. One can criticize these developments, and there is justified fear of green, white, and impact washing (Krlev, 2019). However, this is also an important moment for social economy organizations to become active—which, alas, they mostly seem to miss or ignore. Instead of criticizing such moves by other organizations, now is the time to lead by example. It is very strange to see that a field whose very existence is grounded in purpose, and that has a long track record of creating positive impact and social value, is not positioned at the forefront of debates of how to make purpose and impact a reality for all organizations and fields. Instead, social economy organizations too often remain invisible, even in local settings, and fail to assume civic leadership positions. Part of why this happens, we suppose, relates to the need for

social economy organizations to become better at being truly participatory organizations that engage beneficiaries and also volunteers (see e.g. Wit, Mensink, Einarsson,
& Bekkers, 2017) as co-entrepreneurs and co-innovators throughout the process,
from idea development to scaling. Only in this way can new approaches find broad
acceptance and flourish to increase resilience at a systemic level.

We are aware that this is easier said than done and will not be possible in every
activity and all the time. However, social economy organizations need to find better ways of developing solutions that fully match the problems they are supposed
to address, and also to be perceived and embraced as the leaders of positive social
change they are. The social economy will never be at the forefront of the minds of
people or other sector leaders because of its massive size or the returns it creates—and
for good reason, because the social economy is not there to impress in these ways.
What it can impress with is how it touches and improves the lives of people. Citizens
need to become more aware of what the social economy does for them and others;
they need to identify with it. What would help are dedicated efforts at promotion and
awareness raising—the social economy needs to become more visible (Krlev, 2020b).
The social economy can do this by more proactively seeking coalitions with corporate actors that are located in the boundary areas of the social economy; that is, if
those corporates do not already belong to the social economy, judged by the many
overlaps they have with the social economy's organizational issue field. Such corporate actors, for example, include apparel company Patagonia, which stated that 'earth
is now our only shareholder' after fully transferring company ownership to what the
company calls a 'purpose trust' (Patagonia, 2022), or food producer Danone, who
had the vision to transform fully into a B Corp when it was still under Emmanuel
Faber's leadership (Walt, 2021). Only by crossing these borders, or rather dissolving
them, will the social economy be able to unfold its role as the lead agent of change.

Harness digital technology for collective action

World records have been broken when social economy organizations initiate
processes of mass mobilization by means of digital technologies. The German
WirVsVirus hackathon and later the European EUVsVirus hackathon mobilized
citizens in numbers that were previously unimaginable. Tens of thousands of participants co-engaged in developing responses to the COVID-19 crisis. These responses
were only possible by combining the expertise, experience, and creativity of people
who might otherwise never have crossed paths. These people were brought together
by social economy organizations. The solutions developed during the hackathons
were not only technical in nature, but had a pronounced social character. One among
many new solutions was a counselling service for individuals who had suffered the
death of a loved one when the pandemic was raging (Mair, Gegenhuber, Thäter, &
Lührsen, 2021). We have stressed in our foreword that the sustainability challenges
ahead of us are technological, economic, and social in nature, and that the necessary
technological transformations might not be the hardest part to achieve. In fact, we

witness daily that the roadblocks to a sustainable transformation are foremost political and socially charged. People feel patronized, ignored, or disrespected. They are afraid of losing some of their freedoms. At the same time, several contributions in this book suggest technology can be a key enabler to spur collective social processes (see also Misuraca & Pasi, 2021).

Therefore, social economy organizations need to find better ways of using technology to promote social issues and spur collective action. Technology can help to convene a variety of stakeholders around important issues and develop solutions jointly (solutions not only to societal challenges, but also to the fears of citizens). Policy makers and business leaders, however need to play their part too, in particular when it comes to formalizing and implementing solutions for the long run. A challenge with the solutions developed during the hackathons was that new prototypes faced slow uptake, or that public authorities refused or delayed their implementation. Such roadblocks persisted although digital tracking systems for infections, for instance, could have improved the public sector's crisis management substantially, and much earlier in the timeline of the pandemic. Policy and organizational leaders need to be involved right from the start and throughout collective action processes so that developed solutions can be implemented and formalized swiftly. In this, it is critical to be open and to embrace an uncertainty mindset to make sure there is room for the best innovations and the greatest impact to emerge.

Engage in institutional design

It should have become clear that in many social economy settings, and in contrast to other areas of the economy, regulation after the fact is simply not enough, since some essential practices, structures, and scaling processes might not even materialize if not properly supported. One striking example is the lack of financial infrastructure for social innovation that effectively utilizes public and private funds. Risk–return–impact profiles at present, and without active interventions, simply do not provide social economy organizations enough financial resources to test out, establish, and scale their innovations and impactful activities. Instead of individual policy measures (such as preferential tax treatment for investing socially), policy needs to develop a master plan that takes full account of the spectrum of social economy organizations as well as their innovation and impact profiles. It would need to assume a long-term orientation and a perspective that takes the complexities of social change processes seriously. Propositions exist (e.g., Krlev et al., 2022) and are fully in line with a broader policy agenda of working on grand missions or challenges, rather than being based on a misguided understanding that complex problems can be addressed within certain policy pillars (Mazzucato, 2018). We call for more proactive policy that engages in institutional design rather than merely in regulation (see e.g. Krlev, 2020a). The institutional design process itself should be inclusive of the affected stakeholders. It may otherwise lead to mismatches similar to those we have seen when social economy organizations themselves do not consult and involve their target groups. Portugal Social Innovation—but also other initiatives globally, for instance surrounding social investment or impact measurement practices, as portrayed in this book—can serve as examples of how to put a multi-pronged institutional design into practice. Such new types of support not only should be able to allocate funds more effectively, but would help establish comprehensive social economy, innovation, and impact ecosystems.

Level up social economy science

We have provided rich evidence about the complexities contained in the social economy and about the societal complexities the social economy aims to address. Against this background, social economy science still plays far too small a role in the organization and transitions research fields, and in the social sciences more generally. We therefore suggest levelling up the standing of social economy science in academia. For one, it would substantially expand knowledge about these important issues. However, we suggest the nexus between research (as well as the higher education system more generally) and the social economy should also be fortified for further reasons.

First, a lack of data availability on the social economy makes analytic steps that would be very simple in other fields, such as gauging the size of a field, very demanding (see e.g. Göler von Ravensburg, Krlev, & Mildenberger, 2018; Göler von Ravensburg, Mildenberger, & Krlev, 2021 on challenges in gauging the national social enterprise landscape). Facing such a dearth of data availability and basic research, how are we supposed to judge, for example, the impact of the organizational issue field?

Second, the contributions to this book have sensitized policy makers and managers to the fact that leading social economy organizations, especially those with a strong social change orientation and high levels of participation, is more and not less demanding than leading more mainstream organizations. Because we need to better understand what skills this requires, and which structures and practices are most effective in achieving impactful management, we need a transfer of academic knowledge into the social economy. Since social economy organizations are at the forefront of addressing wicked problems, the need for such a transfer may be even bigger than it already is in other fields (Sharma, Greco, Grewatsch, & Bansal, 2022). The requirements for increasing the knowledge base become exponential when we move from the organizational, to the field, to the societal level, where we meet processes which take on a systems character and aim for profound transitions that involve and affect a multitude of stakeholders. However, for such a transfer to actually happen, we need to re-shape incentive and reward structures in the academic system and support scholars that actively engage in what we call 'impact work' for and with the social economy.

Third, under the pre-condition that researchers make knowledge accessible, actionable, and trustworthy (Kepes, Bennett, & McDaniel, 2014), we also require a greater readiness of social economy organizations to embrace evidence-based management practices. A positive feature of the social economy in this regard may be that it is probably more open to transfers, mutual interaction, and collaborations with science than public or commercial organizations. Ideally, however, as we have stressed throughout the development of this vision, all types of actors would participate jointly to co-create impact. This book is a small yet important testimony of what can emerge when we promote deep exchange between science, policy, and practice.

We sincerely hope that what we outline is not to remain an empty vision, but will become reality. We are convinced that if policy and practice leverage social economy capacities in these ways, we will be able to change the economy profoundly and make society more resilient in view of the major social and environmental sustainability challenges that lie ahead of us.

References

Alix, N., Perret, F., & Séguy, B. (2021). Les Plateformes coopératives: des modèles innovants d'économie sociale dans une société du numérique. In P. Bance, J. Fournier, O. Boned, & Y. Prost (Eds), *Économie publique et économie sociale: Vol. 5. Numérique, action publique et démocratie* (pp. 249–266). Mont-Saint-Aignan: Presses universitaires de Rouen et du Havre.

Audretsch, D. B., Eichler, G. M., & Schwarz, E. J. (2022). Emerging needs of social innovators and social innovation ecosystems. *International Entrepreneurship and Management Journal*, 18(1), 217–254. https://doi.org/10.1007/s11365-021-00789-9

Bapuji, H., Patel, C., Ertug, G., & Allen, D. G. (2020). Corona crisis and inequality: why management research needs a societal turn. *Journal of Management*, 98, 014920632092588. https://doi.org/10.1177/0149206320925881

Barberá-Tomás, D., Castello, I., Bakker, F. G. A. de, & Zietsma, C. (2019). Energizing through visuals: how social entrepreneurs use emotion-symbolic work for social change. *Academy of Management Journal*. Advance online publication. https://doi.org/10.5465/amj.2017.1488

Barman, E. (2015). Of principle and principal: value plurality in the market of impact investing. *Valuation Studies*, 3(1), 9–44. https://doi.org/10.3384/VS.2001-5592.15319

Bauer, A., Wistow, G., Hyanek, V., & Figueroa, M. (2019). Social innovation in healthcare: the recovery approach. In H. K. Anheier, G. Krlev, & G. Mildenberger (Eds), *Social Innovation: Comparative Perspectives* (pp. 130–148). Abingdon: Routledge.

Bernholz, L. (2016). Wiring a new social economy: reflections on philanthropy in the digital age. In S. D. Phillips, J. Harrow, & T. Jung (Eds), *The Routledge Companion to Philanthropy* (pp. 438–451). London: Routledge.

Bernstein, E., Bunch, J., Canner, N., & Lee, M. (2016). Beyond the holacracy hype (July–August). Available at: https://hbr.org/2016/07/beyond-the-holacracy-hype

Berrone, P., Gelabert, L., Massa-Saluzzo, F., & Rousseau, H. E. (2016). Understanding community dynamics in the study of grand challenges: how nonprofits, institutional actors, and the community fabric interact to influence income inequality. *Academy of Management Journal*, 59(6), 1940–1964. https://doi.org/10.5465/amj.2015.0746

Bertello, A., Bogers, M. L. A. M., & Bernardi, P. de (2021). Open innovation in the face of the COVID-19 grand challenge: insights from the Pan-European hackathon 'EUvsVirus'. *R and D Management*, 37(3), 355. https://doi.org/10.1111/radm.12456

Bode, C., Rogan, M., & Singh, J. (2019). Sustainable cross-sector collaboration: building a global platform for social impact. *Academy of Management Discoveries*, 5(4), 396–414. https://doi.org/10.5465/amd.2018.0112

Bothello, J., & Salles-Djelic, M.-L. (2018). Evolving conceptualizations of organizational environmentalism: a path generation account. *Organization Studies*, 39(1), 93–119. https://doi.org/10.1177/0170840617693272

Bouchard, M. J. (2012). Social innovation, an analytical grid for understanding the social economy: the example of the Québec housing sector. *Service Business*, 6(1), 47–59. https://doi.org/10.1007/s11628-011-0123-9

Brammer, S., Branicki, L., & Linnenluecke, M. K. (2020). COVID-19, societalization, and the future of business in society. *Academy of Management Perspectives*, 34(4), 493–507. https://doi.org/10.5465/amp.2019.0053

Brandsen, T., Cattacin, S., Evers, A., & Zimmer, A. (Eds). (2016). *Social Innovations in the Urban Context*. Cham: Springer.

Brandsen, T., & Pestoff, V. (2005). Co-production, the third sector and the delivery of public services: an introduction. *Public Management Review*, 8(4), 493–501.

Brandsen, T., Steen, T., & Verschuere, B. (2018). *Co-production and Co-creation: Engaging Citizens in Public Services*. Abingdon: Routledge.

Bretos, I., Bouchard, M. J., & Zevi, A. (2020). Institutional and organizational trajectories in social economy enterprises: resilience, transformation and regeneration. *Annals of Public and Cooperative Economics*, 91(3), 351–358. https://doi.org/10.1111/apce.12279

Bulkeley, H., Coenen, L., Frantzeskaki, N., Hartmann, C., Kronsell, A., Mai, L., . . . Voytenko Palgan, Y. (2016). Urban living labs: governing urban sustainability transitions. *Current Opinion in Environmental Sustainability*, 22, 13–17. https://doi.org/10.1016/j.cosust.2017.02.003

Busch, C. (2020). *Serendipity Mindset: The Art and Science of Creating Good Luck*. London: Penguin Publishing Group.

Černe, M., Kaše, R., & Škerlavaj, M. (2016). Non-technological innovation research: evaluating the intellectual structure and prospects of an emerging field. *Scandinavian Journal of Management*, 32(2), 69–85. https://doi.org/10.1016/j.scaman.2016.02.001

Cohen, R. (2020). *Impact: Reshaping Capitalism to Drive Real Change*. London: Ebury Press.

Defourny, J., & Nyssens, M. (Eds). (2021). *Social Enterprise in Western Europe: Theory, Models and Practice* (1st ed.). New York: Routledge.

Doh, J. P., Tashman, P., & Benischke, M. H. (2019). Adapting to grand environmental challenges through collective entrepreneurship. *Academy of Management Perspectives*, 33(4), 450–468. https://doi.org/10.5465/amp.2017.0056

Eneqvist, E., Algehed, J., Jensen, C., & Karvonen, A. (2022). Legitimacy in municipal experimental governance: questioning the public good in urban innovation practices. *European Planning Studies*, 30(8), 1596–1614. https://doi.org/10.1080/09654313.2021.2015749

Etzion, D., Gehman, J., Ferraro, F., & Avidan, M. (2017). Unleashing sustainability transformations through robust action. *Journal of Cleaner Production*, 140, 167–178. https://doi.org/10.1016/j.jclepro.2015.06.064

Figueroa, M., Navratil, J., Turrini, A., & Krlev, G. (2019). Social innovation in environmental sustainability: promoting sharing public spaces for bicycle use. In H. K. Anheier, G. Krlev, & G. Mildenberger (Eds), *Social Innovation: Comparative Perspectives* (pp. 149–172). Abingdon: Routledge.

Frantzeskaki, N., & Wittmayer, J. M. (2019). The next wave of sustainability transitions: elucidating and invigorating transformations in the welfare state. *Technological Forecasting and Social Change*, 145(5), 136–140. https://doi.org/10.1016/j.techfore.2018.09.023

Fuster Morell, M., & Espelt, R. (2018). A framework for assessing democratic qualities in collaborative economy platforms: analysis of 10 cases in Barcelona. *Urban Science*, 2(3), 61. https://doi.org/10.3390/urbansci2030061

Gagliardi, D., Psarra, F., Wintjes, R., Trendafili, K., Pineda, J., Haaland, M., . . . Niglia, F. (2020). *New Technologies and Digitisation: Opportunities and Challenges for the Social Economy and Social Economy Enterprises*. Luxembourg: Publications Office of the European Union.

Garud, R., Hardy, C., & Maguire, S. (2016). Institutional entrepreneurship as embedded agency: an introduction to the Special Issue. *Organization Studies*, 28(7), 957–969. https://doi.org/10.1177/0170840607078958

Geels, F. W. (2005). *Technological Transitions and System Innovations: A Co-evolutionary and Socio-technical Analysis*. Cheltenham, UK, Northampton, MA: Edward Elgar.

Geels, F. W., Kern, F., Fuchs, G., Hinderer, N., Kungl, G., Mylan, J., . . . Wassermann, S. (2016). The enactment of socio-technical transition pathways: A reformulated typology and a comparative multi-level analysis of the German and UK low-carbon electricity transitions (1990–2014). *Research Policy*, 45(4), 896–913. https://doi.org/10.1016/j.respol.2016.01.015

Gegenhuber, T., Krlev, G., Scheve, C., Lührsen, R., & Thaeter, L. (2020). *Let the Genie out of the Bottle: A Hackathon to Promote Open Social Innovation in Times of Crisis*. Paper presented at Momentum Kongress. Available at: https://www.momentum-kongress.org/system/files/congress_files/2020/8_paper_thomasgegenhuber.pdf

Gehman, J., Etzion, D., & Ferraro, F. (2022). Robust action: advancing a distinctive approach to grand challenges. In A. A. Gümüsay, E. Marti, H. Trittin-Ulbrich, & C.

Wickert (Eds), *Research in the Sociology of Organizations: Organizing for Societal Grand Challenges* (pp. 259–278). Bingley: Emerald Publishing Limited.

Göler von Ravensburg, N., Krlev, G., & Mildenberger, G. (2018). *Update of the Mapping of Social Enterprises and their Ecosystems in Europe: Country Report Germany.* Brussels.

Göler von Ravensburg, N., Mildenberger, G., & Krlev, G. (2021). Social enterprise in germany: between institutional inertia, innovation and cooperation. In J. Defourny & M. Nyssens (Eds), *Social Enterprise in Western Europe: Theory, Models and Practice* (1st ed.) (pp. 85–101). New York: Routledge.

Gras, D., Conger, M., Jenkins, A., & Gras, M. (2019). Wicked problems, reductive tendency, and the formation of (non-)opportunity beliefs. *Journal of Business Venturing,* 105966. https://doi.org/10.1016/j.jbusvent.2019.105966

Gray, B., & Purdy, J. (2018). *Collaborating for Our Future: Multistakeholder Partnerships for Solving Complex Problems.* Oxford: Oxford University Press.

Grodal, S., & O'Mahony, S. (2017). How does a grand challenge become displaced? Explaining the duality of field mobilization. *The Academy of Management Journal,* 60(5), 1801–1827. https://doi.org/10.5465/amj.2015.0890

Hamann, R., & April, K. (2013). On the role and capabilities of collaborative intermediary organisations in urban sustainability transitions. *Journal of Cleaner Production,* 50(2), 12–21. https://doi.org/10.1016/j.jclepro.2012.11.017

Hansmann, H. (1987). Economic theories of nonprofit organization. In W. W. Powell (Ed.), *The Nonprofit Sector: A Research Handbook* (pp. 27–42). New Haven: Yale University Press.

Hehenberger, L., Mair, J., & Metz, A. (2019). The assembly of a field ideology: an idea-centric perspective on systemic power in impact investing. *The Academy of Management Journal,* 62(6), 1672–1704. https://doi.org/10.5465/amj.2017.1402

Herzog, L., Kellmeyer, P., & Wild, V. (2022). Introduction to the Special Issue 'Digital behavioral technologies, vulnerability, and justice'. *Review of Social Economy,* 80(1), 1–6. https://doi.org/10.1080/00346764.2022.2032293

Hockerts, K. (2015). How hybrid organizations turn antagonistic assets into complementarities. *California Management Review,* 57(3), 83–106. https://doi.org/10.1525/cmr.2015.57.3.83

Kaufmann, L. J., & Danner-Schröder, A. (2022). Addressing grand challenges through different forms of organizing: a literature review. In A. A. Gümüsay, E. Marti, H. Trittin-Ulbrich, & C. Wickert (Eds), *Research in the Sociology of Organizations: Organizing for Societal Grand Challenges* (pp. 163–186). Bingley: Emerald Publishing Limited.

Kepes, S., Bennett, A. A., & McDaniel, M. A. (2014). Evidence-based management and the trustworthiness of our cumulative scientific knowledge: implications for teaching, research, and practice. *Academy of Management Learning & Education,* 13(3), 446–466. https://doi.org/10.5465/amle.2013.0193

Krlev, G. (2019, 18 March). Three elephants in the impact investing room. Available at: https://www.pioneerspost.com/news-views/20190318/three-elephants-the-impact-investing-room

Krlev, G. (2020a). *European Policy for Social Innovation*. Available at: https://euclidnetwork.eu/2020/12/european-policy-for-social-innovation/

Krlev, G. (2020b). Is impact investing becoming too fashionable for its own good? Available at: https://gorgi-krlev.medium.com/is-impact-investing-becoming-too-fashionable-for-its-own-good-3984c7266a12

Krlev, G. (2022a). Let's join forces: institutional resilience and multistakeholder partnerships in crises. *Journal of Business Ethics*. Advance online publication. https://doi.org/10.1007/s10551-022-05231-w

Krlev, G. (2022b). The hiding hand, persistent fragile action, and sustainable development. In M. Hölscher, S. Toepler, R. List, & A. Ruser (Eds), *Civil Society: Concepts, Challenges, Contexts* (pp. 101–115). Heidelberg: Springer.

Krlev, G., Anheier, H. K., & Mildenberger, G. (2019a). Introduction: social innovation—what is it and who makes it? In H. K. Anheier, G. Krlev, & G. Mildenberger (Eds), *Social Innovation: Comparative Perspectives* (pp. 3–35). Abingdon: Routledge.

Krlev, G., Anheier, H. K., & Mildenberger, G. (2019b). Results: the comparative analysis. In H. K. Anheier, G. Krlev, & G. Mildenberger (Eds), *Social Innovation: Comparative Perspectives* (pp. 257–279). Abingdon: Routledge.

Krlev, G., & Lund, A. B. (2020). Social innovation ignored: framing nonprofit activities in European news media. *Voluntas*, 71(5), 752. https://doi.org/10.1007/s11266-020-00224-7

Krlev, G., Mildenberger, G., & Anheier, H. K. (2020). Innovation and societal transformation—what changes when the 'social' comes in? *International Review of Applied Economics*, 34(5), 529–540.

Krlev, G., Sauer, S., Scharpe, K., Mildenberger, G., Elsemann, K., & Sauerhammer, M. (2022). *Financing Social Innovation—International Evidence*. Centre for Social Investment (CSI), University of Heidelberg & Social Entrepreneurship Network Deutschland e.V. (SEND). Available at: https://www.send-ev.de/wp-content/uploads/2022/01/Financing_Social_Innovation.pdf

Lawrence, T. B., Suddaby, R., & Leca, B. (Eds) (2010). *Institutional Work: Actors and Agency in Institutional Studies of Organization*. Cambridge: Cambridge University Press.

Maas Geesteranus, M., Bonnici, F., & Bruin, C. de (2021). *Why 2021 Can and Should Be the Year for Breakthrough Collaboration*. Available at: https://www.weforum.org/agenda/2021/01/why-2021-can-and-should-be-the-year-for-breakthrough-collaboration/

Mair, J., Gegenhuber, T., Thäter, L., & Lührsen, R. (2021). *Learning Report. Open Social Innovation: Gemeinsam Lernen aus #WirvsVirus*. Available at: https://opus4.kobv.de/opus4-hsog/frontdoor/index/index/docId/3782

Mair, J., Marti, I., & Ventresca, M. J. (2012). Building inclusive markets in rural bangladesh: how intermediaries work institutional voids. *Academy of Management Journal*, 55(4), 819–850. https://doi.org/10.5465/amj.2010.0627

Mair, J., & Seelos, C. (2021). Organizations, social problems, and system change: invigorating the third mandate of organizational research. *Organization Theory*, 2(4), 263178772110548. https://doi.org/10.1177/26317877211054858

Markman, G. D., Waldron, T. L., Gianiodis, P. T., & Espina, M. I. (2019). E pluribus unum: impact entrepreneurship as a solution to grand challenges. *Academy of Management Perspectives*, 33(4), 371–382. https://doi.org/10.5465/amp.2019.0130

Mazzucato, M. (2018). *Mission-oriented Research & Innovation in the European Union: A Problem-solving Approach to Fuel Innovation-led Growth*. Brussels: European Commission.

Mensink, W., Cemova, L., Ricciuti, E., & Bauer, A. (2019). Social innovation in community development: self-organisation and refugees. In H. K. Anheier, G. Krlev, & G. Mildenberger (Eds), *Social Innovation: Comparative Perspectives* (pp. 224–254). Abingdon: Routledge.

Micelotta, E., Lounsbury, M., & Greenwood, R. (2017). Pathways of institutional change: an integrative review and research agenda. *Journal of Management*, 43(6), 1885–1910.

Misuraca, G., & Pasi, G. (2021). Shaping the welfare society: unleashing transformation through ICT-enabled social innovation. In F. Davide, A. Gaggioli, & G. Misuraca (Eds), *Emerging Communication: vol. 13. Perspectives for Digital Social Innovation to Reshape the European Welfare Systems* (pp. 45–66). Amsterdam: IOS Press.

Mulgan, G. (2018). *Big Mind: How Collective Intelligence Can Change Our World*. Princeton: Princeton University Press.

Nicholls, A. (2018). A general theory of social impact accounting: materiality, uncertainty and empowerment. *Journal of Social Entrepreneurship*, 9(2), 132–153. https://doi.org/10.1080/19420676.2018.1452785

Nidumolu, R., Ellison, J., Whalen, J., & Billman, E. (2014). The Collaboration Imperative. *Harvard Business Review* (April). Available at: https://hbr.org/2014/04/the-collaboration-imperative-2

OECD (2021). *Building Local Ecosystems for Social Innovation: A Methodological Framework*. Local Economic and Employment Development (LEED) Working Papers (2021/06). Paris.

Ometto, M. P., Gegenhuber, T., Winter, J., & Greenwood, R. (2018). From balancing missions to mission drift: the role of the institutional context, spaces, and compartmentalization in the scaling of social enterprises. *Business & Society*, 58(5), 1003–1046.

Patagonia (2022). Patagonia's next chapter: Earth is now our only shareholder. Available at: https://www.patagoniaworks.com/press/2022/9/14/patagonias-next-chapter-earth-is-now-our-only-shareholder#:~:text=The%20company%20shared%20the%20news,letter%20from%20founder%20Yvon%20Chouinard.

Pel, B., Haxeltine, A., Avelino, F., Dumitru, A., Kemp, R., Bauler, T., . . . Jørgensen, M. S. (2020). Towards a theory of transformative social innovation: a relational framework and 12 propositions. *Research Policy*, 49(8), 104080. DOI: https://doi.org/10.1016/j.respol.2020.104080

Phillips, W., Alexander, E. A., & Lee, H. (2017). Going it alone won't work! The relational imperative for social innovation in social enterprises. *Journal of Business Ethics*, 156, 315–331. https://doi.org/10.1007/s10551-017-3608-1

Pradel-Miquel, M., Cano-Hila, A. B., Hila, A. B. C., & García Cabeza, M. (2020). *Social Innovation and Urban Governance: Citizenship, Civil Society and Social Movements.* Cheltenham: Edward Elgar.

Puranam, P., Alexy, O., & Reitzig, M. (2014). What's 'new' about new forms of organizing? *The Academy of Management Review*, 39(2), 162–180. https://doi.org/10.5465/amr.2011.0436

Quarter, J. (Ed.) (2015). *Social Purpose Enterprises: Case Studies for Social Change.* Toronto: University of Toronto Press.

Rayner, C., & Bonnici, F. (2021). *What Got Us Here Won't Get Us There: The Systems Work of Social Change.* Oxford: Oxford University Press.

Restakis, J. (2010). *Humanizing the Economy: Co-operatives in the Age of Capital.* Gabriola, BC: New Society Publishers.

Rey-Garcia, M., Mato-Santiso, V., & Felgueiras, A. (2020). Transitioning collaborative cross-sector business models for sustainability innovation: multilevel tension management as a dynamic capability. *Business & Society*, 60(10), 000765032094982. https://doi.org/10.1177/0007650320949822

Robertson, B. J. (2015). *Holacracy: The New Management System for a Rapidly Changing World* (1st ed.). New York: Holt.

Rogers, E. M. (2003). *Diffusion of Innovations* (5th ed.). New York: Free Press.

Scheidgen, K., Gümüsay, A. A., Günzel-Jensen, F., Krlev, G., & Wolf, M. (2021). Crises and entrepreneurial opportunities: digital social innovation in response to physical distancing. *Journal of Business Venturing Insights*, 15, e00222. https://doi.org/10.1016/j.jbvi.2020.e00222

Sharma, G., Greco, A., Grewatsch, S., & Bansal, P. (2022). Cocreating forward: how researchers and managers can address problems together. *Academy of Management Learning & Education*, 21(3), 350–368. https://doi.org/10.5465/amle.2021.0233

Smith, G., & Teasdale, S. (2012). Associative democracy and the social economy: exploring the regulatory challenge. *Economy and Society*, 41(2), 151–176. https://doi.org/10.1080/03085147.2012.661627

Smith, W. K., & Besharov, M. L. (2017). Bowing before dual gods: how structured flexibility sustains organizational hybridity. *Administrative Science Quarterly*, 1–44. https://doi.org/10.1177/0001839217750826

Sonpar, K., Handelman, J. M., & Dastmalchian, A. (2009). Implementing new institutional logics in pioneering organizations: the burden of justifying ethical appropriateness and trustworthiness. *Journal of Business Ethics*, 90(3), 345–359. https://doi.org/10.1007/s10551-009-0045-9

Sørensen, E., & Torfing, J. (2012). Collaborative innovation in the public sector. *The Innovation Journal—Public Sector Innovation Journal*, 17(1), 1–14.

Vakili, K., & McGahan, A. M. (2016). Health care's grand challenge: stimulating basic science on diseases that primarily afflict the poor. *The Academy of Management Journal*, 59(6), 1917–1939. https://doi.org/10.5465/amj.2015.0641

Walt, V. (2021). A top CEO was ousted after making his company more environmentally conscious. Now he's speaking out. Available at: https://time.com/6121684/emmanuel-faber-danone-interview/

Weber, C., Weidner, K., Kroeger, A., & Wallace, J. (2017). Social value creation in inter-organizational collaborations in the not-for-profit sector: give and take from a dyadic perspective. *Journal of Management Studies*, 54(6), 929–956. https://doi.org/10.1111/joms.12272

Van Wijk, J., Zietsma, C., Dorado, S., Bakker, F. G. A. de, & Martí, I. (2018). Social innovation: integrating micro, meso, and macro level insights from institutional theory. *Business & Society*, 58(5), 887–918. https://doi.org/10.1177/0007650318789104

Wit, A. de, Mensink, W., Einarsson, T., & Bekkers, R. (2017). Beyond service production: volunteering for social innovation. *Nonprofit and Voluntary Sector Quarterly*, 43, 089976401773465. https://doi.org/10.1177/0899764017734651

Wruk, D., Oberg, A., Klutt, J., & Maurer, I. (2019). The presentation of self as good and right: how value propositions and business model features are linked in the sharing economy. *Journal of Business Ethics*, 159(4), 997–1021. https://doi.org/10.1007/s10551-019-04209-5

Yan, S., Ferraro, F., & Almandoz, J. (2018). The rise of socially responsible investment funds: the paradoxical role of the financial logic. *Administrative Science Quarterly*, 13, 000183921877332. https://doi.org/10.1177/0001839218773324

Ziegler, R., & Jacobi, N. von (2020). Creating fair (economic) space for social innovation? A capabilities perspective. In A. Nicholls & R. Ziegler (Eds), *Creating Economic Space for Social Innovation* (pp. 50–79). Oxford University Press.

Index

For the benefit of digital users, indexed terms that span two pages (e.g., 52–53) may, on occasion, appear on only one of those pages.